COLLEGE ACCOUNTING

SIXTH EDITION

By

J. F. SHERWOOD, C. P. A.

A. B. CARSON, Ph. D., C. P. A.

CLEM BOLING

Published by

SOUTH-WESTERN PUBLISHING COMPANY

Cincinnati 27   New Rochelle, N. Y.   Chicago 5   Dallas 2   San Francisco 3

A20

Library of Congress Catalog Card Number: 57-5069

K257
Printed in the United States of America

PREFACE

•

The conduct of a business — even a small business — may be a complicated matter. In order to provide the owners and managers of an enterprise with information that is essential to the intelligent operation of their business, to measure the progress of the venture year-by-year or month-by-month, and to comply with the requirements of various governmental agencies and taxing authorities, it is essential that orderly and systematic records of business operations be maintained. An understanding of the principles of business accounting is a minimum necessity for anyone who aspires to a successful career in business, in many of the professions, and in numerous branches of government. This textbook was prepared for students of accounting, business administration, and secretarial science. For various reasons, some of them similar and others quite different, each of these groups needs to understand modern financial accounting.

Accounting principles have wide application and adaptability. The same basic principles apply to the keeping of records of the professional practice of a doctor or lawyer, and to the records maintained by a gigantic manufacturing corporation. In the first instance, keeping the records may be only a part of the duties of a secretary. In the latter case, the record keeping may require the full-time efforts of dozens of accountants, auditors, and clerks working with the aid of elaborate mechanical and electronic devices. Each accounting system is adapted to the particular requirements of the individual business, but all have many purposes, principles, and practices in common.

In describing and explaining the principles of business accounting and many of the practices that are followed, a considerable number of forms and documents are illustrated. In the cases of the government forms shown, each is official; in other cases, the forms reproduced are typical and, in many instances, they are so widely used that they have come to be considered "standard." The accounting terminology used in this textbook follows current practice and conforms generally to the recommendations of the Committee on Terminology and the Committee on Accounting Procedure of the American Institute of Accountants.

3

The textbook is organized to facilitate the use of various supplementary learning aids. Each unit consists of one or more study assignments. Workbooks containing correlated practice assignments are available. Each workbook assignment consists of an exercise on principles or theory and one or more practical accounting problems bearing on the subject discussed in the related section of the textbook. Additional accounting problems to be used for either supplementary or remedial work are included in the textbook.

In addition to the workbooks, a choice of practice sets is available. The selection includes sets relating to professional, mercantile, and manufacturing enterprises. The sets provide realistic work designed to test the student's ability to apply his knowledge of the principles of accounting gained from studying the textbook and completing the workbook assignments.

A comprehensive testing program is provided. Analysis tests are provided as an aid in determining the student's qualifications for doing the practice set work satisfactorily. Upon completion of each practice set, a test is used to determine the student's ability to interpret the records and financial statements intelligently. Additional tests are provided for periodic examination purposes.

The authors acknowledge their indebtedness and express their appreciation to the considerable number of business executives, accountants, accounting instructors, and other professional people whose advice and suggestions contributed to the preparation of this textbook.

J. F. S.

A. B. C.

C. B.

TABLE OF CONTENTS

PART I

UNIT ONE — ELEMENTS OF ACCOUNTING............................... 9–26
1 Assets, Liabilities, and Proprietorship
2 The Double-Entry Process

UNIT TWO —ACCOUNTING PROCEDURE................................ 27–48
3 Journalizing Transactions
4 Posting and the Trial Balance
5 The Financial Statements

UNIT THREE —ACCOUNTING FOR MERCHANDISE......................... 49–80
6 Purchases and the Purchases Journal
7 Sales and the Sales Journal
8 Accounting Procedure

UNIT FOUR —ACCOUNTING FOR CASH.................................. 81–116
9 Records of Cash Receipts and Disbursements
10 Banking Procedure
11 The Petty Cash Fund

UNIT FIVE — PAYROLL ACCOUNTING.................................. 117–138
12 Wages and Wage Deductions
13 Payroll Taxes Imposed on the Employer

UNIT SIX — ACCOUNTING FOR A RETAIL STORE........................ 139–184
14 Principles and Procedures
15 Application of Accounting Principles

UNIT SEVEN — THE PERIODIC SUMMARY................................ 185–208
16 End-of-Period Work Sheet
17 The Financial Statements

UNIT EIGHT —ADJUSTING AND CLOSING ACCOUNTS AT END OF ACCOUNTING
PERIOD.. 209–228
18 Adjusting Entries
19 Closing Procedure

UNIT NINE — THE PERSONAL SERVICE ENTERPRISE...................... 229–264
20 Accounting Methods

UNIT TEN — PRACTICAL ACCOUNTING PROBLEMS........................ 265–288

5

PART II

UNIT ELEVEN — ACCOUNTING FOR PROPRIETORSHIP...................... 289–320
    21 The Sole Proprietorship
    22 The Partnership
    23 The Corporation

UNIT TWELVE — ACCOUNTING FOR NOTES AND DRAFTS..................... 321–350
    24 Notes
    25 Drafts and Trade Acceptances

UNIT THIRTEEN — ACCOUNTING FOR PURCHASES............................. 351–376
    26 Purchasing Procedure
    27 Accounting Practice

UNIT FOURTEEN — ACCOUNTING FOR SALES................................... 377–410
    28 Cash Sales and Credit Sales
    29 Installment Sales
    30 Consignment Sales

UNIT FIFTEEN — ACCOUNTING FOR INVENTORY AND PREPAID EXPENSES......... 411–430
    31 Merchandise Inventory
    32 Supplies and Prepayments

UNIT SIXTEEN — ACCOUNTING FOR TANGIBLE FIXED ASSETS................... 431–446
    33 Land, Buildings, and Equipment
    34 Accounting Procedure

UNIT SEVENTEEN — ACCOUNTING FOR A WHOLESALE MERCHANT................. 447–478
    35 Application of Accounting Principles

UNIT EIGHTEEN — ACCOUNTING PROCEDURE AT END OF MONTH................. 479–496
    36 Monthly Adjustment of the Operating Expense Accounts
    37 End-of-Period Work Sheet

UNIT NINETEEN — MONTHLY FINANCIAL STATEMENTS AND PROCEDURE AT END OF
YEAR.. 497–514
    38 The Income Statement
    39 The Balance Sheet
    40 Procedure at End of Year

UNIT TWENTY — PRACTICAL ACCOUNTING PROBLEMS........................ 515–534

PART III

UNIT TWENTY-ONE — THE CORPORATE ORGANIZATION...................... 535–554
    41 Organization and Management
    42 Corporate Records

UNIT TWENTY-TWO — ACCOUNTING FOR CAPITAL STOCK..................... 555–572
    43 Types and Values of Capital Stock
    44 Recording Capital Stock Transactions

UNIT TWENTY-THREE — ACCOUNTING FOR CORPORATION EARNINGS............. 573–586
    45 Earnings Retained in the Business
    46 Earnings Distributed to Stockholders

UNIT TWENTY-FOUR — ACCOUNTING FOR CORPORATION BONDS................ 587–610
    47 Accounting for Bonds Sold and Bond Interest Expense
    48 Accounting for Bonds Retired

UNIT TWENTY-FIVE — ACCOUNTING FOR INTANGIBLE AND WASTING ASSETS...... 611–620
    49 Accounting Procedure

UNIT TWENTY-SIX — THE VOUCHER SYSTEM OF ACCOUNTING................. 621–634
    50 Principles of Voucher Accounting

UNIT TWENTY-SEVEN — ACCOUNTING FOR MANUFACTURERS.................... 635–648
    51 Typical Manufacturing Accounts
    52 The Chart of Accounts and Records of a Manufacturer

UNIT TWENTY-EIGHT — ACCOUNTING FOR MANUFACTURERS (Concluded)........ 649–672
    53 The Work Sheet of a Manufacturer
    54 The Annual Report of a Manufacturer
    55 Closing the Books of a Manufacturer

UNIT TWENTY-NINE — ACCOUNTING FOR BRANCH OPERATIONS................ 673–696
    56 Reciprocal Accounts and Recording Procedure
    57 Work at Close of Fiscal Year
    58 Consolidated Financial Statements

UNIT THIRTY — PRACTICAL ACCOUNTING PROBLEMS..................... 697–716

Unit One

ELEMENTS OF ACCOUNTING

(1) ASSETS, LIABILITIES, AND PROPRIETORSHIP

Importance of Accounting in Business. To attempt to operate a business without keeping records of the transactions and affairs of the enterprise would be comparable to attempting to operate an airplane without a compass and without instruments to show speed, altitude, fuel consumption, oil pressure, and other vital matters. In both cases the absence of indicators of what was happening could be disastrous. The comparison can be carried a step further. Adequate records do not assure successful business operation and adequate instruments do not guarantee a perfect flight and a safe landing, but both the records and the instruments help to accomplish the desired objective in each case.

The individuals who operate or manage a business have the dual objectives of making profit and keeping the enterprise solvent. In attempting to accomplish these two things certain information is necessary. Records are needed concerning such matters as what is bought, what is sold, how much cash or other property is owned, how much is owed to the business, and how much the business owes. At least once a year it is necessary to summarize the results of operations. The total of each type of income and expense must be ascertained and the net income (profit) or net loss computed. Without accounting records this is difficult if not impossible. The amounts of taxes of various sorts — notably income taxes — must be calculated from information supplied by the accounting records. Adequate records are essential in connection with several types of insurance. Data about the past and present are needed in making intelligent plans for the future.

Inasmuch as accounting is so important to the successful conduct of a business enterprise, a knowledge of accounting principles and practices is of value to anyone intending to follow any sort of business career. Accounting is said to be the "language of business." Any individual who intends to engage in any phase of business activity is well advised to learn this language.

9

Accounting vs. Bookkeeping. There is no clear-cut distinction between bookkeeping and accounting; however, bookkeeping is often referred to as the recording branch of accounting. Accounting also involves the summarization and the analysis of the activities of a business enterprise. The person who keeps books of account may be referred to as a bookkeeper. The person who analyzes and interprets accounts as an aid to sound business management may be referred to as an accountant. One person may perform both functions. Some bookkeeping experience is considered essential to success as an accountant. An accountant who offers his services to the public on a fee basis is known as a public accountant. If, after passing an examination, he is certified by the state, he is known as a *certified public accountant* (C.P.A.).

Accounting Elements. If complete records are to be maintained, all transactions and operations that affect the accounting elements should be recorded. The accounting elements consist of *assets*, *liabilities*, and *proprietorship*.

(a) What is owned constitutes assets.

(b) What is owed constitutes liabilities.

(c) Any excess of the amount of assets over the amount of liabilities constitutes proprietorship.

Assets. Anything that is owned which has value to the business is an asset. Property such as money, accounts receivable, notes receivable, merchandise, furniture, fixtures, machinery, buildings, and land are common examples of business assets. *Accounts receivable* are unwritten promises by customers to pay for goods purchased on credit or for services rendered. *Notes receivable* are formal written promises by debtors to pay specified sums in money at some future time.

It is possible to have a business or a professional practice with very few assets. A dentist, for example, may have relatively few assets, such as money, instruments, laboratory equipment, and office equipment. A merchant must have merchandise to sell and store equipment on which to display the merchandise in addition to other assets. A manufacturer must have materials, tools, and machinery in addition to other assets. It will readily be seen that there may be a great variety of assets in varying amounts owned by different businesses.

Liabilities. An obligation of the business to pay a debt of any kind is a business liability. The most common liabilities are accounts payable and notes payable. *Accounts payable* are unwritten promises to pay creditors for property, such as merchandise, supplies, equipment, etc., purchased on credit, or for services rendered. *Notes payable* are formal written promises to pay creditors or lenders specified sums in money at some future time.

Proprietorship. The amount by which the business assets exceed the business liabilities is the proprietorship of the business. The term proprietorship is also known as *net worth* or *capital.* If there are no business liabilities, the proprietorship of the business is equal to the total amount of the business assets.

In visualizing a business that is owned and operated by one person (traditionally called the proprietor) it is essential to realize that a distinction must be made between his business assets and liabilities and any other assets and liabilities that he may have. The proprietor will certainly have various types of personal property, such as clothing; it is probable that he has a home, furniture, and a car. He may own a wide variety of other valuable things that have nothing to do with his business. Likewise the proprietor may owe money for reasons that do not pertain to his business. Amounts owed to merchants from whom food and clothing have been purchased, and amounts owed to doctors and dentists for services received are common examples. Legally there is no distinction between his business and nonbusiness assets nor between his business and nonbusiness liabilities, but since it is to be expected that his formal accounting records for the business will relate to the business only, any nonbusiness assets and liabilities should be excluded.

This distinction between business and nonbusiness assets and liabilities means that the net worth of the business is not necessarily the same thing as the net worth of the proprietor. The difference between the amount of all of his property, including the assets of his business, and the amount of all of his liabilities, including the liabilities of the business, may be very different from the net worth of the business.

Frequent reference will be made to the act of the proprietor in investing money or other property in the business, or the act of withdrawing money or other property from the business. All that is involved in either case is that something is changed from the category of a nonbusiness asset to a business asset or vice versa. It should be apparent that these distinctions are important if the proprietor is to be able to judge the condition and results of the operations of his business apart from his other affairs.

The Accounting Equation. The relationship between the three elements of a business can be expressed in the form of a simple equation:

$$\text{ASSETS} = \text{LIABILITIES} + \text{PROPRIETORSHIP}$$

When the amount of any two of these elements is known, the third can always be calculated. For example, W. C. Taylor has assets in his business on December 31 in the sum of $12,400. His business debts on that date consist of $400 owed for supplies purchased on credit and $500 owed to a bank on a note. The proprietorship element of his business may be calculated by subtraction ($12,400 − $900 ≈ $11,500). These facts about his business can be expressed in equation form as follows:

$$\text{ASSETS } \$12,400 = \text{LIABILITIES } \$900 + \text{PROPRIETORSHIP } \$11,500$$

For Mr. Taylor to increase his proprietary interest in the business, he must increase the assets without increasing the liabilities, or decrease the liabilities without decreasing the assets. To increase his assets and proprietorship without investing more money or other property in the business, he will have to operate his business at a profit. In other words, he will have to operate the business so that the income will exceed the expenses.

If one year later the assets amount to $20,500 and the liabilities $300, the status of the business would be as follows:

$$\text{ASSETS } \$20,500 = \text{LIABILITIES } \$300 + \text{PROPRIETORSHIP } \$20,200$$

The fact that Mr. Taylor's proprietary interest in the business increased by $8,700 (from $11,500 to $20,200) does not prove that he made a profit equal to the increase. He might have invested additional money or other property in the business. Suppose, for example, that he invested additional money during the year in the amount of $3,000. In that event, the remainder of the increase in the proprietorship ($5,700) was due to profit — an excess of income over expenses.

Another possibility is that he had a very profitable year and withdrew assets in an amount less than the amount of profit. For example, his proprietorship might have been increased by $15,000 as a result of profitable operation, and during the year he might have withdrawn a total of $6,300 cash. This series of events could account for the $8,700 increase in proprietorship. It is essential that the business records show the extent to which the change in proprietorship is due to the regular operations of the business and the extent to which increases and decreases in proprietorship are due to the owner's investing and withdrawing assets.

Transactions. The activities of an enterprise are usually referred to as *transactions*. Producing, buying, selling, transporting, and servicing are common transactions. A transaction is an exchange of values. The values are expressed in terms of money. The following typical transactions are analyzed to show that each transaction represents an exchange of values:

TYPICAL TRANSACTIONS	ANALYSIS OF TRANSACTIONS
(a) Purchased equipment for cash, $250.	Money is exchanged for equipment.
(b) Received cash in payment of professional fees, $125.	Professional service is rendered in exchange for money.
(c) Paid office rent, $100.	Money is exchanged for the right to use property.
(d) Paid a debt owed to a creditor, $300.	Money is given in settlement of a debt that may have resulted from the purchase of property on credit or from services rendered by a creditor.
(e) Paid wages in cash, $90.	Money is exchanged for services rendered.
(f) Borrowed $1,000 at the bank giving a 6 per cent interest-bearing note due in 30 days.	A liability known as a note payable is incurred in exchange for money.
(g) Purchased merchandise for cash, $400.	Money is paid in exchange for merchandise.
(h) Purchased merchandise on credit, $200.	A liability known as an account payable is incurred in exchange for merchandise.
(i) Sold merchandise for cash, $140.	Money is received in exchange for merchandise.
(j) Sold merchandise on credit, $185.	Merchandise is exchanged for an asset known as an account receivable.

Effect of Transactions on the Accounting Equation. Each transaction affects one or more of the three elements of the accounting equation. For example, the purchase of a truck for cash represents both an increase and a decrease in assets. The assets are increased because a truck is acquired; the assets are decreased because cash is disbursed. If the truck were purchased on credit, thereby incurring a liability, the transaction would result in an increase in assets (truck) with a corresponding increase in liabilities (accounts payable). Neither of these transactions has any effect upon the proprietorship element of the equation.

The effect of any transaction on the accounting elements may be indicated by addition and subtraction. Assume that on January 1 the status of an enterprise is indicated by the following equation:

ASSETS $19,400 = LIABILITIES $1,900 + PROPRIETORSHIP $17,500

The effect of the following transactions completed during January is shown at the right:

	A $19,400 = L $1,900 + P $17,500
(a) Purchased a truck for $3,000 cash.	
An asset (truck) is increased $3,000:	+ 3,000
An asset (cash) is decreased $3,000:	− 3,000

	Totals	$19,400 =	$1,900 +	$17,500

(b) Purchased office equipment on credit, $1,800.
    An asset (office equipment) is increased $1,800:   + 1,800
    A liability (account payable) is increased $1,800:   + 1,800

	Totals	$21,200 =	$3,700 +	$17,500

(c) Paid $900 to apply on office equipment previously
    purchased on credit.
    An asset (cash) is decreased $900:   − 900
    A liability (account payable) is decreased $900:   − 900

	Totals	$20,300 =	$2,800 +	$17,500

(d) Proprietor withdrew $200 in cash for personal use.
    An asset (cash) is decreased $200:   − 200
    Proprietorship is decreased $200:   −200

	January 31	A $20,100 =	L $2,800 +	P $17,300

After giving effect to the foregoing transactions, the status of the enterprise on January 31 was indicated by the following equation:

ASSETS $20,100 = LIABILITIES $2,800 + PROPRIETORSHIP $17,300

While each transaction affected one or more elements of the equation, the equality of the elements was not disturbed. Changes that take place in the amount of the accounting elements never affect the equality of the elements. As a result of the transactions completed during January, there was an increase of $700 in the total assets, an increase of $900 in the total liabilities, and a decrease of $200 in proprietorship. Despite these changes in the elements their equality was not affected. It is a basic principle of accounting that the total amount of the assets at all times is equal to the sum of the liabilities and the proprietorship.

PRACTICE ASSIGNMENT No. 1. A workbook is provided for use with this textbook. Each practice assignment in the workbook is referred to as a report. The work involved in completing Report No. 1 requires a knowledge of the principles developed in the preceding study assignment. Before proceeding with the following study assignment, complete Report No. 1 in accordance with the instructions given in the workbook.

(2) THE DOUBLE-ENTRY PROCESS

Under the private enterprise system the profit motive is the principal reason individuals engage in business. Money or other property is invested in a business enterprise and transactions are completed with the expectation that a profit will be realized and thus the proprietorship will be increased. Since transactions involve exchanges of values, it is necessary to keep a record of all transactions completed so that the proprietor may ascertain at any time the amount of his assets, the amount of his liabilities, and the net worth or proprietorship of the business.

It is the primary function of accounting to provide a record of the changes in assets, liabilities, and proprietorship which result from transactions. Each transaction must be analyzed to determine what changes occur. The only effect a transaction can have is either to increase or to decrease the amount of the property owned, the debts owed, or the proprietorship. Reference to the transactions analyzed on page 14 will show that in every case a change in any asset was accompanied by a corresponding change either in some other asset, or in some liability, or in proprietorship.

Under the double-entry system of bookkeeping equality of the accounting elements is always maintained. In other words, the total amount of the assets is always equal to the sum of the liabilities and the proprietorship. The double-entry system provides a means of proof. If a transaction is recorded in such manner that the equality of the accounting elements is disturbed, it will be evident that the transaction has been incorrectly recorded. For example, if in recording a transaction the change in one of the elements is properly recorded but the offsetting change in another element is not recorded, the equality of the elements would be disturbed and thus it would be known that an error was made in recording the transaction. In recording any transaction, if an error is made in recording the amount of the change in one of the elements, the equality of the elements will be affected. This will indicate that the records should be checked to discover and correct the discrepancy.

The Account. It has been explained previously that the assets of a business may consist of a number of items, such as money, accounts receivable, notes receivable, merchandise, equipment, buildings, and land. The liabilities may consist of one or more items, such as accounts payable and notes payable. A separate record should be kept of each asset and of each liability. Later it will be shown that a separate record should also be kept of the increases and decreases in proprietorship. The form of record kept for each item is known as an *account*. There are many types of account forms in general use. They may be ruled on sheets of paper and bound in book form or kept in a loose-leaf binder, or they may be ruled on cards and kept in a file of some sort. Following is an illustration of a standard form of account ruling that is widely used:

ACCOUNT

DATE	ITEMS	FOL.	√	DEBITS	DATE	ITEMS	FOL.	√	CREDITS

Standard Account Form

This account form is designed to facilitate the recording of the essential information regarding each transaction. Before recording any transactions in an account, the title of the account should be written on the horizontal line at the top of the form. Each account should be given an appropriate title that will indicate whether it is an asset, a liability, or a proprietorship account. The standard account form is divided into two equal parts or sections which are ruled identically to facilitate recording increases and decreases. The left side is called the debit side, while the right side is called the credit side. The columnar arrangement and headings of the columns on both sides are the same. The Date columns are used for recording the dates of transactions. The Items columns may be used for writing a brief description of a transaction when deemed necessary. The Folio columns and the (√) columns will be discussed later. The columns headed Debits and Credits are used for recording the amounts of transactions.

The three major parts of the standard account form are (1) the title, (2) the debit side, and (3) the credit side. To be able to ascertain the amount of an account at any time, it is only necessary to record the effect of each transaction on the account by entering increases on one side and decreases on the other side. To save time, a "T" form of account is commonly used for instructional purposes. It consists of a two-line drawing resembling the capital letter T and is sometimes referred to as a skeleton form of account.

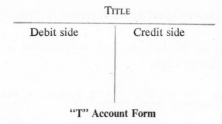

"T" Account Form

Debits and Credits. To debit an account means to record an amount on the left or debit side of the account. To credit an account means to record an amount on the right or credit side of the account. The abbreviation for debit is Dr. and for credit Cr. Sometimes the word *charge* is used as a substitute for debit. Increases in assets are recorded on the left side of the accounts; increases in liabilities or in proprietorship are recorded on the right side of the accounts. Decreases in assets are recorded on the right side of the accounts; decreases in liabilities or in proprietorship are recorded on the left side of the accounts. Recording increases and decreases in the accounts in this manner will reflect the basic equality of assets to liabilities plus proprietorship; at the same time it will maintain equality between the total amounts debited to all accounts and the total amounts credited to all accounts. These basic relationships may be illustrated in the following manner:

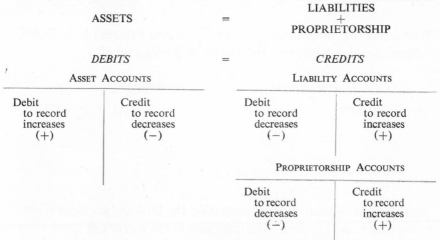

To illustrate the application of the double-entry process, a few transactions will be analyzed and their effect on the accounting elements will be indicated by showing the proper entries in "T" accounts. Certain types of transactions have been selected for this illustration and the transactions are identified by letters; dates are omitted intentionally.

An Increase in an Asset Offset by an Increase in Proprietorship.

Transaction (a). E. S. Walker, an architect, started a business of his own and invested $2,000 in cash.

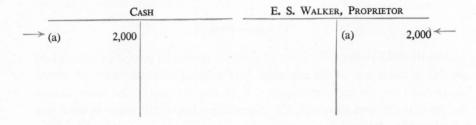

	CASH			E. S. WALKER, PROPRIETOR	
(a)	2,000			(a)	2,000

Analysis: As a result of this transaction the business acquired an asset, Cash. The amount of money invested by Mr. Walker represents his proprietorship in the business, thus the amount of the asset Cash is equal to the proprietorship of the business. Separate accounts are kept for the asset Cash and for the proprietor. To record the transaction properly, the cash account was debited and E. S. Walker's proprietorship account was credited for $2,000.

An Increase in an Asset Offset by an Increase in a Liability.

Transaction (b). Purchased office furniture and fixtures (desk, chairs, file cabinet, drawing table, etc.) for $1,800 on 30 days' credit.

	FURNITURE AND FIXTURES			ACCOUNTS PAYABLE	
(b)	1,800			(b)	1,800

Analysis: As a result of this transaction the business acquired a new asset, Furniture and Fixtures. The debt incurred as a result of purchasing the furniture and fixtures on 30 days' credit represents a liability, Accounts Payable. Separate accounts are kept for furniture and fixtures and for accounts payable. The purchase of furniture and fixtures represents an increase in the assets of the business. Therefore, the asset Furniture and Fixtures was debited and the liability Accounts Payable was credited for $1,800.

An Increase in one Asset Offset by a Decrease in Another Asset.

Transaction (c). Purchased office and drawing supplies (drawing paper, stationery, carbon paper, pencils, etc.) for cash, $250.

OFFICE SUPPLIES		CASH	
→(c)　　　250		(a)　　　2,000	(c)　　　250 ←

Analysis: As a result of this transaction the business acquired a new asset, Office Supplies. However, the cost of this asset is offset by a decrease in the asset Cash. To record the transaction properly, Office Supplies was debited and Cash was credited for $250. (It will be noted that this is the second entry in the cash account; the account was previously debited for $2,000 when Transaction (a) was recorded.)

It is proper to record office supplies as an asset at time of purchase even though they will become an expense when consumed. The procedure in accounting for supplies consumed will be discussed later.

A Decrease in a Liability Offset by a Decrease in an Asset.

Transaction (d). Paid $500 "on account" to the company from whom the office furniture and fixtures were purchased. (See Transaction (b).)

ACCOUNTS PAYABLE		CASH	
→(d)　　500	(b)　　1,800	(a)　　2,000	(c)　　　250 (d)　　　500 ←

Analysis: This transaction resulted in a decrease in the liability Accounts Payable with a corresponding decrease in the asset Cash; hence, it was recorded by debiting Accounts Payable and by crediting Cash for $500. (It will be noted that this is the second entry in the accounts payable account and the third entry in the cash account.)

Income and Expense. The proprietorship element of a business or professional enterprise may be increased in two ways as follows:

(1) The proprietor may invest additional money or other property in the enterprise. Such investments result in an increase in both the assets of the enterprise and the proprietorship, but they do not enrich the proprietor; he merely has more property invested in the enterprise and less property outside of the enterprise.

(2) Income may be derived from sales of goods or services or from other sources.

In most cases business or professional income is the increase in the assets and proprietorship that results from transactions with its customers, clients, or patients. When a lawyer receives money in payment of his legal services, the assets of his legal enterprise are increased with an equal increase in his proprietorship. The reason for the increase in proprietorship is the income derived from services rendered. It is important to realize that the specific thing received — often cash — is not income; the word income does not denote an asset. Instead, it refers to the reason the proprietorship is increased. *Income arises when a transaction causes the proprietorship of a business to be increased apart from an increase due to an investment of assets in the business by the proprietor.*

The proprietorship element of a business or professional enterprise may be decreased in two ways as follows:

(1) The proprietor may withdraw assets (cash or other property) from the enterprise.

(2) Expenses may be incurred in operating the enterprise.

Common examples of expenses are rent for office or store, salaries of employees, telephone service, supplies consumed, and taxes. When an expense is incurred either the assets are reduced or the liabilities are increased. In either event there is a corresponding decrease in proprietorship. *Expense is incurred when a transaction causes the proprietorship of a business to be reduced apart from a reduction due to a withdrawal of assets from the business by the proprietor.*

If, during a specified period of time, the total increases in proprietorship resulting from income exceed the total decreases resulting from expenses, it may be said that the excess represents the *net income* or net profit for the period. On the other hand, if the expenses of the period exceed the income, the excess represents a *net loss* for the period. The time interval used in the measurement of net income or net loss can be chosen by the proprietor. It may be a month, a quarter (three months), a year, or some other period of time. If the accounting period is a year, it is usually referred to as a *fiscal year*. The fiscal year frequently coincides with the *calendar year* ending on December 31.

Transactions involving income and expense always cause a change in the proprietorship element of an enterprise. Such changes could be recorded directly in the proprietor's account by debiting it for expenses and crediting it for income. If this practice were followed, however, the credit side of the proprietor's account would contain a mixture of increases due to investments of assets in the business by the proprietor and income, while the debit side would contain a mixture of decreases due to withdrawals of assets from the business by the proprietor and expenses. In order to calculate the net income or the net loss for each accounting period a careful analysis of the proprietor's account would be required. It is, therefore, better practice to record income and expenses in separate accounts. These are called temporary proprietorship accounts because it is customary to close them at the end of each accounting period by transferring their balances to a summary account. The balance of this summary account then represents the net income or net loss for the period. The summary account is also a temporary account which is closed by transferring its balance to the proprietor's account.

A separate account should be kept for each type of income and for each type of expense. When a transaction produces income the amount of the income should be credited to an appropriate income account. When a transaction involves expense the amount of the expense should be debited to an appropriate expense account. The relationship of these temporary accounts to the proprietor's account and the application of the debit and credit theory to the accounts are indicated in the following diagram:

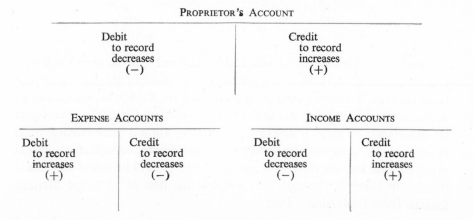

PROPRIETOR'S ACCOUNT

Debit to record decreases (−)	Credit to record increases (+)

EXPENSE ACCOUNTS

Debit to record increases (+)	Credit to record decreases (−)

INCOME ACCOUNTS

Debit to record decreases (−)	Credit to record increases (+)

It is important to recognize that the credit side of any income account is serving temporarily as a part of the credit side of the proprietor's account. Increases in proprietorship are recorded as credits. Thus, increases in proprietorship resulting from income should be credited to income accounts. The debit side of any expense account is serving temporarily as a part of the debit side of the proprietor's account. Decreases in proprietorship are recorded as debits. Thus, decreases in proprietorship resulting from increases in expenses should be debited to expense accounts.

To illustrate the application of the double-entry process in recording transactions that affect income and expense accounts, a few additional transactions completed by E. S. Walker, an architect, will be analyzed and their effect on the accounting elements will be indicated by showing the proper entries in "T" accounts. These transactions represent a continuation of the transactions completed by E. S. Walker in the conduct of his business. (See pages 18 and 19 for Transactions (a) to (d).)

An Increase in an Asset with a Corresponding Increase in Proprietorship Resulting from Income.

Transaction (e). Received $500 in cash from a client for professional services rendered.

CASH				INCOME FROM PROFESSIONAL FEES	
(a)	2,000	(c)	250		
→ (e)	500	(d)	500	(e)	500 ←

Analysis: This transaction resulted in an increase in the asset Cash with a corresponding increase in proprietorship because of income from professional fees. To record the transaction properly, Cash was debited and an appropriate account for the income was credited for $500. Accounts should always be given a descriptive title that will aid in classifying them in relation to the accounting elements. In this case the income account was given the title Income from Professional Fees. (It will be noted that this is the fourth entry in the cash account and the first entry in the account Income from Professional Fees.)

A Decrease in an Asset with a Corresponding Decrease in Proprietorship Resulting from Expense.

Transaction (f). Paid $100 for office rent for one month.

RENT EXPENSE			CASH		
(f)	100	(a)	2,000	(c)	250
		(e)	500	(d)	500
				(f)	100

Analysis: This transaction resulted in a decrease in the asset Cash with a corresponding decrease in proprietorship because of expense. To record the transaction properly, Rent Expense was debited and Cash was credited for $100. (This is the first entry in the rent expense account and the fifth entry in the cash account.)

Transaction (g). Paid bill for telephone service, $17.

TELEPHONE EXPENSE			CASH		
(g)	17	(a)	2,000	(c)	250
		(e)	500	(d)	500
				(f)	100
				(g)	17

Analysis: This transaction is identical with the previous one except that telephone expense rather than rent expense was the reason for the decrease in proprietorship. To record the transaction properly, Telephone Expense was debited and Cash was credited for $17.

The Trial Balance. It is a fundamental principle of double-entry bookkeeping that the amount of the assets is always equal to the sum of the liabilities and proprietorship. In order to maintain this equality in recording transactions the sum of the debit entries must always be equal to the sum of the credit entries. To ascertain if this equality has been maintained, it is customary to take a trial balance periodically. A *trial balance* is a list of all of the accounts showing the title and balance of each account. The balance of any account is the difference between the total debits and the total credits to the account. Preliminary to taking a trial balance the debit and credit amounts in each account should be totaled. This is called *footing* the amount columns. If there is only one item entered in a column, no footing is necessary. To find the balance of an account it is only necessary to ascertain the difference between the footings by subtraction. Since asset and expense accounts are debited for increases these accounts normally have *debit balances*. Since liability, proprietorship, and income accounts are credited to record increases, these accounts normally have *credit balances*. The balance of an account should be entered on the side of the account that has the larger total. The footings and balances of accounts should be written in small figures just below the last entry. A lead pencil is generally used for this purpose. If the footings of an account are equal in amount, the account is said to be *in balance*.

The accounts of E. S. Walker are reproduced on the opposite page. To show the relationship to the fundamental accounting equation the accounts are arranged in three columns under the headings of assets, liabilities, and proprietorship. It will be noted that the cash account has been footed and the balance inserted on the left side. The footings and the balance are printed in italics. It was not necessary to foot any of the other accounts because none of them contained more than one entry on either side. The balance of the accounts payable account is shown on the credit side in italics. It was not necessary to enter the balances of the other accounts because there were entries on only one side of the accounts. A trial balance of these accounts is shown at the bottom of the page. It is not dated because only selected transactions are used in the illustration. Dollar signs are not used when amounts are written in ruled amount columns. The trial balance reveals that the debit and credit totals are equal in amount. This is proof that in recording Transactions (a) to (g) inclusive the total of the debit entries was equal to the total of the credit entries.

Further proof may be obtained by ascertaining that the total assets were equal to the sum of the liabilities and proprietorship at the close of the period. The assets consist of Cash $1,633, Office Supplies $250, and Furniture and Fixtures $1,800, which total $3,683. The only liability account is Accounts Payable amounting to $1,300. The credit balance of the proprietor's account amounts to $2,000. This represents the amount of Mr. Walker's investment in the business at the beginning of the period. To this amount should be added any excess of the income for the period over the expenses for the period. The income from professional fees amounted to $500, while the expenses amounted to a total of $117 (Rent Expense $100 + Telephone Expense $17). Since the income amounted to $500 and the total expenses amounted to $117, the net income for the period was $383. Thus,

ASSETS				LIABILITIES		PROPRIETORSHIP	

ASSETS

CASH

(a)	2,000	(c)	250
(e)	500	(d)	500
1,633	*2,500*	(f)	100
		(g)	17
			867

OFFICE SUPPLIES

(c)	250

FURNITURE AND FIXTURES

(b)	1,800

LIABILITIES

ACCOUNTS PAYABLE

(d)	500	(b)	1,800
			1,300

PROPRIETORSHIP

E. S. WALKER, PROPRIETOR

(a)	2,000

INCOME FROM PROFESSIONAL FEES

(e)	500

RENT EXPENSE

(f)	100

TELEPHONE EXPENSE

(g)	17

E. S. WALKER, ARCHITECT
TRIAL BALANCE

ACCOUNTS	DR. BALANCES		CR. BALANCES	
Cash...............................	1,633	00		
Office Supplies......................	250	00		
Furniture and Fixtures................	1,800	00		
Accounts Payable....................			1,300	00
E. S. Walker, Proprietor..............			2,000	00
Income from Professional Fees.........			500	00
Rent Expense.......................	100	00		
Telephone Expense...................	17	00		
	3,800	00	3,800	00

Mr. Walker's proprietorship was increased to $2,383 at the end of the period. His total assets, liabilities, and proprietorship may now be shown in equation form as follows:

$$\text{ASSETS } \$3,683 = \text{LIABILITIES } \$1,300 + \text{PROPRIETORSHIP } \$2,383$$

PRACTICE ASSIGNMENT No. 2. Refer to the workbook and complete Report No. 2 in accordance with the instructions given therein. The work involved in completing the assignment requires a knowledge of the principles developed in the preceding discussion. Any difficulty experienced in completing the practice assignment will indicate a lack of understanding of these principles. In such event further study should be helpful. After completing the report, you may continue with the textbook discussion in Unit Two until the next report is required.

ACCOUNTING PROCEDURE

(3) JOURNALIZING TRANSACTIONS

Original Records of Transactions. While explaining and illustrating the basic principles of double-entry bookkeeping, the mechanics of collecting and sorting information about business transactions was temporarily ignored. In actual practice the first record of a transaction is made in the form of a business paper, such as a bank check stub, receipt, cash register tape, sales ticket, or a purchase invoice. The information supplied by business papers is an aid in analyzing transactions to determine their effect upon the accounts.

The first formal double-entry record of a transaction is usually made in a *journal*. This procedure is called *journalizing*. It is necessary to analyze each transaction before it can be journalized properly. The purpose of the journal entries is to provide a chronological record of all transactions completed showing the date of each transaction, titles of accounts to be debited and credited, and amounts of the debits and credits. The journal then provides all the information needed in transferring the debits and credits to the proper accounts. The flow of data concerning transactions can be illustrated in the following manner:

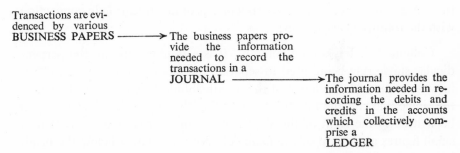

Transactions are evidenced by various BUSINESS PAPERS ——→ The business papers provide the information needed to record the transactions in a JOURNAL ——————→ The journal provides the information needed in recording the debits and credits in the accounts which collectively comprise a LEDGER

Business Papers. The term business papers covers a wide variety of forms and documents. Almost any document that provides information about a business transaction can be called a business paper.

BUSINESS PAPERS

Examples:	Provide Information about:
(a) Check stubs or duplicate copies of checks	Cash disbursements.
(b) Receipt stubs, or duplicate copies of receipts, cash register tapes, or memos of cash register totals	Cash receipts.
(c) Copies of sales tickets or sales invoices issued to customers	Sales of goods or services.
(d) Purchase invoices received from vendors	Purchases of goods or services.

The Journal. While the original record of a transaction usually is a business paper as explained above, the first formal double-entry record of a transaction is made in a journal. For this reason a journal is commonly referred to as a *book of original entry*. A journal may be either a bound book or a loose-leaf book. The ruling of a journal varies with the type and size of a business and the nature of its operations. The simplest form of journal is a two-column journal. A standard form of such a journal is illustrated on the opposite page. It is referred to as a two-column journal because it has only two amount columns. The journal is ruled to facilitate the recording of certain fundamental facts, such as the following:

(a) The date of each transaction.

(b) The titles of the accounts affected by each transaction.

(c) The amount of each transaction.

(d) A description of each transaction.

The ruling of a journal should not only facilitate the recording of transactions in chronological order but it should also provide for recording the effect of each transaction on the accounting elements. In the illustration the columns have been numbered as a means of identification in connection with the following discussion:

Column No. 1 is a date column. It is a double column, the perpendicular single rule being used to separate the month from the day. Thus in writing June 20, the name of the month should be written to the left of the single line and the number representing the day of the month should be written to the right of the single line. The year should be written in small figures at the top of the Date column immediately below the heading and should be repeated at the top of each page and whenever there is a change in the year.

Column No. 2 is generally referred to as a description or an explanation column. It is used to record the titles of the accounts affected by

JOURNAL

DATE	DESCRIPTION	POST. REF.	DEBITS	CREDITS
①	②	③	④	⑤

Standard Two-Column Journal

each transaction, together with a description of the transaction. Two or more accounts are affected by each transaction, and the titles of all accounts affected must be recorded. One line should be used to record the title of each account affected regardless of whether the account is to be debited or credited. The titles of the accounts to be debited are generally written to the extreme left of the column, while the titles of the accounts to be credited are usually indented about one half inch. The description should be written immediately following the debit and credit entries. The description is usually indented about one inch. Reference to the journal reproduced on pages 34 and 35 will help to visualize the arrangement of the copy in the Description column. An orderly arrangement is desirable.

Column No. 3 is a posting reference column — sometimes referred to as a folio column. No entries are made in this column at the time of journalizing the transactions; such entries are made only at the time of posting or transferring the debits and credits to the proper accounts in the ledger. This procedure will be explained in detail later.

Column No. 4 is an amount column in which the amount that is to be debited to any account should be written on the line on which the title of the account appears. In other words, the name of the account to be debited should be written in the Description column and the amount of the debit entry should be written in the left amount column.

Column No. 5 is an amount column in which the amount that is to be credited to any account should be written on the line on which the title of the account appears. In other words, the name of the account to be credited should be written in the Description column and the amount of the credit entry should be written in the right amount column.

Journalizing. Journalizing involves recording the desired information concerning each transaction either (a) at the time the transaction occurs or (b) subsequently, but in the order in which the transactions occur, that is to say, chronologically. In every entry it is essential to record the date of each transaction, the titles of the accounts affected by each transaction, the amount of each transaction, and a brief description of each transaction. Furthermore, the effect of each transaction upon the accounts should be indicated. The only effect a transaction can have on any account is either to increase or to decrease the amount of the account. Before a transaction can be recorded properly, therefore, it must be analyzed in order to determine the following information:

(a) What accounts are affected by the transaction.

(b) What effect the transaction has upon each of the accounts.

(c) How the effect upon the accounts may be recorded.

When it is known what accounts are being kept and when the effect upon the accounts has been determined by analysis, recording a transaction is a relatively simple matter.

The Chart of Accounts. In establishing an accounting system for a new business, the first step is to decide what accounts should be kept. The accounts to be kept depend upon the information needed or desired. Ordinarily it will be found desirable to keep a separate account with each type of asset and each type of liability. Obviously, information will be desired in regard to what is owned and what is owed. A permanent proprietorship or capital account should be kept in order that information may be available as to the proprietor's investment in the business. Furthermore, it is advisable to keep separate accounts with each type of income and each kind of expense. These are the temporary accounts that are used in recording increases and decreases in proprietorship. The specific accounts to be kept in recording the increases and the decreases in proprietorship depend upon the nature and the sources of the income and of the expenses incurred in earning the income.

A professional man or an individual engaged in operating a small business may need to keep relatively few accounts to record the information that he needs or in which he is interested. On the other hand, a large manufacturing enterprise, a public utility, or any large business may need to keep a great many accounts in order that the information required or desired may be available. Regardless of the number of accounts kept, they can be segregated into the three general classes, and they should be grouped according to these classes in the ledger. The usual custom is to arrange the asset accounts first, the liability accounts second, and the proprietorship accounts, including the income and the expense accounts, last. This procedure, however, is not uniform and some variation may be expected in actual practice.

Starting December 1, J. D. Knight engages in the advertising business under the name of The Knight Advertising Agency. He decides to keep his accounts on the calendar year basis, therefore, his first accounting period will be for one month only, that is, the month of December. He employs a combination secretary-bookkeeper and it is decided that a two-column journal and a ledger with standard account ruling will be used. He realizes that he is starting a small business and that he will have need for relatively few accounts. He also realizes that additional accounts may be added as the need arises. Following is a chart of the accounts to be kept at the start:

THE KNIGHT ADVERTISING AGENCY

CHART OF ACCOUNTS

Assets*
　Cash
　Office Supplies
　Office Equipment

Liabilities
　Accounts Payable

Proprietorship
　J. D. Knight, Proprietor
　J. D. Knight, Drawing

Income
　Income from Advertising Fees

Expenses
　Rent Expense
　Salary Expense
　Traveling Expense
　Telephone Expense
　Office Supplies Used
　Miscellaneous Expenses

*Headings are set in italics to distinguish from account titles.

Journalizing Procedure Illustrated. To illustrate journalizing procedure the transactions completed by The Knight Advertising Agency during the month of December will be journalized. A *narrative* of the transactions completed during the month follows. It provides all of the information that is needed in journalizing the transactions. However, some of the transactions are analyzed to explain their effect upon the accounts. The journal of The Knight Advertising Agency is reproduced on pages 34 and 35.

THE KNIGHT ADVERTISING AGENCY

NARRATIVE OF TRANSACTIONS

Tuesday, December 1

Mr. Knight invested $2,500 cash in a business enterprise to be known as The Knight Advertising Agency.

> As a result of this transaction the business acquired an asset, Cash. The amount invested by Mr. Knight represents his capital or his proprietorship in the business. Therefore, the transaction was recorded in the journal by debiting Cash and by crediting J. D. Knight, Proprietor for $2,500. Reference to the first entry in the journal reproduced on page 34 will reveal that the transaction was journalized by recording the date, the titles of the accounts affected, the amounts of the debits and credits, and an explanation of the transaction. The posting references "1" and "5" were not entered at the time of journalizing the transaction but were entered later when the posting was completed.

Paid office rent for December in advance, $100.

> This transaction resulted in a decrease in proprietorship because of expense with a corresponding decrease in the asset Cash. It was recorded in the journal by debiting Rent Expense and by crediting Cash for $100. Reference to the second entry in the journal will reveal that the procedure in recording this transaction was similar to the procedure involved in recording the first transaction. In journalizing any transaction, the date, the titles of the accounts affected, the amounts of the debits and credits, and an explanation of the transaction should be entered.

(Note: Mr. Knight ordered several pieces of office furniture. Since the dealer did not have what Mr. Knight wanted in stock, the articles were ordered from the factory. Delivery is not expected until the latter part of the month; hence, the dealer loaned Mr. Knight some used office furniture for temporary use. No entry is required until the new furniture is received.)

Wednesday, December 2

Purchased office supplies from the A and B Supply Co. on credit, $117.63.

> As a result of this transaction the business acquired a new asset which represents an increase in the total assets. A liability was also incurred because of the purchase on credit. The transaction was recorded by debiting Office Supplies and by crediting Accounts Payable for $117.63. As these supplies are consumed in the course of time they will become an expense of the business, but this may take several months.

Thursday, December 3

Paid the City Telephone Co. $17.50 covering the cost of installing a telephone in the office, together with the first month's service charges payable in advance.

> This expenditure represents a decrease in proprietorship because of expense and a corresponding decrease in the asset Cash. It was recorded in the journal by debiting Telephone Expense and by crediting Cash for $17.50.

Friday, December 4

Paid $5 for a subscription to a trade magazine.

This transaction resulted in a decrease in proprietorship due to expense and a corresponding decrease in the asset Cash. It was recorded in the journal by debiting Miscellaneous Expenses and by crediting Cash for $5.

Monday, December 7

Received $75 from the City Restaurant for services rendered.

This transaction resulted in an increase in the asset Cash with a corresponding increase in proprietorship because of income from advertising fees. It was recorded by debiting Cash and by crediting Income from Advertising Fees for $75. In keeping his accounts Mr. Knight follows the practice of not recording income until it is received in cash. This practice is common to professional and personal service enterprises.

Friday, December 11

Paid $111.71 for traveling expenses incurred in connection with a business trip out of town.

Tuesday, December 15

Paid Virginia Conrad $112.50 covering her salary for the first half of the month.

Miss Conrad is employed by Mr. Knight as his secretary and bookkeeper at a salary of $225 a month. The transaction resulted in a decrease in proprietorship because of salary expense with a corresponding decrease in the asset Cash, hence it was recorded by debiting Salary Expense and by crediting Cash for $112.50. (The matter of payroll taxes is purposely ignored temporarily; this will be discussed in detail in Unit Five.)

Thursday, December 17

Received $265 from The Matthews Manufacturing Co. in payment for services rendered.

Monday, December 21

Mr. Knight withdrew $150 for personal use.

Amounts withdrawn for personal use by the proprietor of a business enterprise represent a decrease in proprietorship and a corresponding decrease in cash. While amounts withdrawn might be recorded as debits to the proprietor's capital account, it is better practice to record withdrawals in a separate account for the reason that such withdrawals are usually made in anticipation of profits. This transaction was recorded in the journal by debiting J. D. Knight, Drawing, and by crediting Cash.

Tuesday, December 22

Received $340 from Wyatt Coal Sales Co. for services rendered.

(*Continued on page 36*)

The Knight Advertising Agency   Page 1

DATE	DESCRIPTION	POST. REF.	DEBITS	CREDITS
'19 Dec. 1	Cash	1	2 5 0 0 0 0	
	J. D. Knight, Proprietor	5		2 5 0 0 0 0
	Original investment			
	in advertising agency.			
1	Rent Expense	8	1 0 0 0 0	
	Cash	1		1 0 0 0 0
	Paid December rent.			
2	Office Supplies	2	1 1 7 6 3	
	Accounts Payable	4		1 1 7 6 3
	A and B Supply Co.			
3	Telephone Expense	11	1 7 5 0	
	Cash	1		1 7 5 0
	Paid telephone bill.			
4	Miscellaneous Expenses	13	5 0 0	
	Cash	1		5 0 0
	Magazine subscription.			
7	Cash	1	7 5 0 0	
	Income from Advertising Fees	7		7 5 0 0
	City Restaurant.			
11	Traveling Expense	10	1 1 1 7 1	
	Cash	1		1 1 1 7 1
	Business trip.			
15	Salary Expense	9	1 1 2 5 0	
	Cash	1		1 1 2 5 0
	Paid secretary's salary.			
17	Cash	1	2 6 5 0 0	
	Income from Advertising Fees	7		2 6 5 0 0
	The Matthews Mfg. Co.			
21	J. D. Knight, Drawing	6	1 5 0 0 0	
	Cash	1		1 5 0 0 0
	Withdrawn for			
	personal use.			
22	Cash	1	3 4 0 0 0	
	Income from Advertising Fees	7		3 4 0 0 0
	Wyatt Coal Sales Co			
23	Miscellaneous Expenses	13	2 5 0 0	
	Cash	1		2 5 0 0
	N. A. A. dues.			
			3 8 1 9 3 4	3 8 1 9 3 4

Model Journal

Page 2

DATE	DESCRIPTION	POST REF	DEBITS	CREDITS
Dec 28	Office Equipment	3	1 6 8 0 1 9	
	Accounts Payable	4		1 6 8 0 1 9
	City Office Furniture Co			
29	Accounts Payable	4	1 1 7 6 3	
	Cash	1		1 1 7 6 3
	Paid A and B Supply Co.			
30	Cash	1	1 1 0 0 0	
	Income from Advertising Fees	7		1 1 0 0 0
	Roscoe Chandler.			
31	Salary Expense	9	1 1 2 5 0	
	Cash	1		1 1 2 5 0
	Paid secretary's salary			
31	Office Supplies Used	12	1 5 0 0	
	Office Supplies	2		1 5 0 0
	Cost of supplies used			
	during December.		≈≈≈≈≈≈	≈≈≈≈≈≈

Model Journal

Wednesday, December 23

Paid $25 for membership dues in the National Association of Advertisers.

Monday, December 28

Received the office furniture ordered December 1. These items were purchased on account from the City Office Furniture Co. Cost: $1,680.19. (The dealer removed the used furniture that had been loaned to Mr. Knight.)

Tuesday, December 29

Paid the A and B Supply Co. $117.63 for the office supplies purchased on December 2.

> This transaction resulted in a decrease in the liability Accounts Payable with a corresponding decrease in the asset Cash, hence it was recorded by debiting Accounts Payable and by crediting Cash for $117.63.

Wednesday, December 30

Received $110 from Roscoe Chandler for services rendered.

Thursday, December 31

Paid Virginia Conrad $112.50 in payment of her salary for the second half of the month.

Office supplies used during the month, $15.

> By referring to the transaction of December 2 it will be noted that office supplies amounting to $117.63 were purchased and were recorded as an asset. By taking an inventory or counting the supplies in stock at the end of the month, Mr. Knight was able to determine that the cost of supplies used during the month amounted to $15. The expenses for the month of December would not be reflected properly in the accounts if the cost of supplies used during the month were not taken into consideration. Therefore, the supplies used were recorded by debiting the expense account, Office Supplies Used, and by crediting the asset account, Office Supplies, for $15.

Proving the Journal. One of the distinctive features of double-entry bookkeeping is that it provides a means of proof. Because a double entry is made for each transaction that is journalized, the equality of debit and credit entries on each page of the journal may be proved merely by totaling the amount columns. The entries made to record the transactions for each day, week, month, or other period may be proved in similar manner. The debits and the credits must always be equal in amount, and proof of equality may be ascertained at any time merely by totaling the amount columns. The total of each column is usually entered in small figures in pencil immediately under the last entry. These pencil totals are commonly called footings. When a page of the journal is filled the footings may be entered just under the last single horizontal ruled line at the bottom of the page as shown in the illustration on page 34. When the page is not filled the footings should be entered immediately under the last entry as shown in the illustration on page 35.

> **PRACTICE ASSIGNMENT No. 3.** *Refer to the workbook and complete Report No. 3. To complete this practice assignment correctly, the principles developed in the preceding discussion must be understood. Review the text assignment if necessary. After completing the report, continue with the following study assignment until the next report is required.*

(4) POSTING AND THE TRIAL BALANCE

The Ledger. A group of accounts constitutes a *ledger*. The account forms may be ruled on sheets of paper or on cards. When ruled on sheets of paper the sheets may be bound in book form or they may be kept in a loose-leaf binder. Usually a separate page is used for each account. The accounts should be classified properly in the ledger, that is, the asset accounts should be grouped together, the liability accounts together, and the proprietorship accounts together. A proper grouping of the accounts in the ledger is an aid in preparing the various reports desired by the proprietor. Mr. Knight decided to keep all of the accounts for The Knight Advertising Agency in a loose-leaf ledger. The chart of accounts was used as a guide in arranging the accounts in the ledger.

Since Mr. Knight makes few purchases on credit, he does not keep a separate account for each creditor. When invoices are received for items purchased on credit, the invoices are checked and recorded in the journal by debiting the proper accounts and by crediting Accounts Payable. Accounts Payable is a summary account, the credit balance of which indicates the total amount owed to creditors. After each invoice is recorded, it is filed in an unpaid invoice file, where it remains until it is paid in full. When an invoice is paid in full, it is removed from the unpaid invoice file and is then filed under the name of the creditor for future reference. The balance of the accounts payable summary account may be proved at any time by ascertaining the total of the unpaid amounts of the invoices.

Posting. The process of recording information in the ledger is known as *posting.* All amounts entered in the journal should be posted to the

(Continued on page 40)

The Knight Advertising Agency

ACCOUNT **Cash** Page 1

DATE	ITEMS	FOLIO	√	DEBITS	DATE	ITEMS	FOLIO	√	CREDITS
19— Dec. 1		1		2 5 0 0 0 0	19— Dec. 1		1		1 0 0 0 0
7		1		7 5 0 0	3		1		1 7 5 0
17		1		2 6 5 0 0	4		1		5 0 0
22		1		3 4 0 0 0	11		1		1 1 1 7 1
30	2,538.16	2		1 1 0 0 0	15		1		1 1 2 5 0
					21		1		1 5 0 0 0
					23		1		2 5 0 0
					29		2		1 1 7 6 3
					31		2		1 1 2 5 0

ACCOUNT **Office Supplies** Page 2

DATE	ITEMS	FOLIO	√	DEBITS	DATE	ITEMS	FOLIO	√	CREDITS
19— Dec. 2	102.63	1		1 1 7 6 3	19— Dec. 31		2		1 5 0 0

ACCOUNT **Office Equipment** Page 3

DATE	ITEMS	FOLIO	√	DEBITS	DATE	ITEMS	FOLIO	√	CREDITS
19— Dec. 28		2		1 6 8 0 1 9					

ACCOUNT **Accounts Payable** Page 4

DATE	ITEMS	FOLIO	√	DEBITS	DATE	ITEMS	FOLIO	√	CREDITS
19— Dec. 29		2		1 1 7 6 3	19— Dec. 2		1		1 1 7 6 3
					28	1,680.19	2		1 6 8 0 1 9

ACCOUNT **J. D. Knight, Proprietor** Page 5

DATE	ITEMS	FOLIO	√	DEBITS	DATE	ITEMS	FOLIO	√	CREDITS
					19— Dec. 1		1		2 5 0 0 0 0

ACCOUNT **J. D. Knight, Drawing** Page 6

DATE	ITEMS	FOLIO	√	DEBITS	DATE	ITEMS	FOLIO	√	CREDITS
19— Dec. 21		1		1 5 0 0 0					

Model Ledger

ACCOUNT *Income from Advertising Fees*   Page 7

DATE	ITEMS	FOLIO	√	DEBITS	DATE	ITEMS	FOLIO	√	CREDITS
					19– Dec. 7		1		75 00
					17		1		265 00
					22		1		340 00
					30		2		110 00

ACCOUNT *Rent Expense*   Page 8

DATE	ITEMS	FOLIO	√	DEBITS	DATE	ITEMS	FOLIO	√	CREDITS
19– Dec. 1		1		100 00					

ACCOUNT *Salary Expense*   Page 9

DATE	ITEMS	FOLIO	√	DEBITS	DATE	ITEMS	FOLIO	√	CREDITS
19– Dec. 15		1		112 50					
31		2		112 50					

ACCOUNT *Traveling Expense*   Page 10

DATE	ITEMS	FOLIO	√	DEBITS	DATE	ITEMS	FOLIO	√	CREDITS
19– Dec. 11		1		111 71					

ACCOUNT *Telephone Expense*   Page 11

DATE	ITEMS	FOLIO	√	DEBITS	DATE	ITEMS	FOLIO	√	CREDITS
19– Dec. 3		1		17 50					

ACCOUNT *Office Supplies Used*   Page 12

DATE	ITEMS	FOLIO	√	DEBITS	DATE	ITEMS	FOLIO	√	CREDITS
19– Dec. 31		2		15 00					

ACCOUNT *Miscellaneous Expenses*   Page 13

DATE	ITEMS	FOLIO	√	DEBITS	DATE	ITEMS	FOLIO	√	CREDITS
19– Dec. 4		1		5 00					
23		1		25 00					

Model Ledger

accounts kept in the ledger in order to summarize the results. Such posting may be done daily or at frequent intervals. The ledger is not a reliable source of information until all the transactions recorded in the journal have been posted.

Since the accounts provide the information needed in preparing accounting reports, a posting procedure that will insure accuracy in maintaining the accounts must necessarily be followed. Posting from the journal to the ledger involves recording the following information in the accounts:

(a) The date of each transaction.
(b) The amount of each transaction.
(c) The page or folio of the journal from which each transaction is posted.

As each entry in the journal is posted to the proper account in the ledger, the page of the ledger on which the account appears should be entered in the Posting Reference column of the journal so as to provide a cross reference between the journal and the ledger.

Reference to the first entry on page 1 of the journal, reproduced on page 34 of this textbook, will show that the debit to Cash was posted to the cash account on page 1 of the ledger, reproduced on page 38 of this textbook, by entering the date and the amount of the debit. The page of the journal was also entered in the Folio column of the ledger and the page of the ledger on which the cash account is kept was entered in the journal as a cross reference. The credit to J. D. Knight, Proprietor was posted to his account which is kept on page 5 of the ledger, reproduced on page 38 of this textbook, by entering the date and the amount of the credit. The page of the journal was entered in the Folio column of the ledger and the page of the ledger on which Mr. Knight's proprietorship account is kept was entered in the journal as a cross reference.

It will be seen from the foregoing discussion that there are four steps involved in posting — three involving information to be recorded in the ledger and one involving information to be recorded in the journal. The date, the amount, and the effect of each transaction are first recorded in the journal. The same information is later posted to the ledger. Posting does not involve an analysis of each transaction to determine its effect upon the accounts. Such an analysis is made at the time of recording the transaction in the journal, and posting is merely transferring the information from the journal to the ledger. In posting, care should be used to record each debit and each credit entry in the proper columns so that the entries will reflect correctly the effect of the transaction on the accounts.

When the posting is completed, the same information is provided in both the journal and the ledger as to the date, the amount, and the effect of each transaction. A cross reference from each book to the other book is also provided. This cross reference makes it possible to trace the entry of December 1 on the debit side of the cash account in the ledger to the journal by referring to the page indicated in the Folio column. The entry of December 1 on the credit side of the account with J. D. Knight, Proprietor may also be traced to the journal by referring to the page indicated in the Folio column. Each entry in the journal may be traced to the ledger by referring to the page numbers indicated in the Posting Reference column of the journal. By referring to pages 34 and 35, it will be seen that the ledger folios were inserted in the Posting Reference column. This was done as the posting was completed.

In posting, care should be used in writing the date as well as the amount of each entry. The year should be written at the top of the Date column and need not be repeated so long as it does not change. The name of the month should be written to the left of the single line and the day of the month should be written to the right of the single line in the Date column. The proper abbreviation may be used for the month and it need not be repeated for subsequent entries during the same month.

The ledger of The Knight Advertising Agency is reproduced on pages 38 and 39. It will be noted that the accounts are arranged in the order in which they appear in the chart of accounts shown on page 31. Each account was kept on a separate page of the ledger and the pages were numbered consecutively.

The Trial Balance. The purpose of a trial balance is to prove the equality of the debit and credit balances. In double-entry bookkeeping, equality of debit and credit balances in the ledger must be maintained. Proof of this equality is obtained periodically by means of a trial balance. A trial balance may be taken daily, weekly, monthly, or whenever desired. Before taking a trial balance, all transactions previously completed should be journalized and the posting should be completed in order that the effect of all transactions may be reflected in the ledger accounts.

Footing Accounts. When an account form similar to the one illustrated on page 16 is used, it is necessary to foot or add the amounts recorded in each account preparatory to taking a trial balance. The footings should be recorded in small figures immediately below the last item in both the debit and the credit amount columns of the account. At the same time the difference between the footings, that is, the balance, should be recorded in small figures in the Items column of the account on the side with the larger footing. In other words, if an account has a debit balance, the balance should be written in the Items column on the debit or left side of the account; if the account has a credit balance, the balance should be written in the Items column on the credit or right side of the account. The balance or difference between the footings should be recorded in the Items column just below the line on which the last regular entry appears and in line with the footing.

Reference to the accounts kept in the ledger shown on pages 38 and 39 will reveal that the accounts have been footed and will show how the footings and the balances are recorded. When only one item has been posted to an account, regardless of whether it is a debit or a credit amount, no footing is necessary.

Care should be used in ascertaining the balances of the accounts. If an error is made in adding the columns or in determining the difference between the footings, the error will be reflected in the trial balance, and considerable time may be required to locate it. Most accounting errors result from carelessness. For example, a careless bookkeeper may write an account balance on the wrong side of an account or may enter figures so illegibly that they may be misread later. Neatness in writing the amounts is just as important as carefulness in determining the footings and the balances. The footings of an account should be written in small figures close to the preceding line so that they will not interfere with the recording of an item on the next ruled line.

Proving the Balances of the Accounts. To prove the balances of the accounts, it is customary to list all of the open accounts in the same order in which they appear in the ledger. The accounts should be kept in the ledger in proper order so that it will not be necessary to rearrange them in listing them for the purpose of a trial balance. If the accounts are not listed in proper order in the trial balance, some confusion in preparing the accounting reports may result.

It is important that the following procedure should be observed in preparing a trial balance:

(a) Head the trial balance, being sure to give the name of the individual, firm, or organization, and the date as of which the trial balance is being taken.

(b) List the account titles in the proper order, showing the page number of the ledger on which each account appears.

(c) Record the account balances in parallel columns, entering debit balances in the left amount column and credit balances in the right amount column.

(d) Add the columns and record the totals, ruling a single line across the amount columns above the totals and a double line below the totals in the manner shown in the illustration below.

If the totals of the trial balance are equal in amount, the equality indicates that the ledger is in balance. In other words, the equality of the totals of the trial balance is an indication that the equality of the debit and the credit amounts has been maintained, not only in journalizing the transactions, but also in posting from the journal to the ledger and in listing the open account balances in the trial balance.

A trial balance may be typewritten on unruled paper, or it may be penwritten on two-column journal ruled paper. The following trial balance of The Knight Advertising Agency is reproduced from penwritten copy.

The Knight Advertising Agency
Trial Balance
December 31, 19-

Accounts	Page	Dr. Balances	Cr. Balances
Cash	1	2 5 3 8 1 6	
Office Supplies	2	1 0 2 6 3	
Office Equipment	3	1 6 8 0 1 9	
Accounts Payable	4		1 6 8 0 1 9
J. D. Knight, Proprietor	5		2 5 0 0 0 0
J. D. Knight, Drawing	6	1 5 0 0 0	
Income from Advertising Fees	7		7 9 0 0 0
Rent Expense	8	1 0 0 0 0	
Salary Expense	9	2 2 5 0 0	
Traveling Expense	10	1 1 1 7 1	
Telephone Expense	11	1 7 5 0	
Office Supplies Used	12	1 5 0 0	
Miscellaneous Expenses	13	3 0 0 0	
		4 9 7 0 1 9	4 9 7 0 1 9

Model Trial Balance

PRACTICE ASSIGNMENT No. 4. Refer to the workbook and complete Report No. 4. To complete this practice assignment correctly, the principles developed in the preceding discussion must be understood. Review the text assignment if necessary. After completing the report, continue with the following study assignment until the next report is required.

(5) THE FINANCIAL STATEMENTS

The transactions completed by The Knight Advertising Agency during the month of December were recorded in a two-column journal. The debits and credits were subsequently posted to the proper accounts in a ledger. At the end of the month a trial balance was taken as a means of proving that the equality of debits and credits had been maintained throughout the journalizing and posting procedures.

While a trial balance may provide much of the information the proprietor of a business may desire, it is primarily a device used by the bookkeeper for the purpose of proof only. While the trial balance of The Knight Advertising Agency taken as of December 31 contains a list of all of the accounts showing the amounts of the debit and credit balances, it does not present all of the information that Mr. Knight may need or desire regarding the results of operations during the month or the status of his business at the end of the month. To meet these needs it is customary to prepare two types of *financial statements*. One is known as an income statement and the other as a balance sheet.

Income Statement. The purpose of an *income statement* is to provide information regarding the results of operations during a specified period of time. It is an itemized statement of the changes in proprietorship resulting from income earned and expenses incurred during the period. Such changes are recorded in temporary proprietorship accounts known as income and expense accounts. Changes in proprietorship resulting from investments or withdrawals of assets by the proprietor are not included in the income statement as they involve neither income nor expense.

A model income statement for The Knight Advertising Agency showing the results of operations for the month ended December 31 is reproduced on page 45. The heading of an income statement consists of the following:

(a) The name of the business.
(b) The title of the statement.
(c) The period of time covered by the statement.

The body of an income statement consists of (a) an itemized list of the sources and amounts of income for the period and (b) an itemized list of the various expenses incurred during the period.

An income statement may be either penwritten or typewritten. The income statement of The Knight Advertising Agency is reproduced from penwritten copy on two-column journal ruled paper.

The Knight Advertising Agency
Income Statement
For Month Ended December 31, 19-

Income:				
Income from Advertising Fees	790 00			
Total Income			790 00	
Expenses:				
Rent Expense	100 00			
Salary Expense	225 00			
Traveling Expense	111 71			
Telephone Expense	17 50			
Office Supplies Used	15 00			
Miscellaneous Expenses	30 00			
Total Expenses			499 21	
Net Income			290 79	

Model Income Statement

In the case of The Knight Advertising Agency the only source of income was income from advertising fees amounting to $790. The total expenses for the month amounted to $499.21. It was found that the income exceeded the expenses to the extent of $290.79. This represents the amount of the net income for the month. If the total expenses had exceeded the total income, the excess would represent a net loss for the month.

The trial balance was the source of the information needed in preparing the income statement. However, it can be seen readily that the income statement provides more information concerning the results of the month's operations than is provided by the trial balance.

The Balance Sheet. The purpose of a *balance sheet* is to provide information regarding the financial condition of a business enterprise as of a specified time or date. It is an itemized statement of the assets, liabilities, and proprietorship at the close of business on the date indicated in the heading.

A model balance sheet for The Knight Advertising Agency showing the status of the business as of December 31 is reproduced on page 46. The heading of a balance sheet consists of the following:

(a) The name of the business.
(b) The title of the statement.
(c) The date of the statement.

The Knight Advertising Agency
Balance Sheet
December 31, 19-

Assets		
Cash		2538 16
Office Supplies		102 63
Office Equipment		1680 19
Total Assets		4320 98

Liabilities		
Accounts Payable		1680 19
Total Liabilities		1680 19
Proprietorship		
J. D. Knight, Proprietor		
Investment, Dec. 1		2500 00
Net Income $290.79		
Less Withdrawals 150.00		
Net Increase	140 79	
Proprietorship, Dec. 31		2640 79
Total Liabilities and Proprietorship		4320 98

Model Balance Sheet — Account Form

The body of a balance sheet consists of an itemized list of (a) the assets, (b) the liabilities, and (c) the proprietorship. A balance sheet may be either penwritten or typewritten. The balance sheet of The Knight Advertising Agency is reproduced from penwritten copy on special ruled paper. It is arranged in account form. Note the similarity of this form of balance sheet to the standard account form illustrated on page 16. The assets are listed on the left side and the liabilities and proprietorship on the right side. The information provided by the balance sheet of The Knight Advertising Agency may be summarized in equation form as follows:

ASSETS $4,320.98 = LIABILITIES $1,680.19 + PROPRIETORSHIP $2,640.79

The trial balance was the source of the information needed in listing the assets and the liabilities in the balance sheet. The amount of the proprietorship may be ascertained simply by subtracting the total liabilities from the total assets. Thus, the amount of Mr. Knight's proprietorship in The Knight Advertising Agency as of December 31 may be computed in the following manner:

Total assets...	$4,320.98
Less total liabilities..	1,680.19
Proprietorship	$2,640.79

Proof of the amount of the proprietorship as calculated above may be ascertained by taking into consideration the following factors:

(a) The amount invested in the enterprise by Mr. Knight on December 1 as shown by his proprietorship account.

(b) The amount of the net income of The Knight Advertising Agency for the month as shown by the income statement.

(c) The total amount withdrawn for personal use during the month as shown by Mr. Knight's drawing account.

The trial balance shows that Mr. Knight's investment in The Knight Advertising Agency on December 1 amounted to $2,500. This is indicated by the credit balance of his proprietorship account. The income statement shows that the net income of The Knight Advertising Agency for the month amounted to $290.79. The trial balance shows that the amount withdrawn by Mr. Knight during the month for personal use amounted to $150. This is indicated by the debit balance of his drawing account. On the basis of this information Mr. Knight's proprietorship in The Knight Advertising Agency as of December 31 may be computed in the manner shown on the following page.

Amount invested in the business December 1...................		$2,500.00
Net income for the month..........................	$290.79	
Less amount withdrawn for personal use during the month.......................................	150.00	140.79
Proprietorship at end of month............................		$2,640.79

PRACTICE ASSIGNMENT No. 5. Refer to the workbook and complete Report No. 5. This practice assignment provides a test of your ability to apply the principles developed in Units One and Two of this textbook. The textbook and the workbook go hand in hand, each serving a definite purpose in the learning process. Inability to solve correctly any problem included in the report indicates that you have failed to master the principles developed in the textbook. After completing the report, you may proceed with the textbook discussion in Unit Three until the next report is required.

ACCOUNTING FOR MERCHANDISE

(6) PURCHASES AND THE PURCHASES JOURNAL

One of the principal divisions of business activity is that of merchandising, that is, buying and selling goods. In this field the retail merchant and the wholesale merchant are important factors. A *retail merchant* is one who sells to the consumer at retail prices. He may buy directly from manufacturers, producers, or importers, or he may buy from jobbers, distributors, or other middlemen at wholesale prices. A *wholesale merchant* is one who sells to retail merchants and large consumers at wholesale prices. He usually buys from the manufacturers, producers, or importers. Thus, a wholesale firm may buy merchandise from various manufacturers, producers, or importers and sell it at wholesale prices to retail dealers who in turn sell to their customers at retail prices.

The retail merchandising business is a broad field of endeavor including such enterprises as grocery and food stores, clothing and dry goods stores, household furniture and furnishing stores, drug stores, hardware and equipment stores, department stores, and many other types of retail stores.

Anyone engaged in a mercantile enterprise must keep records, not only because federal and state laws require it, but in order to operate his business intelligently. Sales should be recorded as income in the period in which the merchandise is sold. However, all of the income from sales does not represent profit. The cost of the goods sold must be taken into consideration in computing the gross profit on sales, and the operating expenses must be taken into consideration in computing the net profit on sales.

In ascertaining the cost of goods sold, it is necessary to take into consideration (a) the amount of any goods on hand at the beginning of the period, (b) the amount of goods purchased during the period, (c) the amount of any goods returned to creditors or suppliers or any allowances received from creditors during the period that resulted in a decrease in the cost of the goods purchased, and (d) the amount of any goods on hand at the end of the period.

To be successful, a merchant should have sufficient capital to acquire the necessary equipment and a stock of merchandise. He should also be able to pay all of his operating expenses and to realize a reasonable profit on the amount of capital invested in the enterprise. Adequate records may not prevent a merchant from failing, but they will increase his chances of succeeding.

The Merchandise Accounts. In recording transactions arising from merchandising, it is desirable to keep at least the following accounts:

(a) Merchandise Inventory.
(b) Purchases.
(c) Purchases Returns and Allowances.
(d) Sales.
(e) Sales Returns and Allowances.

Merchandise Inventory Account. A merchandise inventory account is an asset account in which the cost of goods in stock at the time of taking an inventory is recorded. It is customary to take an inventory of merchandise in stock at the close of each accounting period. The amount of the inventory is then recorded as a debit to Merchandise Inventory. The amount debited to the inventory account at the close of one accounting period also represents the amount of the inventory at the beginning of the succeeding accounting period. In other words, an inventory taken on December 31 of the calendar year represents the inventory both at the close of an old year and at the beginning of a new year.

MERCHANDISE INVENTORY

Debit to record inventory of goods in stock.	

Purchases Account. The purchases account is a temporary account in which the cost of merchandise purchased is recorded. The account should be debited for the cost of all merchandise purchased during the accounting period, whether for cash or on credit. It may also be debited for any transportation charges, such as freight, express, and parcel post charges, that increase the cost of the merchandise purchased.

PURCHASES

Debit to record the cost of merchandise purchased.	

Purchases Returns and Allowances Account. This account is a temporary account in which purchases returns and allowances are recorded. Accounts Payable should be debited and Purchases Returns and Allowances should be credited for the cost of any merchandise returned to creditors or suppliers and for any allowances received from creditors that decrease the cost of the merchandise purchased. Allowances may be received from creditors for merchandise delivered in poor condition or for merchandise that does not meet specifications as to quality, weight, size, color, grade, style, etc.

Purchases Returns and Allowances

	Credit to record returns and allowances.

While purchases returns and allowances might be credited directly to Purchases, it is better to credit Purchases Returns and Allowances. The accounts will then show both gross purchases and the amounts of returns and allowances. If returns and allowances are large in proportion to gross purchases, a weakness in the purchasing operations is indicated. It may be that better sources of supply should be sought or that purchase specifications should be stated more clearly.

Purchase Invoice. (The source of the information needed in recording a purchase transaction is the *purchase invoice*.) A standard purchase invoice form has been widely adopted by merchants, manufacturers, distributors, and other users. It was originally developed by the National Association of Purchasing Agents in collaboration with the Railway Accounting Officers Association, the National Association of Cost Accountants, and the Association of American Railroads. The standard form has been approved by the Division of Simplified Practice of the National Bureau of Standards, U. S. Department of Commerce. The size of the form approved is $8\frac{1}{2}''$ wide by $7''$, $11''$, or $14''$ long. As indicated, the length may vary according to needs. The purchase invoice reproduced on page 52 was prepared on a standard invoice form.

Merchandise may be bought for cash or on credit. When merchandise is bought for cash, the transaction results in an increase in purchases and a decrease in the asset cash; hence it should be recorded by debiting Purchases and by crediting Cash. When merchandise is bought on credit, the transaction results in an increase in purchases with a corresponding increase in the liability accounts payable; hence it should be recorded by debiting Purchases and by crediting Accounts Payable.

	FOR CUSTOMER'S USE ONLY	
INVOICE	REGISTER NO.	VOUCHER NO.

IMPERIAL FURNITURE COMPANY

GRAND RAPIDS, MICHIGAN

F. O. B. CHECKED

TERMS APPROVED *M. S.*	PRICE APPROVED *M. S.*
CALCULATIONS CHECKED *R. M.*	

CUSTOMER'S ORDER NO. & DATE   196

REFER TO INVOICE NO.   23

REQUISITION NO.

TRANSPORTATION

CONTRACT NO.

INVOICE DATE May 2, 19—

FREIGHT BILL NO.	AMOUNT

MATERIAL RECEIVED

SOLD TO   P. A. Mosely
1204 S. Main St.
Lansing, Mich.

5/5 19-   H. Y.   R. C.
DATE   SIGNATURE   TITLE

SATISFACTORY AND APPROVED

SHIPPED TO AND DESTINATION   Same

ADJUSTMENTS

DATE SHIPPED   May 2, 19—   FROM   Grand Rapids   PREPAID OR COLLECT!

ACCOUNTING DISTRIBUTION

CAR INITIALS AND NO.   F. O. B. Grand Rapids

HOW SHIPPED AND ROUTE   Penna. R. R.

AUDITED *B. M.*	FINAL APPROVAL

TERMS   30 days

QUANTITY		DESCRIPTION	UNIT PRICE	AMOUNT
ORDERED	SHIPPED			
2	2	4119 Mhg. Tier Table	21.50	43.00
4	4	662 Mhg. Occasional Table	20.50	82.00
4	4	635 Mhg. Occasional Table	25.50	102.00
4	4	2630 Mhg. Night Stand	22.50	90.00
5	5	2317 Mhg. Coffee Table	13.90	69.50
				386.50

Purchase Invoice

Accounts Payable. In order that the proprietor may know the total amount owed to his creditors at any time, it is advisable to keep a summary ledger account with Accounts Payable. This is a liability account. The credit balance of the account at the beginning of the period represents the total amount owed to creditors. During the period, the account should be credited for the amount of any transactions involving increases and should be debited for the amount of any transactions involving decreases in the amount owed to creditors. At the end of the period, the credit balance of the account again represents the total amount owed to creditors.

It is also necessary to keep some record of the transactions completed with each creditor in order that information may be readily available at all times as to the amount owed to each creditor and as to when each invoice should be paid. The following methods of accounting for credit purchases are widely used:

(a) The invoice method. Under this method it is customary to keep a chronological record of the purchase invoices received and to file them systematically. All other vouchers or documents representing transactions completed with creditors should be filed with the purchase invoices. Special filing equipment facilitates the use of this method.

(b) The ledger account method. Under this method it is customary to keep a chronological record of the purchase invoices received. An individual ledger account with each creditor is also kept. Special equipment may be used in maintaining a permanent file of the invoices and other vouchers or documents supporting the records.

Purchases Journal. All of the transactions of a mercantile enterprise can be recorded in an ordinary two-column general journal. However, in many mercantile enterprises purchase transactions occur frequently, and if most of the purchases are made on credit, such transactions may be recorded advantageously in a special journal. One form of *purchases journal* is illustrated below. The following transactions, representing purchases of merchandise on credit by P. A. Mosely, a retail merchant, during the month of May, are shown recorded in the illustration:

NARRATIVE OF TRANSACTIONS

May 5. Imperial Furniture Co., Grand Rapids; $386.50; Invoice No. 23 dated May 2; terms, 30 days.

    6. A. W. Shaw Co., City; $778.92; Invoice No. 24 dated May 5; terms, 30 days.

  12. Gray Mfg. Co., 420 Spring Street, City; $1,203.60; Invoice No. 25 dated May 12; terms, 10 days.

  29. Dobson Bros., Dayton; $1,398.60; Invoice No. 26 dated May 27; terms, 60 days.

PURCHASES JOURNAL FOR MONTH OF *May* 19—   *Page 9*

DATE OF ENTRY	DATE OF INVOICE	NO. OF INVOICE	FROM WHOM PURCHASED	POST. REF.	AMOUNT	DATE PAID
			AMOUNT FORWARDED			
May 5	May 2	23	Imperial Furniture Co.	✓	386 50	
6	5	24	A. W. Shaw Co.	✓	778 92	
12	12	25	Gray Mfg. Co.	✓	1203 60	
29	27	26	Dobson Bros.	✓	1398 60	
31			Purchases Dr.-Accts. Pay. Cr.	4/20	3767 62	

Model Purchases Journal

It will be noted that in recording each invoice, the following information was entered in the purchases journal:

(a) Date on which the invoice is recorded.

(b) Date of the invoice.

(c) Number of the invoice.
(d) From whom purchased (the creditor).
(e) Amount of the invoice.
(f) Date paid.

When the invoice method of accounting for credit purchases is used, it is not necessary to record the address of the creditor in the purchases journal; neither is it necessary to record the terms in the purchases journal.

With this form of purchases journal, each transaction can be recorded on one horizontal line. As purchase invoices are received, it is customary to number them consecutively. This number should not be confused with the order number or the vendor's number, both of which are usually shown on each purchase invoice.

If an individual ledger account is not kept with each creditor, the purchase invoices should be filed immediately after they have been recorded in the purchases journal. It is preferable that they be filed according to due date in an unpaid invoice file.

If a partial payment is made on an invoice, a notation of the payment should be made on the invoice, which should be retained in the unpaid invoice file until it is paid in full. It is generally considered a better policy to pay each invoice in full. Paying specific invoices in full simplifies record keeping for both the buyer and the seller. If credit is received because of returns or allowances, a notation of the amount of the credit should also be made on the invoice so that the balance due will be indicated.

When an invoice is paid in full, the date of payment should be entered in the purchases journal in the column provided for this purpose. The payment should also be noted on the invoice, which should be transferred from the unpaid invoice file to a paid invoice file.

The unpaid invoice file is usually arranged with a division for each month with folders numbered 1 to 31 in each division. This makes it possible to file the unpaid invoices according to the date they will become due, which facilitates payment of the invoices on or before their due dates. Since certain invoices may be subject to discounts if paid within a specified time, it is important that they be handled in such a manner that payment in time to get the benefit of the discounts will not be overlooked.

The folders in the paid invoice file are usually arranged in alphabetic order, according to the names of creditors. This facilitates the filing of all paid invoices, and all other vouchers or documents representing transactions with creditors, in such a manner that a complete history of the business done with each creditor is maintained.

Posting from the Purchases Journal. Under the invoice method of accounting for credit purchases, individual posting from the purchases journal is not required. When this plan is followed, it is customary to place a check mark in the Posting Reference column of the purchases journal at the time of entering each invoice.

At the end of the month the Amount column of the purchases journal should be footed in small figures, the total entered, and the ruling completed as illustrated. The total credit purchases for the month should then be posted as a debit to Purchases and as a credit to Accounts Payable. A proper cross reference should be provided by entering the page of the purchases journal preceded by the initial "P" in the Folio column of the ledger and by entering the page of the ledger in the Posting Reference column of the purchases journal. The titles of both accounts and the posting references may be entered on one horizontal line of the purchases journal as shown in the illustration. Posting the total in this manner is usually referred to as *summary posting*.

The proper method of completing the summary posting from P. A. Mosely's purchases journal on May 31 is shown in the following illustration of the accounts affected.

ACCOUNT *Accounts Payable* Page 20

DATE	ITEMS	FOLIO	√	DEBITS	DATE	ITEMS	FOLIO	√	CREDITS
					19- May 31		P9		3 7 6 7 6 2

ACCOUNT *Purchases* Page 40

19- May 31		P9		3 7 6 7 6 2					

Under this plan of accounting for credit purchases, the credit balance of the accounts payable account, after the posting is completed, represents the total amount owed to creditors. The balance of the account may be proved by ascertaining the total of the unpaid balances of the invoices kept in the unpaid invoice file.

Schedule of Accounts Payable. It is usually advisable at the end of each month to prepare a list of the creditors showing the name of each creditor and the amount due him. This is known as a *schedule of accounts* *payable.* Such a schedule can be prepared easily by going through the unpaid invoice file and listing the names of the creditors and the amount due to each. Should the total of the schedule not be in agreement with the balance of the summary account with Accounts Payable, it is an indication that an error has been made either in recording the transactions with creditors in the summary account with Accounts Payable or in handling the invoices. If the error is in the summary account, it will usually be revealed by the trial balance. If the trial balance reveals that the debit and the credit balances are equal in amount, it will indicate that the error has probably been made in handling the invoices.

If an individual ledger account is kept with each creditor, all transactions representing either increases or decreases in the amount owed to each creditor should be posted individually to the proper account. The posting may be done by hand or posting machines may be used. If the posting is done by hand, it may be completed either directly from the purchase invoices and other vouchers or documents representing the transactions, or it may be completed from the books of original entry. If the posting is done with the aid of posting machines, it will usually be completed directly from the purchase invoices and other vouchers or documents. The ledger account method of accounting for accounts payable is explained in detail in a subsequent unit.

> *PRACTICE ASSIGNMENT No. 6. Refer to the workbook and complete Report No. 6. To complete this practice assignment correctly, the principles developed in the preceding discussion must be understood. Review the text assignment if necessary. After completing the report, continue with the following study assignment until the next report is required.*

(7) SALES AND THE SALES JOURNAL

On page 50 reference was made to the fact that in recording transactions arising from merchandising it is desirable to keep certain accounts, including accounts for sales and for sales returns and allowances. A discussion of these accounts, together with a discussion of the sales journal, follows.

Sales Account. The sales account is a temporary account in which the income resulting from sales of merchandise is recorded. The account should be credited for the selling price of all merchandise sold during the accounting period, whether for cash or on credit.

SALES

	Credit to record the selling price of merchandise sold.

Sales Returns and Allowances Account. This account is a temporary account in which sales returns and allowances are recorded. Sales Returns and Allowances should be debited and Accounts Receivable should be credited for the selling price of any merchandise returned by customers or for any allowances made to customers that decrease the selling price of the merchandise sold. Such allowances may be granted to customers for merchandise delivered in poor condition or for merchandise that does not meet specifications as to quality, weight, size, color, grade, style, etc.

SALES RETURNS AND ALLOWANCES

Debit to record returns and allowances.	

While sales returns and allowances could be debited directly to Sales, it is better to debit Sales Returns and Allowances. The accounts will then show both gross sales and the amounts of returns and allowances. If returns and allowances are large in proportion to gross sales, a weakness in the merchandising operations is indicated and the trouble should be determined and corrected.

Retail Sales Tax. Retail sales taxes are imposed by most states and by many cities. The term *retail sales tax* refers to a tax imposed upon the sale of tangible personal property at retail. The tax is usually measured by the gross sales price or the gross receipts from sales. The term may also include a tax imposed upon persons engaged in furnishing services at retail in which case it is measured by the gross receipts for furnishing such services. The rates of the tax vary considerably but usually range from 1 per cent to 3 per cent. In most states the tax is a general sales tax. However, in some states the tax is imposed only on specific items, such as automobiles, cosmetics, radios, and playing cards.

To avoid fractions of cents and to simplify the determination of the tax it is permissible in some states to use a sales tax table or schedule which shows the amount of the tax applicable to sales in various brackets. For example, where the rate is 2 per cent the tax may be calculated as shown in the following schedule:

AMOUNT OF SALE	AMOUNT OF TAX
0 to 18¢	None
19¢ to 69¢	1¢
70¢ to $1.18	2¢
$1.19 to $1.69	3¢
$1.70 to $2.18	4¢
and so on	

The amount of the tax imposed under the schedule approximates the legal rate. Retail sales tax reports accompanied by a remittance for the amounts due must be filed periodically, usually monthly or quarterly, depending upon the law of the state or city in which the business is located.

In the case of a retail store operated in a city or state where a sales tax is imposed on merchandise sold for cash or on credit, it is advisable to keep an account with Sales Tax Payable. This is a liability account which should be credited for the

SALES TAX PAYABLE

Debit	Credit
to record payment of tax to the proper taxing authority.	to record tax imposed on sales.

amount of the tax collected or imposed on sales. The account should be debited for the amount of the tax paid to the proper taxing authority. A credit balance in the account at any time indicates the amount of the merchant's liability for taxes collected or imposed.

In Ohio, merchants are required to purchase sales tax stamps. When merchandise is sold, the merchant charges the customer for the tax and gives him canceled tax stamps as a receipt. When this system is used, merchants are required to report periodically the amount of the taxable sales for the period and the amount of tax stamps canceled. If the amount of stamps canceled is less than the tax computed by application of the prescribed rate to the total taxable sales for the period, the merchant is required to pay the difference which constitutes a business expense.

Sales tax accounting may be complicated by such factors as (a) sales returns and allowances and (b) exempt sales. If the tax is recorded at the time the sale is recorded, it will be necessary to adjust for the tax when recording sales returns and allowances. If some sales are exempt from the tax, it will be necessary to distinguish between taxable and nontaxable sales. A common example of nontaxable sales is sales to out-of-state customers.

Sales Ticket. The original record of a sales transaction is the *sales ticket*. Whether merchandise is sold for cash or on credit, a sales ticket should be prepared. When the sale is for cash, the ticket may be printed by the cash register at the time the sale is rung up. However, some stores prefer to use handwritten sales tickets regardless of whether the sale is for cash or on credit. Regardless of the method used in recording cash sales, it is necessary to prepare a handwritten sales ticket or charge slip for every credit sale. Such sales tickets are usually prepared in duplicate or in triplicate. The original copy is for the bookkeeping department.

Sales Ticket

A carbon copy is given to the customer. Where more than one sales-person is employed, each is usually provided with his own pad of sales tickets. Each pad bears a different number that identifies the clerk. The individual sales tickets are also numbered consecutively. This facilitates sorting the tickets by clerks if it is desired to compute the amount of goods sold by each clerk. Reference to the sales ticket reproduced above will show the type of information usually recorded.

When merchandise is sold for cash, the transaction results in an increase in the asset Cash offset by an increase in sales income and an increase in the liability Sales Tax Payable. Such transactions should be recorded by debiting Cash for the amount received and by crediting Sales for the sales price of the merchandise and crediting Sales Tax Payable for the amount of the tax collected. When merchandise is sold on credit, the transaction results in an increase in the asset Accounts Receivable offset by an increase in sales income and an increase in the liability Sales Tax Payable. Such transactions should be recorded by debiting Accounts Receivable for the total amount charged to the customer and by crediting Sales for the amount of the sale and crediting Sales Tax Payable for the amount of the tax imposed.

An alternative procedure that is permissible under some sales tax laws is to credit the total of both the sales and the tax to the sales account in the first place. Periodically — usually at the end of each month — a calculation is made to determine how much of the balance of the sales account is presumed to be tax and an entry is made to remove this amount from the sales account and to transfer it to the sales tax payable account. Suppose, for example, that the tax rate is 2 per cent, and that the sales account includes the tax collected or charged, along with the amount of the sales. In this event, 100/102 of the balance of the account is presumed to be the amount of the sales, and 2/102 of the balance is the amount of the tax. If the sales account had a balance of $10,200, the tax portion would be $200 (2/102 of $10,200). A debit to Sales of $200 would remove this tax portion; the credit would be to Sales Tax Payable.

Accounts Receivable. In order that the proprietor may know the total amount due from charge customers at any time, it is advisable to keep a summary ledger account with Accounts Receivable. This is an asset account. The debit balance of the account at the beginning of the period represents the total amount due from customers. During the period, the account should be debited for the amount of any transactions involving increases and should be credited for the amount of any transactions involving decreases in the amount due from customers. At the end of the period, the debit balance of the account again represents the total amount due from customers.

It is also necessary to keep some record of the transactions completed with each customer in order that information may be readily available at all times as to the amount due from each customer. The following methods of accounting for charge sales are widely used:

(a) The sales ticket method. Under this method it is customary to file the charge sales tickets systematically. All other vouchers or documents representing transactions with customers should be filed with the sales tickets. Special filing equipment facilitates the use of this method. In some cases a chronological record of the charge sales tickets is kept as a means of control.

(b) The ledger account method. Under this method it is customary to keep a chronological record of the charge sales tickets. An individual ledger account with each customer is also kept. Special equipment may be used in maintaining a permanent file of the charge sales tickets and other vouchers or documents supporting the records.

Under either of these methods of accounting for transactions with charge customers it is necessary that a sales ticket or charge slip be made for each sale on credit. In making a charge sales ticket the date, the name and address of the customer, the quantity, a description of the items sold, the unit prices, the total amount of the sale, and the amount of the sales tax should be recorded.

Sales Journal. Transactions involving the sale of merchandise on credit can be recorded in an ordinary two-column general journal. However, in many mercantile enterprises sales transactions occur frequently and if it is the policy to sell merchandise on credit, such transactions may be recorded advantageously in a special journal. If the business is operated in an area where no sales taxes are imposed, all credit sales can be recorded in a *sales journal* with only one amount column designed as follows:

SALES JOURNAL FOR MONTH OF   19--

DATE OF ENTRY	NO. OF SALE	TO WHOM SOLD	POST. REF.	AMOUNT

In an area where a sales tax is imposed, it is better to provide three amount columns as shown in the model sales journal illustrated on page 62. The transactions recorded in the journal were completed by P. A. Mosely, a retail merchant, during the month of May. His store is located in a state that imposes a tax of 2 per cent on the retail sale of all merchandise whether sold for cash or on credit.

It will be noted that the following information regarding each charge sales ticket is recorded in the sales journal:

(a) Date on which the sale is recorded.
(b) Number of the sales ticket.
(c) To whom sold (the customer).
(d) Amount charged to customer.
(e) Amount of sale.
(f) Amount of sales tax.

With this form of sales journal, each transaction can be recorded on one horizontal line. The sales ticket should provide all the information needed in recording the sale.

NARRATIVE OF TRANSACTIONS

May 5. W. H. Hayt, 1330 Hayward Court, City; Sale No. 61; $205, tax $4.10.
      5. W. A. Bain, 1609 Main Street, City; Sale No. 62; $1,175, tax $23.50.
   11. E. M. Hall, 932 Day Street, City; Sale No. 63; $425.50, tax $8.51.
   15. H. B. Boyd, 617 Davis Avenue, City; Sale No. 64; $1,262.75, tax $25.26.
   22. T. L. Britton, 1214 Wabash Street, City; Sale No. 65; $725, tax $14.50.
   26. E. M. Hall; Sale No. 66; $1,165.20, tax 23.30.

Page 14   SALES JOURNAL FOR MONTH OF   *May* 19—

DATE OF ENTRY	NO. OF SALE	TO WHOM SOLD	POST. REF.	ACCOUNTS REC. DR.	SALES CR.	SALES TAX PAY. CR.
		AMOUNTS FORWARDED				
May 5	61	W. H. Hayt	✓	209 10	205 00	4 10
5	62	W. A. Bain	✓	1198 50	1175 00	23 50
11	63	E. M. Hall	✓	434 01	425 50	8 51
15	64	H. B. Boyd	✓	1288 01	1262 75	25 26
22	65	T. L. Britton	✓	739 50	725 00	14 50
26	66	E. M. Hall	✓	1188 50	1165 20	23 30
				5057 62	4958 45	99 17
				(2)	(31)	(18)

Model Sales Journal

If an individual ledger account is not kept with each customer, the charge sales tickets should be filed immediately after they have been recorded in the sales journal. They are usually filed alphabetically under the name of the customer. There are numerous types of trays, cabinets, and files on the market that are designed to facilitate the filing of charge sales tickets by customers. Such devices are designed to save time, to promote accuracy, and to provide a safe means of keeping a record of the transactions with each charge customer.

When a customer makes a partial payment on his account, the amount of the payment should be noted on the most recent charge sales ticket and the new balance should be indicated. Sales tickets paid in full should be receipted and may either be given to the customer or may be transferred to another file for future reference. If a customer is given credit for merchandise returned or because of allowances, a notation of the amount of credit should be made on the most recent charge sales ticket and the new balance should be indicated. If a credit memorandum is issued to a customer, it should be prepared in duplicate and the carbon copy should be attached to the sales ticket on which the amount is noted.

Posting from the Sales Journal. Under the sales ticket method of accounting for charge sales, individual posting from the sales journal is not required. When this plan is followed, it is customary to place a check mark in the Posting Reference column of the sales journal at the time of entering each sale.

At the end of the month the Amount columns of the sales journal should be footed in small figures, the totals entered, and the ruling completed as illustrated. The total of the Accounts Receivable Dr. column must equal the sum of the totals of the Sales Cr. and Sales Tax Payable Cr. columns. The totals should be posted to the general ledger accounts indicated in the column headings. This summary posting should be completed in the following order:

(a) Post the total of the Accounts Receivable Dr. column to the debit of Accounts Receivable.

(b) Post the total of the Sales Cr. column to the credit of Sales.

(c) Post the total of the Sales Tax Payable Cr. column to the credit of Sales Tax Payable.

A proper cross reference should be provided by entering the page of the sales journal preceded by the initial "S" in the Folio column of the ledger and by entering the page of the ledger immediately below the column total of the sales journal. The proper method of completing the summary posting from P. A. Mosely's sales journal on May 31 is shown in the following illustration of the accounts affected.

ACCOUNT *Accounts Receivable*   Page 2

DATE	ITEMS	FOLIO	✓	DEBITS	DATE	ITEMS	FOLIO	✓	CREDITS
19— May 31		S14		5 0 5 7 6 2					

ACCOUNT *Sales Tax Payable*   Page 18

					DATE	ITEMS	FOLIO	✓	CREDITS
					19— May 31		S14		9 9 1 7

ACCOUNT *Sales*   Page 31

					DATE	ITEMS	FOLIO	✓	CREDITS
					19— May 31		S14		4 9 5 8 4 5

Under this plan of accounting for sales on account, the debit balance of the accounts receivable account, after the posting is completed, indicates the amount due from customers. The balance of the account may be proved by ascertaining the total of the unpaid balances of the sales tickets kept in the customers' file.

Schedule of Accounts Receivable. It is usually advisable at the end of each month to prepare a list of customers showing the name of each customer and the amount due from him. This is known as a *schedule of accounts receivable.* Such a schedule can be prepared easily by going through the customers' file and listing the names of the customers and the amount due from each. Should the total not be in agreement with the balance of the summary account with Accounts Receivable, it is an indication that an error has been made either in recording the transactions with customers in the summary account with Accounts Receivable or in handling the charge sales tickets. If the error is in the summary account, it will usually be revealed by the trial balance. If the general ledger accounts are in balance, it will indicate that the error has probably been made in handling the charge sales tickets.

If an individual ledger account is kept with each customer, all transactions representing either increases or decreases in the amount due from each customer should be posted individually to the proper account. The posting may be done by hand or posting machines may be used. If the posting is done by hand, it may be completed either directly from the charge sales tickets and other vouchers or documents representing the transactions, or it may be completed from the books of original entry. If the posting is done with posting machines, it will usually be completed directly from the charge sales tickets and other vouchers or documents.

General Journal. When a purchases journal, a sales journal, and a general journal are used as the only books of original entry, all purchases of merchandise on credit should be recorded in the purchases journal, all sales of merchandise on credit should be recorded in the sales journal, and all other transactions should be recorded in the general journal. All entries in the general journal should be posted individually to the proper accounts in the ledger. At the end of the month, the total credit purchases for the month should be posted in one amount to the debit of Purchases and to the credit of Accounts Payable. At the same time, the total charge sales for the month should be posted in one amount to the debit of Accounts Receivable with credits to Sales for the selling price of the merchandise sold and to Sales Tax Payable for the amount of the tax imposed on the sales. Thus, the use of a purchases journal and a sales journal saves considerable time in posting.

PRACTICE ASSIGNMENT No. 7. Refer to the workbook and complete Report No. 7. To be able to complete this practice assignment correctly, the principles developed in the preceding discussion must be understood. Review the text assignment if necessary. After completing the report, continue with the following study assignment until the next report is required.

(8) ACCOUNTING PROCEDURE

The accounting procedure in recording the transactions of a mercantile enterprise is, in general, the same as that involved in recording the transactions of any other enterprise. In a small mercantile enterprise where the number of transactions is not large and all the bookkeeping may be done by one person, a standard two-column general journal may be used as the only book of original entry. However, if desired, a purchases journal and a sales journal may be used along with the general journal. The purchases journal may be used for keeping a chronological record of purchases of merchandise on credit and the sales journal may be used for keeping a chronological record of sales of merchandise on credit. All of the accounts may be kept in one general ledger which may be either a bound book or a loose-leaf book. The posting from a general journal may be completed daily or periodically; summary posting from the purchases and sales journals is done at the end of the month.

A trial balance should be taken at the end of each month as a means of proving the equality of the account balances. The balance of the summary account with Accounts Receivable should be proved periodically, or at least at the end of each month. This may be done by ascertaining the total of the unpaid sales tickets or charge slips that are kept in a customers' file. Likewise, the balance of the summary account with Accounts Payable should be proved periodically, or at least at the end of each month. This may be done by ascertaining the total of the unpaid invoices that are kept in an unpaid invoice file.

This procedure will be illustrated by (a) recording a narrative of transactions for one month in a purchases journal, a sales journal, and a general journal, (b) by posting to the ledger accounts, (c) by taking a trial balance to prove the equality of the account balances at the end of the month, (d) by preparing a schedule of accounts receivable to prove the balance of the summary account with Accounts Receivable, and (e) by preparing a schedule of accounts payable to prove the balance of the summary account with Accounts Payable.

W. A. Goodman is the owner of a small retail business operated under the name of "The Goodman Store." A purchases journal, a sales journal, and a standard two-column general journal are used as books of original entry. All of the accounts are kept in a general ledger. Individual ledger accounts with customers and creditors are not kept; instead, the purchase invoices and the charge sales tickets are filed in the manner previously described. All sales are subject to a retail sales tax of 2 per cent whether for cash or on credit. All credit sales are payable by the tenth of the following month unless otherwise agreed. A chart of accounts appears below. It includes only the accounts needed to record the transactions completed during March, the first month only of a fiscal year. Certain other accounts would be necessary to record all of the transactions and events for an entire fiscal year and to summarize the temporary accounts at the end of the year.

THE GOODMAN STORE

CHART OF ACCOUNTS

Assets
  Cash
  Accounts Receivable
  Store Supplies
  Prepaid Insurance
  Store Equipment

Liabilities
  Accounts Payable
  Sales Tax Payable

Proprietorship
  W. A. Goodman, Proprietor
  W. A. Goodman, Drawing

Income from Sales
  Sales
    Sales Returns and Allowances

Cost of Sales
  Purchases
    Purchases Returns and Allowances

Expenses
  Rent Expense
  Salary Expense
  Advertising Expense
  Telephone Expense

THE GOODMAN STORE

NARRATIVE OF TRANSACTIONS

Wednesday, March 1

W. A. Goodman started the business with a cash investment of $2,000. Rented a store located at 934 High St. from Acme Realtors and paid one month's rent in advance, $95.

Thursday, March 2

Purchased store equipment on account from the City Store Equipment Co., 1146 Main St., $956.35.

> Since this transaction involved a purchase of store equipment, it was recorded in the general journal. (The purchases journal is used only for recording purchases of merchandise on account.)

Friday, March 3

Received Invoice No. 1 dated March 1 from King and King, 16 York St. for merchandise purchased, $136.95. Terms, 30 days net.

Paid $25 to the Globe Insurance Agency for a fire insurance policy covering store equipment and merchandise for a period of one year from date.

> This transaction represents an exchange of the asset Cash for the asset Prepaid Insurance and it was recorded by debiting Prepaid Insurance and by crediting Cash. It is proper to record prepaid insurance as an asset at the time of purchase even though it will become an expense as it expires. (The method of accounting for expired insurance will be discussed later.)

Saturday, March 4

Purchased store supplies for cash from Apex Supply Co., 621 Broadway, $146.67.

> This transaction was recorded by debiting the asset Store Supplies and by crediting Cash.

Sold merchandise on account to A. Y. Jordan, 115 Spruce St., $16.80, tax 34 cents. Sale No. 1-1.

Sundry cash sales per cash register tape, $32, tax 64 cents.

> On each Saturday the store's total cash sales for the week with tax thereon are recorded, using the cash register tape as the source of the amounts. This transaction was recorded by debiting Cash for the total amount received and by crediting Sales for the selling price of the merchandise and crediting Sales Tax Payable for the amount of the tax imposed on cash sales.

Monday, March 6

Purchased merchandise from Brown Brothers, 820 Park St., for cash, $79.30.

Tuesday, March 7

Sold merchandise on account to James O. Wells, 416 Broad St., $26.05, tax 52 cents. Sale No. 1-2.

Wednesday, March 8

Gave James O. Wells credit for merchandise returned, $9.10, tax 18 cents.

> This transaction increased sales returns and allowances and decreased sales tax payable and accounts receivable. It was recorded in the general journal by debiting Sales Returns and Allowances for the amount of the merchandise returned, by debiting Sales Tax Payable for the amount of the sales tax, and by crediting Accounts Receivable for the total amount of the credit allowed Mr. Wells.

Thursday, March 9

Received Invoice No. 2 dated March 8 from King and King for merchandise purchased, $230. Terms, 30 days net.

Friday, March 10

Sold merchandise on account to R. S. Jones, 61 Maple Ave., $24.10, tax 48 cents. Sale No. 2-1.

Saturday, March 11

Sundry cash sales for week, $115.90, tax $2.32.
Received a check for $17.14 from A. Y. Jordan in payment of merchandise sold to him March 4.

Monday, March 13

Received credit for $12.60 from King and King for merchandise returned by agreement.

> The credit applies to Invoice No. 2, dated March 8. This transaction had the effect of increasing purchases returns and allowances and decreasing accounts payable. It was recorded in the general journal by debiting Accounts Payable and by crediting Purchases Returns and Allowances for the amount of the credit received from King and King.

Tuesday, March 14

Paid Delivery Service, Inc., freight and drayage on merchandise purchased, $27.50.

Wednesday, March 15

Received Invoice No. 3 dated March 13 from Lake View Creamery, Dayton, for merchandise purchased, $30. Terms, 60 days net.
Paid Thomas Jones, salesclerk, semimonthly salary, $87.50.

Thursday, March 16

Paid King and King $136.95 in settlement of Invoice No. 1 dated March 1.

Friday, March 17

Received $17.29 from James O. Wells in payment for merchandise sold March 7 less merchandise returned March 8.

Saturday, March 18

Sundry cash sales for week, $82.50, tax $1.65.

Monday, March 20

Paid City Store Equipment Co. $400 on account.

Tuesday, March 21

Sold merchandise on account to R. S. Jones, $18.95, tax 38 cents. Sale No. 1-3.

Wednesday, March 22

Received Invoice No. 4 dated March 20 from Lake View Creamery for merchandise purchased, $37.50. Terms, 30 days net.

Thursday, March 23

Sold merchandise on account to A. Y. Jordan, $14, tax 28 cents. Sale No. 2-2.

Saturday, March 25

Sundry cash sales for week, $67.40, tax $1.35.

Monday, March 27

Sold merchandise on account to James O. Wells, $39.20, tax 78 cents. Sale No. 2-3.

Tuesday, March 28

Paid The Daily News $15 for advertising.

(*Continued on page 76*)

GENERAL JOURNAL   Page 1

DATE	DESCRIPTION	POST. REF.	DEBITS	CREDITS
19- Mar. 1	Cash	1	2 0 0 0 0 0	
	W. A. Goodman, Proprietor	8		2 0 0 0 0 0
	Original investment.			
1	Rent Expense	14	9 5 0 0	
	Cash	1		9 5 0 0
	Paid store rent for March.			
2	Store Equipment	5	9 5 6 3 5	
	Accounts Payable	6		9 5 6 3 5
	City Store Equipment Co.			
3	Prepaid Insurance	4	2 5 0 0	
	Cash	1		2 5 0 0
	Fire insurance.			
4	Store Supplies	3	1 4 6 6 7	
	Cash	1		1 4 6 6 7
	Apex Supply Co.			
4	Cash	1	3 2 6 4	
	Sales	10		3 2 0 0
	Sales Tax Payable	7		6 4
	Sundry cash sales.			
6	Purchases	12	7 9 3 0	
	Cash	1		7 9 3 0
	Brown Brothers.			
8	Sales Returns and Allowances	11	9 1 0	
	Sales Tax Payable	7	1 8	
	Accounts Receivable	2		9 2 8
	Mdse. retd.- James O. Wells.			
11	Cash	1	1 1 8 2 2	
	Sales	10		1 1 5 9 0
	Sales Tax Payable	7		2 3 2
	Sundry cash sales.			
11	Cash	1	1 7 1 4	
	Accounts Receivable	2		1 7 1 4
	A. Y. Jordan.			
13	Accounts Payable	6	1 2 6 0	
	Purchases Returns & Allowances	13		1 2 6 0
	Mdse. retd.- King and King.			
14	Purchases	12	2 7 5 0	
	Cash	1		2 7 5 0
	Freight and drayage.			
			3 5 1 9 7 0	3 5 1 9 7 0

The Goodman Store — General Journal

Page 2

DATE	DESCRIPTION	POST. REF.	DEBITS	CREDITS
19—				
Mar. 15	Salary Expense	15	8 7 50	
	Cash	1		8 7 50
	Sales clerk's salary.			
16	Accounts Payable	6	1 36 95	
	Cash	1		1 36 95
	King and King – Inv. #1.			
17	Cash	1	1 7 29	
	Accounts Receivable	2		1 7 29
	James O. Wells.			
18	Cash	1	84 15	
	Sales	10		82 50
	Sales Tax Payable	7		1 65
	Sundry cash sales.			
20	Accounts Payable	6	4 00 00	
	Cash	1		4 00 00
	City Store Equipment Co.			
25	Cash	1	68 75	
	Sales	10		67 40
	Sales Tax Payable	7		1 35
	Sundry cash sales.			
28	Advertising Expense	16	1 5 00	
	Cash	1		1 5 00
	Newspaper advertising.			
29	W. A. Goodman, Drawing	9	6 85	
	Cash	1		6 85
	Personal use.			
31	Salary Expense	15	8 7 50	
	Cash	1		8 7 50
	Sales clerk's salary.			
31	Telephone Expense	17	8 63	
	Cash	1		8 63
	Telephone service.			
31	Cash	1	58 75	
	Sales	10		57 60
	Sales Tax Payable	7		1 15
	Sundry cash sales.		9 7 1 37	9 7 1 37

PURCHASES JOURNAL FOR MONTH OF *March* 19—   Page 1

Date of Entry	Date of Invoice	No. of Invoice	From Whom Purchased	Post. Ref.	Amount	Date Paid
			Amount Forwarded			
Mar. 3	Mar. 1	1	King and King	✓	13695	Mar. 16
9	8	2	King and King	✓	23000	
15	13	3	Lake View Creamery	✓	3000	
22	20	4	Lake View Creamery	✓	3750	
31			Purchases Dr. - Accts. Pay. Cr.	12/6	43445	

The Goodman Store — Purchases Journal

SALES JOURNAL FOR MONTH OF *March* 19—   Page 1

Date of Entry	No. of Sale	To Whom Sold	Post Ref	Accounts Rec. Dr.	Sales Cr.	Sales Tax Pay. Cr.
		Amounts Forwarded				
Mar. 4	1-1	A. Y. Jordan	✓	1714	1680	34
7	1-2	James O. Wells	✓	2657	2605	52
10	2-1	R. S. Jones	✓	2458	2410	48
21	1-3	R. S. Jones	✓	1933	1895	38
23	2-2	A. Y. Jordan	✓	1428	1400	28
27	2-3	James O. Wells	✓	3998	3920	78
				14188	13910	278
				(2)	(10)	(7)

The Goodman Store — Sales Journal

GENERAL LEDGER

ACCOUNT *Cash*　　　　　　　　　　　　　　　Page 1

DATE	ITEMS	FOLIO	✓	DEBITS	DATE	ITEMS	FOLIO	✓	CREDITS
19- Mar. 1		J1		2 0 0 0 0 0	19- Mar. 1		J1		9 5 0 0
4		J1		3 2 6 4	3		J1		2 5 0 0
11		J1		1 1 8 2 2	4		J1		1 4 6 6 7
11		J1		1 7 1 4	6		J1		7 9 3 0
17		J2		1 7 2 9	14		J1		2 7 5 0
18		J2		8 4 1 5	15		J2		8 7 5 0
25		J2		6 8 7 5	16		J2		1 3 6 9 5
31	1,281.04	J2		2 3 5 8 7 5	20		J2		4 0 0 0 0
					28		J2		1 5 0 0
					29		J2		6 8 5
					31		J2		8 7 5 0
					31		J2		8 6 3

ACCOUNT *Accounts Receivable*　　　　　　　　Page 2

DATE	ITEMS	FOLIO	✓	DEBITS	DATE	ITEMS	FOLIO	✓	CREDITS
19- Mar. 31	98.17	S1		1 4 1 8 8	19- Mar. 8		J1		9 2 8
					11		J1		1 7 1 4
					17		J2		1 7 2 9

ACCOUNT *Store Supplies*　　　　　　　　　　Page 3

DATE	ITEMS	FOLIO	✓	DEBITS	DATE	ITEMS	FOLIO	✓	CREDITS
19- Mar. 4		J1		1 4 6 6 7					

ACCOUNT *Prepaid Insurance*　　　　　　　　Page 4

DATE	ITEMS	FOLIO	✓	DEBITS	DATE	ITEMS	FOLIO	✓	CREDITS
19- Mar. 3		J1		2 5 0 0					

ACCOUNT *Store Equipment*　　　　　　　　　Page 5

DATE	ITEMS	FOLIO	✓	DEBITS	DATE	ITEMS	FOLIO	✓	CREDITS
19- Mar. 2		J1		9 5 6 3 5					

The Goodman Store — General Ledger

ACCOUNT *Accounts Payable* Page 6

DATE	ITEMS	FOLIO	✓	DEBITS	DATE	ITEMS	FOLIO	✓	CREDITS
19— Mar 13		J1		12 60	19— Mar 2		J1		956 35
16		J2		136 95	31	841.25	P1		434 45
20		J2		400 00					

ACCOUNT *Sales Tax Payable* Page 7

DATE	ITEMS	FOLIO	✓	DEBITS	DATE	ITEMS	FOLIO	✓	CREDITS
19— Mar 8		J1		1 8	19— Mar 4		J1		64
					11		J1		2 32
					18		J2		1 65
					25		J2		1 35
					31		J2		1 15
					31	9.71	S1		2 78

ACCOUNT *W. A. Goodman, Proprietor* Page 8

DATE	ITEMS	FOLIO	✓	DEBITS	DATE	ITEMS	FOLIO	✓	CREDITS
					19— Mar 1		J1		2 000 00

ACCOUNT *W. A. Goodman, Drawing* Page 9

DATE	ITEMS	FOLIO	✓	DEBITS	DATE	ITEMS	FOLIO	✓	CREDITS
19— Mar 29		J2		6 85					

ACCOUNT *Sales* Page 10

DATE	ITEMS	FOLIO	✓	DEBITS	DATE	ITEMS	FOLIO	✓	CREDITS
					19— Mar 4		J1		32 00
					11		J1		115 90
					18		J2		82 50
					25		J2		67 40
					31		J2		57 60
					31		S1		139 10

ACCOUNT *Sales Returns and Allowances* Page 11

DATE	ITEMS	FOLIO	✓	DEBITS	DATE	ITEMS	FOLIO	✓	CREDITS
19— Mar 8		J1		9 10					

The Goodman Store — General Ledger (Continued)

ACCOUNT *Purchases* Page 12

DATE	ITEMS	FOLIO	✓	DEBITS	DATE	ITEMS	FOLIO	✓	CREDITS
19— Mar. 6		J1		79 30					
14		J1		27 50					
31		P1		4 34 45					

ACCOUNT *Purchases Returns and Allowances* Page 13

DATE	ITEMS	FOLIO	✓	DEBITS	DATE	ITEMS	FOLIO	✓	CREDITS
					19— Mar. 13		J1		12 60

ACCOUNT *Rent Expense* Page 14

DATE	ITEMS	FOLIO	✓	DEBITS	DATE	ITEMS	FOLIO	✓	CREDITS
19— Mar. 1		J1		95 00					

ACCOUNT *Salary Expense* Page 15

DATE	ITEMS	FOLIO	✓	DEBITS	DATE	ITEMS	FOLIO	✓	CREDITS
19— Mar. 15		J2		87 50					
31		J2		1 87 50					

ACCOUNT *Advertising Expense* Page 16

DATE	ITEMS	FOLIO	✓	DEBITS	DATE	ITEMS	FOLIO	✓	CREDITS
19— Mar. 28		J2		15 00					

ACCOUNT *Telephone Expense* Page 17

DATE	ITEMS	FOLIO	✓	DEBITS	DATE	ITEMS	FOLIO	✓	CREDITS
19— Mar. 31		J2		8 63					

The Goodman Store — General Ledger (Concluded)

Wednesday, March 29

W. A. Goodman took $6.85 from the cash register to pay a personal bill at the dry cleaner's.

> This decrease in cash was not offset by an increase in any business asset or expense; the transaction was simply a withdrawal of cash for personal use by the proprietor. It was recorded by a debit to W. A. Goodman, Drawing and by a credit to Cash.

Friday, March 31

Paid Thomas Jones' semimonthly salary, $87.50.
Paid $8.63 to the Bell Telephone Co. for service.
Sundry cash sales, $57.60, tax $1.15.

> Inasmuch as this is the last day of the month, the amount of cash sales since March 25, with tax thereon, was recorded.

Journalizing. The transactions completed by The Goodman Store during the month of March were recorded in the general journal reproduced on pages 70 and 71, the purchases journal reproduced on page 72, and the sales journal reproduced on page 72.

Posting. The ledger is reproduced on pages 73 to 75. The posting was completed from the books of original entry in the following order: first, the general journal; second, the purchases journal; and, third, the sales journal. Each entry in the general journal was posted individually to the proper accounts. The only posting that was done from the purchases and sales journals was the summary posting required at the end of the month. The total of the credit purchases was posted in one amount as a debit to Purchases and as a credit to Accounts Payable. The totals of the amount columns in the sales journal were posted to the accounts indicated by the column headings. As each total was posted, the number of the ledger page to which the posting was made was noted below the amount. In all other cases the proper cross references were indicated in the Posting Reference columns of the books of original entry and in the Folio columns of the ledger.

When more than one book of original entry is used, it is advisable to identify each book by means of an initial preceding the page number. The following code was used in conjunction with the page number to indicate the source of each entry in the ledger:

J = General journal

P = Purchases journal

S = Sales journal

The Goodman Store
Trial Balance
March 31, 19-

Accounts	Page	Dr. Balances	Cr. Balances
Cash	1	1 2 8 1 0 4	
Accounts Receivable	2	9 8 1 7	
Store Supplies	3	1 4 6 6 7	
Prepaid Insurance	4	2 5 0 0	
Store Equipment	5	9 5 6 3 5	
Accounts Payable	6		8 4 1 2 5
Sales Tax Payable	7		9 7 1
W. A. Goodman, Proprietor	8		2 0 0 0 0 0
W. A. Goodman, Drawing	9	6 8 5	
Sales	10		4 9 4 5 0
Sales Returns and Allowances	11	9 1 0	
Purchases	12	5 4 1 2 5	
Purchases Returns and Allowances	13		1 2 6 0
Rent Expense	14	9 5 0 0	
Salary Expense	15	1 7 5 0 0	
Advertising Expense	16	1 5 0 0	
Telephone Expense	17	8 6 3	
		3 3 5 8 0 6	3 3 5 8 0 6

Schedule of Accounts Receivable

R. S. Jones	✓	4 3 9 1	
A. Y. Jordan	✓	1 4 2 8	
James O. Wells	✓	3 9 9 8	
		9 8 1 7	

Schedule of Accounts Payable

City Store Equipment Co.	✓		5 5 6 3 5
King and King	✓		2 1 7 4 0
Lake View Creamery	✓		6 7 5 0
			8 4 1 2 5

The Goodman Store — Trial Balance and Schedules

Trial Balance. After the posting was completed, the accounts in the general ledger were footed where necessary and the balances were entered in the Items column on the proper side. The trial balance reproduced on page 77 was taken to prove the equality of the account balances. The balance of the accounts receivable summary account was proved by preparing a schedule of accounts receivable. The information needed in preparing this schedule was obtained from the sales tickets in the customers' file. The balance of the accounts payable summary account was proved by preparing a schedule of accounts payable. The information needed in preparing this schedule was obtained from the invoices in the unpaid invoice file. These schedules are reproduced following the trial balance.

Finding Errors. There are certain types of errors in bookkeeping that a trial balance may not reveal, such as the following:

(a) Failure to record a transaction in the books of original entry.

(b) Failure to post the correct amounts of all debit and credit items recorded in a book of original entry.

(c) Posting an item to the wrong account.

Such errors may be detected by checking to make sure (a) that all transactions have been recorded in the books of original entry, and (b) that all amounts recorded in the books of original entry have been correctly posted to the proper accounts in the ledger.

When the debit and the credit footings of a trial balance are unequal, the trial balance is out of balance. The trial balance can be brought into balance by checking or auditing the accounts and records until the error or errors are found and by making the necessary corrections. There is no standard procedure to be followed in making this check or audit, but it is advisable to follow a definite, logical plan or order of procedure. The following is a suggested plan:

(1) Prove the listing of the accounts in the trial balance by checking the account titles and the amounts with the ledger, making sure that the account balances are correctly listed in position and amount.

(2) Prove the account footings and balances by adding the debit and the credit items and ascertaining the difference between the footings of each account in the ledger.

(3) Prove the posting from the books of original entry to the accounts, checking each item both in the ledger and in the book of original entry.

(4) Prove the equality of the debit and the credit items recorded in each of the books of original entry.

In most cases errors that affect a trial balance will be revealed before the foregoing suggested checking procedure is completed. It should seldom be necessary to carry out the entire four-point program of checking to find errors in a trial balance.

Correcting Errors. When errors are found, corrections should be made. Errors may be made in recording transactions, in footing the columns in books of original entry, in posting, in footing the accounts in the ledger, in subtracting to ascertain the account balances, in listing the account balances in the trial balance, or in footing the trial balance. There are two approved methods of correcting such errors:

(a) By drawing a line through the incorrect item and inserting the correct item.

(b) By drafting a journal entry that will effect the necessary correction and posting the entry to the proper accounts.

An error in footing the columns of the books of original entry, in posting, in footing the accounts in the ledger, in determining the account balances, in listing the accounts in the trial balance, or in footing the trial balance may be corrected by crossing out the incorrect sum and recording the correct amount just above the erroneous amount or wherever it should be recorded. This is the usual plan followed by bookkeepers.

An error in recording a transaction in the books of original entry should preferably be corrected by means of a journal entry. For example, if it is found that in recording a transaction in the general journal, Rent Expense instead of Salary Expense had been debited erroneously for $75 and that the entry was already posted, a correcting entry may be made in the general journal debiting Salary Expense and crediting Rent Expense for $75.

When this journal entry is posted to the proper accounts in the ledger, a notation should be made in the Items column of each account to indicate that the entry is a correcting entry. When the journal entry method of correcting errors is used, it is not necessary to cross out the incorrect entries made originally, because the posting of the correcting entry from the journal accomplishes the desired result. In other words, the posting of the correcting journal entry eliminates the effect of the original error.

Financial Statements. If Mr. Goodman wanted to prepare an income statement for the month of March and a balance sheet as of March 31 for the business, it would be necessary to take into consideration several matters not shown by the records. In order to ascertain the margin of profit on goods sold, it would be necessary to calculate the cost of the goods sold. The purchases account shows the cost of the goods purchased during the month but it does not show the cost of the goods sold. It would be necessary to take an inventory of the unsold merchandise before the cost of the goods sold could be calculated. From the gross profit on goods sold it would be necessary to deduct the total operating expenses. There are certain expenses that have not been recorded. For example, at the beginning of the month insurance on store equipment and merchandise was purchased. Since the insurance policy is for a one-year period, one twelfth of the insurance has expired and, therefore, one twelfth of the original cost should be treated as an expense of the month. The store equipment purchased on March 2 will not last forever. It is necessary to apportion the cost of such assets to the periods they benefit. This process of cost apportionment is called depreciation accounting. If Mr. Goodman were to make up an income statement for the month of March, a proper share of the cost of this equipment would have to be treated as depreciation expense for the month.

Since The Goodman Store has been in operation for only one month and Mr. Goodman does not wish to have financial statements prepared at the end of the month, there is no need for recording the cost of goods sold, the amount of insurance expired, and the amount of depreciation sustained during the month. These matters will be discussed more fully later on when the year-end work of the accountant is considered.

> *PRACTICE ASSIGNMENT No. 8. Refer to the workbook and complete Report No. 8. This practice assignment provides a test of your ability to apply the principles developed in the first three units of this textbook. The textbook and the workbook go hand in hand, each serving a definite purpose in the learning process. Inability to solve correctly any problem included in the report indicates that you have failed to master the principles developed in the textbook. After completing the report, you may proceed with the textbook discussion in Unit Four until the next report is required.*

ACCOUNTING FOR CASH

(9) RECORDS OF CASH RECEIPTS AND DISBURSEMENTS

In the preceding units the fundamental principles of double-entry bookkeeping were introduced and applied to transactions arising from both mercantile and nonmercantile enterprises. A purchases journal, a sales journal, and a general journal were introduced as books of original entry. The procedure in journalizing, posting, and taking a trial balance was illustrated. Another step in developing the theory of accounts is to introduce additional records and accounts that may be used advantageously in recording transactions. This unit is devoted to a discussion of the accounts and records that may be used advantageously in accounting for cash receipts and disbursements.

The Cash Account. Transactions that result in increases in cash are recorded as debits to the cash account; transactions that result in decreases in cash are recorded as credits to the cash account. Normally the cash account will have a debit balance. However, when all of the cash has been paid out, the account will be in balance. A debit balance in the cash account represents either money on hand or in the bank, or both.

Cash Receipts. An accurate record of cash and cash items received should be kept. Cash includes coins and currency. Cash items include checks, drafts, and money orders.

When the amount of cash and the number of cash items received are sufficient to warrant it, a system may be used whereby all such receipts are listed by one individual, who may be the proprietor, a secretary, the cashier, the treasurer, or some other designated employee. Such a list is usually prepared daily in duplicate. One copy goes to the bookkeeper for recording purposes. The other copy is kept with the receipts until the deposit ticket has been prepared and checked with the actual receipts. In preparing a list of cash receipts, the information that is needed to identify each item should be recorded. The list may be either penwritten or typewritten.

The following table shows how a list of cash receipts may be prepared:

DATE	FROM WHOM RECEIVED	NATURE OF REMITTANCE	AMOUNT
19--			
Jan. 2	J. A. Jones	Check	$ 14.20
	Nesmith Bros.	Postal Money Order	24.50
	Orson & Johnson	Currency	20.00
	Hiram Bolsinger	Express Money Order	40.00
	Francis Lyon	Bank Draft	28.75
	Mrs. Frank C. Condon	Cashier's Check	19.25
	Total Cash Receipts...		$146.70

When numerous cash sales are involved, the amounts received are usually recorded in a cash register. The cash register tape provides a list of cash receipts for accounting purposes. If a cash register is not used, some form of receipt in duplicate should be used for each cash transaction. The customer should be given a copy and another copy should be retained for accounting purposes. Under such a plan the bookkeeper may not actually handle any cash; instead he records cash receipts from lists prepared by other persons. This system is sometimes referred to as a method of internal check. It is generally advocated by public accountants as a desirable practice.

Cash Disbursements.   Disbursements may be made in cash or by bank check. When disbursement is made in cash, a receipt or a receipted voucher should be obtained as evidence of the payment. When disbursement is made by bank check, it is not necessary to obtain a receipt since the canceled check that is returned by the bank on which it was drawn serves as a receipt.

Recording Cash Receipts and Disbursements.   In the preceding units, transactions involving the receipt or the disbursement of cash were recorded in the general journal along with other transactions. In many business enterprises, transactions involving the receipt or the disbursement of cash are more numerous than other types of transactions. Because of the frequency of such transactions and the desirability of maintaining a continuous check on cash in order to prove the cash balance at frequent intervals, it may be considered advisable to keep a separate record of cash receipts and cash disbursements.

There are many types of cash records used in recording transactions involving the receipt and the payment of cash. When a separate record is kept of cash receipts only, it is usually referred to as a *cash receipts journal*.

When a separate record is kept of cash payments or disbursements only, it is usually referred to as a *cash payments journal* or a *cash disbursements journal*. When all disbursements are made by check, the journal is sometimes called a *check register*. When cash receipts and cash payments are both recorded in the same book of account, the book is usually referred to as a *cashbook*.

The Cashbook. Cash receipts and cash payments may be recorded on opposite pages of a two-column cashbook. Entering receipts in such a cashbook involves recording the following information:

    (a) Date on which the cash was received.
    (b) Title of the account to be credited.
    (c) A description of the transaction.
    (d) Amount of cash received.

Entries on the left page of the cashbook represent receipts; hence, merely by footing the Amount column and thus ascertaining the total receipts, the aggregate increase in cash for a given period may be determined.

Entering payments in such a cashbook involves recording the following information:

    (a) Date on which the cash was paid.
    (b) Title of the account to be debited.
    (c) A description of the transaction.
    (d) Amount of cash paid.

Entries on the right page of the cashbook represent payments; hence, merely by footing the Amount column and thus ascertaining the total payments, the aggregate decrease in cash for a given period may be determined.

The Cashbook Illustrated. The cashbook reproduced on pages 84 and 85 consists of two pages of a cashbook in which the receipts and the payments of M. B. Roberts for the month of December are recorded. The receipts are recorded on the left page and the payments on the right page. Mr. Roberts is a consulting engineer engaged in professional practice on his own account. Since his income is derived principally from compensation for personal services, he follows the practice of not recording income until it is received in cash and of not recording expenses until they are paid in cash. A narrative of the cash transactions completed by Mr. Roberts during the month of December precedes the illustration.

NARRATIVE OF TRANSACTIONS

Dec. 1. Cash balance, $2,929.50.

1. Paid December rent, $100.

2. Received $120 from Thompson and Whitehead in payment of engineering fees.

4. Paid telephone bill, $16.25.

9. Paid dues in National Association of Consulting Engineers, $15.

12. Gave the Community Chest $15.

15. Paid The Williamson Co. $90 on account.

16. Paid secretary's salary for first half of month, $145.

18. Received $165 from The Lacey Manufacturing Co. in payment of engineering fees.

20. Received $350 from Johnson Bros. in payment of engineering fees.

23. Paid $5 for subscription to a professional magazine.

27. Paid Robbins Furniture Co. $25 on account.

28. Received $200 from The Brown Trucking Co. for engineering fees.

29. Paid Bradfield Bros. Garage $22.50 for gasoline, oil, and storage.

30. Paid secretary's salary for last half of month, $145.

30. Withdrew $200 for personal use.

Page 8   CASH RECEIPTS

DATE	ACCOUNT	DESCRIPTION	POST. REF.	AMOUNT	TOTAL
19— Dec. 1	Balance		✓		2 9 2 9 50
2	Income from Eng. Fees	Thompson & Whitehead	31	1 2 0 0 0	
18	Income from Eng. Fees	The Lacey Mfg. Co.	31	1 6 5 0 0	
20	Income from Eng. Fees	Johnson Bros.	31	3 5 0 0 0	
28	Income from Eng. Fees	The Brown Trucking Co.	31	2 0 0 0 0	
30	Cash Dr.	Total receipts			8 3 5 0 0
					3 7 6 4 50
19— Jan. 1	Balance		✓		2 9 7 5 75

M. B. Roberts' Cashbook (Left page)

It should be remembered that cash transactions only are recorded in a cashbook. Before each transaction is recorded, it is necessary to analyze it to determine whether it represents an increase in cash or a decrease in cash. Increases in cash are recorded on the left or receipts side of the cashbook, while decreases in cash are recorded on the right or payments side. The first transaction of December 1 involved the payment of rent. It had the effect of decreasing cash; therefore it was recorded on the payments side of the cashbook. The transaction of December 2 involved the receipt of cash in payment of engineering fees. It had the effect of increasing cash; therefore it was recorded on the receipts side of the cashbook. The posting references were not entered at the time of recording the transactions in the cashbook but were entered later as the posting was completed.

Advantages of the Cashbook. A study of the cashbook reveals that, for the purpose of recording cash receipts and payments, it offers the following advantages over the general journal:

(a) Since, in most cases, one line only is required to record each transaction in the cashbook, there is a saving of space as well as time.

CASH PAYMENTS   *Page 9*

DATE	ACCOUNT	DESCRIPTION	POST. REF.	AMOUNT	TOTAL
19-		AMOUNTS FORWARDED			
Dec. 1	Rent Expense	Dec. rent	42	1 0 0 0 0	
4	Tel. & Tel. Expense	Telephone bill		1 6 2 5	
9	Misc. Expenses	N.A.C.E. dues		1 5 0 0	
12	Donations	Community Chest		2 5 0 0	
15	Accounts Payable	The Williamson Co.		9 0 0 0	
16	Salary Expense	Secretary		1 4 5 0 0	
23	Misc. Expenses	Magazine sub.		5 0 0	
27	Accounts Payable	Robbins Furn. Co.		2 5 0 0	
29	Auto Expense	Bradfield Bros.		2 2 5 0	
30	Salary Expense	Secretary		1 4 5 0 0	
30	M. B. Roberts, Drawing	Personal Use		2 0 0 0 0	
30	Cash Cr.	Total payments			7 8 8 7 5
30	Balance		✓		2 9 7 5 7 5
					3 7 6 4 5 0

M. B. Roberts' Cashbook (Right page)

(b) Recording cash receipts on the left page and cash payments on the right page of a cashbook facilitates proving the cash balance.

(c) A cashbook makes information more readily available in regard to the total cash receipts, the total cash payments, and the cash balance; it is necessary only to foot the amount columns and to ascertain the difference between the footings to find the cash balance.

(d) A cashbook makes it feasible to employ a bookkeeper to record cash transactions only. This advantage becomes apparent when it is necessary to employ more than one bookkeeper to record all of the transactions of an enterprise.

The use of a cashbook as a book of original entry does not necessarily eliminate the need for using a general journal. There may be some transactions that do not involve the receipt or the payment of cash and that cannot, therefore, be recorded in a cashbook.

For example, if on December 7, M. B. Roberts purchased an adding-listing machine for $150 from the Office Supply Co. on credit, it cannot be recorded in the cashbook because it does not involve the receipt or payment of cash. Neither should it be recorded in the purchases journal which is designed for use in recording merchandise purchases only. It should, therefore, be recorded in the general journal by debiting Office Equipment and by crediting Accounts Payable for $150.

Proving Cash. Cash should be proved frequently. It is customary with most bookkeepers to prove cash before making deposits. Proving cash involves the following procedure:

(a) Ascertaining the total receipts for the period and adding this total to the balance of cash at the beginning of the period. The result is the total amount of cash to be accounted for.

(b) Ascertaining the total payments for the period.

(c) Subtracting the total payments from the sum of (1) the cash balance at the beginning of the period and (2) the total cash receipts for the period. The result is the cashbook balance at the end of the period.

(d) Proving the cashbook balance by counting the undeposited cash on hand and adding it to the amount of the bank balance. The sum of the cash on hand and in the bank should equal the cashbook balance.

Many persons keep a record of deposits and checks issued on the stubs of their checkbooks. If such a record is kept accurately, the bank balance may be ascertained by referring to the checkbook stubs. Some record of the deposits made and of the checks issued should be kept in order that the bank balance may be ascertained readily. If all receipts and payments are properly recorded and the amount columns of the cashbook are footed correctly, the correct cash balance should be indicated. The cash balance may be proved daily, weekly, monthly, or at any time by following the foregoing procedure.

Cash Over and Short. Cashiers and other employees who are required to handle numerous transactions involving cash find it necessary in some instances to make adjustments for the difference between the total amount of cash they have on hand and the amount they should have on hand. For example, a cashier in a restaurant may handle several hundred transactions in the course of a day. In the process of making change, mistakes may occur. At the end of the day the total cash received should agree with the total of the cash sales tickets issued during the day. If the amount received is more or less than the total of the sales tickets, the discrepancy indicates failure to collect the proper amount of all the sales tickets or mistakes in making change. To facilitate adjustments for such discrepancies, it is customary to keep a *cash over and short* account.

In proving cash at the end of the day if a shortage of $5 is found, an adjustment may be made by debiting Cash Over and Short and by crediting Cash for the amount of the shortage. Such an adjusting entry may be made on the payments side of the cashbook.

If an overage in cash of $5 is found, an adjustment may be made by debiting Cash and by crediting Cash Over and Short for the amount of the overage. Such an adjusting entry may be made on the receipts side of the cashbook.

In no case should such an adjusting entry to record either a shortage or an overage in cash be made (a) until a thorough check has been made to verify the balance of the cash account and the accuracy of the cash count, and (b) until the adjusting entry has been properly authorized.

At the end of an accounting period the balance of the cash over and short account may represent either a loss or a gain. If the account has a debit balance, it represents a loss for the period; if the account has a credit balance, it represents a gain for the period.

Footing, Balancing, and Ruling the Cashbook. Reference to the cashbook reproduced on pages 84 and 85 will reveal that the balance at the beginning of the month, amounting to $2,929.50, is recorded in the Total column on the left or receipts side of the cashbook. It should not be recorded in the Amount column, since that column is used to record the receipts of the month. The procedure in balancing this form of cashbook at the end of the month involves the following steps:

(a) The Amount column on the left side of the cashbook is footed and the footing is recorded in small figures in pencil immediately below the horizontal line on which the last entry appears. A single line is then ruled across the Amount column immediately above the footing. The total receipts are then recorded on the next line by writing the date in the Date column; "Cash Dr." in the Account column; "Total receipts" in the Description column; and the amount in the Total column.

(b) The Amount column on the right side of the cashbook is footed and the footing is recorded in small figures in pencil immediately below the horizontal line on which the last entry appears. A single line is then ruled across the Amount column immediately above the footing. The total payments are then recorded on the next line by writing the date in the Date column; "Cash Cr." in the Account column; "Total payments" in the Description column; and the amount in the Total column.

(c) The cashbook balance is then recorded on the next line on the right side of the cashbook by writing the date in the Date column; "Balance" in the Description column; and the amount in the Total column. Since this entry is not to be posted, a check mark is entered in the Posting Reference column.

(d) A single line is next ruled across the Total columns on both sides of the cashbook. This ruled line is drawn on the same horizontal line on both pages. The Total columns are then footed, and the footings are recorded in small figures in pencil immediately below the single ruled line. If the cashbook is in balance, these footings will be equal. After proving the equality of the footings, the amounts are recorded in ink on the next line.

(e) A double line is then ruled immediately below the totals across all of the columns on both sides of the cashbook, except the Account columns and the Description columns. The double rule indicates that the cashbook is in balance at that point.

(f) The balance is either brought down below the double rule on the cash receipts side or is carried forward to the top of the next cash receipts page and entered in the Total column so that it will not be included in the receipts for the ensuing month. A check mark is entered in the Posting Reference column to indicate that the item is not to be posted.

Posting from the Cashbook. The individual posting may be completed daily or periodically. The usual plan is to complete the posting daily, posting the receipts first and the payments second. When transactions have been properly recorded in a cashbook, the information needed for posting purposes is available. For example, refer to M. B. Roberts' cashbook which is reproduced on pages 84 and 85. The December 1 balance is the first item entered on the receipts side. Since this item need not be posted to the cash account, a check mark was placed in the Posting Reference column at the time it was entered.

Each item recorded in the Amount column on the receipts side of a cashbook should be posted to the credit of the account named in the Account column. Each item recorded in the Amount column on the payments side of a cashbook should be posted to the debit of the account named in the Account column. As the posting is completed a proper cross reference should be provided by entering the page of the cashbook preceded by the initial "C" in the Folio column of the ledger and by entering the page of the ledger in the Posting Reference column of the cashbook.

To illustrate the procedure, the accounts with Income from Engineering Fees and Rent Expense are reproduced below. The account with Income from Engineering Fees shows the December 1 balance entered on the credit side followed by the items posted from the receipts side of M. B. Roberts' cashbook. The account with Rent Expense shows the December 1 balance entered on the debit side followed by the item of December 1 posted from the payments side of M. B. Roberts' cashbook. It should be noted that as the posting was completed the page of the cashbook on which the original entry was made was entered in the Folio column of the

ACCOUNT *Income from Engineering Fees*   Page 36

DATE	ITEMS	FOLIO	√	DEBITS	DATE	ITEMS	FOLIO	√	CREDITS
					19-				
					Dec 1	Balance	√		7 4 5 8 75
					2		C8		1 20 0 0
					18		C8		1 6 5 0 0
					20		C8		3 5 0 0 0
					28		C8		2 0 0 0 0

ACCOUNT *Rent Expense*   Page 42

DATE	ITEMS	FOLIO	√	DEBITS					
19-									
Dec 1	Balance	√		1 1 0 0 0 0					
1		C9		1 0 0 0 0					

ledger and the page of the ledger on which the account was kept was entered in the Posting Reference column of the cashbook.

At the end of the month after the Amount columns in the cashbook have been footed and the total receipts and payments determined, the sum of the cash receipts should be posted to the debit of the cash account and the sum of the cash payments should be posted to the credit of the cash account. It will be noted that posting from the cashbook involves both individual and summary posting.

The Combined Cash-Journal. A *combined cash-journal* is a book of original entry combining features of both the general journal and the cashbook. Because it is easy to use and is self-balancing, the combined cash-journal is a popular type of book of original entry that is widely used in personal service and retail merchandising enterprises. A combined cash-journal may be proved at any time merely by footing the amount columns and by comparing the sum of the debit footings with the sum of the credit footings.

Form of Combined Cash-Journal. A combined cash-journal may be a bound book or a loose-leaf book. The blankbook manufacturers produce cash journals with a variety of amount columns, with or without printed headings. Public accountants frequently design cash journals to fit the needs of particular enterprises. In selecting a form of combined cash-journal for a particular enterprise, an effort should be made to obtain the desired number of amount columns to fit the needs of the enterprise.

For a mercantile enterprise that buys and sells merchandise on credit, the simplest form of combined cash-journal that is satisfactory is one similar to that illustrated on page 92. Standard eight-column paper (8 columns divided — 2 left, 6 right) is used in that journal. The Description column should be used to record the account titles affected by the amounts entered in the General Debits and Credits columns. Descriptive information, such as the names of individuals or firms, check numbers, credit memorandum numbers, etc. may also be recorded in the Description column. The account titles should be written at the left of the column, followed by the descriptive information. When an entry is supported by a proper voucher or document, little descriptive information need be recorded since the number of the voucher or document should provide a satisfactory cross reference.

The two amount columns at the left of the Description column are used in recording cash receipts and cash disbursements. All cash receipts should be recorded in the Dr. column and all cash disbursements should be recorded in the Cr. column. These columns serve the same purpose as a cashbook in which receipts are recorded on the left page and disbursements are recorded on the right page.

The first two amount columns at the right of the Description column are used to record transactions that are to be posted individually to accounts kept in the general ledger. In recording such transactions, the proper account title should be recorded in the Description column and the correct amount should be entered in the proper Debit or Credit column. These columns serve the same purpose as an ordinary two-column general journal.

The second pair of amount columns at the right of the Description column are used to record transactions affecting the accounts receivable account, debits being recorded in the left amount column and credits in the right amount column.

The last two amount columns are used to record transactions affecting the accounts payable account, debits being recorded in the left amount column and credits in the right amount column.

Combined Cash-Journal Illustrated. The combined cash-journal used to record the transactions completed by The Goodman Store during the month of March is illustrated on page 92. The narrative of transactions appears in Unit Three beginning on page 66. The combined cash-journal was used in conjunction with a purchases journal and a sales journal. All transactions involving the purchase of merchandise on credit were recorded in the purchases journal and all transactions involving the sale of merchandise on credit were recorded in the sales journal. Both of these journals are illustrated on page 72 in Unit Three. All other transactions are recorded in the combined cash-journal.

Several features of the combined cash-journal should be noted. Most of the entries in this journal required only one line. However, the entries to record cash sales required two lines in each case because each entry involved credits to two accounts. The entry on March 8 required two lines since two debits were involved. Check marks were placed in the Posting Reference column in those entries where individual posting is not required from the General Dr. or Cr. columns. For example, the second transaction of March 11 is recorded as a debit to Cash and as a credit to Accounts Receivable. Since there are no entries in the General Dr. or Cr. columns to be posted individually, a check mark was placed in the Posting Reference column.

COMBINED CASH-JOURNAL FOR MONTH OF *March* 19—   Page 1

Cash Receipts Dr.	Cash Payments Cr.	Date Mo.	Date Day	Description	Post. Ref.	General Debits	General Credits	Accts. Receivable Debits	Accts. Receivable Credits	Accts. Payable Debits	Accts. Payable Credits
				Amounts Forwarded							
200000		Mar.	1	W. A. Goodman, Proprietor	8		200000				
	9500		1	Rent Expense	14	9500					
			2	Store Equipment - City Store Equipment Co.	5	95635					95635
	2500		3	Prepaid Insurance	4	2500					
	14667		4	Store Supplies	3	14667					
3204			4	Sales	10		3200				
				Sales Tax Payable	7		67				
	7930		6	Purchases	12	7930					
			8	Sales Returns and Allowances - James O'Malle	11	910			928		
				Sales Tax Payable	7	18					
11822			11	Sales	10		11590				
				Sales Tax Payable	7		232				
1714			11	A. J. Jordan	1				1714		
			13	King and King - Purchases Returns & Allowances	13		1260			1260	
	2750		14	Purchases	12	2750					
	8750		15	Salary Expense	15	8750					
	13695		16	King and King	1					13695	
1729			17	James O'Malle	1				1729		
8415			18	Sales	10		8250				
				Sales Tax Payable	7		165				
	40000		20	City Store Equipment Co.	1					40000	
6875			25	Store Equipment Co.	10		6740				
				Sales Tax Payable	7		135				
	1500		28	Advertising Expense	16	1500					
	685		29	W. A. Goodman, Drawing	9	685					
	8750		31	Salary Expense	15	8750					
	863		31	Telephone Expense	17	863					
5875			31	Sales	18		5760				
				Sales Tax Payable	7		115				
239694	111590			$1,987.05		1544458	232511		4371	54955	95635
239694	111590					1544458	232511		4371	54955	95635
(1)	(5)					(1)	(1)		(2)	(3)	(6)

Proving a Combined Cash-Journal. To prove a combined cash-journal, it is necessary to foot all of the amount columns and to compare the sum of the debit footings with the sum of the credit footings. The footings should be proved frequently; when the transactions are numerous, it may be advisable to prove the footings daily. Usually, however, it will be sufficient to prove the footings at the end of each week. Some bookkeepers follow the practice of proving the footings before making each bank deposit. The following is a proof of the footings of the combined cash-journal of The Goodman Store at the end of March:

PROOF OF COMBINED CASH-JOURNAL FOOTINGS
MARCH 31, 19--

COLUMN	DR.	CR.
Cash	$2,396.94	$1,115.90
General	1,544.58	2,375.11
Accounts Receivable		43.71
Accounts Payable	549.55	956.35
	$4,491.07	$4,491.07

At the time of proving the footings of the combined cash-journal, it is advisable also to prove the cash balance. To prove the cash balance, it is necessary to count the cash and cash items on hand; also to ascertain the balance in the bank. When a record of the banking transactions is kept on the checkbook stub, it is necessary only to refer to the checkbook stub to ascertain the bank balance at any time.

A proof of the cash balance at the end of March follows.

PROOF OF CASH BALANCE
MARCH 31, 19--

Cash receipts for month	$2,396.94
Less cash payments for month	1,115.90
Cash balance at end of month	$1,281.04
Cash on hand	None
Bank balance per checkbook stub	$1,281.04

There was no cash on hand at the end of the month because all cash received during the month had been deposited in the bank, the last deposit having been made on March 31.

Footing and Ruling a Combined Cash-Journal. A combined cash-journal should be footed and ruled at the end of each month. The footings should first be recorded in small figures in pencil immediately below the last regular entry. After being proved, the totals should be recorded in ink on the next horizontal line, unless the page is filled, in which case the totals should be recorded on the double ruled line at the bottom of the page. If the page is not filled, a single rule should be drawn across all of the amount columns just above the totals and a double rule should be drawn across all of the columns except the Description column, just below the totals.

The cash balance at the beginning of the month should be recorded in the Description column. Inasmuch as The Goodman Store began operations on March 1, there was no beginning balance to be recorded on that date. At the end of the month, the cash balance should be ascertained by adding the total receipts for the month to the beginning balance and by subtracting the total payments for the month. This balance should be recorded in small figures in pencil in the Description column immediately below the last regular entry. The April 1 balance should be entered in the Description column before recording any transactions for April.

When it is necessary to carry forward the totals of a page of a combined cash-journal, each column should be footed and the footings should be proved by ascertaining the equality of the debits and credits. After the footings have been proved, the totals should be recorded in ink and the words "Carried Forward" should be written in the Description column. The totals should then be recorded at the top of the next page by entering the correct total in each Amount column.

Posting from a Combined Cash-Journal. Posting from a combined cash-journal involves both individual posting and summary posting. The individual posting is completed daily or periodically, while the summary posting is usually completed at the end of each month.

Individual Posting. In completing the individual posting from the combined cash-journal of The Goodman Store, each item recorded in the General columns should be posted to the proper account in the general ledger. The account title appears at the left in the Description column. Each item recorded in the General Dr. column should be posted to the debit of the account affected, while each item recorded in the General Cr. column should be posted to the credit of the account affected. Thus, in posting the first entry of March 1, the account of W. A. Goodman, Proprietor should be credited for $2,000. The ledger page should be entered in the Posting Reference column of the combined cash-journal and the combined cash-journal page should be entered in the Folio column of the ledger account to provide a suitable cross reference.

It may or may not be necessary to post individually the amounts entered in the Accounts Receivable Dr. and Cr. columns and the Accounts Payable Dr. and Cr. columns. This will depend upon whether or not individual ledger accounts are kept with customers and with creditors and whether or not the posting is done from the books of original entry or directly from vouchers or other business forms representing the business transactions. Since individual ledger accounts with customers and with creditors are not kept by The Goodman Store, no individual posting from these columns of the combined cash-journal is required.

Summary Posting. The totals of all of the amount columns in the combined cash-journal of The Goodman Store, except the General Dr. and Cr. columns, should be posted to the accounts named in the headings of the columns. This summary posting should be completed after all the amount columns have been footed, the debit and credit footings proved, the totals entered, and the ruling completed. The summary posting from the combined cash-journal should be completed in the following order:

(a) Post the total of the Cash Receipts Dr. amount column to the debit of Cash.

(b) Post the total of the Cash Payments Cr. amount column to the credit of Cash.

(c) Post the total of the Accounts Receivable Dr. amount column to the debit of Accounts Receivable.

(d) Post the total of the Accounts Receivable Cr. amount column to the credit of Accounts Receivable.

(e) Post the total of the Accounts Payable Dr. amount column to the debit of Accounts Payable.

(f) Post the total of the Accounts Payable Cr. amount column to the credit of Accounts Payable.

As the total of each amount column is posted, the ledger page should be entered immediately below the total as a posting reference. Check marks may be placed immediately below the totals of the General Dr. and Cr. amount columns to indicate that these totals are not to be posted.

After completing the summary posting from all of the books of original entry of The Goodman Store, including the purchases journal, the sales journal, and the combined cash-journal, the cash, accounts receivable, and accounts payable accounts appeared as follows:

ACCOUNT *Cash*   *Page 1*

DATE	ITEMS	FOLIO	√	DEBITS	DATE	ITEMS	FOLIO	√	CREDITS
19- Mar. 31	1,281.04	CJ 1		2 3 9 6 9 4	19- Mar. 31		CJ 1		1 1 1 5 9 0

ACCOUNT *Accounts Receivable*   *Page 2*

DATE	ITEMS	FOLIO	√	DEBITS	DATE	ITEMS	FOLIO	√	CREDITS
19- Mar. 31	98.17	S 1		1 4 1 8 8	19- Mar. 31		CJ 1		4 3 7 1

ACCOUNT *Accounts Payable*   *Page 6*

DATE	ITEMS	FOLIO	√	DEBITS	DATE	ITEMS	FOLIO	√	CREDITS
19- Mar. 31		CJ 1		5 4 9 5 5	19- Mar. 31		P 1		4 3 4 4 5
					31	841.25	CJ 1		9 5 6 3 5

The cash account was debited for the total cash receipts for March and was credited for the total cash payments for March, the amounts being posted from the combined cash-journal. The balance of the account, amounting to $1,281.04, indicates the amount of cash on hand at the end of the month.

The accounts receivable account was debited for the total charge sales for March, the amount being posted from the sales journal. The account was credited for the total remittances received from customers during March, the amount being posted from the combined cash-journal. The balance of the account, amounting to $98.17, indicates the amount due from customers at the end of the month.

The accounts payable account was debited for the total payments made to creditors during March, the amount being posted from the combined cash-journal. The account was credited for the total amount of merchandise purchased on credit during the month, the amount being posted from the purchases journal. The account was also credited for the sum of all invoices received during the month representing the purchase on credit of property other than merchandise, the amount being posted from the combined cash-journal. The balance of the account, amounting to $841.25, indicates the amount owed to creditors at the end of the month.

By comparing the foregoing accounts with the corresponding accounts in the ledger reproduced on pages 73 to 75, it will be seen that the use of a combined cash-journal resulted in a saving of time in posting due to the summary posting. It will also be noted that the balances of the accounts are the same in both illustrations.

Other Features of Multicolumn Journals. There is a wide variety of journal forms in common use. The central characteristics of the general journal, the purchases journal, the sales journal, the cashbook, and the combined cash-journal forms that have been illustrated are always present, but numerous variations of detail are found. For example, in the case of cash-journals, it is not uncommon to have a memo column in which the balance of the cash or bank account is noted after each transaction. Sometimes the Date, Description, and Folio columns appear first at the left of the page with all of the Amount columns at the right. The number of Amount columns used in combined cash-journals varies widely.

The accountant chooses the form and arrangement best suited to the needs of each individual business. A variety of so-called "standard" forms can be purchased. Some of these forms have printed column headings; others have just the rulings. Some companies design their own journal forms and have them printed to specification.

> *PRACTICE ASSIGNMENT No. 9. Refer to the workbook and complete Report No. 9. After completing the report, proceed with the textbook discussion until the next report is required.*

(10) BANKING PROCEDURE

A bank is a financial institution that receives deposits, lends money, makes collections, and renders other services, such as providing vaults for the safekeeping of money, securities, and other valuables, or handling trust funds for its customers. Most banks solicit both checking accounts and savings accounts.

Checking Account. A checking account is sometimes referred to as a commercial account. Important factors in connection with a checking account are (a) opening the account, (b) making deposits, (c) making withdrawals, and (d) reconciling the bank balance.

Opening a Checking Account. To open a checking account with a bank, it is necessary to obtain the approval of an official of the bank and to make an initial deposit. Money, checks, bank drafts, money orders, and other cash items will usually be accepted for deposit. Cash is accepted for deposit subject to verification as to amount and validity. Cash items are accepted for deposit subject to their being paid (honored) by their makers when presented for payment by the bank or its agent.

Signature Card. Banks usually require a new depositor to sign his name on a *signature card* or form as an aid in verifying the depositor's signature on checks that he may issue, on cash items that he may endorse for deposit, and on other business papers that he may present to the bank. If desired, a depositor may authorize others to sign his name to checks and to other business forms. Each person who is so authorized is required to sign the depositor's name along with his own signature on a signature card. A signature card is one of the safeguards that a bank uses to protect its own interests as well as the interests of its depositors.

Deposit Ticket. The bank provides a blank *deposit ticket* on which the depositor is required to list the items that are being deposited. A model filled-in deposit ticket is reproduced below.

In preparing a deposit ticket, the name of the depositor and the date should be written in the spaces provided for these purposes. Coins, including pennies, nickels, dimes, quarters, half dollars, and silver dollars, that are to be deposited in considerable quantities should be wrapped in coin wrappers, which the bank will provide. The name of the depositor should be written on the outside of each coin wrapper as a means of identification in the event that a mistake has been made in counting the coins. Paper money should be arranged in the order of the denominations, the smaller denominations being placed on top. The amounts of cash represented by paper money (currency) and by coins should be entered in the amount column of the deposit ticket on the lines provided for these items.

Each additional item to be deposited should be listed on a separate line of the deposit ticket as shown in the illustration at the right. In listing checks on the deposit ticket, the instructions of the bank should be observed in describ-

Deposit Ticket

ing the checks for identification purposes. Formerly it was common practice to list local checks by name of bank and out-of-town checks by name of city. Currently the preferred practice is to identify each check by entering the American Bankers Association (A.B.A.) transit number on the deposit ticket.

The A.B.A. numbers usually appear on checks as shown in the illustration on page 100. The numerator of the fraction is the transit number, while the denominator is the routing symbol. Such identification numbers are assigned to banks by the American Bankers Association. Numbers 1 to 49 are assigned to large cities and numbers 50 to 99 to the states. Number 13 appearing on the check shown is the number assigned to Cincinnati, Ohio, while 1 is the number assigned to the First National Bank.

There are twelve Federal Reserve Bank Districts. Cincinnati is located in the 4th District. If the denominator has three digits, the first digit designates one of the Federal Reserve Districts numbered 1 to 9. The second digit designates the Federal Reserve Bank or Branch serving the territory in which the drawee bank is located. If a bank is located in a city where the head office of the Federal Reserve Bank is located, this fact will be indicated by the figure 1. Branches of the Federal Reserve Bank arranged alphabetically are designated by figures 2 to 5. Thus, the first two digits of number 420 indicate that the First National Bank, Cincinnati, Ohio, is located in the 4th Federal Reserve District and that Cincinnati is served by Branch No. 2 of the Federal Reserve Bank.

The third digit of the denominator serves two purposes: first, it facilitates the separation of items that are receivable for immediate credit from those that are receivable for deferred credit, and second, it facilitates the sorting of items by states in any case where that is convenient. Figure 0 designates items that are receivable for immediate credit if received in time to be cleared on the current day. All other figures designate items that are receivable for deferred credit, and also designate the state in which the drawee bank is located. When a bank is located in one of those Federal Reserve Districts that is numbered 10 to 12, the denominator will have four digits, the first two of which designate the Federal Reserve District in which the bank is located.

Many banks provide special envelopes for the use of depositors in depositing bond coupons. Only one kind of coupon should be placed in each envelope and the amount of the coupons placed in each envelope should be listed separately on the deposit ticket. Thus, if two U. S. Government Bond coupons for $12.50 each are being deposited, they should be enclosed in the envelope provided for that purpose and the total should be listed on the deposit ticket as "U. S. Bond Coupons, $25." If, at the same time, a coupon from an industrial bond is being deposited, it should be placed in a separate envelope.

Endorsements. Items requiring endorsements should be endorsed on the back by the depositor, except postal money orders, which provide space for endorsements on the front. Negotiable instruments, such as checks, notes, and drafts, made payable to the depositor either directly or by prior endorsement, must be endorsed by him before a bank will accept them for deposit. One purpose of such endorsement is to transfer the title of the instrument to the bank. By means of his endorsement the depositor also guarantees the payment of the instrument. Checks and other items submitted for deposit that require endorsements on the back may be endorsed as shown in the illustration below. In endorsing a check, the name of the payee should be written exactly as it appears on the face of the check. Note that the endorsement is written near the left end of the check. The left end is the end that is at the left when the front of the check is held in position for reading. This form of endorsement is known as a *restrictive endorsement*. When so endorsed a check cannot be cashed by anyone other than the bank to whom it is endorsed. Businesses sometimes use a rubber stamp to endorse checks for deposit.

The total of the cash and other items deposited should be entered on the deposit ticket. The deposit ticket, together with the cash and the other items to be deposited, should be delivered to the receiving teller

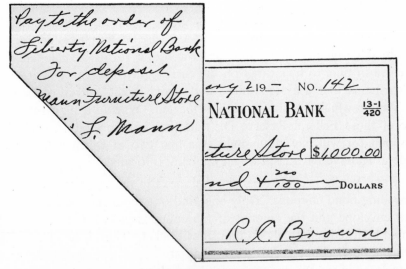

Endorsement for Deposit

of the bank. The teller may enter the date and the amount of the deposit in a passbook that is provided by the bank. If the passbook is not available when a deposit is being made, the deposit ticket may be prepared in duplicate; the teller will receipt the duplicate copy and return it to the depositor to be retained by him until such time as it is convenient to enter the amount of the deposit in his passbook.

Instead of providing the depositor with a passbook, the bank may provide the depositor with a machine-printed receipt for each deposit. Some banks use *automatic teller machines* in preparing the receipts. The use of such machines saves the time of making hand entries in a passbook and eliminates any need for making duplicate copies of deposit tickets. Such machines not only are time-saving machines; they also promote accuracy in the handling of deposits. The deposits handled by each teller during the day may be accumulated so that at the end of the day the total amount of the deposits received by a teller is automatically recorded by the machine and this amount may be proved by counting the cash and cash items accepted for deposit during the day.

Dishonored Checks. Under banking customs the depositor guarantees all items that he deposits and is liable to the bank for the amount involved if, for any reason, any item is not honored when presented for payment. When a check or other cash item is deposited with a bank and is not honored upon presentation to the bank upon which it is drawn, the depositor's bank may charge the amount of the dishonored item to the depositor's account or present it to the depositor for reimbursement. It is not uncommon for checks that have been deposited to be returned to the depositor for various reasons, as indicated on the return notice reproduced below. The most common reason for checks being returned unpaid is "not sufficient funds" (N.S.F.).

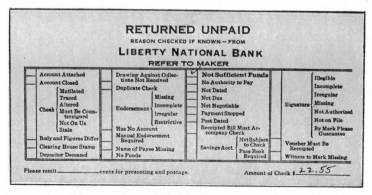

Return Notice

Under the laws of most states, it is illegal for anyone to issue a check on a bank without having sufficient funds on deposit with that bank to redeem the check when it is presented for payment. When a *dishonored check* is charged to the depositor's account, or is redeemed by a check issued by the depositor, an entry should be made in the cashbook debiting the maker of the dishonored check and crediting Cash. If the depositor issues his own check to reimburse the bank, it should be recorded on his checkbook stub. If the dishonored check is charged to the depositor's account by the bank, the depositor should deduct the amount from the balance shown on his checkbook stub, even though he did not issue a check.

Postdated Checks. Sometimes *postdated checks* are issued; that is, they are dated subsequent to the date of issue. Thus, a check issued on March 1 may be dated March 15. The recipient of a postdated check should not deposit it before the date specified on the check. One reason for issuing a postdated check may be that the maker does not have sufficient funds in his bank at the time of issuance to pay it, but he may expect to have a sufficient amount on deposit by the time the check is presented for payment on or after the date of the check. When a postdated check is presented to the bank on which it is drawn and payment is not made, it is handled by the bank in the same manner as any other dishonored check and the payee should treat it as a dishonored check. Generally, it is not good practice to issue postdated checks.

Making Deposits by Mail. Bank deposits may be made either over the counter or by mail. The over-the-counter method of making deposits is generally used. It may not always be convenient, however, for a depositor to make his deposits over the counter, especially if he lives at a great distance from the bank. In such a case it may be more convenient for him to make his deposits by mail. When a depositor makes his deposits by mail, the bank may provide him with a special form of deposit ticket.

Night Deposits. A depositor may find it convenient to use the night deposit safe of his bank. The opening to the night deposit safe is on the exterior of the bank building. Upon signing a night depository contract, the bank supplies the depositor with a key to the door in the opening of the safe, together with a bag that has an identifying number and in which valuables may be placed, and duplicate keys to the bag itself. Once the depositor places his bag in the night deposit safe it cannot be retrieved because it gravitates to a vault in the bank that is accessible to bank employees only. Since only the depositor is provided with keys to his bag, he or his authorized representative must go to the bank to unlock the bag. The depositor may or may not subsequently deposit in his account in the bank the funds that he has placed temporarily in the night deposit safe.

Night deposit banking service is especially valuable to those individuals and concerns that do not have safe facilities in their own places of business and that accumulate cash and other cash items which they cannot take to the bank during banking hours.

Making Withdrawals. The amount deposited in a bank checking account may be withdrawn either by the depositor himself or by any other person who has been properly authorized to make withdrawals from the depositor's account. Such withdrawals are accomplished by the use of checks signed by the depositor or by others having the authority to sign checks drawn on the account.

Checkbook. Banks provide printed forms known as checks for the convenience of their depositors. Such checks are used by depositors to authorize the bank to pay out specified amounts from the funds credited to their accounts. Special forms of checks may be used for payrolls, dividends, or other purposes. Voucher checks are used by many firms. The Federal Reserve Bank of Cleveland stated in a recent bulletin that "roughly 85 per cent of all money payments in the United States are made by check."

Blank checks are often bound in a book with one or more checks to a page. Each check usually contains spaces for recording the following information:

  (a) The number of the check.
  (b) The date of the check.
  (c) The name of the payee.
  (d) The amount the bank is authorized to pay the payee.
  (e) The signature of the drawer — the depositor or his authorized agent.

The stub of a checkbook usually contains blank spaces for recording the same information that is recorded on the checks issued; thus, the completed stubs provide the depositor with a record of all checks issued. Sometimes blank space is also provided on the stub of each check for recording the title of the account to be debited. In any event, sufficient data should be entered on the stub of each check to provide the information needed for recording purposes. Checks should be numbered consecutively, and their stubs should bear identical numbers. The numbers may be penwritten or a numbering machine may be used. It is a good plan to number all stubs and checks before any checks are issued. Frequently businesses have a quantity of blank checks printed with the name and address of the business shown. Usually the checks are prenumbered.

Writing a Check. The stub should be filled in before the check is written. This plan insures the drawer a record of each check issued.

When a depositor withdraws funds personally, the payee of the check should be designated as "Myself," "Cash," "Payroll," "Postage Stamps," or the like. Any one of the foregoing terms will indicate that the check is to be cashed and the money used for a special purpose.

When a depositor desires the bank to pay the money to a third party, he writes the name of that party, referred to as the payee, on the stub and on the check. When the payee presents the check to the bank for payment, he may be required by the bank to identify himself.

The purpose for which a check is drawn is usually recorded on the stub below the name of the payee. The purpose may also be indicated in the lower left-hand corner of the check. Indicating the purpose on the check provides information for the benefit of the payee and provides a specific receipt for the drawer.

The amount is stated on the stub in figures and is stated on the check in both figures and words. If the amount shown on the check in figures does not agree with the amount shown in words, the bank usually will return the check unpaid.

Checks and Stubs

Care must be used in writing the amount on the check in order to avoid any possibility that the payee or a subsequent holder may change the amount. If the instructions given below are followed in the preparation of a check, it will be difficult to change the amount.

(a) The amount shown in figures should be written so that there is no space between the dollar sign and the first digit of the amount.

(b) The amount stated in words should be written beginning at the extreme left on the line provided for this information.

(c) The cents should be written in the form of a common fraction; if the check is for an even number of dollars, use two ciphers or the word "no" as the numerator of the fraction.

(d) A line should be drawn from the amount stated in words to the word "Dollars" on the same line with it, as illustrated on page 104.

Frequently a machine known as a *check writer* is used to write the amount of a check in figures and in words. The use of a check writer is desirable because it practically eliminates the possibility of a change in the amount of a check.

Each check issued by a depositor will be returned to him by the bank on which it is drawn after the check has been paid. Canceled checks are returned to the depositor with the bank statement, which is usually rendered each month. Canceled checks will be endorsed by the payee and any subsequent holders. Canceled checks constitute receipts that the depositor should retain for future reference. They may be pasted to the stubs from which they were removed originally or they may be filed.

Overdraft. As stated previously, it is illegal in most states for a depositor to issue a check against a bank in excess of the amount on deposit. However, it may happen that through an oversight or an error in calculation a depositor will overdraw his checking account. Should this happen the bank may refuse to honor the check or it may honor the check and notify the depositor by mail that he has overdrawn his account. Sometimes an official of the bank will telephone the depositor instead of notifying him by mail. Overdrawing a bank checking account is considered a serious matter and the depositor is expected to make the necessary adjustment without delay.

Recording Bank Transactions. A depositor should keep a record of the transactions he completes with his bank. The usual plan is to keep this record on the checkbook stubs as shown in the illustration on page 104.

It will be noted that the record consists of detailed information concerning each check written and an amount column in which should be recorded (a) the balance brought forward or carried down, (b) the amount of deposits to be added, and (c) the amount of checks to be subtracted. The purpose is to keep a detailed record of deposits made and checks issued and to indicate the balance in the checking account after each check is drawn.

As the amount of each check is recorded in the cashbook, a check mark may be placed immediately after the account title written on the stub to indicate that it has been recorded. When the canceled check is subsequently received from the bank, the amount shown on the stub may be checked to indicate that the canceled check has been received.

Records Kept by a Bank. The usual transactions completed by a bank with a depositor are:

(a) Accepting deposits made by the depositor.

(b) Paying checks issued by the depositor.

(c) Lending money to the depositor.

(d) Discounting commercial paper for the depositor (another type of lending).

(e) Collecting the amounts of various kinds of commercial paper, such as notes and drafts, for the account of the depositor.

The bank keeps an account with each depositor. Each transaction affecting a depositor's account is recorded by debiting or crediting his account, depending upon the effect of the transaction. When a bank accepts a deposit, the account of the depositor is credited for the amount of the deposit. The deposit increases the bank's liability to the depositor.

LIBERTY NATIONAL BANK

CREDIT ADVICE

To The Mann Furniture Store, 12 N. Third St., City

WE HAVE CREDITED YOUR ACCOUNT AS FOLLOWS:

Note - Griffin, Ga.		250 00
	Cost	1 00
		249 00

In receiving items for deposit or collection, this bank acts only as depositor's collecting agent and assumes no responsibility beyond the exercise of due care. All items are credited subject to final payment in cash or solvent credits. This bank will not be liable for default or negligence of its duly selected correspondents nor for losses in transit, and each correspondent so selected shall not be liable except for its own negligence. This bank or its correspondents may send items directly or indirectly to any bank including the payor, and accept its draft or credit as conditional payment in lieu of cash; it may charge back any item at any time before final payment, whether returned or not, also any item drawn on this bank not good at close of business on day deposited. All city checks deposited today will be held at depositor's risk until next day's settlement.

Credit Advice

When the bank pays a check that has been drawn on the bank, it debits the account of the depositor for the amount of the check. If the bank makes a collection for a depositor, the net amount of the collection is credited to his account. At the same time the bank notifies the depositor on a form similar to the one shown on page 106 that the collection has been made.

Bank Statement of Account. Usually at the end of each month a bank renders a statement of account to each depositor similar to that shown below. This statement is a report showing (a) the balance on deposit at the beginning of the month, (b) the amounts of deposits made during the month, (c) the amounts of checks honored during the month,

CHECKS			DEPOSITS		THE LAST AMOUNT IN THIS COLUMN IS YOUR BALANCE	
			BALANCE FORWARD	Sept. 1	8,937.46	
50.00	20.96	85.00		2	8,781.50	
			600.02	4	9,381.52	
641.37	100.00			8	8,640.15	
125.00	10.00		349.65	12	8,854.80	
321.60	129.75	15.00		15	8,388.45	
25.00	152.50		721.30	19	8,932.25	
600.00	39.75	5.00		22	8,287.50	
.50 SC				23	8,287.00	
125.60				26	8,161.40	
			249.00	27	8,410.40	
			591.65	29	9,002.05	
17.65	42.50	98.75		30	8,843.15	

STATEMENT OF YOUR ACCOUNT WITH

LIBERTY NATIONAL BANK

REPORT PROMPTLY ANY CHANGE IN YOUR ADDRESS

The Mann Furniture Store

12 N. Third St.

City

PLEASE EXAMINE AT ONCE AND REPORT ANY DISCREPANCIES OR ERRORS TO OUR AUDITOR WITHIN TEN DAYS.

CHECKS RETURNED 19
SHEET NUMBER 285

Bank Statement

(d) other items charged to the depositor's account during the month, and (e) the balance on deposit at the end of the month. With his monthly bank statement, the depositor also receives all checks paid by the bank during the month, together with any other vouchers representing items charged to his account.

Reconciling the Bank Balance. When a bank statement is received, a depositor should check it immediately with the bank record kept on his check stubs. This procedure is known as *reconciling the bank balance*. The balance shown on the bank statement may not be the same as the amount shown on the check stubs for one or more of the following reasons:

(a) Some of the checks issued during the month may not have been presented to the bank for payment before the statement was prepared.

(b) Deposits made by mail may have been in transit or a deposit placed in the night depository on the last day of the month may not have been recorded by the bank until the following day.

(c) Service charges or other charges may appear on the bank statement that the depositor has not recorded on his check stubs.

(d) The depositor may have erred in keeping his bank record.

(e) The bank may have erred in keeping its account with the depositor.

If a depositor is unable to reconcile his bank balance, he should report the matter to his bank immediately.

Following is a suggested procedure in reconciling the bank balance:

(a) The amount of each deposit recorded on the bank statement should be checked with the amount recorded on the check stubs.

(b) The amount of each canceled check should be compared both with the amount recorded on the bank statement and with the amount recorded on the depositor's check stubs. When making this comparison it is a good plan to check the amount recorded on each check stub to indicate that the canceled check has been returned by the bank.

(c) The amounts of any items listed on a bank statement that represent charges to a depositor's account which have not been entered on the check stubs should be deducted from the balance on the check stubs and should be recorded in the cashbook.

(d) A list of the outstanding checks should be prepared. The information needed in preparing this list may be obtained from the check stubs.

After completing the foregoing steps, the balance shown on the check stubs should equal the balance shown in the bank statement less the total amount of the checks outstanding. A common error on the part of depositors is failure to record the amount of *counter checks* issued. Banks usually provide counter checks for the convenience of their depositors in withdrawing funds for personal use. Such checks are canceled and returned to the depositor with the bank statement so that it is an easy matter for the depositor to detect if he has failed to record such checks.

Following is a reconciliation of the bank balance shown in the statement reproduced on page 107. In making this reconciliation it was assumed that the depositor's check stub indicated a balance of $9,054.52 on September 30, that Checks Nos. 112, 115, and 117 had not been presented for payment and thus were not returned with the bank statement, and that a deposit of $465.92 placed in the night depository on September 30 is not shown on the statement.

Bank Balance, September 30, per Statement....................		$8,843.15
Add: Deposit, September 30.................................		465.92
		$9,309.07
Less Checks Outstanding September 30:		
No. 112...................................	$ 75.00	
No. 115...................................	19.50	
No. 117...................................	160.55	255.05
Corrected Bank Balance, September 30........................		$9,054.02
Check-stub Balance, September 30...........................		$9,054.52
Less: Bank Service Charge.................................		.50
Corrected Check-stub Balance, September 30..................		$9,054.02

Service Charges. A service charge may be made by a bank for the handling of checks and other items. The basis and the amount of such charges vary with different banks in different localities.

When a bank statement indicates that a service charge has been made, the depositor should record the amount of the service charge by debiting an account with Bank Service Charges and by crediting the bank checking account. He should also deduct the amount of such charges from the check-stub balance.

Keeping a Ledger Account with the Bank. As explained previously, a memorandum account with the bank may be kept on the depositor's checkbook stub. The depositor may also keep a ledger account with the bank if desired. The title of such an account usually is the name of the bank. Sometimes more than one account is kept with a bank in which case each account should be correctly labeled. Such terms as "commercial," "executive," and "payroll" are used to identify the accounts.

The bank account should be debited for the amount of each deposit and should be credited for the amount of each check written. The account should also be credited for any other items that may be charged to the account by the bank, including service charges.

When both a cash account and a bank account are kept in the ledger, the following procedure should be observed in recording transactions affecting these accounts:

CASH		LIBERTY NATIONAL BANK	
Debit: For all receipts of cash and cash items.	Credit: (a) For all payments in cash. (b) For all bank deposits.	Debit: For all deposits.	Credit: (a) For all checks written. (b) For all service charges. (c) For all other charges, such as for dishonored checks.

Under this method of accounting for cash and banking transactions, the cash account will be in balance when all cash on hand has been deposited in the bank. To prove the balance of the cash account at any time, it is necessary only to count the cash on hand and to compare it with the cash account balance. To prove the bank account balance, it will be necessary to reconcile the bank balance in the same manner in which it is reconciled when only a memorandum record of bank transactions is kept on the check stubs.

The cash account can be dispensed with when a bank account is kept in the ledger and all cash receipts are deposited in the bank. When this is done, it is advisable to make all disbursements by bank check (except that small expenditures may be made from a petty cash fund as is explained later).

Under this method of accounting, the Cash Receipts Dr. and the Cash Payments Cr. columns of the combined cash-journal may be headed as follows:

BANK	
DEPOSITS DR.	CHECKS CR.

When this form of combined cash-journal is used, all cash receipts should be entered in the Bank Deposits Dr. column and all checks issued should be entered in the Bank Checks Cr. column. Daily, or at frequent intervals, the receipts are deposited in the bank. If all cash received during the month has been deposited before the books are closed at the end of the month, the total bank deposits will equal the total cash receipts for the month. If all disbursements during the month are made by check, the total checks issued will equal the total disbursements for the month.

Savings Account. When a savings account is opened in a bank, a signature card must be signed by the depositor. He is then given a pass-book that he must present at the bank when making deposits or when making withdrawals. By signing the signature card, the depositor agrees to abide by the rules and the regulations of the bank. These rules and regulations vary with different banks and may be altered and amended from time to time. The principal differences between a savings account and a checking account are that interest is paid by the bank on the former and withdrawals from a savings account must be made at the bank by the depositor or his authorized agent. Interest usually is computed on a semiannual basis. The passbook must be presented along with a with-drawal slip when money is drawn from the account. Banks do not as a rule pay interest on the balances in checking accounts. Depositors use checking accounts primarily as a convenient means of making payments while savings accounts are used primarily as a means of accumulating funds with interest.

Savings accounts are not common for businesses. If the assets of a business include money in a bank savings account, there should be a separate account in the ledger with a title that indicates the nature of the deposit. Sometimes the name of the bank is in the title, as, for ex-ample, "Liberty National Bank — Savings Account." When the bank credits interest to the account, the depositor should record the amount in his accounts by a debit to the savings account and by a credit to Interest Income. The interest is income whether withdrawn or not.

PRACTICE ASSIGNMENT No. 10. Complete Report No. 10 in the workbook and submit your working papers to the instructor for approval. After completing the report, continue with the following study assignment until Report No. 11 is required.

(11) THE PETTY CASH FUND

It is a good business policy to deposit in a bank all cash received. When this is done, the total cash receipts and the total bank deposits will be equal. It is also a good policy to make arrangements with the bank so that all checks and other cash items received from customers or others in the usual course of business will be accepted for deposit only. This will cause the business' records of cash receipts and disbursements to agree exactly with the bank's record of deposits and withdrawals. Arrangements may also be made with the bank so that no item will be charged to the depositor's account until a check from the depositor for the proper amount is obtained. For example, arrangement can be made to have dishonored checks presented to the depositor for payment, instead of having them charged to the depositor's account. Service charges too may be paid by check.

When all cash and cash items received are deposited in a bank, an office fund or petty cash fund may be established for paying small items. Such a petty cash fund eliminates the necessity of writing checks for small amounts to pay miscellaneous bills.

Establishing a Petty Cash Fund. To establish a *petty cash fund*, a check should be drawn for the amount that is to be set aside in the fund. The amount may be $25, $50, $100, or any amount considered necessary. The check is usually made payable to "Cash," "Petty Cash," or "Office Fund." When the check is cashed by the bank, the money is placed in a cash drawer, a cash register, or a safe at the depositor's place of business, and a designated individual in the office is authorized to make payments from the fund. The one who is responsible for the fund should be able to account for the amount of the fund at any time. Disbursements from the fund should not be made without a voucher or a receipt. A form of

Petty Cash Voucher

petty cash voucher is shown on page 112. Such a voucher should be used for all expenditures for which no invoice has been received.

The check drawn to establish the petty cash fund may be entered in the combined cash-journal by debiting Petty Cash Fund and by crediting the bank account. When it is necessary to replenish the fund, the petty cashier usually prepares a statement of the expenditures properly classified. A check is then drawn for the exact amount of the total expenditures. This check is recorded in the combined cash-journal by debiting the proper accounts indicated in the statement and by crediting the bank account.

The petty cash fund represents a revolving fund that does not change in amount unless the fund is increased or decreased. The actual amount of cash in the fund plus the total of the petty cash vouchers or receipts should always be equal to the amount originally charged to the petty cash fund.

Petty Cash Disbursements Record. When a petty cash fund is maintained, it is good practice to keep a formal record of all disbursements from the fund. Various types of records have been designed for this purpose. One of the standard forms is illustrated on page 116. The headings of the Distribution columns may vary with each enterprise depending upon the desired classification of the expenditures. It should be remembered that the headings represent accounts that are to be charged for the expenditures. The desired headings may either be printed on the form or may be written in by hand. Sometimes the accounts are numbered and the numbers instead of account titles are used in the headings to represent the accounts to be charged.

The petty cashier should have a voucher for each disbursement made from the petty cash fund. Unless an invoice or receipt is obtained that will serve as a voucher, the petty cashier should provide the necessary voucher. The vouchers should be numbered consecutively.

A model petty cash disbursements record is reproduced on page 116. A narrative of the petty cash transactions completed by M. B. Roberts' secretary, during the month of December, precedes the illustration. Since Mr. Roberts is out of the office much of the time, he considers it advisable to provide a petty cash fund from which his secretary is authorized to make petty cash disbursements not to exceed $5 each.

Proving the Petty Cash Disbursements Record. To prove the petty cash disbursements record, it is first necessary to foot all of the amount columns. The sum of the footings of the Distribution columns should equal the footing of the Total Amount column. After proving the footings, the totals should be recorded and the record should be ruled as shown in the illustration. The illustration shows that a total of $43.60 was paid out during December. Since it was desired to replenish the petty cash fund at this time, the following statement of the disbursements for December was prepared:

STATEMENT OF PETTY CASH DISBURSEMENTS
FOR DECEMBER

Telephone and Telegraph Expense	$ 4.45
Automobile Expense	4.50
Postage	2.40
Donations	6.50
Advertising Expense	4.00
Traveling Expense	3.75
Miscellaneous Expenses	13.00
M. B. Roberts, Drawing	5.00
Total Disbursements	$43.60

The statement of expenditures serves as a voucher authorizing the issuance of a check for $43.60 to replenish the petty cash fund. After footing and ruling the petty cash disbursements record, the balance in the fund and the amount received to replenish the fund may be recorded in the Description column below the ruling as shown in the illustration. It is customary to carry the balance forward to the top of a new page before recording any of the transactions for the ensuing month.

The petty cash disbursements record reproduced on page 116 is an *auxiliary record* that supplements the regular accounting records. No posting is done from this auxiliary record. The total amount of the expenditures from the petty cash fund is entered in the combined cash-journal at the time of replenishing the fund by debiting the proper accounts and by crediting the bank account. The statement of petty cash disbursements provides the information needed in recording the check issued to replenish the petty cash fund. The required posting is done from the combined cash-journal and the posting references are inserted as the posting is completed.

The method of recording the check issued by M. B. Roberts on December 30 to replenish the fund is illustrated on page 116. It is assumed that Mr. Roberts used a combined cash-journal ruled like the one illustrated on page 92. However, the last four amount columns are omitted from the illustration since they are not used in recording this transaction.

The foregoing method of handling a petty cash fund is sometimes referred to as the *imprest method*. It is the method most commonly used.

M. B. ROBERTS, PROPRIETOR
NARRATIVE OF PETTY CASH TRANSACTIONS

Dec. 1. Issued check for $50 payable to Petty Cash, cashed the check, and placed the proceeds in a petty cash fund.

> This transaction was recorded in the combined cash-journal by debiting Petty Cash Fund and by crediting the bank account. A memorandum entry was also made in the Description column of the petty cash disbursements record reproduced on page 116.

During the month of December the following disbursements were made from the petty cash fund:

2. Paid $2 for washing windows. Petty Cash Voucher No. 1.

5. Gave Mr. Roberts $3 to reimburse him for the amount spent in having his automobile repaired. Petty Cash Voucher No. 2.

7. Gave Mr. Roberts $3 to reimburse him for the amount spent in entertaining client at luncheon. Petty Cash Voucher No. 3.

8. Paid $1 for messenger fees. Petty Cash Voucher No. 4.

9. Paid $4 for an announcement in local newspaper. Petty Cash Voucher No. 5.

11. Gave Mr. Roberts $5 for personal use. Petty Cash Voucher No. 6.

> This item was entered in the Amount column provided at the extreme right of the petty cash disbursements record since no special distribution column had been provided for recording amounts withdrawn by the proprietor for personal use.

12. Gave the Red Cross a $5 donation. Petty Cash Voucher No. 7.

14. Paid $1.50 for typewriter repairs. Petty Cash Voucher No. 8.

16. Gave Mr. Roberts $3.75 to reimburse him for traveling expenses. Petty Cash Voucher No. 9.

18. Gave Mr. Roberts $1.50 to reimburse him for the amount spent in having his automobile washed. Petty Cash Voucher No. 10.

20. Paid $3.50 for cleaning office. Petty Cash Voucher No. 11.

22. Paid $1.25 for collect telegram. Petty Cash Voucher No. 12.

23. Gave the Salvation Army a donation of $1.50. Petty Cash Voucher No. 13.

26. Paid $2.40 for postage stamps. Petty Cash Voucher No. 14.

28. Gave Mr. Roberts $3.20 to reimburse him for a long distance telephone call made from a booth. Petty Cash Voucher No. 15.

30. Paid $2 for washing windows. Petty Cash Voucher No. 16.

30. Issued check for $43.60 to replenish the petty cash fund.

> This transaction was recorded in the combined cash-journal by debiting the proper accounts and by crediting the bank account for the total amount of the expenditures.

PETTY CASH DISBURSEMENTS FOR MONTH OF *December* 19—   *Page 1*

Day	Description	Vou. No.	Total Amount	Distribution of Charges								Account	Amount
				T. & T.	Auto Ex.	Postage	Don.	Adv.	Trav. Ex.	Misc.			
	BROUGHT FORWARD												
1	Received in fund	1	$50.00										
2	Washing windows	1	2 00							2 00			
5	Automobile repairs	2	3 00		3 00								
7	Client at luncheon	3	3 00							3 00			
8	Messenger	4	1 00							1 00			
9	Advertising expense	5	4 00					4 00					
11	M. B. Roberts, personal use	6	5 00								M. B. Roberts, Drawing	5 00
12	Red Cross	7	5 00				5 00						
14	Typewriter repairs	8	1 50							1 50			
16	Traveling expenses	9	3 75						3 75				
18	Washing automobile	10	1 50		1 50								
20	Cleaning office	11	3 50							3 50			
22	Collect telegram	12	1 25	1 25									
23	Salvation Army	13	1 50				1 50						
26	Postage stamps	14	2 40			2 40							
28	Long distance call	15	3 20	3 20									
30	Washing windows	16	2 00							2 00			
			43 60	4 45	4 50	2 40	6 50	4 00	3 75	13 00		5 00
30	Balance		$6.40										
30	Received in fund		43.60										
	Total		50.00										

M. B. Roberts' Petty Cash Disbursements Record

COMBINED CASH-JOURNAL

Bank		Date		Description	Post. Ref.	General	
Deposits Dr.	Checks Cr.	Mo.	Day			Debits	Credits
				AMOUNTS FORWARDED			
	43 60	Dec.	30	Telephone and Telegraph Expense		4 45	
				Automobile Expense		4 50	
				Postage		2 40	
				Donations		6 50	
				Advertising Expense		4 00	
				Traveling Expense		3 75	
				Misc. Expenses		13 00	
				M. B. Roberts, Drawing		5 00	

PRACTICE ASSIGNMENT No. 11. Refer to the workbook and complete Report No. 11. This practice assignment provides a test of your ability to apply the principles developed in the first four units of the textbook. After completing the report, you may proceed with the textbook discussion in Unit Five until the next report is required.

PAYROLL ACCOUNTING

(12) WAGES AND WAGE DEDUCTIONS

Importance of Payroll Accounting. Careful and accurate accounting for the earnings of employees is important for several reasons. Every employee has a legal and a moral right to be paid according to the terms of his contract of employment and the provisions of the laws affecting employer-employee relationships. These rights must be respected. If workers are not paid regularly the wages to which they have become entitled, unpleasant consequences of various sorts may ensue. Dissatisfaction, loss of loyalty, inefficiency, and possibly even resignations, friction with unions, or legal involvement may result.

There are still other reasons that require accurate payroll accounting. Various taxes are imposed upon and measured by the earnings of employees. Workmen's compensation insurance is related to payrolls. Retirement benefits, or pensions, vacation pay, sick pay, and other "fringe" benefits may be based upon earnings. Wages constitute a major expense of many business enterprises. Payroll accounting must be timely and accurate; there is little or no margin for error.

Employer-Employee Relationships. An individual may perform services for a business without being an employee. A plumber or an electrician who is called in to make repairs or installations does not become an employee of the business. The same is usually true of lawyers, public accountants, and various consultants who sell their services to the business. These people serve in the capacity of *independent contractors.* They are told what to do, but not how to do it. The compensation they receive for their services is called fees.

An employee, by contrast, is under the control and direction of the employer with regard to both what shall be done and how it shall be done. The distinction between an employee and an independent contractor is important in law. The extent and nature of the responsibilities of a client and a contractor to each other and to various other parties are very different from the obligations that exist when the relationship is that of employer and employee.

117

Types of Compensation. Most employees are paid on the basis of the length of time they work. If they are paid on an hourly basis, their compensation is usually called wages. If they are paid on a monthly or an annual basis, their compensation may be called salaries. However, the words "wages" and "salary" are often used interchangeably.

In some cases the amount of compensation is based upon specific results accomplished. Two examples are (1) payments on a piecework basis and (2) payments to salespeople measured by the amount of their sales. Payments of this latter type are called commissions. Taxable wages include all types of compensation including salaries, fees, bonuses, and commissions. Wages paid in any form other than money are measured by the fair value of the goods, lodging, meals, or other consideration given in payment for services. It is immaterial whether such payments are based on the hour, day, week, month, year, or on a piecework or percentage plan.

Determination of Gross Earnings. An employee's earnings may be based on the time worked, unit output, or sales during the pay period, or on some other basis. The most common basis is the time worked. It is, therefore, necessary to keep a record of the time worked by such employees. Where there are but few employees, a memorandum book or time book may be used satisfactorily. Where there are many employees, time clocks are commonly used to record the time spent on the job each day. In such case a clock card is provided for each employee and the time clock is used to record the time of arrival and the time of departure. Regardless of the method used in ascertaining the amount of time worked by each employee, the total time worked during the payroll period must be computed and recorded in some manner.

Computing Wages. An employee's earnings may be computed on an hourly, weekly, semimonthly, monthly, or other basis. Under the Fair Labor Standards Act, commonly known as the Wages and Hours Law, most employers engaged in interstate commerce are required to pay wages at the rate of time and a half for any time worked in excess of 40 hours in any week. Under the Walsh-Healey Act, employers producing goods under government contract may be required to pay overtime rates for any time worked in excess of eight hours in any day. It is common practice to pay premium rates for working on Sundays and holidays or on night shifts. It is, therefore, necessary to know the hourly rate of pay for regular time and for overtime of all employees whose wages are computed on an hourly basis. Employees who are employed on a regular salary basis may be entitled to premium pay for any overtime. In such cases it is necessary to compute the regular hourly rate of pay before the overtime rate can be computed. For example, an employee whose regular salary is $350 a month may be entitled to overtime pay at the rate of one and a half times his regular hourly rate of pay for any time worked in excess of 40 hours a week. His overtime rate may be computed as follows:

$350 × 12 months = $4,200 annual pay
$4,200 ÷ 52 weeks = $80.77 weekly pay
$80.77 ÷ 40 hours = $2.02 regular hourly rate
$2.02 × 1½ = $3.03 overtime rate

Deductions from Gross Earnings. Most employers of one or more employees are required to withhold a portion of each employee's wages for income and social security taxes. Some states and cities also require employers to withhold taxes from employees' wages. Additional deductions may be made from employees' wages by agreement for such purposes as the following:

(a) Insurance premiums
(b) Pensions
(c) Charitable contributions
(d) Union dues
(e) Savings bonds
(f) Company loans

Withholding Employees' Income Taxes. Employers are required to withhold from the wages of each employee a percentage of the wages in excess of the total amount of the *withholding exemptions* claimed. The total amount of the exemptions claimed is arrived at by multiplying the amount of one withholding exemption by the number of exemptions claimed. The amount of one exemption under present law is shown in the following table:

PERCENTAGE METHOD WITHHOLDING TABLE

Payroll Period	Amount of one withholding exemption
Weekly..................................	$ 13.00
Biweekly...............................	26.00
Semimonthly..........................	28.00
Monthly...............................	56.00
Quarterly..............................	167.00
Semiannual............................	333.00
Annual................................	667.00
Daily or miscellaneous (per day of such period)...............................	1.80

Every employee is required to furnish his employer with a signed with-holding exemption certificate setting forth the number of withholding exemptions claimed. Form W-4 is the official form to be used for this certificate. A model filled-in copy of this form is reproduced below. Reference to this illustration will show that Mr. Mayfield claimed three exemptions including one exemption for himself, one exemption for his wife, and one exemption for a dependent. Assuming that, for the week ended December 15, his earnings amounted to $87.50 and that the with-holding rate is 18 per cent, the amount to be withheld for income tax purposes may be computed as follows:

Total earnings for the week......................................		$87.50
Amount of one exemption.................................	$13	
Number of exemptions claimed............................	3	39.00
Excess of earnings over exemptions............................		$48.50
Rate of tax...		18%
Amount to be withheld.......................................		$ 8.73

In lieu of using the percentage method, an employer may elect to use the "wage bracket method" of determining the amount of the tax to be withheld. This method involves the use of tables in determining the amounts to be withheld. Wage bracket withholding tables covering weekly, biweekly, semimonthly, monthly, and daily or miscellaneous periods are issued by the Internal Revenue Service and copies may be obtained from any District Director of Internal Revenue. A reproduction of a portion of the weekly table appears on page 121. To use this table in

---

FORM W-4
U. S. Treasury Department
Internal Revenue Service

EMPLOYEE'S WITHHOLDING EXEMPTION CERTIFICATE

Print full name ......Richard Alan Mayfield.................................... Social Security No. ..259-08-9112.........

Print home address .....912.Elm.St................................ City .*.............................. State ...*...........

EMPLOYEE:
File this form with your employer. Otherwise, he must withhold U. S. Income tax from your wages without exemption.

EMPLOYER:
Keep this certificate with your records. If the employee is believed to have claimed too many exemptions, the District Director should be so advised.

HOW TO CLAIM YOUR WITHHOLDING EXEMPTIONS

1. If SINGLE, and you claim an exemption, write the figure "1"......................................

2. If MARRIED, one exemption each for husband and wife if not claimed on another certificate.
   (a) If you claim both of these exemptions, write the figure "2"
   (b) If you claim one of these exemptions, write the figure "1" } ....2..
   (c) If you claim neither of these exemptions, write "0"

3. Exemptions for age and blindness (applicable only to you and your wife but not to dependents):
   (a) If you or your wife will be 65 years of age or older at the end of the year, and you claim this exemption, write the figure "1"; if both will be 65 or older, and you claim both of these exemptions, write the figure "2" ....
   (b) If you or your wife are blind, and you claim this exemption, write the figure "1"; if both are blind, and you claim both of these exemptions, write the figure "2" ....

4. If you claim exemptions for one or more dependents, write the number of such exemptions. (Do not claim exemption for a dependent unless you are qualified under instruction 3 on other side.) ....1..

5. Add the number of exemptions which you have claimed above and write the total .... | 3 |

I CERTIFY that the number of withholding exemptions claimed on this certificate does not exceed the number to which I am entitled.

(Date) .....September..1........., 19.==.   (Signed) *Richard A. Mayfield*

Model Filled-in Copy of Withholding Exemption Certificate

---

*When the city and state are omitted from business forms reproduced in this textbook, the student may assume that the city and state in which the school is located apply.

INCOME TAX WITHHOLDING TABLE

If the payroll period with respect to an employee is **Weekly:**

And the wages are—		And the number of withholding exemptions claimed is—										
At least	But less than	0	1	2	3	4	5	6	7	8	9	10 or more
		The amount of income tax to be withheld shall be—										
$0	$13	18% of wages	$0	$0	$0	$0	$0	$0	$0	$0	$0	$0
13	14	$2.40	.10	0	0	0	0	0	0	0	0	0
14	15	2.60	.30	0	0	0	0	0	0	0	0	0
15	16	2.80	.50	0	0	0	0	0	0	0	0	0
16	17	3.00	.70	0	0	0	0	0	0	0	0	0
17	18	3.20	.80	0	0	0	0	0	0	0	0	0
18	19	3.30	1.00	0	0	0	0	0	0	0	0	0
19	20	3.50	1.20	0	0	0	0	0	0	0	0	0
50	51	9.10	6.80	4.50	2.20	0	0	0	0	0	0	0
51	52	9.30	7.00	4.70	2.30	0	0	0	0	0	0	0
52	53	9.50	7.10	4.80	2.50	.20	0	0	0	0	0	0
53	54	9.60	7.30	5.00	2.70	.40	0	0	0	0	0	0
54	55	9.80	7.50	5.20	2.90	.60	0	0	0	0	0	0
55	56	10.00	7.70	5.40	3.10	.80	0	0	0	0	0	0
56	57	10.20	7.90	5.60	3.20	.90	0	0	0	0	0	0
57	58	10.40	8.00	5.70	3.40	1.10	0	0	0	0	0	0
58	59	10.50	8.20	5.90	3.60	1.30	0	0	0	0	0	0
59	60	10.70	8.40	6.10	3.80	1.50	0	0	0	0	0	0
60	62	11.00	8.70	6.40	4.10	1.70	0	0	0	0	0	0
62	64	11.30	9.00	6.70	4.40	2.10	0	0	0	0	0	0
64	66	11.70	9.40	7.10	4.80	2.50	.20	0	0	0	0	0
66	68	12.10	9.80	7.40	5.10	2.80	.50	0	0	0	0	0
68	70	12.40	10.10	7.80	5.50	3.20	.90	0	0	0	0	0
70	72	12.80	10.50	8.20	5.90	3.50	1.20	0	0	0	0	0
72	74	13.10	10.80	8.50	6.20	3.90	1.60	0	0	0	0	0
74	76	13.50	11.20	8.90	6.60	4.30	2.00	0	0	0	0	0
76	78	13.90	11.60	9.20	6.90	4.60	2.30	0	0	0	0	0
78	80	14.20	11.90	9.60	7.30	5.00	2.70	.40	0	0	0	0
80	82	14.60	12.30	10.00	7.70	5.30	3.00	.70	0	0	0	0
82	84	14.90	12.60	10.30	8.00	5.70	3.40	1.10	0	0	0	0
84	86	15.30	13.00	10.70	8.40	6.10	3.80	1.50	0	0	0	0
86	88	15.70	13.40	11.00	8.70	6.40	4.10	1.80	0	0	0	0
88	90	16.00	13.70	11.40	9.10	6.80	4.50	2.20	0	0	0	0
160	170	29.70	27.40	25.10	22.80	20.50	18.20	15.90	13.50	11.20	8.90	6.20
170	180	31.50	29.20	26.90	24.60	22.30	20.00	17.70	15.30	13.00	10.70	8.40
180	190	33.30	31.00	28.70	26.40	24.10	21.80	19.50	17.10	14.80	12.50	10.20
190	200	35.10	32.80	30.50	28.20	25.90	23.60	21.30	18.90	16.60	14.30	12.00
		18 percent of the excess over $200 plus—										
$200 and over		36.00	33.70	31.40	29.10	26.80	24.50	22.20	19.80	17.50	15.20	12.90

Portion of Weekly Income Tax Withholding Table

ascertaining the amount of the tax to be withheld from the wages of Mr. Mayfield for the week ended December 15, it is only necessary to refer to the line showing the tax on wages of "at least $86 but less than $88" and note the amount shown in the column headed "3" exemptions. It will be noted that $8.70 should be withheld. This is 3 cents less than when the tax is computed by the percentage method. Regardless of the method used in computing the amount of the tax to be withheld, the employee is given full benefit for the exemptions claimed plus a standard deduction of approximately 10 per cent. In any event the sum of the taxes withheld from employees' wages only approximates the tax on their actual income up to $5,000 a year derived from wages only. An employee may be required to pay additional taxes. In some cases the amount of the taxes withheld by the employer will be greater than the employee's actual tax liability. In such event he will be entitled to a refund of the excess taxes withheld.

Withholding Employees' F.I.C.A. Taxes. Under the Federal Insurance Contributions Act (F.I.C.A.) payroll taxes are imposed on both employers and employees for old-age and survivors' insurance benefits. The rate and the base of the tax have been changed several times since the law was first enacted and may be changed by Congress any time in the future. For the purpose of this discussion, it will be assumed that the rate is 2 per cent of the taxable wages paid during the taxable year. However, only the first $4,200 of the wages paid to each employee in any calendar year is taxable. Any amount paid in excess of $4,200 is exempt from the tax. The employees' portion of the F.I.C.A. tax must be withheld from their wages by the employer.

While the rate and base of the tax may be changed by Congress at any time, such changes will not affect the accounting principles or methods of recording payroll transactions.

In a few states employers are required to withhold a percentage of the employees' wages for unemployment compensation benefits or for disability benefits. In some states and cities employers are required to withhold a percentage of the employees' wages for income or payroll taxes. Regardless of the number of withholdings required, each employer must comply with the various laws in withholding any taxes based on payrolls and in keeping his payroll records.

If, under agreement with his employees, an employer obligates himself to withhold a portion of the employees' wages for any other purposes, such as insurance, pensions, charitable contributions, union dues, etc., such withholdings must be properly computed and recorded each payday.

Payroll Records. To meet the requirements of the various federal and state laws, it is necessary for employers of one or more employees to keep such records as are necessary to provide the following information:

(a) Each employee's name, address, and social security account number.

(b) The gross amount of each employee's earnings, the time of payment, and the period of service covered by such payment.

(c) The amount of such earnings constituting taxable wages.

(d) The amount of any taxes withheld from each employee's earnings.

Each employee is required to have a social security account number. Form SS-5 is the official form prescribed for filing an application for an account number. A model filled-in copy of this form is reproduced below.

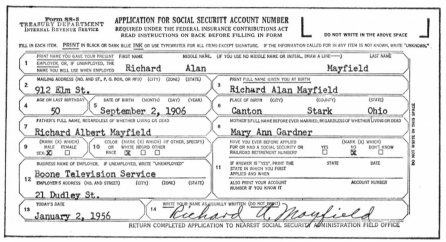

Model Filled-in Application for Social Security Account Number

Every employer subject to any payroll taxes imposed under federal laws is required to keep all records pertinent to these taxes available for inspection by officers of the Internal Revenue Service. Such records should be kept for a period of at least four years.

No specific employment records are prescribed by law for employers, but employers are required to keep records that will enable the government to ascertain whether the taxes for which they are liable are correctly computed and paid. Employers may design their own record forms or they may use one of the many payroll record systems on the market. A variety of payroll systems has been developed for the use of both small and large businesses. Some of these systems involve the use of mechanical or electronic devices. Most employers keep two types of records including

(Continued on page 126)

PAYROLL RECORD

FOR PERIOD ENDING *December 15 19—*

No.	NAME	NO. EXEMP.	TIME RECORD							REGULAR EARNINGS			OVERTIME EARNINGS		
			M	T	W	T	F	S	S	HRS.	RATE	AMOUNT	HRS.	RATE	AMOUNT
1	Adams, John B.	2	8	8	8	8	8			40	1 80	72 00			
2	Grainger, Helen M.	1	8	8	8	8	8			40	1 50	60 00			
3	Gray, James M.	3	8	8	8	8				32	1 60	51 20			
4	Greer, Paul J.	3	8	8	8	8	8	4		40	2 00	80 00	4	3 00	12 00
5	Hall, Peter D.	4	8	8	8	8	8			40	1 80	72 00			
6	Johnson, Carl N.	2		8	8	8	8	4		28	1 80	50 40			
7	Mason, Mary A.	1	8	8	8	8	8	4		40	1 50	60 00	4	2 25	9 00
8	Mayfield, Richard A.	3	8	8	8	8	8	2½		40	2 00	80 00	2½	3 00	7 50
												525 60			28 50

Model Filled-in Payroll Record Form

Left page

PAYROLL RECORD

Total Earnings	F.I.C.A. Taxable Earnings	Employees' F.I.C.A. Taxes	Employees' Income Taxes	Deductions Other Deductions Item	Amount	Net Paid Check No.	Amount
72 00	72 00	1 44	8 50			406	62 06
60 00	60 00	1 20	8 70			407	50 10
51 20	51 20	1 02	2 30			408	47 88
92 00	92 00	1 84	9 80			409	80 36
72 00	72 00	1 44	3 90			410	66 66
50 40	50 40	1 01	4 50			411	44 89
69 00	69 00	1 38	10 10			412	57 52
87 50	none	none	8 70	U.S. Savings Bond	5 00	413	73 80
554 10	466 60	9 33	56 50		5 00		483 27
554 10	466 60	9 33	56 50		5 00		483 27

Model Filled-in Payroll Record Form

DEDUCTIONS

Right page

(a) a payroll record and (b) an employees' earnings record. A payroll record is made up at the end of each pay period. A model filled-in copy of a payroll record form used by the Boone Television Service is illustrated on pages 124 and 125.

The usual source of the information needed in making up a payroll record is the time book or clock cards. Reference to the model filled-in payroll record form reproduced in the illustration will reveal that there are eight employees. Regular deductions are made from the earnings of the employees for F.I.C.A. taxes and federal income taxes. Additional amount columns are provided for use in recording any other deductions that occur frequently enough to justify the use of special columns. Deductions that occur infrequently may be recorded in the columns provided for "Other Deductions." In the case of Richard Mayfield, by agreement, the employer is authorized to withhold $5 on the third payday of each month for U. S. Savings Bonds. When the amount withheld attains the sum of $37.50 a $50 Series E, U. S. Savings Bond is purchased at the bank and delivered to Mr. Mayfield.

The amount entered in the column headed F.I.C.A. Taxable Earnings is the amount subject to the F.I.C.A. tax. Only the first $4,200 of earnings received in any year is subject to this tax. Mr. Mayfield's earnings for the week ended December 15 are exempt from the F.I.C.A. tax because he has already been taxed on earnings totaling $4,200.

After the payroll record has been completed the amount columns should be footed and the footings proved in the following manner:

Regular earnings		$525.60
Overtime earnings		28.50
Total earnings		$554.10
Deductions:		
F.I.C.A. taxes	$ 9.33	
Income taxes	56.50	
Savings bonds	5.00	70.83
Net amount of payroll		$483.27

After proving the footings the totals should be entered in ink and the record should be ruled with single and double lines as shown in the illustration. Employees may be paid in cash or by check. Many businesses draw a single check for the net amount of the payroll and deposit it in a special "payroll" account at the bank. Individual pay checks are then drawn for the amount due each employee. It is customary for the employer to furnish a statement of withholdings to the employee at the time of paying wages. Pay checks with detachable stubs are widely used. A conventional type of pay check with stub attached is reproduced below. The stub should be detached before cashing the check and the stub should be retained by the employee as a permanent record of his earnings and payroll deductions.

Model Filled-in Pay Check

Employees' Earnings Record. An auxiliary record of each employee's earnings is usually kept in order to provide the information needed in preparing the various federal and state reports required of employers. A form similar to the one illustrated on page 129 may be used for this record. This record may be kept in loose-leaf form or on cards, which may be filed alphabetically or numerically for ready reference. The information recorded on this form is obtained from the payroll record. A model filled-in record of Richard Mayfield's earnings for the last half of the year up to December 15 is illustrated. The entry for the pay period ended December 15 is posted from the payroll record illustrated on pages 124 and 125. It will be noted that during the week of August 25 Mr. Mayfield lost one day because of sickness. It is the policy of this business to pay for sick leave at the regular hourly rate of pay, hence Mr. Mayfield's regular earnings for the week amounted to $80 even though he lost one day of work.

The F.I.C.A. taxable wages are listed on a cumulative basis in order that the record will show when the maximum amount of taxable wages is reached. The record shows that during the week of December 8 Mr. Mayfield's cumulative earnings passed the $4,200 mark. While his total earnings for that week amounted to $80, only $20 of such wages was subject to the F.I.C.A. tax of 2 per cent, hence only 40 cents was withheld from his wages for that week. For the remainder of the year his entire earnings will be exempt from F.I.C.A. tax withholding.

The payroll record is a compilation of the earnings of all employees for each pay period, while the earnings record is a compilation of the annual earnings of each employee. The form illustrated on page 129 is designed so that a record of the earnings of the employee for the first half of the year may be kept on one side and a record of the earnings for the last half of the year may be kept on the other side of the form. Thus, at the end of the year the form provides a complete record of the earnings of the employee for the year. It also provides a record of the earnings for each calendar quarter. This is important as will be indicated later when discussing the quarterly returns required of employers.

Withholding Tax Statement. On or before January 31 of each year employers are required by law to furnish to each employee from whose wages income taxes have been withheld, or would have been withheld if such employee had claimed no more than one withholding exemption, a receipt or withholding statement showing the total amount of wages and the amount of tax withheld, if any, during the preceding calendar year. Form W-2 is the official form prescribed for this statement. If a statement on Form W-2 is required for any employee, and his wages were subject to withholding for F.I.C.A. taxes in addition to income taxes, the employer must report the total wages paid and the amounts deducted for both income taxes and F.I.C.A. taxes. The employees' earnings record should provide the information needed in preparing these statements. A model filled-in copy of Form W-2 is reproduced below. The number appear-

Boone Television Service 27-0118774	WITHHOLDING TAX STATEMENT
21 Dudley Street	Federal Taxes Withheld From Wages

Type or print EMPLOYER'S identification number, name, and address above.   **Copy A—For District Director**

SOCIAL SECURITY INFORMATION		INCOME TAX INFORMATION		
$ 4,200.00 Total F.I.C.A. Wages* paid in 19	$ 84.00 F.I.C.A. employee tax withheld, if any	$ 4,800.00 Total Wages* paid in 19	$ 645.60 Federal Income Tax withheld, if any	

⌐
 	
     Richard A. Mayfield   259-08-9112
     912 Elm Street				

 L		EMPLOYER: See instructions on other side.		

Type or print EMPLOYEE'S social security account no., name, and address above.   *Before payroll deductions.
FORM W-2—U. S. Treasury Department Internal Revenue Service

Model Filled-in Withholding Tax Statement

EMPLOYEES' EARNINGS RECORD

19— Period Ending	Worked Days/Hours	Time Lost Days or Hrs	Time Lost Why	Regular Earnings	Overtime Earnings	Total Earnings	F.I.C.A. Taxable Earnings (Cumulative)	F.I.C.A. Taxes	Income Taxes	Other Deductions Item	Other Deductions Amount	Net Paid Check No.	Net Paid Amount
7/7	40			80.00		80.00	2374.00	1.60	7.70			229	70.70
7/14	40			80.00		80.00	2454.00	1.60	7.70			237	70.70
7/21	44			80.00	12.00	92.00	2546.00	1.84	9.30	U.S. Bonds	5.00	245	75.86
7/28	40			80.00		80.00	2626.00	1.60	7.70			253	70.70
8/4	40			80.00		80.00	2706.00	1.60	7.70			261	70.70
8/11	42			80.00	6.00	86.00	2792.00	1.72	8.70			269	75.58
8/18	40			80.00		80.00	2872.00	1.60	7.70	U.S. Bonds	5.00	277	65.70
8/25	32	1	8	80.00		80.00	2952.00	1.60	7.70			285	70.70
9/1	46			80.00	18.00	98.00	3050.00	1.96	10.90			293	85.14
9/8	40			80.00		80.00	3130.00	1.60	7.70			301	70.70
9/15	45			80.00	15.00	95.00	3225.00	1.90	10.20	U.S. Bonds	5.00	309	77.90
9/22	40			80.00		80.00	3305.00	1.60	7.70			317	70.70
9/29	45			80.00	15.00	95.00	3400.00	1.90	10.20			325	82.90
QUARTER TOTAL				1040.00	66.00	1106.00		22.12	110.90		15.00		957.98
10/6	40			80.00		80.00	3480.00	1.60	7.70			333	70.70
10/13	40			80.00		80.00	3560.00	1.60	7.70			341	70.70
10/20	44			80.00	12.00	92.00	3652.00	1.84	9.30	U.S. Bonds	5.00	349	75.86
10/27	42			80.00	6.00	86.00	3738.00	1.72	8.70			357	75.58
11/3	40			80.00		80.00	3818.00	1.60	7.70			365	70.70
11/10	40			80.00		80.00	3898.00	1.60	7.70			373	70.70
11/17	46			80.00	18.00	98.00	3996.00	1.96	10.90	U.S. Bonds	5.00	381	80.14
11/24	43			80.00	9.00	89.00	4085.00	1.78	9.10			389	78.12
12/1	45			80.00	15.00	95.00	4180.00	1.90	10.20			397	82.90
12/8	40			80.00		80.00	4200.00	.40	7.70			405	71.90
12/15	42¾			80.00	7.50	87.50			8.70	U.S. Bonds	5.00	413	73.80
QUARTER TOTAL													
YEARLY TOTAL													

SEX: M ✓ / F

DEPARTMENT: Repair　　OCCUPATION: Service

NAME — LAST: Mayfield　　FIRST: Richard　　MIDDLE: Alan

S.S. ACCOUNTING: 259-08-9112

EMPLOYEE NO.: 8

Model Filled-in Employees' Earnings Record Form

ing after the name of the employer is an identification number assigned by the Social Security Administration. Every employer who pays taxable wages to one or more employees must apply for an *identification number* on or before the seventh day after the date on which employment first occurs. Mr. Sommers, proprietor of the business, duly filed an application on Form SS-4, the official form prescribed for this purpose, and was assigned number 27-0118774. This number must be shown for identification purposes on all reports required of the Boone Television Service under the Federal Insurance Contributions Act.

Withholding statements must be prepared in quadruplicate (four copies). Copy A must be forwarded to the District Director of Internal Revenue with the employer's return of taxes withheld for the fourth quarter of the calendar year. The employee must be furnished with two copies (Copies B and C). Copy D should be retained by the employer for his records. If an employee leaves the service of the employer before the end of the year, the withholding statement must be furnished to the employee not later than 30 days after the last payment of wages is made to the employee.

Accounting for Wages and Wage Deductions. In accounting for wages and wage deductions it is desirable to keep separate accounts for (a) wages earned and (b) wage deductions. Various account titles are used in recording wages, such as Wages, Wage Expense, Salaries, Salary Expense, Salaries and Commissions, etc. The accounts needed in recording wage deductions depend upon what deductions are involved. A separate account should be kept for recording the liability incurred for each type of deduction, such as F.I.C.A. taxes, employees' income taxes, and savings bond deductions.

Wages. This is an expense account which should be debited for the total amount of the gross earnings of all employees for each pay period. Sometimes separate wage accounts are kept for the employees of different departments. Thus, separate accounts might be kept for Office Salaries, Sales Salaries, and Factory Wages.

WAGES	
Debit To record gross earnings of employees for each pay period.	

F.I.C.A. Taxes Payable. This is a liability account which should be credited for (a) the F.I.C.A. taxes withheld from employees' wages and (b) the F.I.C.A. taxes imposed on the employer. The account should be debited for amounts paid to apply on such taxes. When all of the F.I.C.A. taxes have been paid, the account will be in balance.

F.I.C.A. TAXES PAYABLE	
Debit	Credit
To record payment of F.I.C.A. taxes.	To record F.I.C.A. taxes withheld from employees' wages and F.I.C.A. taxes imposed on the employer.

Employees' Income Taxes Payable. This is a liability account which should be credited for the total income taxes withheld from employees' wages. The account should be debited for amounts paid to apply on such taxes. When all of the income taxes withheld have been paid, the account will be in balance.

EMPLOYEES' INCOME TAXES PAYABLE	
Debit	Credit
To record payment of income taxes withheld.	To record income taxes withheld from employees' wages.

Savings Bond Deductions Payable. This is a liability account which should be credited with amounts withheld from employees' wages for the purchase of savings bonds. The account should be debited for the cost of savings bonds purchased.

SAVINGS BOND DEDUCTIONS PAYABLE	
Debit	Credit
To record the cost of savings bonds purchased.	To record amounts withheld for the purchase of savings bonds.

Many employers enter into a program where an agreed amount is withheld from employees' wages to be used in purchasing U. S. Savings Bonds. Each employee who enters into such a program stipulates the amount to be withheld from his wages and the denomination of the bonds desired. The employer withholds the amount specified in the agreement and when a sufficient amount has been withheld to purchase a bond of the desired denomination, it is ordered and delivered to the employee.

Journalizing Payroll Transactions. The payroll record should provide the information needed in recording wages paid. The payroll record illustrated on pages 124 and 125 provided the information needed in drafting the following journal entry* to record the wages paid on December 15:

Dec. 15. Wages......................................	$554.10	
F.I.C.A. Taxes Payable.....................		$ 9.33
Employees' Income Taxes Payable...........		56.50
Savings Bond Deductions Payable...........		5.00
Bank......................................		483.27
Payroll for week ended December 15.		

It will be noted that the above journal entry involves one debit and four credits. Regardless of the number of debits and credits needed to record a transaction, the total debits must be equal to the total credits. When a journal entry involves more than one debit or more than one credit, it is known as a *compound journal entry*.

> **PRACTICE ASSIGNMENT No. 12. Complete Report No. 12 in the workbook and submit your working papers to the instructor for approval. After completing the report, continue with the following study assignment until the next report is required.**

(13) PAYROLL TAXES IMPOSED ON THE EMPLOYER

The employer is liable for the taxes which he is required by law to withhold from the wages of his employees. These taxes include the federal income taxes and the F.I.C.A. taxes which must be withheld from wages paid to employees. Such taxes are not an expense of the employer; nevertheless, the employer is required by law to collect the taxes and he is liable for the taxes until payment is made. Certain taxes are also imposed on the employer for various purposes, such as old-age and survivors' insurance benefits and unemployment compensation benefits. Most employers are subject to payroll taxes imposed under the Federal Insurance Contributions Act (F.I.C.A.) and the Federal Unemployment Tax Act (F.U.T.A.). An employer may also be subject to the payroll taxes imposed under the unemployment compensation laws of one or more states.

Social Security Taxes. All of the payroll taxes imposed on an employer under federal and state social security laws constitute an expense of the employer. In accounting for such taxes at least one expense account should be maintained. The account may be entitled Social Security Taxes.

---

*This journal entry is arranged in skeleton form. The position of the account titles and amounts indicates whether they are debits or credits. It will be noted that the debit item is written to the left and the credit items to the right. Either Bank or Cash may be credited for the net amount paid depending upon which account is being kept. Such entries may be made in either a general journal like the one illustrated on page 34, or in a combined cash-journal like the one illustrated on page 92.

This is an expense account which should be debited for all taxes imposed on the employer under federal and state social security laws. Sometimes separate expense accounts are kept for (a) F.I.C.A. Taxes,

SOCIAL SECURITY TAXES	
Debit	
To record F.I.C.A., F.U.T.A., and State U.C. Taxes imposed on the employer.	

(b) F.U.T.A. Taxes, and (c) State U.C. Taxes. In small business enterprises it is usually considered satisfactory to keep a single expense account for all federal and state social security taxes imposed on the employer.

Employer's F.I.C.A. Tax. The taxes imposed under the Federal Insurance Contributions Act apply equally to employers and to employees. As explained on page 122, both the rate and base of the tax may be changed by Congress at any time. In this discussion it is assumed that the rate is 2 per cent which applies to both the employer and to his employees with respect to taxable wages. Only the first $4,200 of the wages paid to each employee in any calendar year constitutes taxable wages. Any amount of wages paid to an employee during a year in excess of $4,200 is exempt from the F.I.C.A. tax. While the employer is liable both for the taxes withheld from his employees' wages and for the taxes imposed on the business, only the latter constitutes an expense of the business.

Employer's F.U.T.A. Tax. Under the Federal Unemployment Tax Act, a payroll tax is levied on employers for the purpose of aiding and rendering more uniform administration of the various state unemployment compensation laws. For 1956 and subsequent years employers of four or more individuals are subject to this tax. The rate of the tax is 3 per cent of the taxable wages paid during the calendar year. In computing the total amount of the taxable wages, only the first $3,000 of wages paid to an employee during any calendar year should be included. It is important to note that in computing taxable wages under the F.U.T.A. only the first $3,000 of wages paid to any employee during any calendar year should be included, while under the F.I.C.A. only the first $4,200 of wages paid to an employee during any calendar year should be included. It is also important to note that the basis of the tax is the wages paid during the calendar year rather than the wages earned. Sometimes an employee may earn wages in one year that are paid in a different year.

While under the F.U.T.A., the Federal government levies a tax on employers at the rate of 3 per cent of taxable wages, the employer is allowed credit for the amount of taxes paid into state unemployment compensation funds up to a maximum of 90 per cent of the federal tax. Thus, employers who are required to make contributions to state unemployment compensation funds may claim credit up to 2.7 per cent (90 per cent of 3 per cent) of the taxable wages in computing the federal tax of 3 per cent. Since all of the states have enacted unemployment compensation laws most employers are entitled to the full credit of 90 per cent in computing the federal tax. Thus, the net amount of the federal tax imposed on most employers is .3 per cent ($^3/_{10}$ of 1 per cent).

F.U.T.A. Taxes Payable. In recording the federal unemployment tax it is customary to keep a separate liability account entitled F.U.T.A. Taxes Payable. This is a liability account which should be credited for the taxes imposed on employers under the Federal Unemployment Tax Act. The account should be debited for amounts paid to apply on such taxes. When all of the F.U.T.A. taxes have been paid, the account will be in balance.

F.U.T.A. TAXES PAYABLE	
Debit	Credit
To record payment of F.U.T.A. taxes.	To record F.U.T.A. taxes imposed on the employer with respect to wages paid.

State U.C. Taxes. All of the states, territories, and the District of Columbia have enacted unemployment compensation laws providing for the payment of benefits to qualified unemployed workers. The cost of administering the state unemployment compensation laws is borne by the Federal government. Under the federal law an appropriation is made for each year by the Congress from which grants are made to the states to meet the proper administrative costs of their unemployment compensation laws. As a result of this provision the entire amount paid into the state funds may be used for the payment of benefits to qualified workers. While in general there is considerable uniformity in the provisions of the state laws, there are many variations in coverage, rates of taxes imposed, and benefits payable to qualified workers. Not all employers covered by the Federal Unemployment Tax Act are covered by the unemployment compensation laws of the states in which they have employees. Only employers of four or more individuals are covered by the federal law.

The number of employees specified under state laws varies from 1 to 8. However, in many of the states an employer who is covered by the federal law and has one or more individuals employed within the state is covered. Furthermore, under the laws of most states an employer who is covered by the federal law may elect voluntary coverage in states where he has one or more employees, even though he may have less than the number of employees specified by law in that particular state. In any event, it is necessary for each employer to be familiar with the unemployment compensation laws of all the states in which he has one or more employees, and if such employees are covered, he must keep such records and pay such taxes for unemployment compensation purposes as are prescribed by law.

In most states the plan is financed entirely by taxes imposed on employers. However, in a few states employees are also required to contribute and the amount of the tax imposed on the employees must be withheld from their wages.

In most states the maximum tax imposed upon employers is 2.7 per cent of the first $3,000 in wages paid to each employee in any calendar year. However, under the laws of most states there is a merit-rating system which provides a tax-saving incentive to employers to stabilize employment. Under this system an employer's rate may be considerably less than the maximum rate. However, the employer may be allowed credit against the federal tax up to a maximum of 90 per cent. In other words an employer may be entitled to claim the maximum credit against the federal tax even though, due to merit rating, he is taxed at a rate of less than 2.7 per cent by the state. There is, therefore, a strong inducement for employers to do everything possible to stabilize employment and thus to reduce their unemployment tax expense.

There are frequent changes in the state laws with respect to coverage, rates of contributions required, eligibility to receive benefits, amounts of benefits payable, etc., all of which cannot be discussed in detail here. (For the sake of simplification, in the following discussion it will be assumed that a uniform state tax rate of 2.7 per cent of wages paid is imposed upon employers while the federal tax rate is 3 per cent less credit for state contributions up to 2.7 per cent.)

State U.C. Taxes Payable. In recording the taxes imposed under state unemployment compensation laws, it is customary to keep a separate liability account entitled State U.C. Taxes Payable. This is a liability account which should be

STATE U.C. TAXES PAYABLE	
Debit	Credit
To record state contributions paid.	To record liability for state contributions required of employers with respect to wages paid.

credited for the taxes imposed on employers under the state unemployment compensation laws. The account should be debited for the amount paid to apply on such taxes. When all of the state taxes have been paid the account will be in balance. Some employers who are subject to the taxes imposed under the laws of several states keep a separate liability account for the taxes imposed by each state. In the case of small businesses or where an employer is required to make unemployment contributions to only a few states, a single liability account is sufficient.

Journalizing Employers' Payroll Taxes. The payroll taxes imposed on employers may be recorded periodically, such as monthly or quarterly, but it is more common to record such taxes at the time wages are paid so that the employer's liability for such taxes and the expenses incident thereto may be recorded in the same period as the wages to which the taxes relate. The payroll record illustrated on pages 124 and 125 provides the information needed in recording the F.I.C.A. tax imposed on the Boone Television Service with respect to wages paid on December 15. It shows that the F.I.C.A. taxable earnings amounted to $466.60. Assuming that the rate of the tax imposed on the employer was 2 per cent, which is the same as the rate of the tax imposed on the employees, the tax would amount to $9.33.

If the total earnings for the period amounted to $554.10 and only $398.50 were subject to unemployment taxes, the federal and state taxes may be computed as follows:

State U.C. taxes, 2.7% of $398.50..............................		$10.76
F.U.T.A. taxes, 3% of $398.50.........................	$11.96	
Less credit for state taxes............................	10.76	1.20
Total unemployment taxes.......................................		$11.96

The following journal entry may be made to record the payroll taxes imposed on the employer with respect to the wages paid on December 15:

Dec. 15. Social Security Taxes...........................	$21.29	
F.I.C.A. Taxes Payable........................		$ 9.33
F.U.T.A. Taxes Payable.......................		1.20
State U.C. Taxes Payable.....................		10.76
Payroll taxes imposed on employer with respect to wages paid December 15.		

Filing Returns and Paying the Payroll Taxes. If the amount withheld from employees' wages for income tax purposes plus the amount of the taxes imposed on both the employer and the employees under the Federal Insurance Contributions Act during any month is more than $100, it must be paid to a Federal reserve bank or a U. S. depositary within 15 days after the close of the month. However, if desired, the taxes for the last month of a calendar quarter may be remitted to the Director of Internal Revenue at the time of filing the quarterly return which must be filed on or before the last day of the following month. If the total amount of the taxes in any month is less than $100, monthly payment is not required and the total taxes for each calendar quarter may be paid at the time of filing the quarterly return. Most employers make monthly payment of the taxes within 15 days after the close of the month regardless of the amount. When paying the taxes it is necessary to fill in a Federal Depositary Receipt, Form 450, and to send or to take it with the remittance. A model filled-in copy of this form is reproduced below. After validating the receipt, the Federal reserve bank will return it to the taxpayer.

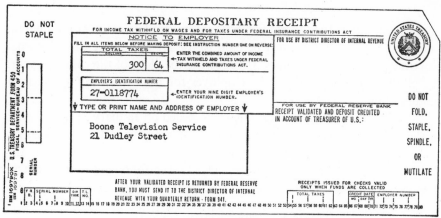

Model Filled-in Federal Depositary Receipt

To illustrate the accounting procedure in recording the payment of employees' income taxes withheld and the F.I.C.A. taxes, it will be assumed that on October 15 Boone Television Service issued a check in payment of the following taxes imposed with respect to wages paid during the month of September:

Employees' income taxes withheld from wages....................		$226.00
F.I.C.A. taxes:		
Withheld from employees' wages......................	$37.32	
Imposed on employer.............................	37.32	74.64
Amount of check...		$300.64

A check for this amount accompanied by a Federal Depositary Receipt, Form 450, was deposited with a Federal reserve bank. This transaction may be recorded as indicated by the following journal entry:

Oct. 15. F.I.C.A. Taxes Payable.......................	$ 74.64	
Employees' Income Taxes Payable..............	226.00	
Bank.....................................		$300.64

    Deposited $300.64 in Federal reserve bank in payment of taxes.

The amount of the tax imposed on employers under the state unemployment compensation laws must be remitted to the proper state office on or before the last day of the month following the close of the calendar quarter.

Each state provides an official form to be used in making a return of the taxes due. Assuming that a check for $139.88 was issued on January 31 in payment of state unemployment compensation taxes imposed on wages paid during the preceding quarter ended December 31, the transaction may be recorded as indicated by the following journal entry:

Jan. 31. State U.C. Taxes Payable.................... $139.88
    Bank.................................... $139.88
      Paid state U.C. taxes.

The amount of the federal tax imposed on employers under the Federal Unemployment Tax Act must be paid to the District Director of Internal Revenue on or before January 31 following the close of the calendar year. An official form is provided the employer for use in making a return of the taxes due.

Assuming that a check for $62.40 was issued on January 31 in payment of the taxes imposed under the Federal Unemployment Tax Act with respect to wages paid during the preceding year ended December 31, the transaction may be recorded as indicated by the following journal entry:

Jan. 31. F.U.T.A. Taxes Payable...................... $ 62.40
    Bank.................................... $ 62.40
      Paid federal unemployment taxes.

PRACTICE ASSIGNMENT No. 13. Complete Report No. 13 in the workbook and submit your working papers to the instructor for approval. After completing the report, you may continue with the textbook discussion in Unit Six until the next report is required.

ACCOUNTING FOR A RETAIL STORE

(14) PRINCIPLES AND PROCEDURES

A business enterprise that purchases and sells goods on credit, maintains a stock of merchandise, and has long-lived assets must account for periodic profit or loss on the accrual basis. This is a necessity both for the sake of measuring the success of the business from the standpoint of the owner and in order to comply with federal and state income tax laws. Several of the features of this type of accounting have been introduced previously. A more detailed consideration of these procedures and the introduction of the other major practices that constitute accrual accounting will be presented in this and the two following units. To make the discussion realistic, it will center around the accounting records of a retail furniture business called The Mann Furniture Store, owned and operated by W. L. Mann. It should be recognized, however, that most of the principles and procedures discussed and illustrated are equally applicable to many other types of businesses.

The discussion will continue to be a blend of accounting principles and bookkeeping practices. It is important to keep in mind that the principles relate to objectives while bookkeeping arrangements are devices to attain the goals. Such procedures as double-entry and the use of business papers, journals, and ledger accounts are employed to make the record-keeping process complete, orderly, and as error-free as possible. While most accounting principles are broad enough to allow considerable flexibility, it is in the area of bookkeeping procedures that wide latitude is found. Within limits, the records for each business can be styled to meet the particular requirements of the management.

The Accrual Basis of Accounting. The *accrual basis of accounting* consists of recording income in the period in which it is earned and expenses in the period in which they are incurred irrespective of whether cash is received or disbursed in connection with such transactions. Income is deemed to be earned when, in exchange for something of value, the right to receive money comes into existence. To a merchant, this normally

139

means the time at which the customer buys the goods and agrees to pay for them. In terms of changes in the accounting elements, income arises or accrues when an increase in a receivable causes an increase in proprietorship. In comparable terms, expense occurs or is incurred when either a reduction in some asset or an increase in a liability causes the proprietorship to be reduced (except in the case of assets withdrawn by the proprietor).

In keeping business records, the accountant must think in terms of time intervals. He must be sure that income and expense are accounted for in the proper fiscal or accounting period. Within a period, the recognition of many types of income and expense at precisely the moment the income or expense arises is not so important nor is it usually practicable. For example, the expense of having a salaried employee literally accrues minute by minute during each work day. If, however, the salary will be paid by the end of the period, no record is made of the expense until it is paid. If, on the other hand, the worker was not paid by the end of the period, the accountant should record the liability and expense at that time. A lag in recording income and expense is not serious within the accounting period, but steps must be taken at the end of the period to be sure that all income earned and expenses incurred are recorded. These steps consist of making what are called *end-of-period adjustments* in the accounts.

The accrual basis of accounting is widely used because it is sound and logical. It involves the period-by-period matching of income with the expenses that caused or aided in producing income. The income from sales, for example, must be matched against the cost of the goods sold and the various expenses that were incurred in conducting the business. A simple matching of cash received from customers during a period with the cash paid for goods purchased in that period would be almost meaningless in most cases. The collections might relate to sales of a prior period and the payments to purchases of the current period, or vice versa. The expense of having most long-lived assets does not arise when the property is acquired; the expense occurs as the usefulness of the property is gradually exhausted. The accrual basis recognizes changes in many types of assets and liabilities in computing net income for a specified period — not just changes in the cash account.

The Chart of Accounts. Mention has already been made of the desirability of keeping the ledger accounts in some sort of order. Usually the accounts for assets, liabilities, and proprietorship are placed first in the order that they appear in the balance sheet, followed by the accounts for

THE MANN FURNITURE STORE

Chart of Accounts

I Assets

  11 Cash

    111 Liberty National Bank

    112 Petty Cash Fund

  12 Receivables

    121 Notes Receivable

    122 Accrued Interest Receivable

    123 Accounts Receivable

      012 Allowance for Bad Debts

  13 Merchandise Inventory

  14 Prepaid Insurance

  15 Stationery and Supplies

  18 Store Equipment

    018 Allowance for Depreciation of Store Equipment

  19 Delivery Equipment

    019 Allowance for Depreciation of Delivery Equipment

II Liabilities

  21 Notes Payable

  22 Accrued Interest Payable

  23 Accounts Payable

  24 Sales Tax Payable

  25 F.I.C.A. Taxes Payable

  26 Employees' Income Taxes Payable

  27 F.U.T.A. Taxes Payable

  28 State U.C. Taxes Payable

III Proprietorship

  31 W. L. Mann, Proprietor

  32 W. L. Mann, Drawing

  33 Income Summary

IV Income from Sales

  41 Sales

    041 Sales Returns and Allowances

V Cost of Sales

  51 Purchases

    051 Purchases Returns and Allowances

  53 Cost of Goods Sold

VI Operating Expenses

  61 Rent Expense

  62 Depreciation Expense

  63 Salaries and Commissions

  64 Social Security Taxes

  65 Heating and Lighting

  66 Stationery and Supplies Used

  67 Telephone and Telegraph Expense

  68 Advertising Expense

  69 Bad Debts Expense

  611 Insurance Expense

  612 Truck Expense

  613 Charitable Contributions

  614 Miscellaneous Expenses

VII Other Income

  71 Interest Income

  72 Purchases Discount

VIII Other Expenses

  81 Interest Expense

Note: Items set in italics indicate classification; they are not account titles.

income and expense in the order that they appear in the income statement. It is common practice to assign numbers to the accounts. Usually the numbering involves an orderly pattern; it becomes a type of code.

The chart of accounts for The Mann Furniture Store showing account numbers appears above. Note that all asset accounts have numbers that begin with 1, liabilities 2, proprietorship 3, income from sales 4, cost of sales 5, operating expenses 6, other income 7, and other expenses 8. Note also that all of the so-called "contra" accounts have numbers that begin with the digit 0 followed by the number of the account or account-group to which each is contra. For example, Allowance for Depreciation of Store Equipment, Account No. 018, is contra to Store Equipment, Account No. 18.

The pattern of numbers or code shown in the illustration is fairly typical of the arrangement used by many businesses. However, numerous variations are possible. Sometimes letters as well as numbers are made a part of the code. When numbers are used, it is not uncommon for special columns in journals to be headed by just the number, rather than the name, of the account involved. In a system of records that requires numerous accounts, the use of account numbers virtually displaces account names for all but statement purposes.

The nature of many of the accounts included in the chart of accounts for The Mann Furniture Store should be apparent as they have been described and their use has been illustrated. However, the chart includes certain accounts that are needed in recording several types of transactions and events that have either not yet been considered, or only briefly mentioned. These accounts will be discussed prior to illustrating the accounting records of The Mann Furniture Store.

Accounting for Notes Receivable and Interest Income. Businesses that sell goods or services on credit sometimes get promissory notes from customers. A *promissory note* is a written promise to pay a certain sum of money on a specified date. Frequently there is also a promise to pay interest at a stated rate. An illustration of an interest-bearing promissory note follows.

Interest-Bearing Promissory Note

When a business receives a promissory note, it acquires an asset called Notes Receivable and there should be an account with this title. While a business might get a note receivable for any of several reasons, only the case of a note received from a customer who owed the business on "open" account will be considered at this point. In such a case the entry to record the receipt of the note would be a debit to Notes Receivable and a credit to Accounts Receivable for the amount of the note. When The

Mann Furniture Store received the note reproduced on page 142, it was recorded as indicated in the following journal entry:

Sept. 15. Notes Receivable............................ $286.50
          Accounts Receivable....................... $286.50
            Received 90-day 6% note from James Marsh.

This is a simple case of an increase in the asset Notes Receivable being offset by a decrease in the asset Accounts Receivable.

The note of James Marsh bears interest at the rate of 6 per cent and is payable in 90 days. Thus the date of maturity is December 14. In counting days, the date of issue is not counted, but the day the note matures is counted. This note will run 15 days in September, 31 days in October, 30 days in November, and 14 days in December. The interest on $286.50 for 90 days at 6 per cent is $4.30. In calculating interest on a daily basis, it is common practice to consider that a year has 360 days. The stated percentage rate of interest is usually the rate per year. Six per cent of $286.50 is $17.19. Ninety days is one fourth of a year; hence, the interest on the note is one fourth of $17.19 or $4.30.

If James Marsh, the maker of the note (the one who promised to pay), pays the amount of the note plus the interest due on December 14, the transaction may be recorded in the books of The Mann Furniture Store as indicated by the following journal entry:

Dec. 14. Liberty National Bank....................... $290.80
          Notes Receivable......................... $286.50
          Interest Income..........................   4.30
            Received check in payment of James Marsh's
            note — principal $286.50, interest $4.30.

Actually the interest income was earned or accrued at the rate of $4^7/_9$ cents a day. However, it would be impractical to record the accrual each day. In this case, the interest was earned and received in the same fiscal period (assuming that the period is the calendar year). Thus, the record of the income could wait until it is received in cash.

Suppose, however, that the note had been dated November 15. In that event the principal amount and interest would not be due until February 13 of the succeeding year. In calculating net income for the year ended December 31, it would be proper to take into consideration the interest that had been earned during that year, even though the money had not been received. From November 15 to December 31 is 46 days. Forty-six times $4^7/_9$ cents is $2.20. That amount has been earned by December 31 and can properly be considered as receivable on that date. Accordingly, it is correct to debit the asset Accrued Interest Receivable and to credit Interest Income for $2.20. In journal form, the entry would appear as follows:

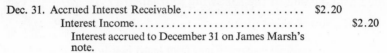

Dec. 31. Accrued Interest Receivable......................	$2.20	
Interest Income...............................		$2.20
Interest accrued to December 31 on James Marsh's note.		

If the business had several interest-bearing notes receivable, the interest accrued on each of them at the end of the accounting period should be calculated and the total amount should be recorded in one entry. This is an adjusting entry of the "accrual" type in contrast to the "write-off" type that is made to record insurance expired, depreciation, and supplies used. The amount of accrued interest receivable will be shown in the balance sheet along with other current receivables. The balance of the interest income account (which will show interest earned during the period without regard to whether any or all of it has been received) will be included in the income statement.

Reference to the chart of accounts for The Mann Furniture Store on page 141 will disclose that Notes Receivable, Account No. 121; Accrued Interest Receivable, Account No. 122; and Interest Income, Account No. 71, are provided to take care of transactions and events relating to notes receivable and to interest income.

Accounting for Bad Debts. Businesses that sell goods or services on credit realize that all of the customers may not pay all they owe. The amounts that cannot be collected are called *bad debts, bad debts expense*, or *loss from bad debts*. The latter designation is slightly misleading because, while the amounts that cannot be collected are certainly losses, they are losses that may reasonably be expected and are accepted in the interest of getting a larger volume of sales by selling on credit. The amount of such losses depends to a large degree upon the credit policy of a business. The seller must avoid the two extremes of either having such a "liberal" credit policy that bad debts become excessive, or having such a "tight" credit policy that he is minimizing bad debt losses at the sacrifice of a larger volume of sales.

It would be possible to wait until it was certain that the amount due from a customer would never be collected to write off the amount by a debit to Bad Debts Expense and by a credit to Accounts Receivable. This procedure is sometimes followed. However, it is considered to be better accounting to estimate the amount of bad debt losses that will eventually result from the sales of a period and to treat the estimated amount of expected losses as an expense of that same period. This is accomplished by using a contra account entitled Allowance for Bad Debts (sometimes called Reserve for Bad Debts or Allowance for Doubtful Accounts). This account is contra to the receivable accounts. At the end of the accounting period, an estimate of the expected bad debt losses is made, and an adjusting entry is made debiting Bad Debts Expense and crediting Allowance for Bad Debts. To illustrate, suppose that in view of past experience, it is expected that there will be a loss of an amount equal to one half of one per cent of the sales on account during the year. If such sales amount to $100,000, the estimated bad debt losses would be $500 which should be recorded as follows:

```
Dec. 31. Bad Debts Expense.........................  $500.00
           Allowance for Bad Debts..................            $500.00
               Bad debts expense provision for the year.
```

This adjustment is of the "write-off" type inasmuch as the effect of the entry is to write off the portion of accounts receivable that is expected to be uncollectible.

The amount of the debit balance in the bad debts expense account is reported in the income statement as an operating expense. The amount of the credit balance in the allowance for bad debts account is reported in the balance sheet as a deduction from the sum of the receivables. This arrangement serves to show the net amount of receivables that is expected to be collected.

It should be apparent that the credit part of the adjusting entry cannot be made directly to one of the receivable accounts because, at the time this entry is made, there is no way of knowing exactly which of the debtors will not pay. Experience gives virtual assurance that some of the amounts due will be uncollectible but only time will reveal which ones.

When it is determined that a certain account will not be collected, an entry should be made to close the account and to charge the loss against the allowance. Suppose, for example, that on April 22 of the next year, it is determined that $85 owed by J. A. Smith cannot be collected. Perhaps he died some time before and it is found that he left no property, or perhaps he became bankrupt, or he left town and cannot be traced. Whatever the circumstance, if it is fairly certain that the amount will not be collected, the following entry should be made:

```
April 22. Allowance for Bad Debts......................  $85.00
            Accounts Receivable.......................            $85.00
                To write off account of J. A. Smith found to be
                uncollectible.
```

The chart of accounts for The Mann Furniture Store includes Allowance for Bad Debts, Account No. 012, and Bad Debts Expense, Account No. 69, to provide for recording bad debts expense and subsequent write-offs.

Accounting for Prepaid Expenses. The term *prepaid expense* is largely self-explanatory. It refers to something that has been bought that is properly considered as an asset when acquired, but which will eventually be consumed or used up and thus become an expense. Prepaid or unexpired insurance and supplies of various sorts are leading examples. At the end of the period, the portion of such assets that has expired or has been consumed must be determined and an entry made debiting the proper expense accounts and crediting the proper prepaid expense accounts.

The chart of accounts for The Mann Furniture Store includes two prepaid expense accounts, Prepaid Insurance, Account No. 14, and Stationery and Supplies, Account No. 15. These accounts are classified as asset accounts in the chart of accounts. The account with Prepaid Insurance should be debited for the amount of insurance purchased. At the end of the year the account should be credited for the amount of the insurance expired with an offsetting debit to Insurance Expense, Account No. 611. The account with Stationery and Supplies should be debited for the amount of stationery and supplies purchased. At the end of the year the account should be credited for the amount of stationery and supplies consumed or used during the year with an offsetting debit to Stationery and Supplies Used, Account No. 66.

Accounting for Depreciation. Depreciation accounting is the process of attempting to allocate the cost of most long-lived assets to the periods benefited by the use of these assets. Most fixed assets eventually become useless to the business either because they wear out or because they become inadequate or obsolete. Sometimes all three of these causes combine to make the assets valueless — except, perhaps, for some small value as scrap or junk.

Generally, in computing depreciation, no consideration is given to what the assets might bring if they were to be sold. Assets of this type are acquired to use and not to sell. During their useful life their resale value is of no consequence unless the business is about to cease. For a going business, the idea is to allocate the net cost of the assets over the years they are expected to serve. By "net cost" is meant original cost less estimated scrap or salvage value. Inasmuch as the possibility of scrap or salvage value is commonly ignored, it is usually the original cost of the assets that is allocated.

It should be apparent that depreciation expense can be no more than an estimate. Usually there is no way of knowing just how long an asset will serve. However, with past experience as a guide, the estimates can be reasonably reliable.

There are several ways of calculating the periodic depreciation write-off. Traditionally, the so-called *straight-line method* has been widely used. With this method, the original cost (or cost less any expected scrap value) of an asset is divided by the number of years the asset is expected to serve to find the amount that is to be considered as depreciation expense each year. It is common practice to express depreciation as a percentage of the original cost of the asset. For example, in the case of an asset with a 10-year life, write off 10 per cent of the original cost each year; for a 20-year asset, write off 5 per cent; etc.

There are some depreciation methods that give larger write-offs in the earlier years of the life of the asset. A change in the Internal Revenue Code in 1954 permits taxpayers to use certain of these methods in the case of newly-acquired assets for income-tax purposes. This event has stimulated the use of these "reducing-charge" methods. ("Reducing-charge" means a successively smaller write-off year by year.) However, the straight-line method has been very popular in the past, and it has a number of virtues including simplicity. It is probable that this method will continue to be used by most businesses. The straight-line method of accounting for depreciation is used by The Mann Furniture Store.

Depreciation expense is recorded by an end-of-period adjusting entry that involves debiting one or more depreciation expense accounts and crediting one or more allowance for depreciation accounts. The latter accounts are contra accounts — contra to the accounts for the assets that are being depreciated. In theory there would be no objection to making the credits directly to the asset accounts themselves (in the same way that the asset accounts for prepaid expenses are credited to record their decreases). However, in order that the original cost of the assets will be clearly revealed, the portions of this cost written off are credited to the contra accounts. The amounts of the credit balances of the contra accounts are reported in the balance sheet as a deduction from the cost of the assets to which they relate.

The credit balances in the allowance for depreciation accounts get larger year by year. When the amounts become equal to the cost of the assets, no more depreciation may be taken.

The difference between the allowance for bad debts account and the allowance for depreciation account should be recognized. Both are credited by adjusting entries at the end of the period. In both cases, the offsetting debits go to expense accounts. In both cases, the balances in the allowance accounts are shown in the balance sheet as subtractions from the amounts of the assets to which they relate. (However, the allowance for bad debts account is debited whenever the anticipated bad debts materialize. The balance of this allowance account does not get continually larger. (If it does, this indicates that the estimate of bad debt losses has been excessive.) In contrast, the credit balances of the allowance for depreciation accounts will get larger year by year — often for many years. The credit balances remain in these accounts for as long as the assets to which they relate are kept in service.)

Since The Mann Furniture Store has two classes of fixed assets that are subject to depreciation, store equipment and delivery equipment, there are two contra accounts, Allowance for Depreciation of Store Equipment, Account No. 018, and Allowance for Depreciation of Delivery Equipment, Account No. 019. While depreciation expense could be classified by the type of asset to which the depreciation relates, just one account, Depreciation Expense, Account No. 62, is used by The Mann Furniture Store.

Accounting for Notes Payable and Interest Expense. Many businesses issue notes promising to pay money. When such notes are issued, the business incurs a liability called Notes Payable and there should be an account with this title. A business may give a promissory note for any of several reasons, but the most usual case is when money is borrowed from a commercial bank.

Bank loans always involve interest. Sometimes the note that the borrower gives does not explicitly promise to pay interest, but the bank will collect interest by *discounting* the note. This means that the borrower gets less cash than the amount he promises to pay back. Suppose, for example, that The Mann Furniture Store gives a noninterest-bearing note dated August 1 to the Liberty National Bank promising to pay $1,000 in 90 days. If the discount rate is 6 per cent, the bank would credit The Mann Furniture Store for only $985. (Interest on $1,000 at 6 per cent for a year is $60. Ninety days is one fourth of a 360-day year, hence the interest or discount would be one fourth of $60 or $15.) The transaction should be recorded as indicated in the following journal entry:

August 1. Liberty National Bank.....................	$985.00	
Interest Expense.........................	15.00	
Notes Payable..........................		$1,000.00
Borrowed from the Liberty National Bank on a $1,000, 90-day note discounted at 6 per cent.		

The entry to record the payment of the note 90 days later would be a debit to Notes Payable and a credit to Liberty National Bank for $1,000.

Unless it happens that short-term borrowing under this type of arrangement is done near the end of the fiscal year, the loan will have been repaid by the end of the period. In such cases all of the interest, even though paid in advance, will be an expense of the period. If it should happen that the money is borrowed in one period to be repaid in the next, and the amount of the discount was charged to Interest Expense as just illustrated, then an adjusting entry with respect to this expense is needed at the end of the period. Part of the amount that was charged to Interest Expense is really an expense of the following period. The exact amount of that part must be calculated and an end-of-period adjusting entry made to defer that part of the expense to the next period. The entry would be a debit to Prepaid Interest and a credit to Interest Expense.

In many cases promissory notes that include a promise to pay interest at a specified rate are given. If a note is given in exchange for a loan of cash, the entry to record the transaction is a debit to Cash (or Bank) and a credit to Notes Payable for the full or "face" amount of the note. When the note and interest are paid, the entry to record the payment involves a debit to Notes Payable for the amount of the note, a debit to Interest Expense for the amount of interest paid, and a credit to Cash (or Bank) for the total amount paid.

If an interest-bearing note payable is outstanding at the end of a fiscal period, an adjusting entry of the accrual type is needed to record the interest expense accrued but not paid and the resulting liability. Suppose, for example, that $2,000 had been borrowed on December 1 and a note promising to pay this amount and interest at the rate of 5 per cent in 90 days had been given to the lender. As of December 31, the borrower has had the use of the $2,000 for 30 days and interest expense of $8.33 (5% of $2,000 for 30 days) has been incurred. The adjusting entry would be as follows:

Dec. 31. Interest Expense................................	$8.33	
Accrued Interest Payable........................		$8.33
Interest accrued on note payable 30 days @ 5 per cent.		

It should be borne in mind that notes payable may arise through transactions other than borrowing money. A business might purchase merchandise or other property and give the seller a note promising later payment. A general creditor (one who is owed "on account") might be given a note as a means of securing an extension of time in which to pay the amount owed to him. In the latter case, an entry would be made debiting Accounts Payable and crediting Notes Payable. This is a simple case of a decrease in the liability Accounts Payable being offset by an increase in the liability, Notes Payable.

The chart of accounts for The Mann Furniture Store includes Notes Payable, Account No. 21; Accrued Interest Payable, Account No. 22; and Interest Expense, Account No. 81. These accounts provide for entries relating to notes payable and interest expense.

Purchases Discount. Purchase invoices representing credit purchases may be subject to discount if paid within a specified time. Retailers may be allowed a discount by wholesalers on invoices that are paid within a specified time, such as five days, ten days, or fifteen days, from the date of the invoice. This is known as a cash discount and it should not be confused with trade discounts.

Trade discounts are the discounts allowed retail dealers from the list or catalog prices of wholesalers. Such trade discounts are usually shown as a deduction on the invoice and only the net amount is recorded as the purchase price. If the invoice is subject to an additional discount for cash, it will be indicated on the invoice under the heading of "Terms." For example, the terms may be specified as "2/10, n/30," which means that if paid within ten days a discount of 2 per cent may be deducted, otherwise the net amount of the invoice is payable within thirty days.

To facilitate the payment of invoices in time to be entitled to any discount offered, Mr. Mann follows the policy of filing each invoice in an unpaid invoice file according to its due date. It is, therefore, only necessary to refer to the file each day to ascertain which invoices are due on that date and which may be subject to discount. Any amount of cash discount deducted when paying an invoice should be recorded as a credit to Purchases Discount, Account No. 72. Thus, if an invoice for $140 is subject to a discount of 2 per cent if paid within ten days and it is paid within the specified time, the payment should be recorded by debiting Accounts Payable for $140, by crediting the bank account for $137.20, and by crediting Purchases Discount for $2.80. The purchases discount account has a credit balance that is usually considered as "other income" or as "financial income." Some accountants, however, prefer to treat purchases discount as a reduction in the cost of merchandise purchased rather than as income.

Accounts with Creditors and Customers. As previously explained, a record of the amounts due to creditors on account of credit purchases and the amounts due from customers on account of charge sales may be kept without maintaining a separate ledger account for each creditor and for each customer. Some retail merchants prefer to keep a separate ledger account for each creditor and for each customer. Even though separate ledger accounts are kept with creditors and customers, it is advisable to keep summary accounts with accounts payable and accounts receivable.

Subsidiary Ledgers. When the character of the enterprise and the volume of business are such that it is necessary to keep relatively few accounts, it may be satisfactory to keep all of the accounts together in a single general ledger, which may be bound or loose-leaf. However, when the volume of business and the number of transactions warrant employment of more than one bookkeeper to keep the records, it may be advisable to subdivide the ledger. In some businesses it is necessary to keep separate accounts with thousands of customers and creditors. In such cases it is usually considered advisable to segregate the accounts with customers and the accounts with creditors from the other accounts and to keep them in separate ledgers. When separate ledgers are kept for creditors and customers, these ledgers are known as *subsidiary ledgers.*

Balance-Column Account Form. A special account form known as the balance-column account form is widely used in keeping the individual accounts with customers and creditors. While the standard account form, shown in the illustration on page 16, may be used satisfactorily for customers' and creditors' accounts, most accountants favor the use of the *balance-column account form* shown below for such accounts. It will be noted that three parallel amount columns are provided for recording debits, credits, and balances. Following each entry the new balance may be ascertained and recorded in the Balance column, or if preferred, the balance may be ascertained and recorded at the end of each month. A Check ($\sqrt{}$) column is provided preceding the amount columns. This column may be used in checking each item recorded in the account.

NAME

ADDRESS

DATE	ITEMS	FOL.	√	DEBITS	CREDITS	BALANCE

Balance-Column Account Form

Control Accounts. When subsidiary ledgers are kept for creditors and for customers, it is customary to keep summary or *control accounts* for the subsidiary ledgers in the general ledger. Thus, if accounts with creditors are kept in a subsidiary accounts payable ledger, a control account for accounts payable should be kept in the general ledger; if accounts with customers are kept in a subsidiary accounts receivable ledger, a control account for accounts receivable should be kept in the general ledger. The use of control accounts in the general ledger makes it possible to take a trial balance of the general ledger accounts without reference to the subsidiary ledgers.

Accounts Payable Control. The accounts payable control account provides a summary of the information recorded in the individual accounts with creditors kept in a subsidiary accounts payable ledger. Transactions affecting creditors' accounts are posted separately to the individual accounts in the subsidiary ledger. These transactions must also be posted separately, or must be summarized periodically and the totals posted, to the control account in the general ledger. The balance of the accounts payable control account may be proved by preparing a schedule of the account balances in the accounts payable ledger.

Accounts with creditors normally have credit balances. If a creditor's account has a debit balance, the balance may be circled or be written in red ink. In preparing the schedule of accounts payable, the total of accounts with debit balances should be deducted from the total of the accounts with credit balances and the difference should agree with the balance of the accounts payable control account.

Accounts Receivable Control. The accounts receivable control account provides a summary of the information recorded in the individual accounts with customers kept in a subsidiary accounts receivable ledger. Transactions affecting customers' accounts are posted separately to the individual accounts in the subsidiary ledger. These transactions must also be posted separately, or must be summarized periodically and the totals posted, to the control account in the general ledger. The balance of the accounts receivable control account may be proved by preparing a schedule of the account balances in the accounts receivable ledger.

Accounts with customers normally have debit balances. If a customer's account has a credit balance, the balance may be circled or be written in red ink. In preparing the schedule of accounts receivable, the total of accounts with credit balances should be deducted from the total of the accounts with debit balances and the difference should agree with the balance of the accounts receivable control account.

Posting from the Books of Original Entry. Posting to the individual accounts with creditors and customers in the subsidiary ledgers may be done either from the books of original entry or directly from vouchers or other documents that represent the transactions. When the posting is done from the books of original entry, each item should, of course, be posted separately to the proper account and as the posting is completed the proper cross reference should be made in the Posting Reference column of the books of original entry and in the Folio column of the ledger. Under this plan the voucher or other document that represents the transaction may be filed after the transaction is recorded in the books of original entry. As each transaction is recorded in the proper book of original entry, care must be taken to enter all of the information that will be needed when posting.

Posting from Vouchers or Other Documents. When the posting is done directly from the vouchers or other documents that represent the transactions, the transactions usually will be recorded first in the proper books of original entry, after which the vouchers or other documents will be referred to the bookkeeper in charge of the creditors' and customers' accounts for immediate posting.

Posting to the Individual Accounts with Creditors. It is necessary to post all items that represent an increase or a decrease in the amount owed to each creditor. Following is a list of vouchers or documents that usually represent transactions completed with creditors. The usual posting reference is also indicated.

VOUCHER OR DOCUMENT	TRANSACTIONS REPRESENTED	POSTING REFERENCE
(a) Purchase invoice No. 1	Purchase	P 1
(b) Credit memo	Return or allowance	CM
(c) Check stub No. 1	Payment on account	Ck 1
(d) Note issued	Temporary settlement of account	N

The purchase invoices are usually numbered consecutively as they are received. These numbers should not be confused with the numbers used by the vendor or creditor. The check stubs should be numbered consecutively to agree with the numbers of the checks issued. As the posting is completed, the proper cross reference should be made in the Folio column of the accounts and on the vouchers or documents. If a loose-leaf ledger is used and accounts with creditors are kept in alphabetic order, the posting may be indicated by means of a distinctive check mark on the voucher or document.

Posting to the Individual Accounts with Customers. It is necessary to post all items that represent an increase or a decrease in the amount owed by each customer. Following is a list of vouchers or documents that usually represent transactions completed with customers. The usual posting reference is also indicated.

VOUCHER OR DOCUMENT	TRANSACTION REPRESENTED	POSTING REFERENCE
(a) Sale ticket No. 1	Sale	S 1
(b) Credit memo No. 1	Return or allowance	CM 1
(c) Remittance received	Collection on account	C
(d) Note received	Temporary settlement of account	N

The sales tickets usually are prepared in duplicate or triplicate and are numbered consecutively. Each salesperson may use a different series of numbers. One copy is retained for the use of the bookkeeper and another copy is given to the customer.

Credit memorandums issued to customers in connection with sales returns or allowances are usually prepared in duplicate and are numbered consecutively. One copy goes to the customer and the other copy is retained for the use of the bookkeeper.

Remittances received from customers may consist of cash or cash items, such as checks, bank drafts, and money orders. When the remittance is in the form of cash, it is customary to issue a receipt. The receipt may be issued in duplicate, in which case the duplicate copy will provide the information needed for the purpose of posting to the customer's account. Sometimes receipt stubs are used to record the information for posting purposes.

When the remittance is in the form of a check, it is not necessary to issue a receipt as the canceled check will serve as a receipt for the customer. Posting to the customer's account may be made directly from the check or from a list of checks received. Sometimes all remittances received daily are listed in such a manner as to provide the information needed for posting purposes. When this plan is followed, the bookkeeper need not handle the remittances at all. Where there is a sufficient number of employees to permit of such an organization, it is advisable to arrange the work so that the bookkeeper who posts to customers' accounts does not handle the remittances. Sometimes, however, the bookkeeper also performs the duties of a cashier, in which case the posting may be done directly to the customers' accounts from the checks, bank drafts, and money orders received.

As the posting is completed, the proper cross reference should be made in the Folio column of the account and on the vouchers or documents. If a loose-leaf ledger is used and accounts with customers are kept in alphabetic order, the posting may be indicated by means of a distinctive check mark or by initialing the voucher or document.

Accountants generally prefer this method of posting to the individual accounts with creditors and customers because it provides better control and promotes accuracy. When a purchase invoice is recorded in a purchases journal by one person and is posted directly from the invoice to the proper creditor's account by another person, it is unlikely that both persons will make the same mistake. Even if the posting is done by the person who also keeps the purchases journal, there is less likelihood of making a mistake than when the posting is done from the purchases journal. If a mistake were made in entering the amount of the invoice in the purchases journal, the same mistake would almost certainly be made in posting from the purchases journal to the creditor's account. The same reasoning may be applied to the recording of sales transactions and all other transactions that affect accounts with creditors and customers.

In most businesses, checks received from customers must be reconciled with the accounts receivable ledger before they can safely be recorded in the books of original entry. It is not uncommon for a firm to receive duplicate checks from customers or checks that are drawn incorrectly as to date, amount, or signature. In some cases, unsigned checks will be received. If a check is not found to be acceptable for any reason, it may be considered advisable to return it to the customer with a letter of explanation.

Statement of Account. When merchandise is sold on credit, it is customary to render a statement of account to each charge customer monthly. Usually the statements are mailed as soon as they can be prepared following the close of each month. In order that statements may be mailed on the first of each month, some firms follow the policy of including transactions completed up to the 25th of the month only. Such statements are an aid to collection. When a remittance is not received from the customer within the usual credit period, a copy of the statement of account may be referred to the credit department for such action as the credit manager may wish to take. A model filled-in copy of a statement of account is reproduced on page 156. This is a statement of the account of

O. H. Roth for the month ended December 31. It shows (a) the balance
at the beginning of the month amounting to $317.73; (b) a charge of
$182.58 for a sale of $179 plus tax of $3.58 made on December 24;
(c) a credit of $100 for cash received on December 26; and (d) the balance
at the close of the month amounting to $400.31.

THE MANN FURNITURE STORE

O. H. Roth

Smith Road

City

PAY
LAST
AMOUNT
IN
BALANCE
COLUMN

DATE	ITEMS	CHARGES	CREDITS	BALANCE
Dec. 1				317.73
24	Mise.	182.58		500.31
26	Cash		100.00	400.31

Receipt will not be mailed unless it is requested.

Statement of Account

*PRACTICE ASSIGNMENT No. 14. Complete Report No. 14 in the
workbook and submit your working papers to the instructor for approval.
After completing the report, continue with the following study assignment
until the next report is required.*

(15) APPLICATION OF ACCOUNTING PRINCIPLES

The accrual basis of accounting as applied to a mercantile enterprise
is illustrated on the following pages by reproducing the records of The
Mann Furniture Store, owned and operated by W. L. Mann. The records
include the following:

(a) Books of original entry

    (1) Combined cash-journal

    (2) Purchases journal

    (3) Sales journal

(b) Books of final entry

    (1) General ledger

    (2) Accounts payable ledger

    (3) Accounts receivable ledger

(c) Auxiliary records

    (1) Petty cash disbursements record

    (2) Checkbook

Combined Cash-Journal. The form of combined cash-journal used is the same as the one illustrated on page 92, except that the first two amount columns are used in recording banking transactions including deposits and checks. These columns serve the same purpose as though they were headed Cash Receipts and Payments. Mr. Mann follows the practice of depositing all cash receipts in a checking account at the Liberty National Bank and of making all disbursements by check (except for the payment of small items, which may be paid from a petty cash fund). For these reasons, a bank account rather than a cash account is kept in the general ledger. The posting to the bank account is from the combined cash-journal, the account being debited for the total receipts (deposits) and being credited for the total payments (checks).

All items entered in the General Debits and Credits columns of the combined cash-journal are posted individually to the proper accounts in the general ledger. No individual posting is required from any of the other amount columns. Instead, the totals of these columns are posted when the summary posting is completed at the end of the month.

Purchases Journal. The form of purchases journal used is the same as the one illustrated on page 53. It was described in detail in Unit Three. All transactions involving the purchase of merchandise on credit are recorded in this journal. Inasmuch as the posting of the credits to the accounts with creditors is done directly from the purchase invoices, the only posting required from the purchases journal is the summary posting of the total purchases for each month. This involves a debit to Purchases, Account No. 51, and a credit to Accounts Payable, Account No. 23.

Sales Journal. The form of sales journal used is the same as the one illustrated on page 62. It was described in detail in Unit Three. All transactions involving the sale of merchandise on credit are recorded in this journal. Inasmuch as the posting of charges to the accounts with customers is done directly from the sales tickets, the only posting required from the sales journal is the summary posting of the total sales for each month. This involves a debit to Accounts Receivable, Account No. 123, and credits to Sales, Account No. 41, and to Sales Tax Payable, Account No. 24.

General Ledger. A general ledger with the accounts arranged in numerical order is used. A chart of the accounts appears on page 141. The standard account form is used for general ledger purposes.

Accounts Payable Ledger. An accounts payable ledger with the accounts for creditors arranged in alphabetic order is used. The balance-column account form is used in this ledger. Posting to the individual accounts with creditors is done directly from the vouchers or other documents. As each item is posted, the balance is extended immediately so that reference to the account of a creditor at any time will reveal the amount owed to that creditor.

Accounts Receivable Ledger. An accounts receivable ledger with the accounts for customers arranged in alphabetic order is used. The balance-column account form is used in this ledger. Posting to the individual accounts with customers is done directly from the vouchers or other documents. As each item is posted, the balance is extended immediately so that reference to the account of any customer will reveal without any delay the amount due from him. This is important since it is frequently necessary to ascertain the status of a particular customer's account before extending additional credit.

Auxiliary Records. As previously stated, certain auxiliary records are used, including a petty cash disbursements record and a checkbook. The form of petty cash disbursements record is similar to that illustrated on page 116. A record of deposits made and checks issued is kept on the check stubs as well as in the combined cash-journal. At the end of each month, when the summary posting from the combined cash-journal has been completed, the balance of the bank checking account in the ledger should be the same as the bank balance recorded on the check stubs.

Accounting Procedure. The books of account containing a record of the transactions completed during the month of December are reproduced on pages 167 to 180. These books include the combined cash-journal, the purchases journal, the sales journal, the petty cash disbursements record, the general ledger, the accounts receivable ledger, and the accounts payable ledger. Before recording any transactions for December, the balance of the bank checking account was entered in the combined cash-journal and the balance in the petty cash fund was entered in the petty cash disbursements record. The balance at the beginning of the month of December is shown in each of the accounts in the general, accounts receivable, and accounts payable ledgers. These balances along with those at the end of the month are summarized in the trial balances and schedules reproduced on pages 181 and 182.

Following is a narrative of the transactions completed during December. Transactions of a type that have not been previously introduced are analyzed to show their effect upon the accounts.

THE MANN FURNITURE STORE

NARRATIVE OF TRANSACTIONS

Monday, December 2

Issued checks as follows:

No. 118, Werk Realty Co., $500, in payment of December rent.

No. 119, Hayes Garage, $58.50, in payment of storage, gasoline and oil, and service.

> Both checks were recorded in the combined cash-journal. Check No. 118 was recorded by debiting Rent Expense and by crediting the bank account. Check No. 119 was recorded by debiting Truck Expense and by crediting the bank account. Note that the account titles and check numbers were written in the Description column. The account numbers were inserted in the Posting Reference column when the individual posting was completed at the end of the week.

Tuesday, December 3

Bought merchandise from the Campbell Furniture Co., Grand Rapids, $79.30, per Invoice No. 21 of November 30. Terms, net 30 days.

> After receiving the merchandise and checking the invoice, the transaction was recorded in the purchases journal. A check mark was placed in the Posting Reference column to indicate that individual posting is not done from the purchases journal. The invoice was then posted directly to the credit of the Campbell Furniture Co. account in the accounts payable ledger, after which the invoice was filed in an unpaid invoice file according to its due date.

Wednesday, December 4

Received check from J. H. Weber, $103.79, in full of account.

> The check was first reconciled with J. H. Weber's account in the accounts receivable ledger. When the check was found to be for the proper amount, it was immediately posted to the customer's account. The check was then recorded in the combined cash-journal by debiting the bank account and by crediting Accounts Receivable. The name of the customer was written in the Description column. Since the check had already been posted to the customer's account, a check mark was placed in the Posting Reference column.

Thursday, December 5

Sold merchandise on credit as follows:

No. 71A, J. H. Weber, 115 Main St., City, $85, tax $1.70.

No. 57B, C. A. Anderson, 165 Willis St., City, $93.50, tax $1.87.

No. 35C, R. O. Burns, Richmond, $435.50, tax $8.71.

Unless otherwise specified, all charge sales are payable on the 10th of the following month. No cash discount is allowed. These transactions were recorded in the sales journal. A check mark was placed in the Posting Reference column to indicate that individual posting is not done from the sales journal. The sales·tickets were then posted directly to the proper customers' accounts in the accounts receivable ledger, after which each ticket was filed under the name of the customer for future reference. The numbers of the sales tickets indicate that there are three salespersons identified by the letters A, B, and C. Each of these persons uses a separate pad of sales tickets numbered consecutively.

Friday, December 6

Issued checks as follows:

No. 120, C. J. Kramer, $53.37, in payment for circulars to be used for advertising purposes.

No. 121, State Treasurer, $183.14, in payment of sales taxes for November.

Both checks were recorded in the combined cash-journal by debiting the proper accounts and by crediting the bank account. Check No. 120 was charged to Advertising Expense and Check No. 121 was charged to Sales Tax Payable. The titles of the accounts to be charged and the check numbers were written in the Description column.

Bought merchandise from the Brookville Furniture Co., Brookville, $356, per Invoice No. 22 of December 6. Terms, net 30 days.

Sold merchandise on credit as follows:

No. 58B, M. D. Wright, 765 E. 9th St., City, $108, tax $2.16.

Saturday, December 7

Cash sales for the week:

SALESPERSON	MERCHANDISE	TAX	TOTAL
A	$ 85.00	$1.70	$ 86.70
B	142.00	2.84	144.84
C	93.00	1.86	94.86
	$320.00	$6.40	$326.40

As each cash sale was completed a sales ticket was prepared. This ticket provided the information needed in recording the sale on the cash register when ringing up the amount of cash received. As each amount was thus recorded it was added to the previous total of cash sales made by each salesperson on a mechanical accumulator in the register. Usually, the total cash sales are recorded daily but to save time and to avoid unnecessary duplication of entries, the total cash sales are here recorded at the end of each week and on the last day of the month. This transaction was recorded in the combined cash-journal by debiting the bank account for $326.40 and by crediting Sales for $320 and Sales Tax Payable for $6.40.

Made petty cash disbursements as follows:

Postage stamps, $5. Petty Cash Voucher No. 47.

Collect telegram, 90 cents. Petty Cash Voucher No. 48.

Messenger fees, $1.50. Petty Cash Voucher No. 49.

All disbursements from the petty cash fund are recorded in the petty cash disbursements record. This record is ruled so as to facilitate the classification of such expenditures. It will be noted that the cost of the postage stamps was recorded as a charge to Stationery and Supplies, Account No. 15, the cost of the telegram to Telephone and Telegraph Expense, Account No. 67, and the messenger fees to Miscellaneous Expenses, Account No. 614.

END-OF-THE-WEEK WORK

(a) Proved the footings of the combined cash-journal. (b) Deposited $430.19 in the Liberty National Bank and proved the bank balance ($7,888.57). (c) Posted each entry individually from the General Dr. and Cr. columns of the combined cash-journal to the proper general ledger accounts. When Check No. 121, issued December 6, was posted to the account with Sales Tax Payable, the account was in balance, hence it was ruled with a double line as illustrated on page 172. (d) Proved the footings of the petty cash disbursements record and proved the balance of the petty cash fund ($92.60). (e) Proved the footings of the sales journal.

Monday, December 9

Issued checks as follows:

No. 122, Brookville Furniture Co., $350, on account.

No. 123, Campbell Furniture Co., $300, on account.

Checks Nos. 122 and 123 were recorded in the combined cash-journal by debiting Accounts Payable and by crediting the bank account, the names of the creditors and the check numbers being written in the Description column. Check marks were placed in the Posting Reference column to indicate that checks issued to creditors are not posted individually from the combined cash-journal. The checks were posted directly to the proper creditors' accounts in the accounts payable ledger from the check stubs.

Tuesday, December 10

Issued Check No. 124 for $172.12 to the Liberty National Bank, a U. S. depositary, in payment of the following taxes:

(a) Employees' income taxes withheld during November		$127.20
(b) F.I.C.A. taxes imposed —		
On employees (withheld during November)	$22.46	
On the employer	22.46	44.92
Total		$172.12

This transaction resulted in decreases in F.I.C.A. taxes payable and in employees' income taxes payable with a corresponding decrease in the bank account, hence it was recorded in the combined cash-journal by debiting F.I.C.A. Taxes Payable for $44.92 and Employees' Income Taxes Payable for $127.20, and by crediting the bank account for $172.12.

Sold merchandise on credit as follows:

No. 75A, James C. Wells, 416 Scott St., City, $62.05, tax $1.24.

Wednesday, December 11

Received the following remittances from customers:

S. A. Burkhart, $200, on account.

E. E. Frank, $100, on account.

F. X. Vance, $15, in full of account.

Thursday, December 12

Made the following disbursements from the petty cash fund:

American Red Cross, $5. Petty Cash Voucher No. 50.
W. L. Mann, $10, for personal use. Petty Cash Voucher No. 51.

Friday, December 13

Received the following invoices for merchandise purchased on credit:

Kearns Furniture Co., Rosemont, $248, per Invoice No. 23 of December 13. Terms, 2/10, n/30.

Robert Mitchell Furniture Co., Arlington, $199.10, per Invoice No. 24 of December 12. Terms, net 30 days.

Saturday, December 14

Cash sales for the week:

SALESPERSON	MERCHANDISE	TAX	TOTAL
A	$ 90.00	$1.80	$ 91.80
B	270.00	5.40	275.40
C	105.00	2.10	107.10
	$465.00	$9.30	$474.30

Issued Check No. 125 payable to Payroll for $869.97.

Mr. Mann follows the policy of paying his employees on the 15th and last day of each month. Since December 15 fell on Sunday, the employees were paid on the 14th. The following statement was prepared from the payroll record:

PAYROLL STATEMENT FOR PERIOD ENDED DECEMBER 15

Total wages and commissions earned during period..........			$969.56
Employees' taxes to be withheld:			
(a) Employees' income taxes...........................		$80.20	
(b) F.I.C.A. taxes, 2%...............................		19.39	99.59
Net amount payable to employees....................			$869.97
Employer's payroll taxes:			
(a) F.I.C.A. taxes, 2% of $969.56......................			$ 19.39
(b) Unemployment compensation taxes —			
State U. C. taxes, 2.7% of $969.56........		$26.18	
F.U.T.A. taxes, 3% of $969.56..........	$29.09		
Less credit for state taxes..............	26.18	2.91	29.09
Total...			$ 48.48

Since no employee's wages during the year have exceeded $3,000, the entire amount of the wages and commissions earned during the period ended December 15 is subject to both the F.I.C.A. and U.C. taxes.

Two entries were required to record the payroll in the combined cash-journal — one to record the total earnings of the employees, the amounts withheld for F.I.C.A. taxes and income taxes, and the net amount paid; the other to record the social security taxes imposed on the employer.

END-OF-THE-WEEK WORK

(a) Proved the footings of the combined cash-journal. (b) Deposited $789.30 in the Liberty National Bank and proved the bank balance ($6,985.78). (c) Posted each entry individually from the General Dr. and Cr. columns of the combined cash-journal to the proper general ledger accounts. When Check No. 124, issued December 10, was posted to the accounts with F.I.C.A. Taxes Payable and Employees' Income Taxes Payable, the accounts were found to be in balance, hence each account was ruled with a double line as illustrated on page 173. (d) Proved the footings of the petty cash disbursements record and proved the balance of the petty cash fund ($77.60). (e) Proved the footings of the sales journal.

Monday, December 16

Issued checks as follows:

No. 126, De Luxe Upholstery Co., $400, on account.
No. 127, Barnes-Wheton Co., $201.70, in full of account.
No. 128, Kearns Furniture Co., $593.76, on account.

Tuesday, December 17

Received the following remittances from customers:

W. A. Newman, $221.95, in full of account.

W. D. Wolfe, $500, on account.

M. D. Wright, $150, on account.

Wednesday, December 18

Sold merchandise on credit as follows:

No. 47C, F. X. Vance, North Bend, $82.05, tax $1.64.

No. 84A, C. E. Perry & Co., Fairmont, $484.20, tax $9.68.

No. 70B, R. R. Philips, 524 Forest Avenue, City, $356.93, tax $7.14.

Thursday, December 19

Made petty cash disbursements as follows:

Advertising, $4. Petty Cash Voucher No. 52.

Supplies, $6. Petty Cash Voucher No. 53.

Miscellaneous expenses, $1.75. Petty Cash Voucher No. 54.

Bought merchandise from Kingston and Welch, 30 State St., City, $196.35, per Invoice No. 25 of December 19. Terms, 2/30, n/60.

Friday, December 20

Received credit memorandum for $24.80 from Robert Mitchell Furniture Co., for merchandise returned; to be applied on Invoice No. 24 received December 13.

This transaction was recorded in the combined cash-journal by debiting Accounts Payable and by crediting Purchases Returns and Allowances. It was also posted directly to the account of the Robert Mitchell Furniture Co. in the accounts payable ledger from the credit memorandum.

Since a page of the combined cash-journal was filled after recording this transaction, the amount columns were footed and the footings proved. The totals were then recorded on the double ruled line at the bottom of the page after which they were carried forward and entered at the top of the next page.

Saturday, December 21

Issued Check No. 129 for $250 to Mr. Mann for personal use. Cash sales for the week:

SALESPERSON	MERCHANDISE	TAX	TOTAL
A	$110.00	$2.20	$112.20
B	164.00	3.28	167.28
C	105.94	2.12	108.06
	$379.94	$7.60	$387.54

END-OF-THE-WEEK WORK

(a) Proved the footings of the combined cash-journal. (b) Deposited $1,259.49 in the Liberty National Bank and proved the bank balance ($6,799.81). (c) Posted each entry individually from the General Dr. and Cr. columns of the combined cash-journal to the proper general ledger accounts. (d) Proved the footings of the petty cash disbursements record and proved the balance of the petty cash fund ($65.85). (e) Proved the footings of the sales journal.

Monday, December 23

Issued Check No. 130 for $243.04 to Kearns Furniture Co. in payment of their invoice of December 13, less 2 per cent discount.

The amount of the check is computed as follows:

Amount of invoice......................	$248.00
Discount, 2 per cent.....................	4.96
Balance due............................	$243.04

This transaction was recorded in the combined cash-journal by debiting Accounts Payable for $248 and by crediting Purchases Discount for $4.96 and crediting the bank account for $243.04. An entry was also made in the purchases journal to record the date of payment of Invoice No. 23. In posting the check directly to the account of the Kearns Furniture Co. in the accounts payable ledger the amount of the check was entered on one line and the amount of the discount on another line.

Tuesday, December 24

Sold merchandise on credit as follows:

No. 81B, J. H. Weber, 115 Main St., City, $417.75, tax $8.36.
No. 58C, O. H. Roth, Smith Road, City, $179, tax $3.58.
No. 59C, E. E. Frank, 875 Blair Ave., City, $298.50, tax $5.97.

Thursday, December 26

Received the following remittances from customers:

R. R. Philips, $200, on account.
O. H. Roth, $100, on account.

Made petty cash disbursements as follows:

Advertising, $3. Petty Cash Voucher No. 55.
Supplies, $4. Petty Cash Voucher No. 56.
Miscellaneous Expenses, $2.90. Petty Cash Voucher No. 57.

Friday, December 27

Issued Credit Memorandum No. 12 for $11.22 to R. R. Philips for merchandise returned. (Sales price of merchandise, $11, tax 22 cents).

Issued Check No. 131 for $170 to The Daily News in payment of advertising bill.

Issued Check No. 132 for $221.95 to the Liberty National Bank for W. A. Newman's check which was returned unpaid (N.S.F.).

> W. A. Newman's check was received on December 17, and was deposited in the bank on December 21. The bank returned the check by messenger with a notice advising that the maker did not have sufficient funds on deposit to redeem the check. Check No. 132 was recorded in the combined cash-journal by debiting Accounts Receivable and by crediting the bank account. The amount of the check was debited immediately to Mr. Newman's account in the accounts receivable ledger.

Saturday, December 28

Cash sales for the week:

SALESPERSON	MERCHANDISE	TAX	TOTAL
A	$144.00	$ 2.88	$146.88
B	211.40	4.23	215.63
C	193.97	3.88	197.85
	$549.37	$10.99	$560.36

Issued checks as follows:

No. 133, The Bell Telephone Co., $17.50, for telephone service.
No. 134, The Union Gas & Electric Co., $44.90, for gas and electricity.

END-OF-THE-WEEK WORK

(a) Proved the footings of the combined cash-journal. (b) Deposited $860.36 in the Liberty National Bank and proved the bank balance ($6,962.78). (c) Posted each entry individually from the General Dr. and Cr. columns of the combined cash-journal to the proper general ledger accounts. (d) Proved the footings of the petty cash disbursements record and proved the balance of the petty cash fund ($55.95). (e) Proved the footings of the sales journal.

(*Continued on page 183*)

Page 52   PURCHASES JOURNAL FOR MONTH OF   *December* 19—

Date of Entry	Date of Invoice	No. of Invoice	From Whom Purchased	Post. Ref.	Amount	Date Paid
			Amount Forwarded			
Dec. 3	Nov. 30	21	Campbell Furniture Co.	✓	7930	
6	Dec. 6	22	Brookville Furniture Co.	✓	35600	
13	13	23	Kearns Furniture Co.	✓	24800	Dec. 23
13	12	24	Robt. Mitchell Furniture Co.	✓	19910	
19	19	25	Kingston and Welch	✓	19635	
30	27	26	Kearns Furniture Co.	✓	21000	
31	30	27	Barnes-Wheton Co.	✓	47760	
			Purchases Dr.-Accts. Pay. Cr.	51/23	176635	

The Mann Furniture Store — Purchases Journal

Page 64   SALES JOURNAL FOR MONTH OF   *December* 19—

Date of Entry	No. of Sale	To Whom Sold	Post. Ref.	Accounts Rec. Dr.	Sales Cr.	Sales Tax Pay. Cr.
		Amounts Forwarded				
Dec. 5	71a	J. H. Weber	✓	8670	8500	170
5	57B	C. A. Anderson	✓	9537	9350	187
5	35C	R. O. Burns	✓	44421	43550	871
6	58B	M. D. Wright	✓	11016	10800	216
10	75a	James C. Wells	✓	6329	6205	124
18	47C	F. X. Vance	✓	8369	8205	164
18	84a	C. E. Perry & Co.	✓	49388	48420	968
18	70B	R. R. Philips	✓	36407	35693	714
24	81B	J. H. Weber	✓	42611	41775	836
24	58C	O. H. Roth	✓	18258	17900	358
24	59C	E. E. Frank	✓	30447	29850	597
				265453	260248	5205
				(123)	(41)	(24)

The Mann Furniture Store — Sales Journal

Page 76

COMBINED CASH-JOURNAL FOR MONTH OF December 19—

Bank Deposits Dr.	Bank Checks Cr.	Mo.	Day	Description	Post. Ref.	General Debits	General Credits	Accts. Receivable Debits	Accts. Receivable Credits	Accts. Payable Debits	Accts. Payable Credits
		Dec.	1	Amounts Forwarded		$2,253.37					
	50000		2	Rent Expense	Ck. #118	50000					
	5850		2	Truck Expense	Ck. #119	5850					
10379			4	J. N. Weber	612				10379		
	5337		6	Advertising Expense	Ck. #120	5337					
	18314		6	Sales Tax Payable	Ck. #121	18314					
32640			7	Sales	41		32000				
			9	Sales Tax Payable	Ck. #122		640		10379		
	35000		9	Brookville Furniture Co.						35000	
	30000		9	Campbell Furniture Co.						30000	
	17212		10	F.I.C.A. Taxes Payable	Ck. #124	4492					
			10	Employees Income Taxes Payable	26	12720					
20000			11	H. Burkhart					20000		
10000			11	E. E. Frank					10000		
1500			11	F. N. Vance					1500		
47430			14	Sales	41		46500				
			14	Sales Tax Payable	24		930				
	86997		14	Salaries and Commissions	Ck. #125	96956					
			14	F.I.C.A. Taxes Payable	25		1939				
			14	Employees Income Taxes Payable	26		8020				
			14	Social Security Taxes	64	4848					
			14	F.I.C.A. Taxes Payable	25		1939				
			14	F.I.C.A. Taxes Payable	27		291				
			16	State U.C. Taxes Payable	28		2618				
	40000		16	DeLuxe Upholstery Co	Ck. #126					40000	
	20170		16	Barnes-Wheaton Co	Ck. #127					20170	
	59376		16	Kearns Furniture Co.	Ck. #128					59376	
22195			17	W. A. Newman					22195		
50000			17	W. D. Wolfe					50000		
15000			17	M. D. Wright					15000		
			20	Robt. Mitchell Furn. Co.—Purchases R & A	051		2489				
209744	362256		20	Carried Forward		98517	97357		129074	187026	

Page 17

COMBINED CASH-JOURNAL FOR MONTH OF December 19—

Bank		Date		Description	Post Ref	General		Accts. Receivable		Accts. Payable	
Deposits Dr.	Checks Cr.	Mo	Day			Debits	Credits	Debits	Credits	Debits	Credits
209144	368256	Dec. 20		Amounts Forwarded	✓	198517	973157		129074	187026	
	25000		21	W. L. Mann, Drawing Ck. 129	32	25000					
38754			21	Sales	41		37994				
				Sales Tax Payable	24						
	24304		23	Mann Furniture Co. - Purchases Discount Ck.130	72		496			24800	
20000			26	R. R. Philips	✓				20000		
10000			26	O. R. Roth	✓				10000		
			27	Sales R. & A. - R. R. Philips C.M. #2	041	1100			1122		
				Sales Tax Payable	24	22					
	17000		27	Advertising Expense Ck. 131	68	17000					
	22195		27	V. A. Newman Ck. 132	✓			22195			
56036			28	Sales	41		54937				
				Sales Tax Payable	24		1099				
	1750		28	Tel. and Tel. Expense Ck. 133	67	1750					
	4490		29	Heating and Lighting Ck. 134	65	4490					
			31	Store Equipment Security Life Co. — Lock Co.	18	40000					40000
19829			31	Sales	41		19440				
				Sales Tax Payable	24		389				
	86941		31	Salaries and Commissions Ck. 135	63	96939					
				F.I.C.A. Taxes Payable	25		1938				
				Employees' Income Taxes Payable	26		8060				
			31	Social Security Taxes	64	48847					
				F.I.C.A. Taxes Payable	25		1939				
				F.I.C.A. Taxes Payable	27		291				
				State U.C. Taxes Payable	28		2617				
	4405		31	W. L. Mann, Drawing Ck. 136	32	1000					
				Stationery and Supplies	15	1500					
				Tel. and Tel. Expense	67	90					
				Advertising Expense	68	700					
				Charitable Contributions	613	500					
				Misc. Expenses	644						
353763	554341					394070	2273117	22195	160196	211826	40000

The Mann Furniture Store — Combined Cash-Journal (Concluded)

PETTY CASH DISBURSEMENTS FOR MONTH OF December 19—

Page 143

DAY	DESCRIPTION	Vou. No.	Total Amount	3 2	15	6 7	6 8	6 13	6 14	DISTRIBUTION OF CHARGES	Account	Amount
	Brought Forward		$100.00									
7	Postage stamps	47	500	500								
7	Collect telegram	48	90			90						
7	Messenger fees	49	150						150			
			$42.60									
12	American Red Cross	50	500		500	90		500				
12	H. L. Mann, Drawing	51	1000/1000	1000/1000								
			$57.60									
19	Advertising	52	400		500	90	400	300	150			
19	Supplies	53	600		600							
19	Misc. expenses	54	175	1000	1100	90	400	300	175			
26	Advertising	55	300				300					
26	Supplies	56	400		400							
26	Misc. expenses	57	290	1000	1500	90	700	500	290			
			44 05	1000	1500	90	700	500	615			
31	Balance		$55.95									
	Rec'd in fund		44.05									
	Total		$100.00									

The Mann Furniture Store — Petty Cash Disbursements Record

GENERAL LEDGER

ACCOUNT *Liberty National Bank*   111

DATE	ITEMS	FOLIO	√	DEBITS	DATE	ITEMS	FOLIO	√	CREDITS
19-- Dec. 1	Balance	√		8 2 5 3 3 9	19-- Dec. 31		CJ 77		5 5 4 3 4 1
31	6,247.61	CJ 77		3 5 3 7 6 3					

ACCOUNT *Petty Cash Fund*   112

19-- Dec. 1	Balance	√		1 0 0 0 0					

ACCOUNT *Notes Receivable*   121

19-- Dec. 1	Balance	√		8 0 1 5 0					

ACCOUNT *Accounts Receivable*   123

19-- Dec. 1	Balance	√		3 5 9 3 5 0	19-- Dec. 31		CJ 77		1 6 0 1 9 6
31		CJ 77		2 2 1 9 5					
31	4,665.02	S 64		2 6 5 4 5 3					

ACCOUNT *Allowance for Bad Debts*   012

					19-- Dec. 1	Balance	√		8 8 5 6

ACCOUNT *Merchandise Inventory*   13

19-- Dec. 1	Balance	√		2 8 5 2 2 4 5					

ACCOUNT *Prepaid Insurance*   14

19-- Dec. 1	Balance	√		4 3 0 7 2					

ACCOUNT *Stationery and Supplies*   15

19-- Dec. 1	Balance	√		1 5 5 0 0					
31		CJ 77		1 5 0 0					

The Mann Furniture Store — General Ledger

ACCOUNT *Store Equipment*   18

DATE	ITEMS	FOLIO	√	DEBITS	DATE	ITEMS	FOLIO	√	CREDITS
19— Dec 1	Balance	√		1 8 5 0 00					
31		CJ77		4 0 0 00					

ACCOUNT *Allowance for Depr. of Store Equipment*   018

DATE	ITEMS	FOLIO	√	DEBITS	DATE	ITEMS	FOLIO	√	CREDITS
					19— Dec 1	Balance	√		3 7 0 00

ACCOUNT *Delivery Equipment*   19

DATE	ITEMS	FOLIO	√	DEBITS	DATE	ITEMS	FOLIO	√	CREDITS
19— Dec 1	Balance	√		1 9 0 0 00					

ACCOUNT *Allowance for Depr. of Delivery Equipment*   019

DATE	ITEMS	FOLIO	√	DEBITS	DATE	ITEMS	FOLIO	√	CREDITS
					19— Dec 1	Balance	√		4 7 5 00

ACCOUNT *Notes Payable*   21

DATE	ITEMS	FOLIO	√	DEBITS	DATE	ITEMS	FOLIO	√	CREDITS
					19— Dec 1	Balance	√		2 0 0 0 00

ACCOUNT *Accounts Payable*   23

DATE	ITEMS	FOLIO	√	DEBITS	DATE	ITEMS	FOLIO	√	CREDITS
19— Dec 31		CJ77		2 1 1 8 26	19— Dec 1	Balance	√		3 0 2 1 51
					31		CJ77		4 0 0 00
					31	3,069 60	P52		6 7 6 4 35

ACCOUNT *Sales Tax Payable*   24

DATE	ITEMS	FOLIO	√	DEBITS	DATE	ITEMS	FOLIO	√	CREDITS
19— Dec 6		CJ76		1 8 3 14	19— Dec 1	Balance	√		1 8 3 14
27		CJ77		2 2	7		CJ76		6 40
					14		CJ76		9 30
					21		CJ77		7 60
					28		CJ77		1 0 99
					31		CJ77		3 89
					31	40.01	S64		5 2 03

The Mann Furniture Store — General Ledger (Continued)

ACCOUNT F. I. C. A. Taxes Payable　　25

DATE	ITEMS	FOLIO	√	DEBITS	DATE	ITEMS	FOLIO	√	CREDITS
19— Dec 10		CJ76		4492	19— Dec 1	Balance	√		4492
					14		CJ76		1939
					14		CJ76		1939
					31		CJ77		1938
					31		CJ77		1939

ACCOUNT Employees' Income Taxes Payable　　26

DATE	ITEMS	FOLIO	√	DEBITS	DATE	ITEMS	FOLIO	√	CREDITS
19— Dec 10		CJ76		12720	19— Dec 1	Balance	√		12720
					14		CJ76		8020
					31		CJ77		8060

ACCOUNT F. U. T. A. Taxes Payable　　27

DATE	ITEMS	FOLIO	√	DEBITS	DATE	ITEMS	FOLIO	√	CREDITS
					19— Dec 1	Balance	√		3706
					14		CJ76		291
					31		CJ77		271

ACCOUNT State U. C. Taxes Payable　　28

DATE	ITEMS	FOLIO	√	DEBITS	DATE	ITEMS	FOLIO	√	CREDITS
					19— Dec 1	Balance	√		6065
					14		CJ76		2618
					31		CJ77		2617

ACCOUNT W. L. Mann, Proprietor　　31

DATE	ITEMS	FOLIO	√	DEBITS	DATE	ITEMS	FOLIO	√	CREDITS
					19— Dec 1	Balance	√		3651731

ACCOUNT W. L. Mann, Drawing.　　32

DATE	ITEMS	FOLIO	√	DEBITS	DATE	ITEMS	FOLIO	√	CREDITS
19— Dec 1	Balance	√		687000					
21		CJ77		25000					
31		CJ77		1000					

The Mann Furniture Store — General Ledger (Continued)

ACCOUNT Sales   41

DATE	ITEMS	FOLIO	√	DEBITS	DATE	ITEMS	FOLIO	√	CREDITS
					19— Dec 1	Balance	√		9 7 8 0 4 15
					7		CJ 76		3 2 0 00
					14		CJ 76		4 6 5 00
					21		CJ 77		3 7 9 94
					28		CJ 77		5 4 9 37
					31		CJ 77		1 9 4 40
					31		S64		1 0 2 6 0 2 48

ACCOUNT Sales Returns and Allowances   041

DATE	ITEMS	FOLIO	√	DEBITS					
19— Dec 1	Balance	√		1 1 3 20					
27		CJ 77		1 1 4 20					

ACCOUNT Purchases   51

DATE	ITEMS	FOLIO	√	DEBITS					
19— Dec 1	Balance	√		6 3 5 5 0 28					
31		P52		1 3 7 6 6 35					

ACCOUNT Purchases Returns and Allowances   051

DATE	ITEMS	FOLIO	√	DEBITS	DATE	ITEMS	FOLIO	√	CREDITS
					19— Dec 1	Balance	√		8 9 50
					20		CJ 76		2 4 80

ACCOUNT Rent Expense   61

DATE	ITEMS	FOLIO	√	DEBITS					
19— Dec 1	Balance	√		5 5 0 0 00					
2		CJ 76		5 0 0 00					

ACCOUNT Salaries and Commissions   63

DATE	ITEMS	FOLIO	√	DEBITS					
19— Dec 1	Balance	√		1 2 3 5 4 40					
14		CJ 76		9 6 9 56					
31		CJ 77		1 4 2 6 9 33					

The Mann Furniture Store — General Ledger (Continued)

ACCOUNT *Social Security Taxes*   64

DATE	ITEMS	FOLIO	√	DEBITS	DATE	ITEMS	FOLIO	√	CREDITS
19- Dec 1	Balance	√		6 1 7 7 2					
14		CJ 76		4 8 4 8					
31		CJ 77		4 8 4 7 (7,847 67)					

ACCOUNT *Heating and Lighting*   65

DATE	ITEMS	FOLIO	√	DEBITS	DATE	ITEMS	FOLIO	√	CREDITS
19- Dec 1	Balance	√		4 8 2 1 0					
28		CJ 77		4 4 9 0 (5,271 00)					

ACCOUNT *Telephone and Telegraph Expense*   67

DATE	ITEMS	FOLIO	√	DEBITS	DATE	ITEMS	FOLIO	√	CREDITS
19- Dec 1	Balance	√		2 1 4 6 5					
28		CJ 77		1 7 5 0					
31		CJ 77		(2,332 15)					

ACCOUNT *Advertising Expense*   68

DATE	ITEMS	FOLIO	√	DEBITS	DATE	ITEMS	FOLIO	√	CREDITS
19- Dec 1	Balance	√		4 7 1 1 2 0					
6		CJ 76		5 3 3 7					
27		CJ 77		1 7 0 0 0					
31		CJ 77		(4,947 57)					

ACCOUNT *Truck Expense*   612

DATE	ITEMS	FOLIO	√	DEBITS	DATE	ITEMS	FOLIO	√	CREDITS
19- Dec 1	Balance	√		4 7 3 6 0					
2		CJ 76		5 8 5 0 (532 10)					

ACCOUNT *Charitable Contributions*   613

DATE	ITEMS	FOLIO	√	DEBITS	DATE	ITEMS	FOLIO	√	CREDITS
19- Dec 1	Balance	√		1 6 0 0 0					
31		CJ 77		5 0 0 (165 00)					

ACCOUNT *Miscellaneous Expenses*   614

DATE	ITEMS	FOLIO	√	DEBITS	DATE	ITEMS	FOLIO	√	CREDITS
19- Dec 1	Balance	√		3 6 9 7 8					
31		CJ 77		(376 15)					

The Mann Furniture Store — General Ledger (Continued)

ACCOUNT *Interest Income*   71

DATE	ITEMS	FOLIO	√	DEBITS	DATE	ITEMS	FOLIO	√	CREDITS
					19- Dec 1	Balance	√		5 1 48

ACCOUNT *Purchases Discount*   72

DATE	ITEMS	FOLIO	√	DEBITS	DATE	ITEMS	FOLIO	√	CREDITS
					Dec 1	Balance	√		2 1 5 71
					23		CJ77		2 4 96

ACCOUNT *Interest Expense*   81

DATE	ITEMS	FOLIO	√	DEBITS	DATE	ITEMS	FOLIO	√	CREDITS
Dec 1	Balance	√		6 2 70					

ACCOUNT

DATE	ITEMS	FOLIO	√	DEBITS	DATE	ITEMS	FOLIO	√	CREDITS

ACCOUNT

DATE	ITEMS	FOLIO	√	DEBITS	DATE	ITEMS	FOLIO	√	CREDITS

ACCOUNT

DATE	ITEMS	FOLIO	√	DEBITS	DATE	ITEMS	FOLIO	√	CREDITS

ACCOUNT

DATE	ITEMS	FOLIO	√	DEBITS	DATE	ITEMS	FOLIO	√	CREDITS

The Mann Furniture Store — General Ledger (Concluded)

NAME   C. A. Anderson
ADDRESS   165 Willis St., City

DATE	ITEMS	FOLIO	√	DEBIT	CREDIT	BALANCE
19— Dec. 5		S 57B		95 37		95 37

NAME   S. A. Burkhart
ADDRESS   2622 Euclid Ave., City

DATE	ITEMS	FOLIO	√	DEBIT	CREDIT	BALANCE
19— Dec. 1	Dr. Balance		√			631 38
11		C			200 00	431 38

NAME   R. O. Burns
ADDRESS   Richmond

DATE	ITEMS	FOLIO	√	DEBIT	CREDIT	BALANCE
19— Dec. 5		S 35C		444 21		444 21

NAME   E. E. Frank
ADDRESS   875 Blair Ave., City

DATE	ITEMS	FOLIO	√	DEBIT	CREDIT	BALANCE
19— Dec. 1	Dr. Balance		√			265 20
11		C			100 00	165 20
24		S 59C		304 47		469 67

NAME   W. A. Newman
ADDRESS   317 Sunshine Ave., City

DATE	ITEMS	FOLIO	√	DEBIT	CREDIT	BALANCE
19— Dec. 1	Dr. Balance		√			221 95
17		C			221 95	- 0 -
27	N. S. F.	Ck. 132		221 95		221 95

NAME   C. E. Perry & Co.
ADDRESS   Fairmont

DATE	ITEMS	FOLIO	√	DEBIT	CREDIT	BALANCE
19— Dec. 1	Dr. Balance		√			103 17
18		S 84Q		493 88		597 05

NAME   R. R. Philips
ADDRESS   524 Forest Ave., City

DATE	ITEMS	FOLIO	√	DEBIT	CREDIT	BALANCE
19— Dec. 1	Dr. Balance		√			306 00
18		S 70B		364 07		670 07
26		C			200 00	470 07
27		C M12			11 22	458 85

The Mann Furniture Store — Accounts Receivable Ledger

NAME *O. H. Roth*
ADDRESS *Smith Road, City*

DATE		ITEMS	FOLIO	√	DEBIT	CREDIT	BALANCE
19— Dec.	1	Dr. Balance	√				317 73
	24		S 58C		182 58		500 31
	26		C			100 00	400 31

NAME *F. V. Vance*
ADDRESS *North Bend*

19— Dec.	1	Dr. Balance	√				15 00
	11		C			15 00	-0-
	18		S 47C		83 69		83 69

NAME *J. H. Weber*
ADDRESS *115 Main St., City*

19— Dec.	1	Dr. Balance	√				103 79
	4		C			103 79	-0-
	5		S 71a		86 70		86 70
	24		S 81B		426 11		512 81

NAME *James C. Wells*
ADDRESS *416 Scott St., City*

19— Dec.	10		S 75a		63 29		63 29

NAME *W. D. Wolfe*
ADDRESS *217 Alpine St., City*

19— Dec.	1	Dr. Balance	√				1178 85
	17		C			500 00	678 85

NAME *M. D. Wright*
ADDRESS *765 E. 9th St., City*

19— Dec.	1	Dr. Balance	√				450 43
	6		S 58B		110 16		560 59
	17		C			150 00	410 59

The Mann Furniture Store — Accounts Receivable Ledger (Concluded)

NAME *Barnes-Wheton Co.*
ADDRESS *Maplewood*

DATE		ITEMS	FOLIO	√	DEBIT	CREDIT	BALANCE
19— Dec.	1	Cr. Balance	√				201 70
	16		Ck 127		201 70		-0-
	31	12/30 - 2/30, n/60	P 27			477 60	477 60

NAME *Brookville Furniture Co.*
ADDRESS *Brookville*

DATE		ITEMS	FOLIO	√	DEBIT	CREDIT	BALANCE
19— Dec.	1	Cr. Balance	√				350 00
	6	12/6 - n/30	P 22			356 00	706 00
	9		Ck 122		350 00		356 00

NAME *Campbell Furniture Co.*
ADDRESS *Grand Rapids*

DATE		ITEMS	FOLIO	√	DEBIT	CREDIT	BALANCE
19— Dec.	1	Cr. Balance	√				601 05
	3	11/30 - n/30	P 21			79 30	680 35
	9		Ck 123		300 00		380 35

NAME *De Luxe Upholstering Co.*
ADDRESS *Pineville*

DATE		ITEMS	FOLIO	√	DEBIT	CREDIT	BALANCE
19— Dec.	1	Cr. Balance	√				800 00
	16		Ck 126		400 00		400 00

The Mann Furniture Store — Accounts Payable Ledger

NAME *Kearns Furniture Co.*
ADDRESS *Rosemont*

DATE	ITEMS	FOLIO	√	DEBIT	CREDIT	BALANCE
'19 Dec. 1	Cr. Balance	√				593 76
13	12/13 - 2/10, n/30	P 23			248 00	841 76
16		Ck.128		593 76		248 00
23		Ck.130		243 04		
23	Discount			4 96		- 0 -
30	12/27 - 2/10, n/30	P 26			210 00	210 00

NAME *Kingston and Welch*
ADDRESS *30 State St., City*

DATE	ITEMS	FOLIO	√	DEBIT	CREDIT	BALANCE
'19 Dec. 19	12/19 - 2/30, n/60	P 25			196 35	196 35

NAME *Robert Mitchell Furniture Co.*
ADDRESS *Arlington*

DATE	ITEMS	FOLIO	√	DEBIT	CREDIT	BALANCE
'19 Dec. 1	Cr. Balance	√				475 00
13	12/12 - n/30	P 24			199 10	674 10
20		C M		24 80		649 30

NAME *Security Safe & Lock Co.*
ADDRESS *Chicago*

DATE	ITEMS	FOLIO	√	DEBIT	CREDIT	BALANCE
'19 Dec. 31	12/30 - 2/30, n/60	CJ 77			400 00	400 00

The Mann Furniture Store — Accounts Payable Ledger (Concluded)

The Mann Furniture Store
Trial Balances

Accounts	Nos.	November 30, 19— Dr. Balances	November 30, 19— Cr. Balances	December 31, 19— Dr. Balances	December 31, 19— Cr. Balances
Liberty National Bank	111	825339		624761	
Petty Cash Fund	112	10000		10000	
Notes Receivable	121	80150		80150	
Accounts Receivable	123	359350		486802	
Allowance for Bad Debts	012		8856		8856
Merchandise Inventory	13	2852245		2852245	
Prepaid Insurance	14	43072		43072	
Stationery and Supplies	15	15500		17000	
Store Equipment	18	185000		225000	
Allowance for Depr. of Store Equipment	018		37000		37000
Delivery Equipment	19	190000		190000	
Allowance for Depr. of Delivery Equipment	019		47500		47500
Notes Payable	21		200000		200000
Accounts Payable	23		302151		306960
Sales Tax Payable	24		18314		9001
F.I.C.A. Taxes Payable	25		4492		7755
Employees' Income Taxes Payable	26		12720		16080
F.U.T.A. Taxes Payable	27		3706		4288
State U.C. Taxes Payable	28		6065		11300
W. L. Mann, Proprietor	31		3651731		3651731
W. L. Mann, Drawing	32	687000		713000	
Sales	41		9780415		10231534
Sales Returns and Allowances	041	11320		12420	
Purchases	51	6355028		6531663	
Purchases Returns and Allowances	051		8950		11430
Rent Expense	61	550000		600000	
Salaries and Commissions	63	1235440		1429335	
Social Security Taxes	64	61772		71467	
Heating and Lighting	65	48210		52700	
Telephone and Telegraph Expense	67	21465		23305	
Advertising Expense	68	471120		494157	
Truck Expense	612	47360		53210	
Charitable Contributions	613	16000		16500	
Miscellaneous Expenses	614	36978		37593	
Interest Income	71		5148		5148
Purchases Discount	72		21571		22067
Interest Expense	81	6270		6270	
		14108619	14108619	14570650	14570650

The Mann Furniture Store — Trial Balances

The Mann Furniture Store
Schedule of Accounts Receivable

Customers	November 30, 19-	December 31, 19-
C. A. Anderson		9 5 3 7
S. A. Burkhart	6 3 1 3 8	4 3 1 3 8
R. O. Burns		4 4 4 2 1
E. E. Frank	2 6 5 2 0	4 6 9 6 7
W. A. Newman	2 2 1 9 5	2 2 1 9 5
C. E. Perry & Co.	1 0 3 1 7	5 9 7 0 5
R. R. Philips	3 0 6 0 0	4 5 8 8 5
O. H. Roth	3 1 7 7 3	4 0 0 3 1
F. L. Vance	1 5 0 0	8 3 6 9
J. H. Weber	1 0 3 7 9	5 1 2 8 1
James C. Wells		6 3 2 9
W. D. Wolfe	1 1 7 8 8 5	6 7 8 8 5
M. D. Wright	4 5 0 4 3	4 1 0 5 9
	3 5 9 3 5 0	4 8 6 8 0 2

The Mann Furniture Store — Schedule of Accounts Receivable

The Mann Furniture Store
Schedule of Accounts Payable

Creditors	November 30, 19-	December 31, 19-
Barnes-Wheton Co	2 0 1 7 0	4 7 7 6 0
Brookville Furniture Co	3 5 0 0 0	3 5 6 0 0
Campbell Furniture Co.	6 0 1 0 5	3 8 0 3 5
De Luxe Upholstering Co.	8 0 0 0 0	4 0 0 0 0
Kearns Furniture Co	5 9 3 7 6	2 1 0 0 0
Kingston and Welch		1 9 6 3 5
Robert Mitchell Furniture Co.	4 7 5 0 0	6 4 9 3 0
Security Safe and Lock Co.		4 0 0 0 0
	3 0 2 1 5 1	3 0 6 9 6 0

The Mann Furniture Store — Schedule of Accounts Payable

Monday, December 30

Received invoice from Kearns Furniture Co., Rosemont, $210, for merchandise purchased per Invoice No. 26 of December 27. Terms, 2/10, n/30.

Tuesday, December 31

Received the following invoices:

Barnes-Wheton Co., Maplewood, $477.60, merchandise purchased per Invoice No. 27 of December 30. Terms, 2/30, n/60.

Security Safe & Lock Co., Chicago, $400, safe purchased per invoice of December 30. Terms, 2/30, n/60.

The invoice received from the Barnes-Wheton Co. was recorded in the purchases journal in the usual manner. The invoice received from the Security Safe & Lock Co. was recorded in the combined cash-journal by debiting Store Equipment and by crediting Accounts Payable. In this enterprise the purchases journal is used only for recording invoices covering merchandise purchased on credit.

Cash sales:

SALESPERSON	MERCHANDISE	TAX	TOTAL
A	$ 72.00	$1.44	$ 73.44
B	62.40	1.25	63.65
C	60.00	1.20	61.20
	$194.40	$3.89	$198.29

Issued Check No. 135 payable to Payroll for $869.41.

PAYROLL STATEMENT FOR PERIOD ENDED DECEMBER 31

Total wages and commissions earned during period.........			$969.39
Employees' taxes to be withheld:			
(a) Employees' income taxes.........................		$80.60	
(b) F.I.C.A. taxes, 2%.............................		19.38	99.98
Net amount payable to employees..................			$869.41
Employer's payroll taxes:			
(a) F.I.C.A. taxes, 2% of $969.39.....................			$ 19.39
(b) Unemployment compensation taxes —			
State U.C. taxes, 2.7% of $969.39		$26.17	
F.U.T.A. taxes, 3% of $969.39............	$29.08		
Less credit for state taxes..............	26.17	2.91	29.08
Total..			$ 48.47

Since no employee's wages during the year have exceeded $3,000, the entire amount of the wages and commissions earned during the period ended December 31 is subject to both the F.I.C.A. and U.C. taxes.

The reason the F.I.C.A. tax imposed on the employer is 1 cent more than the sum of the F.I.C.A. taxes withheld from employees' wages is due to fractions. The amounts withheld from the employees is based on their individual wages, while the amount of the tax imposed on the employer is based on the total wages of all employees.

Issued Check No. 136 for $44.05 to replenish the petty cash fund.

The following statement of the petty cash disbursements for December served as a voucher authorizing the issuance of the check to replenish the petty cash fund:

STATEMENT OF PETTY CASH DISBURSEMENTS FOR DECEMBER

W. L. Mann, Drawing	$10.00
Stationery and Supplies	15.00
Telephone and Telegraph Expense	.90
Advertising Expense	7.00
Charitable Contributions	5.00
Miscellaneous Expenses	6.15
Total Disbursements	$44.05

Before the above statement was prepared the petty cash disbursements record was proved by footing the amount columns, the totals were entered in ink, and the record was ruled with single and double lines. The balance was then brought down below the double rules. The amount received to replenish the fund was added to the balance and the total, $100, was entered in the Description column.

The amount of the check issued was entered in the combined cash-journal by debiting the proper accounts and by crediting the bank account. It should be remembered that no posting is done from the petty cash disbursements record; the proper accounts will be charged for the petty cash disbursements when the posting is completed from the combined cash-journal.

ROUTINE END-OF-THE-MONTH WORK

(a) Proved the footings and entered the totals in the combined cash-journal and the sales journal. (b) Deposited $198.29 in the Liberty National Bank and proved the bank balance ($6,247.61). (c) Completed the individual posting from the General Dr. and Cr. columns of the combined cash-journal. (d) Completed the summary posting of the columnar totals of the combined cash-journal, the purchases journal, and the sales journal to the proper accounts in the general ledger. (e) Ruled the purchases and sales journals. (f) Prepared a trial balance and schedules of accounts receivable and accounts payable.

PRACTICE ASSIGNMENT No. 15. Complete Report No. 15 in the workbook and submit your working papers to the instructor for approval. After completing this report, continue with the textbook discussion in Unit Seven until the next report is required.

THE PERIODIC SUMMARY

(16) END-OF-PERIOD WORK SHEET

One of the major reasons for keeping accounting records is to accumulate information that will make it possible to prepare periodic summaries of both (a) the income and expenses of the business during a specified period, and (b) the assets, liabilities, and net worth of the business at a specified date. A trial balance of the general ledger accounts will provide most of the information that is required for these summaries (the income statement and the balance sheet). However, the trial balance does not supply the data in a form that is easily interpreted, nor does it reflect changes in the accounting elements that have not been represented by ordinary business transactions. Therefore, at the end of a fiscal period it is necessary, first, to determine the kind and amounts of changes that the accounts do not reflect and to adjust the accounts accordingly and, second, to recast the information into the form of an income statement and a balance sheet. These two steps are often referred to as the "periodic summary."

Nature and Function of the Work Sheet. In most cases the accountant is under some pressure to produce the income statement and the balance sheet as soon as possible after the period has ended. In response to this need for haste, it is common practice to use a *work sheet* to aid in the preparation of the statements.

The work sheet, sometimes called a *working trial balance*, is prepared on multi-column paper. The trial balance of the general ledger is placed on the work sheet first. Space is provided to make any needed adjustments of the account balances, to show the adjusted amounts, and to classify the adjusted amounts as between those that will be reported in the income statement and those that will be reported in the balance sheet. The accountant can then prepare the formal statements from the work sheet. After preparing the statements, the various adjustments are actually recorded in the books and the income and expense accounts are closed so as to set the stage for the records of the next period.

Work sheets are not financial statements; they are devices to facilitate the preparation of financial statements. Ordinarily it is only the accountant who uses (or even sees) a work sheet.

A Work Sheet for a Mercantile Business. While an end-of-period work sheet can be in any of several forms, a common and widely-used arrangement involves ten amount columns. The amount columns are used in pairs. The first pair of amount columns is for the trial balance. The data to be recorded consist of the title, number, and debit or credit balance of each account. Debit balances should be entered in the left amount column and credit balances in the right amount column. The second pair of amount columns is used to record needed end-of-period adjustments. The third pair of amount columns is used to show the account balances as adjusted. This pair of amount columns is headed "Adjusted Trial Balance" because its purpose is to ascertain that the debit and credit account balances as adjusted are equal in amount. The fourth pair of amount columns is for the adjusted balances of the expense and income accounts. This pair of columns is headed "Income Statement" since the amounts shown will be reported in that statement. The fifth, and last, pair of amount columns is headed "Balance Sheet" and shows the adjusted account balances that will be reported in that statement.

To illustrate the preparation and use of the end-of-period work sheet, the example of the accounts of The Mann Furniture Store will be continued. The journals and ledgers for this business for the month of December were reproduced in the preceding unit. In this unit the income statement for the year and the balance sheet at the end of the year will be reproduced, showing the use of a work sheet as a device for summarizing the data to be presented in those statements.

The Work Sheet for The Mann Furniture Store. The end-of-year work sheet for this business is reproduced on pages 192 and 193. Following is a description and discussion of the steps that were followed in the preparation of this work sheet. Each step should be studied carefully with frequent reference to the work sheet itself.

Trial Balance Columns. The trial balance of the general ledger accounts as of December 31 was entered in the first pair of amount columns. This trial balance is the same as the one shown on page 181 except that all of the account titles, with the exception of Income Summary, Account No. 33, were included in the listing even though certain of the accounts had no balance at this point. Two lines were allowed for Cost of Goods Sold, Account No. 53, since this account receives two debits and two credits in the adjustment process.

The debit and credit amount columns were footed and the footings were entered in small figures in pencil. Obviously the footings should be equal. If not, the cause of any discrepancy must be found and corrected before the preparation of the work sheet can proceed.

Adjustments Columns. The second pair of amount columns on the work sheet was used to record certain adjustments that were necessary to reflect various changes that had occurred during the year in some of the accounting elements. In this case, adjustments were needed (1) to record the calculated cost of goods sold during the year and the amount of the year-end inventory; (2) to record the amounts of interest income earned but not collected, and interest expense incurred but not paid; (3) to record the portions of prepaid insurance expired and stationery and supplies used during the year; (4) to record the estimated depreciation expense for the year; and (5) to record the estimated amount of expected bad debt losses.

Ten complete entries involving ten debits and eleven credits were made in the adjustment pair of columns to reflect these changes. When an account was debited, the amount was entered on the same horizontal line as the account title and in the debit column of the adjustment pair. Amounts credited were entered, of course, in the credit column. Each such entry made on the work sheet was identified by a small letter in parentheses to facilitate cross reference. Following is an explanation of each of the entries:

Entry (a): The beginning inventory of merchandise in stock was transferred to cost of goods sold by debiting Cost of Goods Sold, Account No. 53, and by crediting Merchandise Inventory, Account No. 13, for $28,522.45. This amount was the calculated cost of the inventory at the end of the previous year (the beginning of the year under consideration). This amount had been standing as a debit to the account since the accounts were adjusted as of December 31 a year ago.

Entry (b): The balance of the purchases account was transferred to cost of goods sold by debiting Cost of Goods Sold, Account No. 53, and by crediting Purchases, Account No. 51, for $65,316.63. This amount was the gross cost of goods purchased during the year.

Entry (c): The balance of the account for purchases returns and allowances was transferred to cost of goods sold by debiting Purchases Returns and Allowances, Account No. 051, and by crediting Cost of Goods Sold, Account No. 53, for $114.30. At this point Cost of Goods Sold had two debits and one credit; the debit excess represented the cost of goods available for sale during the year.

Entry (d): This entry recorded the calculated cost of the merchandise on hand December 31 — often referred to as the year-end inventory. The calculation is based on a physical count of the merchandise in stock at the close of the year. The cost of the merchandise in stock was recorded by debiting Merchandise Inventory, Account No. 13, and by crediting Cost of Goods Sold, Account No. 53, for $32,453.16. At this point the difference between the debits and credits to Cost of Goods Sold, $61,271.62, was the calculated cost of goods sold during the year.

Entry (e): This entry recorded the accrued interest income that had been earned but not received by debiting Accrued Interest Receivable, Account No. 122, and by crediting Interest Income, Account No. 71, for $18.70. The December 31 trial balance shows that Notes Receivable had a debit balance of $801.50. This was the amount of a 6 per cent, six-month note dated August 13, signed by Frank Zeigler. From August 13 to December 31 was 140 days. Interest at the rate of 6 per cent per year on $801.50 for 140 days is $18.70.

Entry (f): This entry recorded the accrued interest expense that had been incurred but not paid by debiting Interest Expense, Account No. 81, and by crediting Accrued Interest Payable, Account No. 22, for $40.56. The December 31 trial balance shows that Notes Payable had a credit balance of $2,000. This related to a 5 per cent, six-month note dated August 7, payable to the Liberty National Bank. From August 7 to December 31 was 146 days. Interest at the rate of 5 per cent per year on $2,000 for 146 days is $40.56.

Entry (g): This entry recorded the insurance expense for the year by debiting Insurance Expense, Account No. 611, and by crediting Prepaid Insurance, Account No. 14, for $215.36. The December 31 trial balance shows that Prepaid Insurance had a debit balance of $430.72. This amount was the cost of a two-year policy dated January 2 of the year under consideration. Accordingly, by December 31 one year had elapsed and, thus, one half of the premium paid had become an expense.

Entry (h): This entry recorded the calculated cost of the stationery and supplies used during the year by debiting Stationery and Supplies Used, Account No. 66, and by crediting Stationery and Supplies, Account No. 15, for $110. The December 31 trial balance shows that Stationery and Supplies had a debit balance of $170. This amount was the sum of the cost of stationery and supplies on hand at the start of the year (if any) plus the cost of stationery and supplies purchased during the year. A physical count of the stationery and supplies on hand December 31 was made and its cost ascertained to be $60. Accordingly, stationery and supplies that cost $110 ($170 − $60) had been used during the year.

Entry (i): This entry recorded the calculated depreciation expense for the year by debiting Depreciation Expense, Account No. 62, for $818.33 and by crediting Allowance for Depreciation of Store Equipment, Account No. 018, for $185 and crediting Allowance for Depreciation of Delivery Equipment, Account No. 019, for $633.33. The December 31 trial balance shows that Store Equipment had a debit balance of $2,250. This balance represented the $1,850 cost of various items of property that had been owned the entire year plus the $400 cost of the safe that was purchased on December 31. Mr. Mann follows the policy of not calculating any depreciation on assets that have been owned for less than a month. Thus, depreciation expense for the year on store equipment related to property that had been owned for the entire year. Its cost was $1,850. This equipment is being depreciated at the rate of 10 per cent a year. Ten per cent of $1,850 is $185.

The December 31 trial balance shows that the delivery equipment account had a debit balance of $1,900. This was the cost of a delivery truck that had been owned the entire year. The truck is being depreciated at the rate of $33\frac{1}{3}$ per cent per year. Thirty-three and one-third per cent of $1,900 is $633.33.

Entry (j): This entry recorded the estimated bad debts expense for the year by debiting Bad Debts Expense, Account No. 69, and by crediting Allowance for Bad Debts, Account No. 012, for $572.28. Guided by past experience, Mr. Mann estimated that bad debt losses will be approximately one per cent of the total sales on account for the year. Investigation of the records revealed that such sales amounted to $57,228. One per cent of $57,228 is $572.28.

After making the required entries in the Adjustments columns of the work sheet, the columns were footed to prove the equality of the debit and credit entries and the footings were entered in small figures in pencil.

Adjusted Trial Balance Columns. The third pair of amount columns of the work sheet was used for the *adjusted trial balance*. To ascertain the balance of each account after making the required adjustments, it was necessary to take into consideration the amounts recorded in the first two pairs of amount columns. When an account balance was not affected by entries in the Adjustments columns, the balance recorded in the Trial Balance columns was extended to the Adjusted Trial Balance columns.

When an account balance was affected by an entry in the Adjustments columns, the balance recorded in the Trial Balance columns was increased or decreased, as the case may be, by the amount of the adjusting entry. For example, Allowance for Depreciation of Store Equipment was listed in the Trial Balance columns with a credit balance of $370. Since there was a credit entry of $185 in the Adjustments columns, the amount extended to the Adjusted Trial Balance Cr. column was ascertained by addition to be $555 ($370 + $185). Prepaid Insurance was listed in the Trial Balance columns with a debit balance of $430.72. Since there was a credit entry of $215.36 in the Adjustments columns, the amount to be extended to the Adjusted Trial Balance Dr. column was ascertained by subtraction to be $215.36 ($430.72 − $215.36).

The Adjusted Trial Balance columns were footed to prove the equality of the debit and credit balances and the footings were entered in small figures in pencil.

Income Statement Columns. The fourth pair of amount columns of the work sheet was used to show the account balances that will be reported in the income statement. Debit balances were entered in the left column and credit balances in the right column. Accounts with debit balances included Sales Returns and Allowances, Cost of Goods Sold, and all expense accounts. Accounts with credit balances included Sales, Interest Income, and Purchases Discount.

The Income Statement amount columns were footed and the footings were entered in small figures in pencil. The difference between the footings of these columns constitutes the amount of the net increase or the net decrease in proprietorship due to net income or net loss during the accounting period. If the total of the credit balances exceeds the total of the debit balances, the difference represents the net increase in proprietorship due to net income; if the total of the debit balances exceeds the total of the credit balances, the difference represents the net decrease in proprietorship due to net loss.

Reference to the Income Statement columns of The Mann Furniture Store work sheet will show that the total of the credit balances amounted to $102,606.19 and the total of the debit balances amounted to $90,997.72. The difference, amounting to $11,608.47, was the amount of the net income for the year.

Balance Sheet Columns. The fifth pair of amount columns of the work sheet was used to show the account balances that will be reported in the balance sheet. The Balance Sheet columns were footed and the footings were entered in small figures in pencil. The difference between the footings of these columns, likewise, constitutes the amount of the net income or the net loss for the accounting period. If the total of the debit balances exceeds the total of the credit balances, the difference represents a net income for the accounting period; if the total of the credit balances exceeds the total of the debit balances, the difference represents a net loss for the period. This difference should be the same as the difference between the footings of the Income Statement columns.

Reference to the Balance Sheet columns of the work sheet will show that the total of the debit balances amounted to $56,044.35 and the total of the credit balances amounted to $44,435.88. The difference of $11,608.47 represented the amount of the net income for the year.

Totaling and Ruling the Work Sheet. After all of the amount columns have been footed and the footings proved, the totals should be entered in ink. The difference between the totals of the Income Statement columns and the totals of the Balance Sheet columns should be recorded on the next horizontal line below the totals. If the difference represents net income, it should be so labeled and recorded in the debit column of the Income Statement pair and in the credit column of the Balance Sheet pair of columns. If, instead, a net loss has been the result, the amount should be so designated and entered in the credit column of the Income Statement pair and in the debit column of the Balance Sheet pair of columns. Finally, the totals of the Income Statement and Balance Sheet columns, after the net income (or net loss) has been recorded, are entered in ink, and a double line is ruled immediately below the totals.

Proving the Work Sheet. The work sheet provides proof of the arithmetical accuracy of the data it summarizes. The totals of the Trial Balance columns, the Adjustments columns, and the Adjusted Trial Balance columns must balance in each case. The amount of the difference between the totals of the Income Statement columns must be exactly the same as the amount of the difference between the totals of the Balance Sheet columns.

It is important to understand just why the same amount must be inserted to balance the Income Statement pair and the Balance Sheet pair of columns. The reason is found in the basic difference between the balance sheet accounts and the income statement accounts, and in an understanding of the real nature of net income (or net loss). The reality of net income is that the assets have increased, or that the liabilities have decreased,

(*Continued on page 194*)

The Mann Furniture Store
Work Sheet for Year Ended December 31, 19—

Accounts	Trial Balance Dr. Balances	Trial Balance Cr. Balances	Adjustments Debits	Adjustments Credits	Adj. Trial Balance Dr. Balances	Adj. Trial Balance Cr. Balances	Income Statement Dr. Balances	Income Statement Cr. Balances	Balance Sheet Dr. Balances	Balance Sheet Cr. Balances
Liberty National Bank 111	624761				624761				624761	
Petty Cash Fund 112	10000				10000				10000	
Notes Receivable 121	80150				80150				80150	
Accrued Interest Receivable 122			(a) 1870		1870				1870	
Accounts Receivable 123	486802				486802				486802	
Allowance for Bad Debts 012		8856		(a) 57228		66084				66084
Merchandise Inventory 13	3274521 45		32453 16	(a) 3274521 45	3245316				3245316	
Prepaid Insurance 14	43072			(a) 2/536	2/536				2/536	
Stationery and Supplies 15	17000			(a) 11000	6000				6000	
Store Equipment 15	225000				225000				225000	
Allowance for Depr of 16		37000		(b) 18500		55500				55500
Delivery Equipment 19	190000				190000				190000	
Allowance for Depr of 016		47500		(c) 63333		110833				110833
Notes Payable 21		200000				200000				200000
Accrued Interest Payable 22				(f) 4056		4056				4056
Accounts Payable 23		306960				306960				306960
Fed. Tax Payable 24		9001				9001				9001
F.I.C.A. Taxes Payable 25		7755				7755				7755
Employees Income Tax Pay. 26		16080				16080				16080
F.U.T.A. Taxes Payable 27		4288				4288				4288
State U.C. Taxes Payable 28		11300				11300				11300
W. L. Mann, Proprietor 31		3651731				3651731				3651731
W. L. Mann, Drawing 32	713000				713000				713000	
Sales 41		1023 1534				1023 1534		1023 1534		
Sales Returns & Allowances 041	12420				12420		12420			

Account	No.								
Purchases	51	6531663							
Purchases Returns & Allowances	52		1143.0			1143.0			
Cost of Goods Sold	53		2852245	1143.0	6127162		6127162		
			6531663	3245316					
Rent Expense	61	600000			600000		600000		
Depreciation Expense	62		81833		81833		81833		
Salesmen's Commission	63	1429335			1429335		1429335		
Social Security Tax	64	71467			71467		71467		
Heating and Lighting	65	52700			52700		52700		
Stationery and Office Supplies	66			11000	11000		11000		
Tel. and Tel. Expense	67	23305			23305		23305		
Advertising Expense	68	494157			494157		494157		
Bad Debts Expense	69			57228	57228		57228		
Insurance Expense	611			21536	21536		21536		
Truck Expense	612	53210			53210		53210		
Charitable Contributions	613	16500			16500		16500		
Misc. Expense	614	37593			37593		37593		
Interest Income	71		5148	1870		7018			7018
Purchases Discount	72		22067			22067			22067
Interest Expense	81								

or that some combination of both events has taken place during a period of time. Day by day these changes have been recorded in the asset and liability accounts in order that they may be kept up to date. However, the effect of the changes on the net worth element is not recorded in the permanent proprietorship account. Instead, the changes are recorded in the temporary proprietorship accounts — the income and expense accounts.

Thus, at the end of the period after the accounts have been adjusted, each of the asset and liability accounts reflects the amount of that element *at the end of the period.* If, however, there have been no capital investments during the period and any withdrawals have been charged to a drawing account, the balance of the proprietor's capital account is the amount of the net worth *at the beginning of the period.* (All of the changes in proprietorship are shown in the income and expense accounts and in the drawing account.)

As applied to the work sheet, this must mean that the Balance Sheet column totals are out of balance by the amount of the change in proprietorship that is due to net income or net loss for the period involved. If there was net income, the assets, in total, are either that much larger, or the liabilities are that much smaller, or some combination of such changes has resulted. In other words, the asset and liability accounts reflect the net income of the period, but the proprietor's capital account, at this point, does not. It is only after the temporary accounts are closed at the end of the period and the net amount of the income for the period has been transferred to the proprietor's capital account that the latter account reflects the net income of the period.

The proprietor's capital account lacks two things to bring its balance up to date (like the balances of the asset and liability accounts): (1) the decrease due to any withdrawals during the period which is reflected in the debit balance of the drawing account, and (2) the increase due to any net income for the period. On the work sheet the debit balance of the drawing account is extended to the debit column of the Balance Sheet pair. Thus, all that is needed to cause the Balance Sheet pair of columns to be equal is the amount of the net income for the year — the same amount that is the difference between the totals of the Income Statement pair of columns.

PRACTICE ASSIGNMENT No. 16. Complete Report No. 16 in the workbook and submit your working papers to the instructor for approval. After completing the report, continue with the following study assignment until the next report is required.

(17) THE FINANCIAL STATEMENTS

The financial statements usually consist of (a) an income statement and (b) a balance sheet. The purpose of an income statement is to provide a summary of the results of operations over a specified period of time. It provides information as to the sources of income, types of expenses, and the amount of the net income or the net loss for the period. The purpose of a balance sheet is to provide information regarding the status of a business at a stated time. It shows the kinds and amounts of assets and liabilities, and the net worth of the business at a specified point of time — usually at the close of business on the last day of the fiscal period.

The Income Statement. A formal statement of the results of the operation of a business for a specified period of time is called an income statement. Other titles commonly used for this statement include *profit and loss statement, income and expense statement, revenue and expense statement, operating statement*, and *report of earnings*. Whatever the title, the purpose of the statement or report is to show the types and amounts of income and expenses that the business had during the period involved, and the resulting net income or net loss for the period.

Importance of the Income Statement. The income statement is now generally considered to be the most important financial statement of a business. A business cannot exist indefinitely unless it has profit or net income. The income statement is essentially a "report card" of the enterprise. The statement provides a basis for judging the over-all effectiveness of the management. Decisions as to whether to continue a business, to expand it, or to contract it are often based upon the results as reported in the income statement. Actual and potential creditors are interested in income statements because one of the best reasons for extending credit or for making a loan is that the business is profitable.

Various government agencies are interested in income statements of businesses for one or more of several reasons. Regulatory bodies are concerned with the income of the enterprises they regulate, because a part of the regulation usually relates to the prices, rates, or fares that may be charged. If the enterprise is either exceptionally profitable or unprofitable, some change in the allowed prices or rates may be needed. Income tax authorities, both federal and local, have an interest in business income statements. Income determination for tax purposes differs somewhat from the calculation of net income for other purposes, but, for a variety of reasons, the tax authorities are interested in both sets of calculations.

Form of the Income Statement. The form of the income statement depends, in part, upon the type of business. For merchandising businesses, the so-called "ladder type" is commonly used. This name is applied because the final net income is calculated on a step-by-step basis. The amount of gross sales is shown first with sales returns and allowances deducted. The difference is *net sales*. Cost of goods sold is next subtracted to arrive at *gross profit* (sometimes called *gross margin*). The portion of the statement down to this point is sometimes called the "trading section." Operating expenses are next listed and the total of their amounts is subtracted to arrive at the amount of the *net operating profit*. Finally, the amounts of any "other" income are added and any "other" expenses are subtracted to arrive at the final amount of net income (or net loss).

It is essential that the statement be properly headed. The name of the business (or of the individual if a professional practice, or if the proprietor operates a business in his own name) should be shown first. The name of the statement is then shown followed by the period of time that the statement covers. It is common practice to state this as, for example, "Year Ended December 31, 19--" (or whatever the period and ending date happen to be).

The income statement may be penwritten or typewritten. The income statement for The Mann Furniture Store for the Year Ended December 31, 19-- is reproduced in penwritten form on page 197. The information needed in preparing the statement was obtained from the work sheet shown on pages 192 and 193.

Income Statement Analysis. There are various procedures employed to assist in the interpretation of income statements. One device is to present income statements for two or more comparable periods in comparative form. If the figures for two periods are shown in adjacent columns, a third column showing the amount of increase or decrease in each element may be shown. This will call attention to changes which may be of significance.

Another analytical device is to express all, or at least the major, items on the statement as a per cent of total net sales and then compare these percentages for two or more periods. For example, if the net sales of $102,191.14 for The Mann Furniture Store for the year just ended are treated as 100 per cent, the cost of goods sold which amounted to $61,271.62 was equal to 59.96 per cent of net sales; the gross profit on sales which amounted to $40,919.52 was equal to 40.04 per cent of net sales; operating expenses which amounted to $29,498.64 were equal to

The Mann Furniture Store
Income Statement
For the Year Ended December 31, 19-

Operating Income:			
Sales			1023153 4
Less Sales Returns & Allowances			1242 0
Net Sales			1021911 4
Less Cost of Goods Sold:			
Merchandise Inventory, January 1	285224 5		
Purchases	653166 3		
Total	938390 8		
Less Purchases Returns & Allowances	1143 0		
Merchandise Available for sale	937247 8		
Less Merchandise Inventory, December 31	324531 6	612716 2	
Gross Profit on Sales			409195 2
Operating Expenses:			
Rent Expense	60000 0		
Depreciation Expense	8183 3		
Salaries and Commissions	142933 5		
Social Security Taxes	7146 7		
Heating and Lighting	5270 0		
Stationery and Supplies Used	1100 0		
Telephone and Telegraph Expense	2330 5		
Advertising Expense	49415 7		
Bad Debts Expense	5722 8		
Insurance Expense	2153 6		
Truck Expense	5321 0		
Charitable Contributions	1650 0		
Miscellaneous Expenses	3759 3		
Total Operating Expenses			294986 4
Net Operating Income			114208 8
Other Income:			
Interest Income	701 8		
Purchases Discount	2206 7		
Total Other Income			2908 5
			117117 3
Other Expenses:			
Interest Expense			1032 6
Net Income			116084 7

28.87 per cent of net sales; net operating income which amounted to $11,420.88 was equal to 11.18 per cent of net sales; and the net income which amounted to $11,608.47 was equal to 11.36 per cent of net sales. It is obvious that a comparison of these percentages with the same data for one or more prior years would reveal trends that would surely be of interest — and perhaps real concern — to the management of the business.

The Balance Sheet. A formal statement of the assets, liabilities, and proprietorship of a business at a specified date is known as a balance sheet. The title of the statement had its origin in the equality of the elements, that is, in the balance between the sum of the assets and the sum of the liabilities and proprietorship. Sometimes the balance sheet is called a *statement of assets and liabilities* or a *statement of condition.* Various other similar titles are occasionally used.

Importance of the Balance Sheet. The balance sheet of a business is of considerable interest to various parties for several reasons. The owner or owners of a business are interested in the kind and amount of assets and liabilities, and the amount of the net worth or capital element.

Creditors of the business are interested in the financial condition of the enterprise, particularly as it pertains to the claims they have and the prospects for prompt payment. Potential creditors or possible lenders are concerned about the financial position of the business. Their decision as to whether to extend credit or to make loans to the business may depend, in large part, upon the condition of the enterprise as revealed by a balance sheet.

Persons considering buying an ownership interest in a business are considerably interested in the character and amount of the assets and liabilities, though this interest is probably secondary to their concern about the future profit possibilities.

Finally, various regulatory bodies are interested in the financial condition of the businesses that are under their jurisdiction. Examples of regulated businesses include banks, insurance companies, public utilities, railroads, and airlines.

Form of the Balance Sheet. Traditionally, balance sheets have been presented either in *account form* or in *report form.* When the account form is followed, the assets are shown on the left side of the page (or on the left of two facing pages) and the liabilities and proprietorship on the right. This form roughly parallels the debit-side and credit-side arrangement of the standard ledger account. The balance sheet of The Mann

Furniture Store as of December 31, 19- - is shown in account form on page 200. The data for the preparation of the statement were secured from the work sheet.

When the report form of the balance sheet is followed, the assets, liabilities, and proprietorship elements are exhibited in that order on the page. The balance sheet of The Mann Furniture Store is shown in report form on page 201. This arrangement is generally superior when the statement is typed on regular letter-size paper (8½" x 11").

Whichever form is used, it is essential that the statement have the proper heading. This means that three things must be shown: (1) The name of the business must be given (or name of the individual if the business or professional practice is carried on in the name of an individual), followed by (2) the name of the statement — usually just "Balance Sheet," and, finally (3) the date — month, day, and year. Sometimes the expression "as of close of business December 31, 19--" (or whatever date is involved) is included. It must be remembered that a balance sheet relates to a particular moment of time.

In comparing the penwritten balance sheet in account form with the typewritten statement in report form, attention is directed to a small matter of technique. Since the penwritten copy is on paper that has columnar rulings, no dollar signs ($) were used. In the case of the statement on unruled paper, dollar signs were placed before the first amount in each column and before each total. These illustrations reflect a general rule of form that is followed in all illustrations in this textbook.

Classification of Data in the Balance Sheet. The purpose of the balance sheet and of all other accounting statements and reports is to convey as much information as possible. This aim is furthered by some classification of the data being exhibited. As applied to balance sheets, it has become almost universal practice to classify both assets and liabilities as between those that are called "current" and those that are called "fixed."

Current Assets. Current assets include cash and all other assets that may be reasonably expected to be converted into cash during the normal operating cycle of the business as a result of regular operations. In a mercantile business the current assets usually will include cash, temporary investments, receivables, such as accounts receivable and notes receivable, and the merchandise inventory. Prepaid expenses, such as unexpired insur-

(*Continued on page 202*)

The Mann Furniture Store
Balance Sheet
December 31, 19—

Assets			
Current Assets:			
Cash			634761
Notes Receivable	80150		
Accrued Interest Receivable	1870		
Accounts Receivable	486802		
Total		568822	
Less Allow. for Bad Debts		66084	502738
Merchandise Inventory			3245316
Prepaid Insurance			21536
Stationery and Supplies			6000
Total Current Assets			4410351
Fixed Assets:			
Store Equipment		225000	
Less Allowance for Depr.		55500	169500
Delivery Equipment		190000	
Less Allowance for Depr.		110833	79167
Total Fixed Assets			248667
Total Assets			4659018

Liabilities			
Current Liabilities:			
Notes Payable	200000		
Accrued Interest Payable	4056		
Accounts Payable	306960		
Sales Tax Payable	9001		
F.I.C.A. Taxes Payable	7755		
Employees Income Taxes Pay.	16080		
F.U.T.A. Taxes Payable	4288		
State U. Taxes Payable	11300		
Total Current Liabilities			559440
Proprietorship			
W. L. Mann, Proprietor			
Proprietorship, Jan. 1			3651731
Net Income	1160847		
Less Withdrawals	713000	447847	
Proprietorship, Dec. 31			4099578
Total Liabilities & Proprietorship			4659018

Model Balance Sheet — Account Form

THE MANN FURNITURE STORE
BALANCE SHEET
DECEMBER 31, 19--

ASSETS

Current Assets:

Cash..		$ 6,347.61	
Notes Receivable.............................	$ 801.50		
Accrued Interest Receivable..................	18.70		
Accounts Receivable..........................	4,868.02		
Total......................................	$ 5,688.22		
Less Allowance for Bad Debts...............	660.84	5,027.38	
Merchandise Inventory........................		32,453.16	
Prepaid Insurance............................		215.36	
Stationery and Supplies......................		60.00	
Total Current Assets......................			$44,103.51

Fixed Assets:

Store Equipment..............................	$ 2,250.00		
Less Allowance for Depreciation............	555.00	$ 1,695.00	
Delivery Equipment...........................	$ 1,900.00		
Less Allowance for Depreciation............	1,108.33	791.67	
Total Fixed Assets........................			2,486.67
Total Assets..................................			$46,590.18

LIABILITIES

Current Liabilities:

Notes Payable................................	$ 2,000.00	
Accrued Interest Payable.....................	40.56	
Accounts Payable.............................	3,069.60	
Sales Tax Payable............................	90.01	
F.I.C.A. Taxes Payable.......................	77.55	
Employees' Income Taxes Payable..............	160.80	
F.U.T.A. Taxes Payable.......................	42.88	
State U.C. Taxes Payable.....................	113.00	
Total Current Liabilities..................		$ 5,594.40

PROPRIETORSHIP

W. L. Mann, Proprietor

Proprietorship, January 1....................		$36,517.31	
Net Income...................................	$11,608.47		
Less Withdrawals..........................	7,130.00	4,478.47	
Proprietorship, December 31..................			40,995.78
Total Liabilities and Proprietorship.........			$46,590.18

Model Balance Sheet — Report Form

ance and unused stationery and supplies, are also generally treated as current assets. This is not because such items will be converted into cash, but because they will probably be consumed in a relatively short time.

The asset Cash may be represented by one or more accounts, such as bank checking accounts, bank savings accounts, and a petty cash fund. Reference to The Mann Furniture Store balance sheet will show that cash is listed at $6,347.61. Reference to the work sheet will show that this is made up of two items including the balance in the checking account at the Liberty National Bank, $6,247.61, and the amount of the petty cash fund, $100.

Temporary investments refer to those assets that have been acquired to use money that would otherwise be temporarily idle and unproductive. Such investments usually take the form of corporation stocks, bonds, or notes, or any of several types of government bonds. Quite often the policy is to invest in securities that can be liquidated in a short time with little chance of loss. So-called *marketable securities* are often favored. Assets of the same type may be owned by a business for many years, but they would not be classed as temporary investments. It is the matter of intention that indicates whether the investments are to be classed as temporary and be included in the current assets or considered as long-term investments and either be included in the fixed-asset classification or in a separate classification entitled *Permanent Investments*.

Reference to the balance sheet of The Mann Furniture Store on pages 200 and 201 reveals that the current assets of this business consisted of cash, notes receivable, accrued interest receivable, accounts receivable, merchandise inventory, prepaid insurance, and stationery and supplies.

Fixed Assets. Property that is used in the operation of a mercantile business may include such assets as land, buildings, office equipment, store equipment, and delivery equipment. Such assets are called *fixed assets*. Of these assets only land is really permanent; however, all of these assets have a useful life that is comparatively long. For this reason these assets are termed "fixed."

Reference to the balance sheet of The Mann Furniture Store will show that the fixed assets of the business consist of store equipment and delivery equipment. In each case, the amount of the allowance for depreciation is shown as a deduction from the cost of the equipment. The difference represents the *book value* of the equipment. This is the amount that should be written off as depreciation expense in future periods.

Current Liabilities. Current liabilities include those obligations that will be paid in the normal operating cycle of the business from funds provided by the current assets. As of December 31, the current liabilities of The Mann Furniture Store consisted of notes payable, accrued interest payable, accounts payable, sales tax payable, F.I.C.A. taxes payable, employees' income taxes payable, F.U.T.A. taxes payable, and state U.C. taxes payable.

Fixed Liabilities. Fixed liabilities include those obligations that do not mature within the normal operating cycle of the business. The most common of the fixed liabilities is mortgages payable.

A mortgage payable is a debt or an obligation that is secured by a *mortgage,* which provides for the conveyance of certain property upon failure to pay the debt at maturity. When the debt is paid, the mortgage becomes void. It will be seen, therefore, that a mortgage payable differs little from an account payable or a note payable except that the creditor holds the mortgage as security for the payment of the debt. Usually debts secured by mortgages run for a longer period of time than ordinary notes payable or accounts payable. A mortgage payable should be classed as a fixed liability only in case the maturity date extends beyond a year or beyond the normal operating cycle of the business. In other words, only long-time indebtedness should be classed as a fixed liability. The Mann Furniture Store has no fixed liabilities.

Proprietorship. As previously explained, accounts representing the proprietorship element may constitute either permanent or temporary proprietorship accounts.

Permanent Proprietorship Accounts. The permanent proprietorship accounts kept in recording the operations of a particular enterprise depend upon the type of legal organization, that is, whether the enterprise is organized as a sole proprietorship, as a partnership, or as a corporation.

In the case of a sole proprietorship, one or more accounts representing the proprietor's interest or equity in the assets may be kept. Reference to the chart of accounts, shown on page 141, will reveal that the following accounts are classified as proprietorship accounts:

Account No. 31, W. L. Mann, Proprietor

Account No. 32, W. L. Mann, Drawing

Account No. 33, Income Summary

Account No. 31 reflects the amount of Mr. Mann's proprietorship. It may be increased by additional investments or by failing to withdraw cash or other assets in an amount as large as the net income of the enterprise; it may be decreased by withdrawals in excess of the amount of the net income or by sustaining a net loss during one or more fiscal periods. Usually there will be no changes in the balance of this account during the accounting period, in which case the balance represents the proprietor's investment in the business as of the beginning of the accounting period and until such time as the books are closed at the end of the accounting period.

Account No. 32 is Mr. Mann's drawing account. This account is charged for any withdrawals of cash or other property for personal use. In a sense it is a temporary account in which is kept a record of the proprietor's personal drawings during the accounting period. Such drawings ordinarily are made in anticipation of earnings rather than as a withdrawal of capital. The balance of the account, as shown by the trial balance at the close of an accounting period, represents the total amount of the proprietor's drawings during the period.

Reference to the work sheet shown on pages 192 and 193 will reveal that the balance of Mr. Mann's drawing account is listed in the Dr. column of the Balance Sheet columns. When a drawing account has a debit balance, it is customary to list it in the Dr. column; however, it represents a deduction from proprietorship. The balance is listed in the Dr. column because there is no provision on a work sheet for making deductions except by listing items in opposite columns. Since the balance of the proprietor's capital account is listed in the Cr. column of the Balance Sheet columns, the listing of the balance of the proprietor's drawing account in the Dr. column is equivalent to deducting it from the balance of the proprietor's capital account.

Account No. 33 is used only at the close of the accounting period for the purpose of summarizing the temporary proprietorship accounts. Sometimes this account is referred to as a *clearing account*. No entries should appear in the account before the books are closed at the end of the accounting period.

The proprietorship section of the balance sheet of The Mann Furniture Store is arranged to show the major changes that took place during the year in the proprietary element of the business. Mr. Mann's proprietary interest in the business amounted to $36,517.31 at the beginning of the period. His interest was increased $11,608.47 as the result of profitable operations, and decreased $7,130 as the result of withdrawals during the year. Thus, the proprietorship element of the business on December 31 amounted to $40,995.78.

Balance Sheet Analysis. The information provided by a balance sheet can be analyzed in several ways to assist in judging the financial condition and soundness of the business. A few of the major analytical procedures will be briefly considered.

A balance sheet as of one date may be compared with a balance sheet as of another date to ascertain the amount of the increase or the decrease in any of the accounts or groups of accounts. Sometimes balance sheets as of two or more dates are prepared in comparative form by listing the amounts as of different dates in parallel columns. Thus, if balance sheets as of the close of two succeeding calendar years are compared, it is possible to ascertain the amount of the increase or the decrease during the intervening period in any of the accounts or groups of accounts listed thereon. If such a comparison reveals an increase in accounts receivable, it may indicate that collections during the later period were not as favorable as they were during the preceding period. If the comparison reveals an increase in accounts payable, it may indicate an inability to pay current bills because of insufficient cash. If the comparison reveals an increase in the current assets without a corresponding increase in the liabilities, it may indicate an improved financial position or status.

Too much emphasis should not be placed upon an increase or a decrease in cash. Some individuals are inclined to judge the results of operations largely by the cash balance. This practice may, however, be misleading. The net results of operations can be properly determined only by comparison of all the assets and the liabilities. The ability of a business to meet its current obligations may be determined largely by an analysis of the current assets, particularly those assets that are sometimes referred to as the quick assets. *Quick assets* include cash and all other current assets that are readily convertible into cash, such as temporary investments in the form of marketable securities.

The relation of an account, a group of accounts, or an accounting element to another account, group of accounts, or accounting element may be referred to as the *ratio*. For example, if the total current assets amount to twice as much as the total current liabilities, the ratio thereof is said to be 2 to 1. Ratios may be expressed in percentages or on a basis of units. Fractions of units may be expressed by means of common fractions or decimals, as for example $7\frac{3}{4}$ to 1 or 7.75 to 1.

In an enterprise where capital invested is a material income-producing factor, such as is the case in a merchandising enterprise, the ratio of the current assets to the current liabilities may be important. Reference to the balance sheet shown on pages 200 and 201 reveals that the total current assets amount to $44,103.51 and the total current liabilities amount to $5,594.40, a ratio of nearly 8 to 1. The total assets amount to $46,590.18 and the total liabilities amount to $5,594.40, a ratio of nearly $8\frac{1}{3}$ to 1. These ratios are sufficiently high to indicate a very favorable financial condition.

Banks often consider the ratio of current assets to current liabilities when considering the advisability of making a loan. It is not expected that the fixed assets will be sold to realize sufficient funds with which to pay a short-time loan. If the balance sheet indicates that a sufficient amount of cash will not be realized from the collection of accounts receivable or from the sales of service or merchandise to repay a loan at maturity, the bank may consider the loan inadvisable.

Ratio analysis may be helpful to the prospective investor in evaluating the securities of a corporation, such as bonds and capital stock. Financial writers frequently refer to the ratios of various items in discussing the balance sheets of corporations. This fact will be readily noted in reading financial magazines or the financial pages of newspapers.

The amount invested in current assets as shown by the balance sheet is often said to represent the amount of the *working capital*. The excess of the amount of the current assets over the amount of the current liabilities represents the net working capital.

It is difficult to estimate what the ratio of current assets to current liabilities should be, because of the variations in enterprises and industries. A 2 to 1 ratio of current assets to current liabilities may be more than sufficient in some enterprises but entirely insufficient in others. In the milk business, for example, a 1 to 1 ratio of current assets to current liabilities is considered satisfactory. The reasons are that very little capital is tied up in an inventory, the amount of accounts receivable is comparatively small, and the terms on which the milk is purchased from farmers are such that settlements are slow and comparatively large amounts are due to farmers at all times. Another reason is that a large amount of capital is invested in fixed assets, such as equipment for treating the milk and for delivering it to customers.

Generally speaking, the ratio of the current assets to the current liabilities should be maintained at from 2 to 1 to 5 to 1. While a standard ratio cannot be established for all enterprises, a knowledge of the working capital requirements of a particular enterprise will be helpful in determining what the ratio of current assets to current liabilities should be.

A comparison of the relationships between certain amounts in the income statement and the balance sheet may be informative. The leading example of this type is the ratio of net income to proprietorship of the business. The net worth of The Mann Furniture Store was $36,517.31 on January 1. The net income for the year of $11,608.47 was nearly 32 per cent of this amount. In other words, the ratio of net income to the amount invested in the enterprise was nearly 1 to 3. A comparison of this ratio with the ratio of net income to capital invested in prior years should be of interest to the proprietor. It may also be of interest to compare the ratio of the net income of The Mann Furniture Store to the amount of capital invested by Mr. Mann with other stores of comparable nature and size. It is important to note, however, that the net income of The Mann Furniture Store was computed without regard to any salary or other compensation for the services of Mr. Mann.

Turnover. A merchant is usually interested in ascertaining the rate of *turnover* for each accounting period. This has reference to the number of times the merchandise available for sale is turned during the accounting period. The rate of turnover is ascertained by dividing the cost of sales for the period by the average inventory. Where an inventory is taken only at the end of each accounting period, the average inventory for the period may be ascertained by adding the beginning and ending inventories together and dividing by two. The turnover of The Mann Furniture Store for the year ended December 31 may be computed as follows:

Beginning inventory	$28,522.45
Ending inventory	32,453.16
Cost of sales for the period	61,271.62

$28,522.45 + $32,453.16 ÷ 2 = $30,487.81, average inventory
$61,271.62 ÷ $30,487.81 = 2, rate of turnover

This indicates a turnover of approximately two times the average inventory for the year. In the retail furniture business, a turnover of from 2½ to 3 times the average inventory is considered normal. It is evident, therefore, that the rate of turnover of The Mann Furniture Store is a little below normal. A careful analysis of the theory involved in computing the rate of turnover will indicate that the greater the turn-over the smaller the profit need be on each dollar of sales in order to produce a satisfactory gross profit on sales.

PRACTICE ASSIGNMENT No. 17. Complete Report No. 17 in the workbook and submit your working papers to the instructor for approval. After completing the report, you may continue with the textbook discussion in Unit Eight until the next report is required.

ADJUSTING AND CLOSING ACCOUNTS AT END OF ACCOUNTING PERIOD

(18) ADJUSTING ENTRIES

As explained in the preceding unit, the adjustment of certain accounts at the end of the accounting period is required because of changes that have occurred during the period that are not reflected in the accounts. In preparing the work sheet for The Mann Furniture Store (reproduced on pages 192 and 193), adjustments were made for the following purposes:

(a) To transfer the amount of the merchandise inventory at the beginning of the accounting period to the cost of goods sold account.

(b) To transfer the balance of the purchases account to the cost of goods sold account.

(c) To transfer the balance of the purchases returns and allowances account to the cost of goods sold account.

(d) To record the calculated cost of the merchandise inventory at the end of the accounting period.

(e) To record the amount of interest accrued on notes receivable.

(f) To record the amount of interest accrued on notes payable.

(g) To record the amount of insurance expired during the year.

(h) To record the amount of stationery and supplies used during the year.

(i) To record the estimated amount of depreciation of fixed assets for the year.

(j) To record the amount of bad debt losses expected to result from the charge sales made during the year.

The effect of these adjustments was reflected in the financial statements reproduced on pages 197 and 200. To bring the ledger into agreement with the financial statements, the adjustments should be recorded in the proper accounts. It is customary, therefore, at the end of each accounting period to journalize the adjustments and to post them to the accounts affected.

Journalizing the Adjusting Entries. Adjusting entries may be recorded in either a general journal or a combined cash-journal. If the entries are made in a combined cash-journal, the only amount columns used are the General Dr. and Cr. columns. A portion of a page of a combined cash-journal showing the adjusting entries of The Mann Furniture Store is reproduced below. It should be noted that when the adjusting entries are recorded in the combined cash-journal, they are entered in exactly the same manner as they would be entered in a general journal. Since the heading "Adjusting Entries" explains the nature of the entries, a separate explanation of each adjusting entry is unnecessary. The information needed in journalizing the adjustments was obtained from the Adjustments pair of amount columns of the work sheet reproduced on pages 192 and 193. The account numbers were not entered in the Posting Reference column at the time of journalizing; they were entered as the posting was completed.

Page 78   COMBINED CASH-JOURNAL FOR MONTH OF   December 19—

| DATE | | DESCRIPTION | POST. REF. | GENERAL | |
MO.	DAY			DEBITS	CREDITS
		AMOUNTS FORWARDED			
Dec	31	Adjusting Entries			
		Cost of Goods Sold	53	2852245	
		Merchandise Inventory	13		2852245
		Cost of Goods Sold	53	6531663	
		Purchases	51		6531663
		Purchases Returns & Allowances	051	11430	
		Cost of Goods Sold	53		11430
		Merchandise Inventory	13	3245316	
		Cost of Goods Sold	53		3245316
		Accrued Interest Receivable	122	1870	
		Interest Income	71		1870
		Interest Expense	81	4056	
		Accrued Interest Payable	22		4056
		Insurance Expense	611	21536	
		Prepaid Insurance	14		21536
		Stationery and Supplies Used	66	11000	
		Stationery and Supplies	15		11000
		Depreciation Expense	62	81833	
		Allowance for Depr.-Store Equip.	018		18500
		Allowance for Depr.-Del. Equip.	019		63333
		Bad Debts Expense	69	57228	
		Allowance for Bad Debts	012		57228

ACCRUED INTEREST RECEIVABLE   Account No. 122

19 --			
Dec. 31		CJ78	18.70

ALLOWANCE FOR BAD DEBTS   Account No. 012

		19 --			
		Dec. 1 Balance		✓	88.56
		31		CJ78	572.28
					660.84

MERCHANDISE INVENTORY   Account No. 13

19 --				19 --			
Dec. 1 Balance		✓	28,522.45	Dec. 31		CJ78	28,522.45
Dec. 31		CJ78	32,453.16				

PREPAID INSURANCE   Account No. 14

19 --				19 --			
Dec. 1 Balance		✓	430.72	Dec. 31		CJ78	215.36
	215.36						

STATIONERY AND SUPPLIES   Account No. 15

19 --				19 --			
Dec. 1 Balance		✓	155.00	Dec. 31		CJ78	110.00
31		CJ77	15.00				
	60.00		*170.00*				

ALLOWANCE FOR DEPRECIATION OF STORE EQUIPMENT   Account No. 018

		19 --			
		Dec. 1 Balance		✓	370.00
		31		CJ78	185.00
					555.00

ALLOWANCE FOR DEPRECIATION OF DELIVERY EQUIPMENT   Account No. 019

		19 --			
		Dec. 1 Balance		✓	475.00
		31		CJ78	633.33
					1,108.33

ACCRUED INTEREST PAYABLE   Account No. 22

		19 --			
		Dec. 31		CJ78	40.56

PURCHASES   Account No. 51

19—				19—			
Dec. 1 Balance		✓	63,550.28	Dec. 31		CJ78	65,316.63
31		P52	1,766.35				
			65,316.63				
			65,316.63				65,316.63

PURCHASES RETURNS AND ALLOWANCES   Account No. 051

19—				19—			
Dec. 31		CJ78	114.30	Dec. 1 Balance		✓	89.50
				20		CJ76	24.80
							114.30
			114.30				114.30

COST OF GOODS SOLD   Account No. 53

19—				19—			
Dec. 31 Beg. inventory		CJ78	28,522.45	Dec. 31 Pur. Ret. & Al.		CJ78	114.30
31 Purchases		CJ78	65,316.63	31 End. inventory		CJ78	32,453.16
	61,271.62		93,839.08				32,567.46

DEPRECIATION EXPENSE   Account No. 62

19—			
Dec. 31		CJ78	818.33

STATIONERY AND SUPPLIES USED   Account No. 66

19—			
Dec. 31		CJ78	110.00

BAD DEBTS EXPENSE   Account No. 69

19—			
Dec. 31		CJ78	572.28

INSURANCE EXPENSE   Account No. 611

19—			
Dec. 31		CJ78	215.36

INTEREST INCOME   Account No. 71

		19—			
		Dec. 1 Balance		✓	51.48
		31		CJ78	18.70
					70.18

INTEREST EXPENSE   Account No. 81

19—			
Dec. 1 Balance		✓	62.70
31		CJ78	40.56
			103.26

Posting the Adjusting Entries. The adjusting entries should be posted individually to the proper general ledger accounts. The accounts of The Mann Furniture Store that were affected by the adjusting entries are reproduced in type on pages 211 and 212. The entries in the accounts for transactions made prior to posting the adjusting entries are the same as appeared in the accounts reproduced in script on pages 171 to 176. The number of the combined cash-journal page on which the adjusting entries were recorded was entered in the Folio column of the general ledger and the account numbers were entered in the Posting Reference column of the combined cash-journal as the posting was completed. This provided a cross reference in both books.

Cost of Goods Sold Account. Cost of Goods Sold is a summary account that is used only at the close of an accounting period. In order that this account may provide detailed information, it is customary to write a brief description of each entry in the Items column of the summary account. For example, in posting the adjusting entry made to transfer the amount of the beginning inventory to Cost of Goods Sold, the notation "Beginning Inventory" was written in the Items column on the debit side of the account. As each adjusting entry was posted to Cost of Goods Sold, similar descriptive information was entered in the Items column of the summary account. After posting the adjusting entries, the balance of the account represents the cost of the goods sold during the period. This balance is the same as the cost of goods sold shown in the work sheet reproduced on pages 192 and 193, and in the income statement reproduced on page 197.

Ruling the Merchandise Inventory Account. After posting the adjusting entry required to transfer the amount of the beginning inventory to the cost of goods sold account, the merchandise inventory account was in balance. Since there was only one amount recorded on each side of the account, it was ruled by drawing a double line below the amounts across all columns except the Items columns. In posting the entry to record the inventory at the end of the period, the debit to the merchandise inventory account was recorded on the next horizontal line below the double line.

Ruling the Purchases Account. After posting the entry required to transfer the amount of the purchases for the period to the cost of goods sold account, the purchases account was in balance. The account was ruled as shown on page 212. When more than one item is recorded on either side of an account, the ruling should be completed by drawing a single line across the amount columns only on the line below the amount in the column with the most entries and, after entering the totals on the next horizontal line, by ruling a double line across all columns except the Items columns. When the accounts are ruled in this manner, the single ruling denotes addition and the double ruling denotes balancing or closing. (The ruling of the purchases returns and allowances account follows the same pattern.)

PRACTICE ASSIGNMENT No. 18. Complete Report No. 18 in the workbook and submit your working papers to the instructor for approval. Continue with the following study assignment until Report No. 19 is required.

(19) CLOSING PROCEDURE

After the adjusting entries are posted, all of the temporary proprietorship accounts should be closed. The temporary proprietorship accounts include all income accounts, all expense accounts, and the proprietor's drawing account. This process is often called "closing the accounts" or "closing the books," but it is only the temporary proprietorship accounts that are closed.

The purpose of closing is to transfer the balances of the temporary proprietorship accounts to the permanent proprietorship account. This could be accomplished by simply debiting or crediting each account involved with an offsetting credit or debit to the permanent proprietorship account. However, it is considered to be better practice to transfer the balances of all of the income and expense accounts to a summarizing account called Income Summary (sometimes called Profit and Loss Summary or just Profit and Loss). Then, the resulting balance of the income summary account (which will be the amount of net income or net loss for the period) is transferred to the permanent proprietorship account. Note that Cost of Goods Sold and Income Summary have the common characteristic of being summarizing accounts used only at the end of the period.

The last step is to transfer the balance of the proprietor's drawing account to the permanent proprietorship account. After this is done, only the asset accounts, the liability accounts, and the permanent proprietorship account have balances. If there has been no error, the sum of the balances of the asset accounts (less balances of any contra accounts) will be equal to the sum of the balances of the liability accounts plus the balance of the permanent proprietorship account. The accounts will agree exactly with what is shown by the balance sheet as of the close of the period. Reference to the balance sheet of The Mann Furniture Store reproduced on page 200 will show that the assets, liabilities, and proprietorship as of December 31 may be expressed in equation form as follows:

ASSETS $46,590.18 = LIABILITIES $5,594.40 + PROPRIETORSHIP $40,995.78

Journalizing the Closing Entries. Closing entries, like adjusting entries, may be recorded in either a general journal or a combined cash-journal. If the entries are made in a combined cash-journal, the only amount columns used are the General Dr. and Cr. columns. A portion of a page of a combined cash-journal showing the closing entries for The Mann Furniture Store is reproduced on page 216. Since the heading "Closing Entries" explains the nature of the entries, a separate explanation of each closing entry is unnecessary. The information required in preparing the closing entries was obtained from the work sheet illustrated on pages 192 and 193.

The first closing journal entry was made to close the income accounts. The income accounts included Sales, Interest Income, and Purchases Discount. Since these accounts have credit balances, each account must be debited for the amount of its balance in order to close it. The debits to these three income accounts are offset by a credit of $102,606.19 to Income Summary.

The second closing journal entry was made to close Sales Returns and Allowances, Cost of Goods Sold, and all of the expense accounts. Since these accounts have debit balances, each account must be credited for the amount of its balance to close it. The credits to these accounts are offset by a debit of $90,997.72 to Income Summary.

When the first two closing journal entries are posted, all of the income and expense accounts will be closed (in balance) and Income Summary will have a credit balance of $11,608.47. This is the net amount of the increase in proprietorship during the period due to profitable operations.

The third closing journal entry was made to close the income summary account. Since this account has a credit balance, it must be debited to close it. The offsetting entry is a credit of $11,608.47 to W. L. Mann, Proprietor.

The fourth closing journal entry was made to close W. L. Mann's drawing account. Since this account has a debit balance, it must be credited to close it. The offsetting entry is a debit of $7,130 to W. L. Mann, Proprietor. This is the amount of the decrease in proprietorship during the period due to Mr. Mann's withdrawals.

The account numbers shown in the Posting Reference column were not entered at the time of journalizing the closing entries; they were entered as the posting was completed.

216   ADJUSTING AND CLOSING ACCOUNTS AT END OF PERIOD   [Unit 8

COMBINED CASH-JOURNAL FOR MONTH OF *December* 19—   *Page 79*

DATE MO.	DAY	DESCRIPTION	POST. REF.	GENERAL DEBITS	GENERAL CREDITS
		AMOUNTS FORWARDED			
Dec.	31	Closing Entries			
		Sales	41	10 23 15 34	
		Interest Income	71	70 18	
		Purchases Discount	72	2 20 67	
		Income Summary	33		10 26 06 19
		Income Summary	33	9 09 97 72	
		Sales Returns & Allowances	041		1 24 20
		Cost of Goods Sold	53		6 1 27 1 62
		Rent Expense	61		6 00 00 0
		Depreciation Expense	62		8 18 33
		Salaries and Commissions	63		14 29 3 35
		Social Security Taxes	64		7 14 67
		Heating and Lighting	65		5 27 00
		Stationery and Supplies Used	66		1 10 00
		Telephone and Telegraph Expense	67		2 33 05
		Advertising Expense	68		4 94 1 57
		Bad Debts Expense	69		5 72 28
		Insurance Expense	611		2 15 36
		Truck Expense	612		5 32 10
		Charitable Contributions	613		1 65 00
		Miscellaneous Expenses	614		3 75 93
		Interest Expense	81		1 03 26
		Income Summary	33	1 16 08 47	
		W. L. Mann, Proprietor	31		1 16 08 47
		W. L. Mann, Proprietor	31	7 13 00 0	
		W. L. Mann, Drawing	32		7 13 00 0

Posting the Closing Entries. If the closing entries for The Mann Furniture Store were posted to the income summary account in the usual manner, it would appear as follows after the posting was completed:

ACCOUNT *Income Summary*   33

DATE	ITEMS	FOLIO	√	DEBITS	DATE	ITEMS	FOLIO	√	CREDITS
19— Dec. 31		CJ 79		9 09 97 72	19— Dec. 31		CJ 79		10 26 06 19
31		CJ 79		1 16 08 47					
				10 26 06 19					10 26 06 19

In order that the income summary account may provide more detailed information and correlate more closely with the income statement, it is customary to identify the accounts that are being closed by itemizing them in the summary account. For example, in the first closing entry, the sales, interest income, and purchases discount accounts are closed by transferring their balances to the income summary account. In posting the entry, Sales should be debited and Income Summary should be credited for $102,315.34; Interest Income should be debited and Income Summary should be credited for $70.18; and Purchases Discount should be debited and Income Summary should be credited for $220.67. It is also good practice to write a brief description of each entry in the Items column of the summary account. For example, in posting the entry required to close the sales account, it is well to write "Sales" in the Items column on the credit side of the income summary account. As the posting is completed the proper cross references should be inserted in the Posting Reference column of the combined cash-journal and in the Folio column of the ledger. After all of the closing entries have been posted in the manner suggested, the accounts affected appear as shown on pages 218 to 221. A comparison of the income summary account shown on page 218 with the same account shown on page 216 should reveal clearly the advantages of the recommended method of posting the closing entries.

Ruling the Closed Accounts. After posting the closing entries all of the temporary proprietorship accounts of The Mann Furniture Store were in balance and they were ruled in the manner illustrated on pages 218 to 221. Following is the recommended procedure:

(1) Where there are two or more items posted to either side of an account, foot the amounts to ascertain that the total debits are equal to the total credits.

(2) Rule a single line across the debit and credit amount columns immediately below the last amount entered on the side with the most entries.

(3) Enter the totals of the debit and credit amount columns in ink on the next line.

(4) Rule a double line immediately below the totals extending through all but the Items columns.

If an account has only one item on each side, double ruling is sufficient. Note the ruling of the account with Depreciation Expense on page 219. If a page is not filled, it may be used for recording the transactions of the succeeding period.

ACCOUNT *W. L. Mann, Proprietor* — 31

DATE	ITEMS	FOLIO	√	DEBITS	DATE	ITEMS	FOLIO	√	CREDITS
19— Dec. 31		CJ 79		7 1 3 0 0 0	19— Dec. 1	Balance	√		3 6 5 1 7 3 1
					31		CJ 79		1 1 6 0 8 4 7

ACCOUNT *W. L. Mann, Drawing* — 32

DATE	ITEMS	FOLIO	√	DEBITS	DATE	ITEMS	FOLIO	√	CREDITS
19— Dec. 1	Balance	√		6 8 7 0 0 0	19— Dec. 31		CJ 79		7 1 3 0 0 0
21		CJ 77		2 5 0 0 0					
31		CJ 77		~~1 6 8 9 8~~					
				7 1 3 0 0 0					7 1 3 0 0 0

ACCOUNT *Income Summary* — 33

DATE	ITEMS	FOLIO	√	DEBITS	DATE	ITEMS	FOLIO	√	CREDITS
19— Dec. 31	Sales R. & A.	CJ 79		1 2 4 2 0	19— Dec. 31	Sales	CJ 79		1 0 2 3 1 5 3 4
31	Cost of Goods Sold	CJ 79		6 1 2 7 1 6 2	31	Interest Income	CJ 79		7 0 1 8
31	Rent Expense	CJ 79		6 0 0 0 0 0	31	Pur. Discount	CJ 79		2 2 0 6 7
31	Depr. Expense	CJ 79		8 1 8 3 3					~~1 0 2 6 0 6 1 9~~
31	Sal. and Com.	CJ 79		1 4 2 9 3 3 5					
31	S. S. Taxes	CJ 79		7 1 4 6 7					
31	Heating & Lighting	CJ 79		5 2 7 0 0					
31	Sta. & Sup.	CJ 79		1 1 0 0 0					
31	Tel. & Tel.	CJ 79		2 3 3 0 5					
31	Adv. Expense	CJ 79		4 9 4 1 5 7					
31	Bad Debts Expense	CJ 79		5 7 2 2 8					
31	Insurance Exp.	CJ 79		2 1 5 3 6					
31	Truck Expense	CJ 79		5 3 2 1 0					
31	Char. Contrib.	CJ 79		1 6 5 0 0					
31	Misc. Expense	CJ 79		3 7 5 9 3					
31	Int. Expense	CJ 79		~~9 0 1 9 3 2 6~~					
31	W. L. Mann, Prop.	CJ 79		~~1 1 6 0 8 4 7~~					
				1 0 2 6 0 6 1 9					1 0 2 6 0 6 1 9

ACCOUNT *Sales* — 41

DATE	ITEMS	FOLIO	√	DEBITS	DATE	ITEMS	FOLIO	√	CREDITS
19— Dec. 31		CJ 79		1 0 2 3 1 5 3 4	19— Dec. 1	Balance	√		9 7 8 0 4 1 5
					7		CJ 76		3 2 0 0 0
					14		CJ 76		4 6 5 0 0
					21		CJ 77		3 7 9 9 4
					28		CJ 77		5 4 9 3 7
					31		CJ 77		1 9 4 4 0
					31		S 64		~~2 4 9 2 4 8~~
				1 0 2 3 1 5 3 4					1 0 2 3 1 5 3 4

ACCOUNT *Sales Returns and Allowances* 041

DATE	ITEMS	FOLIO	√	DEBITS	DATE	ITEMS	FOLIO	√	CREDITS
19— Dec. 1	Balance	√		1 1 3 20	19— Dec. 31		CJ 79		1 2 4 20
27		CJ 77		1 1 00					
				1 2 4 20					1 2 4 20

ACCOUNT *Cost of Goods Sold* 53

DATE	ITEMS	FOLIO	DEBITS	DATE	ITEMS	FOLIO	CREDITS
19— Dec. 31	Beg. Inventory	CJ 78	2 8 5 2 2 45	19— Dec. 31	Pur. R. & A.	CJ 78	1 1 4 30
31	Purchases	CJ 78	6 5 3 1 6 63	31	End. Inventory	CJ 78	3 2 4 5 3 1 6
				31		CJ 79	6 1 2 7 1 6 2
			9 3 8 3 9 08				9 3 8 3 9 08

ACCOUNT *Rent Expense* 61

DATE	ITEMS	FOLIO	√	DEBITS	DATE	ITEMS	FOLIO	√	CREDITS
19— Dec. 1	Balance	√		5 5 0 0 00	19— Dec. 31		CJ 79		6 0 0 0 00
2		CJ 76		5 0 0 00					
				6 0 0 0 00					6 0 0 0 00

ACCOUNT *Depreciation Expense* 62

DATE	ITEMS	FOLIO	DEBITS	DATE	ITEMS	FOLIO	CREDITS
19— Dec. 31		CJ 78	8 1 8 33	19— Dec. 31		CJ 79	8 1 8 33

ACCOUNT *Salaries and Commissions* 63

DATE	ITEMS	FOLIO	DEBITS	DATE	ITEMS	FOLIO	CREDITS
19— Dec. 1	Balance	√	1 2 3 5 4 40	19— Dec. 31		CJ 79	1 4 2 9 3 35
14		CJ 76	9 6 9 56				
31		CJ 77	9 6 9 39				
			1 4 2 9 3 35				1 4 2 9 3 35

ACCOUNT *Social Security Taxes* 64

DATE	ITEMS	FOLIO	DEBITS	DATE	ITEMS	FOLIO	CREDITS
19— Dec. 1	Balance	√	6 1 7 72	19— Dec. 31		CJ 79	7 1 4 67
14		CJ 76	4 8 48				
31		CJ 77	4 8 47				
			7 1 4 67				7 1 4 67

ACCOUNT *Heating and Lighting* — 65

DATE	ITEMS	FOLIO	√	DEBITS	DATE	ITEMS	FOLIO	√	CREDITS
19— Dec 1	Balance	√		482 10	19— Dec 31		CJ 79		527 00
28		CJ 77		44 90					
				527 00					527 00

ACCOUNT *Stationery and Supplies Used* — 66

DATE	ITEMS	FOLIO	√	DEBITS	DATE	ITEMS	FOLIO	√	CREDITS
19— Dec 31		CJ 78		110 00	19— Dec 31		CJ 79		110 00

ACCOUNT *Telephone and Telegraph Expense* — 67

DATE	ITEMS	FOLIO	√	DEBITS	DATE	ITEMS	FOLIO	√	CREDITS
19— Dec 1	Balance	√		214 65	19— Dec 31		CJ 79		233 05
28		CJ 77		17 50					
30		CJ 77		90					
				233 05					233 05

ACCOUNT *Advertising Expense* — 68

DATE	ITEMS	FOLIO	√	DEBITS	DATE	ITEMS	FOLIO	√	CREDITS
19— Dec 1	Balance	√		4711 20	19— Dec 31		CJ 79		4941 57
6		CJ 76		53 37					
27		CJ 77		170 00					
31		CJ 77		7 00					
				4941 57					4941 57

ACCOUNT *Bad Debts Expense* — 69

DATE	ITEMS	FOLIO	√	DEBITS	DATE	ITEMS	FOLIO	√	CREDITS
19— Dec 31		CJ 78		572 28	19— Dec 31		CJ 79		572 28

ACCOUNT *Insurance Expense* — 611

DATE	ITEMS	FOLIO	√	DEBITS	DATE	ITEMS	FOLIO	√	CREDITS
19— Dec 31		CJ 78		215 36	19— Dec 31		CJ 79		215 36

ACCOUNT Truck Expense   612

DATE	ITEMS	FOLIO	√	DEBITS	DATE	ITEMS	FOLIO	√	CREDITS
Dec 1	Balance	✓		4 7 3 60	Dec 31		CJ 79		5 3 2 10
2		CJ 76		5 8 50					
				5 3 2 10					5 3 2 10

ACCOUNT Charitable Contributions   613

DATE	ITEMS	FOLIO	√	DEBITS	DATE	ITEMS	FOLIO	√	CREDITS
Dec 1	Balance	✓		1 6 0 00	Dec 31		CJ 79		1 6 5 00
31		CJ 77		5 00					
				1 6 5 00					1 6 5 00

ACCOUNT Miscellaneous Expenses   614

DATE	ITEMS	FOLIO	√	DEBITS	DATE	ITEMS	FOLIO	√	CREDITS
Dec 1	Balance	✓		3 6 9 78	Dec 31		CJ 79		3 7 5 93
31		CJ 77		6 15					
				3 7 5 93					3 7 5 93

ACCOUNT Interest Income   71

DATE	ITEMS	FOLIO	√	DEBITS	DATE	ITEMS	FOLIO	√	CREDITS
Dec 31		CJ 79		7 0 18	Dec 1	Balance	✓		5 1 48
					31		CJ 78		1 8 70
				7 0 18					7 0 18

ACCOUNT Purchases Discount   72

DATE	ITEMS	FOLIO	√	DEBITS	DATE	ITEMS	FOLIO	√	CREDITS
Dec 31		CJ 79		2 2 0 67	Dec 1	Balance	✓		2 1 5 71
					23		CJ 77		4 96
				2 2 0 67					2 2 0 67

ACCOUNT Interest Expense   8.1

DATE	ITEMS	FOLIO	√	DEBITS	DATE	ITEMS	FOLIO	√	CREDITS
Dec 1	Balance	✓		6 2 70	Dec 31		CJ 79		1 0 3 26
31		CJ 78		4 0 56					
				1 0 3 26					1 0 3 26

Balancing and Ruling Open Accounts. After the temporary proprietor-ship accounts have been closed, the open accounts may be balanced and ruled in order to prepare them to receive entries for the next fiscal period. The open accounts include the asset accounts, the liability ac-counts, and the permanent proprietorship account. Prior to ruling the open accounts the balance should be entered on the side which has the smaller total. The effect of this entry is to equalize the total debits and credits. The account should then be ruled with single and double lines in the manner suggested on page 217. The balance should then be brought down below the ruling on the proper side of the account. However, if the page is filled, the balance may be carried forward to the top of a new page. In carrying the balance down or forward, as the case may be, care must be taken to be sure that it is entered on the side which originally had the larger total.

There is no need for balancing and ruling an open account that has entries on only one side of the account. To illustrate the procedure in balancing and ruling open accounts, the following accounts of The Mann Furniture Store are reproduced on page 223:

> Liberty National Bank, Account No. 111
> Accounts Payable, Account No. 23
> **W.** L. Mann, Proprietor, Account No. 31

In the case of the account with the Liberty National Bank, the balance of the account amounting to $6,247.61 was entered on the credit side, the totals were entered in ink, the account was ruled with single and double lines, and the balance was brought down below the ruling on the debit side. Note that in bringing the December 31 balance down below the ruling, it was entered as of January 1 to indicate that it was the balance at the beginning of a new accounting period.

In the case of the account with Accounts Payable, the balance amount-ing to $3,069.60 was entered on the debit side, the totals were entered in ink, the account was ruled with single and double lines, and the balance was brought down below the ruling on the credit side as of January 1.

In the case of the account with W. L. Mann, Proprietor, the balance amounting to $40,995.78 was entered on the debit side, the totals were entered in ink, the account was ruled with single and double lines, and the balance was brought down below the ruling on the credit side as of January 1. This balance represents the proprietorship or net worth of the business on that date.

Formerly it was common practice to use red ink in balancing and rul-ing accounts. Any losses were also entered in red ink. This was the origin of the expression "in the red" to describe a loss. Accountants sometimes

ACCOUNT *Liberty National Bank*   *111*

DATE	ITEMS	FOLIO	✓	DEBITS	DATE	ITEMS	FOLIO	✓	CREDITS
19— Dec. 1	Balance	✓		8 2 5 3 3 9	19— Dec. 31		CJ77		5 5 4 3 4 1
31		CJ77	6,247.61	3 5 3 7 6 3	31	Balance	✓		6 2 4 7 6 1
				1 1 7 9 1 0 2					1 1 7 9 1 0 2
19— Jan. 1	Balance	✓		6 2 4 7 6 1					

ACCOUNT *Accounts Payable*   *23*

DATE	ITEMS	FOLIO		DEBITS	DATE	ITEMS	FOLIO		CREDITS
19— Dec. 31		CJ77		2 1 1 8 2 6	19— Dec. 1	Balance	✓		3 0 2 1 5 1
31	Balance	✓	3,069.60	3 0 6 9 6 0	31		CJ77		4 0 0 0 0
					31		P52		1 7 6 4 3 5
				5 1 8 7 8 6					5 1 8 7 8 6
					19— Jan. 1	Balance	✓		3 0 6 9 6 0

ACCOUNT *W. L. Mann, Proprietor*   *31*

DATE	ITEMS	FOLIO		DEBITS	DATE	ITEMS	FOLIO		CREDITS
19— Dec. 31		CJ79		7 1 3 0 0 0	19— Dec. 1	Balance	✓		3 6 5 1 7 3 1
31	Balance	✓	40,995.78	4 0 9 9 5 7 8	31		CJ79		1 1 6 2 8 4 7
				4 8 1 2 5 7 8					4 8 1 2 5 7 8
					19— Jan. 1	Balance	✓		4 0 9 9 5 7 8

use a different color of pencil or ink to indicate that an amount is a deduction in preparing various reports or in correcting various records.

Sometimes a balance-column account form is used for the general ledger accounts. In such case, the balance of each account is entered after each item is posted. When an account is in balance, a cipher is entered in the Balance column and no ruling of the account is required.

Trial Balance After Closing. A trial balance of the open accounts in the general ledger, after the temporary proprietorship accounts have been closed, is usually referred to as a *post-closing trial balance*. The purpose of this post-closing trial balance is to prove that the general ledger is in balance at the beginning of a new accounting period. Obviously it is advisable to ascertain that the ledger is in balance before any transactions for the new accounting period are recorded.

The post-closing trial balance should contain the same accounts and amounts as appear in the Balance Sheet columns of the work sheet, except that (a) the proprietor's drawing account is omitted because it has been closed, and (b) the proprietor's capital account has been adjusted for the amount of the net income and the amount of his drawings.

A post-closing trial balance of the general ledger of The Mann Furniture Store is shown on page 224. Some accountants advocate that the post-closing trial balance should be dated as of the close of the old accounting period, while others advocate that it should be dated as of the beginning of the new accounting period. In this illustration the trial balance is dated December 31, the end of the period.

THE MANN FURNITURE STORE

POST-CLOSING TRIAL BALANCE

December 31, 19 - -

ACCOUNTS	NOS.	DR. BALANCES	CR. BALANCES
Liberty National Bank....................	111	$ 6,247.61	
Petty Cash Fund.........................	112	100.00	
Notes Receivable........................	121	801.50	
Accrued Interest Receivable..............	122	18.70	
Accounts Receivable.....................	123	4,868.02	
Allowance for Bad Debts.................	012		$ 660.84
Merchandise Inventory...................	13	32,453.16	
Prepaid Insurance.......................	14	215.36	
Stationery and Supplies..................	15	60.00	
Store Equipment........................	18	2,250.00	
Allowance for Depr. of Store Equipment....	018		555.00
Delivery Equipment......................	19	1,900.00	
Allowance for Depr. of Delivery Equipment..	019		1,108.33
Notes Payable	21		2,000.00
Accrued Interest Payable.................	22		40.56
Accounts Payable........................	23		3,069.60
Sales Tax Payable.......................	24		90.01
F.I.C.A. Taxes Payable...................	25		77.55
Employees' Income Taxes Payable..........	26		160.80
F.U.T.A. Taxes Payable..................	27		42.88
State U. C. Taxes Payable................	28		113.00
W. L. Mann, Proprietor..................	31		40,995.78
		$48,914.35	$48,914.35

Reversing Entries for Accrual Adjustments. In addition to balancing and ruling the open accounts at the close of a fiscal period to make ready for recording the transactions of the succeeding fiscal period, many accountants reverse the adjusting entries for accruals. The purpose of such reversing entries (sometimes called "readjusting entries") is to facilitate the recording of the transactions of the succeeding fiscal period in a routine manner and to assure that the proper amount of income will be credited to the period in which earned and that the proper amount of expenses will be charged to the period in which incurred.

When cash is received in payment of interest, the routine manner of recording the transaction is to debit Cash (or Bank) and to credit Interest Income. If any portion of such interest were accrued in the preceding fiscal period and the adjusting entry had not been reversed at the beginning of the current fiscal period, the amount credited to Interest Income would not represent the proper amount of interest income earned in the current period. If, however, the adjusting entry at the end of the preceding period had been reversed, the interest income account would be debited for the amount accrued and, after recording the interest collected in the current period as a credit to Interest Income, the balance of the account would represent the correct amount of income from interest earned.

When cash is disbursed in payment of interest, the routine manner of recording the transaction is to debit Interest Expense and to credit Cash (or Bank). If any portion of such interest were accrued in the preceding fiscal period and the adjusting entry had not been reversed at the beginning of the current fiscal period, the amount debited to Interest Expense would not represent the proper amount of interest expense incurred in the current period. If, however, the adjusting entry at the end of the preceding period had been reversed, the interest expense account would be credited for the amount accrued and, after recording the interest paid in the current period as a debit to Interest Expense, the balance of the account would represent the correct amount of the interest expense incurred in the current period.

Journalizing the Reversing Entries. Reversing entries, like adjusting and closing entries, may be recorded in either a general journal or a combined cash-journal. If the entries are made in a combined cash-journal, the only amount columns used are the General Dr. and Cr. columns. A portion of a page of a combined cash-journal showing the reversing entries of The Mann Furniture Store is reproduced below. Usually the reversing entries are made immediately after closing the books at the end of an accounting period. However, it is customary to date the entries as of the first day of the succeeding accounting period. Thus, the reversing entries for The Mann Furniture Store are dated January 1. Since the heading "Reversing Entries" explains the nature of the entries, a separate explanation of each reversing entry is unnecessary. Following is a discussion of each of the reversing entries:

Page 80	COMBINED CASH-JOURNAL FOR MONTH OF	*January* 19—			
DATE			**POST.**	**GENERAL**	
MO.	**DAY**	**DESCRIPTION**	**REF.**	**DEBITS**	**CREDITS**
		AMOUNTS FORWARDED			
Jan.	1	Reversing Entries			
		Interest Income	71	1 8 7 0	
		Accrued Interest Receivable	122		1 8 7 0
		Accrued Interest Payable	22	4 0 5 6	
		Interest Expense	81		4 0 5 6

The Mann Furniture Store — Reversing Entries

(a) **Accrued Interest Receivable.** Reference to the adjusting entries reproduced on page 210 will reveal that Accrued Interest Receivable, Account No. 122, was debited and Interest Income, Account No. 71, was credited for $18.70 to record the interest accrued on the 6 per cent interest-bearing note of Frank Zeigler for $801.50. To reverse the adjusting entry it was necessary to debit Interest Income, Account No. 71, and to credit Accrued Interest Receivable, Account No. 122, for $18.70. The accounts affected by this entry are reproduced below.

ACCOUNT   *Accrued Interest Receivable*   122

DATE	ITEMS	FOLIO	√	DEBITS	DATE	ITEMS	FOLIO	√	CREDITS
19- Dec 31		CJ78		18 70	19- Jan 1		CJ80		18 70

ACCOUNT   *Interest Income*   71

DATE	ITEMS	FOLIO	√	DEBITS	DATE	ITEMS	FOLIO	√	CREDITS
19- Dec 31		CJ79		70 18	19- Dec 1	Balance	√		51 48
					31		CJ78		18 70
				70 18					70 18
19- Jan 1		CJ80		18 70					

It will be noted that, after posting the reversing entry, the account with Accrued Interest Receivable is in balance and the account with Interest Income has a debit balance of $18.70. If Frank Zeigler pays the amount due when his note matures on February 13, his remittance will amount to $825.55 (principal of note $801.50, plus interest at 6 per cent for six months, $24.05). To record the receipt of this remittance it is only necessary to debit Liberty National Bank for $825.55 and to credit Notes Receivable, Account No. 121, for $801.50 and Interest Income, Account No. 71, for $24.05. After posting this entry the interest income account will have a credit balance of $5.35 ($24.05 minus $18.70). This balance represents the amount of interest earned in the year in which the note matures. If the adjusting entry had not been reversed, it would be necessary to make an analysis before recording the remittance received from Mr. Zeigler on February 13 in order to determine the amount of interest accrued in the preceding year and the amount of interest earned in the current year. This would reveal that it would be necessary to credit Accrued Interest Receivable for $18.70 and Interest Income for $5.35, in order that each year might receive credit for the proper amount of interest income. When the adjustment is reversed, the need for this analysis is eliminated.

The reversal procedure is particularly useful if the year-end adjustment for interest earned but not collected related to interest accrued on several notes or other interest-bearing assets. When the adjustment is reversed, all future collections of interest can be credited to the interest income account without any concern as to when the amount was earned. The portion of any collections that was earned in the new period will automatically emerge as the balance of the interest income account.

(b) **Accrued Interest Payable.** In the adjusting entries for The Mann Furniture Store, Interest Expense, Account No. 81, was debited and Accrued Interest Payable, Account No. 22, was credited for $40.56 to record the interest accrued on the 5 per cent interest-bearing note for $2,000 issued to the Liberty National Bank August 7. To reverse the adjusting entry it was necessary to debit Accrued Interest Payable, Account No. 22, and to credit Interest Expense, Account No. 81, for $40.56. The accounts affected by this entry are reproduced below.

ACCOUNT *Accrued Interest Payable*   22

DATE	ITEMS	FOLIO	√	DEBITS	DATE	ITEMS	P	FOLIO	√	CREDITS
19- Jan. 1		CJ80		40 56	19- Dec. 31				CJ78		40 56

ACCOUNT *Interest Expense*   81

DATE	ITEMS	FOLIO	√	DEBITS	DATE	ITEMS	P	FOLIO	√	CREDITS
19- Dec. 31	Balance	√		62 70	19- Dec. 31				CJ79		1 03 26
31		CJ78		40 56							
				1 03 26						1 03 26
					19- Jan. 1				CJ80		40 56

It will be noted that, after posting the reversing entry, the account with Accrued Interest Payable is in balance and the account with Interest Expense has a credit balance of $40.56. If the note for $2,000 plus interest is paid when due on February 7, the remittance will amount to $2,050 (principal of note $2,000, plus interest at 5 per cent for six months, $50). To record the payment it is only necessary to debit Notes Payable, Account No. 21, for $2,000 and Interest Expense, Account No. 81, for $50 and to credit Liberty National Bank for $2,050. After posting this entry the interest expense account will have a debit balance of $9.44 ($50 minus $40.56). This balance represents the amount of interest expense incurred in the year in which the note matures. If the adjusting entry had not been reversed, it would be necessary to make an analysis before recording the payment on February 7 in order to determine the amount of interest accrued in the preceding year and the amount of interest expense incurred in the current year. This would reveal that it would be necessary to debit Accrued Interest Payable for $40.56 and Interest Expense for $9.44 in order that each year might be charged with the proper amount of interest expense. When the adjustment is reversed, the need for this analysis is eliminated.

The reversal procedure is particularly useful if the year-end adjustment for interest expense incurred but not paid related to interest accrued on several interest-bearing obligations. When the adjustment is reversed, all future payments of interest can be debited to the interest expense account without any concern as to when the amount paid was incurred. The portion of any payments that is an expense of the new period will automatically emerge as the balance of the interest expense account.

From the foregoing discussion it will be seen that by reversing the adjusting entries made on December 31 for accrued interest receivable and accrued interest payable, it will be possible to record the interest collected on February 13 amounting to $24.05 and the interest paid on February 7 amounting to $40.56 in an ordinary routine manner.

The Accounting Cycle. This unit completes an accounting cycle. The term *accounting cycle* refers to the steps involved in recording the effect of all of the transactions and events completed during an accounting period, beginning with the entries in the books of original entry and ending with the reversing entries. The following is a brief summary of the various steps involved in an accounting cycle:

(1) Journalizing the transactions.
(2) Posting to the ledger accounts.
(3) Taking a trial balance.
(4) Determining the needed adjustments.
(5) Completing a work sheet.
(6) Preparing an income statement and a balance sheet.
(7) Journalizing and posting the adjusting and closing entries.
(8) Taking a post-closing trial balance.
(9) Journalizing and posting the reversing entries.

PRACTICE ASSIGNMENT No. 19. Complete Report No. 19 in the workbook and submit your working papers to the instructor for approval. After completing the report you may continue with the textbook discussion in Unit Nine until the next report is required.

Unit Nine

THE PERSONAL SERVICE ENTERPRISE

(20) ACCOUNTING METHODS

A personal service enterprise is one in which the principal source of income is compensation for personal services rendered. There are two types of personal service enterprises:

(a) Professional enterprises.
(b) Business enterprises.

Professional enterprises include law, medicine, surgery, dentistry, public accounting, engineering, architecture, art, sculpture, and education. The principal source of income of individuals engaged in such professions is usually the compensation received in payment for the personal services rendered.

Business enterprises of the personal service type include real estate, insurance, advertising, transportation, storage, entertainment, brokerage, and many other enterprises in which the income is derived chiefly from personal services rendered. Mercantile enterprises are not classified as personal service enterprises for the reason that their principal source of income is from the sale of merchandise rather than from compensation received for services rendered.

The Cash Basis of Accounting for a Personal Service Enterprise. The most logical way to determine the periodic profit or loss of a business undertaking is to follow the principles and practices that have been described as accrual accounting. For a merchant, this is the only basis that provides reasonable approximations of operating results period by period. When the proprietor's personal services rather than merchandise are being sold, however, the so-called "cash basis" of accounting will usually suffice.

Accounting for income on the cash basis means that, in most cases, no record of income is made in the accounts until cash is received for the services rendered. This may mean that the proprietor renders the services in one period and accounts for the income received in the succeeding period. He may take the view that, in most cases, he has no income until it is received in such form that it can be spent; he cannot "spend" an account receivable. If he were to account for income on the accrual basis, it might mean that he would have to pay an income tax on income that, according to his point of view, has not been received.

In view of these considerations, the cash basis of accounting for the income of a personal service enterprise is widely used. It is acceptable for federal and state income tax purposes. Actually, certain events other than the receipt of cash are accounted for as income under this basis. Any property or service that is accepted in lieu of cash for services rendered is treated as income to the extent of its fair market value at the time received. Any amounts *constructively received* are also treated as income. Income is constructively received when it is credited to a person's account or is set apart so he can draw upon it. For example, when interest on a savings account is credited to the depositor's account, such interest is income to the depositor even though it is not actually received in cash or is not immediately withdrawn.

Accounting for expenses on the cash basis generally means that expenses are not recorded in the accounts until paid in cash. This may mean that an expense is really incurred in one period and recorded in the accounts in the succeeding period. In the case of many expenses of a recurring nature, however, this is deemed to be a minor objection. If, for example, twelve monthly telephone bills of about the same amount must be paid during each year, little importance is attached to the fact that the bill that is paid and recorded as an expense in January was really for service in December.

When accounts are kept on the cash basis, no adjustments of the accrual type or deferral type are made at the end of the period. However, the write-off type of adjustments are made. Under the cash basis, the disbursement of cash, or incurrence of debt, for long-lived assets is not recorded as an expense. Accounts are maintained for such assets as office furniture and equipment. If supplies are purchased in substantial quantities, they are treated as prepaid expenses and are recorded as assets. At the end of the period the accounts are adjusted to record depreciation of fixed assets and to record the consumption of any other items that originally had been recorded as prepaid expenses. The expression "cash basis" as applied to income and expense accounting is actually something of a misnomer. The term really means that most, but not all, income and expenses are accounted for when cash is received and disbursed.

While not relative to personal service enterprises alone, it is appropriate to mention in passing that some businesses follow practices best described as a blend of the cash basis and the accrual basis of accounting. The majority of income and expense items may be accounted for on a cash receipts and disbursements basis during the year. At the end of the year, however, the accounts are adjusted to record accruals of income and expense so that the financial statements reflect accrual accounting. In other cases, purchases, sales, and certain types of income and expense are accounted for on the accrual basis, while some types of recurrent expenses and incidental income are not recorded until cash is disbursed or received. Thus, a workable compromise between technical accuracy and practical expediency is reached.

Application of Principles. As an aid in applying the principles involved in keeping the accounts of a personal service enterprise on the cash basis, a system of accounts for J. C. Allen, an attorney at law, will be described. While certain distinctive problems may arise in keeping the accounts of any specific enterprise, it will be found that the general principles are the same in all cases; hence, the system of accounts used by Mr. Allen may readily be adapted to the needs of any personal service enterprise regardless of whether it is of a professional or a business nature.

Chart of Accounts. Mr. Allen's chart of accounts is reproduced on the following page. Reference to this chart will show that each account is given a number as well as an appropriate title. All account numbers beginning with 1 represent assets; 2, liabilities; 3, proprietorship; 4, income; and 5, expenses. Account numbers beginning with 0 represent *contra accounts* used to record the estimated decrease in certain assets caused by depreciation or other factors. This system of numbering accounts permits the addition of new accounts as they are needed without disturbing the numerical order of the accounts. Some of Mr. Allen's accounts are peculiar to the legal profession. A discussion of these accounts and certain other accounts that have not previously been introduced follows.

Advances on Behalf of Clients, Account No. 14. In handling a legal case, a lawyer may incur certain costs and expenses on behalf of his client. The bar associations consider it unethical for lawyers to stand or absorb such expenses personally. While it is not considered unethical for a lawyer to take a case on a *contingent fee* basis, it is considered unethical for him to incur expenses contingently on behalf of his client. Expenses of this type may include court filing fees, the cost of obtaining depositions,

CHART OF ACCOUNTS FOR J. C. ALLEN, ATTORNEY AT LAW

I *Assets*
  11 First National Bank
  12 Petty Cash Fund
  13 Notes Receivable
  14 Advances on Behalf of Clients
  16 Office Equipment
      016 Allowance for Depreciation
          of Office Equipment
  17 Law Library
      017 Allowance for Depreciation
          of Law Library
  18 Automobile
      018 Allowance for Depreciation
          of Automobile

II *Liabilities*
  21 Accounts Payable
  22 Employees' Income Taxes Payable
  23 F.I.C.A. Taxes Payable

III *Proprietorship*
  31 J. C. Allen, Proprietor
  32 J. C. Allen, Drawing
  33 Income Summary

IV *Income*
  411 Legal Fees
  412 Collection Fees

V Expenses
  511 Rent Expense
  512 Telephone and Telegraph Expense
  513 Salaries
  514 Social Security Taxes
  515 Stationery and Supplies
  516 Depreciation Expense
  517 Automobile Expenses
  518 Charitable Contributions
  519 Miscellaneous Expenses

Note: Items in italics represent headings and not account titles.

fees charged by accountants employed to make audits, and other similar expenses incurred on behalf of a client in handling his case. When a lawyer incurs expenses on behalf of a client, he usually charges such expenses to an account entitled Advances on Behalf of Clients. At the same time a record of the charges is made in the client's account on a case docket as will be explained later.

Advances on Behalf of Clients is an asset account. It should be debited for any expenses incurred on behalf of clients and should be credited for remittances received from clients in settlement of such charges. After all posting is completed, the balance of the account represents the aggregate amount due from clients on account of advances made on their behalf.

Law Library, Account No. 17. It is not uncommon for a lawyer to invest a considerable amount in a library of legal publications. Such a library constitutes an asset that should be treated in the same manner as other fixed assets that are subject to depreciation. The library account should be debited for the cost of the books purchased and should be credited for the cost of any books sold or discarded.

Allowance for Depreciation of Law Library, Account No. 017. Legal publications are subject to depreciation. The estimated amount of depreciation sustained each year should be recorded by debiting Depreciation Expense, Account No. 516, and by crediting Allowance for Depreciation of Law Library, Account No. 017. The allowance account is a contra account. To ascertain the book value of a law library it is necessary to subtract the balance of the allowance account from the balance of the library account. It is customary to show this deduction in the balance sheet, extending the difference as the book value of the library.

Accounts Payable, Account No. 21. A lawyer may incur liability in the form of accounts payable as a result of the following types of transactions:

(a) Purchases of equipment or other property on credit.
(b) Collections made for or on behalf of clients.

When equipment or other property is purchased on credit, the transaction should be recorded by debiting the proper asset account and by crediting Accounts Payable for the cost of the property. Even though the accounts are kept on the cash basis, property may be purchased on credit; such transactions should be recorded immediately in order that both the assets and the liabilities will be reflected in the accounts. This is particularly important where the property purchased is subject to depreciation, because depreciation is an expense that is not accounted for on a cash-disbursement basis.

When collections are made for or on behalf of clients, the transactions should be recorded by debiting the bank account and by crediting (a) Collection Fees for the amount of the lawyer's commission and (b) Accounts Payable for the proceeds, represented by the difference between the amount collected and the amount of the lawyer's commission. When the proceeds are remitted to a client, the transaction should be recorded by debiting Accounts Payable and by crediting the bank account.

Mr. Allen does not keep a separate ledger account with each creditor. Purchase invoices representing the purchase of equipment or other property on credit are recorded in the combined cash-journal by debiting the proper asset account and by crediting Accounts Payable. The invoices are then filed in an unpaid invoice file where they are held until they are paid, at which time they are transferred to a paid invoice file. This is a method of handling invoices that is widely used by individuals engaged in personal service enterprises.

Legal Fees, Account No. 411. This account is an income account that is credited for cash received from clients in payment of legal fees. When the accounts are kept on the cash basis, no income is recorded in this account until it is received in cash or other property accepted in lieu of cash.

Collection Fees, Account No. 412. One source of income for many lawyers is fees charged clients for collecting accounts from their customers, patients, or clients. The collection fees account is an income account that should be credited for the commissions or fees received for collections made on behalf of clients. When a lawyer makes a collection in partial or in full settlement of an account, the transaction should be recorded by debiting the bank account for the amount received, by crediting Collection Fees for the amount of his commission, and by crediting Accounts Payable for the balance. Thus, if Lawyer A undertakes to collect an account amounting to $100 for Client B on a commission basis of 15 per cent, the following entry should be made when a remittance is received in payment of the account:

Bank..	$100.00	
Collection Fees.......................................		$15.00
Accounts Payable.....................................		85.00

When Lawyer A remits the proceeds, amounting to $85, to Client B, an entry should be made as follows:

Accounts Payable......................................	$85.00	
Bank..		$85.00

If desired, a special account may be opened at the bank in which all cash, checks, and other cash items received in settlement of collection cases may be deposited. Some lawyers consider it advisable to segregate such deposits from the deposits in their regular checking account. When a separate bank account is maintained for this purpose, all checks drawn in favor of clients for the purpose of remitting the proceeds of collections should be credited to that account instead of to the regular checking account.

Stationery and Supplies, Account No. 515. Reference to the chart of accounts for J. C. Allen on page 232 will reveal that this account is classified as an expense account. When the income and expense accounts are kept on the cash basis and stationery and supplies are purchased in relatively small quantities for current use, it is common practice to charge the cost to an expense account at time of payment. Mr. Allen follows this practice.

Books of Account. Mr. Allen uses the following books of account:

(a) General books
    Combined cash-journal
    General ledger

(b) Auxiliary records
    Petty cash disbursements record
    Lawyers' case docket
    Lawyers' collection docket

Combined Cash-Journal. The form of combined cash-journal that is best suited to the needs of an individual engaged in a personal service enterprise differs somewhat from the form of combined cash-journal that is best suited to the needs of a mercantile enterprise. Reference to Mr. Allen's combined cash-journal reproduced on page 238 reveals that he uses standard eight-column paper (8 columns divided — 2 left, 6 right). The columnar arrangement of Mr. Allen's combined cash-journal is as follows:

    (a) First National Bank
        (1) Deposits, Dr.
        (2) Checks, Cr.

    (b) General
        (3) Debits
        (4) Credits

    (c) Income
        (5) Legal Fees, Cr.
        (6) Collection Fees, Cr.

    (d) Wage Deductions
        (7) Employees' Income Taxes Payable, Cr.
        (8) F.I.C.A Taxes Payable, Cr.

The account numbers are also indicated in the headings. This is an aid in completing the summary posting at the end of each month.

Mr. Allen's principal sources of income are (a) legal fees and (b) collection fees. Since separate accounts are kept for each of these sources of income, it is desirable to provide a separate amount column in the combined cash-journal for recording the income from each source. Any income derived from other sources is recorded in the General Cr. column.

The last two amount columns are used for recording the amounts withheld from the wages paid to Mr. Allen's employees for federal income taxes and F.I.C.A. taxes. Under the laws of some states it would also be necessary to withhold a percentage of the employees' wages for disability benefits or unemployment compensation purposes. Mr. Allen is not a resident of one of these states; hence, no such withholding is required in his case. Since Mr. Allen's accounts are kept on the cash basis, the F.I.C.A. taxes imposed upon him as an employer should not be recorded until the tax is paid. When payment is made, the tax should be recorded in the combined cash-journal by debiting Social Security Taxes and by crediting the bank account.

Following is a narrative of transactions completed by Mr. Allen during the month of December. These transactions are recorded in the combined cash-journal reproduced on page 238.

J. C. ALLEN, ATTORNEY AT LAW

NARRATIVE OF TRANSACTIONS

Monday, December 2

Issued Check No. 201 for $90, payable to J. H. Walker, for the December office rent.

Tuesday, December 3

Issued Check No. 202 for $4.09 to the Public Service Electric Co. for electricity consumed during November.

> The amount of this check was charged to Miscellaneous Expenses, Account No. 519, for the reason that no separate expense account for electric service is maintained.

Received $20 from Mrs. Laura Womack for services rendered in preparing an abstract of title.

> Because the cash received from Mrs. Womack will be deposited in Mr. Allen's regular checking account, the transaction was recorded by debiting First National Bank, Account No. 11, and by crediting Legal Fees, Account No. 411. Since individual posting of this entry is not required, a check mark was placed in the Posting Reference column.

Wednesday, December 4

Mr. Allen reports that he has been engaged by Dependable Motors, Inc., 1401 Reading Road, City, to represent it in a lawsuit against George Maher, 3450 May St., City, at a minimum fee of $110 and costs, and that he has received a check for $50 as a retainer. Case No. 103.

> The amount received as a retainer constitutes income realized on the cash basis. Case Docket No. 103 is reproduced on page 241. This docket is an auxiliary record of information designed to supplement the information recorded in the regular books of account and to facilitate the handling of the case.

Issued Check No. 203 for $12.50 to Miss Clara Hazelton, a public stenographer, for stenographic services.

Issued Check No. 204 for $14.95 to the Bell Telephone Co. for the November service invoice.

Thursday, December 5

Received a check for $100 from W. R. Halsey in payment of the balance due on Case No. 94.

Received a check for $90 from the Automotive Accessories Co. in full payment of Case No. 96.

Friday, December 6

Issued Check No. 205 for $19.12 to Harry's Friendly Service Station in payment of the December 1 statement, covering gasoline, oil, and services rendered during November.

Received for collection from The H. & S. Pogue Co., Fourth and Race Streets, City, a statement of its account with S. L. Hale, 1642 Paxton Road, City, for $130. This account is over eighteen months past due. Collection fee, 25%; no suit without further instructions. Collection No. 51.

> Inasmuch as Mr. Allen's books are kept on the cash basis, no entry in the regular books of account is required for this transaction. Collection Docket No. 51 is reproduced on page 243. This docket is an auxiliary record of information designed to supplement the information recorded in the regular books of account and to facilitate handling the account.

Saturday, December 7

Proved the footings of the combined cash-journal. Deposited $260 in the First National Bank and proved the bank balance ($2,699.37).

> The individual posting was completed at this time. As each item was posted from the General columns of the combined cash-journal to the proper ledger account, the account number was entered in the Posting Reference column.

Monday, December 9

Received $20 from The Keith Co. for services rendered in connection with preparing a mortgage.

> *The waved lines appearing at this point in the combined cash-journal indicate omission of the transactions completed on the days between December 9 and 31.*

Tuesday, December 31

Issued Check No. 215 for $36.80 to Robert Hamilton, part-time law clerk, in payment of one half month's salary amounting to $40, less 80 cents withheld for F.I.C.A. taxes, and $2.40 withheld for federal income taxes.

Issued Check No. 216 for $68.80 to the office secretary, in payment of one half month's salary amounting to $80, less $1.60 withheld for F.I.C.A. taxes, and $9.60 withheld for federal income taxes.

> Since Mr. Allen has less than four employees, he is not subject to the social security taxes imposed under the Federal Unemployment Tax Act. Neither is he required to make contributions to a state unemployment compensation fund because he is located in a state that does not require contributions from employers of less than four employees.

(*Continued on page 239*)

COMBINED CASH-JOURNAL FOR MONTH OF December 19—

First National Bank		Date		Description	Post. Ref.	General		Income		Wage Deductions	
Deposits 11 Dr.	Checks 11 Cr.	Mo.	Day			Debits	Credits	Legal Fees 411 Cr.	Collection Fees 412 Cr.	Emp'l I.T. Pay. 22 Cr.	F.I.C.A. Taxes Pay. 23 Cr.
				Amounts Forwarded $2,580.03 ✓							
	9000	Dec	1	Rent Expense #201	511 ✓	9000					
	409		2	Miscellaneous Expenses #202	519 ✓	409					
2000			3	Mrs. Laura Womack, abstract	✓			2000			
5000			3	Dependable Motors Inc. Case 103	✓			5000			
	1250		4	Miscellaneous Expense #203	519 ✓	1250					
	1495		4	Tel. and Tel. Expense #204	512 ✓	1495					
10000			5	W. R. Halsey Case #94	✓			10000			
9000			5	Automotive Accessories Co. Case #96	✓			9000			
	1912		6	Automobile Expenses #205	517 ✓	1912					
2000			9	The Keith Co. mortgage $2,097.37	✓			1600			
2000								2000			
3680			31	Salaries #215	513	4000				240	80
6880			31	Salaries #216	513	8000				960	160
2905			31	Advances on behalf of clients #217	14	800					
				J. C. Allen, Drawing	32	500					
				Tel. and Tel. Expense	512	135					
				Stationery and Supplies	515	295					
				Automobile Expense	517	200					
				Charitable Contributions	518	200					
				Miscellaneous Expenses	519	773					
				$2,909.95		136955	48799	7500	1651	2400	420
137545	134810					(✓)	(✓)	(411)	(412)	(22)	(23)
(11)	(11)										

Combined Cash-Journal for a Personal Service Enterprise

Issued Check No. 217 for $29.05 to replenish the petty cash fund.

The following statement provided the information needed in recording this transaction in the combined cash-journal:

STATEMENT OF PETTY CASH DISBURSEMENTS FOR DECEMBER

Advances on Behalf of Clients	$ 8.00
J. C. Allen, Drawing	5.00
Telephone and Telegraph Expense	1.35
Stationery and Supplies	2.95
Automobile Expenses	2.00
Charitable Contributions	2.00
Miscellaneous Expenses	7.75
Total Disbursements	$29.05

Proved the footings, entered the totals, and ruled the combined cash-journal. Proved the bank balance ($2,607.38).

The individual posting from the General columns of the combined cash-journal was completed at this time. Since this is the end of the month, the summary posting of the totals of the special columns was also completed. As the summary posting was completed, the account numbers were written immediately below the totals of the columns in the combined cash-journal.

General Ledger. The general ledger used by a personal service enterprise may be either a bound book or a loose-leaf book. Either the standard account form or the balance account form may be used. The standard account form is generally preferred for general ledger accounts. The accounts should be arranged in the general ledger in the order in which they appear in the chart of accounts. If the accounts are numbered they should, of course, be arranged in numerical order. Inasmuch as the combined cash-journal is the only book of original entry used by Mr. Allen, all posting to the general ledger accounts is from this journal. Proof of equality of the general ledger account balances is ascertained at the end of each month by taking a trial balance. Mr. Allen's trial balance as of December 31 is reproduced in the first two amount columns of his work sheet illustrated on page 245.

Auxiliary Records. Auxiliary records are used to record information which is supplemental to that recorded in the regular books of account. In addition to the regular books of account, Mr. Allen uses a petty cash disbursements record, a case docket, and a collection docket, as auxiliary records.

Petty Cash Disbursements Record. Mr. Allen maintains a petty cash fund amounting to $50. The form of the petty cash disbursements record used by Mr. Allen is the same as that illustrated on page 170. Accounts

Nos. 14, 32, 512, 515, 517, 518, and 519 are inserted in the headings of the Distribution columns to facilitate classification of the expenditures.

Lawyers' Case Docket. Lawyers usually use a form known as a *case docket* to maintain a memorandum record of each legal case with a client from the time it is accepted until final disposition. A model filled-in copy of a case docket is reproduced on page 241. This docket provides a history of the case of Dependable Motors, Inc., plaintiff, vs. George Maher, defendant. It also provides a record of the charges and credits to the account of the client — Dependable Motors, Inc. The upper part of the form is designed to facilitate recording the legal information that may be needed in handling the case. The lower part of the form is designed to facilitate keeping a memorandum account with the client.

When a lawyer keeps his accounts on the cash basis he does not keep a summary account with clients in the general ledger as accounts receivable. However, it is necessary to keep a memorandum account with each client. The account form on the case docket serves this purpose. The client's account should be charged for —

(a) Fees for services rendered.

(b) Advances on behalf of the client, such as court costs and other expenses paid on his behalf.

The fees to be charged for services may be agreed upon in advance, in which case they may be recorded when opening the memorandum account on the case docket. Otherwise, the fees are not recorded until the case is settled and the amount determined.

The client's account should be credited for —

(a) Payments received for services.

(b) Payments received as reimbursement for advances made on behalf of the client.

In the illustration on page 241 the client, Dependable Motors, Inc., is charged for the following:

December 4. Amount of the fee agreed upon at the time the case was taken, $110.

December 9. Amount advanced in payment of suit fee, $3.

The account is credited for the following:

December 4. Amount received as a retainer, $50.

January 2. Amount received in payment of balance due on account, $63.

LAWYERS' CASE DOCKET

IN THE *Common Pleas* COURT   COURT FILE NO. *A 10905*

COUNTY *Hamilton, State of Ohio*   OFFICE FILE NO. *103*

PARTIES	NATURE OF CASE
Dependable Motors, Inc *1401 Reading Road* *City*	ACTION *Lawsuit*
	AMOUNT *Minimum fee, $110.00 with costs*
vs. PLAINTIFF	
George Maher	ATTORNEYS FOR PLAINTIFF
	ATTORNEYS FOR DEFENDANT
DEFENDANT	

DATE	PROCEEDINGS IN CAUSE AND DISPOSITION OF CASE
Dec 9	*Suit filed*

DATE OF JUDGMENT   AMOUNT $

DATE	DESCRIPTION	✓	CHARGES	DATE	DESCRIPTION	✓	CREDITS
Dec 4	*Case Received*	✓	110.00	*Dec 4*	*Retainer*	*cg*	50.00
9	*Suit Fee*	*pc*	3.00	*Jan 2*	*In full*	*cg*	63.00

Lawyers' Case Docket

Lawyers' Collection Docket.   Lawyers who handle collections for clients usually use a form known as a *collection docket* to maintain a record of the essential data pertaining to collections. A model filled-in copy of a collection docket is reproduced on page 243. This docket provides a history of the case of The H. & S. Pogue Co., creditor, vs. S. L. Hale, debtor. It also provides a record of the amounts collected from the debtor and the amounts paid to the creditor.

Lawyers take most collection cases on a percentage basis. The charges for collection services are thus based on the collections actually made. Since a lawyer's only compensation for making collections usually is a percentage of the amount collected, any expenses incurred in making collections should be charged to the usual expense accounts of the lawyer and not to the client. However, if a client has agreed to stand any expenses incident to a law suit, such as court costs, the amounts paid by the lawyer should be charged to the client's account just the same as amounts advanced on behalf of clients in handling other legal cases.

In the illustration the following transactions are shown recorded on the collection docket for The H. & S. Pogue Co.:

January 6. Collected $40 from S. L. Hale, debtor.
January 9. Collected $90 from S. L. Hale, debtor.
January 13. Paid $97.50 to The H. & S. Pogue Co., creditor.

The amounts received from the creditor in payment of the lawyer's commission is also recorded on the collection docket. Since his commission of 25 per cent was actually deducted from the amounts collected from the debtor, it will be noted that the amounts deducted are entered as follows:

January 6. $10.
January 9. $22.50.

Work at the Close of the Fiscal Period.   The work required at the close of the fiscal period in keeping the accounts for a personal service enterprise is similar to that required for any other enterprise. The accounts should be analyzed and any required adjustments made. An income statement and a balance sheet should be prepared. The temporary accounts should be closed. A work sheet is an aid in compiling and classifying the information needed in preparing the financial statements and in drafting the adjusting and closing entries.

A Work Sheet for a Personal Service Enterprise.   The work sheet reproduced on page 245 is based on the accounts of J. C. Allen, an attorney

LAWYERS' COLLECTION DOCKET   No. 51

DEBTOR *S. L. Hale*

ADDRESS *1642 Paxton Road, City*

BUSINESS

CREDITOR *The H. & S. Pogue Co.*

ADDRESS *Fourth and Race Streets, City*

REC'D CLAIM FROM

ATTORNEY FOR DEBTOR

CALLS ON DEBTOR

CORRESPONDENCE

DATE CLAIM REC'D *Dec. 6* 19—

DATE DISPOSED OF *Jan. 14* 19—

TOTAL AMOUNT $ *130.00*

AMOUNT COLLECTED $ *130.00*

FEES $ *32.50*

EXPENSE $

AMOUNT REMITTED $ *97.50*

CHECK NO. *231*

RECEIVED FROM CREDITOR

DATE	FOR	AMOUNT
Jan. 6—	*Com.*	*10.00*
Jan. 9—	*Com.*	*22.50*

RECEIVED FROM DEBTOR				PAID TO CREDITOR			
DATE	AMOUNT	DATE	AMOUNT	CHECK NO.	AMOUNT	CHECK NO.	AMOUNT
Jan. 6—	*40.00*			*231*	*97.50*		
9—	*90.00*						

REMARKS: *Statement of account. Collection fee, 25%. No suit without further instructions.*

Lawyers' Collection Docket

at law. His accounts are kept on the cash basis and the work sheet reflects the results of operations for the year ended December 31. It will be noted that the form of this work sheet is the same as the work sheet for a mercantile enterprise reproduced on pages 192 and 193. Mr. Allen's trial balance as of December 31 was copied in the first pair of amount columns.

The required adjustments of certain account balances were entered in the second pair of amount columns. When the accounts are kept on the cash basis, few adjustments are required; usually, however, it is necessary to make adjustment for the amount of depreciation sustained during the period. Other adjustments may also be necessary.

In preparing the work sheet for Mr. Allen, the only adjustments required were those needed to record the amount of depreciation sustained during the accounting period. He estimated that he had sustained depreciation as follows:

(a) Office equipment, 10 per cent a year.
(b) Law library, 5 per cent a year.
(c) Automobile, 25 per cent a year.

These rates indicate that Mr. Allen estimated that his office equipment had a useful life of ten years, his law library twenty years, and his automobile four years. He had also ascertained that he would be permitted to claim such depreciation as an allowable deduction in his income tax return for each year during the life of the property.

The basis for computing the depreciation is the original cost of the assets. The calculations were as follows:

Office Equipment, 10% of $1,600	$ 160.00
Law Library, 5% of $2,000	100.00
Automobile, 25% of $3,200	800.00
Total Depreciation	$1,060.00

The depreciation was recorded on the work sheet by debiting Depreciation Expense for $1,060, and by crediting Allowance for Depreciation of Office Equipment for $160, Allowance for Depreciation of Law Library for $100, and Allowance for Depreciation of Automobile for $800.

After entering the required adjustments on the work sheet and proving the footings, the adjusted account balances were extended to the Adjusted Trial Balance columns. After proving the footings of the Adjusted Trial Balance columns, the account balances were classified by extending the balance of each account to the proper column. The net income for the period was then ascertained by footing the Income Statement columns

J. C. Allen, Attorney at Law
Work Sheet for Year Ended December 31, 19—

Accounts	Acct. No.	Trial Balance Dr.	Trial Balance Cr.	Adjustments Debits	Adjustments Credits	Adj. Trial Balance Dr.	Adj. Trial Balance Cr.	Income Statement Dr.	Income Statement Cr.	Balance Sheet Dr.	Balance Sheet Cr.
First National Bank	11	2607 38				2607 38				2607 38	
Petty Cash Fund	12	50 00				50 00				50 00	
Advances on Behalf of Clients	14	8 00				8 00				8 00	
Office Equipment	16	1600 00				1600 00				1600 00	
Allow. for Depr. of Office Equip.	016		420 00		160 00		580 00				580 00
Law Library	17	2000 00				2000 00				2000 00	
Allow. for Depr. of Law Library	017		400 00		100 00		500 00				500 00
Automobile	18	3200 00				3200 00				3200 00	
Allow. for Depr. of Automobile	018		1200 00		800 00		2000 00				2000 00
Accounts Payable	21		50 00				50 00				50 00
Employees Income Tax Pay.	22		57 60				57 60				57 60
F.I.C.A. Taxes Payable	23		14 40				14 40				14 40
J. C. Allen, Proprietor	31		3441 98				3441 98				3441 98
J. C. Allen, Drawing	32	4826 50				4826 50				4826 50	
Legal Fees	411		12841 75				12841 75		12841 75		
Collection Fees	412		576 30				576 30		576 30		
Rent Expense	511	1080 00				1080 00		1080 00			
Telephone & Telegraph Exp.	512	64 75				64 75		64 75			
Salaries	513	2880 00				2880 00		2880 00			
Social Security Taxes	514	57 60				57 60		57 60			
Stationery and Supplies	515	232 65				232 65		232 65			
Depreciation Expense	516			1060 00		1060 00		1060 00			
Automobile Expenses	517	251 28				251 28		251 28			
Charitable Contributions	518	42 00				42 00		42 00			
Miscellaneous Expenses	519	101 87				101 87		101 87			
		19002 03	19002 03	1060 00	1060 00	20062 03	20062 03	5770 15	13418 05	14291 88	6643 98
Net Income								7647 90			7647 90
								13418 05	13418 05	14291 88	14291 88

and by ascertaining the difference between the footings. This difference amounted to $7,647.90. The Balance Sheet columns were then footed and the difference ascertained. This difference, amounting to $7,647.90, represents the net increase in proprietorship due to net income for the period. When the work sheet is correctly prepared, the difference between the footings of the Balance Sheet columns will always be the same as the difference between the footings of the Income Statement columns.

The Financial Statements of a Personal Service Enterprise. The proprietor of a personal service enterprise wants periodic income statements and balance sheets for the same reasons as the owner of a mercantile business. An income statement for J. C. Allen's law practice for the year ended December 31 is reproduced below and a balance sheet as of December 31 on page 247. Both statements are in report form. The source of the information needed in preparing the statements was the end-of-period work sheet.

Adjusting Entries for a Personal Service Enterprise. To bring the ledger accounts into agreement with the financial statements, any adjusting entries made on the work sheet should be journalized and posted to the proper accounts. Reference to Mr. Allen's work sheet on page 245 reveals that adjustments were made for the estimated depreciation sustained on office equipment, law library, and automobile. The adjusting journal entry to record this depreciation was made in the combined cash-journal as shown

J. C. ALLEN, ATTORNEY AT LAW

INCOME STATEMENT

FOR YEAR ENDED DECEMBER 31, 19--

Professional Income:

Legal Fees	$12,841.75	
Collection Fees	576.30	
Total Professional Income		$13,418.05

Professional Expenses:

Rent Expense	$ 1,080.00	
Telephone and Telegraph Expense	64.75	
Salaries	2,880.00	
Social Security Taxes	57.60	
Stationery and Supplies	232.65	
Depreciation Expense	1,060.00	
Automobile Expenses	251.28	
Charitable Contributions	42.00	
Miscellaneous Expenses	101.87	
Total Professional Expenses		5,770.15
Net Income		$ 7,647.90

Model Income Statement for a Professional Enterprise

```
                    J. C. ALLEN, ATTORNEY AT LAW
                            BALANCE SHEET
                          DECEMBER 31, 19--
                               ASSETS
```

Current Assets:			
Cash		$2,657.38	
Advances on Behalf of Clients		8.00	
Total Current Assets			$2,665.38
Fixed Assets:			
Office Equipment	$1,600.00		
Less Allowance for Depreciation	580.00	$1,020.00	
Law Library	$2,000.00		
Less Allowance for Depreciation	500.00	1,500.00	
Automobile	$3,200.00		
Less Allowance for Depreciation	2,000.00	1,200.00	
Total Fixed Assets			3,720.00
Total Assets			$6,385.38

```
                            LIABILITIES
```

Current Liabilities:			
Accounts Payable		$ 50.00	
Employees' Income Taxes Payable		57.60	
F.I.C.A. Taxes Payable		14.40	
Total Current Liabilities			$ 122.00

```
                          PROPRIETORSHIP
```

J. C. Allen, Proprietor			
Proprietorship, January 1		$3,441.98	
Net Income	$7,647.90		
Less Withdrawals	4,826.50	2,821.40	
Proprietorship, December 31			6,263.38
Total Liabilities and Proprietorship			$6,385.38

Model Balance Sheet for a Professional Enterprise

on page 248. It will be noted that only the General Dr. and Cr. amount columns were used. The adjusting entries were posted individually to the proper general ledger accounts. As the posting was completed the account numbers were entered in the Posting Reference column of the journal and the journal page was entered in the Folio column of the ledger to provide a proper cross reference. After posting the adjusting entries, the balances of the allowance for depreciation accounts were the same as the balances shown in the Balance Sheet columns of the work sheet and in the balance sheet. The balance of the depreciation expense account was the same as the balance shown in the Income Statement columns of the work sheet and in the income statement.

Closing Entries for a Personal Service Enterprise. To close the temporary proprietorship accounts of Mr. Allen, it was necessary to transfer the balance of each account to an income summary account. This was done by means of journal entries in the combined cash-journal as illustrated below. It will be noted that after closing the income and the expense accounts into Income Summary, the balance of the income summary account was closed into J. C. Allen's permanent proprietorship account. The balance of Mr. Allen's drawing account was also closed into his permanent proprietorship account. The work sheet was the source of the information needed in drafting the closing journal entries. The closing entries were posted individually to the proper general ledger accounts.

COMBINED CASH-JOURNAL FOR MONTH OF *December* 19–

DATE MO.	DAY	DESCRIPTION	POST. REF.	GENERAL DEBITS	GENERAL CREDITS
		AMOUNTS FORWARDED			
Dec. 31		Adjusting Entries			
		Depreciation Expense	516	1 0 6 0 00	
		Allow. for Depr. - Office Equip.	016		1 6 0 00
		Allow. for Depr. - Law Library	017		1 0 0 00
		Allow. for Depr. - Automobile	018		8 0 0 00
	31	Closing Entries			
		Legal Fees	411	1 2 8 4 1 75	
		Collection Fees	412	5 7 6 30	
		Income Summary	33		1 3 4 1 8 05
		Income Summary	33	5 7 7 0 15	
		Rent Expense	511		1 0 8 0 00
		Tel. and Tel. Expense	512		6 4 75
		Salaries	513		2 8 8 0 00
		Social Security Taxes	514		5 7 60
		Stationery and Supplies	515		2 3 2 65
		Depreciation Expense	516		1 0 6 0 00
		Automobile Expenses	517		2 5 1 28
		Charitable Contributions	518		4 2 00
		Misc. Expenses	519		1 0 1 87
		Income Summary	33	7 6 4 7 90	
		J. C. Allen, Proprietor	31		7 6 4 7 90
		J. C. Allen, Proprietor	31	4 8 2 6 50	
		J. C. Allen, Drawing	32	3 1 6 6 2 60	3 1 6 6 2 60

Adjusting and Closing Entries

In posting to the income summary account the accounts being closed were identified in the following manner:

INCOME SUMMARY			Account No. 33
19—		19—	
Dec. 31 Rent Expense	1,080.00	Dec. 31 Legal Fees	12,841.75
31 Tel. & Tel. Expense	64.75	31 Collection Fees	576.30
31 Salaries	2,880.00		*13,418.05*
31 Social Security Taxes	57.60		
31 Stationery & Supplies	232.65		
31 Depreciation Expense	1,060.00		
31 Automobile Expenses	251.28		
31 Charitable Contributions	42.00		
31 Misc. Expenses	101.87		
31 J. C. Allen, Prop.	7,647.90		
	13,418.05		
	13,418.05		13,418.05

As the posting was completed the account numbers were entered in the Posting Reference column of the journal and the journal page was entered in the Folio column of the ledger to provide a proper cross reference. After posting the closing entries all of Mr. Allen's temporary proprietorship accounts were in balance and the balance of his permanent proprietorship account represented the net worth of his legal practice as of the close of the year.

Post-Closing Trial Balance. After posting the closing entries, it is advisable to take a post-closing trial balance to prove the equality of the debit and credit balances. The post-closing trial balance of Mr. Allen's ledger follows:

J. C. ALLEN, ATTORNEY AT LAW
POST-CLOSING TRIAL BALANCE
DECEMBER 31, 19--

First National Bank	$2,607.38	
Petty Cash Fund	50.00	
Advances on Behalf of Clients	8.00	
Office Equipment	1,600.00	
Allowance for Depreciation of Office Equipment		$ 580.00
Law Library	2,000.00	
Allowance for Depreciation of Law Library		500.00
Automobile	3,200.00	
Allowance for Depreciation of Automobile		2,000.00
Accounts Payable		50.00
Employees' Income Taxes Payable		57.60
F.I.C.A. Taxes Payable		14.40
J. C. Allen, Proprietor		6,263.38
	$9,465.38	$9,465.38

Accounting for Investments. The proprietor of any type of business or professional practice may make investments in real or personal property. Surplus funds may be invested in real estate or in securities, such as stocks and bonds. Under a savings program, a regular amount may be invested periodically in U. S. Savings Bonds. It is necessary to keep an adequate record of all investments. The income earned and the expenses incurred should be properly recorded. It is also necessary to record any gain or loss resulting from the sale of any property held as an investment. Such records can be kept entirely independent of the proprietor's main business or professional practice. However, it is not uncommon for a proprietor to expand the records of his regular business or profession to include his investment activities. This is often done as a matter of convenience. The proprietor may have a full-time or a part-time bookkeeper for his regular business or profession. If a record of his investments is made a part of his regular business records and is kept by a competent bookkeeper, it is likely to be more complete and accurate. No great problem is involved in adding whatever accounts are needed to provide a record of the assets, liabilities, income, and expenses relating to any investment activities. Any needed auxiliary records can be maintained. The items in the financial statements — particularly the income statement — can be appropriately classified so as to distinguish between the amounts that relate to the main business and those that relate to the investment activities of the proprietor.

Accounting for Investments in Real Property. Real estate, sometimes called *real property*, includes land, whether laid out in town lots or otherwise, buildings, structures, improvements, and fixtures of whatever kind thereon, and all rights and privileges belonging or appertaining thereto. Real estate may consist of either city property or farm property.

In accounting for the cost of real property, it is advisable to keep separate accounts for the land and the buildings because the land is not subject to depreciation. When real property is acquired, the total cost should be allocated between the land and the buildings. For example, if apartment property is purchased as an investment at a cost of $75,000, the cost should be allocated between the lot and the building on a reasonable basis. The lot might be valued at $5,000 and the building at $70,000. It is necessary to take into consideration the depreciation sustained on buildings in computing the gain or loss resulting from a sale or an exchange of the property.

Land. When land is purchased as an investment, whether it be city lots, farm land, or undeveloped land, a land account should be debited for the cost. The usual plan is to open an account for such land with a title that is descriptive of the land in respect to its location. For example, the title of an account representing a city lot might be "Lot No. 10, Observatory Subdivision." After the account is debited for the original cost of the land, it should be debited for any additional expenditures constituting improvements, such as the cost of assessments for sidewalks, streets, sewers, highways, or other permanent improvements that tend to enhance the value of the land.

Example: Dr. A. C. Dolan purchased Lot No. 14 in Fairview Subdivision as an investment, paying $4,000 cash for it. Subsequently expenditures for improvements were made as follows:

Assessment for paving street..................................	$1,000.00
Assessment for sidewalk.....................................	200.00
Assessment for sewer.......................................	100.00

All of the costs incurred are shown recorded in the following "T" account:

LOT NO. 14, FAIRVIEW SUBDIVISION

Cost	4,000.00
Street assessment	1,000.00
Sidewalk "	200.00
Sewer "	100.00

When such land is sold, the account should be credited for the total cost including the original cost and subsequent expenditures for improvements. Any gain resulting from the sale should be recorded in a separate account entitled Gain from Sale of Fairview Property. Any loss resulting from the sale should be recorded in a separate account entitled Loss from Sale of Fairview Property. The land account will then be in balance after the sale is recorded.

Buildings. Accounting for buildings is somewhat more complicated than accounting for land, although the general principles are the same. When real property is acquired through purchase, the value allocated to any buildings located on the land should be recorded in separate accounts. Thus, in the case of city property it may be necessary to keep separate accounts with the lot, the residence, and the garage (if the garage is separate from the residence). In the case of farm property it may be necessary to keep separate accounts with the land, the house, the barn, and other buildings.

If any loss is sustained that is deductible for income tax purposes, the amount of that loss must be ascertained. Unless the cost of real property is allocated separately to the land and the buildings at the time of purchase and separate accounts are maintained with each, it may be difficult subsequently to arrive at the information needed in (a) computing the gain or the loss derived from the sale or exchange of each type of property, or (b) determining, either for the purpose of an insurance settlement or for income tax purposes, the amount of a fire loss sustained.

Another important reason for keeping separate accounts with different buildings is that the type of construction largely determines the rate of depreciation. Obviously, a frame building may depreciate more rapidly than one of brick, concrete, or metal construction.

When buildings are used for business purposes or are held for investment purposes, the depreciation sustained on such buildings is a business expense and is an allowable deduction for income tax purposes.

Example: Dr. Dolan had an apartment building constructed on Lot No. 14, Fairview Subdivision at a total cost of $24,000. Dr. Dolan borrowed $10,000, giving a mortgage on the land and building as security. The building was estimated to have a useful life of forty years; hence, each year Dr. Dolan charged off depreciation at the rate of $2\frac{1}{2}$ per cent, recording the depreciation by debiting an account entitled Depreciation of Fairview Apartment Building and by crediting an account entitled Allowance for Depreciation of Fairview Apartment Building for $600. After depreciation had been charged off for three years, the building and the allowance accounts appeared on his ledger as shown in the following "T" accounts:

FAIRVIEW APARTMENT BUILDING

24,000.00	

ALLOWANCE FOR DEPRECIATION OF FAIRVIEW APARTMENT BUILDING

	Depr. first year	600.00
	Depr. second year	600.00
	Depr. third year	600.00

Real Property Income. When real property is held as an investment and income is derived from rentals, a separate account should be kept for recording the rent received. If other income is received from such property, it should be recorded in separate accounts. For example, if income is derived from advertising privileges, such as billboards erected on the property, a separate account of such income should be kept.

Real Property Expenses. A separate account should be kept for each type of expense sustained in connection with the ownership of real property. In accounting for real property expenses, such as taxes, insurance, depreciation, repairs, and interest on money borrowed to purchase the property, it is necessary to consider the purpose for which the property was purchased or is used. Certain expenses, such as insurance premiums, repairs, and depreciation, are deductible in computing net income for the purpose of the income tax when they apply to property purchased for investment purposes or property owned for business purposes. On the other hand, such expenses are not deductible when they apply to property used by a taxpayer for residential purposes. The purpose for which property is acquired determines whether or not certain expenses represent business expenses or personal expenses.

Net Income from Real Estate Investment. If the proper accounts have been kept, a summary of the income and expenses connected with the ownership of the property can be prepared at the end of each year in the following manner:

INVESTMENT INCOME — FAIRVIEW APARTMENT PROPERTY

Rent income...		$3,600.00
Operating expenses:		
Depreciation.....................................	$600.00	
Repairs..	100.00	
Taxes..	500.00	
Insurance..	60.00	
Interest on mortgage.............................	500.00	
Wages of caretaker...............................	480.00	
Gas and electricity...............................	400.00	
Total Operating Expenses.........................		2,640.00
Net income — Fairview apartment property............		$ 960.00

If the foregoing summary is included in the regular income statement of Dr. Dolan, it should be inserted immediately following the net income from his profession. Thus, his investment income will be shown separately from his professional income.

At the end of each year the income and expense accounts relating to the property should be closed into a specific income summary account for such property. For example, the income and expense accounts relating to the Fairview Apartment Property owned by Dr. Dolan may be closed by means of the journal entry shown at the top of the following page.

Rent Income — Fairview Apartment Property..........	$3,600.00	
Depreciation of Fairview Apartment Building.........		$600.00
Repairs to Fairview Apartment Building.............		100.00
Taxes on Fairview Apartment Property..............		500.00
Insurance on Fairview Apartment Property...........		60.00
Interest on Mortgage — Fairview Apartment Property.		500.00
Wages of Caretaker—Fairview Apartment Property...		480.00
Gas and Electricity — Fairview Apartment Building...		400.00
Income Summary — Fairview Apartment Property....		960.00

In posting the closing entry to the income summary account, it is good policy to identify the accounts being closed by itemizing them in the income summary account in the following manner:

INCOME SUMMARY — FAIRVIEW APARTMENT PROPERTY

Depreciation	600.00	Rent Income	3,600.00
Repairs	100.00		*960.00*
Taxes	500.00		
Insurance	60.00		
Interest on Mortgage	500.00		
Wages of Caretaker	480.00		
Gas and Electricity	400.00		
	2,640.00		

The Fairview Apartment Property income summary account should be closed by transferring its balance to the regular income summary account.

Accounting for the Sale of Real Property. When real property is sold, all accounts pertaining to it should be closed and the gain or loss on the sale should be recorded. Suppose, for example, that after having owned the apartment house for three years, Dr. Dolan sold it for $32,500. The purchaser assumed (took over) the mortgage, amounting to $10,000, and paid Dr. Dolan $22,500 cash. The total cost of the land was $5,300 and the book value of the apartment building was $22,200 ($24,000 − $1,800). Thus, the gain on the sale was $5,000 ($32,500 − $5,300 − $22,200). The sale should be recorded as indicated by the following journal entry:

Cash	$22,500.00	
Mortgage Payable....................	10,000.00	
Allowance for Depreciation of Apartment Building......	1,800.00	
Lot No. 14, Fairview Subdivision....................		$ 5,300.00
Fairview Apartment Building......................		24,000.00
Gain on Sale of Fairview Property..................		5,000.00
Sold Fairview apartment property.		

Any gain or loss realized from the sale of real property should be recorded in a separate account. Such gain or loss represents capital gain or capital loss which should be reported separately for income tax purposes. Following the sale of real property held as an investment, the temporary accounts that relate to the property may be closed into a specific summary account without waiting until the end of the year. Such summary account should be given a title that identifies it with the property. At the end of the year, this special summary account should be closed by transferring its balance to the regular summary account.

Accounting for Investments in Securities. Securities purchased for investment purposes may include bonds and stocks. Income may be derived from the interest received on bonds or from the dividends received on stocks.

Bonds. Bonds may be divided into two general classes: namely, public bonds and corporation bonds. Public bonds are those issued by some government or government agency. Traditionally, only the obligations of the Federal government are called "government" bonds even though obligations of states, counties, cities, and other jurisdictions logically deserve to be considered as government bonds. The major obligations of the Federal government are U. S. Savings Bonds, U. S. Treasury Bonds, and U. S. Treasury Notes. From time to time, Congress authorizes various federal agencies and authorities to issue bonds. State bonds are obligations of the respective states. Municipal bonds are obligations of the respective municipalities. Bonds are issued by other subdivisions of states also, including school districts, conservancy districts, counties, and townships. All such bonds are considered public bonds.

Private corporations may issue bonds as a means of borrowing money. Corporation bonds may be secured by a mortgage on specific assets of the corporation. Many different types of corporation bonds are issued.

The accounting procedure in recording bonds purchased for investment purposes is the same with all types of bonds. To illustrate the accounting procedure in recording bonds purchased as an investment and held for income purposes, U. S. Savings Bonds, U. S. Treasury Bonds, and corporation bonds will be considered.

U. S. Savings Bonds. Since 1935 the Federal government has been issuing savings bonds. These bonds are of two general types. The non-interest-bearing bonds that are issued at a discount and are redeemable, at the option of the owner, at increasing fixed values are known as *appreciation bonds*. The interest-bearing bonds that are issued at par value and are redeemable, at the option of the owner, at fixed redemption values are known as *current income bonds*. Currently Series E, H, J, and K Bonds are being issued. The Series E and J Bonds are appreciation bonds; the H and K Bonds are current income bonds.

The purchase of U. S. Savings Bonds of the Series E and J type should be recorded by debiting Government Bonds and by crediting Cash for the cost price. Thus, if a $1,000 Series E Bond is purchased at the issue price of $750, the transaction should be recorded as indicated in the following journal entry:

Government Bonds...............................	$750.00	
Cash..		$750.00
Purchased a $1,000 U. S. Savings Bond, Series E.		

The appreciation or increase in the value of Series E and J Bonds may, at the option of the owner, be treated either as current income or deferred income for income tax purposes. If the purchaser of Series E and J Bonds elects to treat the appreciation as current income, an entry should be made each year to record the amount of the increased value or increment resulting from the accumulation of interest. For example, the redemption value of a $1,000 Series E Bond at the end of the second year is $760, an increase of $10 over its original cost. This increase in the value of the bond should be recorded as indicated in the following journal entry:

Government Bonds...............................	$10.00	
Interest Income................................		$10.00
Increased redemption value of a $1,000 U. S. Savings Bond, Series E.		

Upon maturity, when all appreciation has been recorded, the total debits to the bond account should equal the maturity value of the bond. When the bond is redeemed, the transaction should be recorded by debiting Cash and by crediting Government Bonds for $1,000.

If the purchaser of a $1,000 Series E Bond for $750 prefers to treat the appreciation as deferred income, the appreciation need not be recorded until the bond is redeemed. If the bond is redeemed at maturity, the transaction should be recorded as indicated in the following journal entry:

Cash...	$1,000.00	
Government Bonds..............................		$750.00
Interest Income...............................		250.00
Redeemed a $1,000 U. S. Savings Bond, Series E.		

Treating the appreciation in Series E and J Bonds as current income is advantageous taxwise to many buyers because it results in a more uniform distribution of the income over the life of the bonds instead of treating the entire amount as income in the year in which the bonds are redeemed.

Since U. S. Savings Bonds of the Series H and K type are not issued at a discount, they cannot be purchased for less than their face value.

Thus, when a $1,000 Series H Bond is purchased, the transaction should be recorded by debiting Government Bonds and by crediting Cash for $1,000. The interest on these bonds is paid semiannually by U. S. Treasury checks, which are mailed direct to the registered owner. When such checks are received, they should be recorded by debiting Cash and by crediting Interest Income.

U. S. Treasury Bonds. U. S. Treasury Bonds may be subscribed for at the time of original issue or they may be purchased subsequently at the prevailing market price through banks and brokerage houses or from private holders. The accounting procedure in recording the purchase of these bonds differs only slightly from the procedure in recording U. S. Savings Bonds that are purchased at a discount. The face value of U. S. Treasury Bonds is constant, and the government pays the interest on the bonds at a fixed rate. The interest is payable semiannually. The bonds are issued in various denominations.

When U. S. Treasury Bonds are subscribed for and obtained at the original issue price, they should be recorded by debiting Government Bonds and by crediting Cash for the cost of the bonds. The cost will be the par value of the bonds, that is, the value specified on the face of the bonds.

When U. S. Treasury Bonds are purchased subsequent to date of issue, the transaction should be recorded similarly, that is, by debiting Government Bonds and by crediting Cash for the cost of the bonds. Because of market conditions, the cost may be more or less than the par value of the bonds. The quoted market prices of U. S. Treasury Bonds do not include either commission charges or accrued interest.

When the bonds are purchased through a bank or a brokerage firm, it will be necessary for the purchaser to pay a commission. The commission represents a part of the cost of the bonds and should be so recorded. If an individual purchases a U. S. Treasury $3\frac{1}{4}$ per cent, $1,000 Bond, to mature in 1983, at a total cost of $1,081.60, including the bank's or the broker's commission, the transaction should be recorded as indicated in the following journal entry:

Government Bonds...............................	$1,081.60	
Cash...		$1,081.60
Purchased a $1,000 U. S. Treasury Bond.		

The foregoing entry is based on the assumption that no interest had accrued on the bond at the time of purchase. If interest amounting to

$7.53 had accrued, the total cost would be increased proportionately and the transaction should be recorded as indicated in the following journal entry:

Government Bonds...............................	$1,081.60	
Interest Income...................................	7.53	
Cash...		$1,089.13
Purchased a $1,000 U. S. Treasury Bond.		

The amount charged to Interest Income represents the amount paid for the right to receive the interest already accrued on the bond at the time of purchase. By charging the accrued interest to Interest Income, that account will show the proper amount of income earned when it is credited later for the full amount of the interest collected.

Interest on U. S. Treasury Bonds, which is payable semiannually, should be recorded by debiting Cash and by crediting Interest Income for the amount of the interest received.

When a bond is sold prior to maturity or when it is redeemed upon maturity, the transaction should be recorded by debiting Cash for the proceeds received and by crediting Government Bonds for the cost of the bond. If the amount received for the bond is more than the original cost of the bond, the excess represents a profit that should be recorded by crediting Gain on Government Bonds. If the amount received for the bond is less than the original cost of the bond, the difference represents a loss that should be recorded by debiting Loss on Government Bonds.

If the U. S. Treasury Bond, referred to previously as having cost $1,081.60, were sold through a broker and the proceeds amounted to $1,124.50 after deducting the broker's commission, the transaction should be recorded as indicated in the following journal entry:

Cash..	$1,124.50	
Government Bonds.............................		$1,081.60
Gain on Government Bonds......................		42.90
Sold a $1,000 U. S. Treasury Bond.		

The foregoing entry is based on the assumption that no interest had accrued on the bond at the time of sale. If interest amounting to $9 had accrued at the time of sale, the selling price would be increased proportionately and the transaction should be recorded as indicated in the following journal entry:

Cash..	$1,133.50	
Interest Income.................................		$ 9.00
Government Bonds.............................		1,081.60
Gain on Government Bonds......................		42.90
Sold a $1,000 U. S. Treasury Bond.		

The additional amount received because of the interest accrued at the time of the sale is recorded as a credit to Interest Income. Any interest accrued prior to the sale of the bond represents earned income that is realized when the bond is sold. It should be understood that the broker's commission is treated as a deduction from the selling price of the bond and that only the net proceeds are recorded. The gain is the difference between the total cost and the net amount received from the sale of the bond, less any accrued interest.

Other Government Bonds. Government bonds may include bonds issued by the states or any of their subdivisions, such as counties, townships, municipalities, and school districts. Such bonds may be accounted for in the same manner as U. S. Treasury Bonds, that is, all such bonds may be charged to Government Bonds at cost at the time of purchase. When such bonds are sold prior to maturity or are redeemed at maturity, Government Bonds may be credited for the cost and any gain that is realized may be credited to Gain on Government Bonds or any loss sustained may be debited to Loss on Government Bonds.

Corporation Bonds. The purchase of bonds issued by private corporations should be recorded by debiting Corporation Bonds and by crediting Cash for the cost of the bonds. The cost is the purchase price regardless of whether the price paid is more or less than the par value or the face value of the bonds. If the bonds are purchased through a bank or a brokerage firm and a commission is paid, the commission should be treated as a part of the cost of the bonds.

Corporation bonds generally bear interest at a fixed rate payable annually or semiannually. When interest on corporation bonds is received, it should be recorded by debiting Cash and by crediting Interest Income for the amount of the interest received.

When a corporation bond is sold prior to maturity or is redeemed at maturity and the net amount received is greater than the cost, the transaction should be recorded by debiting Cash for the net amount received and by crediting (a) Corporation Bonds for the cost of the bonds and (b) Gain on Corporation Bonds for the difference between the cost and the proceeds of the sale.

When a corporation bond is sold prior to maturity or is redeemed at maturity and the net amount received is less than the cost, the transaction should be recorded by debiting (a) Cash for the net amount received and (b) Loss on Corporation Bonds for the difference between the cost and the proceeds of the sale, and by crediting Corporation Bonds for the cost of the bonds.

If the bonds are sold through a bank or a brokerage firm and a commission is paid, the commission should be treated as a deduction from the selling price and the net proceeds only should be recorded.

Example: January 15—Purchased a 4 per cent, $1,000 Union Terminal Company Bond through a broker and paid a total of $1,072.25, including the broker's commission.

July 15 — Sold the Union Terminal Company Bond purchased on January 15 through a brokerage firm and received a check for the net proceeds amounting to $1,125.18.

The foregoing transactions should be recorded as indicated in the following journal entries:

```
Jan. 15.  Corporation Bonds.......................   $1,072.25
              Cash...................................              $1,072.25
                  Purchased a $1,000 Union Terminal Com-
                  pany Bond.
July 15.  Cash....................................    1,125.18
              Corporation Bonds......................              1,072.25
              Gain on Corporation Bonds..............                  52.93
                  Sold a $1,000 Union Terminal Company
                  Bond.
```

The entries for the transactions of January 15 and July 15 assume that there was no interest accrued on the bond either at the time of the purchase or at the time of the sale. Any interest accrued on the bond at the time of purchase should be recorded by debiting Interest Income. The purchase price would be increased in proportion to the amount of the interest accrued; hence, the credit to Cash would be correspondingly increased. Any interest accrued at the time of the sale should be recorded by crediting Interest Income. The selling price would be increased in proportion to the amount of the interest accrued; hence, the debit to Cash would be correspondingly increased.

Corporation Stocks. The ownership of a private corporation is evidenced by certificates of stock, commonly known as capital stock. Shares of capital stock may be purchased as an investment. There are two principal classes of capital stock, known as common stock and preferred stock. The *common stock* of a corporation is stock that has no preference as to dividends or to assets in the event of the liquidation of the corporation. The *preferred stock* of a corporation is stock that has a preferred or prior claim on either dividends or on assets in the event of liquidation. Some preferred stock issues have both types of preference. In considering the relative merits of common stock and preferred stock, careful consideration should be given to all of the factors involved. While preferred stock is generally considered to be a more conservative investment than common stock, it may not, in a particular case, be a better investment than the common stock of the same company. The mere designation of stock as preferred does not necessarily indicate that it is more desirable than common stock.

Capital stock, whether common or preferred, may or may not have a designated par value. If capital stock has par value, the value will be stated on the stock certificate; if it has no par value, that fact will be stated on the stock certificate.

If a corporation has the authority to issue 100 shares of common capital stock with par value of $100 per share and all of the stock is sold at its par value, the corporation's capital will amount to $10,000. The owner of each share of stock will actually own 1/100 of the corporation, and the owner of 10 shares of stock will own 1/10 of the corporation.

The par value of capital stock should not be confused with its market value, as these values may differ materially. The par value is the stated value expressed on the stock certificate, while the market value is the price at which the stock may be purchased or sold in the open market. Investors are primarily interested in the market value of the share of capital stock that they may own or may desire to purchase.

Interest is not paid on capital stock. Income from capital stock is derived from dividends received rather than from interest received. In this respect capital stock differs materially from bonds that may be issued by the same corporation. The fact should not be overlooked that the ownership of capital stock represents direct ownership of a portion of the issuing corporation. On the other hand, the ownership of bonds puts the bondholder in the position of a creditor who has loaned money to the issuing corporation and who has received in return the promise of the corporation to redeem its bonds at a specified date and to pay, in the meantime, a specified rate of interest on the bonds.

When capital stock is purchased as an investment, it may be recorded by debiting an investment account entitled Corporation Stocks and by crediting Cash for the amount paid for the stock. If desired, a separate account may be kept for each company's stock purchased. For example, if an investor should purchase common stock of the General Motors Corporation, he might open a separate account for the stock under the title of General Motors Corporation Common Stock. If he also invested money in the common stock of the U. S. Steel Corporation, he might open an additional account for that stock under the title of U. S. Steel

Corporation Common Stock. The usual plan, however, is to keep a summary account only entitled Corporation Stocks for all capital stock purchased for investment purposes. Such a summary account should be debited at the time of purchase for the cost price of capital stock bought, and should be credited at the time of sale for the cost price of capital stock sold. If the stock is sold at a profit, the profit may be recorded by crediting a separate account entitled Gain on Corporation Stocks. If the stock is sold at a loss, the loss may be recorded by debiting an account entitled Loss on Corporation Stocks.

If an individual purchases 100 shares of the common stock of the Master Motors Corporation through a brokerage company at a total cost of $4,950 and pays cash for it, the transaction may be recorded as indicated in the following journal entry:

Corporation Stocks...............................	$8,950.00	
Cash..		$8,950.00
Purchased 100 shares of Master Motors common stock.		

If a dividend amounting to $1 per share is received while the stock is owned, the transaction may be recorded as indicated in the following journal entry:

Cash...	$100.00	
Dividends Received.................................		$100.00
Dividends received on 100 shares of Master Motors common stock.		

If the stock is subsequently sold and the net proceeds of the sale amount to $9,150, the transaction may be recorded as indicated in the following journal entry:

Cash..	$9,150.00	
Corporation Stocks.............................		$8,950.00
Gain on Corporation Stocks......................		200.00
Sold 100 shares of Master Motors common stock.		

Record of Stocks and Bonds. When investments in securities, such as bonds and capital stock, are sufficiently numerous to justify keeping a detailed record of them, special forms similar to the one reproduced on page 263 may be used for this purpose. Such forms are produced by the leading manufacturers of loose-leaf forms and may usually be obtained through local stationery stores. The forms are so designed that all necessary information may be recorded conveniently thereon. A separate sheet should be used for keeping a record of each bond and of each stock certificate owned. A description of the bond or stock certificate, together

RECORD OF STOCKS AND BONDS

NAME *U. S. Treasury Bond*

DESCRIPTION *#40019 K*

DATE OF ISSUE *June 15, 1944* DATE OF MATURITY *June 15, 1969* INTEREST OR DIVIDEND *2½* PAYABLE *J & D* SEMI-ANNUALLY ✔

DENOMINATION *$1,000.00*

DATE 19__	OF WHOM PURCHASED	DATE 19__	SOLD TO	CERTIFICATE OR BOND NOS.	MATURITY	PAR VALUE	PRICE PAID	TOTAL COST	SOLD FOR	INTEREST OR DIVIDENDS EARNED	LOSS OR GAIN
June	Subscription			40019 K	6/15/69	1,000	1,000	1000 00			

with information regarding its purchase and sale, may be recorded on the front of the form as shown in the illustration. The back of the form is ruled to facilitate recording interest or dividends received during the period of ownership.

This type of record is usually regarded as an auxiliary or memorandum record, and the information recorded on it is supplementary to the information recorded in the regular books of account.

Exhibiting Investment Income in the Income Statement. As explained on page 253, a summary of the income and expenses connected with real property owned as an investment should be shown separately in the income statement following the net income derived from a business or profession. Other investment income derived from the ownership of securities, such as stocks and bonds, should also be shown separately in the income statement. For example, if an attorney has investments in both apartment property and securities and the accounts for such investments are kept in the same books as the accounts for his profession, his income statement should be arranged so as to show, first, the net professional income, second, the net income from the apartment property, third, the income from other investments, such as interest income and dividends received, and finally, the total net income.

Income and Self-Employment Taxes. The discussion of accounting for the income and expenses of a business enterprise in this and the previous units has included frequent references to income tax considerations. It is important to note that an unincorporated business owned by one person is not taxed. The proprietor — not the business — is subject to income taxes. He, of course, must report the amounts of business income and expenses in his personal tax return regardless of the amount of money or other property he has actually withdrawn from the business during the year. As mentioned earlier, in the case of a sole proprietorship, there is no legal distinction between the business and the proprietor.

In order to bring a large class of self-employed individuals into the federal social security program, the law requires all self-employed persons (except those specifically exempted) to pay a self-employment tax. The current rate is 3 per cent of the "self-employment income" up to a maximum of $4,200. The rate and base of the tax may be changed by Act of Congress at any time. In general, *self-employment income* means the net income of a trade or business conducted by a single proprietor or a partner's distributive share of the net income of a partnership whether or not distributed. Earnings of less than $400 from self-employment is ignored.

A taxable year for the purpose of the tax on self-employment income is the same as the taxpayer's taxable year for federal income tax purposes. The self-employment tax is reported along with the regular federal income tax. For calendar-year taxpayers, the tax return and full or final payment is due on April 15 following the close of the year. Like the personal income tax, the self-employment tax is treated as a personal expense of the proprietor. If the taxes are paid with business funds, the amount should be charged to the proprietor's drawing account.

PRACTICE ASSIGNMENT No. 20. Complete Report No. 20 in the workbook and submit your working papers to the instructor for approval. You will then be given instructions as to the work to be done next.

PRACTICAL ACCOUNTING PROBLEMS

The problems in this unit are supplementary to those in the workbook. They are numbered to indicate the unit of the textbook with which they correlate. For example, Problems 1-A and 1-B correlate with Unit One. Loose-leaf stationery should be used in solving these problems. The paper required includes plain ruled paper, two-column, three-column, and four-column journal paper, cash-journal paper, ledger paper, and work sheet paper.

Problem 1-A

O. A. Sargent is a civil engineer. As of December 31 he owned the following property that related to his business: Cash, $619; office equipment, $1,000; and an automobile, $1,990. At the same time he owed business creditors $280.

REQUIRED: (a) On a basis of the foregoing information, compute the amount of the accounting elements and show them in equation form. (b) Assuming that during the ensuing year there is an increase in Mr. Sargent's business assets of $1,400 and a decrease in his business liabilities of $30, indicate the changes in the accounting elements by showing them in equation form after the changes have occurred.

Problem 1-B

J. B. Brown, a C.P.A. who has been employed by a large national firm of certified public accountants, decides to go into business for himself. His business transactions for the first month of operations were as follows:

(a) Mr. Brown invested $3,000 cash in the business.
(b) Paid office rent for one month, $80.
(c) Purchased office equipment from the City Supply Co., $1,560, on account.
(d) Paid telephone bill, $11.

(e) Received $450 for service rendered to the Green Grocery.

(f) Paid $500 to the City Supply Co. on account.

(g) Received $275 for services rendered to the Ajax Garage.

(h) Paid $225 salary to office secretary.

REQUIRED: (a) On a plain sheet of paper rule eight "T" accounts and enter the following titles: Cash, Office Equipment, Accounts Payable, J. B. Brown, Proprietor, Income from Professional Fees, Rent Expense, Telephone Expense, and Salary Expense. (b) Record the above transactions directly in the accounts. (c) Foot the accounts and enter the balances where necessary. (d) Prepare a trial balance of the accounts, using a sheet of two-column journal paper.

Problem 2-A

Following is a narrative of the transactions completed by P. G. Thomas, a consulting engineer, during the first month of his business operations:

Oct. 1. Mr. Thomas invested $2,000 cash in the business.
　1. Purchased office furniture and fixtures for $850 cash.
　2. Paid office rent, $95.
　3. Paid $13.65 for installation of telephone and for one month's service charge.
　4. Purchased stationery and supplies on account from Edwards Brothers, $165.42.
　5. Received $175 from The Progress Laundry for consulting services rendered.
　6. Paid $5 for subscription to a professional engineering magazine. (Charge Miscellaneous Expenses.)
　8. Received $60 from The Mill Supply Co. for professional services rendered.
　9. Paid $25 to Dr. W. J. Samuel, a dentist, for dental service performed for Mrs. Thomas.
　　　(NOTE: This is equivalent to a withdrawal of $25 by Mr. Thomas for personal use. Charge to his drawing account.)
　13. Paid $42.87 for a plane ticket for a business trip.
　15. Paid other traveling expenses, $35.90.
　19. Received $240 from Suburban Machine Co. for professional services rendered.
　20. Paid $165.42 to Edwards Brothers in full of account.
　31. Paid $200 monthly salary to secretary.

REQUIRED: Journalize the foregoing transactions, using a sheet of two-column journal paper. Number the pages and use both sides of the sheet, if necessary. Select the account titles from the following chart of accounts:

Chart of Accounts

Assets
  Cash
  Stationery and Supplies
  Furniture and Fixtures

Liabilities
  Accounts Payable

Proprietorship
  P. G. Thomas, Proprietor
  P. G. Thomas, Drawing

Income
  Income from Professional Fees

Expenses
  Rent Expense
  Telephone Expense
  Traveling Expenses
  Salary Expense
  Miscellaneous Expenses

After journalizing the transactions, prove the equality of the debits and credits by footing the amount columns. Enter the footings in pencil immediately under the line on which the last entry appears.

Problem 2-B

L. J. RADCLIFFE, CERTIFIED PUBLIC ACCOUNTANT

Trial Balance

June 30, 19 —

Cash	$ 912.43	
Office Equipment	475.00	
Automobile	1,800.00	
Accounts Payable		$ 231.23
L. J. Radcliffe, Proprietor		2,200.00
L. J. Radcliffe, Drawing	1,500.00	
Income from Professional Fees		3,400.00
Rent Expense	600.00	
Telephone Expense	72.50	
Electric Expense	50.00	
Automobile Expenses	197.20	
Miscellaneous Expenses	84.10	
Charitable Contributions	140.00	
	$5,831.23	$5,831.23

L. J. Radcliffe is a certified public accountant engaged in practice on his own account.

Narrative of Transactions for July

July 1. (Saturday) Paid one month's rent, $100.
   3. Paid electric bill, $7.50.
   3. Paid telephone bill, $7.10.
   5. Received $275 from United Dairy Farmers in payment of services rendered.
   7. Paid a garage bill, $21.25.
  10. Received $80 from the Vernon Manor Hotel in payment of services rendered.
  12. Paid Shillito's Department Store, $29.75. (Charge to Mr. Radcliffe's drawing account.)
  15. Mr. Radcliffe withdrew $125 for personal use.

July 17. Paid the Underwood Typewriter Co. $75 on account.
   19. Received $110 from Dot Food Stores in full for services rendered.
   24. Gave the American Red Cross $10.
   26. Paid the American Institute of Accountants $40 for annual member-
      ship dues.
   29. Received $47.50 from Master Motor Sales Co. in payment of profes-
      sional services.
   31. Mr. Radcliffe withdrew $90 for personal use.

REQUIRED: (a) Journalize the July transactions, using a sheet of two-
column journal paper. Number the pages and use both sides of the sheet,
if necessary. (b) Open the necessary accounts, using the standard account
form of ledger paper. Allow one page for each account and number the
accounts consecutively. Record the July 1 balances as shown in the June 30
trial balance and post the journal entries for July. (c) Foot the ledger
accounts, enter the balances, and prove the balances by taking a trial balance as of July 31. Use a sheet of two-column journal paper for the trial
balance.

Problem 2-C

THE K. S. ERWIN AGENCY

TRIAL BALANCE

January 31, 19 _ _

Cash...	$1,986.14	
Stationery and Supplies............................	256.67	
Office Furniture and Fixtures.......................	1,412.00	
Notes Payable.....................................		$ 600.00
Accounts Payable..................................		314.19
K. S. Erwin, Proprietor............................		2,653.86
K. S. Erwin, Drawing..............................	304.60	
Income from Professional Fees......................		972.18
Rent Expense......................................	125.00	
Telephone Expense.................................	18.16	
Salary Expense....................................	240.00	
Traveling Expenses................................	165.19	
Stationery and Supplies Used.......................	13.42	
Miscellaneous Expenses............................	19.05	
	$4,540.23	$4,540.23

REQUIRED: (a) Prepare an income statement for The K. S. Erwin Agency
showing the results of operations for the month of January. (b) Prepare
a balance sheet in account form showing the financial condition of the
agency as of January 31. Use a sheet of two-column journal paper for
the income statement. Two sheets of two-column journal paper may be
used for the balance sheet. List the assets on one sheet and the liabilities
and proprietorship on the other sheet.

Problem 3-A

Mrs. Helen Smith decides to open a dress shop under the name of Helen's Shop. The books of original entry include a purchases journal, a sales journal, and a two-column general journal. This problem involves the use of the purchases journal and the general journal only. The following selected transactions were completed during the month of October:

Oct.   1. Invested $4,500 in the business.

      2. Received Invoice No. 362 dated October 1 from Fashions, Inc. for merchandise purchased, $75.10. Terms, 30 days net.

      3. Received Invoice No. 363 dated October 1 from White Brothers for merchandise purchased, $182.14. Terms, 10 days net.

      5. Purchased a cash register for cash, $39.14. (Debit Furniture and Fixtures.)

      7. Received Invoice No. 364 dated October 4 from Stevens, Inc. for merchandise purchased, $89.06. Terms, 30 days net.

    10. Purchased merchandise for cash, $55.15.

    11. Received Invoice No. 365 dated October 8 from Fashions, Inc. for merchandise purchased, $131.16. Terms, 30 days net.

    12. Paid White Brothers $182.14 in full for Invoice No. 363 dated October 1.

    13. Returned defective merchandise to Fashions, Inc., $26.62.

    17. Received invoice dated October 15 from the National Store Furniture Co. for showcases purchased, $1,432.18. Terms, 15 days net.

    22. Received Invoice No. 366 dated October 18 from White Brothers for merchandise purchased, $247.86. Terms, 10 days net.

    25. Purchased merchandise for cash, $89.16.

    28. Received Invoice No. 367 dated October 26 from Kay Paul for merchandise purchased, $42.50. Terms, 30 days net.

Required: (a) Record each transaction in the proper journal using the following account titles:

Cash	Helen Smith, Proprietress
Furniture and Fixtures	Purchases
Accounts Payable	Purchases Returns and Allowances

For the purchases journal, use a sheet of paper ruled like that shown in the illustration on page 53. For the general journal, use a sheet of two-column journal paper. (b) Prove the general journal by footing the amount columns. Foot the purchases journal, enter the total, and rule. (c) Open the necessary accounts using the standard account form of ledger paper. Allow one page for each account and number the accounts consecutively. Post the purchases journal and general journal entries for October, foot the accounts, and enter the balances. (d) Take a trial balance as of October 31, using a sheet of two-column journal paper.

Problem 3-B

M. C. Clark decides to open a men's clothing store under the name of The Westvale Store. The books of original entry include a sales journal, a purchases journal, and a two-column general journal. This problem involves the use of the sales journal and general journal only. The following selected transactions were completed during the month of July:

July 1. Invested $6,750 in the business.
       2. Sold merchandise on account to A. M. Zeitlin, $16.50, tax 33 cents. Sale No. 104.
       5. Sold merchandise on account to D. F. Murray, $46.95, tax 94 cents. Sale No. 105.
       6. A. M. Zeitlin returned goods for credit. Sale price $5.10, tax 10 cents.
       9. Sold merchandise on account to C. J. Brown, $18.13, tax 36 cents. Sale No. 106.
      13. Received $11.63 from A. M. Zeitlin in payment of account.
      14. Sold merchandise on account to N. F. Franks, $22.05, tax 44 cents. Sale No. 107.
      19. A customer returned some merchandise purchased earlier in the day for cash. Sales price, $7.95, tax 16 cents.
      22. Received $18.49 from C. J. Brown in payment of account.
      26. Sold merchandise on account to Benson Davis, $13.50, tax 27 cents. Sale No. 108.
      28. Sold merchandise on account to D. F. Murray, $4.90, tax 10 cents. Sale No. 109.
      31. Total cash sales for month, $615.80, tax $12.32.

REQUIRED: (a) Record each transaction in the proper journal using the following account titles:

Cash	M. C. Clark, Proprietor
Accounts Receivable	Sales
Sales Tax Payable	Sales Returns and Allowances

For the sales journal, use a sheet of paper ruled like that shown in the illustration on page 62. For the general journal, use a sheet of two-column journal paper. (b) Prove the general journal by footing the amount columns. (c) Prove the sales journal by footing the amount columns and ascertaining that the totals of the debit and credit columns are equal in amount. Enter the totals and rule. (d) Open the necessary accounts using the standard account form of ledger paper. Allow one page for each account and number the accounts consecutively. Post the sales journal and the general journal entries for July, foot the accounts, and enter the balances. (e) Take a trial balance as of July 31, using a sheet of two-column journal paper.

Problem 3-C

Samuel E. Oliver is engaged in a retail merchandising business operating under the name of The SEO Store. He keeps a purchases journal, a sales journal, and a two-column general journal as books of original entry. The standard account form of general ledger is used. Individual accounts with customers and creditors are not kept in ledger form; however, the purchase invoices and sales tickets are filed in such a manner that the amounts due to creditors and due from customers may be ascertained at any time. All charge sales are payable by the tenth of the following month. Following is a trial balance taken as of March 31:

THE SEO STORE
TRIAL BALANCE

March 31, 19--

Cash	$ 1,074.00	
Accounts Receivable	1,785.00	
Merchandise Inventory	11,000.00	
Store Equipment	580.00	
Accounts Payable		$ 1,868.31
Sales Tax Payable		25.69
Samuel E. Oliver, Proprietor		4,500.00
Samuel E. Oliver, Drawing	700.00	
Sales		24,400.00
Sales Returns and Allowances	212.50	
Purchases	13,400.00	
Purchases Returns and Allowances		106.00
Rent Expense	450.00	
Advertising Expense	120.00	
Gas and Electric Expense	60.00	
Telephone and Telegraph Expense	36.00	
Salary Expense	1,425.00	
Miscellaneous Expenses	57.50	
	$30,900.00	$30,900.00

NARRATIVE OF TRANSACTIONS FOR APRIL

Apr. 1. (Saturday) Paid the rent for April in advance, $150.
3. Paid the following bills:
   Gas and electric bill, $21.50.
   Telephone bill, $10.75.
4. Received Invoice No. 71 dated April 1 from C. M. Janis, 124 Spring St., for merchandise purchased, $195. Terms, 30 days net.
4. Sold merchandise on credit to R. A. Stratton, 120 Main St., $26.50, tax 53 cents. Sale No. 41.
6. Sold merchandise on credit to the Clinton Hotel, 20 Broadway, $80.25, tax $1.61. Sale No. 42.
8. Sundry cash sales, $178, tax $3.56.
10. Paid the following creditors on account:
    Cramer Bros., $136.50.
    Samuels & Co., $225.40.

Apr. 11. Received the following remittances from customers to apply on account:

        Sterling Hotel, $76.50.

        C. L. Woodward, $52.

        Mrs. D. E. Carter, $47.50.

  12. Received Invoice No. 72 dated April 10 from Harrison & Lang, Detroit, for merchandise purchased, $230. Terms, 30 days net.

  13. Paid $25.69 to State Treasurer for March sales tax.

  13. Made credit sales as follows:

        No. 43, Mrs. D. E. Carter, Kingston, $84.75, tax $1.70.

        No. 44, Sterling Hotel, 200 Locust, $52.75, tax $1.06.

        No. 45, Mrs. O. M. Lawton, 125 E. Fourth St., $60, tax $1.20.

  14. Paid $27.50 for newspaper advertising.

  15. Sundry cash sales, $142.50, tax $2.85.

  15. Paid semimonthly salaries, $237.50.

  17. Samuel E. Oliver withdrew $100 for personal use.

  18. Made charge sales as follows:

        No. 46, L. C. Byrd, 604 Race St., $79.10, tax $1.58.

        No. 47, Mrs. G. R. Martin, 25 E. Fourth St., $39.10, tax 78 cents.

        No. 48, Clinton Hotel, 20 Broadway, $71.56, tax $1.43.

  19. Received Invoice No. 73 dated April 17 from Cramer Bros., City, for merchandise purchased, $225.40. Terms, 30 days net.

  20. Gave the Clinton Hotel credit for $12.24 on account of merchandise returned. (Sales price, $12, tax 24 cents.)

  21. Received credit from Cramer Bros. for $17.80 on account of merchandise returned.

  22. Sundry cash sales, $143.70, tax $2.87.

  24. Received Invoice No. 74 dated April 22 from Samuels & Co., Cleveland, for merchandise purchased, $92.50. Terms, 30 days net.

  25. Made charge sales as follows:

        No. 49, C. L. Woodward, 121 Elm St., $54.40, tax $1.09.

        No. 50, Sterling Hotel, City, $76.15, tax $1.52.

  26. Allowed credit for $4.28 to L. C. Byrd for merchandise returned. (Sales price, $4.20, tax 8 cents.)

  27. Paid Davis Bros. $69.50 on account.

  27. Received $163.20 from Clinton Hotel to apply on account.

  28. Purchased store equipment on account from the Carew Supply Co., 16 John St., $70. Terms, 60 days net.

  28. Paid freight and drayage on merchandise purchased, $18.

  29. Sundry cash sales, $156.40, tax $3.13.

  29. Paid semimonthly salaries, $237.50.

  29. Samuel E. Oliver withdrew $75 for personal use.

REQUIRED: (a) Journalize the April transactions. Foot the purchases and sales journals, enter the totals, and rule. Prove each page of the general journal by footing the debit and credit columns. (b) Open the necessary general ledger accounts. Allow one page for each account and number the accounts consecutively. Record the April 1 balances as shown in the March 31 trial balance, complete the individual posting from the general journal, and complete the summary posting from the purchases and sales journals. Foot the accounts and enter the balances. (c) Take a trial balance using a sheet of two-column journal paper.

Problem 4-A

U. A. Noble is an advertising counselor. The books of original entry for his business include a two-page cashbook and a two-column general journal. He uses the standard account form of general ledger. Following is the trial balance of his business taken as of November 30:

U. A. NOBLE, ADVERTISING COUNSELOR

TRIAL BALANCE

November 30, 19—

Cash..	$1,736.14	
Office Equipment....................................	370.00	
Accounts Payable....................................		$ 57.79
U. A. Noble, Proprietor.............................		2,470.00
U. A. Noble, Drawing................................	2,175.00	
Income from Fees....................................		4,620.00
Rent Expense..	825.00	
Telephone and Telegraph Expense.....................	102.50	
Electric Expense....................................	64.75	
Salaries..	1,687.50	
Charitable Contributions............................	145.00	
Miscellaneous Expenses..............................	41.90	
	$7,147.79	$7,147.79

NARRATIVE OF TRANSACTIONS FOR DECEMBER

Dec.　1. (Friday) Paid December office rent in advance, $75.

1. Paid electric bill, $5.42.
2. Paid telephone bill, $9.50.
2. Received a check from Gilmartin Appliance Co. for $150 in payment of services rendered.
4. Received payment from Hughes Mercantile Co. for services rendered, $195.
7. Donated $5 to the American Red Cross.
7. Paid $4.50 for cleaning office.
9. Received check for $215 from Laughlin Directory Co. for advertising counsel.
11. Mr. Noble withdrew $150 for personal use.
15. Paid secretary's salary for the half month, $115.
18. Purchased office furniture on credit from Mandel Furniture Co., $300.
19. Paid $2 for having the office windows washed.
20. Received $125 from Walters Provision Co. for services rendered.
22. Paid traveling expenses while on business trip out of city, $17.50.
23. Donated $10 to the Community Chest.
26. Paid Mandel Furniture Co. $50 on account.

Dec. 28. Mr. Noble withdrew $75 for personal use.

    30. Paid secretary's salary for the half month, $115.

REQUIRED: (a) Journalize the December transactions. For the cashbook use two sheets of two-column journal paper. Number the pages and record the receipts on page 2 and the payments on page 3. (b) Open the necessary ledger accounts. Allow one page for each account and number the accounts consecutively. Record the December 1 balances, and post the cashbook and general journal entries. Balance and rule the cashbook. (c) Take a trial balance.

Problem 4-B

J. C. Hilliard engages in the retail clothing business under the name of The Hilliard Clothing Store. He uses a purchases journal, a sales journal, an eight-column combined cash-journal (8 columns divided — 2 left, 6 right), and a general ledger with standard account form of ruling. Since the store is located in an area where no tax is imposed on retail sales, he uses a single-column sales journal like the one illustrated on page 61. Merchandise is sold both for cash and on credit, all credit sales being due on the tenth of the following month. Ledger accounts are not kept with individual creditors and customers. Unpaid purchase invoices are filed numerically according to due dates. When paid they are filed alphabetically, under creditors, in another file. Sales tickets are filed alphabetically until payment is received.

THE HILLIARD CLOTHING STORE
CHART OF ACCOUNTS

Assets
  Cash
  Accounts Receivable
  Store Equipment

Liabilities
  Accounts Payable

Proprietorship
  J. C. Hilliard, Proprietor
  J. C. Hilliard, Drawing

Income from Sales
  Sales
  Sales Returns and Allowances

Cost of Sales
  Purchases
  Purchases Returns and Allowances

Expenses
  Rent Expense
  Advertising Expense
  Telephone Expense
  Salary Expense
  Miscellaneous Expenses

NARRATIVE OF TRANSACTIONS FOR MARCH

Mar. 1. (Wednesday) Mr. Hilliard invested $4,000 cash in the business.

    1. Paid one month's rent in advance, $100.

    2. Paid $8 for telephone service.

    3. Received Invoice No. 1 dated March 1 from Kahn Tailoring Co. for merchandise purchased on credit, $275.50.

Mar. 4. Received Invoice No. 2 dated March 2 from Ed. V. Price & Co. for merchandise purchased on credit, $436.50.
6. Sold merchandise on credit to W. W. Griffith, $49.50. Sale No. 1.
7. Sold merchandise on credit to W. H. Gaddis, $92. Sale No. 2.
8. Purchased store equipment from George Tull on credit, $95.
9. Sold merchandise on credit to W. W. Hilligoss, $72. Sale No. 3.
10. Sold merchandise on credit to F. A. Munson, $102. Sale No. 4.
13. Sold merchandise on credit to George Gould, $120. Sale No. 5.
14. Gave W. W. Griffith credit for merchandise returned, $9.
15. Mr. Hilliard withdrew $125 in cash for personal use.
15. Paid salesclerk's semimonthly salary in cash, $90.
16. Received credit for $20 from Kahn Tailoring Co. for merchandise returned by agreement.
17. Paid $22.75 for newspaper advertising.
20. Received Invoice No. 3 dated March 17 from Goodall Co. for merchandise purchased on credit, $362.50.
21. Paid freight and drayage on merchandise purchased, $12.65.
22. Received $40.50 from W. W. Griffith in payment of the merchandise sold him on March 6.
23. Paid George Tull $95 in full for store equipment purchased on March 8.
24. Paid $3 for window washing.
25. Sold merchandise on credit to John Smysor, $122. Sale No. 6.
27. Received $50 from W. W. Hilligoss on account.
27. Purchased a second-hand checkwriter for $20 cash.
28. Paid $21.25 for advertising matter.
28. Received credit for $12.25 from Goodall Co., allowance on defective merchandise.
28. Received Invoice No. 4 dated March 23 from M. Born Co. for merchandise purchased on credit, $397.35.
29. Paid Kahn Tailoring Co., $255.50, balance due on invoice of March 1.
29. Sold merchandise on credit to J. A. Flint, $69.75. Sale No. 7.
30. Received $75 from W. H. Gaddis on account.
31. Sundry cash sales for the month, $1,256.13.
31. Paid salesclerk's semimonthly salary in cash, $90.
31. Mr. Hilliard withdrew $100 in cash for personal use.
31. Paid Ed. V. Price & Co. $436.50 in full settlement of invoice of March 2.

Required: (a) Journalize the foregoing transactions. Foot, total, and rule the journals. Enter the cash balance in the Description column of the combined cash-journal. (b) Using the chart of accounts as a guide, open the necessary ledger accounts. Allow one page for each account and number the accounts consecutively. Complete the individual posting from the combined cash-journal. Complete the summary posting from the purchases journal, sales journal, and combined cash-journal. (c) Take a trial balance as of March 31.

Problem 4-C

M. P. Carroll, a merchant, completed the following transactions with the Harris Trust and Savings Bank during the month of October:

Oct. 2. (Monday) Balance in bank per record kept on check stubs........	$1,900.00
2. Deposit..............	1,000.00
2. Check No. 108.......	208.80
2. " " 109.......	20.00
3. " " 110.......	450.00
4. " " 111.......	101.00
5. " " 112.......	150.00
6. " " 113.......	75.00
7. " " 114.......	165.50
7. " " 115.......	40.00
7. " " 116.......	38.00
7. Deposit..............	248.65
10. Check No. 117.......	445.23

Oct. 11. Check No. 118.......	$ 60.00
11. " " 119.......	49.50
13. " " 120.......	457.74
14. " " 121.......	48.10
14. " " 122.......	273.42
14. Deposit..............	341.38
16. Check No. 123.......	150.00
18. " " 124.......	256.01
21. " " 125.......	94.75
21. Deposit..............	791.00
24. Check No. 126.......	141.32
25. " " 127.......	103.88
27. " " 128.......	279.77
28. " " 129.......	38.00
30. " " 130.......	567.43
30. Deposit..............	815.24

REQUIRED: (a) A record of the bank account as it would appear on the check stubs. (b) A reconciliation of the bank statement for October which indicated a balance of $1,666.92 on October 31 with Checks Nos. 116, 126, 129, and 130 outstanding, and a service charge of 65 cents.

Problem 4-D

William Ellis, a contractor, had a balance of $50 in his petty cash fund as of June 1. During June the following petty cash transactions were completed:

June 2. (Friday) Paid for repairs on a typewriter, $1.25. Petty Cash Voucher No. 44.

6. Paid for telegram, $2.95. Petty Cash Voucher No. 45.

8. Donated $5 to the Community Chest fund. Petty Cash Voucher No. 46.

9. Paid garage for washing car, $1.50. Petty Cash Voucher No. 47.

12. Gave Mr. Ellis' son, $2. (Charge William Ellis, Drawing.) Petty Cash Voucher No. 48.

14. Paid for postage stamps, $3. Petty Cash Voucher No. 49.

17. Paid for newspaper for month, $1.32. Petty Cash Voucher No. 50.

22. Paid for window washing, $2. Petty Cash Voucher No. 51.

27. Paid $1 to the Parent-Teachers Association for dues. (Charge William Ellis, Drawing.) Petty Cash Voucher No. 52.

28. Paid for car lubrication, $1.50. Petty Cash Voucher No. 53.

29. Donated $10 to the American Red Cross. Petty Cash Voucher No. 54.

30. Rendered report of petty cash expenditures for month and received the amount needed to replenish the petty cash fund.

REQUIRED: (a) Record the foregoing transactions in a petty cash disbursements record, distributing the expenditures as follows:

William Ellis, Drawing   Charitable Contributions
Automobile Expenses   Miscellaneous Expenses
Telephone and Telegraph Expense

(b) Prove the petty cash disbursements record by footing the amount columns and proving the totals. Enter the totals and rule the amount columns with single and double lines. (c) Prepare a statement of the petty cash disbursements for June. (d) Bring down the balance in the petty cash fund below the ruling in the Description column. Enter the amount received to replenish the fund and record the total.

Problem 5-A

Following is a summary of the hours worked, rates of pay, and other relevant information concerning the employees of The Precision Machine Shop, D. A. Maxwell, Proprietor, for the week ended Saturday, November 8. Employees are paid at the rate of time and one half for all hours worked in excess of 8 in any day or 40 in any week.

No.	NAME	EXEMPTIONS CLAIMED	HOURS WORKED M T W T F S						REGULAR HOURLY RATE	CUMULATIVE EARNINGS JAN. 1–NOV. 2
1	Gray, John A............	4	8	8	8	8	8	4	$1.90	$4,105
2	Hilby, Peter F............	3	8	9	8	8	0	0	2.10	4,364
3	Johnson, William R.......	4	8	8	8	8	8	0	2.05	4,160
4	Lucas, Robert B..........	2	8	8	8	8	8	4	1.80	2,517
5	Miller, Thomas N.........	1	0	8	8	8	8	4	2.00	3,115
6	Sweeney, Ralph C........	1	8	8	8	8	8	0	2.00	3,764

Thomas N. Miller has authorized his employer to withhold $3.75 a week from his pay to be used in purchasing savings bonds for him.

REQUIRED: (a) Using plain ruled paper size 8½″ by 11″, rule a payroll record form similar to that reproduced on pages 124 and 125 and insert the proper columnar headings. Enter on this form the payroll for the week ended Saturday, November 8. Refer to the Wage Bracket Withholding Table on page 121 to determine the amounts to be withheld from the wages of each worker for income tax purposes. Two per cent of the taxable wages of each employee should be withheld for F.I.C.A. taxes. Checks Nos. 613 through 618 were issued to the employees. Complete the payroll record by footing the amount columns, proving the footings, entering the totals, and ruling. (b) Assuming that the wages were paid on November 12, record the payment on a sheet of two-column general journal paper.

Problem 5-B

The Midtown Store employs fifteen people. They are paid by checks on the 15th and last day of each month. The entry to record each payroll includes a record of the amounts withheld. The expense and liabilities arising from the employer's payroll taxes are recorded on each payday.

Following is a narrative of the transactions completed during the month of January that related to payrolls and payroll taxes:

Jan. 15. Payroll for first half of month:

Total salaries...		$1,680.00
Less amounts withheld:		
F.I.C.A. taxes..............................	$ 33.60	
Employees' income taxes.....................	154.10	187.70
Net amount paid.....................................		$1,492.30

15. Social security taxes imposed on employer:

F.I.C.A. taxes, 2%
State U.C. taxes, 2.7%
F.U.T.A. taxes, 3% less credit for state U.C. taxes.

28. Deposited $382.90 in Federal reserve bank in payment of the following December taxes:

F.I.C.A. taxes, $95.80.
Employees' income taxes withheld, $287.10.

28. Paid state U. C. taxes for quarter ended December 31, $53.60.

28. Paid F.U.T.A. taxes for year ended December 31, $135.

31. Payroll for last half of month:

Total salaries...		$1,710.00
Less amounts withheld:		
F.I.C.A. taxes..............................	$ 34.20	
Employees' income taxes.....................	165.60	199.80
Net amount paid.....................................		$1,510.20

31. Social security taxes imposed on employer:
All salaries taxable; rates same as on January 15.

REQUIRED: (a) Journalize the foregoing transactions, using two-column general journal paper. (b) Foot the debit and credit amount columns as a means of proof.

Problem 7-A

P. H. O'Brien is engaged in business as a retail electrical supplies dealer. Merchandise is sold for cash and on credit. At the top of the following page is a reproduction of the Trial Balance columns of his work sheet for the current year ended December 31.

REQUIRED: Prepare a ten-column work sheet making the necessary entries in the Adjustments columns to record the following:

(1) Cost of goods sold:
(Merchandise inventory, end of year, $6,377.)

(2) Accruals:
Interest accrued on notes receivable, $7.
Interest accrued on notes payable, $9.17.

P. H. O'BRIEN

ACCOUNTS	TRIAL BALANCE	
	DR. BALANCES	CR. BALANCES
Cash....................................	2,732.96	
Notes Receivable........................	700.00	
Accrued Interest Receivable..............		
Accounts Receivable.....................	2,162.00	
Allowance for Bad Debts.................		24.86
Merchandise Inventory...................	5,364.00	
Prepaid Insurance.......................	280.00	
Stationery and Supplies..................	90.00	
Store Equipment........................	2,200.00	
Allowance for Depreciation of Store Equipment.......		220.00
Delivery Equipment.....................	1,800.00	
Allowance for Depreciation of Delivery Equipment....		450.00
Notes Payable..........................		1,100.00
Accrued Interest Payable.................		
Accounts Payable.......................		3,312.10
Sales Tax Payable.......................		40.00
Employees' Income Taxes Payable.........		102.50
F.I.C.A. Taxes Payable..................		30.00
P. H. O'Brien, Proprietor...............		12,666.50
P. H. O'Brien, Drawing.................	2,000.00	
Sales..................................		25,717.50
Sales Returns and Allowances............	89.50	
Cost of Goods Sold.....................		
Purchases..............................	18,115.65	
Purchases Returns and Allowances........		92.15
Rent Expense...........................	1,500.00	
Advertising Expense.....................	420.00	
Salaries................................	6,000.00	
Social Security Taxes....................	120.00	
Insurance Expense......................		
Stationery and Supplies Consumed........		
Depreciation Expense....................		
Bad Debts Expense......................		
Charitable Contributions................	125.00	
Miscellaneous Expenses..................	60.00	
Interest Income........................		17.50
Interest Expense........................	14.00	
	43,773.11	43,773.11

(3) Prepaid expenses:
  Prepaid insurance unexpired, $140.
  Stationery and supplies on hand, $30.

(4) Depreciation:
  Store equipment, 10% a year, $220.
  Delivery equipment, 25% a year, $450.

(5) Bad debts expense:
  (Increase allowance for bad debts $40 to provide for estimated loss.)

Note: Problems 7-B and 8-A are based on P. H. O'Brien's work sheet; hence, if those problems are to be solved, the work sheet should be retained for reference until after they are solved, when the solutions of all three problems may be submitted to the instructor.

Problem 7-B

Refer to the work sheet for P. H. O'Brien (based on Problem 7-A) and from it prepare the following financial statements:

(a) An income statement for the year ended December 31.

(b) A balance sheet in account form as of December 31.

Problem 8-A

Refer to the work sheet for P. H. O'Brien (based on Problem 7-A) and draft the general journal entries required:

(a) To adjust the general ledger accounts so they will be in agreement with the financial statements.

(b) To close the temporary proprietorship accounts on December 31.

(c) To reverse the accrual adjustments as of January 1.

Problem 8-B (Complete cycle problem)

R. C. Watson is engaged in a mercantile business on a sole proprietorship basis. He calls his business "Watson's Store." He keeps a purchases journal, sales journal, combined cash-journal, and general ledger. For his combined cash-journal, he uses eight-column paper (8 columns divided — 2 left, 6 right) with headings arranged as follows:

Cash
   (1) Receipts, Dr.
   (2) Payments, Cr.

General
   (3) Debits
   (4) Credits

Accounts Receivable
   (5) Debits
   (6) Credits

Accounts Payable
   (7) Debits
   (8) Credits

The standard account form of ledger ruling is used. Individual accounts with customers and creditors are not kept in ledger form; however, the purchase invoices and sales tickets are filed in such a manner that the amounts due to creditors and due from customers can be ascertained at any time. At the end of the eleventh month of the current year, his trial balance appeared as shown on the following page.

NARRATIVE OF TRANSACTIONS FOR DECEMBER

Dec. 1. (Friday) Purchased merchandise from Evans Bros., Clinton, $650. Invoice No. 31, dated November 30. Terms, 2/10, n/30.

    2. Paid the December rent, $300. Check No. 64.

    2. Paid the telephone bill, $13.50. Check No. 65.

    4. Paid J. R. Miller $721.50 in full of December 1 balance. Check No. 66.

WATSON'S STORE
TRIAL BALANCE
November 30, 19—

Cash..	$ 5,139.50	
Notes Receivable.............................	1,800.00	
Accounts Receivable...........................	2,739.90	
Allowance for Bad Debts........................		$ 69.60
Merchandise Inventory.........................	20,800.00	
Prepaid Insurance............................	475.00	
Stationery and Supplies........................	80.00	
Store Equipment..............................	1,900.00	
Allowance for Depr. of Store Equipment...........		380.00
Notes Payable................................		1,200.00
Accounts Payable..............................		1,601.30
Sales Tax Payable.............................		152.15
Employees' Income Taxes Payable.................		122.50
F.I.C.A. Taxes Payable.........................		45.90
F.U.T.A. Taxes Payable.........................		38.70
State U.C. Taxes Payable.......................		63.45
R. C. Watson, Proprietor.......................		31,900.00
R. C. Watson, Drawing.........................	3,700.00	
Sales..		83,680.00
Sales Returns and Allowances...................	126.40	
Purchases....................................	63,200.00	
Purchases Returns and Allowances................		141.10
Rent Expense.................................	3,300.00	
Advertising Expense............................	2,400.00	
Salaries and Commissions......................	12,900.00	
Social Security Taxes..........................	645.00	
Miscellaneous Expenses........................	293.90	
Purchases Discount............................		110.00
Interest Income...............................		9.00
Interest Expense..............................	14.00	
	$119,513.70	$119,513.70

Dec. 5. Sold merchandise on credit to A. F. Wade, 32 Main St., City, $350, tax $7. Sale No. 101.

6. Purchased merchandise from the Dixon Supply Co., Maryville, $975. Invoice No. 32, dated December 5. Terms, 30 days.

7. Received $175 from Russell Long in full payment of his account.

8. Paid Evans Bros. $637 in settlement of their invoice of November 30, less 2% discount. Check No. 67.

8. Received $212.16 from H. L. Beck in full payment of his account.

9. Sold merchandise on credit to C. A. Jordan, Dayton, $241.50, tax $4.83. Sale No. 102.

11. Purchased merchandise from the Campbell Mfg. Co., City, $1,621.90. Invoice No. 33, dated December 9. Terms, 30 days.

12. Sold merchandise on credit to R. E. Keith, 201 King St., City, $325.70, tax $6.51. Sale No. 103.

13. Issued Check No. 68 to the Second National Bank, a U. S. Depositary, in payment of the following taxes:

(a) Employees' income taxes withheld during November......		$122.50
(b) F.I.C.A. taxes —		
On employees (withheld during November)....	$22.95	
On the employer...........................	22.95	45.90
Total...		$168.40

Dec. 14. Sold merchandise on credit to D. R. Brown, 738 High St., City, $625, tax $12.50. Sale No. 104.

15. Issued Check No. 69 payable to State Treasurer for $152.15 for November sales tax.

18. R. C. Watson withdrew $60 for personal use. Check No. 70.

19. Gave R. E. Keith credit for $20.40 because a part of the merchandise sold him on the twelfth was returned. (Sales price, $20, tax 40 cents.)

20. Sold merchandise on credit to A. F. Wade, 32 Main St., $212.50, tax $4.25. Sale No. 105.

21. Purchased merchandise from the White Mfg. Co., City, $1,487.25. Invoice No. 34, dated December 20. Terms, 30 days.

22. Received $311.81 from R. E. Keith in full of Sale No. 103.

23. Paid bill for advertising, $115. Check No. 71.

26. Sold merchandise on credit to L. D. Marvin, 159 Jackson St., City, $735, tax $14.70. Sale No. 106.

26. Purchased merchandise from Evans Bros., Clinton, $975.40. Invoice No. 35, dated December 23. Terms, 2/10, n/30.

26. Received a check for $200 from A. F. Wade to apply on account.

27. Sold merchandise on credit to R. E. Keith, 201 King St., City, $362.75, tax $7.26. Sale No. 107.

27. Sent the Campbell Mfg. Co. a check for $500 to apply on account. Check No. 72.

28. Sold merchandise on credit to S. T. Gross, 218 Seventh St., City, $913.45, tax $18.27. Sale No. 108.

28. Purchased store equipment from the Centerville Supply Co., Centerville, $210. Terms, 60 days net.

29. Received $246.33 from C. A. Jordan in payment of Sale No. 102.

29. Received credit from Evans Bros. for $45 because a part of the merchandise purchased on the twenty-sixth was returned by agreement.

29. Sold merchandise on credit to C. A. Jordan, Dayton, $487.10, tax $9.74. Sale No. 109.

30. Sundry cash sales for month, $2,047.20, tax $40.94.

30. Issued Check No. 73 payable to Payroll for $1,051.23.

PAYROLL STATEMENT FOR MONTH ENDED DECEMBER 31

Total wages and commissions earned during period................		$1,201.00
Employees' taxes to be withheld:		
(a) Employees' income taxes...........................	$125.75	
(b) F.I.C.A. taxes @ 2%.............................	24.02	149.77
Net amount payable to employees..................		$1,051.23
Employer's payroll taxes:		
(a) F.I.C.A. taxes @ 2%.............................		$ 24.02
(b) U.C. taxes —		
State @ 2.7%................................	$ 32.43	
Federal (3% less credit for state contributions).....	3.60	36.03
Total...		$ 60.05

(In addition to recording the amounts withheld from employees' wages for income tax purposes and for F.I.C.A. taxes, the social security taxes imposed on the employer should also be recorded.)

REQUIRED: (a) Journalize the December transactions. (b) Open the necessary general ledger accounts and record the December 1 balances, using the November 30 trial balance as the source of the needed information. Complete the individual and summary posting from the books of original entry. (c) Take a trial balance of the general ledger accounts. (d) Prepare a ten-column work sheet making the required adjustments for the following:

(1) Cost of goods sold:
 (Merchandise inventory, end of year, $33,700.)

(2) Accruals:
 Interest accrued on notes receivable, $24.
 Interest accrued on notes payable, $12.

(3) Prepaid expenses:
 Prepaid insurance unexpired, $317.
 Stationery and supplies on hand, $25.

(4) Depreciation:
 Store equipment, 10% a year, $190.

(5) Bad debts expense:
 (Increase allowance for bad debts $105.68 to provide for estimated loss.)

In recording the required adjustments on the work sheet, it will be necessary to add the following account titles to those already appearing in the trial balance:

Cost of Goods Sold (Allow 2 lines)
Accrued Interest Receivable
Accrued Interest Payable
Insurance Expense
Stationery and Supplies Consumed
Depreciation Expense
Bad Debts Expense

(e) Prepare an income statement for the year ending December 31 and a balance sheet in report form as of December 31. (f) Record the adjusting entries in the combined cash-journal and post. (g) Record the closing entries in the combined cash-journal and post. (h) Balance and rule the accounts that are in balance after the adjusting and closing entries have been posted; also balance and rule the cash account, and rule the merchandise inventory account. (i) Take a post-closing trial balance. (j) Record the necessary reversing entries as of January 1 in the combined cash-journal. Post and rule the accounts that are closed.

Problem 9-A

Carl Smith is an architect engaged in professional practice on his own account. Since his income consists entirely of compensation for personal services rendered, he keeps his accounts on the cash basis. His trial balance for the current year ending December 31 is as follows:

CARL SMITH

TRIAL BALANCE

December 31, 19—

Cash	$ 1,917.53	
Office Equipment	960.00	
Allowance for Depr. of Office Equipment		$ 96.00
Automobile	1,820.00	
Allowance for Depr. of Automobile		227.50
Accounts Payable		380.26
Employees' Income Taxes Payable		42.60
F.I.C.A. Taxes Payable		13.50
Carl Smith, Proprietor		2,864.20
Carl Smith, Drawing	4,250.00	
Income from Professional Fees		8,959.49
Rent Expense	1,200.00	
Salaries	1,800.00	
Automobile Expenses	203.00	
Social Security Taxes	36.00	
Charitable Contributions	120.00	
Miscellaneous Expenses	277.02	
	$12,583.55	$12,583.55

REQUIRED: (a) Prepare a ten-column work sheet making the necessary entries in the Adjustments columns to record the depreciation of the following assets:

Office equipment, 10%, $96.
Automobile, 25%, $455.

(b) Prepare the following financial statements:

(1) An income statement for the year ended December 31.
(2) A balance sheet in report form as of December 31.

Problem 9-B

Fred Bullock operates an airline charter service, specializing in day and night airplane service. A trial balance of his general ledger accounts appears on the following page.

REQUIRED: (a) Prepare a ten-column work sheet making the necessary adjustments to record the depreciation of fixed assets as follows:

PROPERTY	RATE OF DEPRECIATION	AMOUNT OF DEPRECIATION
Office equipment................	10%	$ 125
Airplane equipment..............	20%	11,920

(b) Prepare an income statement for the year ended December 31.

(c) Prepare a balance sheet in report form as of December 31.

(d) Using two-column general journal paper, draft the entries required:

(1) To adjust the general ledger accounts so that they will be in agreement with the financial statements.

(2) To close the temporary proprietorship accounts on December 31.

FRED BULLOCK

TRIAL BALANCE

December 31, 19—

Cash...	$ 5,982.23	
Office Equipment..............................	1,250.00	
Allowance for Depreciation of Office Equipment.......		$ 250.00
Airplane Equipment.............................	59,600.00	
Allowance for Depreciation of Airplane Equipment....		23,840.00
Notes Payable..................................		1,200.00
Accounts Payable...............................		1,490.50
Employees' Income Taxes Payable..................		200.00
F.I.C.A. Taxes Payable..........................		40.00
Fred Bullock, Proprietor.........................		21,500.00
Fred Bullock, Drawing...........................	4,200.00	
Traffic Income.................................		42,781.26
Rent Expense..................................	2,800.00	
Salaries.......................................	8,000.00	
Office Expense.................................	700.00	
Airplane Expense...............................	8,455.13	
Social Security Taxes...........................	160.00	
Charitable Contributions.........................	100.00	
Miscellaneous Expenses..........................	54.40	
	$91,301.76	$91,301.76

Problem 9-C

Isaac Miller is the sole proprietor of a dry cleaning establishment. Since his income consists of compensation for services rendered, he keeps his accounts on the cash basis. He does not extend credit to customers but operates on a cash-on-delivery basis. The Trial Balance columns of his work sheet for the current year ended December 31 are reproduced on the following page.

(a) Complete the work sheet making the necessary adjusting entries to record the depreciation of fixed assets as follows:

Office equipment, 10% a year, $50.

Cleaning equipment, 8% a year, $144.

Delivery truck, 30% a year, $276.

(b) Prepare an income statement for the year ended December 31.

(c) Prepare a balance sheet as of December 31 in report form.

(d) Using two-column general journal paper, draft the entries required to record the adjusting and closing entries.

ISAAC MILLER
WORK SHEET FOR YEAR ENDED DECEMBER 31, 19—

ACCOUNTS	TRIAL BALANCE	
	DR. BALANCES	CR. BALANCES
Security National Bank..........................	3,156.40	
Office Equipment...............................	500.00	
Allowance for Depreciation of Office Equipment......		50.00
Cleaning Equipment.............................	1,800.00	
Allowance for Depreciation of Cleaning Equipment....		144.00
Delivery Truck.................................	920.00	
Allowance for Depreciation of Delivery Truck........		276.00
Accounts Payable...............................		205.34
Employees' Income Taxes Payable..................		107.06
F.I.C.A. Taxes Payable...........................		20.46
Isaac Miller, Proprietor..........................		3,808.22
Isaac Miller, Drawing............................	3,162.45	
Dry Cleaning Income............................		9,308.85
Pressing Income................................		3,989.51
Rent Expense...................................	2,080.00	
Heat, Light, and Power..........................	1,303.67	
Salaries..	4,112.50	
Delivery Expense................................	414.43	
Depreciation Expense............................		
Social Security Taxes............................	82.25	
Miscellaneous Expenses..........................	377.74	
	17,909.44	17,909.44

Problem 9-D

L. J. Martin, who is engaged in business as a furrier, occasionally invests surplus funds in securities, including government bonds and corporation bonds and stocks. Following is a narrative of such transactions that were completed during the current year:

Feb. 1. Issued a check for $2,400 in payment of 100 shares of National Acme Co. common stock purchased at $24 a share, including the broker's commission.

     15. Issued a check for $750 in payment of a $1,000 Series E, U. S. Savings Bond.

Mar. 15. Purchased a $1,000, 3% U. S. Treasury Bond for $1,000.

May 15. Issued a check for $1,020 in payment of a $1,000 Columbia Electric Co. 3½% Bond due in 1960, including the broker's commission (no interest accrued).

July 1. Redeemed a $500 Series E, U. S. Savings Bond at maturity. Original cost $375. (Since Mr. Martin has not elected to treat the annual appreciation in savings bonds as current income, the total appreciation in the value of the bond amounting to $125 should be recorded as interest income when the bond is redeemed.)

Sept. 15. Cashed a $12.50 coupon on a 2½%, $1,000 U. S. Treasury Bond due today.

Nov. 15. Received a check for $17.50 in payment of the semiannual interest on a 3½%, $1,000 Bond of the Columbia Electric Co.

Dec. 15. Received a check for $100 in payment of a dividend at $1 a share on 100 shares of common stock of the National Acme Co.

REQUIRED: Record the foregoing transactions on a sheet of two-column general journal paper and foot the amount columns to prove the equality of the debits and credits.

Problem 9-E

Dr. William Krummel is a surgeon. He keeps his accounts on the cash basis, using a combined cash-journal and a general ledger as his principal books of account. For his combined cash-journal, he uses standard eight-column paper with headings arranged as follows:

Cash
    (1) Receipts, Dr.
    (2) Payments, Cr.

General
    (3) Debits
    (4) Credits

Professional Fees
    (5) Cash Service, Cr.
    (6) Patients' Accts., Cr.

Wage Deductions
    (7) Employees' Income Taxes Payable, Cr.
    (8) F.I.C.A. Taxes Payable, Cr.

Dr. Krummel has two employees as follows:

Mary Brammel, nurse. Semimonthly salary, $125. Deductions: (a) $2.50 for F.I.C.A. taxes; (b) $12.70 for federal income taxes.

Lillian Randall, secretary. Semimonthly salary, $100. Deductions: (a) $2 for F.I.C.A. taxes; (b) $13.20 for federal income taxes.

Since Dr. Krummel has less than four employees, he is not subject to the federal tax imposed for unemployment compensation purposes. Neither is he required to make contributions to a state unemployment compensation fund because he is located in a state that does not require contributions of employers of less than four employees.

All professional expenses applicable to the office are charged to Office Expenses. These include rent, electricity, telephone and telegraph expense, janitor service, laundry, etc.

From time to time, Dr. Krummel invests his surplus funds in real and personal property. In addition to the account titles given in the headings of the combined cash-journal, the following accounts will be affected in recording the transactions that were completed during the month of August:

Government Bonds   Interest Income
Corporation Bonds   Dividends Received
Notes Receivable   Office Expenses
Lot 1416 Sycamore St.   Interest Expense
Building — Paxton Subdivision   Salaries
Notes Payable   Gain on Sale of Government Bonds
Mortgages Payable   Gain on Sale of Real Estate

NARRATIVE OF TRANSACTIONS FOR AUGUST

Aug. 1. (Tuesday) Cash balance, $12,450.

  3. Paid office rent for August in advance, $125.

  4. Paid telephone bill, $14.50.

  5. Paid electric bill, $17.25.

  7. Received $300 from Mrs. J. B. Thornton in payment of statement rendered for professional fees.

  8. Purchased a U. S. Savings Bond for $75.

  10. Received a check for $20 in payment of a quarterly dividend of 40 cents a share on 50 shares of Kroger Grocery & Baking Co. common stock.

  14. Received $400 from H. B. Brand in payment of statement rendered for professional fees.

  15. Purchased one $1,000 Bell Telephone of Pennsylvania, 5% Bond, for $1,205, including the broker's commission.

  15. Paid the semimonthly salaries of the nurse and secretary, withholding the proper amounts for F.I.C.A. taxes and employees' income taxes.

  16. Sold one $1,000 U. S. Treasury, $2\frac{7}{8}$% Bond, receiving $1,090 after deducting the broker's commission. (Dr. Krummel had purchased this bond at the issue price of $1,000.)

  17. Dependable Building Co. completed the construction of a house on Dr. Krummel's Lot 43, Paxton Subdivision. Contract price $21,500. Paid $11,000 down and executed a mortgage for $10,500 in favor of Dependable Building Co.

  18. Received from John Duncan a check for $1,500 in payment of lot located at 1416 Sycamore St. (Original cost, $1,200).

  19. Paid note due today at the Liberty National Bank. Principal, $750; interest, $15.

  21. Received $15 in cash in payment of consultation fees.

  22. Received $430 in payment of a note; principal, $400; interest, $30.

  23. Paid the Industrial Savings Bank $202.07 to release Lot 43, Paxton Subdivision from the mortgage held on the lot. Principal, $200; interest, $2.07.

  31. Paid the semimonthly salaries of the nurse and secretary, withholding the proper amounts for F.I.C.A. taxes and employees' income taxes.

REQUIRED: (a) Record the foregoing transactions using a sheet of eight-column combined cash-journal paper. (b) Foot the amount columns, prove the footings, record the totals, and rule the combined cash-journal.

ACCOUNTING FOR PROPRIETORSHIP

(21) THE SOLE PROPRIETORSHIP

Proprietorship is a term commonly used in referring to the ownership of an enterprise. Ownership or proprietorship of an enterprise may be vested in one individual, in two or more partners, or in a group of stockholders, depending upon the legal organization of the enterprise. If an enterprise is owned by one individual, it is known as a sole proprietorship; if owned by two or more partners, it is known as a partnership; if owned by a group of stockholders, it is known as a corporation.

In small mercantile enterprises and in personal service enterprises the sole proprietorship form of organization predominates. The medical and dental professions, for example, are composed largely of individuals who are engaged in practice as sole proprietors. One reason for the popularity of the sole proprietorship form of organization is that it is easily organized, involving no formal or legal agreement with others as to ownership or conduct. Anyone may engage in a lawful enterprise merely by complying with state and local laws.

Organization of a Sole Proprietorship. When engaging in an enterprise as a sole proprietor, an individual decides the amount he will invest and the nature of the property to be invested. The original investment may consist of cash only, or of cash and any other property that is owned, such as merchandise, office equipment, store equipment, and delivery equipment. The property invested is usually segregated from any other property that may be owned by the proprietor. An individual may engage in more that one enterprise and may operate each enterprise separately as a sole proprietorship. In such cases, it is preferable to keep separate records of the activities of each enterprise.

In comparison with other forms of business organization, the sole proprietorship offers certain advantages, such as the following:

   (a) Simplicity of organization.
   (b) Freedom of initiative and industry.
   (c) Fewer required government reports.
   (d) Strong incentive to individual enterprise.

The sole proprietorship form of organization has some disadvantages, of which the following are most significant:

(a) The amount of available capital may be limited.
(b) The amount of credit may be restricted.
(c) The proprietor is solely responsible for all debts incurred.

Accounting Procedure. In general, the accounting procedure in recording the ordinary operating transactions of an enterprise is not affected by the type of organization. Whether an enterprise is operated as a sole proprietorship by an individual, as a partnership by two or more partners, or as a corporation by stockholders through directors and officers has little bearing on the accounting procedure in recording the routine transactions arising from the ordinary operations of the business. However, the proprietorship accounts required depend largely upon the type of organization.

Proprietorship Accounts. There are two types of proprietorship accounts as follows: (a) permanent proprietorship accounts, and (b) temporary proprietorship accounts.

In a sole proprietorship, the owner's capital account is the only permanent proprietorship account. The account is usually given the name of the owner of the enterprise followed by "Proprietor" or "Capital."

The temporary proprietorship accounts are those in which increases and decreases in proprietorship arising from the transactions completed during an accounting period are recorded. The proprietor's personal or drawing account and all of the income and expense accounts are temporary accounts. At the end of each year, it is customary to close the temporary income and expense accounts by transferring their balances to one or more summary accounts. In a nonmercantile type of enterprise, the only summary account kept may be Income Summary. In a mercantile type of enterprise, the summary accounts kept will usually include Cost of Goods Sold and Income Summary. In the closing process, Cost of Goods Sold is debited for (a) the amount of the merchandise inventory at beginning of the year and (b) the amount of the purchases for the year; it is credited for (a) the amount of purchases returns and allowances for the year and (b) the merchandise inventory at end of the year. The balance of the account, representing the cost of goods sold during the year, is in turn transferred to the debit of Income Summary. The balances of all income and expense accounts are also transferred to Income Summary after which the balance of this summary account represents the net income or net loss for the year. The cost of goods sold account and the income summary account are the most temporary of all accounts; they are used only at the end of the year in summarizing the income and expense accounts.

Opening Entries. An individual may invest cash and other property in a sole proprietorship enterprise. Certain liabilities may attach to the property invested. If the investment consists solely of cash, the opening entry will involve a debit to Cash or the bank account and a credit to the proprietor's capital account for the amount invested.

If cash and other property, such as office equipment, store equipment, or other equipment, are invested, the opening entry will involve a debit to Cash or the bank account for the amount of cash invested, debits to appropriate equipment accounts for the amount of the other property invested, and a credit to the proprietor's capital account for the total amount of the investment.

If, at the time of organizing an enterprise, there are any liabilities, such as accounts payable, notes payable, or mortgages payable, applicable to the property invested, appropriate accounts representing the liabilities should be credited and the proprietor's capital account should be credited only for the excess of the amount of the assets invested over the aggregate amount of the liabilities. In other words, the proprietor's capital account should be credited for his *equity* in the assets invested.

EXAMPLE: F. W. Scott decides to engage in a mercantile business and invests cash amounting to $4,500, office equipment amounting to $600, store equipment amounting to $400, and delivery equipment amounting to $900. He owes $200 on the office equipment, and there is a mortgage amounting to $400 on the delivery equipment. The opening entry in general journal form to record Scott's investment is as follows:

Bank *	$4,500.00	
Office Equipment	600.00	
Store Equipment	400.00	
Delivery Equipment	900.00	
Accounts Payable		$ 200.00
Mortgage Payable		400.00
F. W. Scott, Proprietor		5,800.00
Investment in business.		

---

*The bank account is debited for the amount of cash invested for the reason that it is the usual custom of business firms to deposit all cash receipts in the bank and to make all disbursements by check. Under this plan a cash account is not kept in the general ledger. Instead, all receipts are debited to the bank account and all disbursements are credited to the bank account. This method of accounting for cash is followed consistently throughout this textbook. It should be understood, however, that a cash account and one or more bank accounts may be kept in the general ledger, if desired.

It may become advisable to install a new set of books for a going enterprise that is being operated as a sole proprietorship. The proprietor may realize that his accounting system is out of date, inadequate, or incomplete. The principles involved in installing a new set of books are much the same as in opening the books for a new enterprise. Before opening the new books, financial statements should be prepared and the old books should be closed. The balance sheet and the schedules of accounts receivable and accounts payable will then provide the information needed in opening the new books.

EXAMPLE: F. W. Scott decided, after operating for a period of five years, to install a new set of books. Financial statements were prepared and the old books were closed in the usual manner. The balance sheet prepared at that time appeared as follows:

F. W. SCOTT

BALANCE SHEET

December 31, 19—

ASSETS			LIABILITIES		
Cash..............		$ 4,750.00	Notes Payable.....	$1,000.00	
Accounts Rec......	$3,800.00		Accounts Payable...	3,200.00	
Less Allow. for					
Bad Debts.....	400.00	3,400.00	Total Liabilities....		$ 4,200.00
Mdse. Inventory....		6,950.00			
Office Equipment...	$1,600.00		PROPRIETORSHIP		
Less Allow. for					
Depreciation...	400.00	1,200.00	F. W. Scott, Prop...		14,300.00
Store Equipment...	$1,200.00				
Less Allow. for					
Depreciation...	300.00	900.00			
Delivery Equipment	$2,900.00				
Less Allow. for					
Depreciation ..	1,600.00	1,300.00			
			Total Liabilities and		
Total Assets.......		$18,500.00	Proprietorship....		$18,500.00

Mr. Scott's balance sheet provides the information needed in journalizing the opening entry. Assuming that the new set of books is being installed as of January 1, the proper opening entry in general journal form is as shown at the top of the opposite page.

After opening the necessary accounts in the general ledger, the opening journal entry should be posted in the usual manner. It should be noted that each asset account is debited for the amount shown in the balance sheet and each liability account is credited for the amount shown

Jan. 1. Bank	$4,750.00	
Accounts Receivable	3,800.00	
Merchandise Inventory	6,950.00	
Office Equipment	1,600.00	
Store Equipment	1,200.00	
Delivery Equipment	2,900.00	
Notes Payable		$ 1,000.00
Accounts Payable		3,200.00
Allowance for Bad Debts		400.00
Allowance for Depr. of Office Equipment		400.00
Allowance for Depr. of Store Equipment		300.00
Allowance for Depr. of Delivery Equipment		1,600.00
F. W. Scott, Proprietor		14,300.00
Opening a new set of books.		

in the balance sheet. These amounts represent the balances of the accounts. The accounts for allowance for bad debts and allowances for depreciation are also credited for their balances. Mr. Scott's capital account is credited for his equity in the business. Entering the balances of the accounts with customers in the accounts receivable ledger may be done directly from a schedule of accounts receivable. Entering the balances of the accounts with creditors in the accounts payable ledger may be done directly from a schedule of accounts payable.

Proprietary Transactions Completed During the Accounting Period. Certain types of transactions may be referred to as proprietary transactions because they affect either the proprietor's drawing account or his capital account. The following are typical proprietary transactions:

(a) Periodic withdrawals of cash for personal use of proprietor.
(b) Payment of proprietor's personal or family bills with business cash.
(c) Withdrawal of cash or other assets by the proprietor intended as a partial liquidation of the business.
(d) Investment of cash or other assets by proprietor intended as a permanent increase in assets and capital.

Cash withdrawn periodically by the proprietor for personal use is usually charged to his personal or drawing account on the assumption that such amounts represent withdrawals in anticipation of profits. Such withdrawals are sometimes regarded as salary or compensation for personal services rendered; however, they represent charges to the proprietor's personal or drawing account and should not be treated as an operating expense of the enterprise.

The payment of personal or family bills or accounts with business funds should be recorded as a withdrawal of cash by the proprietor. It is not unusual for an individual engaged in a business or professional enterprise as a sole proprietor to pay all personal and family or household bills by issuing checks against the same bank account as that used for business expenditures of the enterprise. However, care should be used in recording all checks issued, and those representing personal or family expenditures should be charged to the proprietor's personal or drawing account, while those representing business expenditures should be charged to the proper expense, asset, or liability accounts.

A sole proprietor may, at any time, withdraw a portion of the cash or other assets invested in his business or he may make additional investments in the business in the form of cash or other property. Withdrawals, considered to be decreases in the permanent invested capital, should be charged to his capital account; investment of additional capital should be credited to his capital account.

Disposition of the Balance of the Income Summary Account at End of Accounting Period. It is customary to close the temporary proprietorship accounts at the end of each year. As the temporary accounts are closed, their balances are usually transferred to an account entitled Income Summary. The difference between the footings of the income summary account represents the amount of the net income or the net loss for the year. If the summary account has a credit balance, it represents net income; if the account has a debit balance, it represents net loss. The simplest way to dispose of the balance of the income summary account after it has served its purpose at the end of the accounting period is to transfer its balance to the proprietor's capital account by means of a journal entry. If the income summary account has a credit balance, the journal entry will involve a debit to Income Summary and a credit to the proprietor's capital account for the amount of the net income. If the income summary account has a debit balance, the journal entry will involve a debit to the proprietor's capital account and a credit to Income Summary for the amount of the net loss.

The proprietor's drawing account is usually closed at the end of each year by transferring its balance to the proprietor's capital account. The drawing account usually has a debit balance and it may be closed by means of a journal entry debiting the proprietor's capital account and crediting the drawing account for the amount of its balance.

After transferring the balances of the income summary account and the proprietor's drawing account to the proprietor's capital account, the balance of the proprietor's capital account represents the proprietor's equity in the enterprise at the end of the year.

Proprietary Accounts in the Balance Sheet. The method of exhibiting the proprietary interest of the owner of the business in the balance sheet is shown on pages 200, 201, and 247. There may be some variation in the account titles used by different enterprises; however, the final results should be the same since the balance sheet is an exhibit of the accounting elements, including (a) the assets, (b) the liabilities, and (c) the proprietorship. The proprietorship section of the balance sheet should be arranged to show the proprietor's equity in the business at the beginning of the accounting period, the net increase or the net decrease in his equity during the period, and his equity or the net worth of the business at the end of the period.

PRACTICE ASSIGNMENT No. 21. Complete Report No. 21 in the workbook and submit your working papers to the instructor for approval. Then continue with the following study assignment until Report No. 22 is required.

(22) THE PARTNERSHIP

When two or more individuals engage in an enterprise as co-owners, the organization is known as a partnership. This form of organization is prevalent in practically all types of enterprises; however, it is more popular among personal service enterprises than among mercantile enterprises. For example, the partnership form of organization is quite common in the legal and public accounting professions.

Organization of a Partnership. The Uniform Partnership Act stipulates that "a partnership is an association of two or more persons who carry on, as co-owners, a business for profit." The partners may, by agreement, unite their capital, labor, skill, or experience in the conduct of a business for their mutual benefit. While under certain circumstances a partnership may be formed by means of an oral or an implied agreement, it is desirable that a partnership agreement be evidenced by a written contract. Such a contract is known as *articles of copartnership*. There is no standard form of partnership agreement, but there are certain provisions that are uniformly desirable, such as the following:

(a) Date.
(b) Names of the partners.
(c) Nature of the business.
(d) Duration of the agreement.
(e) Name and location of the firm.
(f) Investment of each partner.
(g) Basis on which profits or losses are to be shared by the partners.
(h) Accounting methods.
(i) Limitation of partners' rights.
(j) Salary allowances.
(k) Duties of partners.
(l) Unusual restraints upon the partners.

(m) Division of assets upon dissolution of the partnership.

(n) Signatures of the partners.

The articles of copartnership reproduced on page 297 constitute a partnership agreement drawn in the usual form.

The partnership form of organization offers certain advantages similar to those of the sole proprietorship. Additional advantages include the following:

(a) The ability and the experience of the partners are combined in one enterprise.

(b) More capital may be raised because the resources of the partners are combined.

(c) Credit may be improved because each general partner is personally liable for partnership debts.

There are some disadvantages that are peculiar to the partnership form of organization, including the following:

(a) Each partner is individually liable for all the debts of the partnership. The liability of each partner is not limited to a pro-rata share of the partnership debts; he is personally liable for all debts of the partnership to the same extent as if he were the sole proprietor. Under the laws of some states, certain partners may limit their liability; at least one partner, however, must be a general partner who is responsible for all the debts of the partnership.

(b) A partner cannot transfer his interest in the partnership without the consent of the other partners.

(c) Termination of the partnership agreement, bankruptcy of the firm, or death of one of the partners dissolves the partnership.

Accounting Procedure. In accounting for the operations of a partnership, it is necessary to keep a separate capital account for each partner. It is also customary to keep a separate personal or drawing account for each partner. While no new principles are involved in keeping these accounts, care should be used in drafting the opening entry and in recording any transactions thereafter that affect the respective interests of the partners.

Opening Entries. When two or more individuals engage in an enterprise as partners, each may invest cash and other property. Certain liabilities may be assumed by the partnership, such as accounts payable, notes payable, and mortgages payable. In opening the books for a partnership, it is customary to draft a separate journal entry to record the investment of each partner. The proper asset accounts should be debited for the amounts invested, the proper liability accounts should be credited for the amounts assumed, and the partner's capital account should be credited for his equity in the assets. The opening entries for Bryant &

(*Continued on page 298*)

ARTICLES OF COPARTNERSHIP

𝕿his Contract, *Made and entered into on the*......first..............................*day of* ....July........*19--- by and between*..J. A. Bryant, of Chicago, Illinois, Party of the First Part, and W. L. Wood, of the same city and state, Party of the Second Part.

    WITNESSETH: That the said parties have this day formed a copartnership for the purpose of engaging in and conducting......a wholesale auto accessories.. *business under the following stipulations which are made a part of this contract:*

    FIRST: The said copartnership is to continue for a term of...twenty-five years................. *from date hereof.*

    SECOND: The business shall be conducted under the firm name of..Bryant & Wood...................

    THIRD: The investments are as follows:..Each partner, $15,000 in cash...............

    FOURTH: All profits or losses arising from said business are to be shared as follows:..Equally..........

    FIFTH: A systematic record of all transactions is to be kept in a double entry set of books, which are to be open for the inspection of each partner. The accounts are to be kept on the accrual basis.

    On..June 30 of each year..................*hereafter a statement of the business is to be made, the books closed and each partner credited with his share of the gain. A statement may be made at such other time as the partners agree upon.*

    SIXTH: Each partner is to devote his entire time and attention to the business and to engage in no other business enterprise without the written consent of the other.

    *SEVENTH: Each partner is to receive a salary of $*400.00...*per month, the same to be treated as an operating expense in computing net profit. Neither partner is to withdraw from the business an amount in excess of his salary without the written consent of the other.*

    EIGHTH: The duties of each partner are defined as follows:..J. A. Bryant as senior partner is to act as general manager and to have general supervision of the business. W. L. Wood is to serve as purchasing agent and sales manager, with supervision of the merchandise stock. Each partner is to attend to such other duties as are deemed necessary for the successful operation of the business.

    NINTH: Neither partner is to become surety or bondsman for anyone without the written consent of the other.

    TENTH: In case of death, incapacity, or withdrawal of either partner, the business is to be conducted for the remainder of the fiscal year by the surviving partner, and the profits for the year allocated to the withdrawing partner to be determined by the ratio of the time he was a partner during the year to the whole year.

    ELEVENTH: In case of dissolution, the assets are to be divided between the partners in the ratio of the capital invested at the time of dissolution.

    IN WITNESS WHEREOF, The parties aforesaid have hereunto set their hands and affixed their seals on the day and year above written.

J. A. Bryant
W. L. Wood

Articles of Copartnership

Wood based on the articles of copartnership reproduced on page 297 may be made in general journal form as follows:

```
Bank............................................. $15,000.00
    J. A. Bryant, Partner............................            $15,000.00
        J. A. Bryant invested $15,000 in cash.

Bank.............................................  15,000.00
    W. L. Wood, Partner.............................             15,000.00
        W. L. Wood invested $15,000 in cash.
```

If, instead of investing $15,000 in cash, Bryant were to invest office equipment valued at $600 on which he owes $200, delivery equipment valued at $1,900 on which he owes $400 represented by a mortgage, and $13,100 in cash, the proper opening entry in general journal form to record his investment would be as follows:

```
Bank............................................. $13,100.00
Office Equipment..................................    600.00
Delivery Equipment................................  1,900.00
    Accounts Payable...............................           $   200.00
    Mortgage Payable...............................               400.00
    J. A. Bryant, Partner..........................            15,000.00
        J. A. Bryant's investment in partnership.
```

Sometimes two or more individuals who have been engaged in business as sole proprietors form a partnership for the purpose of combining their businesses. Their respective balance sheets may be the basis for the opening entries to record the investments of such partners. For example, on April 1, C. E. Palmer and A. G. Sawyer form a partnership under the firm name of Palmer and Sawyer to continue the conduct of the businesses which they have been operating as sole proprietors. They agree to invest the assets shown in their respective balance sheets. It is also agreed that the partnership shall assume the liabilities shown in their respective balance sheets. Each partner is to receive credit for his equity in the assets invested by him, and the profits and losses are to be shared on the basis of Palmer, two fifths, and Sawyer, three fifths. In case of dissolution, the assets are to be distributed between the partners on the basis of their respective capital ratios at the time of dissolution. The balance sheets reproduced on page 299 were made a part of the partnership agreement.

Since the partnership is taking over the fixed assets at their book value, the cost of such property should be adjusted for prior accumulated depreciation up to the date of the transfer. Thus, the cost of the store equipment contributed by Palmer should be adjusted for the depreciation accumulated prior to the organization of the partnership. The adjusted value is the difference between the cost of $1,200 and the accumulated depreciation of $319, or $881. Likewise, the cost of the office equip-

C. E. PALMER

BALANCE SHEET

March 31, 19—

ASSETS			LIABILITIES		
Cash.............		$ 1,033.00	Notes Payable.....	$ 1,000.00	
Accounts Rec......	$1,771.32		Accounts Payable..	3,231.60	
Less Allow. for					
Bad Debts.....	137.52	1,633.80	Total Liabilities....		$ 4,231.60
Mdse. Inventory...		6,875.86	PROPRIETORSHIP		
Store Equipment...	$1,200.00		C. E. Palmer, Prop.		6,192.06
Less Allow. for					
Depreciation...	319.00	881.00			
			Total Liabilities and		
Total Assets.......		$10,423.66	Proprietorship...		$10,423.66

A. G. SAWYER

BALANCE SHEET

March 31, 19—

ASSETS			LIABILITIES		
Cash.............		$ 1,136.30	Notes Payable.....	$ 2,000.00	
Accounts Rec......	$1,700.00		Accounts Payable..	3,243.00	
Less Allow. for					
Bad Debts.....	200.00	1,500.00	Total Liabilities....		$ 5,243.00
Mdse. Inventory...		9,517.22	PROPRIETORSHIP		
Supplies..........		91.90	A. G. Sawyer, Prop.		8,702.42
Office Equipment...	$ 800.00				
Less Allow. for					
Depreciation...	200.00	600.00			
Store Equipment...	$1,500.00				
Less Allow. for					
Depreciation...	400.00	1,100.00			
			Total Liabilities and		
Total Assets.......		$13,945.42	Proprietorship...		$13,945.42

ment and the store equipment contributed by Sawyer should be adjusted for the depreciation accumulated prior to the organization of the partnership. The adjusted value of the office equipment is $600 and the store equipment $1,100.

·Since it cannot be determined which of the accounts receivable may prove to be uncollectible in whole or in part, the amount of the accounts receivable cannot be adjusted for the accumulated allowance for bad debts. It is, therefore, necessary to record the full amount of accounts receivable as a debit and the amount of the allowance for bad debts as a credit in journalizing each partner's investment in the books of the partnership.

The proper entries in general journal form to record the partners' investments are as follows:

April 1. Bank..	$1,033.00	
Accounts Receivable............................	1,771.32	
Merchandise Inventory..........................	6,875.86	
Store Equipment................................	881.00	
Notes Payable..............................		$1,000.00
Accounts Payable............................		3,231.60
Allowance for Bad Debts.....................		137.52
C. E. Palmer, Partner.......................		6,192.06
C. E. Palmer's investment in partnership.		
1. Bank..	1,136.30	
Accounts Receivable............................	1,700.00	
Merchandise Inventory..........................	9,517.22	
Supplies..	91.90	
Office Equipment...............................	600.00	
Store Equipment................................	1,100.00	
Notes Payable..............................		2,000.00
Accounts Payable............................		3,243.00
Allowance for Bad Debts.....................		200.00
A. G. Sawyer, Partner.......................		8,702.42
A. G. Sawyer's investment in partnership.		

Had the fixed assets of Palmer and Sawyer been taken over by the partnership at any value other than their book value, the assets should be recorded in the books of the partnership at the value agreed upon. For example, if it had been agreed that the store equipment invested by Palmer was to be valued at $1,000 instead of its book value, Store Equipment should be debited for $1,000 instead of $881, and Palmer's capital account should be credited for $6,311.06 instead of $6,192.06. Thus, the book value of the store equipment as shown in Palmer's balance sheet of March 31 would be ignored and the store equipment would be recorded in the books of the partnership at the value agreed upon between the partners. Such agreed value represents the cost of the store equipment to the partnership.

It will be observed that the ratio of the partners' investments in the partnership is not exactly the same as their profit-and-loss-sharing ratio. The basis on which profits and losses are to be shared is a matter of agreement between the partners and it is not necessarily the same as their investment ratio. It should be recognized that there are factors other than capital invested that may enter into a profit-and-loss-sharing agreement. For example, one partner may contribute most of the capital but may render no services, while the other partner may contribute less capital but may devote his full time to the partnership; therefore, they may agree to share the profits equally.

Admitting a New Partner. A new partner may be admitted to a partnership by agreement among the partners. For example, Palmer and

Sawyer may admit W. H. Walker as a partner and agree to share profits and losses on the basis of their capital ratio. If his investment consisted of cash only, the proper entry to admit him to the partnership would involve a debit to the bank account and a credit to his capital account for the amount invested. If Walker has been operating a business of his own as a sole proprietor and his business is taken over by the partnership, his balance sheet will serve as a basis for drafting the opening entry. Assume that, as of July 1, Walker was admitted to the partnership. The assets listed in his balance sheet are taken over, his liabilities are assumed, and he is given credit for his equity in the assets. His balance sheet follows:

W. H. WALKER

BALANCE SHEET

June 30, 19—

ASSETS			LIABILITIES		
Cash.............		$ 2,865.46	Notes Payable.....	$ 2,900.00	
Accounts Rec......	$4,580.00		Accounts Payable..	2,419.65	
Less Allow. for					
Bad Debts.....	345.43	4,234.57	Total Liabilities....		$ 5,319.65
Mdse. Inventory...		7,747.25	PROPRIETORSHIP		
			W. H. Walker, Prop.		9,527.63
			Total Liabilities and		
Total Assets.......		$14,847.28	Proprietorship...		$14,847.28

The proper entry in general journal form to admit Walker as a partner is as follows:

July 1. Bank......................................	$2,865.46	
Accounts Receivable..........................	4,580.00	
Merchandise Inventory........................	7,747.25	
Notes Payable............................		$2,900.00
Accounts Payable...........................		2,419.65
Allowance for Bad Debts....................		345.43
W. H. Walker, Partner......................		9,527.63
W. H. Walker admitted to partnership.		

The admission of a new partner calls for the dissolution of the old partnership and the creation of a new partnership. A new partnership agreement should be drawn including all the usual provisions.

Goodwill. Some business organizations are able to earn consistently profits that are very large in relation to the amount of the recorded assets that they possess. This excess earning power may be due to exceptional management, good location, or one or more of several other factors. When such a condition exists, the business is said to possess *goodwill*. Because of the fact that goodwill is difficult to measure and may not be permanent, accountants do not favor its formal recognition as an asset unless it has been purchased.

For example, suppose that Palmer and Sawyer purchased the business of W. H. Walker for $12,134.54 cash, acquiring all his business assets except cash and assuming all his liabilities. If the book value ($11,981.82) of the assets purchased from Walker was considered to be their fair value, Palmer and Sawyer paid $5,472.37 more for the business than the net value of the assets acquired. This amount may be considered to be the price paid for the goodwill of Walker's business. The transaction could be recorded as follows:

July 1. Accounts Receivable............................	$4,580.00	
Merchandise Inventory.........................	7,747.25	
Goodwill....................................	5,472.37	
Notes Payable..............................		$ 2,900.00
Accounts Payable...........................		2,419.65
Allowance for Bad Debts....................		345.43
Bank......................................		12,134.54
Purchased W. H. Walker's business.		

It is permissible to record goodwill if a new partner is taken into a firm and is allowed a capital interest in excess of the net assets he invests. For example, suppose that, instead of purchasing Walker's business, Palmer and Sawyer had agreed to take him into the firm as a partner and to give him a capital interest of $15,000 for his business (including his business cash). Walker's investment might be recorded as follows:

July 1. Bank..	$2,865.46	
Accounts Receivable..........................	4,580.00	
Merchandise Inventory.........................	7,747.25	
Goodwill....................................	5,472.37	
Notes Payable..............................		$ 2,900.00
Accounts Payable...........................		2,419.65
Allowance for Bad Debts....................		345.43
W. H. Walker, Partner......................		15,000.00
W. H. Walker admitted to partnership.		

Goodwill is considered to be an *intangible asset*. When goodwill is recorded in the accounts, it is usually reported in the balance sheet as the last item in the asset section.

Compensation of Partners. The compensation of partners may be in the form of salaries, royalties, commissions, bonuses, or other compensation. The amount of each partner's compensation and the method of accounting for it should be stated in the partnership agreement. For example, in the articles of copartnership shown on page 297, it is stipulated that each partner is to receive a salary of $400 a month. When all partners receive the same salaries and when profits and losses are shared equally, it is immaterial whether the salaries are treated as an expense of the partnership or as withdrawals of anticipated profits. Under the federal income tax law, salaries or other compensation paid to partners for services rendered may not be claimed as a deduction from gross income in the income tax return of the partnership unless such salaries are guaranteed. In this event, the amounts may be treated as deductions. (The partners, of course, must report such income in their individual returns.) However, apart from income tax considerations, the partnership agreement may provide that partners' salaries are to be treated as an operating expense in computing the net income or the net loss to be shared by the partners.

If partners' salaries are not treated as an expense of the partnership, it is not necessary to keep a salary account for each partner. Amounts withdrawn by the partners as compensation for services may simply be charged to their respective drawing accounts. If partners' salaries are treated as an operating expense, it is usually advisable to keep a separate salary account for each partner. For example, the salaries specified in the partnership agreement between J. A. Bryant and W. L. Wood are to be treated as an operating expense. If the salaries are paid regularly, such as monthly or semimonthly, it will be necessary only to debit each partner's salary account and to credit the bank account. Instead of paying partners' salaries regularly in cash, they may be credited to the partners' drawing accounts. The partners may then draw against such salaries at will. Under this plan the proper entry to record each partner's salary on each payday is to debit his salary account and to credit his drawing account for the proper amount.

Allocation of Partnership Profits and Losses. The partnership agreement should specify the basis on which profits and losses are to be shared by the partners. In the absence of an agreement between the partners, profits and losses must be shared equally regardless of the ratio of the partners' investments. If the partnership agreement specifies how profits are to be shared, but does not specify how losses are to be shared, the losses must be shared on the same basis as that indicated for the profits.

After closing the temporary accounts into Income Summary at the end of the accounting period, the balance of the summary account represents either net income or net loss. If the account has a credit balance, it represents net income; if the account has a debit balance, it represents net loss.

The balance of the income summary account should be allocated in accordance with the partnership agreement. If the account has a credit balance, the entry to close requires a debit to Income Summary and credits to either the partners' drawing or capital accounts for the proper share of the net income in each case. Because the partners may formally or informally agree that they will not withdraw any of their permanent investments without mutual consent, it may be preferable to credit their drawing accounts with their respective shares of net income. Any credit balances in partners' personal or drawing accounts can be reduced by withdrawals without restriction.

Dissolution of a Partnership. As previously explained, dissolution of a partnership may be brought about through bankruptcy or the death of one of the partners. A partner cannot retire from the partnership before its termination without the consent of his partners. To do so would constitute a violation of the partnership agreement and would make him liable to his partners for any loss resulting from his retirement.

By agreement, a partner may retire and be permitted to withdraw assets equal to or more or less than the amount of his proprietary interest in the partnership. The book value of a partner's interest is shown by the credit balance of his capital account after all profits or losses have been allocated in accordance with the agreement and the books are closed. Should the retiring partner withdraw cash or other assets equal to the credit balance of his capital account, the transaction will have no effect upon the capital of the remaining partners.

Suppose, for example, that sometime after W. H. Walker had been taken into the partnership of Palmer and Sawyer, he expressed a desire to retire and his partners agreed to his withdrawal of cash equal to the amount of his equity in the assets of the partnership. After closing the temporary proprietorship accounts into Income Summary and after allocating the net income and closing the partners' drawing accounts, the partners' capital accounts had credit balances as follows:

C. E. Palmer	$ 7,000.00
A. G. Sawyer	9,000.00
W. H. Walker	10,000.00

This indicates that the book value of Walker's interest in the partnership amounts to $10,000. If this amount is withdrawn in cash, the entry in general journal form to record the transaction in the books of the partnership is as follows:

W. H. Walker, Partner	$10,000.00	
Bank		$10,000.00
W. H. Walker retired, withdrawing $10,000 in settlement of his equity.		

While the transaction involves a decrease in the asset Cash with a corresponding decrease in the aggregate capital of the partnership, it does not affect the equity of the remaining partners. Thus, Palmer still has an equity of $7,000 and Sawyer, $9,000, in the partnership assets.

If a retiring partner agrees to withdraw less than the book value of his interest in the partnership, the effect of the transaction will be to increase the capital accounts of the remaining partners. To record such a transaction it is necessary to debit the retiring partner's account for the amount of its credit balance, to credit the assets withdrawn, and to credit the remaining partners' accounts for the difference between the value of the assets withdrawn and the credit balance of the retiring partner's account.

Thus, if Walker had agreed to withdraw only $8,000 in settlement of his equity in the assets of the partnership, the transaction should be recorded in the books of the partnership as follows:

W. H. Walker, Partner...........................	$10,000.00	
Bank...		$8,000.00
C. E. Palmer, Partner...........................		875.00
A. G. Sawyer, Partner...........................		1,125.00

W. H. Walker retired, withdrawing $8,000 in settlement of his equity.

The difference between Walker's equity in the assets of the partnership and the amount of cash withdrawn is $2,000. This difference is divided between the remaining partners on a basis of their profit-and-loss-sharing agreement which happens to be the same as their capital ratio. Thus, Palmer is credited for 7/16 of $2,000, or $875, while Sawyer is credited for 9/16 of $2,000, or $1,125.

If a partner is permitted to withdraw more than the book value of his interest in the partnership, the effect of the transaction is to decrease the capital accounts of the remaining partners. Thus, if Palmer and Sawyer had agreed to Walker's withdrawal of $12,000 in settlement of his equity in the assets of the partnership, the transaction should be recorded in the books of the partnership as follows:

W. H. Walker, Partner...........................	$10,000.00	
C. E. Palmer, Partner...........................	875.00	
A. G. Sawyer, Partner...........................	1,125.00	
Bank...		$12,000.00

W. H. Walker retired, withdrawing $12,000 in settlement of his equity.

The excess of the amount of cash withdrawn over Walker's equity in the partnership is divided between the remaining partners on a basis of their profit-and-loss-sharing agreement. Thus, Palmer is debited for 7/16 of $2,000, or $875, while Sawyer is debited for 9/16 of $2,000, or $1,125.

When a partner retires from the business his interest may be purchased by one or more of the remaining partners or by an outside party. If he sells his interest to one of the remaining partners, his equity is merely transferred to the other partner. Thus, if instead of withdrawing cash in settlement of his equity in the partnership, Walker sells his interest to Palmer, the only entry required to record the transaction on the books of the partnership is as follows:

W. H. Walker, Partner.............................	$10,000.00	
C. E. Palmer, Partner.............................		$10,000.00
C. E. Palmer purchased W. H. Walker's interest in the partnership.		

The amount paid Walker for his interest is immaterial to the firm. Any profit or loss resulting from the transaction is a personal gain or loss affecting the individual parties to the transaction but not the firm. If Walker should sell his interest to an outside party who is admitted to the partnership, the only entry needed to record the transaction is an entry to transfer Walker's interest to the new partner. Thus, a journal entry should be made debiting Walker's capital account and crediting the capital account of the new partner for $10,000.

Partnership Accounts in the Balance Sheet. The method of exhibiting the proprietary interests of the partners in the balance sheet of a partnership is similar to that of a sole proprietorship except that the proprietary interest of each partner should be shown separately. Following is an illustration of the proprietorship section of a balance sheet for a partnership which is operated on the basis of a fiscal year ending June 30.

PROPRIETORSHIP

J. A. Bryant, Partner			
Proprietorship, July 1 (Beginning of Year).........		$15,000.00	
Net Income (½ of $3,779.40)...........	$1,889.70		
Less Withdrawals...................	1,126.60	763.10	
Proprietorship, June 30 (End of Year).............			$15,763.10
W. L. Wood, Partner			
Proprietorship, July 1 (Beginning of Year).........		$15,000.00	
Net Income (½ of $3,779.40)...........	$1,889.70		
Less Withdrawals...................	1,127.35	762.35	
Proprietorship, June 30 (End of Year).............			15,762.35
Total Proprietorship..............................			$31,525.45

PRACTICE ASSIGNMENT No. 22. Complete Report No. 22 in the workbook and submit your working papers to the instructor for approval. Then continue with the following study assignment until Report No. 23 is required.

(23) THE CORPORATION

A private corporation is an artificial person created by law for an expressed purpose, combining the capital of its stockholders for their mutual benefit. It differs from a sole proprietorship or a partnership from the standpoints of organization, ownership, and distribution of net income.

Organization of a Corporation. In order to incorporate an enterprise, a charter must be obtained from the state in which the corporation is to be formed. The persons who file application for a charter or for a certificate of incorporation are known as the *incorporators*. Such persons must be competent to contract, some or all of them must be citizens of the state in which the application is filed, and usually each incorporator is required to be a subscriber for one or more shares of the capital stock. All of the incorporators must sign the application for the charter.

The procedure in incorporating an enterprise must conform to the laws of the state in which it is desired to incorporate. The laws of the different states vary considerably in their provisions relating to the organization of corporations. Persons desiring to incorporate a company should acquaint themselves with the laws of the state in which they wish to incorporate, as it will be necessary to comply with the laws of that state. The following excerpts from the laws of one of the states will illustrate the procedure to be observed in forming a corporation:

"Private corporations may be created by the voluntary association of three or more persons for the purposes authorized by law and in the manner hereinafter mentioned.
"A charter must be prepared, setting forth:

1. The name of the corporation;
2. The purpose for which it is formed;
3. The place or places where the business is to be transacted;
4. The term for which it is to exist;
5. The number of directors or trustees, and the names and residences of those who are appointees for the first year; and
6. The amount of the capital stock, if any, and the number of shares into which it is divided.

"It must be subscribed by three or more persons, two of whom must be citizens of this State, and must be acknowledged by them, before an officer duly authorized to take acknowledgments of deeds.

"The certificate of incorporation shall also set forth the minimum amount of capital with which the corporation will commence business, which shall not be less than $1,000. The certificate of incorporation may also contain any provision which the incorporators may choose to insert for the management of the business and for the conduct of the affairs of the corporation, and any provisions creating, defining, limiting, and regulating the powers of the corporation, the directors and the stockholders, or any class of the stockholders.

"The affidavit of those who executed the charter shall be furnished to the Secretary of State, showing:

1. The name, residence, and post-office address of each subscriber to the capital stock of such company;
2. The amount subscribed by each, and the amount paid by each;
3. The cash value of any property received, with its description, location, and from whom and the price at which it was received; and
4. The amount, character, and value of labor done, and from whom and the price at which it was received."

The Charter. After articles of incorporation or a petition for a charter has been filed, and other conditions, such as the payment of incorporation fees, have been fulfilled, the document is examined by a court or an administrative officer. If the instrument is satisfactory and the other requirements have been met, a license, a certificate of incorporation, or a charter is issued and recorded or filed as required by the particular statute of the state concerned. An illustration of a charter issued to a corporation under the laws of the State of Texas is shown on page 309. While, as previously stated, the provisions of law governing corporation organization vary in different states, in general they include all the important factors peculiar to a corporation, such as name, purpose, duration, location, and capitalization.

Ownership of a Corporation. Ownership of a corporation is represented by capital stock, and the owners of the stock are known as *stockholders*.

Subscriptions to the capital stock of a corporation may be made before or after incorporation. A subscription made before incorporation is an agreement to subscribe for stock. It is a contract entered into between the subscriber and the incorporator or promoter and not between the subscriber and the corporation. The corporation, as such, does not exist until after articles of incorporation have been filed with the secretary of state or other proper official. A subscription to capital stock after incorporation is a contract between the subscriber and the corporation.

Stockholders. All parties holding stock of a corporation, or whose subscriptions for stock have been accepted, are known as stockholders. In order to possess all of the rights of a stockholder of record, the party holding stock must have his ownership duly recorded in the books of the issuing company. If a party purchases stock from a stockholder, such stock must be transferred in the books of the issuing company before the purchaser is entitled to have a certificate of stock in his own name, to vote, or to share in any dividends declared.

Directors. The stockholders elect a *board of directors* that is charged with the management and direction of corporate affairs. It will readily be seen that it would be impracticable for all the stockholders of a large corporation to meet periodically or at special times to decide upon questions in connection with the direction and management of affairs; hence,

(*Continued on page 310*)

<table>
<tr><td>THE STATE OF TEXAS
COUNTY OF DALLAS</td><td>} KNOW ALL MEN BY THESE PRESENTS:</td></tr>
</table>

That we, the subscribers hereto, citizens of the State of Texas, under the provisions of the Revised Statutes of the State of Texas, do hereby form and incorporate ourselves into a voluntary association and corporation to transact a mercantile business and particularly to purchase and sell goods, wares, and merchandise used for said business, having all the authority, express or implied, by the Statutes of the State of Texas, and to that end we do hereby adopt and subscribe the following, to-wit:

CHARTER

Article 1. This corporation shall be named and known as THE BRYANT COM-PANY, INC., *by which name it shall contract and be contracted with, sue and be sued, and transact all other business.*

Article 2. This corporation is formed for the purpose of transacting a mercantile business and particularly to purchase and sell goods, wares, and merchandise usually offered for sale by wholesale and retail merchants engaged in such business.

Article 3. The place of business of this corporation shall be Dallas County, Texas, the principal office being at Dallas in Dallas County, Texas, and said corporation having the right, power, and authority to operate and do business anywhere in the State of Texas.

Article 4. Said corporation shall exist for a term of fifty years.

Article 5. The business of this corporation shall be transacted by not less than three and not more than twenty-one directors, who shall be elected by the stockholders annually on the last Tuesday of July, the following named stockholders being hereby declared to be directors for the first year:

J. A. BRYANT
W. L. WOOD
RICHARD SMITH

Article 6. The capital stock of this corporation shall consist of five hundred (500) shares with a par value of One Hundred Dollars ($100) each, all common voting stock, all of which has been in good faith subscribed, and one half thereof has been paid for in cash, as shown by affidavit hereto attached.

Article 7. This corporation when created reserves to itself, and for and on behalf of its stockholders, all rights, powers, and privileges granted by the laws of the State of Texas at this time, with the right to accept all laws hereafter passed granting additional powers.

IN TESTIMONY WHEREOF, witness our signatures this 28th day of June, A. D. 19--.

(Signed) J. A. BRYANT
W. L. WOOD
RICHARD SMITH

THE STATE OF TEXAS }
COUNTY OF DALLAS

BEFORE ME, the undersigned authority, a Notary Public in and for Dallas County, Texas, on this day personally appeared J. A. Bryant, W. L. Wood, and Richard Smith, all known to me to be the persons whose names are subscribed to the foregoing instrument and acknowledged to me that they each executed the same for the purposes and considera-tion therein expressed.

GIVEN UNDER MY HAND AND SEAL OF OFFICE this 28th day of June, A. D. 19--.

(Signed) ALLEN JONES
Notary Public in and for
Dallas County, Texas

Charter of a Corporation

the stockholders elect a board of directors that is responsible to the stockholders for the proper management of the corporate affairs. The directors are held to be the agents of the corporation.

A board of directors usually consists of three or more stockholders. Where the board is composed of a large number of persons, it is customary to appoint an *executive committee* of from three to five members of the board, who are given authority to administer the affairs of the corporation.

Officers. The board of directors elects the officers. Usually a president, vice-president, secretary, and treasurer are elected as executive officers. One person may hold two positions; for instance, the same person may serve both as secretary and treasurer. All the officers are responsible to the board of directors and receive their instructions from the board. They have no authority whatever other than to perform the duties imposed by the by-laws of the corporation and the statutes of the state. Generally they are liable for fraud or misrepresentation, or for exceeding the rights and powers conferred by the by-laws of the company or the statutes of the state.

Capital Stock. The charter obtained by a business corporation specifies the amount of capital stock that it is authorized to issue. The state authorizes a corporation to issue a certain number of shares of stock, and it is illegal for a company to issue a greater number of shares than is authorized in its charter. A certificate of stock issued to J. A. Bryant by The Bryant Company, Inc., with the stub completed is reproduced on page 311. It will be noted that the stub of the stock certificate book provides information as to the number of shares issued and the date of issue.

Capital stock may or may not have *par value.* Par value is a technical legal matter whose practical significance is not very great in most cases. In general, par represents the smallest amount that the corporation can accept in exchange for a share of stock when it is originally issued without the buyer of the stock incurring some liability to the corporation. In many states par-value stock cannot be sold originally by the corporation for less than par value. In most states it is possible for corporations to issue stock that has no par value.

If the corporation has only one type of capital stock, it is called *common stock.* The stockholders own the corporation "in common." Among other things, they have the right to vote for directors and upon certain other matters, the right to receive *dividends* representing a share of any

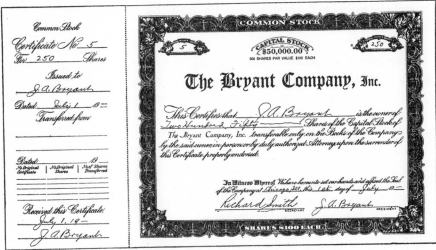

Certificate of Stock with Stub Attached

earnings, and the right to share in the distribution of the assets if the corporation is dissolved. In all cases these rights are in direct proportion to the number of shares of stock owned.

Some corporations have more than one class or type of stock. The classes differ with respect to the rights which go with the ownership of the stock. In addition to common stock, a corporation may have one or more types of *preferred stock*. Stock of this type may entitle the holder to receive a limited share of the earnings before the common stockholders receive any dividends and may involve a first or "prior" claim upon assets in the event the corporation is dissolved. Sometimes preferred stock has a "preference" as to both dividends and assets. Frequently preferred stockholders do not have voting rights.

If a corporation has only one class of common stock outstanding, the *book value* per share of such stock is equal to the total capital of the corporation (assets less liabilities) divided by the number of shares outstanding. If the corporation also has preferred stock outstanding, the book value per share of common stock will be the total capital less the portion of net worth that is allocated to the preferred stock, divided by the number of shares of common stock outstanding.

It is not to be expected that the book value per share and the *market value* per share will be the same. The latter is influenced by a number of factors, particularly the corporation's chances for success in the future. Market value is easy to determine if the corporation's stock is listed and actively traded on an organized stock exchange. If not, market value can only be estimated. In most cases the par value (if any), the book value, and the market value of the stock of a corporation differ in amount.

Corporate Transactions. The ordinary operating transactions of a corporation are similar to those of a sole proprietorship or of a partnership operating a business of like nature. Corporate transactions are those involving capital stock or those that affect the net worth of the corporation in some other way. Following are a few typical corporate transactions:

    (a) Capital stock subscriptions.
    (b) Payments received to apply on capital stock subscriptions.
    (c) Issuance of capital stock to subscribers.
    (d) Transfer of capital stock from one stockholder to another stockholder.
    (e) Declaration and payment of dividends.

Corporate Accounts. Following is a list of the major accounts that are peculiar to the corporate form of organization:

ACCOUNT	CLASSIFICATION
Capital Stock	Capital
Subscriptions Receivable	Asset
Capital Stock Subscribed	Capital
Retained Earnings (sometimes called *Earned Surplus*)	Capital
Dividends Payable	Liability

One of the features of accounting for corporate net worth is the distinction that is usually maintained in the records between capital that is due to investments by stockholders and capital that results from the retention of income. In the case of certain types of corporate transactions, this distinction as to the source of the capital is not evident, but in most cases the difference is reflected in the accounts. If the corporation exchanges its stock for cash or other property equal in amount to the par value of the shares issued, the transaction should be recorded by debiting the proper asset account and by crediting Capital Stock. If there is more than one type of capital stock, there should be an account for each type.

Sometimes a corporation obtains *subscriptions* to its stock wherein each subscriber agrees to buy a certain number of shares at an agreed price — possibly par, if the stock has par value — and to pay for the shares at or within a specified time, either in full at one time or in installments over a period of time. If, for example, a subscription were received for 100 shares at a price of $25 each (assumed to be the par value of the shares in this case), the transaction should be recorded by debiting Subscriptions Receivable and by crediting Capital Stock Subscribed for $2,500. Collections of the subscription should be debited to Cash (or whatever was accepted in lieu of cash) and credited to Subscriptions Receivable. When the subscription is paid in full the stock will be issued and an entry should be made debiting Capital Stock Subscribed and crediting Capital Stock for $2,500. As long as Subscriptions Receivable has a balance representing an amount that is expected to be collected, the account is treated as an asset and should be so exhibited in the balance sheet. Capital Stock Subscribed is a capital account, the balance of which indicates the amount that eventually will be added to Capital Stock.

At the end of each accounting period, the balance of the income summary account is transferred to the retained earnings account. If a corporation is operated at a loss, the amount of the net loss which is transferred from the income summary account to the retained earnings account might result in the retained earnings account having a debit balance. In such event, this balance is termed a *deficit* and it will appear as a negative element in the capital section of the corporation's balance sheet.

A decision on the part of the directors of a corporation to pay a dividend is commonly referred to as a *declaration of dividends*. When dividends are declared and such dividends are payable in cash at a later date, it is customary to record the declaration by debiting Retained Earnings and by crediting Dividends Payable. The dividends payable account will have a credit balance until all dividends declared have been paid in full, after which the account will be in balance. When dividends are paid immediately upon being declared, there is no need for setting up an account with Dividends Payable. Usually the dividends are not paid for sometime after being declared by the directors; in the meantime, the amount of the dividends declared represents a liability of the corporation that should be listed in the balance sheet as Dividends Payable.

Accounting Procedure. Following is a narrative of corporate transactions with illustrative journal entries:

(1) The Bryant Company, Inc. was incorporated with an authorized issue of 500 shares of common capital stock, par value $100 per share. At the time of incorporation, subscriptions had been received as follows:

J. A. Bryant... 250 shares
W. L. Wood... 125 shares
Richard Smith.. 125 shares

The stock was subscribed for at par value and one half of the subscription price was paid in cash, the balance to be paid on demand.

To record this transaction it is necessary (a) to record the stock subscriptions received, and (b) to record the cash received to apply on the subscription price. These entries may be made in journal form as follows:

(a)

Subscriptions Receivable............................	$50,000.00	
Capital Stock Subscribed...........................		$50,000.00
Received subscriptions to capital stock at par as follows:		

<blockquote>
J. A. Bryant, 250 shares
W. L. Wood, 125 shares
Richard Smith, 125 shares
</blockquote>

(b)

Bank...	25,000.00	
Subscriptions Receivable..........................		25,000.00
Received cash on account of subscriptions to capital stock as follows:		

<blockquote>
J. A. Bryant, $12,500
W. L. Wood, $6,250
Richard Smith, $6,250
</blockquote>

(2) Received cash from subscribers to capital stock to complete payment of balances due as follows:

<blockquote>

J. A. Bryant......................................	$12,500.00
W. L. Wood.......................................	6,250.00
Richard Smith....................................	6,250.00

</blockquote>

This transaction involves an increase in the asset Cash and a decrease in the asset Subscriptions Receivable. The transaction may be recorded in journal form as follows:

Bank...	$25,000.00	
Subscriptions Receivable..........................		$25,000.00
Received cash in payment of the balance due from subscribers to capital stock as follows:		

<blockquote>
J. A. Bryant, $12,500
W. L. Wood, $6,250
Richard Smith, $6,250
</blockquote>

(3) Issued certificates of stock to the following subscribers who had paid their subscriptions in full:

<blockquote>

J. A. Bryant.....................................	250 shares
W. L. Wood......................................	125 shares
Richard Smith...................................	125 shares

</blockquote>

Usually certificates of stock are not issued until subscriptions are paid in full. In this case the subscribers have paid their subscriptions in full and the stock certificates have been issued.　The transaction may be recorded in journal form as follows:

Capital Stock Subscribed............................	$50,000.00	
Capital Stock*....................................		$50,000.00
Capital stock issued to subscribers as follows:		
J. A. Bryant, 250 shares		
W. L. Wood, 125 shares		
Richard Smith, 125 shares		

After posting all of the foregoing entries, the capital stock account will have a credit balance of $50,000 that represents the par value of the capital stock outstanding.

(4) J. A. Bryant returned his stock certificate for 250 shares and requested that 50 shares be transferred to J. M. Fields and that a new certificate for 200 shares be issued to himself.

This transaction indicates that Bryant has sold 50 shares of his stock to Fields.　Transferring capital stock from one stockholder to another involves the cancellation of an old certificate and the issuance of new certificates for the proper number of shares.　In this case, it is necessary to cancel the original certificate for 250 shares issued to Bryant and to issue two new certificates, one to Fields for 50 shares and one to Bryant for 200 shares.　The transaction has no effect upon the assets, liabilities, or capital of the corporation.　It is merely a transfer of stock between stockholders and the only entry required is a transfer entry in the records kept of stock issued by the corporation.

(5) The board of directors at its annual meeting held on June 15 voted to pay a cash dividend of $5 per share, the dividend to be paid on July 1 to stockholders of record June 15.

The credit balance of the income summary account is usually transferred to the credit of the retained earnings account. The board of directors has the right to decide when dividends shall be paid to stockholders. After dividends have been declared, they constitute a liability of the corporation, and this liability should be recorded at the time the dividend is declared.　The transaction may be recorded in journal form as follows:

June 15. Retained Earnings............................	$2,500.00	
Dividends Payable........................		$2,500.00
Dividend declared by the directors.		

---

*When both common stock and preferred stock are authorized in the charter of a corporation, separate accounts should be kept for each class of stock.　A memorandum entry of the number of shares authorized should be entered in the Items column of each capital stock account.

Dividends may be paid immediately upon being declared or at some later date. The larger corporations usually do not pay dividends until sometime after the date of declaration. The directors usually specify that the dividends shall be paid to the stockholders of record as of a certain date. This means that only stockholders who have their stock recorded in their names on that date are entitled to receive dividends. Any stockholder who acquires stock after that date is not entitled to share in the dividend previously declared. To record the payment of the dividend declared in transaction No. 5, it is necessary to debit Dividends Payable and to credit the bank account as in the following journal entry:

July   1.   Dividends Payable......................... $2,500.00
                Bank.................................... $2,500.00
                   Paid dividend declared June 15.

This transaction has the effect of decreasing the liability Dividends Payable $2,500 with a similar decrease in the asset Cash. After the transaction is posted, the dividends payable account will be in balance.

Incorporating a Sole Proprietorship. The legal steps involved in incorporating a sole proprietorship are the same as in organizing a new corporation. Usually the sole proprietor becomes the principal stockholder in the corporation and transfers his assets to the corporation in exchange for capital stock. His liabilities may also be assumed by the corporation. The same books of account may be continued or an entirely new set of books may be installed. Suppose, for example, that The Scott Company, Inc. was organized to take over the business formerly conducted by F. W. Scott as a sole proprietorship. Scott subscribes for 200 shares of the capital stock at $100 per share and transfers his equity in the assets ($14,300) listed in his balance sheet of December 31 (reproduced on page 292) to apply on his subscription.

If Scott plans to continue to use the same set of books with any modifications needed in view of the change to the corporate form of enterprise, the entries to record his subscription and its partial payment by the transfer of his business assets and liabilities to the corporation would be as follows:

Subscriptions Receivable........................... $20,000.00
     Capital Stock Subscribed......................... $20,000.00
        F. W. Scott subscribed for 200 shares of stock at par.

F. W. Scott, Proprietor............................ 14,300.00
     Subscriptions Receivable.........................   14,300.00
        Assets and liabilities of F. W. Scott transferred to
        corporation at book value.

When these entries are posted, Scott's proprietorship account will be in balance. The following corporate accounts will take the place of Scott's proprietorship account in the general ledger:

Capital Stock
Subscriptions Receivable
Capital Stock Subscribed

If, instead of using the same books of account that were used by Scott, a new set of books is installed by the corporation, a journal entry should be made to record the transfer of the accounts of the sole proprietorship to the corporation. If the fixed assets are being taken over at their book value, it is customary to record them in the books of the corporation at their net value after making adjustment for prior accumulated depreciation. If the fixed assets are being taken over at any value other than their book value, they should be recorded in the books of the corporation at the value agreed upon. Such value represents the cost of the assets to the corporation. The accounts of Scott may be transferred to The Scott Company, Inc. by means of the following general journal entry in the books of the corporation:

Bank..	$4,750.00	
Accounts Receivable................................	3,800.00	
Merchandise Inventory..............................	6,950.00	
Office Equipment...................................	1,200.00	
Store Equipment....................................	900.00	
Delivery Equipment.................................	1,300.00	
Notes Payable.................................		$1,000.00
Accounts Payable...............................		3,200.00
Allowance for Bad Debts........................		400.00
Subscriptions Receivable........................		14,300.00
Assets and liabilities of F. W. Scott transferred to corporation at book value.		

Assuming that Scott paid the balance due on his subscription and that a stock certificate for 200 shares was issued to him, the transactions should be recorded in the books of the corporation as follows:

Bank..	$ 5,700.00	
Subscriptions Receivable........................		$ 5,700.00
Cash received from F. W. Scott in payment of balance due on subscription to capital stock.		
Capital Stock Subscribed...........................	20,000.00	
Capital Stock..................................		20,000.00
Issued 200 shares of common capital stock to F. W. Scott.		

Incorporating a Partnership. A partnership may be terminated by incorporation and the partners may become stockholders of the corporation. The same books of account may be continued or a new set of books may be installed by the corporation. Suppose, for example, that The James Company, Inc. is organized with an authorized capital of $50,000 to take over the business formerly conducted by James and Snyder, partners. The partners subscribe for capital stock of the corporation as follows:

J. O. James, 150 shares @ $100 a share............................ $15,000.00
M. W. Snyder, 100 shares @ $100 a share......................... 10,000.00

James and Snyder, as individuals, are to receive credit toward their subscriptions for their respective equities in the assets of the partnership.

The following balance sheet for the partnership was prepared at the time of incorporating the business:

JAMES & SNYDER
BALANCE SHEET
DECEMBER 31, 19--

ASSETS			LIABILITIES		
Cash..............		$ 4,600.00	Notes Payable.....	$2,000.00	
Notes Receivable...	$ 750.00		Accounts Payable..	3,738.75	
Accounts Rec......	3,800.00				
	$4,550.00		Total Liabilities....		$ 5,738.75
Less Allow. for					
Bad Debts.....	300.00	4,250.00	PROPRIETORSHIP		
			J. O. James, Partner		7,246.50
Mdse. Inventory...		9,800.00	M. W. Snyder,		
Office Equipment...	$1,600.00		Partner.........		7,364.75
Less Allow. for					
Depreciation...	500.00	1,100.00			
Delivery Equipment	$1,200.00				
Less Allow. for					
Depreciation...	600.00	600.00			
			Total Liabilities and		
Total Assets.......		$20,350.00	Proprietorship...		$20,350.00

The subscriptions to the capital stock should be recorded as indicated in the following general journal entry:

Subscriptions Receivable........................... $25,000.00
Capital Stock Subscribed.......................... $25,000.00
    Received subscriptions to capital stock as follows:
        J. O. James, 150 shares
        M. W. Snyder, 100 shares

If the books of the partnership are to be continued in use by the corporation, the transfer of the partners' equities to the corporation may be made by means of the following general journal entry:

J. O. James, Partner................................	$7,246.50	
M. W. Snyder, Partner.............................	7,364.75	
Subscriptions Receivable..........................		$14,611.25
Assets and liabilities of James and Snyder transferred to corporation at book value.		

When this entry is posted, the partners' accounts will be in balance. If, instead of using the same books of account as were used by James and Snyder, a new set of books is installed by the corporation, the following journal entry in the books of the corporation is required to transfer the accounts of the partnership to the corporation:

Bank..	$4,600.00	
Notes Receivable..................................	750.00	
Accounts Receivable...............................	3,800.00	
Merchandise Inventory.............................	9,800.00	
Office Equipment..................................	1,100.00	
Delivery Equipment................................	600.00	
Notes Payable....................................		$ 2,000.00
Accounts Payable.................................		3,738.75
Allowance for Bad Debts...........................		300.00
Subscriptions Receivable...........................		14,611.25
Assets and liabilities of James and Snyder transferred to corporation at book value.		

It will be noted that the fixed assets of James and Snyder are recorded in the books of the corporation at their net book value after making adjustments for prior accumulated depreciation. Had the fixed assets been taken over at any value other than their book value, they should be recorded in the books of the corporation at the value agreed upon.

Assuming that James and Snyder paid the balance due on their subscriptions and that stock certificates were issued to them, the transactions should be recorded in the books of the corporation as follows:

Bank..	$10,388.75	
Subscriptions Receivable..........................		$10,388.75
Received cash from subscribers as follows:		
J. O. James, $7,753.50		
M. W. Snyder, $2,635.25		
Capital Stock Subscribed...........................	25,000.00	
Capital Stock....................................		25,000.00
Issued common capital stock to subscribers.		

Corporate Accounts in the Balance Sheet. In preparing a balance sheet for a corporation the corporate accounts are usually grouped together under the heading of "Capital" following the liabilities. This is known as the capital section of the balance sheet and it serves exactly the same purpose as the proprietorship section of the balance sheet for a sole proprietorship or for a partnership. At the end of the first year of operations, the capital section of the balance sheet of The James Company, Inc. appeared as follows:

CAPITAL

Capital Stock (500 shares authorized; 250 shares issued)..........	$25,000.00
Retained Earnings..	4,000.00
Total Capital...	$29,000.00

It should be understood that, because of differences in capital structure, there may be considerable variation in the capital section of balance sheets prepared for different corporations. If more than one kind of capital stock is issued, each kind should be listed separately. There may be retained earnings or a deficit at the end of the year. A deficit should be shown as a deduction from the par or stated value of the capital stock in arriving at the total capital of a corporation.

PRACTICE ASSIGNMENT No. 23. Complete Report No. 23 in the workbook and submit your working papers to the instructor for approval. Then continue with the following study assignment in Unit Twelve until Report No. 24 is required.

Unit Twelve

ACCOUNTING FOR NOTES AND DRAFTS

(24) NOTES

Negotiable Instruments. "An unconditional, written promise or order to pay a sum certain in money to a designated person or to his order, or to bearer, on demand or at a fixed or determinable future time"* is a *negotiable instrument.* The essential elements of negotiability are as follows:

(a) The instrument must be in writing and it must be signed by the party executing it.

(b) It must contain an unconditional promise or order to pay a sum certain in money.

(c) It must be payable to a designated person, or to his order, or to bearer.

(d) It must be payable either on demand or at a fixed or determinable future time.

The most commonly used negotiable instruments may be divided into three classes as follows:

(a) Checks.

(b) Notes.

(c) Drafts and trade acceptances.

Ordinary bank checks are negotiable instruments. Certified checks and cashier's checks are also negotiable instruments. A *certified check* is an ordinary check that has been certified by the bank on which it is drawn. Either the drawer or the payee of a check may have it certified. When a bank certifies a check, the amount is charged to the depositor's account immediately and the money is held in a special account until the check is presented for payment. The method of accounting for a certified check is the same as for an ordinary check so far as the drawer is concerned.

A *cashier's check* is a draft drawn by the cashier of a bank on its own funds. Anyone may purchase a cashier's check. If an ordinary bank check is issued in payment of a cashier's check, the method of accounting

---

*Uniform Negotiable Instruments Act.

for the check issued is identical with the method of accounting for a check issued for any other purpose.

Money orders and *travelers' checks* are similar to ordinary bank checks in that they constitute a written order for payment of a sum certain in money on demand. Postal money orders may be purchased from any post office; they constitute an order for the payment of a specified amount of money by any post office on demand. Express money orders may be purchased from any office of the American Express Company; they constitute an order for the payment of a specified amount of money by any office of the American Express Company. Travelers' checks may be purchased from banks, American Express Company offices, and the offices of certain other transportation companies.

Negotiable notes may be received and issued in the ordinary course of business. Notes received are commonly referred to as notes receivable, while notes issued are commonly referred to as notes payable. Notes may or may not be interest bearing. Interest is the amount charged for the use of money. It is similar to rent charged for the use of property. In some cases the interest is payable in advance, that is, it must be prepaid. Usually, however, the interest is payable at maturity of the note, or periodically until the note matures and is paid.

Calculating Interest. In calculating interest on notes, it is necessary to take the following factors into consideration:

(a) The principal or face amount.

(b) The time.

(c) The rate of interest.

The principal is the face amount or principal sum specified in a note. It is the base on which the interest is calculated.

The period elapsing from the date of a note to the date of its maturity, or to the interest payment date, is the time for which the interest is computed. Thus, if a note is payable in 60 days with interest, the interest should be computed for the 60-day period. On the other hand, if a note is dated March 1 and is due May 1, the period for which the interest should be computed is 61 days.

When the time in a note is specified by months, the interest should be calculated on a basis of months rather than days. For example, if a note is payable 3 months from date, the interest should be calculated on a basis of 3 months or $\frac{1}{4}$ of a year. However, when the due date is specified in a note, the time should be computed by ascertaining the exact number of days elapsing from the date of the note to the date of its maturity and the interest should be computed on the basis of such number of days. For example, if a note is dated April 1 and the due date is specified as July 1, the time should be computed in the following manner:

Days in April..............	30
Date of note, April.........	1
Days remaining in April.....	29
Days in May...............	31
Days in June...............	30
Note matures on July.......	1
Total time in days..........	91

In this computation it will be noted that the date of maturity was counted but the date of the note was not counted. If the due date had been specified as "3 months after date" instead of July 1, the interest should be computed on a basis of 90 days, instead of 91 days.

In the case of long-term notes, the interest may be payable periodically, such as semiannually or annually.

The rate of interest is usually expressed in the form of a percentage, such as 4 per cent or 6 per cent. Ordinarily the rate is an annual percentage rate, but in some cases the rate is quoted on a monthly basis, such as 1 per cent a month. A rate of 1 per cent a month is equivalent to a rate of 12 per cent a year payable monthly. When a note is interest bearing but the rate is not specified, it is subject to the legal rate, which varies under the laws of different states.

In computing interest it is customary to consider 360 days as a year. Most banks and business firms follow this practice. However, the Federal Reserve System uses 365 days as a year in computing interest on notes rediscounted by member banks. Following is an illustration of the difference in computing interest under the two methods:

FACTORS
(a) Principal of note.............. $500
(b) Time...................... 60 days
(c) Rate of interest.............. 6%

COMPUTATIONS

360-day year	*365-day year*
6% of $500 = $30	6% of $500 = $30
60/360 of $30 = $5	60/365 of $30 = $4.93

It will be noted that under both methods, the time for which the interest is being computed is used as the numerator while the number of days in the year is used as the denominator. The following formula may be applied in computing interest regardless of whether it is being computed on the basis of a 360-day year or a 365-day year:

PRINCIPAL × RATE × TIME (IN YEARS) = AMOUNT OF INTEREST

The 60-Day, 6 Per Cent Method. There are many short cuts that may be used in computing interest on the basis of a 360-day year. The interest on any amount for 60 days at 6 per cent can be ascertained by simply moving the decimal point in the amount two places to the left. The reason for this is that 60 days is ⅙ of a year and the interest on any amount at 6 per cent for ⅙ of a year is the same as the interest at 1 per cent for a year. Thus, the interest on $241.30 for 60 days at 6 per cent is $2.41.

The 60-day, 6 per cent method may be used advantageously in many cases even though the actual time may be more or less than 60 days. The following examples will serve to illustrate this fact:

(a)	(b)
FACTORS	FACTORS
(a) Principal of note, $1,000	(a) Principal of note, $1,000
(b) Time, 30 days	(b) Time, 120 days
(c) Rate of interest, 6%	(c) Rate of interest, 6%
CALCULATION	CALCULATION
When the decimal point is moved two places to the left the result is $10	When the decimal point is moved two places to the left the result is $10
30 days = ½ of 60 days, hence the interest amounts to ½ of $10 or $5	120 days = 2 times 60 days, hence the interest amounts to 2 times $10 or $20

The 60-day, 6 per cent method may also be used advantageously when the actual rate is more or less than 6 per cent. The following examples will serve to illustrate this fact:

(a)	(b)
FACTORS	FACTORS
(a) Principal of note, $1,000	(a) Principal of note, $1,000
(b) Time, 30 days	(b) Time, 120 days
(c) Rate of interest, 3%	(c) Rate of interest, 8%
CALCULATION	CALCULATION
Interest at 6% for 60 days = $10	Interest at 6% for 60 days = $10
Interest at 6% for 30 days = $5	Interest at 6% for 120 days = $20
Interest at 3% = ½ of $5 or $2.50	Interest at 8% = 1⅓ times $20 or $26.67

Sometimes it is advantageous to ascertain the interest for 6 days at 6 per cent and to use the result as a basis for calculating the actual interest. The interest on any sum for 6 days at 6 per cent may be ascertained by simply moving the decimal point three places to the left; thus, the interest on $1,000 at 6 per cent for 6 days is $1. If the actual time were 18 days instead of 6 days, the interest would be three times $1 or $3. This method differs from the 60-day, 6 per cent method only in that 6 days is used in the basic computation instead of 60 days. In other words, the interest is first calculated for 6 days at 6 per cent and then the result is used as the basis for calculating the interest for the actual time and at the actual rate specified in the note.

Published tables are available for reference use in ascertaining the amount of interest on stated sums at different rates for any length of time. Such tables are widely used by financial institutions and may also be used by other firms. The fact that published tables are available for reference use does not lessen the importance of being able to compute interest accurately and speedily.

Present Value. The present value or *present worth* of a note is its value on any day between the date of the instrument and the maturity of the instrument. If a note is interest bearing, the present value may be ascertained by adding the accrued interest to the face of the note. If a note is noninterest bearing, the present value may be ascertained by subtracting from its face, interest at the discount rate for the time elapsing from the date as of which the present value is computed to the date of maturity.

It may be necessary to ascertain the present value of a note (a) when it is being transferred for credit or (b) when it is being sold for cash. The following note is reproduced in order that it may be used to illustrate the method of calculating the present value of a note:

The following alternate transactions involving the foregoing note indicate the reason for ascertaining its present value:

(a) May 16, Robert Clarkson transferred the note to Bryant & Wood, who agreed to allow him credit for its present value.

(b) May 16, Robert Clarkson sold the note to the Liberty National Bank at a discount of 7 per cent.

In transaction (a) the note is transferred for credit at its present value. The factors involved in computing its present value are as follows:

FACTORS
(a) Principal of note, $286.50
(b) Time interest has accrued, 40 days (April 6 to May 16)
(c) Rate of interest, 6%

CALCULATION
Interest accrued on $286.50 at 6% for 40 days = $1.91
$286.50 + $1.91 = $288.41, present value

In transaction (b) the note was sold to the Liberty National Bank at a discount of 7 per cent. Such a transaction is often referred to as *discounting a note*. It is the custom of banks to calculate the discount on the maturity value of a note. The amount of the discount is then subtracted from the maturity value to find the present value of the note.

FACTORS
(a) Principal of note, $286.50
(b) Time from date of note to date of maturity, 90 days (April 6 to July 5)
(c) Rate of interest, 6%
(d) Time from date of discount to date of maturity, 50 days (May 16 to July 5)
(e) Rate of discount, 7%

CALCULATION
Interest on $286.50 at 6% for 90 days = $4.30
$286.50 + $4.30 = $290.80, maturity value
Discount on $290.80 at 7% for 50 days = $2.83
$290.80 − $2.83 = $287.97, present value

The interest is computed on the face of the note, while the discount is computed on the maturity value of the note. Bank discount should not be confused with either trade discount or cash discount. Trade discount is a discount from the list price of merchandise, while cash discount is a discount allowed for payment of an invoice within a specified time. Bank discount is regarded as interest collected in advance on a loan. Discounting a note receivable at the bank is a method of borrowing money and using the note as security. Since the party discounting the note must endorse it, he is liable for its maturity value in case the maker does not pay it at maturity.

Accounting for Notes Receivable. The following types of transactions involve notes receivable:

(a) Notes received in exchange for merchandise or other property.
(b) Notes received from customers in order to obtain an extension of time on their obligations.
(c) Notes received as security for cash loans.
(d) Notes transferred prior to maturity.
(e) Notes discounted prior to maturity.
(f) Notes paid at maturity.
(g) Notes renewed at maturity.
(h) Notes dishonored.

Notes Received in Exchange for Merchandise or Other Property. A note may be accepted in exchange for merchandise or other property. For example, Bryant & Wood accepted a 60-day, 5 per cent interest-bearing note for $101.48 in exchange for radios sold Robinson Bros. on April 29. This transaction was recorded in the books of Bryant & Wood by debiting Notes Receivable and by crediting Sales, Dept. B, for $101.48.

Notes Received from Customers to Obtain an Extension of Time for Payment. When a customer wishes to obtain an extension of time on his indebtedness, he may be willing to issue a note for all or part of the amount due. A merchant may be willing to accept a note from a customer who desires an extension of time for the reason that the note is a written acknowledgment of a debt and, if cash is needed before the note matures, it may be possible to discount the note at a bank.

R. E. Brand owes Bryant & Wood $422.36 on open account. The account is past due and Bryant & Wood insist upon a settlement. Mr. Brand offers to give them his 60-day, 6 per cent interest-bearing note. Bryant & Wood accept the note, dated April 10. It was recorded in their books as indicated by the following general journal entry:

```
April 10.  Notes Receivable.............................  $422.36
              Accounts Receivable.........................            $422.36
                Received note from R. E. Brand.
```

If, instead of tendering a note for the full amount, Mr. Brand tendered a check for $22.36 and a note for the balance and Bryant & Wood accepted the check and the note, the transaction should be recorded in their books as indicated by the following general journal entry:

```
April 10.  Bank........................................  $ 22.36
           Notes Receivable.............................   400.00
              Accounts Receivable.........................            $422.36
                Received check and note from R. E. Brand.
```

Notes Received from Employees. Loans to employees may be evidenced by notes receivable. For example, Bryant & Wood might loan Robert Jackson, an employee, $100 on his 90-day, 4 per cent note. Such a transaction may be recorded in their books as indicated by the following general journal entry:

```
April  1.  Notes Receivable..............................  $100.00
              Bank.......................................            $100.00
                Loaned Robert Jackson $100.
```

If it is the practice of a firm to make frequent loans to employees, it is generally considered advisable to keep a separate account for such notes.

An appropriate title for such an account is Notes Receivable from Employees.

Notes Transferred Prior to Maturity. In order to obtain an extension of time a customer may tender a note that he has accepted from another party. For example, R. E. Brand might have tendered to Bryant & Wood a note that he had accepted from James B. Roberts and agreed to pay the balance of his account in cash. Bryant & Wood might have agreed to accept the note for credit at its present value. Assume, for example, that the face of the note amounted to $350, that it is dated March 1, and that it is due in 90 days with interest at 6 per cent. If Bryant & Wood accept this note on April 15, its present value may be computed as follows:

```
March 1 to April 15 = 45 days
$350 at 6% for 45 days = $2.63, interest accrued
$350 + $2.63 = $352.63, present value of note
```

The amount to be paid in cash is the difference between the amount of Mr. Brand's account, $422.36, and the present value of the note, $352.63, or $69.73. The transaction should be recorded in the books of Bryant & Wood as indicated by the following general journal entry:

```
April 15.  Bank......................................  $ 69.73
           Notes Receivable...........................   350.00
           Interest Income............................     2.63
               Accounts Receivable.......................          $422.36
               Received note for $350 and check for $69.73
               from R. E. Brand.
```

The amount charged to Interest Income represents the amount paid for the right to receive the interest already accrued on the note prior to April 15. By charging the accrued interest to Interest Income, that account will show the proper amount of income earned when it is credited later for the full amount of the interest collected.

Notes Discounted Prior to Maturity. As previously explained, a note may be discounted at a bank prior to its maturity. It sometimes happens that a merchant is in need of funds to be used as working capital and, in order to obtain the necessary funds, he may discount at a bank one or more notes that he owns. Suppose, for example, that on May 1 Bryant & Wood discounted at the Liberty National Bank the note received from Robinson Bros. on April 29 and received credit for the proceeds. The rate of discount was 6 per cent. The proceeds were computed as follows:

```
Face value of note.............................................  $101.48
Interest at 5% for 60 days.....................................      .85
Maturity value of note.........................................  $102.33
```

```
Discount period May 1 to June 28 = 58 days
$102.33 at 6% for 58 days = 99¢
$102.33 − 99¢ = $101.34, proceeds
```

Since the note had been accepted originally by Bryant & Wood at its face value of $101.48 and the proceeds from discounting the note amounted to only $101.34, the difference of 14 cents represents interest expense. This transaction should be recorded in the books of Bryant & Wood as indicated by the following general journal entry:

May 1. Bank..	$101.34	
Interest Expense................................	.14	
Notes Receivable............................		$101.48
Discounted Robinson Bros.' note at the bank.		

If the interest on the note had amounted to more than the bank discount, the difference would represent a gain which should be credited to Interest Income.

Contingent Liability on Notes Discounted. In discounting Robinson Bros.' note at the bank it was necessary for Bryant & Wood to endorse the note. This endorsement had the effect of guaranteeing payment of the note at maturity, because Bryant & Wood would have to pay it if Robinson Bros. should fail to pay it. This liability is known as a *contingent liability* for the reason that Bryant & Wood's liability is contingent upon the failure of Robinson Bros. to pay the note at maturity.

In preparing a balance sheet, it is customary to ascertain the sum of any notes that have been discounted but have not been paid by the makers and to indicate that the sum represents a contingent liability. This is usually indicated by means of a footnote to the balance sheet. The usual plan is to place an asterisk (*) after the amount of the asset, Notes Receivable, and to state the amount of the contingent liability in a footnote. For example, if the notes receivable amounted to $12,000 and notes discounted but not yet paid amounted to $2,000, the following statement should be added to the balance sheet in a footnote:

Contingent liability on notes discounted, $2,000.

If a note that was discounted at a bank is not paid at maturity, the bank will immediately inform the party who endorsed the note and look to him for payment.

Sometimes a separate account is kept with Notes Receivable Discounted. In this case notes receivable that are discounted are credited to the notes receivable discounted account instead of being credited to the notes receivable account. A record is kept of the due date of notes discounted and when it is ascertained that a note has been paid by the maker, an entry is made debiting Notes Receivable Discounted and crediting Notes Receivable. When a separate account with notes receivable discounted is kept, the balance of the account should be shown as a deduction from notes receivable on the asset side of the balance sheet, although it is sometimes listed as a liability under the heading of Contingent Liabilities.

Notes Paid at Maturity. When notes receivable mature, they may be collected by the payee or he may leave them at his bank for collection. If the maker of a note resides in another locality, the note may be forwarded to a bank in his locality for collection. It is customary for banks to charge a fee for making such collections.

Usually the maker is notified a few days before the maturity of a note in order that he may know the due date and the amount payable. From the foregoing discussion it will be seen that the payment may be received directly from the maker or from a bank with whom the note has been left for collection. If Robert Jackson pays his note in full plus the interest when it matures, Bryant & Wood should record the transaction in their books as indicated by the following general journal entry:

June 30. Bank..	$101.00	
Notes Receivable............................		$100.00
Interest Income..............................		1.00
Received $101 from Robert Jackson in payment of his note for $100 and interest $1.		

If Bryant & Wood left R. E. Brand's note for $422.36 at the Liberty National Bank for collection and on June 10 received the notice of collection reproduced below, the transaction should be recorded in their books as indicated by the following general journal entry:

June 10. Bank..	$426.03	
Collection Expense...........................	.55	
Notes Receivable............................		$422.36
Interest Income..............................		4.22
Received credit for the proceeds of R. E. Brand's note collected by the bank.		

CREDIT ADVICE	**LIBERTY NATIONAL BANK**		
	To Bryant & Wood, 542 S. Dearborn St., Chicago, Ill.		
	WE HAVE CREDITED YOUR ACCOUNT AS FOLLOWS:		
	R. E. Brand's note	422	36
	Interest for 60 days @ 6%	4	22
		426	58
	Less collection charge		55
	Net Proceeds	426	03

In receiving items for deposit or collection, this bank acts only as depositor's collecting agent and assumes no responsibility beyond the exercise of due care. All items are credited subject to final payment in cash or solvent credits. This bank will not be liable for default or negligence of its duly selected correspondents nor for losses in transit, and each correspondent so selected shall not be liable except for its own negligence. This bank or its correspondents may send items directly or indirectly to any bank including the payor, and accept its draft or credit as conditional payment in lieu of cash; it may charge back any item at any time before final payment, whether returned or not, also any item drawn on this bank not good at close of business on day deposited.
All city checks deposited today will be held at depositor's risk until next day's settlement.

Notes Renewed at Maturity. If the maker of a note is unable to pay the amount due at maturity, he may be permitted to renew the note in whole or in part. If, instead of paying his note for $100 at maturity, Robert Jackson were permitted to pay the interest and renew the note for another 90 days at the same rate of interest, the transaction should be recorded in the books of Bryant & Wood as indicated by the following general journal entry:

June 30.	Notes Receivable (new note)....................	$100.00	
	Bank..	1.00	
	Notes Receivable (old note)..................		$100.00
	Interest Income.............................		1.00

Received a new note for $100 from Robert Jackson in renewal of his note due today and $1 in cash in payment of the interest on the old note.

Notes Receivable Register. When many notes are received in the usual course of business, it may be advisable to keep an auxiliary record of such notes that will provide more detailed information than can be provided in a ledger account. Such an auxiliary record is usually known as a notes receivable register. One form of a notes receivable register is reproduced at the bottom of pages 332 and 333. The notes recorded in the illustration were those received by Wilson & Jones during the period indicated by the record.

The information recorded in the register is obtained directly from the notes received. The notes are numbered consecutively as they are entered in the register. This number should not be confused with the maker's number. The due date of each note is calculated and entered in the proper When Due column. The interest to maturity is calculated and entered in the Interest Amount column. When a note is discounted, the name of the bank at which it is discounted and the date are entered in the Discounted columns. When a remittance is received in payment of a note, the date is entered in the Paid column.

Notes Receivable Account. The information recorded in the notes receivable account should agree with that entered in the notes receivable register. The account shown on page 332 contains a record of the notes that were entered in the notes receivable register of Wilson & Jones. It should be noted that the identity of each note is indicated by the number assigned to the note. If the notes are not numbered, the identity of each note should be indicated by writing the name of the maker in the Items column of the account.

NOTES RECEIVABLE

19—				19—			
Mar. 28	No. 1		180.00	May 27	No. 1		180.00
30	No. 2		200.00	29	No. 4		492.50
30	No. 3		250.00	29	No. 2		200.00
Apr. 1	No. 4		492.50	29	No. 3		250.00
May 15	No. 5		350.00	29	No. 7		300.00
18	No. 6		286.50				*1,422.50*
18	No. 7		300.00				
25	No. 8		218.60				
29	No. 9		200.00				
		1,055.10	*2,477.60*				

Proving the Notes Receivable Account. Periodically, usually at the end of each month, the notes receivable account should be proved by comparing the balance of the account with the total of the notes owned as shown by the notes receivable register. Following is a schedule of the notes owned on May 31:

SCHEDULE OF NOTES OWNED

No. 5........................	$ 350.00
No. 6........................	286.50
No. 8........................	218.60
No. 9........................	200.00
Total.......................	$1,055.10

It will be noted that the total of this schedule is the same as the balance of the notes receivable account reproduced above.

NOTES RECEIVABLE REGISTER

DATE RECEIVED	NO.	BY WHOM PAYABLE	WHERE PAYABLE		DATE MADE
			BANK OR FIRM	ADDRESS	MO. DAY YEAR
Mar. 28	1	W. O. Booker	City Bank	Troy	Mar 28 19–
30	2	C. M. Martin	First National Bank	Detroit	Mar 30 19–
30	3	A. W. Whitten	Union Bank	Dexter	Mar 30 19–
Apr. 1	4	J. A. Robbins	State National Bank	Erie	Apr 1 19–
May 15	5	R. E. Branch	City National Bank	City	May 15 19–
18	6	James Mariner	State Bank	Mason	Apr 6 19–
18	7	Williams & Allison	City National Bank	City	May 18 19–
25	8	Jason & Cox	Union Bank	Clinton	Apr 28 19–
29	9	A. W. Whitten	″ ″	Dexter	May 29 19

(Left page)

Endorsement of Notes. A promissory note is usually payable to a specified person or firm, though some notes are made payable to "Bearer." If the note is payable to the order of a specified party, he must *endorse* the note to transfer the promise to pay to another party. The two major types of endorsements are (1) the *blank endorsement* and (2) the *full endorsement*. When the payee signs his name only on the left end of the back of the note, he is endorsing it in blank. If, instead, he precedes his signature with the words "Pay to the order of" followed by the name of a specified party, he is giving a full endorsement. The legal effect of both types of endorsement is much the same except that a blank endorsement makes the note payable to the bearer, while a full endorsement serves to identify the party to whose order payment is to be made.

Under certain circumstances the maker of a note may arrange for an additional party to join in the promise to pay, either as a *cosigner* or as an endorser of the note. In the first instance, this other party signs his name below that of the maker of the note on the face of the instrument. In the second case, the other party makes a blank endorsement on the back of the note. This is called an *accommodation endorsement*. In either event the payee of the note has two persons to look to for payment. This presumably adds security to the note.

If a partial payment is made on a note, it is common practice to record the date of the payment and the amount paid on the back of the note. This is called endorsing the payment.

On page 334 is a reproduction of the back of a promissory note originally made payable to the order of M. A. Allen. The maker of the note (whoever he was) was able to get C. O. Barclay to become an accommoda-

NOTES RECEIVABLE REGISTER

TIME	WHEN DUE													AMOUNT	INTEREST		DISCOUNTED		PAID	REMARKS
	J	F	M	A	M	J	J	A	S	O	N	D		RATE	AMOUNT	BANK	DATE		
60 d's					27								18000	6%	180			May 27	
60 d's					29								20000	—				May 29	Sent for Coll 5/22
60 d's					29								25000	6%	250			May 29	Renewal for $200
90 d's						30							49250	6%	739	Liberty Nat'l.	May 29		
60 d's							14						35000	6%	350				
90 d's							5						28650	6%	430				
60 d's							17						30000	—		Liberty Nat'l	May 29		
60 d's					27								21860	—					
60 d's						28							20000	6%	200				Renewal of Note #3

(Right page)

tion endorser. Later, the payee, Allen, transferred the note to R. L. Foley by a full endorsement. On April 15, $100 was paid on the note.

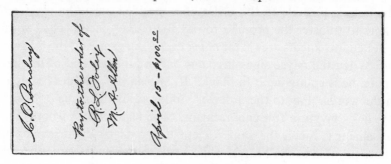

Endorsements on Note

Dishonored Notes. Should the maker fail to pay or renew a note at maturity and it is not deemed collectible, the usual practice is to charge the note to the allowance for bad debts account. Before making such an entry, however, every reasonable effort should be made to collect the principal and the accrued interest from the maker or any endorser. It should be remembered that each endorser is liable for the full amount of the note, plus any accrued interest. Assuming that A. W. Whitten failed to pay his note of May 29, which was a renewal of his note of March 30, and it is deemed uncollectible, it may be charged off by Wilson & Jones in the manner indicated in the following general journal entry:

Allowance for Bad Debts................................ $200.00
Notes Receivable...................................... $200.00
A. W. Whitten's dishonored note charged off.

If Mr. Whitten's note had been discounted at the bank prior to maturity and he failed to pay it at maturity, Wilson & Jones would be liable for the face of the note plus any accrued interest. When the note is redeemed by Wilson & Jones it should be recorded on their books by debiting Notes Receivable for the face of the note, debiting Interest Expense for the accrued interest, and by crediting the bank for the total amount paid (or charged to their account by the bank). Subsequently the note may be charged off as a bad debt as indicated above.

Sometimes a separate allowance for bad notes is provided, but usually the allowance for bad debts is intended to provide for losses on both accounts receivable and notes receivable.

Some accountants would advocate that the note be charged back to Mr. Whitten's account in order that his account might provide a complete history of the firm's dealings with him. While there are no objections to such a procedure, the same results may be accomplished by simply making a notation in Mr. Whitten's account to the effect that the note was not paid when due and that it has been charged off as a bad debt. Such information will be of value to the credit manager should Mr. Whitten seek additional credit at any time in the future.

Accounting for Notes Payable. The following types of transactions involve notes payable:

    (a) Notes issued in exchange for merchandise or other property.
    (b) Notes issued to creditors in order to obtain an extension of time on accounts payable.
    (c) Notes issued as security for cash loans.
    (d) Notes paid at maturity.
    (e) Notes renewed at maturity.

Notes Issued in Exchange for Merchandise or Other Property. A note may be issued in exchange for merchandise, fixed assets, or other property. For example, Bryant & Wood issued a 30-day, 6 per cent interest-bearing note for $75 to the Modern Machine Co. in exchange for store equipment purchased on April 1. This transaction was recorded in the books of Bryant & Wood by debiting Store Equipment and by crediting Notes Payable for $75.

Notes Issued to Creditors to Obtain an Extension of Time for Payment. When a firm wishes to obtain an extension of time for the payment of an obligation, a note for all or part of the amount due may be tendered to and accepted by the creditor. Assume, for example, that Bryant & Wood owe Williams & Co. $291.50 and by agreement on May 14 a check on the Liberty National Bank for $41.50 and a 90-day, 5 per cent interest-bearing note for $250 are issued. This transaction should be recorded in the books of Bryant & Wood as indicated by the following general journal entry:

May 14. Accounts Payable.............................	$291.50	
Bank.......................................		$ 41.50
Notes Payable..............................		250.00
Issued check for $41.50 and note for $250 to Williams & Co.		

Notes Issued as Security for Cash Loans. Many firms experience periods in which receipts from customers in the usual course of business are not adequate to finance their operations. During such periods, therefore, it may be necessary to borrow money from banks. Business firms commonly borrow money from banks on short-term notes as an aid in financing their business operations. Assume, for example, that on May 15 Bryant & Wood borrow $1,000 from the Liberty National Bank on a

60-day, 6 per cent interest-bearing note. The transaction should be recorded as indicated in the following general journal entry:

May 15.	Bank.....................................	$1,000.00	
	Notes Payable............................		$1,000.00
	Borrowed $1,000 at the bank on a 60-day, 6% note.		

Notes Paid at Maturity. When a note payable matures, payment may be made directly to the holder or to a bank where the note was left for collection. The maker will know who the payee is but he may not know who the holder is at maturity because the payee may have transferred the note to another party or he may have left it with a bank for collection. When a note is left with a bank for collection, it is customary for the bank to mail the maker a notice of maturity. For example, the Modern Machine Co. might forward the note of Bryant & Wood for $75 dated April 1 to the Liberty National Bank for collection and the bank might notify Bryant & Wood by sending them a notice similar to the one reproduced below.

LIBERTY NATIONAL BANK

April 25,   19--

We hold a note signed by you on which there will be due on the   1st   *day of*   May   *19--*   *Principal* $ 75.00

Interest $ .38

TOTAL $ 75.38

PLEASE BRING THIS NOTICE WITH YOU

To   Bryant & Wood

542 S. Dearborn St., City

CHECKS ON OTHER BANKS NOT RECEIVED UNLESS CERTIFIED

Notice of Maturity

If, upon receipt of this notice, Bryant & Wood issued a check to the bank for $75.38 in payment of the note and interest, the transaction should be recorded in their books as indicated by the following general journal entry:

May 1.	Notes Payable.................................	$75.00	
	Interest Expense................................	.38	
	Bank...		$75.38
	Paid note issued to the Modern Machine Co. April 1, plus interest.		

Notes Renewed at Maturity. If the maker is unable to pay a note in full at maturity, he may arrange to renew all or a part of the note. For example, on August 12 Bryant & Wood might pay the interest, amounting to $3.13, and $50 on the principal of the note for $250 issued to Williams & Co. on May 14 and give them a new note for $200 with interest at 5 per cent payable in 60 days. This transaction should be recorded as indicated in the following general journal entry:

Aug. 12. Notes Payable (old note)........................ $250.00
          Interest Expense..............................   3.13
          Bank... $ 53.13
          Notes Payable (new note)....................   200.00
          Issued a check for $53.13 and a note for $200 to
          Williams & Co. in settlement of a note for $250
          plus interest.

Notes Payable Register. Where many notes are issued in the usual course of business, it may be advisable to keep an auxiliary record of such notes that will provide more detailed information than can be provided in a ledger account. Such an auxiliary record is usually known as a notes payable register. One form of a notes payable register is reproduced at the top of pages 338 and 339. The notes recorded in the illustration were those issued by Wilson & Jones during the period indicated by the record.

The information recorded in the register may be obtained directly from the note before it is mailed or given to the payee, or from a note stub. Blank notes are usually made up in pads with stubs attached on which spaces are provided for recording such essential information as Amount, Payee, Where Payable, Date, Time, Rate of Interest, and Number. The due date of each note is calculated and entered in the proper When Due column of the register. The interest at maturity is also calculated and entered in the Interest Amount column. When a note is paid, the date is entered in the Paid column.

Notes Payable Account. The information recorded in the notes payable account should agree with that recorded in the notes payable register. The following account contains a record of the notes that were entered in the notes payable register of Wilson & Jones.

NOTES PAYABLE

19—			19—			
June 13	No. 1	150.00	Mar. 15	No. 1		150.00
			May 16	No. 2		378.65
			20	No. 3		1,000.00
			22	No. 4		200.00
			22	No. 5		200.00
			29	No. 6		2,500.00
					4,278.65	*4,428.65*

NOTES PAYABLE REGISTER

| DATE ISSUED | | NO. | TO WHOM PAYABLE | WHERE PAYABLE | | | DATE MADE | | |
				BANK OR FIRM	ADDRESS		MO.	DAY	YEAR
Mar.	15	1	Dalton & Co.	Union Bank		Springfield	Mar.	15	19—
May	16	2	Woods Bros.	City National Bank		Canton	May	16	19—
	20	3	City National Bank	"	"	City	May	20	19—
	22	4	Luce Motor Car Co.	"	"	"	May	22	19—
	22	5	" "	"	"	"	May	22	19—
	29	6	City National Bank	"	"	"	May	29	19—

(Left page)

Proving the Notes Payable Account. Periodically, usually at the end of each month, the notes payable account should be proved by comparing the balance of the account with the total notes outstanding as shown by the notes payable register. Following is a schedule of the notes outstanding on May 31:

SCHEDULE OF NOTES OUTSTANDING

No. 2...........................	$ 378.65
No. 3...........................	1,000.00
No. 4...........................	200.00
No. 5...........................	200.00
No. 6...........................	2,500.00
Total........................	$4,278.65

It will be noted that the total of this schedule is the same as the balance of the notes payable account.

Accrued Interest Receivable. While interest on a note literally accrues day by day, it is impractical to keep a daily record of such accruals. If the life of a note receivable is entirely within the accounting period, no record need be made of interest until the amount is received.

If, however, the business owns some interest-bearing notes receivable at the end of the accounting period, neither the net income for the period nor the assets at the end of the period will be correctly stated unless the interest accrued on notes receivable is taken into consideration. It is, therefore, customary to adjust the accounts by debiting Accrued Interest Receivable and by crediting Interest Income for the amount of interest that has accrued to the end of the period. The amount of the accrual may

NOTES PAYABLE REGISTER

TIME	WHEN DUE												AMOUNT	INTEREST		PAID	REMARKS
	J	F	M	A	M	J	J	A	S	O	N	D		RATE	AMOUNT		
90 d/s.					13								15000	—		June 13	
60 d/s						15							37865	6%	379		
90 d/s							18						100000	6%	1500		
3 mos.							12						20000	6%	300		
6 mos.									12				20000	6%	600		
60 d/s						18							250000	5%	2043		

(Right page)

be computed by reference to the notes themselves or to the record provided by a notes receivable register. Suppose, for example, that at the end of a fiscal year ending June 30, a business owns four interest-bearing notes. The amount of each note, the date of issue, the rate of interest, the number of days from issue date to June 30, and the interest accrued on June 30 are shown in the following schedule:

SCHEDULE OF ACCRUED INTEREST ON NOTES RECEIVABLE

PRINCIPAL	DATE OF ISSUE	RATE OF INTEREST	DAYS FROM ISSUE DATE TO JUNE 30	ACCRUED INTEREST JUNE 30
$350.00	April 15	6%	76	$4.43
$200.00	May 4	5%	57	1.58
248.50	May 31	6%	30	1.24
500.00	June 15	6%	15	1.25

Total accrued interest on notes receivable..................$8.50

The entry, in general journal form, to record the interest accrued on June 30 is as follows:

June 30. Accrued Interest Receivable........................ $8.50
        Interest Income................................... $8.50
        Interest accrued on notes receivable as of June 30.

In preparing the financial statements at the end of the year, the balance of the interest income account (which includes $8.50 interest earned but not yet received) should be reported in the income statement, while the balance of the account with Accrued Interest Receivable should be reported in the balance sheet as a current asset.

After posting the adjusting entry, the debit balance in the accrued interest receivable account reflects the amount of interest accrued on June 30. The actual amount accrued will change as time elapses. On July 1, the start of the new period, a reversing entry should be made to transfer the balance of the accrued interest receivable account to the interest income account. All collections of interest should be credited to Interest Income without regard to the period in which the interest was earned; the portions of any interest collections that represent income of the new period will automatically show up as a part of the final credit balance in the interest income account.

Accrued Interest Payable. Neither the expenses of a period nor the liabilities at the end of the period will be correctly stated unless the interest accrued on notes payable is taken into consideration. The mechanics of calculating the amount of interest accrued on notes payable is the same as in the case of notes receivable. If a notes payable register is kept, it should provide the information needed in computing the amount of interest accrued on notes payable. If the total amount of such accrued interest was calculated to be $23.18, and the fiscal period ended June 30, the proper adjusting entry may be made in general journal form as follows:

```
June 30.  Interest Expense...................................    $23.18
              Accrued Interest Payable........................            $23.18
          Interest accrued on notes payable as of June 30.
```

In preparing the financial statements at the end of the year, the balance of the interest expense account (which includes $23.18 interest incurred but not yet paid) should be reported in the income statement, while the balance of the account with Accrued Interest Payable should be reported in the balance sheet as a current liability.

After posting the adjusting entry, the credit balance of the accrued interest payable account reflects the amount of interest accrued on June 30. The actual amount accrued will change as time elapses. On July 1, the start of the new period, a reversing entry should be made to transfer the balance of the accrued interest payable account to the interest expense account. All payments of interest should be debited to Interest Expense without regard to the period in which the interest was incurred; the portions of any payments that represent an expense of the new period will automatically show up as a part of the final debit balance in the interest expense account.

PRACTICE ASSIGNMENT No. 24. Complete Report No. 24 in the workbook and submit your working papers to the instructor for approval. Then continue with the following study assignment until Report No. 25 is required.

(25) DRAFTS AND TRADE ACCEPTANCES

A draft is "an unconditional order in writing addressed by one person to another, signed by the person giving it, requiring the person to whom it is addressed to pay on demand, or at a fixed or determinable future time, a sum certain in money to order or to bearer."* Apart from ordinary checks there are two kinds of drafts as follows:

(a) Bank drafts.

(b) Commercial drafts.

Bank Drafts. A bank draft is a check drawn by a bank on funds that it has deposited in another bank. For example, a Chicago bank having funds deposited in a New York bank may draw against such funds by ordering the New York bank to pay a specified sum to a designated third party. Anyone may obtain a bank draft from a bank by paying the bank a sum equal to the amount of the desired draft plus the service charge. Below is a reproduction of a bank draft drawn by the Liberty National Bank of Chicago on the Chase National Bank of New York in favor of Bryant & Wood. Banks usually have funds on deposit in other banks located in other cities and can, therefore, issue bank drafts payable in such cities.

A bank draft differs from a cashier's check in that it is drawn on funds deposited in another bank. Both may be signed by the cashier of the

payee

LIBERTY NATIONAL BANK		
	CHICAGO __April 17,_____19--	
PAY TO THE ORDER OF __Bryant & Wood_____		$ 200.00
Two Hundred and no/100 - **Dollars**		
To Chase National Bank		
New York, N. Y.		*J. E. John, Jr.*
		Cashier.

drawer

drawee

Bank Draft

*Uniform Negotiable Instruments Act.

bank that issues them. If it is a cashier's check, it is a draft on the bank drawing the draft. If it is a bank draft, it is a draft on another bank in which the drawer has funds on deposit.

If an ordinary check is issued in payment of a bank draft, it should be recorded in the usual manner. If it is issued in payment of a draft that is to be sent to a creditor in payment of his account, it should be recorded by debiting Accounts Payable for the amount of the draft, by debiting an expense account for the amount of any service charge, and by crediting the bank for the total amount of the check issued. One reason for using a bank draft in remitting to a creditor may be that the debtor is unknown to the creditor and has not established credit. Usually, ordinary checks will be accepted by a creditor, subject to payment upon presentation. However, ordinary checks may not be acceptable in the case of out-of-town cash purchases. In such cases bank drafts, cashier's checks, or certified checks may be used to advantage. All are negotiable instruments and the bank on which they are drawn is responsible for payment; hence, the credit of the purchaser or debtor is not involved.

Commercial Drafts. A commercial draft is a formal demand by one party for payment by another party to a third party. The party making the demand is known as the *drawer;* the party on whom the draft is drawn is known as the *drawee;* the party to whom the draft is payable is known as the *payee.* Usually the payee is a bank or other collecting agency for the drawer.

In both commercial drafts and bank drafts there are three parties involved — the drawer, the drawee, and the payee. In the case of a commercial draft the payee is usually a bank while the other parties are individuals or firms other than banks. In the case of a bank draft, the drawer and the drawee are banks while the payee is an individual or firm other than a bank.

There are three types of commercial drafts as follows:

(a) Sight drafts.
(b) Time drafts.
(c) Trade acceptances.

Sight Drafts. A commercial draft that is made payable upon presentation is known as a *sight draft.* It indicates that the amount is either due or past due and that the drawer is demanding payment at once. A model filled-in copy of a sight draft is reproduced on page 343. The drawer of this draft is Canton Bros.; the drawee is J. A. Barton; the payee is the City National Bank of Utica. It should be noted that the draft is pay-

Sight Draft with Stub

able at sight. While a draft is a demand for payment, the drawee is not required to honor it upon presentation. If the draft is honored upon presentation, it must be paid at once. If Mr. Barton refuses payment upon presentation, the draft is said to be dishonored and it will then be returned to the drawer by the bank with a statement to the effect that Mr. Barton refused to honor it.

Until it is accepted by the drawee, a sight draft is an order rather than a written promise "to pay a sum certain in money." If it is accepted, it must be paid immediately, since it is payable on sight. Accounting for sight drafts, therefore, differs from accounting for other negotiable instruments. A memorandum record is ordinarily all that is required at the time a sight draft is drawn. This record may be a stub of the draft, similar to the stub attached to the sight draft reproduced above, or it may be a notation in the ledger account of a customer on whom a sight draft is drawn. If the draft is dishonored, a notation to this effect should be made either on the stub of the original draft or in the ledger account. It should be noted that the accounts of the drawer are not affected either by the drawing of a sight draft or by the failure of the drawee to honor it. On the other hand, if the drawee accepts the draft by paying it at sight, the drawer will in due time receive a remittance from the bank to whom it was made payable. Upon receipt of this remittance, an entry should be made in the books of the drawer debiting the bank account for the amount of the remittance received, debiting Collection Expense for the amount of the bank's service charge, and crediting Accounts Receivable for the amount of the draft.

The most common uses of sight drafts are as follows:

(a) To aid in collecting accounts receivable.
(b) To facilitate the handling of C.O.D. freight shipments.

Before a draft is drawn as a collection device, it is customary to obtain permission from the drawee to draw the draft. Permission may be requested in advance, or the drawee may be notified that unless payment of an account is made by a specified date, a sight draft will be drawn. In either case the drawee is notified in advance that a sight draft may be drawn on him. When the draft is drawn, it is usually made payable to a bank located in the same city as the drawee. The bank is instructed to present the draft and to remit the proceeds. When the draft is presented, the drawee must either pay it immediately or refuse to pay it. Refusal to pay the draft may be embarrassing to a person who wants to maintain a good credit record. A debtor who enjoys a high credit rating with his bank and with his creditors is seldom confronted with a sight draft. Should a sight draft be drawn on him by mutual agreement, he will have no hesitancy in accepting it by paying it at sight.

Order Bill of Lading — Sight Draft Attached. Some firms prefer to make C.O.D. freight shipments by means of an *order bill of lading* with a sight draft attached. Under this plan title to the property covered by the bill of lading does not pass to the buyer until he surrenders the original copy and obtains possession of the property. The order bill of lading instructs the freight agent at the destination to hold the merchandise

EUREKA TIRE & RUBBER COMPANY
246 DEVONSHIRE STREET
CLEVELAND, OHIO

DIRECTORS
HUBERT L. CARTER, TREAS.
GEORGE H. LOWE, PRES.
JOHN C. KENNEDY, SECY.
C. A. YOUNG
F. W. POWER
W. L. CARTER
E. A. CARTER
W. H. DUNBAR

No. C **2393**

DATE	August 14, 19--
YOUR ORDER	A 3517
OUR ORDER	875
SALESMAN	Reid

Sold to   Bryant & Wood
542 S. Dearborn St.
Chicago, Ill.

VIA C.C.C. & ST. L. R.R.   TERMS   C.O.D.

DESCRIPTION	QUANTITY ORDERED	SHIPPED	EXCISE TAX	UNIT PRICE	EXTENSION	TOTAL
6.00-16 4-Ply Black Tires	12	12	1.05	13.80	165.60	
6.70-15 6-Ply Black Tires	12	12	1.27	22.85	274.20	
7.10-15 4-Ply White-Black Tires	12	12	1.16	21.75	261.00	
6.00-16 Heavy Duty Tubes	18	18	.23	2.14	38.52	739.32
				Federal excise tax		45.90
				Total		785.22

C.O.D. Purchase Invoice

$ 785.22   CLEVELAND   August 14,   19 --

- - - - - - At Sight - *Pay to the*

Order of   First National Bank, Chicago, Illinois

Seven hundred eighty-five and 22/100 - - - - - - - - - - - - - - - - - - *Dollars*

WITH EXCHANGE

Value received and charge the same to account of

To   Bryant & Wood | EUREKA TIRE & RUBBER CO.

No. 21   Chicago, Illinois | *C. H. Tallent*

Sight Draft

until the original copy of the bill of lading has been presented by the consignee. At the time of making shipment the shipper draws a sight draft for the amount of the invoice and attaches to it the original copy of the order bill of lading. The draft is made payable to a bank located in the same city as the consignee. The bill of lading is transferred to this bank by endorsement, and both the draft and the original copy of the bill of lading are mailed to the bank.

Upon receipt of the draft and the order bill of lading, the bank presents the draft to the consignee for payment. After paying the draft, the consignee will be given the original copy of the order bill of lading. By presenting this bill of lading to the freight agent he may then obtain the property consigned to him. In handling this transaction the bank acts as an agent of the seller or consignor and collects the amount specified in the draft before delivering the bill of lading to the consignee.

To illustrate the use of the order bill of lading, it is assumed that Bryant & Wood placed a purchase order with the Eureka Tire & Rubber Co., shipment to be made by freight, C.O.D. Upon receipt of the order, the Eureka Tire & Rubber Co. billed the merchandise ordered and mailed the original copy of the invoice to Bryant & Wood so that they would know the amount. The purchase invoice received by Bryant & Wood is reproduced on page 344.

At the time of making shipment, the Eureka Tire & Rubber Co. drew a sight draft on Bryant & Wood for the amount of the invoice and mailed this draft to the First National Bank of Chicago with the original copy of the order bill of lading attached. The draft is reproduced above and the original copy of the order bill of lading is reproduced on page 346. It will be noted that the merchandise is consigned to the order of

Uniform Domestic Straight Bill of Lading, adopted by Carriers in Official, Southern, Western and Illinois Classification Territories, March 15, 1922, as amended August 1, 1930 and June 15, 1941

UNIFORM ORDER BILL OF LADING
ORIGINAL

Shipper's No.

THE NEW YORK CENTRAL RAILROAD   Company   Agent's No.

RECEIVED, subject to the classifications and tariffs in effect on the date of issue of this Bill of Lading.

At **Cleveland**   **August 14,** 19-- From **Eureka Tire & Rubber Company**

the property described below, in apparent good order, except as noted (contents and condition of contents of packages unknown), marked, consigned, and destined as indicated below, which said company (the word company being understood throughout this contract as meaning any person or corporation in possession of the property under the contract) agrees to carry to its usual place of delivery at said destination, if on its own road or its own water line, otherwise to deliver to another carrier on the route to said destination. It is mutually agreed, as to each carrier of all or any of said property over all or any portion of said route to destination, and as to each party at any time interested in all or any of said property, that every service to be performed hereunder shall be subject to all the conditions not prohibited by law, whether printed or written, herein contained, including the conditions on back hereof, which are hereby agreed to by the shipper and accepted for himself and his assigns.

The surrender of this Original ORDER Bill of Lading properly indorsed shall be required before the delivery of the property. Inspection of property covered by this bill of lading will not be permitted unless provided by law or unless permission is indorsed on this original bill of lading or given in writing by the shipper.

Consigned to ORDER OF **Eureka Tire & Rubber Co., 246 Devonshire St., Cleveland, Ohio**

Destination **Chicago** ___ State of **Ill.** ___ County of **Cook**

Notify **J. A. Bryant**

At **542 S. Dearborn St., Chicago** ___ State of **Ill.** ___ County of **Cook**

Route **NYC**

Delivering Carrier **NYC** ___ Car Initial ___ Car No.

NO. PACKAGES	DESCRIPTION OF ARTICLES, SPECIAL MARKS AND EXCEPTIONS	*WEIGHT (Subject to Correction)	CLASS or RATE	CHECK COLUMN	
20	bundles, 54 Tires	800#			Subject to Section 7 of conditions, if this shipment is to be delivered to the consignee without recourse on the consignor, the consignor shall sign the following statement: The carrier shall not make delivery of this shipment without payment of freight and all other lawful charges. *S. A. Brown* Signature of Consignor.
					If charges are to be prepaid, write or stamp here, "To be Prepaid."
					Received $ to apply in prepayment of the charges on the property described hereon.
					Agent or Cashier. Per (The signature here acknowledges only the amount prepaid.)
					Charges Advanced: $

*If the shipment moves between two ports by a carrier by water, the law requires that the bill of lading shall state whether it is "carrier's or shipper's weight."
Note.—Where the rate is dependent on value, shippers are required to state specifically in writing the agreed or declared value of the property

The agreed or declared value of the property is hereby specifically stated by the shipper to be not exceeding $ ___ per ___

EUREKA TIRE & RUBBER CO. Shipper, Per *S. A. B.* AGENT ___ PER ___ **1**
Permanent postoffice address of shipper ___ **Cleveland**

Order Bill of Lading

the Eureka Tire & Rubber Co. It was necessary, therefore, for the shipper to endorse the bill of lading before mailing it to the First National Bank of Chicago.

Time Drafts. A commercial draft that is made payable at a fixed or determinable future time is known as a *time draft*. It indicates that the amount is not yet due or that the drawer is willing to allow additional time in which to make payment. When accepted, a time draft becomes a negotiable promise to pay.

Time drafts may be made payable as follows:

(a) On a specified date.
(b) At a specified number of days after sight.
(c) At a specified number of days after date.

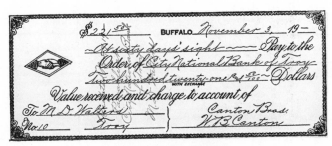

Time Draft with Stub

If a time draft is made payable on a specified date, it becomes a promise to pay when accepted by the drawee and will be due on the date specified.

If a time draft is made payable at 30 days after sight, it becomes a promise to pay when accepted and will be due 30 days after the date of acceptance.

If a time draft is made payable at 30 days after date, it becomes a promise to pay when accepted and will be due 30 days after the date of the draft.

The time draft reproduced above is payable 60 days after sight. After the draft was drawn, it was removed from the stub and sent to the City National Bank of Troy, the payee, with instructions to present it to M. D. Walters, the drawee, for acceptance. When the bank presented the draft to the drawee, he accepted it by writing his acceptance across the face and adding his signature as shown below. This procedure is sometimes referred to as honoring the draft. When Canton Bros. received the honored draft from the City National Bank of Troy, they recorded the draft in the same manner as if it had been a 60-day noninterest-bearing note. Thus the transaction was recorded by debiting Notes Receivable and by crediting Accounts Receivable for $221.50. Had Mr. Walters refused to accept

Honored Time Draft

the draft, the bank would have returned it to Canton Bros. with a notation to the effect that it had not been honored.

An auxiliary record of time drafts may be kept in note registers in the same manner as notes receivable and notes payable. An accepted time draft involves the same obligation as a note payable on the part of the drawee and is the same as a note receivable on the part of the drawer.

Trade Acceptances. A trade acceptance is similar to a time draft. It is a formal demand on the drawee by the drawer for the payment of a specified amount at a fixed or determinable future time. Its use is limited to transactions arising out of the purchase of goods. When accepted, it becomes a negotiable promise that is similar to a note. The drawer of a trade acceptance may designate any bank or trust company as the payee, or the trade acceptance may be made payable directly to the drawer. The trade acceptance reproduced below is made payable to the drawer.

Following are some of the advantages claimed for trade acceptances:

(a) They are intended to be self-liquidating. They arise out of the purchase of merchandise and it is assumed that the proceeds of the sales of such merchandise will provide the funds with which to pay the acceptances when they mature.

(b) Trade acceptances receivable possess the same legal status as notes receivable; hence, they are preferable to open accounts receivable.

(c) The use of trade acceptances relieves a merchant of the burden of financing his customers through extending credit on open account. If necessary, trade acceptances can be discounted at a bank more readily and with less expense than accounts receivable may be assigned.

(d) Experience indicates that the loss on trade acceptances will be less than on open accounts receivable.

Trade Acceptance with Stub

Honored Trade Acceptance

When merchandise is sold on trade acceptance terms, it is customary to bill the merchandise in the usual way, indicating that the terms are "trade acceptance." The sales invoice is recorded in the usual manner by debiting Accounts Receivable and by crediting Sales. A trade acceptance is drawn on the customer and is attached to the sales invoice. The following transactions and illustrations will explain the procedure more fully:

May 12. Canton Bros., Buffalo, sold merchandise to J. B. Martin, Jamestown, amounting to $378.65; terms, 60-day trade acceptance.

May 15. Canton Bros. received from J. B. Martin the honored trade acceptance reproduced above.

The merchandise was billed and the sales invoice was recorded in the sales journal in the same manner as other charge sales. The trade acceptance reproduced on page 348 was prepared and attached to the invoice, both being mailed to J. B. Martin. A carbon copy of the sales invoice was used for posting purposes, J. B. Martin's account in the accounts receivable ledger being debited for the amount of the sale and the terms being indicated in the Items column.

The honored trade acceptance reproduced above was recorded in the manner indicated in the following general journal entry:

Notes Receivable.....................................	$378.65	
Accounts Receivable...............................		$378.65
Received a trade acceptance from J. B. Martin.		

The trade acceptance was also entered in the notes receivable register of Canton Bros.

When J. B. Martin received the sales invoice from Canton Bros., he honored the trade acceptance and recorded the transaction in his invoice record by debiting Purchases and by crediting Notes Payable. If preferred, the invoice may be recorded in the invoice record in the same manner as other credit purchases and the trade acceptance may be recorded in the general journal by debiting Accounts Payable and by crediting Notes Payable.

PRACTICE ASSIGNMENT No. 25. Complete Report No. 25 in the workbook and submit your working papers to the instructor for approval. Then continue with the next study assignment in Unit Thirteen until Report No. 26 is required.

ACCOUNTING FOR PURCHASES

(26) PURCHASING PROCEDURE

In many firms all incoming invoices covering credit purchases, whether they represent purchases of merchandise, supplies, or other property, are recorded in one journal. Many firms also prefer to keep the merchandise accounts on a departmental basis in order that more information may be available and better control may be exercised.

Property purchased may consist of: (a) merchandise bought for resale; (b) supplies, such as letterheads and envelopes for office use, catalogues and circulars for advertising purposes, wrapping paper and twine for use in wrapping and shipping, and cleaning supplies; or (c) fixed assets, such as office equipment, store equipment, and delivery equipment, bought for use in operating the business.

The use of a properly designed columnar journal facilitates recording all incoming invoices in one journal regardless of whether they represent purchases of merchandise, supplies, or fixed assets. Such a journal also facilitates a proper classification of essential data and makes summary posting possible.

Merchandise for resale and other property for use in the operation of a business enterprise may be purchased for cash or on credit. In one enterprise the buying may be done by the proprietor, or by an employee, and it may require only a part of his time. In a large enterprise a purchasing department may be maintained with a manager in charge who will devote his entire time to buying. The successful operation of such a purchasing department requires an efficient organization and proper equipment. There should be a definite procedure for handling and recording the operations of the department.

The Purchase Requisition. Requests to purchase merchandise or other property may come to the purchasing agent or the purchasing department from any department of an enterprise. A form commonly known as a *purchase requisition* may be used for this purpose. Purchase requisitions should be numbered serially to prevent the loss or misuse of any

PURCHASE REQUISITION

BRYANT & WOOD

CHICAGO

REQUISITION
No. D-129

Required for Department_____A_____   Date Issued __March 27, 19--__

Advise Mr.__Wood_____on delivery   Date Required __April 15, 19--__

QUANTITY	DESCRIPTION
28	6.00-16 4-Ply Black Tires
48	6.70-15 6-Ply Black Tires
24	7.10-15 4-Ply White-Black Tires
40	6.00-16 Heavy Duty Tubes
60	6.70-15 Heavy Duty Tubes

Approved by __J. A. Bryant__   Requisition Placed by __W. L. Wood__

PURCHASING AGENT'S MEMORANDUM

Purchase Order No.___196___   Issued to___The Cole Tire Co.

Date___March 27, 19--___   Buffalo

Purchase Requisition

of the forms. Usually they are prepared in duplicate, the original going to the purchasing department and the duplicate copy being retained in the department in which the requisition originates. Sometimes the requisitions are prepared in triplicate so as to provide a copy for the receiving clerk, though in many organizations the receiving clerk is supplied with a copy of the purchase order rather than a copy of the purchase requisition.

A model filled-in purchase requisition form is reproduced above. The requisition specifies merchandise wanted in Department A. The mercantile business conducted by Bryant & Wood is organized into two departments. Requisitions for merchandise originate with the heads of these departments. After the purchase requisition shown in the illustration was approved by Bryant, an order was placed with The Cole Tire Co., manufacturers of tires and tubes, as indicated by the purchasing agent's memorandum at the bottom of the form. The purchase requisition, when approved, is the purchasing department's authority to order the merchandise or other property described in the requisition.

The Purchase Order. A written order for the merchandise or other property specified in the requisition is known as a *purchase order*. A purchase order may be prepared on a printed stock form, on a specially designed form, or on an order blank supplied by the vendor. Purchase orders should be numbered serially. Often they are prepared with multiple copies. The original copy goes to the *vendor* — the person or firm from

PURCHASE ORDER　　　　　　No. **196**

BRYANT & WOOD

CHICAGO

To　The Cole Tire Co.　　　　　　　　Date　March 27,　　　　19--

　　　Buffalo　　　　　　　　　　　Ship Via　Pa. R. R.

　　　　　　　　　　　　　　　　　F. O. B.　Buffalo

Deliver　by Apr. 15,　19--　　　　　　Terms　2/10 - n/30

QUANTITY	DESCRIPTION	PRICE
28	6.00-16 4-Ply Black Tires	13.80
48	6.70-15 6-Ply Black Tires	22.85
24	7.10-15 4-Ply White-Black Tires	21.75
40	6.00-16 Heavy Duty Tubes	2.14
60	6.70-15 Heavy Duty Tubes	2.40

J. A. Bryant

Purchase Order

whom the merchandise or other property is ordered. Sometimes the duplicate copy also goes to the vendor. If this is the case, this copy — called the "acknowledgment copy" — will have a space for the vendor to sign to indicate his acceptance of the order thereby creating a formal contract. The signed acknowledgment copy is then returned to the ordering firm. Normally a copy of the purchase order is sent to the department that requisitioned the purchase. In many organizations a copy of the purchase order is sent to the receiving clerk. The procedure followed by some firms requires that the accounting department receive a copy of the purchase order to provide a basis for verifying the charges made by the vendor. A variety of practices are followed with respect to requisitioning purchases, placing orders, checking goods received and charges made, recording purchases, and paying vendors. Each organization adopts procedures best suited to its particular needs.

A model filled-in copy of a purchase order is reproduced above. The quantity and the description of the merchandise ordered are the same as were specified in the purchase requisition reproduced on page 352. The unit prices shown in the purchase order are those quoted by the vendor and it is expected that the merchandise will be billed at such prices.

The Purchase Invoice. A bill rendered for property or service is commonly referred to as an *invoice*. From the viewpoint of the seller, it is considered a *sales invoice*; from the viewpoint of the buyer, it is considered a *purchase invoice*.

THE COLE TIRE COMPANY

BUFFALO

			FOR CUSTOMER'S USE ONLY		
			REGISTER NO. *74*	VOUCHER NO.	
CUSTOMER'S ORDER NO. & DATE 196 March 27, 19—		REFER TO INVOICE NO. 4251	F. O. B. CHECKED *M. S.*		
REQUISITION NO.			TERMS APPROVED *M. S.*	PRICE APPROVED *M. S.*	
CONTRACT NO.		INVOICE DATE March 30, 19— VENDOR'S NOS.	CALCULATIONS CHECKED *M. S.*		
			TRANSPORTATION *385745*	*$57.95*	
SOLD TO	Bryant & Wood 542 S. Dearborn St. Chicago, Illinois		FREIGHT BILL NO.	AMOUNT	
			MATERIAL RECEIVED *4/10* 19—	*H. K.*	*R. C.*
SHIPPED TO AND DESTINATION	Same		DATE	SIGNATURE	TITLE
			SATISFACTORY AND APPROVED		
DATE SHIPPED March 31, 19— FROM Buffalo		PREPAID OR COLLECT?	ADJUSTMENTS		
CAR INITIALS AND NO. F. O. B. Buffalo					
HOW SHIPPED AND ROUTE Pa. R.R.			ACCOUNTING DISTRIBUTION *Act. no. 53*		
TERMS 2/10, n/30			AUDITED *C. B.*	FINAL APPROVAL *H. B.*	

DESCRIPTION		QUANTITY ORDERED	SHIPPED	EXCISE TAX	UNIT PRICE	EXTENSION	TOTAL
6.00-16	4-Ply Black Tires	28	28	1.05	13.80	386.40	
6.70-15	6-Ply Black Tires	48	48	1.27	22.85	1,096.80	
7.10-15	4-Ply White-Black	24	24	1.16	21.75	522.00	
6.00-16	Heavy Duty Tubes	40	40	.23	2.14	85.60	
6.70-15	Heavy Duty Tubes	60	*50	.25	2.40	120.00	2,210.80
				Federal excise tax			142.40
*10 tubes back ordered. Will ship April 15.				Total			2,353.20

Purchase Invoice

A purchase invoice may be received before or after delivery of the merchandise or other property ordered. As invoices are received, it is customary to number them consecutively. These numbers should not be confused with the vendor's number, which represents his sale number. After being numbered, each purchase invoice should be checked with the carbon copy of the purchase order to ascertain that the quantity, the description, the prices, and the terms agree and that the method of shipment and the date of delivery conform to the instructions and specifications. An approval form may be printed on the invoice form. Otherwise, a separate approval form may be used, or approval may be stamped on the invoice by means of a rubber stamp. If a separate approval form is used, it may be stapled to or be pasted on the invoice form.

A model filled-in purchase invoice on a standard invoice form is reproduced above. The portion of the form headed "For Customer's Use Only" was filled in by the purchasing department of Bryant & Wood after the invoice was received. After the invoice is approved, it should be filed with the carbon copies of the purchase order and the purchase requisition until the merchandise is received.

When the merchandise is received, the contents of the shipment may be checked with a carbon copy of the purchase order by the receiving clerk or he may prepare an independent report of the contents for the purchasing department. In the latter case the receiving clerk's report will be checked with a carbon copy of the purchase order by a clerk in the purchasing department. After the merchandise has been received and the invoice has been approved by the purchasing department, the invoice is usually referred to the accounting department where the extensions and the amounts are verified and the invoice is recorded. After the invoice is recorded by entering it in the invoice record and by posting it to the account of the creditor in the accounts payable ledger, it is usually filed in an unpaid invoice file.

Back Orders. Sometimes the vendor is unable to ship immediately a part or all of the merchandise ordered. He may, however, render an invoice immediately for the complete order and indicate thereon what has been back ordered and when such items will be shipped. Reference to the purchase invoice reproduced on page 354 will show that 60 6.70-15 Heavy Duty Tubes were ordered but only 50 were shipped immediately by The Cole Tire Co. Notice of this shortage was indicated on the invoice.

Trade Discounts. Many manufacturers and wholesalers quote list prices subject to trade discounts. This makes possible the publication of catalogues with quotations of prices that will not be subject to frequent changes. Some firms, such as those dealing in hardware and jewelry, publish catalogues listing thousands of items. Such catalogues are expensive, and considerable loss might be involved where price changes occur if it were not for the fact that discount rates may be changed without changing the list or catalogue prices. This practice also has the advantage of permitting retail dealers to display catalogues to their customers without revealing the cost price of the merchandise.

When an invoice is subject to a trade discount, the discount is usually shown as a deduction from the total amount of the invoice. For example, if the invoice shown on page 354 had been subject to a trade discount of 25 per cent, the discount might be stated in the body of the invoice in the manner shown at the top of page 356.

In recording the invoice the amount to be entered is the net amount after deducting the discount; trade discounts should not be entered in the accounts of either the seller or the buyer, as they represent merely a reduction in the price of the merchandise.

Sometimes a series or chain of trade discounts is allowed. For example, the list prices may be subject to discounts of 25, 10, and 5 per cent. In computing the total discount where two or more trade discounts are

Description	Quantity Ordered	Shipped	Excise Tax	Unit Price	Extension	Total
6.00-16 4-Ply Black Tires	28	28	1.05	13.80	386.40	
6.70-15 6-Ply Black Tires	48	48	1.27	22.85	1,096.80	
7.10-15 4-Ply White-Black	24	24	1.16	21.75	522.00	
6.00-16 Heavy Duty Tubes	40	40	.23	2.14	85.60	
6.70-15 Heavy Duty Tubes	60	*50	.25	2.40	120.00	2,210.80
				Less 25% discount		552.70
						1,658.10
				Federal excise tax		142.40
				Total		1,800.50

*10 tubes back ordered. Will ship April 15.

allowed, each discount is computed separately on the successive net amounts. For example, if the gross amount of an invoice is $100 and discounts of 25, 10, and 5 per cent are allowed, the net amount should be computed as follows:

Gross amount of invoice...	$100.00
Less 25%..	25.00
Balance...	$ 75.00
Less 10%..	7.50
Balance...	$ 67.50
Less 5%...	3.38
Net Amount..	$ 64.12

In recording this invoice only the net amount, or $64.12, should be entered.

Cash Discounts. Many firms follow the practice of allowing cash discounts as an inducement for prompt payment of invoices. The terms of payment should be indicated on the invoice. It will be noted that the terms specified on the invoice reproduced on page 354 are "2/10, n/30." This means that a discount of 2 per cent will be allowed if payment is made within 10 days from the date of the invoice, that is, if payment is made by April 9.

Should the invoice be paid on or before April 9, 2 per cent, or $44.22, may be deducted from the cost price of $2,210.80 and a check for $2,308.98 may be issued in full settlement of the invoice. After April 9 no discount will be allowed and the total amount, or $2,353.20, must be paid not later than 30 days after the date of the invoice, that is, by April 29.

Cash discounts are usually ignored at the time of recording purchase invoices, even though it may be the policy of a firm to pay all invoices in time to get the benefit of any cash discounts offered. For example, the invoice reproduced on page 354 should be recorded by debiting the proper accounts and by crediting Accounts Payable for $2,353.20. The discount taken at time of payment on or before April 9 will be entered at the time of recording the check issued in settlement of the invoice. Thus, cash discounts are treated as income rather than as a reduction in the cost of merchandise purchased.

Sometimes an invoice is subject to both trade and cash discounts. In such case the trade discount should be deducted from the gross amount of the invoice before the cash discount is computed. For example, if the invoice reproduced in on page 354 had been subject to a trade discount of 25 per cent and the terms were 2/10, n/30, the net amount payable within 10 days from the date of the invoice should be computed in the following manner:

Amount of invoice (not including excise tax)......................	$2,210.80
Less trade discount, 25%......................................	552.70
Amount subject to discount....................................	$1,658.10
Less cash discount, 2%.......................................	33.16
	$1,624.94
Add federal excise tax..	142.40
Net amount payable..	$1,767.34

Usually an invoice must be paid in full within the time specified in order to obtain the benefit of any cash discount offered. However, in some instances, the purchaser may be allowed the usual cash discount for partial payment of an invoice within the time specified. Thus if, instead of paying the invoice of The Cole Tire Co. in full, Bryant & Wood had made a payment of $300 on the invoice by April 9, The Cole Tire Co. might agree to allow them the cash discount of 2 per cent. In such case the amount of the discount should be computed in the following manner:

100% = amount for which Bryant & Wood should receive credit
100% − 2% = 98%
98% = $300
$300 ÷ 98% = $306.12
$306.12 − $300 = $6.12 discount

This transaction should be recorded in the books of Bryant & Wood by debiting Accounts Payable for $306.12, by crediting Purchases Discount for $6.12, and by crediting the bank account for $300.

Federal Excise Taxes. A federal excise tax on tires and inner tubes made wholly or in part of rubber is imposed on manufacturers, producers, or importers. The base of the tax is the total weight in pounds of the tires and tubes. It is the custom of manufacturers of tires and inner tubes to list the excise tax separately on the invoice as shown on page 354. The tax may be passed on to wholesalers, retailers, or consumers, provided the tax is stated separately on all invoices. Such taxes are in no case subject to discount.

Terms. The following terms are commonly used in connection with purchase invoices:

30 days	The amount of the invoice must be paid within 30 days from its date.
2/10, n/30	A discount of 2% will be allowed if payment is made within 10 days from the date of the invoice; otherwise, the total amount of the invoice must be paid within 30 days from its date.
2/E.O.M., n /60	A discount of 2% will be allowed if payment is made before the end of the month; otherwise, the total amount of the invoice must be paid within 60 days of its date.
C.O.D.	Collect on delivery. The amount of the invoice must be paid at the time the merchandise is delivered.
F.O.B. Shipping Point	Free on board at point of origin of the shipment. Under such terms the buyer must pay all transportation charges and assume all risks from the time the merchandise is accepted for shipment by the carrier.
F.O.B. Destination	Free on board at destination of the shipment. The seller will pay the transportation charges and will assume all responsibility for the merchandise until it reaches the carrier's delivery point at destination.

Miscellaneous Forms. In addition to the forms previously discussed, there are a number of miscellaneous forms, such as bills of lading, freight bills, drayage bills, and credit memorandums, that may be used in connection with the purchase of merchandise and other property. It is important that the function of these forms be understood in order that they may be properly handled.

Bills of Lading. The desired method of shipment is usually specified in the purchase order and the actual method of shipment is indicated in the purchase invoice. When shipment is made by freight via railroad or truck, the shipper is given a receipt that is known as a *bill of lading*.

A bill of lading is usually prepared in triplicate. The first copy is referred to as the original, the second copy as the shipping order, and the third copy as the memorandum. The freight agent signs all three copies, returning the original and the memorandum to the shipper and retaining the shipping order. The shipper in turn may send the original or the memorandum copy to the buyer and retain the other copy for his files.

(Uniform Domestic Straight Bill of Lading, adopted by Carriers in Official, Southern, Western and Illinois Classification territories, March 15, 1922, as amended August 1, 1930, and June 15, 1941.)

UNIFORM STRAIGHT BILL OF LADING--ORIGINAL--NOT NEGOTIABLE   Shipper's No.

Pa. R. R.   **Company**   Agent's No.

RECEIVED, subject to the classifications and tariffs in effect on the date of the issue of this Bill of Lading,

at BUFFALO_____   March 31, 19--   FROM **THE COLE TIRE COMPANY**

the property described below, in apparent good order, except as noted (contents and condition of contents of packages unknown), marked, consigned, and destined as indicated below, which said company (the word company being understood throughout this contract as meaning any person or corporation in possession of the property under the contract) agrees to carry to its usual place of delivery at said destination, if on its own road or its own water line, otherwise to deliver to another carrier on the route to said destination. It is mutually agreed, as to each carrier of all or any of said property over all or any portion of said route to destination, and as to each party at any time interested in all or any of said property, that every service to be performed hereunder shall be subject to all the conditions not prohibited by law, whether printed or written, herein contained, including the conditions on back hereof, which are hereby agreed to by the shipper and accepted for himself and his assigns.

(Mail or street address of consignee—For purposes of notification only.)

Consigned to ___Bryant & Wood___   542 S. Dearborn

Destination ___Chicago___   State of ___Illinois___   County of ___

Route ___

Delivering Carrier ___   Car Initial ___   Car No. ___

No. Packages	Description of Articles, Special Marks and Exceptions	*WEIGHT (Sub. to Cor.)	Class or Rate	Ck. Col.	Subject to Section 7 of conditions, if this shipment is to be delivered to the consignee without recourse on the consignor, the consignor shall sign the following statement: The carrier shall not make delivery of this shipment without payment of freight and all other lawful charges.
50	bundles, 100 Tires	2768#			
4	cartons, 90 Tubes	252#			
					Per ___ (Signature of Consignor) If charges are to be prepaid, write or stamp here, "To be Prepaid."

†The fibre boxes used for this shipment conform to the specifications set forth in the box maker's certificate thereon, and all other requirements of Rule 41 of the Consolidated Freight Classification.

‡Shipper's imprint in lieu of stamp; not a part of bill of lading approved by the Interstate Commerce Commission.

*If the shipment moves between two ports by a carrier by water, the law requires that the bill of lading shall state whether it is "carrier's or shipper's weight." Note.—Where the rate is dependent on value, shippers are required to state specifically in writing the agreed or declared value of the property. The agreed or declared value of the property is hereby specifically stated by the shipper to be not exceeding ___ per ___

Received $ ___ to apply in prepayment of the charges on the property described hereon.

Agent or Cashier

Per ___ (The signature here acknowledges only the amount prepaid.)

Charges Advanced: $ ___

THE COLE TIRE CO., Shipper, Per ___*alfB.*___   ___Agent, Per ___

Permanent post-office address of shipper BUFFALO.

Straight Bill of Lading

The merchandise or other property is delivered to the freight agent in cases, cartons, bundles, or packages; hence, the description in the bill of lading may differ from the description in the purchase invoice. In addition to describing the merchandise in the bill of lading, the number of packages and the weight of each are indicated. The freight rate depends upon the type of merchandise being shipped, the distance it is being shipped, and the weight of the shipment. The rate on a carload (C.L.) is lower than the rate on less than a carload (L.C.L.).

A model filled-in bill of lading is reproduced above. This is known as a *straight bill of lading*, under the terms of which title to the merchandise passed to Bryant & Wood when the merchandise was delivered to the transportation company. When Bryant & Wood present a copy of this bill of lading to the local agent of the railroad, or otherwise identify themselves, they will be entitled to receive the merchandise.

C.O.D. Purchases. Merchandise or other property may be purchased on C.O.D. terms. C.O.D. shipments may be received by parcel post, express, or freight. When such shipments are received by parcel post or express, the consignee must pay for the property at the time of delivery. The bill may include transportation charges and C.O.D. fees. In any event, the total amount paid represents the cost of the property purchased.

Make checks payable to	FREIGHT BILL					

THE PENNSYLVANIA RAILROAD COMPANY   CHICAGO   FRONT AND BUTLER STS.

Dr., For Charges on Articles Transported:

SECTION   FREIGHT BILL NO.

DATE April 2, 19--

CONSIGNEE 29 X   ROUTE   385745

DESTINATION Bryant & Wood, Chicago, Ill.   Point of Origin to Destination)

Way-Billed From	Way-Bill Date and No.	Full Name of Shipper	Car Initials and No.
Buffalo	1829 Mar. 31	The Cole Tire Co.	C 29475
Point and Date of Shipment	Connecting Line Reference	Previous Way-Bill Reference	Original Car Initials and No.

Original paid freight bills must be surrendered for overcharges to be refunded and must accompany claims for overcharge, loss or damage.

NUMBER OF PACKAGES, ARTICLES AND MARKS	WEIGHT	RATE	FREIGHT	ADVANCES	TOTAL
50 Bundles, 100 Tires	2768#	1.86	51.48		51.48
4 Cartons, 90 Tubes	252#	1.86	4.69		4.69
					56.17
				Tax	1.69

TOTAL PREPAID:

RECEIVED PAYMENT   TOTAL   57.86

FREIGHT AGENT

F. B. Kline

Freight Bill

When C.O.D. shipments are made by freight, the amount to be collected by the transportation company should be entered immediately below the description of the merchandise on the bill of lading. A copy of the sales invoice may be inserted in an envelope which can be pasted to the outside of the package, carton, or case. The transportation company will then collect the amount specified at the time of delivering the merchandise and will in turn remit to the shipper.

Freight Bills. At the time merchandise or other property is delivered to a transportation company for shipment, an agent of the transportation company prepares a document known as a *waybill*. The waybill describes the shipment, shows the point of origin and destination, and indicates any special handling that may be required. The original is forwarded to the agent of the transportation company at the station to which the shipment is consigned. When the shipment arrives at the destination a bill for the transportation charges is prepared. This is called a *freight bill*. Usually the consignee is required to pay the freight bill before he can obtain the property.

A reproduction of a freight bill appears above. A comparison of this freight bill with the bill of lading reproduced on page 359 will show that it contains the same description of the shipment. In addition, however, the freight charges (including the federal tax) are shown.

Trucking companies usually make what is known as "store-door delivery." Freight shipments made by railroad may also be delivered to the consignee's place of business at no extra charge. In case such service is not rendered by the transportation company, it may be necessary for the consignee to employ a drayage company to transport the merchandise from the freight station to his place of business. In this case the drayage company will submit a bill for the services rendered. This is known as a *drayage bill*.

Credit Memorandums. Ordinarily the buyer expects to receive the merchandise or other property ordered and to pay for it at the agreed price in accordance with the terms specified in the purchase invoice. However, part or all of the merchandise or other property may be returned to the vendor for various reasons, such as the following:

(a) It may not conform to the specifications in the purchase order.

(b) A mistake may have been made in placing the order and the vendor may give permission for it to be returned.

(c) It may have been delayed in shipment and, as a result, the buyer cannot dispose of it. This sometimes happens with seasonable goods.

In some cases where the merchandise received is unsatisfactory or the prices charged are not in accord with an existing agreement or with previous quotations, an adjustment may be made that is referred to as an *allowance*.

When merchandise is returned to the supplier for credit, a charge-back invoice is usually issued for the purchase price of the merchandise returned. Upon receipt of the merchandise, the supplier will usually issue

CREDIT MEMORANDUM

THE COLE TIRE CO.

BUFFALO

DATE ___April 8, 19--___

To ___Bryant & Wood___

___542 S. Dearborn___

___Chicago, Ill.___

WE CREDIT YOUR ACCOUNT AS FOLLOWS:

DESCRIPTION	QUANTITY	EXCISE TAX	UNIT PRICE	EXTENSION	TOTAL
6.70-15 6-Ply Black Tires	2	1.27	22.85	45.70	45.70
			Federal excise tax		2.54
			Total credit		48.24

Credit Memorandum

a credit memorandum for the amount of the credit allowed. A model filled-in credit memorandum is reproduced on page 361. This form indicates that The Cole Tire Co. has given Bryant & Wood credit for the return of two 6.70-15 6-ply Black Tires.

Standard Forms. Standard purchase order and invoice forms have been widely adopted by merchants, manufacturers, distributors, and other users. The standard invoice form was originally developed by The National Association of Purchasing Agents in collaboration with The Railway Accounting Officers Association, The National Association of Cost Accountants, and The Association of American Railroads. The forms developed by these associations have been approved by the Division of Simplified Practice of The National Bureau of Standards, U. S. Department of Commerce. The size of the forms approved is 8½ inches wide by 7, 11, or 14 inches long. As indicated, the length may vary according to needs. As there naturally is a considerable variation in the number of items ordered at various times, an invoice form 7 inches long may be satisfactory in one case and not satisfactory in other cases. The purchase invoice shown on page 354 was prepared on a standard invoice form.

> *PRACTICE ASSIGNMENT No. 26. Complete Report No. 26 in the workbook and submit your working papers to the instructor for approval. Then continue with the following study assignment until Report No. 27 is required.*

(27) ACCOUNTING PRACTICE

When all incoming invoices covering purchases on credit are recorded in one journal, regardless of whether the invoices represent the purchase of merchandise or other property, provision should be made for a proper classification of the debits and the credits. If the merchandise accounts are kept on a departmental basis, a separate column should be provided for recording the merchandise purchased for each department. The use of special columns for this purpose will facilitate summary posting. General Ledger Dr. and Cr. columns should also be provided for recording items that must be posted individually to the general ledger accounts. If individual accounts with creditors are kept in a subsidiary ledger, a summary or control account for accounts payable must be kept in the general ledger.

The procedure in recording all incoming invoices in one journal and of keeping the merchandise accounts on a departmental basis will be illustrated (a) by recording chronologically in an invoice record a narrative of selected transactions, (b) by posting directly from the purchase invoices to the individual accounts of creditors kept in a subsidiary accounts payable ledger, (c) by posting from the invoice record to the proper general ledger accounts, and (d) by preparing a schedule of accounts payable as a means of proving the accounts payable control account.

Bryant & Wood are engaged in the wholesale tire and accessories business as partners. Two departments are maintained — Dept. A, tires and tubes, and Dept. B, radios and batteries. Separate merchandise accounts are kept for each department in order that the gross operating profit for each department may be computed separately. In addition to separate departmental purchases accounts and sales accounts, separate departmental accounts are kept for transportation charges and for returns and allowances. A separate account is kept also for any federal excise taxes that are billed separately, as is the custom of manufacturers of tires and tubes. Following is a list of these accounts:

41 Sales, Dept. A
    041 Sales Returns and Allowances, Dept. A
42 Sales, Dept. B
    042 Sales Returns and Allowances, Dept. B
51 Purchases, Dept. A
    051 Purchases Returns and Allowances, Dept. A
52 Purchases, Dept. B
    052 Purchases Returns and Allowances, Dept. B
53 Transportation In, Dept. A
54 Transportation In, Dept. B
166 Prepaid Federal Excise Tax

Invoice Record. The form of the invoice record used by Bryant & Wood is illustrated on page 365. It will be noted that a special column is provided for recording the federal excise tax on tires and tubes. This facilitates recording the tax and makes possible summary posting of the total tax incurred each month. A narrative of the transactions that have been entered in the invoice record precedes the illustration. It will be helpful to check each transaction and to note how it was entered in the invoice record.

Corrected Purchase Invoices. If a corrected purchase invoice is received before the original invoice has been entered in the invoice record, the original invoice may be canceled and the corrected invoice may be entered in the usual manner.

If a corrected purchase invoice is received after the original invoice has been entered in the invoice record and has been posted to the individual account of the creditor, the corrected invoice may be entered either in the invoice record or in the general journal. The proper entry will depend upon whether or not the amount of the corrected invoice is more or less than the amount of the original invoice. The corrected invoice should be attached to the original invoice.

If the amount of the corrected invoice is more than the amount of the original invoice, the increase should be recorded by debiting the proper account, depending upon whether merchandise or other property was purchased, and by crediting Accounts Payable. The amount of the increase should then be posted to the credit of the proper creditor's account in the subsidiary accounts payable ledger.

If the amount of the corrected invoice is less than the amount of the original invoice, the decrease should be recorded by debiting Accounts Payable and by crediting the proper account. The amount of the decrease should then be posted to the debit of the proper creditor's account.

NARRATIVE OF TRANSACTIONS

April 1. (Saturday) Received the following purchase invoices:

No. 101, The Cole Tire Co., Buffalo; tires and tubes, $2,210.80, federal excise tax, $142.40; terms, March 30 — 2/10, n/30; freight collect.

No. 102, Pushin Auto Supply Co., Dayton; radios, $397.65; terms, March 29 — 2/10, n/30; freight collect.

No. 103, Chatfield Paper Co., City; store supplies, $56.80; terms, March 31 — 30 days.

No. 104, Modern Machine Co., City; store equipment, $75; terms, April 1 — 30-day note with interest at 6%.

5. Received a corrected purchase invoice from Pushin Auto Supply Co. for $407.65. (See Purchase Invoice No. 102.)

25. Received the following purchase invoices:

No. 121, Hood Tire Co., Cleveland; tires and tubes, $885.75, federal excise tax, $87.60; terms, April 21 — 2/10, n/60; freight prepaid and added to invoice, $32.10.

No. 122, Western Auto Supply Co., Chicago; radios and batteries, $727.70; terms, April 22 — 1/10, n/30; freight prepaid and added to invoice, $14.

No. 123, Acme Supply Co., City; office supplies, $46; terms, April 24 — 30 days.

No. 124, The Office Equipment Co., Philadelphia; office equipment, $244; terms, April 22 — 2/10, n/30; freight prepaid and added to invoice, $17.50.

29. Received a corrected purchase invoice from the Acme Supply Co. for $40. (See Purchase Invoice No. 123.)

Page 34

INVOICE RECORD FOR MONTH OF April 19—

| DEBITS | | | | | | | | | | CREDITS | | | | |
Purchases Dept. A	Dept. B	Federal Excise Tax	Gen. Ledger Act. No.	Gen. Ledger Amount	✓	Day	Date of Inv.	Inv. No.	Name	Accounts Payable	✓	Gen. Ledger Act. No.	Gen. Ledger Amount	✓
									AMOUNTS FORWARDED					
2210 80		142 40				1	3/30	101	The Cole Tire Co.	2353 20	✓			
	397 65					1	3/29	102	Pushin Auto Supply Co.	397 65	✓			
			161	5480		1	3/31	103	Chatfield Paper Co.	54 80	✓			
			17	7500	✓	1	4/1	104	Modern Machine Co.			25	7500	✓
1000						5	3/29	102	Pushin Auto Supply Co. (correction)	1000	✓			
8 8875		8760	53	3710	✓	25	4/21	121	Hood Tire Co.	1005 45	✓			
	74770		54	1400	✓	25	4/22	122	Western Auto Supply Co.	741 70	✓			
			163	4600	✓	25	4/24	123	Acme Supply Co.	46 00	✓			
			19	7650	✓	25	4/22	124	The Office Equipment Co.	76 50	✓			
		23000	27	600		29	4/24	123	Acme Supply Co. (corrected inv.)	487 30	✓	163	600	✓
		23000								487 30			8100	
3 09688	1 17395	23000		49140										
2 09655	1 13535	23000		(1)						(27)			(1)	
(51)	(52)	(66)												

Proving the Invoice Record. The invoice record may be footed and the footings may be proved at any time by comparing the sum of the debit footings with the sum of the credit footings. The footings of Bryant & Wood's invoice record were proved as of April 30 in the following manner:

COLUMN HEADINGS	DEBITS	CREDITS
Purchases, Dept. A	$3,096.55	
Purchases, Dept. B	1,135.35	
Federal Excise Tax	230.00	
General Ledger	491.40	
Accounts Payable		$4,872.30
General Ledger		81.00
Totals	$4,953.30	$4,953.30

Ledgers. The ledgers used by Bryant & Wood include a general ledger with standard ruling and a subsidiary accounts payable ledger with balance-column ruling. The accounts affected by the transactions entered in the invoice record reproduced on page 365 are shown in skeleton form on pages 367 to 369. The March 31 balances are recorded in the accounts as of April 1. An accounts payable control account is kept in the general ledger.

Posting Procedure. Posting to Bryant & Wood's general ledger and accounts payable ledger involves both individual posting and summary posting. After each purchase invoice was entered in the invoice record, it was immediately posted to the proper creditor's account in the accounts payable ledger. The posting was done directly from the invoice, the invoice number being inserted in the Folio column.

While the posting to creditors' accounts may be done from the invoice record, there are certain advantages in posting directly from the purchase invoices. For example, the invoice provides all the information needed in posting, whereas, if the posting were done from the invoice record, it would be necessary to enter in the invoice record all the information needed in posting, regardless of whether or not it served any other purpose. Furthermore, if an error were made in entering an invoice in the invoice record, it would probably be carried over into the accounts payable ledger through the posting, whereas if the posting is done directly from the invoice, it is not likely that the same error would be made twice.

Posting directly from incoming invoices to the creditors' accounts in the accounts payable ledger is not only efficient; it also provides a sound method of internal check and control. One bookkeeper may enter the invoices in the invoice record and complete such posting as is required

(*Continued on page 370*)

General Ledger

S<small>TORE</small> S<small>UPPLIES</small>   Account No. 161

19--						
April	1	Balance	√	70.00		
	1		I34	56.80		
				126.80		

O<small>FFICE</small> S<small>UPPLIES</small>   Account No. 163

19--					19--			
April	1	Balance	√	47.50	April 29		I34	6.00
	25		I34	46.00				
		87.50		*93.50*				

P<small>REPAID</small> F<small>EDERAL</small> E<small>XCISE</small> T<small>AX</small>   Account No. 166

19--					
April	1	Balance	√	1,472.97	
	30		I34	230.00	
				1,702.97	

S<small>TORE</small> E<small>QUIPMENT</small>   Account No. 17

19--					
April	1	Balance	√	360.00	
	1		I34	75.00	
				435.00	

O<small>FFICE</small> E<small>QUIPMENT</small>   Account No. 19

19--					
April	1	Balance	√	600.00	
	25		I34	261.50	
				861.50	

NOTES PAYABLE   Account No. 25

19--			
April	1 Balance	√	400.00
	1	I34	75.00
			475.00

ACCOUNTS PAYABLE   Account No. 27

19--				19--		
April 29		I34	6.00	April 1 Balance	√	636.57
				30	I34	4,872.30
				5,502.87		*5,508.87*

PURCHASES, DEPT. A   Account No. 51

19--			
April	1 Balance	√	24,232.64
	30	I34	3,096.55
			27,329.19

PURCHASES, DEPT. B   Account No. 52

19--			
April	1 Balance	√	18,500.00
	30	I34	1,135.35
			19,635.35

TRANSPORTATION IN, DEPT. A   Account No. 53

19--			
April	1 Balance	√	180.00
	25	I34	32.10
			212.10

TRANSPORTATION IN, DEPT. B   Account No. 54

19--			
April	1 Balance	√	210.00
	25	I34	14.00
			224.00

Accounts Payable Ledger

ACME SUPPLY CO., CITY

DATE	ITEMS	FOL.	DEBITS	CREDITS	BALANCE
19--					
April 1	Cr. Balance	✓			79.50
25	4/24 — 30 ds.	P123		46.00	125.50
29	Corrected invoice	P123	6.00		119.50

CHATFIELD PAPER CO., CITY

19--					
April 1	Cr. Balance	✓			21.75
1	3/31 — 30 ds.	P103		56.80	78.55

THE COLE TIRE CO., BUFFALO

19--					
April 1	Cr. Balance	✓			98.82
1	Mdse. 3/30 — 2/10, n/30	P101		2,210.80	
1	Fed. excise tax	P101		142.40	2,452.02

HOOD TIRE CO., CLEVELAND

19--					
April 1	Cr. Balance	✓			125.00
25	Mdse. 4/21 — 2/10, n/60	P121		885.75	
25	Fed. excise tax	P121		87.60	
25	Freight prepaid	P121		32.10	1,130.45

THE OFFICE EQUIPMENT CO., PHILADELPHIA

19--					
April 25	4/22 — 2/10, n/30	P124		244.00	
25	Freight prepaid	P124		17.50	261.50

PUSHIN AUTO SUPPLY CO., DAYTON

19--					
April 1	Cr. Balance	✓			84.50
1	3/29 — 2/10, n/30	P102		397.65	482.15
5	Corrected invoice	P102		10.00	492.15

WESTERN AUTO SUPPLY CO., CHICAGO

19--					
April 1	Cr. Balance	✓			227.00
25	Mdse. 4/22 — 1/10, n/30	P122		727.70	
25	Freight prepaid	P122		14.00	968.70

from the invoice record to the general ledger accounts, while another book-keeper may post directly from the invoices to the creditors' accounts in the accounts payable ledger. Thus the work is divided between two employees. Proof of the accuracy of their work is obtained periodically by preparing a schedule of accounts payable and comparing its total with the balance of the accounts payable control account that is kept in the general ledger.

Posting to the accounts of creditors in the accounts payable ledger may be done either with a pen or with a machine. The use of posting machines for this purpose may be justifiable where there are a large number of accounts and a large number of transactions involved.

In addition to ordinary posting machines there are electric accounting machines that may be used not only as an aid in keeping accounts with creditors, but also in keeping a record of invoices and in preparing a schedule of accounts payable at the end of each accounting period. The use of mechanical devices in accounting for the operations of a business enterprise does not change the fundamental principles of double-entry bookkeeping. The primary purpose of this course is to develop these fundamentals.

Individual Posting. Each invoice entered in the Accounts Payable Cr. column of the invoice record was posted individually to the proper creditor's account in the accounts payable ledger shown on page 369. In the case of invoices involving federal excise taxes and prepaid transportation charges, the amounts of the merchandise or other property purchased, the federal excise taxes, and the transportation charges were posted separately. For example, in posting the invoice of March 30 received from The Cole Tire Co., the amount of the merchandise, $2,210.80, and the amount of the federal excise taxes, $142.40, were posted separately to the account of The Cole Tire Co.

In posting the invoice of April 22 received from the Western Auto Supply Co., the amount of the merchandise, $727.70, and the amount of the freight prepaid, $14, were posted separately to the account of the Western Auto Supply Co. The reason for posting the excise taxes and the transportation charges as separate items is that the excise taxes and the transportation charges are never subject to discount; only the amount of the merchandise purchased may be subject to discount. Since the individual posting to the accounts payable ledger was done directly from the invoices, a check mark was placed in the Check ($\sqrt{}$) column following the Accounts Payable column of the invoice record at the time of entering the invoices.

It was also necessary to post individually each item entered in the General Ledger Dr. and Cr. columns of the invoice record. Usually this posting is completed daily. As each item was posted, a check mark was placed in the Check ($\sqrt{}$) column following the Amount column of the invoice record and the number of the invoice was entered in the Folio column of the ledger account preceding the amount posted.

Summary Posting. The summary posting is usually completed at the end of each month and involves the following procedure:

(a) The total of the column headed Purchases — Dept. A was posted to the debit of Purchases, Dept. A, Account No. 51, in the general ledger.

(b) The total of the column headed Purchases — Dept. B was posted to the debit of Purchases, Dept. B, Account No. 52, in the general ledger.

(c) The total of the column headed Federal Excise Tax was posted to the debit of Prepaid Federal Excise Tax, Account No. 166, in the general ledger.

(d) The total of the column headed Accounts Payable was posted to the credit of Accounts Payable, Account No. 27, in the general ledger.

As the total of each column was posted, the account number was written immediately below the total in the invoice record and the page of the invoice record was written in the Folio column of the general ledger as a cross reference. A check mark was placed below the totals of the General Ledger Dr. and Cr. columns in the invoice record to indicate that those totals need not be posted.

Schedule of Accounts Payable. The balance of the accounts payable control account may be proved any time after all posting is completed by preparing a schedule of the accounts with creditors from the accounts payable ledger. The following schedule was prepared from the accounts payable ledger of Bryant & Wood at the end of April and the total was checked with the balance of the accounts payable control account in the general ledger as a means of proof:

SCHEDULE OF ACCOUNTS PAYABLE
APRIL 30, 19--

Acme Supply Co.	$ 119.50
Chatfield Paper Co.	78.55
The Cole Tire Co.	2,452.02
Hood Tire Co.	1,130.45
The Office Equipment Co.	261.50
Pushin Auto Supply Co.	492.15
Western Auto Supply Co.	968.70
Total	$5,502.87

Cash Purchases. Bryant & Wood follow the practice of entering only credit purchases in their invoice record. Cash purchases are entered in the record of checks issued, by debiting the proper departmental purchases accounts and by crediting the bank account. Usually cash purchases are not posted to the individual accounts of creditors. However, if it is desired to post cash purchases to the individual accounts of creditors, such transactions may be entered in both the invoice record and in the record of checks issued. In other words, invoices received in connection with cash purchases may be recorded in the same manner as invoices for credit purchases, if desired.

C.O.D. Purchases. When property is purchased on C.O.D. terms, the total amount paid represents the cost of the property. Since payment must be made before possession of the property can be obtained, it is customary to treat such transactions the same as cash purchases. Thus the check issued in payment is entered in the check record by debiting the proper account and by crediting the bank account. The proper account to debit depends upon the kind of property purchased. If merchandise is purchased, the proper departmental purchases account should be debited for the cost of the merchandise and the proper departmental transportation account should be debited for the amount of any transportation charges paid. If fixed assets are purchased, the proper equipment account should be debited for the total cost, including the C.O.D. fees and any transportation charges; likewise, if supplies are purchased, the proper supply account should be debited for the total cost of the supplies, including C.O.D. fees and any transportation charges.

Transportation Charges. Express charges and freight charges may be prepaid by the shipper or may be paid by the buyer at the time of delivery. Parcel post charges must be prepaid by the shipper. Store-door delivery of freight shipments may be made by the transportation companies. However, when freight shipments are not delivered to the buyer's place of business by the transportation company, the buyer must either call for the goods at his freight station or must employ a drayman to deliver the goods to his place of business.

Transportation Charges Prepaid. If the transportation charges are prepaid by the shipper, the amount may or may not be added to the invoice, depending upon the terms of sale. If the shipper has quoted prices f.o.b. destination, it is understood that the prices quoted include transportation charges either to the buyer's place of business or to his freight station and that no additional charge will be made for any transportation charges paid by the shipper.

If the shipper has quoted prices f.o.b. point of shipment, it is understood that the prices quoted do not include the transportation charges and that the buyer will be expected to stand the transportation costs. If shipment is made prepaid, the transportation charges will be added to the invoice and the shipper will be reimbursed by the buyer when the invoice is paid.

Transportation Charges Collect. If prices are quoted f.o.b. point of shipment and shipment is made collect, the buyer must pay the transportation charges before obtaining possession of the shipment. Such transportation charges represent an addition to the cost of the merchandise or other property purchased. The method of recording the transportation charges in this case is the same as if the charges had been prepaid by the shipper and added to the invoice.

If prices are quoted f.o.b. point of destination but for some reason shipment is made collect, the buyer must pay the transportation charges before he can obtain possession of the shipment. In such cases the transportation charges paid by the buyer should be recorded as a debit to the account of the creditor from whom the merchandise or other property was ordered. In other words, the payment of the transportation charges in such case should be treated the same as a partial payment on the account of the shipper.

Transportation Accounts. As explained in Unit Three, transportation charges applicable to merchandise purchased may be recorded by debiting the purchases account. However, it is common practice to record transportation charges on incoming merchandise in a separate account, which may be entitled Transportation In or Transportation on Purchases. This account is treated as a subdivision of the purchases account and the balance must be taken into consideration in computing the cost of goods sold at the close of each accounting period.

The merchandise accounts of Bryant & Wood are kept on a departmental basis, with separate accounts for Purchases and for Transportation In being kept for Departments A and B. The only time transportation charges are entered in the invoice record is when they are prepaid by the shipper and are added to the invoice. For example, in recording Invoice No. 121, the freight prepaid amounting to $32.10 was charged to Transportation In, Dept. A, Account No. 53. In recording Invoice No. 122, the freight prepaid amounting to $14 was charged to Transportation In, Dept. B, Account No. 54. On all shipments by freight collect, the transportation charges will be entered in the check record. For example, when the freight charges applicable to Invoice No. 101 are paid, the amount of the check issued will be entered in the check record as a debit to Transportation In, Dept. A, Account No. 53, and as a credit to the bank account.

As a further illustration of the proper method of recording transportation charges on merchandise purchased, it will be assumed that Bryant & Wood ordered radios and batteries from the Western Auto Supply Co. under the following alternative conditions:

(a) Total amount of invoice, $500; terms, March 1 — 1/10, n/30; f.o.b. point of shipment; freight collect, $20.

(b) Total amount of invoice, $520; terms, March 1 — 1/10, n/30; f.o.b. point of shipment; freight prepaid, $20.

(c) Total amount of invoice, $520; terms, March 1 — 1/10, n/30; f.o.b. destination; freight prepaid, $20.

(d) Total amount of invoice, $520; terms, March 1 — 1/10, n/30; f.o.b. destination; freight collect, $20.

Recording transaction (a) involves an entry in the invoice record for the amount of the invoice and an entry in the check record for the amount of the check issued in payment of the freight charges. The effect of both entries is the same as in the following general journal entries:

Purchases, Dept. A.	$500.00	
Accounts Payable.		$500.00
Transportation In, Dept. A.	20.00	
Bank.		20.00

Recording transaction (b) involves an entry in the invoice record only. The effect of this entry is indicated by the following general journal entry:

Purchases, Dept. A.	$500.00	
Transportation In, Dept. A.	20.00	
Accounts Payable.		$520.00

Recording transaction (c) involves an entry in the invoice record only. The effect of this entry is indicated by the following general journal entry:

Purchases, Dept. A.	$520.00	
Accounts Payable.		$520.00

Recording transaction (d) involves an entry in the invoice record for the amount of the invoice and an entry in the check record for the amount of the check issued in payment of the freight charges. The effect of these entries is indicated by the following general journal entries:

```
Purchases, Dept. A......................................  $520.00
    Accounts Payable......................................          $520.00
Accounts Payable......................................   20.00
    Bank.................................................           20.00
```

It will be noted that in recording transactions (a) and (b) Purchases, Dept. A is debited for $500 and Transportation In, Dept. A is debited for $20. In recording transactions (c) and (d) Purchases, Dept. A is debited for $520. Thus the total cost of the merchandise purchased is the same in all four transactions.

Transportation charges applicable to fixed assets, such as office equipment, store equipment, or delivery equipment, should be treated as an addition to the cost of such equipment. For example, in entering the invoice of April 22 received from The Office Equipment Co. in the invoice record of Bryant & Wood, the total amount of the invoice, $261.50, including transportation charges amounting to $17.50, was charged to Office Equipment, Account No. 19. It is immaterial whether the freight charges are prepaid by the shipper and added to the invoice or whether shipment is made collect. If the freight is prepaid and added to the invoice, the total cost, including the invoice price and the transportation charges, may be recorded as a debit to the office equipment account in one amount. On the other hand, if shipment is made collect, the amount of the invoice should be posted in one amount and the freight charges in a separate amount as debits to the office equipment account.

Parcel Post Insurance. Merchandise or other property shipped by parcel post mail may be insured against loss or damage in transit. Such insurance may be purchased from the government through the post office, may be purchased from private insurance companies, or may be carried by the shipper at his own risk. If the cost of insurance is charged to the customer and is added to the invoice, it represents an addition to the price of the merchandise or other property purchased. Thus, if an invoice is received for merchandise purchased and the merchandise is billed at a total cost of $100 plus postage amounting to $1 and insurance amounting to 25 cents, the total cost of the merchandise is $101.25. The purchaser may indicate in placing an order that he does not want the merchandise insured. When the purchaser indicates that he does not want merchandise insured when shipment is made by parcel post, he indicates that he is willing to assume the risk for any loss or damage sustained in transit. Title to merchandise ordinarily passes to the purchaser when it is placed in the hands of the post office for delivery.

The cost of insurance is seldom recorded separately in the books of the buyer, but is either charged directly to the purchases account or is included with transportation charges and is charged to Transportation In.

Purchases Returns and Allowances. When a credit memorandum is received as a result of merchandise returned for credit or because of an allowance made by the seller, it should be recorded by debiting Accounts Payable and by crediting the proper merchandise account. The individual account of the creditor should also be debited for the amount of the credit memorandum.

The proper merchandise account to credit for the amount of a credit memorandum received depends upon the classification of the merchandise accounts. Bryant & Wood keep separate purchases, purchases returns and allowances, and transportation accounts for Departments A and B; therefore, any credit memorandums received by them should be recorded in their books by crediting the proper departmental account for purchases returns and allowances. For example, if a credit memorandum for $175 is received from the Western Auto Supply Co. for batteries returned, it should be recorded as indicated in the following general journal entry:

```
Accounts Payable......................................  $175.00
     Purchases Returns and Allowances, Dept. B ...........          $175.00
```

The credit memorandum should also be posted to the debit of the individual account of the Western Auto Supply Co. in the subsidiary accounts payable ledger.

PRACTICE ASSIGNMENT No. 27. Complete Report No. 27 in the workbook and submit your working papers to the instructor for approval. Then continue with the next study assignment in Unit Fourteen until Report No. 28 is required.

ACCOUNTING FOR SALES

(28) *CASH SALES AND CREDIT SALES*

The organization of a sales department and the procedure in handling incoming purchase orders may vary widely depending upon many factors, such as the nature of the merchandise sold, the volume of sales, the methods of selling, the terms, etc. The incoming purchase order must be interpreted, terms determined, credit approved, a sales invoice prepared, goods packed and shipped or delivered, and collection made before the sales transaction has been entirely completed.

Merchandise may be sold either at retail or at wholesale prices. In selling directly to the customer through retail stores, it is customary to prepare sales tickets, which constitute the original record of the sale. In the wholesale merchandising field, sales may be made by mail or through salesmen; in either case, purchase orders received constitute the basis for sales transactions. The terms on which merchandise is sold affect the procedure in handling orders and in recording the sales transactions.

Terms of Sale. The terms on which sales are made vary widely in the retail and the wholesale merchandising fields. The bases on which sales may be made are as follows:

(a) For cash.
(b) On account.
(c) C.O.D.
(d) On approval.
(e) On installment.
(f) On consignment.

Cash Sales. Some firms sell merchandise for cash only, while others sell merchandise either for cash or on credit. In department stores and certain other retail establishments the usual procedure in handling cash sales is for salesclerks to prepare sales tickets in duplicate or in triplicate; one copy is given to the customer and another copy is sent to the accounting department for recording purposes. The cash received is recorded in a cash register. At the end of each day the amount of cash received is checked with the cash register tape. It may also be checked with the total of the sales tickets.

Sales on Account. Sales on account are often referred to as "charge sales" because the seller exchanges merchandise for the buyer's promise to pay which, in accounting terms, means that the asset Accounts Receivable is increased by a debit or charge. Selling goods on account is common practice at both the wholesale and retail stages in the distribution process. Firms that sell goods on account should investigate the financial reliability of those to whom they sell. A business of some size may have a separate credit department whose major function is to establish credit policies and to pass upon requests for credit from persons and firms who wish to buy goods on account. Seasoned judgment is needed to avoid both the pitfall of following a credit policy that is so stringent that profitable business may be refused, or a credit policy that is so liberal that bad debt losses may become excessive.

Generally, no goods are delivered until the salesclerk has assured himself that the buyer has established credit — that he "has an account" with the company. In the case of wholesale merchants who commonly secure a large portion of their orders through the mail, by phone, or by telegraph, this confirmation of the buyer's status can be handled as a matter of routine before the goods are shipped or delivered. There is no pressing problem in this respect because the buyer is not personally waiting for the merchandise.

C.O.D. Sales. Merchandise or other property may be sold on C.O.D. terms; that is, *collect on delivery*. Under such terms payment must be made at the time the goods are delivered by the seller or his agent. The agent may be an employee of the seller, a messenger, the post office, an express company, a railroad company, a trucking company, a steamship company, or any common carrier.

In wholesale merchandising, C.O.D. sales are usually recorded in the same manner as charge sales. When such sales are made to out-of-town customers, the merchandise is usually delivered by parcel post, express, or freight.* If shipment is made by parcel post or express, the post office or the express company will collect for the merchandise before giving the customer possession of it and, in turn, will remit to the seller by means of a money order. When the money order is received by the seller, it is handled in the same manner as a remittance received from any other customer in full or part payment of his account.

---

*The method of making C.O.D. shipments by freight and of collecting for the merchandise before it is delivered was explained in the preceding unit under the heading of C.O.D. Purchases.

In retail merchandising, C.O.D. sales are usually recorded as cash sales. The C.O.D. sales tickets are segregated each day and a C.O.D. list is prepared for control purposes. The merchandise is then delivered to the customer and the sale price is collected upon delivery. When the money is turned in by the driver or other agent of the seller, he is given credit for the collection on the C.O.D. list and the sale is then recorded in the same manner as cash sales. If, for any reason, the customer refuses to accept the merchandise, it is returned to stock and the sale is canceled. It should be understood that, under this plan of handling C.O.D. sales, title to the merchandise does not pass to the customer until it is delivered and paid for; therefore, the merchandise is considered to be a part of the inventory of the seller until payment is received. Usually retail merchants who sell merchandise on C.O.D. terms make their own deliveries and collections; however, delivery may be made through the post office or any common carrier.

Sales on Approval. When sales are made on approval, the customer is given the right to return the goods within a specified time; hence, the sale is not complete until it is known whether the customer will retain the goods or return them. Such sales may be handled as ordinary charge sales, and any returns may be handled like ordinary sales returns. On the other hand, sales on approval may be handled the same as ordinary cash sales. Under this plan a memorandum record of the sale is kept until such time as it is definitely known that the goods will be retained by the customer. The customer must either pay for the goods or return them by a specified date. If the sale is not recorded until payment is received, it may be treated the same as an ordinary cash sale.

Sales on approval should not be confused with *will call sales*. Will call sales may be made for cash or on credit, but in either case the customer agrees to call for the goods.

Sometimes a deposit is made by the buyer with the understanding that merchandise will be held until some future date, at which time he will call for the merchandise or at his request the merchandise will be delivered to him. Accounting for such deposits is not uniform, but the usual plan is to record the deposits in the same manner as cash sales. At the same time a charge sales ticket is prepared for the balance due, and the charge sale is recorded by debiting a special accounts receivable control account and by crediting the proper sales account. Individual accounts with such customers may be kept in a special subsidiary ledger. Some retail stores refer to this ledger as a *will call ledger*.

Instead of calling for the merchandise, the customer may request delivery on a C.O.D. basis, in which case a C.O.D. slip is made for the proper amount. When the remittance is received, it is recorded in the same manner as if the customer had called for the merchandise and paid cash.

At the end of the accounting period the total amount due from customers who have made deposits on will call sales is treated in the same manner as ordinary accounts receivable. The cost of the merchandise that is being held for future delivery is not included in the inventory because it is considered to be the property of the customer.

Procedure in Handling Incoming Purchase Orders. In the field of wholesale merchandising, sales usually result from purchase orders received by mail, telephone, telegram, or cablegram. Purchase orders received by mail may be written on the purchase order form, letterhead, or other stationery of the buyer or on an order blank furnished by the seller. Orders received by telephone should be carefully recorded on forms provided for that purpose. The procedure in handling purchase orders varies widely with different firms; nevertheless, it is important that there be a well-organized plan for handling orders. The purpose of such a plan should be to promote efficiency and to maintain an internal check that will tend to prevent mistakes in handling orders.

Interpretation. Each purchase order received should be interpreted as to (a) identity of the customer and (b) quantity and description of items ordered. Orders may be received from old or new customers. Sometimes it is difficult to identify a new customer, particularly where there has been no previous correspondence with him or where he has not been contacted by a salesman. In some cases the identity of the items ordered involves considerable difficulty because customers frequently are careless in describing the merchandise wanted. Different items of merchandise may be specified by name, stock number, or code word. Care should be used to make sure that the stock number or the code word agrees with the description of the item. Code words are commonly used in ordering by telegram or by cablegram.

Transportation. In handling each purchase order, it is necessary to determine how shipment will be made and how the transportation charges will be handled. Shipment may be made by parcel post, express, or freight. Parcel post packages may be insured. Express shipments may be made by rail or air. Freight shipments may be made by rail, air, truck, or water. The transportation charges on parcel post shipments must be prepaid. The transportation charges on express and freight shipments may be prepaid by the shipper or may be paid by the consignee upon receipt of the shipment. When transportation charges are prepaid by the shipper, they may or may not be added to the invoice, depending upon whether prices have been quoted f.o.b. point of shipment or f.o.b. point of destination.

If shipment is to be made by freight, it is also necessary to determine the routing of the shipment. The buyer may specify how he prefers to have shipment made, in which case his request usually is granted. Where the buyer does not indicate any preference, the shipper must determine whether to ship by rail, truck, air, or water, and must also frequently exercise a choice of transportation companies. Shipment to certain points may be made via different trucking companies, airlines, or railroads.

Credit Approval. All purchase orders received that involve credit in any form should be referred to the credit department or the credit manager for approval before being billed or shipped. Even C.O.D. orders should be approved by the credit department, because some customers have a reputation for not accepting C.O.D. shipments, in which case they are returned to the shipper at the latter's expense. Customers who abuse the C.O.D. privilege may be required thereafter to send cash with the order, either in full or part payment. Some firms follow a policy of requiring part payment in cash with all orders for merchandise to be shipped C.O.D. It is a good business policy on the part of anyone to establish credit with those from whom he purchases merchandise.

Checking Accuracy of Purchase Orders. The unit prices specified on purchase invoices should be checked, the proper extensions should be made, and the total should be recorded. This operation may be performed by special clerks with the aid of calculating machines.

Billing. The next step in the handling of a purchase order is billing or preparing the sales invoice.

The purchase order reproduced on page 382 was received by the Kruse Hardware Co. The information recorded in the spaces provided by the rubber stamp impression shows that the order was received on May 9, that the credit of the purchaser was approved by the credit department, and that the goods were billed on the same day the order was received. After the goods were billed, the purchase order was filed alphabetically under the name of the customer for future reference.

In the case of a wholesale merchant, the sales invoice is usually prepared on a typewriter or a billing machine. Any desired number of copies may be prepared with the aid of carbon paper. At least three copies usually are considered necessary, the original copy going to the customer as an

PURCHASE ORDER

No. 229

R. W. AURNER

328 Main Street

CLINTON

To Kruse Hardware Company

Riverside

Date   May 8,   19--

Ship Via Insured Parcel Post

F. O. B.

Deliver May 15,   19--

Terms   2/10, n/30

QUANTITY	DESCRIPTION	PRICE
3	#8466 G. E. Clocks	1.50
3	#74190 G. E. Clocks	2.65
1 doz.	Lufkin Spring Joint Rules	9.20
½ doz.	#5009 Paper Holders	8.57
2 doz.	2½# Rutland Patching Plaster	2.20
20 boxes	#1 Insulated Staples (50)	.07

Received May 9. 19 -

Credit   O.K. J.M.

Billed   May 9, 19 -

C. M. Morris

Purchase Order Received

acknowledgment of his order, the duplicate copy going to the accounting department for recording purposes, and the triplicate copy going to the shipping department as authority for packing and shipping the merchandise. The duplicate copy of the sales invoice reproduced on page 383 is based on the purchase order received from R. W. Aurner reproduced above. Sales invoices should be numbered consecutively.

Additional copies of the sales invoice may serve the following purposes:

(a) One copy may go to the salesman in whose territory the sale is made.

(b) One copy may go to a branch office, if the sale is made in a territory served by such an office.

(c) One copy may serve as a label to be pasted on the carton or package in which shipment is made. Usually this copy is perforated so that only that part containing the name and the address of the consignee is used as the label.

Parcel Post Insurance. Merchandise shipped by parcel post mail may be insured against loss or damage in transit. Such insurance may be purchased from a post office or from a private insurance company, or the risk may be assumed by the shipper.

If parcel post insurance is purchased from the government through the post office, it is necessary only to attach the required amount of stamps to cover the additional charge for the insurance and to obtain a receipt at the time of mailing the package. The rate depends upon the value of

```
                                                        1146

                                           May 9, 19—

          R. W. Aurner
          328 Main St.
          Clinton


          Insured Parcel Post          2/10,n/30

  3              #8466 G. E. Clocks                    1.50      4.50
  3              #74190 G. E. Clocks                   2.65      7.95
  1 doz.         Lufkin Spring Joint Rules             9.20      9.20
  ½ doz.         #5009 Paper Holders                   8.57      4.29
  2 doz.         2½# Rutland Patching Plaster          2.20      4.40
  20 boxes       #1 Insulated Staples (50)              .07      1.40
                                                               31.74
                                           Postage & Ins.        .84
                                                               32.58
```

Carbon Copy of Sales Invoice for Accounting Department

the parcel. If the parcel is lost or the merchandise is damaged in transit, the government will reimburse the shipper upon receipt of claim and proof of loss.

The cost of government insurance is usually accounted for in the same manner as ordinary postage. The total value of stamps purchased is recorded by debiting Postage Stamps and by crediting the bank account. Usually a memorandum record of the stamps used on parcel post shipments is kept until the end of the month, when the total is recorded by debiting Transportation Out and by crediting Postage Stamps.

When a government insured parcel post shipment is lost or damaged in transit, the amount of the loss should be ascertained and should be recorded by debiting an account with Loss on Parcel Post Shipments and by crediting Accounts Receivable in the general ledger. At the same time a credit entry should be made in the proper customer's account in the subsidiary accounts receivable ledger. A claim should then be filed with the post office for the value of the shipment. When a remittance is received from the post office in settlement of the claim, it should be recorded by debiting the bank account and by crediting Loss on Parcel Post Shipments.

When parcel post insurance is purchased from a private insurance company, a parcel post insurance coupon book is purchased. As each coupon is used, the stub is filled in as shown on page 384. It is necessary to

Name___ R. W. Aurner_____

Address___ 328 Main St._____
_____ Clinton_____

Mdse.___ Miscellaneous_____

Date___ 5/9/19--_____ Value, $ 31.74_____

Unreg.___✔___ Reg._____ Gov't Ins._____

COMMERCE
Insurance Company
GLENS FALLS, NEW YORK

THIS SHIPMENT IS INSURED
IN THE EVENT OF LOSS OR DAMAGE PLEASE
NOTIFY THE SHIPPER IMMEDIATELY.

Parcel Post Insurance Coupon with Stub

enclose the required number of coupons in each insured package. The number of coupons required to insure a parcel depends upon the value of the parcel and whether or not it is shipped by registered mail and/or insured parcel post. If the parcel is lost or the merchandise is damaged in transit, the insurance company will reimburse the shipper upon receipt of claim and proof of loss.

The cost of a book of coupons purchased from a private insurance company should be charged to a parcel post insurance account. The value of the coupons used in insuring each parcel is usually entered on the invoice as an additional charge to the customer and should be credited to the parcel post insurance account.

When a privately insured parcel post shipment is lost or damaged in transit, the amount of the loss should be ascertained and should be recorded by debiting an account with Loss on Parcel Post Shipments and by crediting Accounts Receivable in the general ledger. At the same time a credit entry should be made in the proper customer's account in the subsidiary accounts receivable ledger. A claim should then be filed with the insurance company for the value of the shipment. When a remittance is received from the insurance company in settlement of the claim, it should be recorded by debiting the bank account and by crediting Loss on Parcel Post Shipments. If the parcel post insurance account has a debit balance, it indicates that all of the coupons purchased have not been used. This balance is usually listed among the current assets on the balance sheet as prepaid parcel post insurance.

If parcel post insurance is carried by the shipper at his own risk, the premium charged the customer is usually the same as for government insurance. The amounts charged to customers for insurance are usually accumulated until the end of the month, when the total is recorded as a credit to Parcel Post Insurance. Any losses sustained on insured parcel post shipments should be recorded by debiting Parcel Post Insurance and by crediting Accounts Receivable in the general ledger and crediting the proper customers' accounts in the subsidiary accounts receivable ledger. If, at the close of the accounting period, the parcel post insurance account has a debit balance, it indicates that the losses sustained during the period have exceeded the total premiums charged to customers. If the account has a credit balance, it indicates that the value of the premiums charged to customers has exceeded the total losses sustained. While a debit balance should be treated as a loss, it does not follow that a credit balance should be treated as a gain unless it is known that no insured parcels are still in transit. It is usually considered satisfactory, however, to close the account into Income Summary at the end of each accounting period.

Discounts. Any trade discounts allowed on sales are usually shown as a deduction from the total of the sales invoice. Such discounts should not be entered in the accounts of the seller, as they represent merely a reduction in the selling price of the merchandise.

Any cash discounts offered should be indicated in the terms. Retail merchants seldom allow cash discounts, but wholesale merchants commonly allow cash discounts as an inducement for prompt payment of sales invoices. Cash discounts should be ignored at the time of recording sales invoices, for it cannot be known at that time that the customers will pay the invoices in time to earn the discounts offered. Any cash discount that is deducted from an invoice by the customer when making payment represents an expense rather than a deduction from sales; hence, it is customary to record cash discounts on sales in a separate account that is usually entitled Sales Discount.

Returns and Allowances. Merchandise may be returned by the purchaser for credit or he may ask for an allowance representing a reduction in the price of the merchandise. If credit is given or an allowance is made for merchandise returned, it is customary to issue a credit memorandum for the amount involved. A model filled-in copy of a credit memorandum was reproduced on page 361.

Accounting Procedure. When the merchandise accounts are kept on a departmental basis and all sales invoices covering charge sales are recorded in a columnar sales record, provision should be made for a proper classification of the debits and the credits. A separate column should be provided for recording the charge sales of each department so as to facilitate summary posting of the totals periodically. General Ledger Dr. and Cr. columns should also be provided for recording items that must be posted individually to the general ledger accounts. If individual accounts with customers are kept in a subsidiary ledger, a summary or control account for accounts receivable must be kept in the general ledger.

The procedure in recording all charge sales invoices in one journal and of keeping the merchandise accounts on the departmental basis will be illustrated (a) by recording a narrative of selected transactions chronologically in a sales record, (b) by posting from carbon copies of the sales invoices directly to the individual accounts of customers kept in a subsidiary accounts receivable ledger, (c) by posting from the sales record to the proper general ledger accounts, and (d) by preparing a schedule of accounts receivable as a means of proving the balance of the accounts receivable control account.

Bryant & Wood are engaged in the wholesale tire and accessories business as partners. Separate departments are maintained as follows:
Department A — Tires and tubes
Department B — Radios and batteries

Separate departmental accounts are kept for sales and for sales returns and allowances as follows:
41 Sales, Dept. A
    041 Sales Returns and Allowances, Dept. A
42 Sales, Dept. B
    042 Sales Returns and Allowances, Dept. B

All charge sales are made on uniform terms of 2/10, n/30. Unless otherwise specified, freight and express shipments are made on a basis of transportation charges collect. In the case of parcel post shipments, the postage is added to the invoice as an additional charge to the customer. When the invoices are entered in the sales record, the prepaid transportation charges are credited to Transportation Out, Account No. 619, in the General Ledger column. Any federal excise taxes that are billed to customers must be stated separately on the sales invoices, and the amount of the tax should be credited to Prepaid Federal Excise Tax, Account No. 166.

Sales Record. The form of the sales record used by Bryant & Wood is illustrated on page 389. A special column is provided for recording the federal excise tax on tires and tubes. This facilitates recording the tax and makes possible summary posting of the total tax billed to customers each month. All of the sales of Bryant & Wood are to dealers. The merchandise is "intended for resale." Accordingly, Bryant & Wood are not required to collect retail sales taxes.

Corrected Sales Invoices. If a corrected sales invoice is issued before the original invoice has been entered in the sales record, the original invoice may be canceled and the corrected invoice may be entered in the usual manner.

If a corrected sales invoice is issued after the original sales invoice has been entered in the sales record and has been posted to the individual account of the customer, the corrected invoice may be entered either in the sales record or in the general journal. The proper entry will depend upon whether or not the amount of the corrected invoice is more or less than the amount of the original invoice. A copy of the corrected invoice should be attached to the copy of the original invoice.

If the amount of the corrected invoice is more than the amount of the original invoice, the increase should be recorded by debiting Accounts Receivable and by crediting the proper departmental sales account. The amount of the increase should also be posted to the debit of the proper customer's account in the subsidiary accounts receivable ledger.

If the amount of the corrected invoice is less than the amount of the original invoice, the decrease should be recorded by debiting the proper departmental sales account and by crediting Accounts Receivable. The amount of the decrease should also be posted to the credit of the proper customer's account in the subsidiary accounts receivable ledger.

Proving the Sales Record. The sales record may be footed and the footings may be proved at any time by comparing the sum of the debit footings with the sum of the credit footings. The footings of Bryant & Wood's sales record were proved as of April 30 in the following manner:

Column Headings	Debits	Credits
General Ledger.....................................	$ 180.98	
Accounts Receivable...............................	970.72	
Sales, Dept. A.....................................		$ 577.07
Sales, Dept. B.....................................		493.01
Federal Excise Tax.................................		41.69
General Ledger....................................		39.93
Totals...	$1,151.70	$1,151.70

Ledgers. The ledgers used by Bryant & Wood include a general ledger with standard ruling and a subsidiary accounts receivable ledger with balance-column ruling. The accounts affected by the transactions entered in the sales record reproduced on page 389 are shown in skeleton form on pages 391 and 392. The March 31 balances are recorded in the accounts as of April 1. An accounts receivable control account is kept in the general ledger.

NARRATIVE OF TRANSACTIONS

The following selected transactions are shown recorded in the sales record reproduced on page 389.

April 1. (Saturday) Made charge sales as follows:

       No. 81, Reading Garage; tires and tubes, $78.11, federal excise tax, $5.76; batteries, $48.10; freight collect.

       No. 82, Woodlawn Motor Co.; tires and tubes, $103.20, federal excise tax, $6.90; radio, $41.30; express collect.

       No. 83, Lang's Auto Service; tires and tubes, $71.05, federal excise tax, $5.93; express collect.

       No. 84, Triangle Motor Co.; radio, $49.84; postage added to invoice, 84 cents.

       No. 85, Ideal Garage; batteries, $34.65; insured parcel post, 89 cents.

  5. Sent Triangle Motor Co. a corrected invoice for Sale No. 84, amounting to $51.58.

 25. Made charge sales as follows:

       No. 141, Adair Service Station; tires and tubes, $169.90, federal excise tax, $11.25; batteries, $83.40; freight collect.

       No. 142, Woodlawn Motor Co.; tires and tubes, $154.81, federal excise tax, $11.85; radio, $82.60; freight collect.

       No. 143, Ideal Garage; radio, $50.74; less credit for radio returned, $41.30.

 29. Sent Woodlawn Motor Co. a corrected invoice for Sale No. 142; tires and tubes, $154.81, federal excise tax, $11.85; radio, $44.40.

 29. Sold Robinson Bros., radios, $101.48 and received 60-day, 5% interest-bearing note. (Sale No. 144.)

Posting Procedure. The use of a general ledger and an accounts receivable ledger involves both individual posting and summary posting. After each sales invoice was entered in the sales record, it was immediately posted to the proper customer's account in the accounts receivable ledger. The posting was done directly from the invoice, the invoice number being inserted in the Folio column.

While the posting to customers' accounts might be done from the sales record, there are certain advantages in posting directly from the sales invoice. For example, the invoice provides all the information needed in posting, whereas, if the posting were done from the sales record, it would be necessary to enter in the sales record all the information needed in

(*Continued on page 390*)

SALES RECORD FOR MONTH OF April 19—

Page 65

DEBITS				DAY	NAME	SALE NO.	SALES		CREDITS			
GENERAL LEDGER			ACCOUNTS RECEIVABLE				DEPT. A	DEPT. B	FEDERAL EXCISE TAX	GENERAL LEDGER		
Acct. No.	AMOUNT	✓	AMOUNT ✓							Acct. No.	AMOUNT	✓
					AMOUNTS FORWARDED							
			13.97 ✓	1	Reading Garage	81	7.11	48.10	576			
			15.14 ✓	1	Woodlawn Motor Car	82	103.70	41.30	690			
			74.93 ✓	1	Lange Auto Service	83	71.05		593			
			50.68 ✓	1	Triangle Motor Co.	84		49.44		619		✓
			35.54 ✓	1	Roland Garage	85		34.65		619		✓
			90 ✓	5	Triangle Motor Co.	86		90				
			26.55 ✓	25	Acme Service Station	141	169.90	83.40	1175			
			14.92 ✓	25	Woodlawn Motor Co.	142	154.81	126.0	1125			
042	4130 ✓		9.44 ✓	25	Roland Garage	143		50.74		133	3120	✓
42	3520 ✓			29	Woodlawn Motor Car	142						
131	10.148 ✓			29	Robinson Bros.	144						
	18.098		87.072				577.07	493.61	4169		3993	
	(✓)		(33)				(41)	(42)	(44)		(✓)	

posting whether or not it served any other purpose. Furthermore, if an error were made in entering an invoice in the sales record, it would probably be carried over into the accounts receivable ledger through the posting, whereas, if the posting were done directly from the invoice, it is not likely that the same error would be made twice.

Posting directly from the sales invoices to the customers' accounts in the accounts receivable ledger is not only efficient; it also provides a sound method of internal check and control. One bookkeeper may enter the invoices in the sales record and may complete such posting as is required from the sales record to the general ledger accounts, while another bookkeeper may post directly from the sales invoices to the customers' accounts in the accounts receivable ledger. Thus the work is divided between two employees. Proof of the accuracy of their work is obtained periodically by preparing a schedule of accounts receivable and comparing its total with the balance of the accounts receivable control account that is kept in the general ledger.

Posting to the accounts of customers in the accounts receivable ledger may be done either with a pen or with a machine. Posting machines are widely used for this purpose and are justifiable where there are a large number of accounts and a large number of transactions involved.

In addition to ordinary posting machines there are electric accounting machines that may be used not only as an aid in keeping accounts with customers, but also in keeping a record of the sales invoices and in preparing a schedule of accounts receivable at the end of each accounting period.

Some firms use the "micro-film" method of accounting for charge sales. Under this method it is customary to keep a chronological record of charge sales in the same manner as in other methods of accounting. An individual account of the transactions with each customer is also kept until the end of the month, when it is photographed. The film is then filed as a permanent record of the business done with each customer, while the individual account becomes the customer's monthly statement.

Individual Posting. Each sales invoice entered in the Accounts Receivable Dr. column of the sales record was posted individually to the proper customer's account in the accounts receivable ledger shown on page 392. In the case of sales invoices involving federal excise taxes or prepaid transportation charges, the amount of the merchandise sold, the amount of the federal excise taxes, and the amount of the prepaid transportation charges were posted separately. For example, in posting

(Continued on page 393)

General Ledger

NOTES RECEIVABLE   Account No. 131

19--					
April 1 Balance	√	600.00			
29	S65	101.48			
		701.48			

ACCOUNTS RECEIVABLE   Account No. 133

19--			19--		
April 1 Balance	√	1,753.55	April 29	S65	38.20
30	S65	970.72			
2,686.07		*2,724.27*			

PREPAID FEDERAL EXCISE TAX   Account No. 166

19--			19--		
April 1 Balance	√	1,454.29	April 30	S65	41.69
30	I34	248.68			
1,661.28		*1,702.97*			

SALES, DEPT. A   Account No. 41

			19--		
			April 1 Balance	√	36,400.00
			30	S65	577.07
					36,977.07

SALES, DEPT. B   Account No. 42

19--			19--		
April 29	S65	38.20	April 1 Balance	√	27,100.00
			30	S65	493.01
		27,554.81			*27,593.01*

SALES RETURNS AND ALLOWANCES, DEPT. B   Account No. 042

19--					
April 1 Balance	√	275.00			
25 Returns	S65	41.30			
		316.30			

TRANSPORTATION OUT   Account No. 619

			19--		
			April 1	S65	.84
			1	S65	.89
					1.73

Accounts Receivable Ledger

ADAIR SERVICE STATION, 209 Main St., City

DATE	ITEMS	FOL.	DEBITS	CREDITS	BALANCE
19--					
April 1	Dr. Balance	√			185.25
25	Mdse.	S141	253.30		
25	Fed. excise tax	S141	11.25		449.80

IDEAL GARAGE, Oakland

DATE	ITEMS	FOL.	DEBITS	CREDITS	BALANCE
19--					
April 1	Dr. Balance	√			493.79
1	Mdse.	S85	34.65		
1	Postage	S85	.89		529.33
25		S143	9.44		538.77

LANG'S AUTO SERVICE, 397 High St., Paris

DATE	ITEMS	FOL.	DEBITS	CREDITS	BALANCE
19--					
April 1	Dr. Balance	√			76.70
1	Mdse.	S83	71.05		
1	Fed. excise tax	S83	5.93		153.68

READING GARAGE, Roselawn

DATE	ITEMS	FOL.	DEBITS	CREDITS	BALANCE
19--					
April 1	Dr. Balance	√			500.00
1	Mdse.	S81	126.21		
1	Fed. excise tax	S81	5.76		631.97

TRIANGLE MOTOR CO., Melbourne

DATE	ITEMS	FOL.	DEBITS	CREDITS	BALANCE
19--					
April 1	Dr. Balance	√			399.81
1	Mdse.	S84	49.84		
1	Postage	S84	.84		450.49
5	Corrected invoice	S84	.90		451.39

WOODLAWN MOTOR CO., Pinewood

DATE	ITEMS	FOL.	DEBITS	CREDITS	BALANCE
19--					
April 1	Dr. Balance	√			98.00
1	Mdse.	S82	144.50		
1	Fed. excise tax	S82	6.90		249.40
25	Mdse.	S142	237.41		
25	Fed. excise tax	S142	11.85		498.66
29	Corrected invoice	S142		38.20	460.46

Sales Invoice No. 81, Reading Garage was debited separately for the amount of the merchandise sold, $126.21, and for the amount of the federal excise tax, $5.76. In posting Sales Invoice No. 84, the Triangle Motor Co. was debited separately for the amount of the merchandise sold, $49.84, and for the amount of the postage, 84 cents. The reason for posting the excise tax and the transportation charges as separate items is that the excise tax and the transportation charges are never subject to discount; only the amount of the merchandise sold is subject to discount. As each invoice was posted directly to the proper account in the accounts receivable ledger, a check mark was placed in the Check ($\sqrt{}$) column following the Accounts Receivable column in the sales record.

It was also necessary to post each item entered in the General Ledger Dr. and Cr. columns of the sales record. Usually this posting is completed daily. As each item was posted, a check mark was placed in the Check ($\sqrt{}$) column following the Amount column of the sales record and the page number of the sales record was entered in the Folio column of the ledger account preceding the amount posted.

Summary Posting. The summary posting is usually completed at the end of each month and involves the following procedure:

(a) The total of the column headed Accounts Receivable was posted to the debit of Accounts Receivable, Account No. 133, in the general ledger.

(b) The total of the column headed Sales, Dept. A was posted to the credit of Sales, Dept. A, Account No. 41, in the general ledger.

(c) The total of the column headed Sales, Dept. B was posted to the credit of Sales, Dept. B, Account No. 42, in the general ledger.

(d) The total of the column headed Federal Excise Tax was posted to the credit of Prepaid Federal Excise Tax, Account No. 166, in the general ledger.

It will be noted that the account with Prepaid Federal Excise Tax is debited for the excise tax on merchandise purchased and is credited for the excise tax on merchandise sold; thus, the balance of the account represents the amount of the excise tax on the inventory of merchandise in stock. When all merchandise that is subject to the excise tax has been sold, the account will be in balance.

As the total of each column was posted, the account number was written immediately below the total in the sales record and the page of the sales record was written in the Folio column of the general ledger as a cross reference. A check mark was placed below the totals of the General Dr. and Cr. columns in the sales record to indicate those totals need not be posted.

Schedule of Accounts Receivable. The balance of the accounts receivable control account may be proved any time after all posting is completed by preparing a schedule of the accounts with customers from the accounts receivable ledger. The following schedule was prepared from the ledger of Bryant & Wood at the end of April and the total was checked with the balance of the accounts receivable control account in the general ledger as a means of proof:

SCHEDULE OF ACCOUNTS RECEIVABLE

APRIL 30, 19--

Adair Service Station..	$ 449.80
Ideal Garage...	538.77
Lang's Auto Service..	153.68
Reading Garage..	631.97
Triangle Motor Co..	451.39
Woodlawn Motor Co..	460.46
Total..	$2,686.07

Cash Sales. Bryant & Wood follow the practice of entering charge sales only in their sales record. Cash sales are entered in the record of cash receipts by debiting the bank account and by crediting the proper departmental sales accounts. Cash sales are not posted to the individual accounts of customers. In a wholesale business there are relatively few cash sales, as most of the business is usually done on a credit basis.

C.O.D. Sales. Bryant & Wood follow the practice of recording C.O.D. sales in the same manner as credit sales. Since they are engaged in a wholesale business, a relatively large percentage of their sales are to out-of-town customers; hence, several days may elapse from the date of sale until the date payment is received. C.O.D. sales are therefore recorded in the sales record in the same manner as ordinary sales. When the remittance is received from the post office, express company, trucking company, railroad company, or other common carrier, it is entered in the record of cash receipts in the same manner as other remittances received from customers to apply on account.

Transportation Charges. In the case of parcel post shipments, the postage must, of course, be prepaid. If such packages are insured, the total amount of the postage and the insurance is added to the invoice. Bryant & Wood follow the practice of making all express and freight shipments with transportation charges collect, unless the customer requests that they be prepaid and added to the invoice. Since most shipments are made collect, it is not deemed necessary to provide a special column in the sales record for recording transportation charges prepaid; instead, they are entered in the General Ledger Cr. column as a credit to Transportation Out, Account No. 619.

When the express and freight charges are prepaid, the payments are entered in the record of checks issued by debiting Transportation Out and by crediting the bank account. The amount of postage stamps used on parcel post shipments is recorded by debiting Transportation Out and by crediting Postage Stamps. Usually a memorandum record of the stamps used is kept until the end of the month, when an entry is made for the total. The transportation out account should be in balance after all posting is completed at the end of the month, provided all prepaid transportation charges were charged to customers' accounts. If, however, any shipments are made f.o.b. destination, the transportation charges represent a selling expense. In this case the transportation out account will have a debit balance, which represents the amount of the expense incurred as a result of prepaying transportation charges on shipments made f.o.b. destination.

Where numerous shipments are made by parcel post, express, and freight and the transportation charges are prepaid and charged to customers, it is advisable to provide a special credit column in the sales record for entering the transportation charges. All transportation charges on outgoing shipments that are prepaid and added to the invoices and charged to customers should be entered in this column. At the end of the month when the summary posting is completed, the total of the column should be posted to the credit of Transportation Out.

Sales Returns and Allowances. When a credit memorandum is issued to a customer for the value of merchandise returned for credit or because of an allowance made on merchandise sold, it should be recorded by debiting the proper merchandise account and by crediting Accounts Receivable. The individual account of the customer should also be credited for the amount of the credit memorandum.

The proper merchandise account to debit for the amount of a credit memorandum issued depends upon the classification of the merchandise accounts. If all sales transactions are recorded in a single sales account, that account should be debited for the amount of any credit memorandums issued that represent the value of merchandise returned by customers or the amount of any allowances made on merchandise sold.

Bryant & Wood keep separate departmental accounts for sales and for sales returns and allowances; therefore, any credit memorandums issued by them should be recorded in their books by debiting the proper departmental account for sales returns and allowances. For example, if a credit memorandum for $38.20 is issued to the Woodlawn Motor Co. for a radio returned for credit, it should be recorded as indicated in the following general journal entry:

Sales Returns and Allowances, Dept. B...................... $38.20
   Accounts Receivable..................................... $38.20
      Issued credit memorandum to Woodlawn Motor Co.

The credit memorandum should also be posted to the credit of the individual account of the Woodlawn Motor Co. in the subsidiary accounts receivable ledger.

If transactions involving the issuance of credit memorandums are numerous, a special sales returns and allowances journal may be used to advantage. Such a journal should be designed similar to the sales record reproduced on page 389, except that there should be columns provided on the debit side for recording departmental sales returns and allowances and a column provided on the credit side for recording accounts receivable. The effect of an entry to record credit allowed for merchandise returned is the reverse of an entry to record merchandise sold; therefore, if a special journal is used, its columnar arrangement should be the reverse of the columnar arrangement of the sales record.

PRACTICE ASSIGNMENT No. 28. Complete Report No. 28 in the workbook and submit your working papers to the instructor for approval. Then continue with the following study assignment until Report No. 29 is required.

(29) INSTALLMENT SALES

Personal property, such as automobiles, refrigerators, freezers, washing machines, sewing machines, radios, television sets, phonographs, musical instruments, furniture, and many other types of merchandise are marketed extensively on the *installment basis*. This is equally true of many types of real property (real estate). The installment basis refers to a sales arrangement wherein the buyer secures physical possession of the property in return for his promise to pay for the property by a number of fractional payments at regular intervals over a period of time. Frequently a so-called *down payment* is made at the time the buyer enters into the contract and secures physical possession of the property. Merchants who sell personal property on the installment basis usually protect themselves from loss in case of default by adopting one of the following plans:

(a) Title to the property is retained by the vendor until the purchaser has completely performed his part of the transaction.

(b) Title is conveyed to the purchaser immediately, subject to a lien for the unpaid portion of the sales price.

(c) Title is conveyed to the purchaser immediately, but at the same time the purchaser executes a conveyance to the vendor in the form of a chattel mortgage.

(d) Title is conveyed to a trustee, pending performance of the contract and subject to its provisions.

A firm may be more lenient in extending credit to customers who buy on the installment basis for the reason that title to the merchandise is retained by the vendor until it is fully paid for. It is customary to require a down payment representing a part of the selling price. Some firms that sell merchandise on the installment basis mark up their prices in order to obtain a higher margin of profit. One reason for this practice is that credit is extended for a longer period of time. In selling merchandise on ordinary credit terms, it may be the custom to extend credit for no more than thirty days, whereas in selling merchandise on the installment basis, credit may be extended for as long a period as a year or more on at least a part of the sales price.

Accounting for Installment Sales. Sales on the installment basis, or the "installment plan" as it is sometimes called, can be accounted for on either (a) the conventional accrual basis or (b) the installment basis. If the accrual basis is used, the profit on installment sales is accounted for in the same manner as the profit on ordinary charge sales. If the installment basis is used, the profits are accounted for in the period in which the installments are collected rather than in the period in which the sales are made. Following is a more detailed discussion of the two methods:

(a) Accrual Basis. When installment sales are accounted for on the accrual basis, they should be recorded in the same manner as charge sales, that is, by debiting Accounts Receivable and by crediting Sales. Usually an installment sales contract will be executed at the time of the sale and a notation of the terms will be made in the individual account of the customer in the subsidiary accounts receivable ledger. Under this plan, any anticipated loss on deferred installments should be provided for in the same manner as on ordinary charge sales, that is, through an allowance for bad debts. Since the dealer usually retains title to the merchandise until the final installment is paid, he can recover the merchandise in case of failure to make payments as agreed. Any loss sustained will be the difference between the amount charged the customer under the contract and the total amount collected in installments plus the amount re-

SALES RECORD FOR MONTH OF *APRIL*, 19 – –

| DEBITS | | | | | | | | CREDITS | | | | | |
| GENERAL LEDGER | | ACCOUNTS REC. √ | INST. ACCTS. REC. √ | DAY | NAME | SALE NO. √ | SALES | | INST. SALES | | GENERAL LEDGER | | |
ACCT. NO.	AMOUNT √						DEPT. A	DEPT. B	DEPT. A	DEPT. B	ACCT. NO.	AMOUNT √	
					Amounts Forwarded								
			500 00 √	20	C. H. Andrews				500 00				

alized from the resale of the repossessed merchandise. Any losses sustained should be charged to the allowance for bad debts account.

(*b*) *Installment Basis.* When installment sales are accounted for on the installment basis, a control account for installment accounts receivable should be kept in the general ledger and the individual accounts of installment customers should be kept in a subsidiary installment accounts receivable ledger. To facilitate the recording of transactions affecting installment accounts receivable, it is advisable to provide a special debit column in the sales record for installment accounts receivable and a special credit column for installment sales. If the business is departmentalized, a separate installment sales column should be provided for each department. Such a sales record is illustrated on this page.

This form of sales record may be used in recording both installment sales and ordinary credit sales. After each installment sales invoice is recorded in the sales record, it should be posted directly to the individual account of the customer in the subsidiary installment accounts receivable ledger. Sometimes a special account form is used for this ledger. Such an account from is reproduced on page 399.

At the end of the month when the summary posting is being completed, the total of the installment accounts receivable column of the

| COLLECTION DAY | 1 | 2 | 3 | 4 | 5 | 6 | 7 | 8 | 9 | 10 | 11 | 12 | 13 | 14 | 15 | 16 | 17 | 18 | 19 | ⑳ | 21 | 22 | 23 | 24 | 25 | 26 | 27 | 28 | 29 | 30 | 31 |

INSTALLMENT LEDGER

TERMS: $25   WEEKLY   SEMI-MONTHLY   MONTHLY ✓   NAME *C. H. Andrews*

OCCUPATION *Salesman* COLLECTION DAY *20th*   ADDRESS *4410 St. Johns Place*

KEEPS HOUSE ✓   ROOMS   BOARDS   HOW LONG   REMOVED

MARRIED ✓   HUS. NAME

OWN PROPERTY   WHERE

EMPLOYED AT   HOW LONG   REFERENCE *The Second National Bank*

CHARGES					PAYMENTS								
DATE	REMARKS	FOLIO	AMOUNT	DATE	FOLIO	AMOUNT	BALANCE	DATE	FOLIO	AMOUNT	BALANCE
Apr. 20	Furniture	8	500 00	Apr. 20	C	25 00	475 00				

Installment Sales Account Form

sales record should be posted to the debit of the installment accounts receivable control account in the general ledger. The totals of the departmental sales columns should also be posted to the credit of the proper departmental sales accounts in the general ledger.

To facilitate the recording of payments received to apply on installment accounts receivable, a special column should be provided in the record of cash receipts. After each payment is recorded in this journal, it should be posted directly to the credit of the individual customer's account in the installment accounts receivable ledger. At the end of the month when the summary posting is being completed, the total of this column should be posted to the credit of the installment accounts receivable control account in the general ledger.

At the end of the year the percentage of gross profit to be realized on the total installment sales should be determined, and this rate should be applied to the sum of the down payments and the installment payments collected during the year to find the gross profit realized on the installment sales for the year. The difference between the gross profit to be realized and the gross profit actually realized on the basis of installments collected should be treated as an unrealized profit applicable to installment accounts receivable. The procedure in computing the gross profit on installment sales realized during the accounting period may be summarized as follows:

(1) Ascertain the gross profit to be realized on installment sales by deducting the cost of the merchandise sold on installment terms from the total installment sales.

(2) Ascertain the percentage of gross profit to be realized on installment sales by dividing the gross profit to be realized by the total installment sales.

(3) Apply this rate of gross profit to the sum of the down payments and the installment payments collected during the year to ascertain the amount of the gross profit actually realized.

To illustrate, assume that on April 20 a furniture dealer sold an article that cost $400 to C. H. Andrews for $500 under a sales contract calling for a down payment of $25 and monthly installments of $25 each. The effect of these transactions on the accounts of the dealer is indicated by the following general journal entries:

Purchases..	$400.00	
Accounts Payable..............................		$400.00
Purchased furniture.		
Installment Accounts Receivable...................	500.00	
Installment Sales.............................		500.00
Sold furniture on installment basis.		
Bank..	25.00	
Installment Accounts Receivable...............		25.00
Down payment. (Each monthly installment collected subsequently should be recorded in like manner.)		

The gross profit realized on the installments collected during the year may be computed in the following manner:

First Step. Ascertain gross profit to be realized.

Total installment sales...........................	$500.00
Less cost of goods sold.........................	400.00
Gross profit to be realized.......................	$100.00

Second Step. Ascertain percentage of gross profit to be realized.

Gross profit to be realized, $100 ÷ total installment sales, $500 = 20%.

Third Step. Apply rate of gross profit to payments collected during year.

Amount of down payment collected................	$ 25.00
Amount of monthly installments collected (8 × $25)...............	200.00
Total collections during year......................	$225.00
Percentage of gross profit realized................	20%
Gross profit realized.............................	$ 45.00

When the installment sales account is closed at the end of the year the gross profit realized should be credited to Realized Gross Profit on Installment Sales and the remainder of the gross profit to be realized should be credited to Unrealized Gross Profit on Installment Sales. Following is an illustrative general journal entry:

Installment Sales......................................	$500.00	
Cost of Goods Sold..................................		$400.00
Realized Gross Profit on Installment Sales..............		45.00
Unrealized Gross Profit on Installment Sales............		55.00

      Closing the installment sales account and transferring the gross profit to the proper accounts.

In preparing the balance sheet at the end of the year, the balance of the installment accounts receivable account, amounting to $275, should be classified as a current asset, while the unrealized gross profit on installment sales, amounting to $55, should be listed as a *deferred credit* immediately following the current liabilities.

In preparing the income statement at the end of the year the gross profit realized on installment sales, amounting to $45, should be included in arriving at the total gross profit on sales. Sometimes a schedule of profits realized on installment sales is prepared to accompany the income statement. Such a schedule is illustrated below.

PROFITS REALIZED ON INSTALLMENT SALES

For PERIOD ENDED DECEMBER 31, 19--

Installment Sales..	$500.00
Less Cost of Goods Sold.......................................	400.00
Gross Profit to be Realized.......................................	$100.00
Less Unrealized Gross Profit on Installment Sales................	55.00
Gross Profit Realized on Installment Sales.........................	$ 45.00

If this information is not provided in a schedule, it should be embodied in the income statement so that the information will be available to those concerned.

    PRACTICE ASSIGNMENT No. 29. Complete Report No. 29 in the workbook and submit your working papers to the instructor for approval. Then continue with the following study assignment until Report No. 30 is required.

(30) CONSIGNMENT SALES

Produce may be shipped to commission merchants on consignment; merchandise may be shipped to dealers on consignment. Title to produce and merchandise so consigned is retained by the shipper, known as the *consignor*, until the goods are sold by the merchant or dealer, known as the *consignee*. At the time the goods are shipped to the consignee, an *invoice of shipment* is rendered. While this invoice of shipment may be similar to a sales invoice, it should be understood that a consignment shipment is not a sale. The function of the invoice of shipment is to notify the consignee of the quantity and to provide a description of the items in the shipment. Unit prices may or may not be extended on the invoice of shipment depending upon whether the produce or the merchandise is to be sold at current market prices or at prices stipulated by the consignor.

Produce, such as livestock, poultry, eggs, fresh fruits, and vegetables, is widely marketed on the consignment basis. Such shipments are usually made to commission merchants on consignment to be sold at the prevailing market prices. At the time of remitting for the produce, the consignee renders a statement of consignment sales, sometimes referred to as an *account sales*, showing the amount of the sales, the amounts of the expenses charged to the consignor, and the amount of the net proceeds. Expenses charged to the consignor may include transportation charges, storage, insurance, and other similar expenses incurred in handling the consigned goods. If the consignee is allowed a commission on sales or a discount from the selling price, the amount of his commission or discount will also be deducted in arriving at the amount of the net proceeds to be remitted to the consignor.

Incandescent lamps (light bulbs), radio and television tubes, electric motors, garden seeds, and many other products are also widely marketed on the consignment basis. Such goods are usually shipped to dealers or other agents on consignment to be sold at prices stipulated by the consignor. Instead of receiving a commission, the consignee may be allowed certain discounts from the consignor's list prices based upon the consignee's volume of sales.

Invoice of Shipment. A model filled-in copy of an invoice of shipment covering incandescent lamps shipped by a wholesale distributor to a retail hardware store on consignment is reproduced on page 403. The original copy of the invoice of shipment goes to the consignee and a duplicate copy is retained by the consignor as his record of the shipment. Note that the invoice of shipment provides the dealer with detailed information

THE QUEEN CITY ELECTRIC CO.

AGENT OF

LAMP DEPARTMENT

UNIVERSAL ELECTRIC
COMPANY

YOUR ORDER NO.	YOUR ORDER DATE	TERMS AS PER YOUR CONTRACT	DATE SHIPPED	INVOICE DATE	INVOICE NO.
	6/6/19—		6/7/19—	6/7/19—	G1 7939

CHARGE
TO

     OAKWOOD HARDWARE CO.
     OAK ST.
     CITY

SHIPPED TO   OAKWOOD HARDWARE CO.

QUANTITY	SPECIFICATION ABBREVIATIONS OR WATTS-VOLT-BULB-BASE-FINISH	UNIT LIST PRICE	AMOUNT	TOTAL
	CHARGE YOUR LAMP CONSIGNMENT ACCOUNT			
48	25 A	.13	6.24	
48	60 A	.14	6.72	
24	75 A	.16	3.84	
24	100 A	.16	3.84	
24	10 S11/W	.21	5.04	25.68

CONSIGNMENT OF ELECTRIC LAMPS TO BE HELD BY THE AGENT, AND TO BE SOLD OR
DISTRIBUTED ONLY IN ACCORDANCE WITH THE EXISTING CONTRACT WITH THE AGENT.

Invoice of Shipment

relative to the merchandise that has been charged to his account, including specifications of the items, the quantities, the unit list prices, the extended amount of each item, and the total amount of the shipment.

The duplicate copy of the invoice of shipment provides the information needed by the consignor in recording merchandise shipped on consignment. The invoice may be recorded in the general journal, or a special consignment shipments record may be kept if desired. Accounts with consignees may be kept in the general ledger; or, if preferred, a subsidiary consignment ledger may be kept with a control account in the general ledger.

Statement of Consignment Sales. Periodically, usually at the end of each month, the consignor mails the consignee a partially completed statement of merchandise consigned to him. This statement shows (a) the value of the consigned merchandise in the consignee's hands at the beginning of the month, (b) a summary of the consignment shipments made during the month, and (c) the total amount of consigned merchandise for which the consignee must account. On the basis of an inventory taken at the end of the month, the consignee completes the statement by calculating (a) the volume of the sales he has made of consigned merchandise during the month, (b) his compensation, and (c) the amount of the proceeds he should remit to the consignor.

A model filled-in statement of consignment sales is reproduced on page 405. In the statement reproduced, the balance forwarded from the previous month's statement, amounting to $348.92, represents the amount charged to the consignee at the beginning of June. The items listed in the body of the statement indicate the value of the merchandise shipped to the consignee during June. The amount listed on line 1 of the agent's monthly report, $447.46, is the sum of the items listed in the body of the statement. This includes the balance forwarded from the previous statement plus the sum of the shipments during the month. The basic compensation indicated in the statement is based on a contract agreement between the consignor and the consignee.

Accounting for Consignment Sales. As previously explained, produce and merchandise may be consigned to a commission merchant or a dealer to be sold at the prevailing market prices or at stipulated prices. Because of varying conditions, methods of accounting for consignment sales are not uniform.

Consigned Merchandise to be Sold at Market Prices. Produce or merchandise that is shipped on consignment to be sold at prevailing market prices may be charged to the consignee at wholesale prices or no charge at all may be made. In the latter case a memorandum record of the shipment will be kept by the consignor. Merchandise that is shipped on consignment to be sold at stipulated prices may be billed to the consignee either at wholesale prices or at retail prices. The principal effect of such shipments is to transfer the goods from one place to another, with the consignor retaining title to the goods. It is advisable, of course, to keep some record of the consignments in order that the location and the cost of the goods may be determined at any time. The cost of the goods out on consignment must be included in the consignor's inventory, although it is customary to list the inventory of consigned goods separately in the balance sheet, using the same method of costing that is used in inventorying ordinary merchandise in stock.

When a statement of consignment sales is received from a commission merchant, the sales should be recorded on the books of the consignor. The

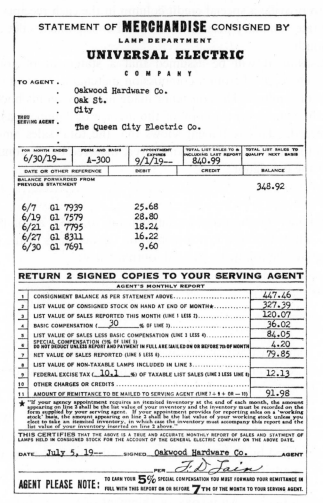

Statement of Consignment Sales

proper entries will vary depending upon the method of accounting for consignment shipments. Usually a separate account will be kept for consignment sales so that such sales may be recorded separately from ordinary sales. If it is desired to record consignment sales in the sales record along with ordinary charge sales, it may be advisable to provide a special credit column to facilitate the summary posting of the total consignment sales at the end of each month. If it is customary for the consignee to remit the proceeds at the time of rendering a statement of consignment sales, the entire transaction may be entered in the record of cash receipts in much the same manner as ordinary cash sales. It may be advisable, however, to provide a special credit column in the cash receipts record so as to facilitate summary posting of the total consignment sales at the end of each month.

To illustrate, it will be assumed that a statement of consignment sales has been received from a commission merchant covering the sale of a shipment of poultry. The consignor made no entry on his books for the shipment; he simply kept a copy of the invoice of shipment as a memorandum record. This statement shows that the total sales amounted to $1,200 and that the following expenses were incurred by the consignee and charged to the consignor:

Transportation charges.....................................	$145.00
Commission..	120.00

A remittance for the proceeds, amounting to $935, accompanied the statement. The effect of this transaction on the accounts of the consignor is indicated by the following general journal entry:

Transportation Out..................................	$145.00	
Commission..	120.00	
Bank..	935.00	
Consignment Sales.................................		$1,200.00
Received statement of consignment sales.		

Since a remittance for the amount of the proceeds was received with the statement, the transaction may be recorded completely in the record of cash receipts.

Consigned Merchandise to be Sold at Stipulated Prices. When merchandise is shipped on consignment to a dealer under contract to be sold at prices stipulated by the consignor, an entirely different accounting procedure may be advisable.

Consignor's Books. An invoice of shipment of lamps to the Oakwood Hardware Co. by The Queen City Electric Co. is reproduced on page 403. This invoice was recorded in the books of The Queen City Electric Co. as indicated by the following general journal entry:

Oakwood Hardware Co., Consignee......................	$25.68	
Consignment Shipments.............................		$25.68
Invoice of shipment No. 7939.		

The Queen City Electric Co. follows the practice of charging the consigned merchandise to the consignee and crediting Consignment Shipments at list or retail prices. A separate account may be kept in the general ledger for each consignee, or these accounts may be kept in a subsidiary ledger with a control account in the general ledger. An account is also kept in the general ledger for consignment shipments. The accounts with the consignees are not ordinary accounts receivable because the consignees are not obligated to pay for the merchandise unless it is sold. The Queen City Electric Co., therefore, follows the practice of treating the accounts with the consignees and with consignment shipments as memorandum or offsetting accounts that are never shown in the balance sheet. On the other hand, some firms follow the practice of treating the consignees' accounts as an asset and the account with consignment shipments as *deferred income* to be shown as offsetting or contra items in the balance sheet.

A statement of consignment sales received from the Oakwood Hardware Co. is reproduced on page 405. It shows that in addition to the shipment of June 7, which amounted to $25.68, four other shipments from The Queen City Electric Co., were received during the month. When this statement was received by The Queen City Electric Co., the following entries were made to record consigned merchandise sold by the Oakwood Hardware Co. and the remittance received in payment of the proceeds:

Consignment Shipments................................	$120.07	
Consignment Sales.....................................		$120.07
Consigned merchandise sold by Oakwood Hardware Co. during June.		
Bank...	91.98	
Commission on Consignment Sales.......................	36.02	
Discount Allowed on Consignment Sales..................	4.20	
Federal Excise Tax....................................		12.13
Oakwood Hardware Co., Consignee......................		120.07
Statement of consignment sales received from Oakwood Hardware Co. with remittance of $91.98 in payment of proceeds.		

The first entry was made to record the June sales of merchandise consigned to the Oakwood Hardware Co. The second entry was made to record the remittance received from the Oakwood Hardware Co. in payment of the proceeds for June sales of consigned merchandise.

The amount credited to Federal Excise Tax is the amount of the tax collected by the consignee and remitted to the consignor. The Queen City Electric Co. follows the practice of debiting Federal Excise Tax for the amount of the tax billed separately on invoices received from the manufacturer and crediting Federal Excise Tax for the amount of tax collected by the consignee.

Assuming that the Oakwood Hardware Co. was the only consignee to whom merchandise was shipped on consignment, the consignment accounts would appear in the general ledger of The Queen City Electric Co., after the June transactions were posted, as illustrated on the following page.

OAKWOOD HARDWARE CO., CONSIGNEE

19--			19--	
June 1 Balance		348.92	June 30	120.07
7		25.68		
19		28.80		
21		18.24		
27		16.22		
30		9.60		
	327.39	*447.46*		

CONSIGNMENT SHIPMENTS

19--		19--		
June 30	120.07	June 1 Balance		348.92
		7		25.68
		19		28.80
		21		18 24
		27		16.22
		30		9.60
			327.39	*447.46*

It should be noted that the debit balance of the account with the Oakwood Hardware Co., Consignee is the same as the credit balance of the account with Consignment Shipments. This balance represents the June 30 inventory of merchandise consigned to the Oakwood Hardware Co.

Consignee's Books. At the time of receiving the invoice of shipment reproduced on page 403, the Oakwood Hardware Co. recorded the transaction in its books as indicated by the following general journal entry:

Consigned Merchandise.................................. $25.68
    The Queen City Electric Co., Consignor................. $25.68
        Invoice of shipment No. 7939.

Other invoices of shipment received from the same consignor during the month were recorded in like manner. The account with The Queen City Electric Co. is not an ordinary account payable as there is no obligation to pay for the consigned merchandise unless it is sold. The Oakwood Hardware Co. follows the practice of treating the accounts with consignors and with consigned merchandise as memorandum or offsetting accounts that need not appear in the balance sheet.

As the consigned merchandise was sold by the Oakwood Hardware Co., the sales were recorded by debiting the bank account or Accounts Receivable, depending upon whether the sales were for cash or on account, and by crediting Sales for the selling price and crediting Federal Excise Tax for the amount of the tax added to the selling price of the merchandise. At the end of the month an inventory of the consigned merchandise was taken and the statement of consignment sales, reproduced on page 405, was completed by filling in the agent's monthly report at the bottom of the form. This statement, together with a remittance for $91.98, was then mailed to The Queen City Electric Co. prior to July 7 in order to get the benefit of the special 5 per cent compensation allowed. This transaction was recorded in the books of the Oakwood Hardware Co. as indicated by the following general journal entries:

```
Sales.................................................   $120.07
    Consigned Merchandise................................           $120.07
        Consigned merchandise sold during June.

The Queen City Electric Co...........................    120.07
Federal Excise Tax...................................     12.13
    Discount Received on Consignment Sales..............              4.20
    Commission on Consignment Sales....................             36.02
    Bank.............................................               91.98
        Statement of consignment sales rendered to The Queen
        City Electric Co. with remittance of $91.98 in payment of
        proceeds.
```

The first entry was made to record the June sales of merchandise consigned by The Queen City Electric Co. After this entry was posted, the balance of the sales account represented the amount of the regular sales of other merchandise during the month. The second entry was made to record the check issued in payment of the proceeds for June sales of consigned merchandise.

THE QUEEN CITY ELECTRIC CO., CONSIGNOR

19--		19--		
June 30	120.07	June 1 Balance		348.92
		7		25.68
		19		28.80
		21		18.24
		27		16.22
		30		9.60
			327.39	*447.46*

CONSIGNED MERCHANDISE

19--			19--	
June 1 Balance		348.92	June 30	120.07
7		25.68		
19		28.80		
21		18.24		
27		16.22		
30		9.60		
	327.39	*447.46*		

Assuming that The Queen City Electric Co. is the only company from which merchandise is received on consignment, the consignment accounts would appear in the general ledger of the Oakwood Hardware Co., after the June transactions were posted, as illustrated on page 409.

It should be noted that the debit balance of the account with Consigned Merchandise is the same as the credit balance of the account with The Queen City Electric Co., Consignor. This balance represents the June 30 inventory of merchandise consigned by The Queen City Electric Co.

The federal excise tax imposed on electric light bulbs is a manufacturer's tax that is passed on to the ultimate consumer. The tax was recorded in the books of the Oakwood Hardware Co. as a credit to Federal Excise Tax at the time of recording sales of electric light bulbs. When the June statement of consignment sales was rendered to The Queen City Electric Co., the federal excise tax collected, amounting to $12.13, was included in the remittance and was recorded as a debit to Federal Excise Tax. Thus the account with Federal Excise Tax in the books of the Oakwood Hardware Co. was in balance after recording the tax included in the June settlement. While the actual rate of the tax is 10 per cent, the total tax collected amounted to 10.1 per cent of sales. The difference is accounted for by fractions of cents. For example, if one electric light bulb were sold for 19 cents, the tax collected would amount to 2 cents which is slightly more than 10 per cent of the sales price.

PRACTICE ASSIGNMENT No. 30. Complete Report No. 30 in the workbook and submit your working papers to the instructor for approval. Then continue with the next study assignment in Unit Fifteen until Report No. 31 is required.

ACCOUNTING FOR INVENTORY AND PREPAID EXPENSES

(31) MERCHANDISE INVENTORY

The calculation of periodic net income for a firm engaged in the purchase and sale of merchandise involves several problems that do not arise in the case of a personal service enterprise. The basic task is to apportion reasonably the cost of all of the goods available for sale during the period (opening inventory plus purchases) between the amount that should be considered as the cost of goods sold during the period and the amount that should be related to the goods on hand (merchandise inventory) at the end of the period. The routine bookkeeping procedure, using accounts for Purchases, Purchases Returns and Allowances, Merchandise Inventory, and Cost of Goods Sold, has been described in detail previously. Certain difficulties that arise in determining the cost to be assigned to goods unsold at the end of the period remain to be considered.

Taking a Physical Inventory. In many cases there is no record to show the quantity and cost of the merchandise on hand. Lacking such a record, the first step in attempting to apportion merchandise costs between sold and unsold goods consists of counting the goods that are on hand at the end of the period. This process is called *taking an inventory* or *taking a physical inventory*.

Taking a physical inventory of a stock of merchandise can be a sizable task. Frequently it must be done after regular business hours. Some firms close down for a few days to take inventory. The ideal time to count the goods is when the quantity on hand is the smallest. The fiscal year used by many businesses was selected so as to start and end at the time that the stock of goods is normally at its lowest point. This may be termed a *natural business year*.

It would be desirable if everything on hand could be counted within a few hours. Sometimes extra help is employed so as to make the count in as short a time as possible. Even if this is done, however, the taking of an inventory may require several days. If regular business is carried on during

411

this time, special records must be kept of additions to and subtractions from the stock during the period of the count. In this way a reckoning of the quantities of goods that were on hand at the end of the last day of the fiscal period can be made.

Various procedures are followed in taking an inventory so as to be sure that no items are missed and that no items are counted more than once. It is customary for persons taking inventory to work in pairs; one counts the items and "calls out" the information to the other who records it. Usually such information is recorded on a form commonly known as an *inventory sheet*. The sheet is arranged to provide space to show the description of each type of item, the quantity on hand, the cost per unit, and the extension — the amount that results from multiplying the quantity times the unit cost. (The cost per unit can be determined and the extensions completed after the count has been made.) Inventory sheets commonly provide spaces (a) to note the date of the count, (b) to record the location of the items listed, and (c) to record the names or initials of the person who did the counting, the person who recorded the count, the person who entered the costs or prices, the person who made the extensions, and the person who checked the information. A reproduction of part of an inventory sheet is shown below. Two extension columns are provided to facilitate the showing of subtotals.

In taking a physical inventory care must be exercised to be sure that only the goods that are the property of the firm are counted. Goods that have been sold and are awaiting delivery, and goods held on consignment must not be included in the count. It is also important to be sure to include goods that are owned on the date of the count which may not be in the store or warehouse. Examples are goods out on consignment and goods which

INVENTORY *May 31,* 19 — Page *1*				
Sheet No. *1*			Priced by *R. H.*	
Called by *P. G. S.*	Department *A*		Extended by *R. H.*	
Entered by *M. M.*	Location *Storeroom*		Examined by *N. W. B.*	

Description	Quantity	Unit	Price	Extensions	
Table Lamp	20	ea.	9 60	192 00	
Wall Rack	18	ea.	2 20	39 60	
Bookcase	7	ea.	26 90	188 30	
End Table	13	ea.	6 30	81 90	
Desk	6	ea.	22 75	136 50	
Total					948 62

Inventory Sheet

may have been recorded as purchased but which have not been received. Such goods are said to be *in transit* (on their way in a freight car, truck, ship, or airplane). Goods which have arrived but have not yet been unloaded must also be counted.

Assigning Cost to the Inventory. After the quantities of goods that are owned at the end of the period have been determined by count, the next step is to decide how much cost should be assigned to each unit. At first glance, this would seem to be an easy, though perhaps a time-consuming, job. If all purchases of the same article had been made at the same price per unit, reference to any purchase invoice covering such items would show the unit cost. The unit cost times the number of units in the inventory would give the total cost to be assigned to that merchandise. However, it is frequently the case that identical articles have been purchased at different times at different costs per unit. The question then arises as to which unit cost should be assigned to the goods in the inventory. Often there is no way of knowing exactly which price was paid for the specific goods that are on hand. As a workable solution to this problem, one of several different bases of inventory costing must be followed. The most common bases are (1) first-in, first-out costing, (2) average costing, and (3) last-in, first-out costing.

First-In, First-Out Costing. Over the years, the most commonly used method of allocating cost between goods sold during a period and goods unsold at the end of the period has been to assume that the goods first bought were first sold. Accordingly, the items on hand at the end of the period are considered to be those most recently purchased. This is known as the *first-in, first-out* method. (It is frequently referred to as the "FIFO" method, the abbreviation secured by using the first letter of each of the four words.) To illustrate how this method works, assume the following circumstances with respect to a particular article of merchandise:

On hand at start of period, 100 units assigned a cost of $1.01 each......	$ 101.00
Purchased during period:	
First purchase, 500 units @ $1.11 each.........................	555.00
Second purchase, 400 units @ $1.16 each.......................	464.00
Last purchase, 600 units @ $1.20 each.........................	720.00
Total cost of 1,600 units available for sale.........................	$1,840.00

On hand, end of period, 400 units

If it is assumed that the units first purchased were first sold, then the 400 units left at the end of the period were those purchased last at a cost of $1.20 each. Accordingly, the total cost to be assigned to these units would be $480 (400 units x $1.20). The cost assigned to the units sold would be $1,360 ($1,840 – $480).

First-in, first-out costing gained its popularity because of two features: (1) Whenever a merchant is able to control the flow of merchandise, he will see to it that the old goods move out first. Thus, FIFO costing is often in harmony with what actually happened; the newest goods are those on hand and they are assigned their actual cost. (2) FIFO costing assigns the most recent or most current costs to the ending inventory. The amount of that inventory is shown on the balance sheet among the current assets.

Another reason for widespread use of FIFO costing is the reluctance of accountants to change a method of accounting of long standing and thus to destroy the comparability of their calculations over a period of years. Consistency is considered an important virtue in accounting. Firms that have used the FIFO method successfully are reluctant to abandon it.

Average Costing. Another method of allocating merchandise cost between goods sold and those in the inventory is on the basis of the average cost of identical units. In the example on page 413, the total cost of the 1,600 units that were available for sale during the period was $1,840. Dividing $1,840 by 1,600 units results in an average cost of $1.15 per unit. (This is actually what is called a *weighted average* because the quantities involved as well as the unit costs were taken into consideration.) On the average-cost basis, the 400 units in the ending inventory would be assigned a total cost of $460 (400 x $1.15). The cost assigned to the units sold would be $1,380 ($1,840 − $460).

The logical appeal of using the average basis to assign cost between goods sold and goods on hand is apparent. In this example, one fourth (400) of the total units available (1,600) were unsold. The average cost basis assigns one fourth ($460) of the total cost ($1,840) to these goods.

Last-In, First-Out Costing. A third method of allocating cost between goods sold and goods on hand is to assume that all of the sales were made from the goods most recently purchased. This is called the *last-in, first-out* or "LIFO" method. As applied to the data shown on page 413, this would mean that the 400 units on hand at the end of the period would be presumed to comprise the 100 units that were on hand at the start of the period with an assigned cost of $1.01 per unit plus 300 of the units from the first purchase at a cost of $1.11 each. Therefore, the cost assigned to the inventory would be calculated as follows:

100 units @ $1.01.............. $101
300 units @ $1.11.............. 333

Total.................... $434

The cost allocated to the units sold would be $1,406 ($1,840 − $434).

The LIFO method is sometimes justified on the grounds that the physical movement of goods may be actually last-in, first-out. There are, however, better reasons to justify it. One persuasive argument is that the method causes the most recent purchase costs to be matched against the current sales. It is sometimes claimed that the method does not charge the cost of the units sold to current operations but, rather, the cost to replace the units sold is treated as the cost of sales. In periods of changing prices and costs, this is deemed to give better income measurement.

Another argument in favor of the LIFO method is that a going business must keep a minimum or base quantity of inventory on hand at all times. While this portion of the inventory is considered to be a current asset, it is, in reality, more like a fixed asset. Fixed assets are carried at original cost. Therefore, it is logical to assign original cost to the base amount of inventory. LIFO substantially accomplishes this result.

LIFO gained popularity in recent years because it was approved for federal income tax purposes. In a period of rising prices, its use will result in a smaller net income than would be obtained by using the FIFO or average method and, thus, lower income taxes. Even though income calculated on a LIFO basis during a period of falling prices will be higher, it is contended that the consistent use of the LIFO method for the entire life of a business will cause total income taxes to be less than otherwise because of the progressive nature of the federal income tax. (An income tax is progressive when successive segments of income are taxed at successively higher rates.)

Opponents of the LIFO method argue that it causes old, out-of-date inventory costs to be shown in the balance sheet. The theoretical and practical virtues of FIFO and LIFO are the subject of much debate.

Comparison of Methods. To compare the results obtained by the use of the three inventory costing methods discussed, assume that the 1,200 units that were sold brought $2,200 and that operating expenses for the period were $600. (The amount of the income from sales and the amount of operating expenses will not be affected by the method used to apportion cost between goods sold and goods unsold.) The tabulation on page 416 contrasts calculated net income and the cost assigned to the ending inventory under each costing method. Bear in mind that the example relates to a period when costs were rising.

	FIFO COSTING	AVERAGE COSTING	LIFO COSTING
Sales..............................	$2,200	$2,200	$2,200
Cost of Goods Sold..................	1,360	1,380	1,406
Gross Profit......................	$ 840	$ 820	$ 794
Operating Expenses..................	600	600	600
Net Income......................	$ 240	$ 220	$ 194
Cost Assigned to Ending Inventory.....	$ 480	$ 460	$ 434

Note that, in every case, the total cost of goods available for sale ($1,840) was apportioned between goods sold and goods on hand at the end of the period. It is common practice to describe the procedures that have been discussed as methods of inventory valuation. It should be apparent, however, that what is involved is also a process of valuing the cost of goods sold. Actually, the term valuation is misleading; what is involved is, essentially, *cost apportionment*.

Cost or Market, Whichever is Lower. There is a well-established tradition in accounting that unrealized profits or income should not be recorded except in very unusual cases. If the value of an asset increases, no formal record of the fact is entered on the books because the gain has not been actually realized. However, in most cases, if the value or usefulness of an asset declines, it is generally proper to consider that an expense or a loss has been incurred and to make appropriate record of the fact even though the loss has not been realized. This is called the *rule of conservatism*. The rule says to "provide for all losses, but anticipate no gains." The rule is not entirely consistent, but it has the force of tradition behind it.

This rule has a special application in connection with the allocation of cost to ending inventories of merchandise. When either the FIFO or average basis is followed in allocating cost, the unit cost that is determined for the ending inventory is not used if it is more than the replacement cost per unit of the goods. In that event, the goods are assigned a cost equal to their replacement cost or "market" price. (This means the market in which the goods are purchased, not the market in which they are sold.) This is referred to as the rule of "cost or market, whichever is lower."

To illustrate the application of the rule, suppose that, in the case of the example that has been used, the replacement cost or price of the items in question was $1.14 on the last day of the period. This is less than the FIFO cost per unit ($1.20) or the average cost per unit ($1.15). Accordingly, the 400 units that comprise the ending inventory would be assigned a total cost of $456 (400 × $1.14) and the cost of goods sold would be $1,384 ($1,840 − $456). Gross profit and net income would be reduced accordingly. Actually what is called cost of goods sold will then include an amount that can be described as a loss due to a decline in the replacement cost of unsold goods.

Since the merchandise will probably be sold for considerably more than either market or cost (however calculated), the reason for following so conservative a practice may be questioned. The purpose in using the cost-or-market, whichever-is-lower rule is to carry the goods into the next period with an assigned cost that will result in no less than the average or normal percentage of margin when the units are sold in the new period. If replacement cost has fallen, competition may cause some reduction in selling price.

To adhere strictly to the rule, the lower of cost or market should be used for each item in the inventory; it is not simply a matter of using the lower of total cost or total replacement cost (market). The cost-or-market rule does not apply when cost has been calculated on the LIFO basis. Special applications of the rule have been developed to take care of nonreplaceable, damaged, or shopworn goods.

In ascertaining the cost to be assigned to goods in an inventory, it is proper to assign to the unsold goods a fair share of any transportation costs that have been incurred on goods purchased. In all cases cost means cost at the buyer's place of business; not cost at the supplier's shipping point. In some cases, transportation charges are an important portion of the total cost of merchandise acquired.

Estimated Allocation of Merchandise Cost: The Gross Profit Method. The taking of a physical inventory may be such a sizable task that it is not attempted more than once a year. If so-called *interim* income statements and balance sheets are to be prepared, the allocation of the cost of goods available for sale during the interim period between goods sold and the amount on hand at the end of the period must be estimated. One way of doing this is to use what is called the *gross profit method*. The amount of sales during the period is reduced by what is considered to be the normal percentage of gross profit or gross margin to determine the estimated cost of goods sold. Deducting this amount from the total cost of goods available for sale gives the estimated amount of the ending inventory.

To illustrate, assume that a firm normally has a gross margin of 40 per cent on sales. At the start of its fiscal year, the balance in the merchandise inventory account was $35,000. Net purchases for the first month of the year amounted to $25,000. Net sales for the month amounted to $58,000. (1) What was the estimated cost of goods sold during the month? (2) What was the estimated amount of the merchandise inventory at the end of the month?

(1) Since gross profit is assumed to have been 40% of sales, cost of goods sold has been 60% of sales (100% − 40%).
Therefore, cost of goods sold = 60% of $58,000 (net sales for the month), or $34,800.

(2) Cost of goods available for sale was $60,000 (opening inventory of $35,000 plus net purchases of $25,000).
Inventory at the end of the month would be equal to goods available for sale, $60,000, less estimated cost of goods sold, $34,800, or $25,200.

The computed amounts are only reasonable if the normal mark-up on sales has prevailed during the period and is expected to prevail during following periods when the goods in the inventory will be sold. This type of calculation can be used to check the general reasonableness of the amount of an inventory that has been computed on the basis of a physical count. Any sizable difference in the two calculations might serve to call attention to a possible mistake in the count, in costing the items, or a marked variation in the realized rate of gross profit. The gross profit method can also be used to estimate the cost of an inventory that may have been destroyed by fire or otherwise. Such a calculation might be useful in negotiating an insurance settlement.

The Retail Method of Inventory. Many retail merchants use a variation of the gross profit method to calculate cost of goods sold and ending inventory for interim-statement purposes. The procedure employed is called the *retail method of inventory*. It necessitates keeping records of the prices at which purchased goods were marked to sell. This information, together with the record of cost of goods purchased, will make it possible to compute the ratio between cost and sales or retail prices. When sales are subtracted from the retail prices of all goods available for sale, the result is the estimated retail value of the ending inventory. Multiplying this amount by the ratio of cost to selling price gives the calculated cost of the ending inventory.

Following is an example of the calculation of the cost of an ending inventory of merchandise by the retail method:

	COST	RETAIL
Inventory, start of period	$31,800	$45,000
Net purchases during period	20,700	30,000
Merchandise available for sale	$52,500	$75,000
Less: Sales for period		50,000
Inventory, end of period, at retail		$25,000
Ratio of cost to retail prices of merchandise available for sale ($52,500 ÷ $75,000)		70%
Inventory, end of period, at cost (70% of $25,000)	$17,500	

The foregoing example was simplified by assuming that there were no changes in the prices at which the goods were marked to sell. In practice, such changes are commonplace and the calculation must take such adjustments into consideration.

Perpetual Inventories. Firms that deal in certain types of merchandise sometimes find it feasible to keep up-to-date records of the quantities and cost of goods on hand at all times. This type of record is referred to as a *perpetual inventory*. The general ledger account for Merchandise Inventory is somewhat like the account for Cash or Bank; chronological records of additions and subtractions are maintained. The balance of the account shows the cost of the goods that should be on hand.

When a perpetual inventory is kept, the merchandise inventory account in the general ledger is usually a control account. A subsidiary ledger with an account for each type of goods is maintained. These accounts are often in the form of cards which provide spaces to show additions, subtractions, and the balance after each change. Goods sold can be assigned cost on either a FIFO, an average, or a LIFO basis. The day-to-day costing of sales on either the average or LIFO basis will give results that differ somewhat from those obtained when LIFO or average costing is done at the end of the period. (The results will be the same if the FIFO basis is used.) Perpetual inventories do not eliminate the need for taking periodic physical inventories. The records must be checked from time to time to discover and correct any errors. However, it is not always necessary to count everything at substantially the same time. The stock can be counted and the records verified by groups of items, by departments, or by sections.

A business that sells a wide variety of rather low-cost goods (such as five-and-ten-cent stores) will not find it practical to keep a perpetual inventory. By contrast, a business that sells relatively few high-cost items (an automobile dealer, for example) can maintain such a record without incurring prohibitive clerical cost.

Firms of many types often keep supplementary or auxiliary records of goods in terms of quantities only. This is called a *stock record*. Stock records serve as a guide in purchasing operations, help to reveal any shortages, and provide information as to the goods on hand to serve as a basis for assigning merchandise cost for interim-statement purposes.

PRACTICE ASSIGNMENT No. 31. Complete Report No. 31 in the workbook and submit your working papers to the instructor for approval. Then continue with the following study assignment until Report No. 32 is required.

(32) SUPPLIES AND PREPAYMENTS

Office supplies, store supplies, advertising materials, fuel, and other supplies may be purchased during an accounting period but may not be wholly consumed in the same period. The premium on insurance covering merchandise, equipment, and buildings may be prepaid, but the term of the policy may extend beyond the accounting period in which the service was contracted for. Rent and interest may be paid in advance, but the expense may not be wholly incurred in the same accounting period. The cost of unused supplies on hand at the close of an accounting period and of prepaid items not incurred during the accounting period should be treated as current assets. Such items represent temporary assets that will become expenses in the period in which they are consumed or used.

When the accounts are kept on the accrual basis, it is necessary to adjust certain accounts at the close of each accounting period for the following:

(a) The amounts of any supplies or services purchased during the period that were recorded as assets at time of purchase and that were consumed or used during the period.

(b) The amounts of any supplies or services purchased during the period that were recorded as expenses at time of purchase and that were not consumed or used during the period.

Asset Method of Accounting for Supplies and Prepayments. Supplies, such as office supplies, store supplies, advertising supplies, fuel, and postage, that may be purchased in one accounting period but may not be wholly consumed in the same period are usually recorded as assets at the time of purchase.

Office Supplies. Office supplies may consist of letterheads and envelopes, pencils, carbon paper, ink, notebooks, typewriter ribbons, rubber bands, paper clips, and other miscellaneous supplies that are normally consumed in the operation of an office. Transactions arising from the the purchase of such supplies on credit should be entered in the invoice record. When such supplies are purchased for cash, the transactions should be entered in the record of checks issued. In either case, the purchases are posted to an account with Office Supplies in the general ledger.

At the end of each accounting period an inventory of the unused office supplies on hand is taken and an adjusting entry is made to record the amount of the office supplies consumed during the period. For example, if on December 31 the office supplies account has a debit balance of $300 and an inventory reveals that the cost of the supplies on hand amounts to $100, it is apparent that the supplies consumed during the period amounted to $200. The required adjustment may be made as indicated in the following general journal entry:

Office Supplies Consumed.............................	$200.00	
Office Supplies.......................................		$200.00
Office supplies consumed during period.		

After this entry is posted, the office supplies account will have a debit balance of $100, which should be listed in the balance sheet as a current asset. The account with Office Supplies Consumed will have a debit balance of $200, which should be listed in the income statement as an operating expense.

Store Supplies. Store supplies may consist of wrapping paper and twine, corrugated board, paper bags and other containers, cleaning supplies, and other miscellaneous supplies that are normally consumed in the operation of a store. Transactions arising from the purchase of such supplies should be recorded in the same manner as transactions arising from the purchase of office supplies; that is, purchases should be recorded by debiting Store Supplies and by crediting Accounts Payable or the bank account, depending upon whether they are purchased on credit or for cash.

At the end of each accounting period an inventory of the unused store supplies on hand is taken and an adjusting entry is made to record the amount of the store supplies consumed during the period. The method of adjusting the store supplies account is the same as the method of adjusting the office supplies account.

For example, if on December 31 the store supplies account has a debit balance of $240 and an inventory reveals that the cost of the supplies on hand amounts to $70, it is apparent that the supplies consumed during the period amounted to $170. The required adjustment may be made as indicated in the following general journal entry:

Store Supplies Consumed.............................	$170.00	
Store Supplies.......................................		$170.00
Store supplies consumed during period.		

After the adjusting entry is posted, the debit balance of the store supplies account represents an asset that should be listed in the balance sheet as a current asset. At the same time the debit balance of the account with Store Supplies Consumed represents an expense that should be listed in the income statement as an operating expense.

Advertising Supplies. Advertising supplies may consist of catalogues, circulars, price lists, order blanks, and other miscellaneous supplies that are normally consumed in the advertising program. Transactions arising from the purchase of such supplies should be recorded in the same manner as transactions arising from the purchase of other supplies; that is, purchases should be recorded by debiting Advertising Supplies and by crediting Accounts Payable or the bank account, depending upon whether they are purchased on credit or for cash.

At the end of each accounting period an inventory of the unused advertising supplies on hand is taken and an adjusting entry is made to record the amount of the advertising supplies consumed during the period. The method of adjusting the advertising supplies account is the same as the method of adjusting the office supplies and store supplies accounts.

For example, if on December 31 the advertising supplies account has a debit balance of $375 and an inventory reveals that the cost of the supplies on hand amounts to $125, it is apparent that the supplies consumed during the period amounted to $250. The required adjustment may be made as indicated in the following general journal entry:

Advertising Supplies Consumed...........................	$250.00	
Advertising Supplies.................................		$250.00
Advertising supplies consumed during period.		

After the adjusting entry is posted, the debit balance of the advertising supplies account represents an asset that should be listed in the balance sheet as a current asset. At the same time the debit balance of the account with Advertising Supplies Consumed represents an expense that should be listed in the income statement as an operating expense.

Postage Stamps. The cost of postage stamps purchased is usually recorded by debiting Postage Stamps and by crediting the bank account. Usually a check is made payable to Postage and, after it is cashed at the bank, the money is used to purchase stamps in the desired denominations. Some of the stamps may be used on parcel-post packages and the balance on ordinary mail. A memorandum record of the stamps used on parcel-post packages may be kept until the end of the month, when the total is recorded by debiting Transportation Out and by crediting Postage Stamps. Usually no record is kept of the stamps used on ordinary mail each day, but periodically the unused stamps are counted and their total amount is ascertained. The difference between the amount of the unused stamps on hand and the debit balance of the postage stamps account represents the amount of the stamps used on ordinary mail.

If the account with Postage Stamps is debited (a) for the amount of the stamps on hand at the beginning of the month, $15, and (b) for the amount of stamps purchased during the month, $85, and is credited for the amount of the stamps used on parcel-post packages during the month, $40, the account will have a debit balance of $60 at the end of the month. If, at that time, the amount of the unused stamps on hand is found to be $25, the difference, or $35, represents the amount of the stamps that must have been used on ordinary mail during the month. It is, therefore, necessary to adjust the accounts in order to record the decrease in the asset Postage Stamps to an amount that is in agreement with the inventory of unused stamps and to record the increase in postage expense resulting from the stamps used on ordinary mail during the month. The required adjustment may be made as indicated in the following general journal entry:

Postage...	$35.00	
Postage Stamps......................................		$35.00
Amount of stamps used on ordinary mail.		

After the adjusting entry is posted, the account with Postage Stamps will have a debit balance of $25, which represents an asset that should be listed in the balance sheet as a current asset. The account with Postage will have a debit balance of $35, representing an expense that should be listed in the income statement as an operating expense.

In addition to buying postage stamps, a firm may make a deposit under the permit system that entitles the firm to a certain amount of postage. Sometimes postage meters are used. In this case, a certain amount of postage is paid for and the meter is set so that the postage may be used as needed. Regardless of whether postage stamps are purchased, whether a deposit is made under the permit system, or whether metered postage is purchased, the accounting procedure may be the same. The prepaid postage may be charged to an account with postage stamps, and when the stamps are used or the postage is consumed, the amount should be charged to the proper expense accounts.

Insurance. Insurance against loss from fire, water, windstorm, burglary, and other casualties is a form of protection provided by insurance companies. A contract under which an insurance company, the insurer, agrees to protect the owner of property, the insured, from loss on such property is known as an *insurance policy*. The amount that the insured is required to pay for such protection is known as the *premium*. The premium is usually stated as a specified rate per $1,000 of insurance for one or more years. If the rate is quoted on a basis of one year, it is known as the *annual rate*. If it is quoted for a longer period than one year, it is known as the *term rate*. Since insurance is usually purchased for a period of one or more years and the premium must be paid in advance by the policyholder, the amount paid is usually charged to an account with Prepaid Insurance, which is classified as a current asset.

Expired Insurance. The asset value of prepaid insurance decreases day by day, but it is not customary to keep a daily record of expired insurance. Instead the usual plan is to record, at the close of each accounting period, the total amount of expired insurance applicable to each period. Thus an entry may be made at the end of each month to record the amount of the insurance expired during the month.

Many firms keep an auxiliary record of insurance policies similar to the one reproduced below. The left page is used to record the essential information with respect to each policy. It also provides the information needed in distributing the insurance premium on each policy in the columns provided on the right page. To ascertain the amount of the expired premium to be entered in the column provided for each month, it is only necessary to divide the total premium by the number of months in the term of the policy. Thus, if the premium amounts to $15

INSURANCE POLICY REGISTER

DATE OF POLICY		POLICY No.	NAME OF INSURANCE COMPANY	PROPERTY INSURED	AMOUNT OF INSURANCE		TERM	PREMIUM	
19—									
Jan.	1	63428	Union Fire & Theft Ins. Co.	Truck — Fire & Theft	3000	00	1 yr.	45	00
	1	26731	Merchants Insurance Co.	Truck — Property Damage	5000	00	1 yr.	24	00
	1	439128	Globe Insurance Co.	Merchandise	5000	00	2 yrs.	74	88
	1	91027	U. S. Fire Insurance Co.	Office Equipment	3000	00	3 yrs.	108	00
July	1	86329	Standard Insurance Co.	Merchandise	5000	00	1 yr.	45	00
Nov.	1	361892	National Insurance Co.	Store Equipment	2000	00	2 yrs.	60	00
								356	88

(Left page)

and the term of the policy is one year, the amount of insurance expired monthly will be $1.25 ($15 ÷ 12 months). The total of each monthly column is the amount of insurance expired during the month. Before this amount can be recorded, it is necessary to make a proper distribution of the insurance expense. It will be noted that the total insurance expired during the month of January amounted to $11.87.

The insurance expired during January was distributed as follows:

Expired insurance on merchandise..................................	$ 3.12
Expired insurance on delivery equipment...........................	5.75
Expired insurance on office equipment.............................	3.00
Total...	$11.87

The amount of the expired insurance was therefore recorded as indicated by the following general journal entry:

Expired Insurance on Merchandise...........................	$3.12	
Expired Insurance on Delivery Equipment.....................	5.75	
Expired Insurance on Office Equipment.......................	3.00	
Prepaid Insurance.......................................		$11.87
Insurance expired during January.		

INSURANCE POLICY REGISTER

JAN.	FEB.	MAR.	APR.	MAY	JUNE	JULY	AUG.	SEPT.	OCT.	NOV.	DEC.	EXPIRED	UNEXPIRED
3 75	3 75	3 75	3 75	3 75	3 75	3 75	3 75	3 75	3 75	3 75	3 75	45 00	
2 00	2 00	2 00	2 00	2 00	2 00	2 00	2 00	2 00	2 00	2 00	2 00	24 00	
3 12	3 12	3 12	3 12	3 12	3 12	3 12	3 12	3 12	3 12	3 12	3 12	37 44	37 44
3 00	3 00	3 00	3 00	3 00	3 00	3 00	3 00	*12 40				36 40	
11 87	11 87	11 87	11 87	11 87	11 87								
						3 75	3 75	3 75	3 75	3 75	3 75	22 50	22 50
						15 62	15 62	25 02	12 62				
										2 50	2 50	5 00	55 00
										15 12	15 12	170 34	114 94

Policy #91027 canceled August 31.

(Right page)

INSURANCE POLICY REGISTER

DATE OF POLICY	POLICY No.	NAME OF INSURANCE COMPANY	PROPERTY INSURED	AMOUNT OF INSURANCE	TERM	PREMIUM
19 —						
Jan. 1	439128	Globe Insurance Co.	Merchandise	5000 00	1 yr.	37 44
July 1	86329	Standard Insurance Co.	Merchandise	5000 00	6 mos.	22 50
Nov. 1	361892	National Insurance Co.	Store Equipment	2000 00	22 mos.	55 00

(Left page)

After the expired insurance is recorded for each month during the year, the balance of the prepaid insurance account at the end of the year should be the same as the total of the unexpired insurance premium column in the insurance policy register.

At the beginning of each year, it is necessary to forward the data in the insurance policy register as shown in the illustration at the top of this page. The left page only of the register is reproduced in this illustration. In bringing forward the data, the unexpired term of the policy and the amount of the unexpired premium are recorded; thus, the information needed in computing the amount of the premium to be charged off each month is available. For example, the unexpired premium on Policy No. 439128 amounted to $37.44 and the policy had one year to run; therefore, one twelfth of the unexpired premium, or $3.12, should be charged off during each month of the ensuing year. The unexpired premium on Policy No. 86329 amounted to $22.50 and the policy had six months to run; therefore, one sixth of the unexpired premium, or $3.75, should be charged off during each of the next six months. The unexpired premium on Policy No. 361892 amounted to $55 and the policy had twenty-two months to run; therefore, one twenty second of the unexpired premium, or $2.50, should be charged off each month during the ensuing year. At the time of forwarding the amount of unexpired insurance to a new page, the total of the Premium column should be in agreement with the debit balance of the prepaid insurance account.

Canceled Insurance. Either the insurance company or the policyholder may cancel an insurance policy at any time before expiration of the policy. If a policy is canceled, the insured is entitled to receive a refund of that part of the premium applicable to the unexpired period. The amount of the refund will depend upon whether the policy is canceled at the instigation of the insurance company or at the request of the policyholder. When the policy is canceled by the insurance company, the premium for the expired period is computed on a pro-rata basis. When the policy is canceled at the request of the policyholder, the premium for the expired period is usually canceled on a *short-term rate* basis. To record the amount refunded, it is only necessary to debit the bank account and to credit the prepaid insurance account. At the same time an entry should be made in the insurance policy register to indicate that the policy was canceled and to record the additional cost of insurance due to the short-term rate charged. This increased cost should be recorded in the column for the month in which the refund was received.

Policy No. 91027, purchased on January 1, was canceled on August 31. The insurance company refunded $71.60 in September and the loss of $12.40, representing the difference between the short-term rate and the annual rate, was recorded in the September column. It could not be recorded in the August column because the amount of the loss was not known until the amount of the refund was received in September.

Prepaid Interest. Sometimes interest is prepaid on a note payable. When this is done and the note does not mature in the same accounting period, the amount of interest paid may be recorded as a charge to a prepaid interest account, which should be classified as a current asset.

At the end of the accounting period the amount of the interest expense actually incurred during the period should be calculated and an adjusting entry should be made to transfer that portion of the interest from the prepaid interest account to an interest expense account. For example, on December 1 a note for $1,000 due in three months with interest at 6 per cent was issued to a bank and the interest amounting to $15 was paid in advance. On December 31 it was ascertained that one third of the interest expense was incurred during the current accounting period; therefore, an adjustment should be made as indicated in the following general journal entry:

Interest Expense...	$5.00	
Prepaid Interest...		$5.00
Prepaid interest transferred to Interest Expense.		

After this entry is posted, the prepaid interest account will have a debit balance of $10, which should be listed in the balance sheet as a current asset. The debit balance of the interest expense account should be listed in the income statement under the heading of "Other Charges."

One advantage of using the asset method of accounting for supplies and prepayments is that the adjusting entries that are required at the end of the period are of the amortization, or write-off, type. Such adjustments do not need to be reversed at the start of the new period.

Expense Method of Accounting for Supplies and Prepayments. Supplies and services that may not be wholly consumed in the period in which they are purchased may be recorded as expenses at the time of purchase. Under this method of accounting, it is necessary to adjust the accounts at the end of each accounting period in order that the unused portions may be recorded as assets. For example, if office supplies purchased during an accounting period are charged to an account with Office Supplies Expense, it will be necessary to adjust the account at the end of the period for the value of the unused supplies on hand. If Office Supplies Expense had been charged for a total of $200 during the period and an inventory taken at the end of the period showed that the unused supplies on hand amounted to $75, it would be necessary to adjust the accounts as indicated by the following general journal entry:

```
Unused Office Supplies....................................    $75.00
    Office Supplies Expense.................................             $75.00
        Office supplies on hand.
```

After this entry is posted, the account with Office Supplies Expense will have a debit balance of $125 that should be listed in the income statement as an operating expense. The account with Unused Office Supplies will have a debit balance of $75 that should be listed in the balance sheet as a current asset.

If the expense method is followed, the adjustments made at the end of the period are known as *deferral adjustments* — they defer expenses to the next period. Adjustments of this type should be reversed at the start of the new period. In this case, the effect of the adjusting, closing, and reversing procedure is to remove the proper amount from an expense account at the end of the period, transfer the remaining amount to the income summary account, and transfer the amount that was deferred back to the expense account at the start of the new period.

A detailed comparison of the asset and expense methods of accounting for supplies and prepaid items is shown in parallel columns on the following page.

Accounting for Prepaid Expenses

Asset Method   **Expense Method**

TRANSACTION. March 1. Purchased office supplies, $200. Terms, 30 days.

JOURNAL ENTRY   JOURNAL ENTRY

Mar. 1. Office Supplies....... $200   Mar. 1. Office Supplies Expense $200
    Accounts Payable.. $200   Accounts Payable.. $200
    Purchased office   Purchased office
    supplies on   supplies on
    credit.   credit.

ADJUSTMENT DATA. December 31. Inventory of unused office supplies on hand, $75.

JOURNAL ENTRY   JOURNAL ENTRY

Dec. 31. Office Supplies Con-   Dec. 31. Unused Office Supplies $75
    sumed............. $125   Office Supplies Expense $75
    Office Supplies.... $125   Unused office
    Office supplies   supplies on hand.
    consumed during
    period.

LEDGER ACCOUNTS   LEDGER ACCOUNTS

OFFICE SUPPLIES (An asset account)   OFFICE SUPPLIES EXPENSE

Mar. 1	*75*	200	Dec. 31	125

Mar. 1	*125*	200	Dec. 31	75

OFFICE SUPPLIES CONSUMED   UNUSED OFFICE SUPPLIES
(An expense account)   (An asset account)

Dec. 31	125		Dec. 31	75

ACCOUNTS PAYABLE   ACCOUNTS PAYABLE

	Mar. 1	200		Mar. 1	200

The balance of the account with Office Supplies, amounting to $75, should be listed as a current asset in the balance sheet, while the balance of the account with Office Supplies Consumed, amounting to $125, should be listed as an operating expense in the income statement.

The balance of the account with Office Supplies Expense, amounting to $125, should be listed as an operating expense in the income statement, while the balance of the account with Unused Office Supplies, amounting to $75, should be listed as a current asset in the balance sheet. As of the start of the new period, the adjusting entry should be reversed so as to transfer the deferred amount back to the expense account.

The final results are the same under both methods of accounting, but the adjusting entries required at the close of each accounting period differ. Reversing or readjusting entries are advisable if the expense method is used.

Under the asset method, adjusting entries are made periodically to record the amounts consumed or used during the period; under the expense method, entries are made periodically to record the asset value of the amounts to be deferred to a succeeding accounting period. Regardless of which method is used in accounting for supplies and prepaid items, it is advisable to follow a consistent policy.

PRACTICE ASSIGNMENT No. 32. Complete Report No. 32 in the workbook and submit your working papers to the instructor for approval. Then continue with the next study assignment in Unit Sixteen until Report No. 33 is required.

ACCOUNTING
FOR TANGIBLE FIXED ASSETS

(33) LAND, BUILDINGS, AND EQUIPMENT

There are many types of business assets that are acquired with the expectation that they will serve for a number of accounting periods. Long-lived assets of this type are called fixed assets or capital assets. Such assets can be classified in various ways. From a legal standpoint all property is either *real property* or *personal property*. Real property (realty or real estate) includes land and anything attached to the land; personal property includes everything that can be owned except real property. In nearly all cases, any real property owned by a business is considered to be a fixed asset. (The exception relates to cases where real estate is acquired as a short-term investment.) Many kinds of personal property are treated as fixed assets. Furniture, equipment, motor vehicles, machinery, patents, and copyrights are common examples of personal property that is owned and used in business for a number of accounting periods.

Another way of classifying long-lived assets is on the basis of tangibility. All real property has physical tangibility. The same is true of such personal property as furniture, equipment, and machinery. The major examples of *intangible* long-lived assets are patents, copyrights, leaseholds, leasehold improvements, franchises, trade-marks, and goodwill. These latter assets have no physical tangibility though they do have existence in either an economic or a legal sense.

Sometimes firms possess assets in the form of capital stock of other firms, or bonds or long-term notes of other firms or of governments. It is logical to classify such assets as intangibles; however, because of their special nature, they are usually classified as "Investments." If it is expected that they will be owned for a long time, they will be considered long-term investments and will be exhibited in the balance sheet under some such heading. If the investments are temporary in nature, they are treated as current assets.

431

For accounting purposes, a common classification of long-lived or fixed assets is on the basis of how the original cost of the property is handled in the process of computing net income period by period. The cost of land used only as a site for a store, a factory, a warehouse, a parking lot, etc. is normally left undisturbed in the accounts for as long as the land is owned. Such land does not depreciate. Tangible property, such as buildings, furniture, and equipment are usually called depreciable assets. This is because their value or usefulness is exhausted as time passes. In calculating net income period by period, a portion of the cost of such assets is charged off as depreciation expense. In a similar fashion, the cost of such intangible properties as patents, copyrights, and leaseholds is gradually charged off as expense to the periods benefited by the ownership of the assets. As applied to these assets, however, the periodic write-off is termed *amortization* (in contrast to depreciation of the tangible assets). Actually, the meaning of the word amortization is broad enough to include depreciation, but custom dictates that the write-off of the cost of most tangible fixed assets shall be called depreciation, while the write-off of the cost of intangibles shall be called amortization.

Finally, there are certain long-lived assets whose physical substance is consumed in the operation of a business. Common examples include mines, stands of timber, and oil and gas wells. These are called *wasting assets*. As might be expected, an effort is made to allocate the cost of such property to the periods in which the assets are consumed or exhausted. In this case, however, the periodic write-off is called *depletion*.

Relatively few nonmanufacturing businesses own intangible assets and wasting assets. Tangible fixed assets, such as land, buildings, and various types of equipment, are more common. The major features of accounting for these types of property will be considered in this unit. For the sake of brevity, and in conformity with common practice, such items will be referred to as simply "fixed assets" though it will be understood that those under consideration in this unit are all in the "tangible" category.

Acquisition of Fixed Assets. Fixed assets may be bought for cash or on credit. The amount at which fixed assets should be recorded is the total cost when acquired and ready for operation or use. The cost may include the purchase price, transportation charges, installation costs, and any other costs that are incurred up to the point of making the assets available for use. In some cases interest may be included in the cost. For example, if money is borrowed for the purpose of constructing a building or other facilities, it is considered sound accounting to add the interest incurred during the period of construction to the cost of such building or facilities.

It is important that the cost of depreciable assets be properly accounted for, because the total cost becomes the basis for the periodic depreciation charge.

Transactions involving the purchase of fixed assets may be recorded in the appropriate book of original entry by debiting the proper asset accounts and by crediting the bank account for the amount paid, or by crediting the proper liability account, such as Accounts Payable, Notes Payable, or Mortgages Payable, for the obligations incurred.

Additions or improvements representing an increase in the value of fixed assets should be recorded by debiting the proper asset accounts and by crediting the bank account or the proper liability account. For example, if an addition to a building is constructed, the total cost incurred should be debited to the building account. In the same manner, such improvements as the installation of partitions, shelving, hardwood floors, a sprinkler system, air conditioning, or any other improvements that increase the usefulness of property should be recorded by debiting the proper asset accounts for the cost of the improvements. The cost of landscaping grounds surrounding an office or factory building, constructing new driveways, planting trees and shrubbery, and similar improvements should all be capitalized by debiting the proper asset accounts. Assessments for street improvements, sidewalks, sewers, flood prevention, parks, etc. represent improvements in, or enhancement of the value of, the land. They should be recorded by debiting the land account.

Depreciation. The central task in attempting to calculate income or loss on a periodic basis is to allocate income to the period in which it is earned and to assign costs and expenses to the periods that are benefited. Fixed assets last a relatively long time and, accordingly, benefit a number of periods. The process of recording the depreciation of most fixed assets is carried on in an effort to allocate their cost to the periods that they benefit or serve.

Causes of Depreciation. Depreciation is the loss of useful value of an asset. There are two types of depreciation:

(1) Physical Depreciation. This term refers to the loss of useful value because of deterioration from age and from wear and tear. This type of depreciation is generally continuous, though not necessarily uniform from period to period. Assets exposed to the elements may wear out at a fairly uniform rate. Assets not exposed to the elements may slowly deteriorate whether in use or not, but the speed at which they deteriorate is likely to be related to the extent that they are used.

(2) *Functional Depreciation.* This term refers to loss of useful value because of inadequacy or obsolescence. The growth of a business may result in some of its fixed assets becoming inadequate. The assets remain capable of doing the job for which they were acquired, but the job has become too big for them. Assets may become obsolete because of a change in the demand for products or services or because of the development of new methods, processes, or equipment.

Calculating the Amount of Depreciation for a Period. The net cost of an asset should be apportioned over the periods the asset will serve. Net cost means original cost less scrap or residual value. Scrap or residual value is difficult to predict in most cases. Quite often, the assumption is that the scrap value will be zero. The major problem connected with depreciation accounting, however, is to attempt to foretell either how many periods the asset will serve or how many units of service the asset will provide. If it were possible to know that a machine would function 100,000 hours, it would be easy to decide that 5 per cent of its net cost should be charged to the first year when it was used 5,000 hours. Likewise, a certain knowledge that an asset would last 10 years and equally serve each of those years would solve the problem of how to apportion its cost. Unfortunately, there is no way of knowing exactly how long an asset will last or exactly what its output will be. All that can be done is to make estimates based upon experience. In attempting to make such estimates the accountant may be assisted by data relating to assets previously owned by the business or he may be guided by the experience of others. Statistics supplied by trade associations and government agencies may help. Opinions of engineers or appraisal companies may be sought. Past experience with respect to physical depreciation may be a very good guide for the future. Past events, however, are not much help in attempting to predict depreciation caused by inadequacy or obsolescence. Uncertainty surrounds all depreciation calculations.

Methods of Calculating Depreciation. There are several different ways of calculating the amount of depreciation to be recorded each period. The most commonly used methods are the following:

(1) Straight-line method.

(2) Unit-of-output method.

(3) Declining-balance method.

(4) Sum-of-the-year's-digits method.

Federal income tax laws and regulations do not prescribe any particular depreciation method. They generally allow the taxpayer to use any method that is reasonable under the circumstances and that is consistently applied.

Straight-Line Method. With the straight-line method, the net cost of an asset is apportioned equally over its estimated useful life in terms of months or years. For example, assume that a frame building cost $26,000. It is expected to last 20 years. The estimated residual or scrap value is $500. The amount of depreciation each year, then, would be $1,275. This is computed as follows:

$$\frac{\$26,000 - \$500}{20} = \$1,275$$

The annual rate of depreciation would be 4.904 per cent ($1,275 ÷ $26,000). As a practical matter, the estimated scrap value probably would be ignored, since it is relatively so small, and a depreciation rate of 5 per cent would be used. In this event the annual charge would be $1,300 (5% of $26,000).

A month is usually the smallest period that is considered in depreciation accounting. An asset purchased before the fifteenth of the month is considered to have been owned for the full month. Assets purchased after the middle of the month are considered to have been acquired on the first of the next month.

The difference between the cost of an asset and the total amount of its cost that has been charged off as depreciation is its book value at that particular time. When the straight-line method is used, the book value of the asset decreases uniformly period by period. Shown on a graph, the book value over a number of periods is downward-sloping, but perfectly straight line. That is how the method got its name.

The straight-line method of calculating depreciation closely reflects the facts in many cases. The method has the outstanding advantage of simplicity. Since depreciation is based upon estimates in any case, many businessmen and accountants feel that the use of more complicated procedures is not warranted. The calculation of depreciation on a straight-line basis is the most widely used method.

Depreciation can be calculated on each asset or on each group of substantially identical assets. It is possible to calculate a *composite rate* to be applied to a number of assets that may include various types of property. For example, suppose that the general ledger account Office Furniture included the following:

ITEM	QUANTITY	ESTIMATED LIFE, YEARS	TOTAL COST
Desks	10	20	$2,000
Chairs	25	15	1,500
Tables	4	12	420
Filing Cabinets	20	15	960
			$4,880

The depreciation rates for the four types of office furniture would be, respectively, 5, $6\frac{2}{3}$, $8\frac{1}{3}$, and $6\frac{2}{3}$ per cent. The total depreciation for a year would be calculated as follows:

Desks	$2,000 x 5%	= $100
Chairs	1,500 x $6\frac{2}{3}$%	= 100
Tables	420 x $8\frac{1}{3}$%	= 35
Filing Cabinets	960 x $6\frac{2}{3}$%	= 64
	$4,880	$299

The average or group rate would be $299 ÷ $4,880, or 6.127 per cent, which probably would be rounded to 6 per cent. As long as the relative proportion of the types of items in the groups stays about the same, and no reason arises to alter the estimated life of any of the items, the composite rate of 6 per cent can be applied to the group total to determine the annual depreciation write-off.

When depreciation is calculated on the basis of a group or composite rate, no attempt is made to relate the depreciation to specific units. No depreciation is recorded in the subsidiary record (if any) for each individual unit. Therefore, when disposition is made of a unit, its original cost, less any scrap or trade-in value, is charged to the allowance for depreciation account for the appropriate group. No gain or loss is recognized upon the disposition of a unit.

Unit-of-Output Method. The unit-of-output or unit-of-production method of depreciation is suitable and preferable in many cases. If it is possible to estimate the number of units of service or output that can be secured from an asset, then it is logical to prorate the net cost of the asset to the periods it serves on the basis of the use or output during each period. Obviously such a measure of service does not exist in the case of many assets. In the case of certain types of machinery, equipment, and vehicles, however, the unit-of-output method may be used.

For example, a company may have found from experience that it usually can obtain 100,000 miles of service from certain types of trucks before they become so worn out that the need for extensive repairs and replacements makes it advisable for the company to dispose of them. Suppose a new truck of this type is purchased. The cost of the truck (apart from tires, which are separately depreciated on the basis of a shorter life) is $4,600. The company expects that the truck can be traded in for $1,600 after 100,000 miles. The estimated net cost to be charged to operations during the life of the truck is, therefore, $3,000. The estimated depreciation per mile is 3 cents ($3,000 ÷ 100,000 miles). If the truck was driven 32,000 miles the first year, the depreciation charge for that year with respect to that truck would be $960 (32,000 × .03).

Declining-Balance Method. Many fixed assets require repairs and parts replacements to keep them in service. Such expenses usually increase as the assets grow older. Some accountants believe that depreciation expense should be higher in early years to offset the higher repair and maintenance expenses of the later years. Another reason advanced in support of this method of depreciation is the contention that many, if not most, assets contribute proportionately more to the business during the years that the assets are comparatively new. For these reasons, it may be desirable to calculate depreciation in a way that will give larger write-offs in the early years of the life of the unit. One way to accomplish this result is to apply a fixed or uniform rate to the book value of the property each year. As the book value diminishes year by year, the depreciation charges are successively smaller. This method is called the *declining-balance* or *fixed-percentage-of-diminishing-value* method.

The popularity of this method was increased by a change in the Internal Revenue Code in 1954 which permitted taxpayers to calculate depreciation on new assets acquired after December 31, 1953 using a rate no more than twice the straight-line rate. (Prior to this time, the law did not allow a deduction greater than $1\frac{1}{2}$ times the amount computed by using straight-line depreciation.)

Suppose, for example, that an asset with a cost of $1,000 and an expected life of 5 years is to be depreciated on the declining-balance basis. Assume that the company wishes to handle depreciation in the same way for income tax and other purposes. Accordingly, since the straight-line rate would be 20 per cent (100% ÷ 5 years), the company could use a rate of 40 per cent (2 × 20%). The annual depreciation, balance in the allowance for depreciation account, and book value at the end of each year would be as follows:

YEAR	ANNUAL DEPRECIATION	ALLOWANCE FOR DEPRECIATION END OF YEAR	BOOK VALUE END OF YEAR
0			$1,000.00
1	$400.00	$400.00	600.00
2	240.00	640.00	360.00
3	144.00	784.00	216.00
4	86.40	870.40	129.60
5	51.84	922.24	77.76

It is not possible to write off the original amount entirely by taking a fixed percentage only of the remainder. However, it is possible to abandon this method in later years and to write off the book value at that time on a straight-line basis over the remaining years. For example, at the end of the third year the book value of the asset was $216. One half of this amount, or $108, could be taken as the depreciation charge in both the fourth and fifth years so as to write off the entire cost. (It may be, of course, that there is no wish to write off the entire cost; the intention may be to depreciate down to an estimated salvage or scrap value. If such scrap or salvage value is expected to be approximately $75 or $80 for the asset in the example, there would be no need to change the method of depreciation.)

Sum-of-the-Year's-Digits Method. Another method of achieving successively smaller amounts of depreciation year by year is known as the *sum-of-the-year's-digits* method. This method is similar in effect to the declining-balance method, except that it results in complete depreciation of an asset at the end of its useful life. The write-off each year is based on a schedule of fractions obtained by listing the digits that comprise the estimated life of the asset and adding these digits to get the denominator for all of the fractions. The largest digit is used as the numerator for the first year, the next largest digit as the numerator for the second year, etc. For example, suppose that the estimated life of the asset is 5 years. $5 + 4 + 3 + 2 + 1 = 15$. Therefore, write off $5/15$ of the original cost the first year, $4/15$ the second year, $3/15$ the third year, etc. As applied to an asset costing $1,000, the results would be as follows:

YEAR	ANNUAL DEPRECIATION	ALLOWANCE FOR DEPRECIATION END OF YEAR	BOOK VALUE END OF YEAR
0			$1,000.00
1	$333.33	$333.33	666.67
2	266.67	600.00	400.00
3	200.00	800.00	200.00
4	133.33	933.33	66.67
5	66.67	1,000.00	0

This method likewise gained popularity when the Internal Revenue Act passed in 1954 specifically allowed its use in depreciating new assets acquired after December 31, 1953. A comparison of write-offs under this method with those obtained under the declining-balance method (see page 437) reveals that both methods will write off about $2/3$ of the cost of an asset during the first half of its estimated life.

PRACTICE ASSIGNMENT No. 33. Complete Report No. 33 in the workbook and submit your working papers to the instructor for approval. Then continue with the following study assignment until Report No. 34 is required.

(34) ACCOUNTING PROCEDURE

Fixed Asset Accounts and Records. The number of accounts for tangible fixed assets that will be kept in the general ledger and the nature and extent of any other fixed-asset records will depend upon the number of such assets, the type of information required by the management, and, in the case of all but land, the sort of depreciation procedure that is to be followed. If there are very few fixed assets, a separate account for each one with a related depreciation account (except for land, which is not subject to depreciation) can be kept in the general ledger. In such a case, the periodic depreciation for each one would be calculated and recorded separately.

If the business has a considerable number of depreciable fixed assets, it is likely that there will be relatively few accounts for them in the general ledger. Summary accounts will be kept for each major class of assets, such as one account for buildings, one for machinery and equipment, one for office furniture and equipment, one for delivery trucks, etc. Each of these summary accounts will have a related allowance for depreciation account. It is highly desirable that such summary accounts be supported by some sort of either supplementary or subsidiary records of the items that comprise the general ledger account totals. If depreciation is calculated on what is called the *unit basis* (meaning a separate calculation and record of depreciation for each unit), it is common practice to maintain a subsidiary record of each unit. Such records are commonly in the form of cards. Space is provided on the card to show the details about the asset including the cost of the unit (the entry being subsidiary to the debit in the general ledger asset account) and the amount of depreciation taken each period. (These entries are subsidiary to the credits in the general ledger allowance for depreciation accounts.) Space is also provided to record matters relating to the disposition of the asset. A typical fixed asset record card of this type is shown on page 440. Following is a narrative of the transactions that were recorded on the card:

January 7, 1955. Purchased Underwood Typewriter, No. 6200625, from the Office Supply Co., City, for $150.

December 31, 1955. Depreciation of typewriter at annual rate of 20 per cent, $30.

December 31, 1956. Depreciation of typewriter at annual rate of 20 per cent, $30.

July 1, 1957. Sold typewriter for $80 cash.

Before the sale of the typewriter on July 1, 1957 was recorded, the depreciation sustained for the half year, amounting to $15, was recorded by debiting Depreciation of Office Equipment and by crediting Allowance

FIXED ASSET RECORD

Description   Typewriter   Account   Office Equipment

Age when acquired New   Estimated life 4 years   Estimated salvage value $30   Rate of annual depreciation 20%

COST				DEPRECIATION RECORD			
Date Purchased	Description	Amount		Year	Rate	Amount		Total to date	
1955				19 55	20%	30	00	30	00
Jan. 7	Underwood Typewriter	150	00	19 56	20%	30	00	60	00
	#6200625			19 57	20%	15	00	75	00
	Office Supply Co.			19					
	City			19					
				19					
				19					
				19					
				19					
				19					
				19					
				19					

SOLD, EXCHANGED, OR DISCARDED						
Date	Explanation	Amount Realized	More than ✓ Less than	Book Value	Debit Allowance	
1957						
July 1	Sold	80 00	✓	5 00	75 00	

Fixed Asset Record

for Depreciation of Office Equipment. The amount of this depreciation was also entered on the record card. The sale was then recorded as indicated by the following general journal entry:

Bank..	$80.00	
Allowance for Depreciation of Office Equipment.............	75.00	
Office Equipment.......................................		$150.00
Gain on Sale of Office Equipment.......................		5.00
Sold Underwood typewriter #6200625.		

The sale was also entered on the record card, after which the card was transferred from a file of assets owned to a file of assets sold, exchanged, or discarded. Such an asset record, when properly kept, will provide all the information needed in claiming the proper amount of depreciation of fixed assets as a deduction from gross income in the annual income tax returns. The gain resulting from the sale of the typewriter for $5 more than its book value represents taxable income, which must be reported in the income tax return for the year in which the sale was made.

In some accounting systems, no effort is made to calculate separately the periodic depreciation on each unit. Instead, depreciation is calculated by groups of assets. The grouping is usually by similar types of assets and similarity of average length of life. If this procedure is followed, there will be relatively few summary asset and related allowance for depreciation accounts in the general ledger, and there are not likely to be very extensive subsidiary records. No record is kept of the periodic depreciation on each unit; depreciation is calculated for each group as a whole, using an average or composite rate. Even if the group procedure is followed, however, it is desirable to have some sort of an individual record for each asset that will show its acquisition date, cost, location, and date and nature of disposition.

Recording Depreciation. It has been seen that depreciation usually is recorded at the end of the period along with other necessary adjusting entries. One or more depreciation expense accounts may be debited, and one or more allowance for depreciation accounts may be credited. The number of each of these accounts that will be used will depend upon the degree of detail that is desired in the general ledger accounts and for the periodic statements. Usually there is one depreciation expense account for each major type of asset, such as Depreciation of Buildings, Depreciation of Furniture and Fixtures, Depreciation of Delivery Equipment, etc. A business that classifies expenses on a departmental basis may use a considerable number of depreciation expense accounts.

In the normal course of events, the only entries in the allowance for depreciation accounts are those made at the end of each period to record the depreciation for the period then ended. When some disposition is made of a depreciable asset, however, such as its sale, exchange, retirement, or destruction by fire, depreciation should be recorded for the interval between the date of the last regular adjustment of the accounts and the date of the disposition of the asset, usually to the nearest full month. The entry to record the disposition will include a credit to the asset account for the cost of the asset and a debit to the related allowance for depreciation account for the amount of the recorded depreciation on the asset.

Disposition of Fixed Assets. A fixed asset may be disposed of in any one of the following ways:

(a) It may be discarded or retired.
(b) It may be sold.
(c) It may be exchanged or traded in for property of like kind or for other property.

Discarding or Retiring Fixed Assets. A fixed asset may be discarded or retired whether or not it has been fully depreciated. If it has been fully depreciated, no gain or loss will be sustained. If it has not been fully depreciated, the book value of the discarded asset will represent a loss. Such a loss may be the result of underestimating the depreciation of the asset for the period of time that it has been in use, or it may be the result of obsolescence. Often it is better to scrap an obsolete machine and to buy a new one even though a loss is sustained on the old machine.

On July 16, Bryant & Wood discarded parcel-post scales that had no exchange or sale value. The fixed asset record indicated that the scales originally cost $80 and that depreciation amounting to a total of $60 had been recorded as a credit to the allowance for depreciation of store equipment account.

This transaction involved a loss of $20 resulting from the discard of the asset, which had a book value of $20. The transaction should be recorded as indicated by the following general journal entry:

Loss on Discarded Store Equipment......................	$20.00	
Allowance for Depreciation of Store Equipment..............	60.00	
Store Equipment..		$80.00
Discarded parcel-post scales.		

When this entry is posted, the debit of $60 to the allowance account and the credit of $80 to the store equipment account will have the effect of eliminating the parcel-post scales from the balances of these accounts. The debit of $20 to Loss on Discarded Store Equipment records the loss sustained.

When a fixed asset is discarded after it has been fully depreciated, no gain or loss will result from the transaction, but the discarded asset should be eliminated from the account balances by debiting the allowance account and by crediting the asset account for the original cost of the asset.

Selling Fixed Assets. If a fixed asset is sold, it is necessary to know its book value before the proper amount of any gain or loss resulting from the transaction can be determined. The book value of an asset is the difference between its cost and the amount of depreciation recorded. Thus, if an adding machine that cost $150 depreciates at the rate of 10 per cent a year and the annual depreciation is recorded by debiting Depreciation of Office Equipment and by crediting Allowance for Depreciation of Office Equipment, the book value of the adding machine at the end of three years will be $105, the difference between the cost price of the adding machine and the credit balance of the allowance account. When a fixed asset is sold at its book value, no gain or loss results from the transaction; when it is sold for more than its book value, the difference represents a gain; when it is sold for less than its book value, the difference represents a loss.

Assuming that the adding machine was sold at the end of three years for $110 cash, the transaction should be recorded as indicated by the following general journal entry:

Bank..	$110.00	
Allowance for Depreciation of Office Equipment............	45.00	
Office Equipment.......................................		$150.00
Gain on Sale of Office Equipment.......................		5.00
Sold adding machine.		

When this entry is posted, the debit of $45 to the allowance account will offset the amount recorded previously as a credit to the allowance account because of the estimated depreciation of the adding machine over a period of three years. The amount credited to Office Equipment will offset the purchase price previously recorded as a debit to Office Equipment. These entries have the effect of completely eliminating the old adding machine from the office equipment and allowance accounts. The gain realized from the sale of the adding machine for $5 more than its book value is recorded as gain on sale of office equipment. This gain should be listed under the heading of "Other Income" in the income statement and must be included in gross income in the income tax return.

If the adding machine referred to on the preceding page was sold at the end of three years for $100 instead of $110, there would be a loss of $5 instead of a gain of $5. The transaction should be recorded as indicated by the following general journal entry:

Bank..	$100.00	
Allowance for Depreciation of Office Equipment............	45.00	
Loss on Sale of Office Equipment........................	5.00	
Office Equipment.....................................		$150.00
Sold adding machine.		

When this entry is posted, the debit of $45 to the allowance account and the credit of $150 to the office equipment account will eliminate the old adding machine from the account balances. The loss resulting from the sale of the old adding machine for $5 less than its book value will be recorded as a loss on sale of office equipment. This loss should be listed under the heading of "Other Charges" in the income statement and may be claimed as a deduction from gross income in the income tax return.

Exchange of Fixed Assets. A fixed asset may be exchanged or traded in for property of like kind or for other property. The *exchange allowance* may be equal to the book value of the property exchanged or it may be more or less than the book value. The federal income tax law should be taken into consideration in recording transactions involving exchanges of property held for productive use in trade or business or held for investment. The following is quoted from the income tax regulations:

"No gain or loss is recognized if (1) a taxpayer exchanges property held for productive use in his trade or business, together with cash, for other property of like kind for the same use, such as a truck for a new truck or a passenger automobile for a new passenger automobile to be used for a like purpose, or (2) a taxpayer who is not a dealer in real estate exchanges city real estate for a ranch or farm, or improved real estate for unimproved real estate, or (3) a taxpayer exchanges investment property and cash for investment property of a like kind."

To avoid confusion in preparing income tax returns and to eliminate the need for making adjustments in computing the taxable income, it is generally deemed advisable to record transactions involving exchanges of property in such a manner as to conform to the income tax regulations.

Regardless of the amount of the allowance received for old property exchanged for new property of like kind, the new property acquired should be recorded at cost. To find the cost, it is necessary to take into consideration (a) the book value of the old property given in exchange plus (b) the amount paid in cash or to be paid in cash.

A delivery truck costing $2,800 was charged to a delivery equipment account and depreciation amounting to $840 was credited to an allowance account each year for three years. The book value of the truck after three years was $280 as shown by the following computation:

Cost of truck...	$2,800.00
Less amount charged off as depreciation.......................	2,520.00
Book value..	$ 280.00

If this truck is traded in on a new truck to be used for a similar purpose and $2,400 is paid in cash, the cost of the new truck is $2,680 ($2,400 + $280). This transaction should be recorded as indicated in the following general journal entry:

Delivery Equipment (new truck)........................	$2,680.00	
Allowance for Depreciation of Delivery Equipment.......	2,520.00	
Delivery Equipment (old truck).....................		$2,800.00
Bank..		2,400.00
Purchased a new truck.		

When this journal entry is posted, the cost of the old truck will be eliminated from the delivery equipment account and that account will be charged for the cost of the new truck, which constitutes the basis for future depreciation charges. The amount of the depreciation of the old truck will also be eliminated from the allowance account. It will be seen that no gain or loss was recognized in recording the transaction; hence, the method of accounting conforms to the income tax regulations.

Some accountants prefer to take into consideration the amount of the exchange allowance rather than the book value of an asset given in exchange in determining the cost of the new asset acquired. However, if this practice is followed, it will be necessary to adjust the accounts in preparing the annual income tax return. These adjustments can become quite complicated where there are frequent transactions involving the exchange of fixed assets. It is, therefore, generally preferable from a practical standpoint to follow the income tax regulations in recording such transactions.

In any transaction involving an exchange in which property is exchanged for property not of like kind, any gain or loss resulting from the transaction should be recorded, since it must be taken into consideration in preparing the income tax return. Any gain resulting from such an exchange is taxable and must be reported; any loss sustained may be claimed as a deduction.

A typewriter costing $150 was charged to an office equipment account and depreciation on the typewriter amounting to $30 was credited to an allowance account each year for two years. At the end of two years the typewriter was traded in on a new cash register costing $400. The trade-in allowance amounted to $115, the balance being paid in cash. Since this transaction did not involve an exchange of property for other property of like kind, any gain realized or loss sustained will be recognized for income tax purposes; hence, it should be recorded in the same manner as it would be if the typewriter had been sold for $115 and the proceeds applied on the purchase of the new cash register. The transaction should therefore be recorded as indicated in the following general journal entry:

Store Equipment..	$400.00	
Allowance for Depreciation of Office Equipment............	60.00	
Office Equipment.....................................		$150.00
Bank..		285.00
Gain on Sale of Office Equipment......................		25.00
Purchased a new cash register.		

When this entry is posted, the debit of $60 to the allowance account will offset the amount recorded previously as a credit to the allowance account because of the estimated depreciation of the typewriter over a period of two years. The amount credited to Office Equipment will offset the purchase price of the typewriter previously recorded as a debit to Office Equipment. These entries have the effect of completely eliminating the old typewriter from the office equipment and allowance accounts. The gain realized on the old typewriter is recorded as a gain on sale of office equipment. Had the trade-in allowance been less than the book value of the typewriter, the difference would represent a loss that should be charged to Loss on Sale of Office Equipment.

Fully Depreciated Fixed Assets. A fixed asset is said to be fully depreciated when the recorded depreciation is equal to the cost of the asset less its scrap or salvage value, if any. When an asset is fully depreciated, no further depreciation should be recorded. Since the rate of depreciation is based on its estimated useful life, an asset may be continued in use after it is fully depreciated. In this case, the cost of the asset and an equal amount in the allowance for depreciation are usually retained in the accounts, although some accountants prefer to adjust the accounts when a fixed asset has been fully depreciated so as to remove the cost of the asset and the total amount of depreciation from the accounts. This adjustment should be made when a fully depreciated asset is scrapped. The adjustment involves a debit to the proper allowance account and a credit to the proper fixed asset account for the cost of the asset.

In some states a taxable value is placed on a fully depreciated fixed asset if the asset is continued in use. Under such circumstances, the taxable value of the fully depreciated asset should be stated in the fixed asset record as a guide in preparing the property tax schedule. The taxable values of fully depreciated fixed assets and the book value of other fixed assets should be listed so that the total taxable value of the fixed assets may be ascertained.

Depreciation in the Statements. Most accountants and businessmen consider depreciation to be an operating expense and so classify it in the income statement. There may be as much subclassification as the management desires. Depreciation of delivery equipment, for example, may be classed as a selling expense, while depreciation of office furniture and equipment may be classed as an office or general administrative expense.

In view of the close relationship between fixed asset accounts and their allowance for depreciation, the preferred practice in the preparation of balance sheets is to show the amount of the allowance as a deduction from the cost of the asset. The difference, representing book value, is extended to be included in the asset total.

Allowance for depreciation, like allowances for bad debts, are sometimes called asset valuation accounts. An allowance for depreciation, however, only values the asset in a very limited and remote sense. The difference between the cost of the asset and the balance of the depreciation allowance account is not expected to have any relation to the market value of the asset. Such assets are not intended for sale. What they might bring, if sold, is usually of no consequence. Those who understand accounting interpret the difference between the gross amount of the assets and the related allowances for depreciation as being simply costs not yet charged to operations. Some companies are using this or a similar phrase in their balance sheets.

PRACTICE ASSIGNMENT No. 34. Complete Report No. 34 in the workbook and submit your working papers to the instructor for approval. Then continue with the next study assignment in Unit Seventeen until Report No. 35 is required.

Unit Seventeen

ACCOUNTING
FOR A WHOLESALE MERCHANT

(35) APPLICATION OF ACCOUNTING PRINCIPLES

In a wholesale merchandising enterprise, the merchandise handled is usually purchased directly from the manufacturers, importers, or producers, and is sold to retailers and distributors, who in turn sell to consumers at retail prices. The wholesaler usually buys in large quantities and has storage facilities to enable him to carry a large stock of merchandise from which he may supply his customers in the desired quantities. The wholesaler may purchase the goods he handles for cash or on credit and, likewise, he may sell the goods for cash or on credit. A large percentage of the wholesale business is on a credit basis.

The books of account and the auxiliary records of a wholesale merchant will vary depending upon a number of factors, such as the following:

- (a) Type of business organization.
- (b) Nature of the business.
- (c) Volume of business.
- (d) Office equipment.
- (e) Information desired on the part of the management and others concerned with the operation of the business.

Type of Business Organization. A wholesale merchandising enterprise may be conducted as a sole proprietorship, a partnership, or a corporation. So far as the sole proprietorship and the partnership forms of organization are concerned, there are no distinctive records to be kept. Under the corporate form of organization, certain corporate records, such as a minute book, a stock certificate record, and a stockholders' ledger, may be kept. The type of organization will usually affect the chart of accounts also. In the case of a sole proprietorship, it may be necessary to keep two accounts for the proprietor — one for recording his capital and the other for recording his personal transactions. In the case of a partnership, it is necessary to keep separate accounts for each partner. In the case of a corporation, it is necessary to keep separate accounts for capital stock, retained earnings, and dividends payable.

447

Nature of the Business. The system of accounts may vary considerably, depending upon the nature of the business enterprise; for example, the transactions of a mercantile enterprise may be quite different from the transactions of a service enterprise. The sources of income and the types of expenses incurred may vary with the nature of the business. Some businesses are of such a nature that it is advisable to keep the accounts on a departmental basis in order that the results of operating each department may be ascertained. In some businesses it is customary to buy and sell for cash only; in some it is customary to buy and sell for both cash and on credit; and in others it may be customary to sell on the installment basis. The accounts of a mercantile enterprise selling on the installment basis may be kept on either the usual accrual basis or the installment basis.

Volume of Business. The size of a firm and the volume of its business are important factors in determining the extent to which the records and the accounts should be subdivided. Obviously, the records and the accounts of a firm doing a million-dollar business annually will vary considerably from those of a firm doing a $50,000 business. In a big business with numerous departments, there will be a demand for more statistical information and a greater need for adequate control.

In most cases there is a fairly direct relationship between the size of a business and the number of persons engaged in keeping its accounting records. When several persons are required, the work must be divided in some logical fashion. Generally, this means that a separate record or book of original entry will be kept for each major type of business transaction, and that the books of final entry (the ledgers) will be subdivided. For example, a journal may be provided to record purchases, another journal to record sales, another to record cash receipts, another to record checks drawn, and a general journal to record transactions that cannot be recorded in special journals. It is likely that there will be one or more subsidiary ledgers to record the details about some of the elements that are shown in summary in certain of the general ledger accounts. Each employee engaged in accounting activity will specialize in keeping one of these records.

A functional division of the accounting has the following advantages:

(a) Provides for a better internal check and control.

(b) Makes possible an equitable distribution of work among several employees.

(c) Provides for a more detailed classification of transactions in the books of original entry.

(d) Facilitates summary posting periodically to the general ledger.

Office Equipment.   The accounting system is certain to be affected by the use of various types of office machines.   In recent years there has been a great expansion in the use of various types of accounting, calculating, and other office machines.   In the modern office of a big business enterprise, it is not uncommon in these times to find a large share of the accounting work being done with the aid of mechanical devices, including posting machines, electric accounting machines, and photographic equipment.   Many large companies are using electronic data-processing equipment.

Regardless of the extent to which machines are used in the accounting department, the fundamental principles involved in keeping the accounts continue to apply.   A knowledge of accounting theory on the part of those employed in the accounting department is just as essential as if no machines were used.

Information Desired.   The accounting system must be designed to provide the management and others concerned with the operation of a business with the desired information.   The management not only will wish to know where the business stands financially from time to time, but also will surely want to know the results of operations over given periods of time.   The accounting department may be required to supply much information of a statistical nature as well as the usual accounting reports.   For example, the manager of the purchasing department may expect the accounting department to keep detailed stock records of all merchandise handled.   The accounts must be kept so as to provide all the information needed for all the various tax reports required by the federal, state, and local governments.   In recent years there has been a tremendous increase in the number of tax reports and in the amount of tax information that must be furnished.   Many large firms have found it necessary to organize a tax accounting department separate from the general accounting department.   The work of the tax accounting department may be confined to the handling of federal and state social security tax reports, or the scope of its work may be extended to all tax reports including income taxes, sales taxes, excise taxes, property taxes, corporation franchise taxes, etc.

Application of Principles.   Bryant & Wood are partners conducting a wholesale automobile accessory business.   The merchandise handled consists of (a) tires and tubes and (b) radios and batteries.   The merchandise is purchased from various manufacturers and producers and is sold to local dealers and distributors.   Most of the merchandise is purchased on credit, but occasionally goods may be purchased for cash.   The merchandise is sold both for cash and on credit. On credit purchases the terms may vary considerably. Most of the firms from whom Bryant & Wood buy allow discounts ranging from 1 to 3 per cent for cash in from 10 to 30 days. On credit sales the terms usually are 2 per cent discount for cash in 10 days, net 30 days.

The records maintained by Bryant & Wood consist of the following:

(a) Books of original entry
  (1) Invoice record
  (2) Sales record
  (3) Record of cash receipts
  (4) Record of checks drawn
  (5) General journal

(b) Books of final entry
  (1) General ledger
  (2) Accounts receivable ledger
  (3) Accounts payable ledger
  (4) Operating expense ledger

(c) Auxiliary records
  (1) Petty cash disbursements record
  (2) Stock record
  (3) Fixed asset record
  (4) Notes receivable register
  (5) Insurance policy register
  (6) Daily bank statement

Invoice Record. A comparison of Bryant & Wood's invoice record reproduced on page 470 with the invoice record reproduced on page 365 will reveal that they are identical. This form of invoice record was described in detail in Unit Thirteen.

Sales Record. A comparison of Bryant & Wood's sales record reproduced on page 471 with the sales record reproduced on page 389 will reveal that they are identical. This form of sales record was described in detail in Unit Fourteen.

Record of Cash Receipts. Bryant & Wood keep a columnar record of cash receipts. Reference to the record of cash receipts reproduced on page 472 will reveal that General Ledger Dr. and Cr. columns are provided. In addition, special amount columns are provided for (a) Sales Discount Dr., (b) Bank Dr., (c) Accounts Receivable Cr., and (d) Cash Sales, Depts. A and B, Cr. All cash and cash items received are recorded by debiting the bank account immediately. This practice is usually followed where it is the custom to deposit all cash receipts in a bank and to make all disbursements by check.

Proving the Record of Cash Receipts. The record of cash receipts may be footed and the footings may be proved daily or periodically by comparing the sum of the debit footings with the sum of the credit footings. When a page is filled, the amount columns should be footed, the footings should be proved, and the totals should be carried forward to the top of the next page. It is customary to start a month at the top of a new page.

Posting from the Record of Cash Receipts. Completing the posting from the record of cash receipts involves both individual posting and summary posting. Individual posting is required from the General Ledger Dr. and Cr. columns. This posting is usually done daily. As each item is posted, a check mark should be entered in the Check ($\sqrt{}$) column following the Amount column of the record of cash receipts; the initials "CR" and the page number of the record of cash receipts should be entered in the Folio column of the proper general ledger account preceding the amount posted.

The summary posting is usually completed at the end of each month and involves the following procedure:

(a) The total of the column headed Sales Discount should be posted to the debit of Sales Discount, Account No. 82, in the general ledger.

(b) The total of the column headed Bank should be posted to the debit of Liberty National Bank, Account No. 111, in the general ledger.

(c) The total of the column headed Accounts Receivable should be posted to the credit of Accounts Receivable, Account No. 133, in the general ledger.

(d) The total of the column headed Cash Sales, Dept. A, should be posted to the credit of Sales, Dept. A, Account No. 41, in the general ledger.

(e) The total of the column headed Cash Sales, Dept. B, should be posted to the credit of Sales, Dept. B, Account No. 42, in the general ledger.

As the total of each column is posted, the account number should be written immediately below the total in the record of cash receipts; the page number of the record of cash receipts should be entered in the Folio column of the proper general ledger account as a cross reference. A check mark should be placed below the totals of the General Ledger Dr. and Cr. columns to indicate that these totals need not be posted.

Record of Checks Drawn. Bryant & Wood keep a columnar record of checks drawn. Reference to the record of checks drawn reproduced on pages 473 and 474 will reveal that General Ledger Dr. and Cr. columns are provided. In addition, special amount columns are provided for (a) Operating Expenses Dr., (b) Accounts Payable Dr., (c) Purchases Discount Cr., and (d) Bank Cr.

Proving the Record of Checks Drawn. The record of checks drawn may be footed and the footings may be proved daily or periodically by comparing the sum of the debit footings with the sum of the credit footings. When a page is filled, the amount columns should be footed, the footings should be proved, and the totals should be carried forward to the top of the next page. It is customary to start a month at the top of a new page.

Posting from the Record of Checks Drawn. Completing the posting from the record of checks drawn involves both individual posting and summary posting. Individual posting is required from the General Ledger Dr. and Cr. columns. This posting is usually done daily. As each item is posted, a check mark should be entered in the Check ($\sqrt{}$) column following the Amount column of the record of checks drawn; the initials "CD" and the page number of the record of checks drawn should be entered in the Folio column of the ledger account preceding the amount posted.

Individual posting is also required from the Operating Expenses Dr. column. This posting is usually done daily. As each item is posted, a check mark should be entered in the Check ($\sqrt{}$) column following the Amount column of the record of checks drawn; the initials "CD" and the page number of the record of checks drawn should be entered in the Folio column of the proper operating expense ledger account preceding the amount posted.

The summary posting is usually completed at the end of each month and involves the following procedure:

(a) The total of the Operating Expenses Amount column should be posted to the debit of Operating Expenses, Account No. 61, in the general ledger.

(b) The total of the column headed Accounts Payable should be posted to the debit of Accounts Payable, Account No. 27, in the general ledger.

(c) The total of the column headed Purchases Discount should be posted to the credit of Purchases Discount, Account No. 72, in the general ledger.

(d) The total of the column headed Bank should be posted to the credit of Liberty National Bank, Account No. 111, in the general ledger.

As the total of each column is posted, the account number should be written immediately below the total in the record of checks drawn; the page number of the record of checks drawn should be entered in the Folio column of the proper general ledger account as a cross reference. A check mark should be placed below the totals of the General Ledger Dr. and Cr. columns to indicate that these totals need not be posted.

General Journal. Bryant & Wood use a columnar general journal. Reference to the general journal reproduced on page 475 will reveal that General Ledger Dr. and Cr. columns are provided. In addition, special amount columns are provided for (a) Operating Expenses Dr., (b) Accounts Payable Dr., (c) Accounts Payable Cr., and (d) Accounts Receivable Cr. The general journal is used for recording all transactions that cannot be recorded in the special journals. It is also used for recording the adjusting, closing, and reversing entries.

Proving the General Journal. The general journal may be footed and the footings may be proved daily or periodically by comparing the sum of the debit footings with the sum of the credit footings. When a page is filled, the amount columns should be footed, the footing should be proved, and the totals should be carried forward to the top of the next page. It is customary to start a month at the top of a new page.

Posting from the General Journal. Completing the posting from the general journal involves both individual posting and summary posting. Individual posting is required from the General Ledger Dr. and Cr. columns. This posting is usually done daily. As each item is posted, a check mark should be entered in the Check ($\sqrt{}$) column following the Amount column of the general journal; the initials "GJ" and the page number of the general journal should be entered in the Folio column of the proper general ledger account preceding the amount posted.

Individual posting is also required from the Operating Expenses Dr. column. As each item is posted, a check mark should be entered in the Check ($\sqrt{}$) column following the Amount column of the general journal; the initials "GJ" and the page number of the general journal should be entered in the Folio column of the proper operating expense ledger account preceding the amount posted.

The summary posting is usually completed at the end of each month and involves the following procedure:

(a) The total of the Operating Expenses Amount column should be posted to the debit of Operating Expenses, Account No. 61, in the general ledger.

(b) The total of the debit column headed Accounts Payable should be posted to the debit of Accounts Payable, Account No. 27, in the general ledger.

(c) The total of the credit column headed Accounts Payable should be posted to the credit of Accounts Payable, Account No. 27, in the general ledger.

(d) The total of the column headed Accounts Receivable should be posted to the credit of Accounts Receivable, Account No. 133, in the general ledger.

As the total of each column is posted, the account number should be written immediately below the total in the general journal; the page number of the general journal should be entered in the Folio column of the proper general ledger account as a cross reference. A check mark should be placed below the totals of the General Ledger Dr. and Cr. columns to indicate that these totals need not be posted.

General Ledger. Bryant & Wood use a general ledger containing standard ledger ruled paper. The accounts are arranged in this ledger in numerical order. A chart of the accounts is reproduced on page 455. It will be noted that the accounts are numbered and classified. It will also be noted that the account for charitable contributions is classified as one of the "Other Expenses" (nonoperating), while in the chart of accounts for The Mann Furniture Store it is classified as one of the "Operating Expenses" (see page 141). There is a difference of opinion among accountants as to which is the preferred classification of charitable contributions.

All posting to the general ledger accounts is done from the books of original entry. As each item is posted, the page of the journal from which it is posted is entered in the Folio column of the account.

Accounts Receivable Ledger. Bryant & Wood use an accounts receivable ledger containing balance-column ledger ruled paper. The accounts are arranged in this ledger in alphabetic order. A control account for accounts receivable (Account No. 133) is kept in the general ledger. At the end of each month it is customary to prepare a schedule of the accounts receivable, the total of which should be the same as the balance of the accounts receivable control account.

Posting to the customers' accounts in the accounts receivable ledger may be done either from the books of original entry or directly from

BRYANT & WOOD

CHART OF GENERAL LEDGER ACCOUNTS

I Assets

  11 Cash
    111 Liberty National Bank
    112 Petty Cash Fund
  12 Government Bonds

  13 Receivables
    131 Notes Receivable
    132 Accrued Interest Receivable
    133 Accounts Receivable
      013 Allowance for Bad Debts
  14 Mdse. Inventory, Dept. A
  15 Mdse. Inventory, Dept. B

  16 Supplies and Prepayments
    161 Store Supplies
    162 Advertising Supplies
    163 Office Supplies
    164 Postage Stamps
    165 Prepaid Insurance
    166 Prepaid Federal Excise Tax
  17 Store Equipment
    017 Allow. for Depr. of Store Equipment
  18 Delivery Equipment
    018 Allow. for Depr. of Delivery Equipment
  19 Office Equipment
    019 Allow. for Depr. of Office Equipment

II Liabilities

  21 F.I.C.A. Taxes Payable
  22 F.U.T.A. Taxes Payable
  23 State U. C. Taxes Payable
  24 Employees' Income Taxes Payable
  25 Notes Payable
  26 Accrued Interest Payable
  27 Accounts Payable
  28 Accrued Property Taxes Payable

III Proprietorship

  31 J. A. Bryant, Partner
  311 J. A. Bryant, Drawing
  32 W. L. Wood, Partner
  321 W. L. Wood, Drawing
  33 Income Summary

IV Income from Sales

  41 Sales, Dept. A
    041 Sales R. & A., Dept. A
  42 Sales, Dept. B
    042 Sales R. & A., Dept. B

V Cost of Sales

  51 Purchases, Dept. A
    051 Purchases R. & A., Dept. A
  52 Purchases, Dept. B
    052 Purchases R. & A., Dept. B
  53 Transportation In, Dept. A
  54 Transportation In, Dept. B
  55 Cost of Goods Sold, Dept. A
  56 Cost of Goods Sold, Dept. B

VI Operating Expenses

  61 Operating Expenses

VII Other Income

  71 Interest Income
  72 Purchases Discount

VIII Other Expenses

  81 Interest Expense
  82 Sales Discount
  83 Charitable Contributions
  84 Collection Expense

Note: Items in italics represent headings and not account titles.

vouchers or other documents that represent the transactions. The accountant for Bryant & Wood follows the latter practice.

Accounts Payable Ledger. Bryant & Wood use an accounts payable ledger containing balance-column ledger ruled paper. The accounts are arranged in this ledger in alphabetic order. A control account for accounts payable (Account No. 27) is kept in the general ledger. At the end of each month it is customary to prepare a schedule of the accounts payable, the total of which should be the same as the balance of the accounts payable control account.

Posting to creditors' accounts in the accounts payable ledger may be done either from the books of original entry or directly from vouchers or other documents that represent the transactions. The accountant for Bryant & Wood follows the latter practice.

Operating Expense Ledger. Bryant & Wood use an operating expense ledger containing balance-column ledger ruled paper. The accounts are arranged in this ledger in numerical order. A chart of the accounts follows:

BRYANT & WOOD

Chart of Operating Expense Ledger Accounts

Selling Expenses
- 611 Advertising Expense
- 612 Salaries of Store Clerks
- 613 Wages of Truck Driver
- 614 W. L. Wood, Salary
- 615 W. L. Wood, Traveling Exp.
- 616 Gas and Oil for Truck
- 617 Repairs on Truck
- 618 Garage Rent
- 619 Transportation Out
- 620 Expired Insurance on Mdse.
- 621 Expired Ins. on Del. Equip.
- 622 Expired Ins. on Store Equip.
- 623 Store Supplies Consumed
- 624 Postage
- 625 Depreciation of Store Equip.
- 626 Depreciation of Del. Equip.
- 627 Miscellaneous Selling Expense

Administrative Expenses
- 631 Rent
- 632 J. A. Bryant, Salary
- 633 Office Salaries
- 634 Light and Water
- 635 Telephone and Telegrams
- 636 Bad Debts Expense
- 637 Property Taxes
- 638 Office Supplies Consumed
- 639 Postage
- 640 Expired Ins. on Office Equip.
- 641 Depreciation of Office Equip.
- 642 Social Security Taxes
- 643 Miscellaneous Gen. Expense

A control account for operating expenses (Account No. 61) is kept in the general ledger. At the end of each month, after any needed adjustments in the operating expense accounts are made, it is customary to prepare a schedule of the operating expenses. The total of this schedule should be the same as the balance of the operating expense control account.

All posting to the operating expense accounts is done from the books of original entry. As each item is posted, the page of the journal from which it is posted is entered in the Folio column of the account.

Auxiliary Records. Bryant & Wood keep certain auxiliary records, including a petty cash disbursements record, a stock record, a fixed asset record, a notes receivable register, an insurance policy register, and a daily bank statement. The form of the petty cash disbursements record is similar to that shown on page 116. Their record of petty cash disbursements for May is reproduced on page 476. The form of the fixed asset record is not shown. Since Bryant & Wood use the group method of depreciation accounting, the fixed asset record does not show the periodic depreciation on each unit. The form of the notes receivable register is similar to that shown on pages 332 and 333. The form of the insurance policy register is similar to that shown on pages 424 and 425.

Stock Record. Bryant & Wood keep a stock record as a means of control and as an aid to good business management. Many merchants follow a practice of having financial statements prepared monthly even though the accounts may be kept on the basis of an annual accounting period. Usually it is impractical to take a physical inventory monthly; hence, a merchant may rely on his stock record for ascertaining the inventories needed for monthly statements. Even though a stock record or perpetual inventory is kept, it is advisable to take a physical inventory at the end of each year, at which time the stock records should be adjusted for any discrepancies that may be found to exist.

One form of stock record is shown below. The information needed in keeping such a record is obtained from the purchase invoices, sales invoices, charge-back invoices, and credit memorandums. In recording receipts,

STOCK RECORD									
DATE	INV. NO.	RECEIVED	ISSUED	BALANCE	DATE	INV. NO.	RECEIVED	ISSUED	BALANCE
19— Apr.1				50					
5	S810		2	48					
11	S811		7	41					
15	S812		3	38					
18	P89	12		50					
20	Cm23	2		52					
25	S813		25	27					
26	S814		7	20					
27	CB14		4	16					
28	P90	24		40					
30	Totals	38	48	40					

ARTICLE	DESCRIPTION	MINIMUM	DEPT.
White–Black Tire	7.10-15 4-Ply	45	A

Stock Record

sales, returns, and balances, only quantities are entered. Minimum quantities are indicated and, whenever the quantity in stock reaches the minimum, the purchasing department is notified.

Daily Bank Statement. Bryant & Wood keep a daily record of banking transactions known as a daily bank statement. Their May statement is reproduced on page 477. It will be noted that in addition to providing amount columns for recording the total deposits each day, the total checks written each day, and the bank balance at the end of each day, provision is made for a monthly bank reconciliation. This statement eliminates the need for keeping a record of the bank balance on the stubs of the checkbook.

Checkbook. Bryant & Wood use a checkbook bound with three checks to a page with stubs attached. The purpose of the stubs is to provide spaces for recording the information needed in recording the checks in the record of checks drawn and in posting to the accounts with creditors in the accounts payable ledger.

Accounting Procedure. The accounts of Bryant & Wood are being kept on the basis of a fiscal year ending June 30. However, monthly work sheets are used to facilitate the preparation of monthly financial statements. The operating expense accounts are adjusted at the end of each month. No formal adjustment of income accounts and other expense accounts is made until June 30, the end of the fiscal year when the accounts are finally closed. The books of original entry, including the invoice record, the sales record, the record of cash receipts, the record of checks drawn, and the general journal, are reproduced in the illustrations on pages 470 to 475, inclusive. The only auxiliary records reproduced are the petty cash disbursements record, page 476, and the daily bank statement, page 477. The general and subsidiary ledgers are not reproduced. Following is a narrative of the May transactions that are shown recorded in the illustrations:

BRYANT & WOOD
WHOLESALE DEALERS IN AUTOMOBILE ACCESSORIES
NARRATIVE OF TRANSACTIONS

Monday, May 1

Issued Check No. 430 for $300 to H. H. Davids in payment of the May rent.

Received a check for $418.65 from W. O. Davenport in payment of our invoice of April 21 for $426.50, less 2% discount.

Before recording the check received from W. O. Davenport, it was reconciled by referring to his account in the accounts receivable ledger. The account showed that on April 21 he had been charged for merchandise amounting to $392.38 and for federal excise tax amounting to $34.12. A discount of 2% is allowed for cash in ten days, but of course the excise tax is not subject to any discount. The amount of his remittance was therefore verified in the following manner:

Merchandise sold...	$392.38
Less 2% discount...	7.85
	$384.53
Plus federal excise tax......................................	34.12
Net amount due...	$418.65

When the check was found to be for the proper amount, it was posted immediately to the credit of the account with W. O. Davenport in the accounts receivable ledger, the amount of the check, $418.65, being entered on one line and the amount of the discount, $7.85, being entered on the next line. The check was then entered in the record of cash receipts by debiting the bank account for the amount of the check, $418.65, by debiting Sales Discount for the amount of the discount, $7.85, and by crediting Accounts Receivable for the total of the invoice, $426.50. A check mark was placed in the Check ($\checkmark$) column following the amount entered in the Accounts Receivable column to indicate that the posting to W. O. Davenport's account had been completed.

Made charge sale as follows:

No. 815, W. O. Davenport, Jackson; tires and tubes, $148.76, federal excise tax, $12.94; radio and batteries, $84.20; express collect; terms, 2/10, n/30.

The information needed by the bookkeeper in recording each sale is obtained from a carbon copy of the sales invoice prepared by the billing clerk. As this invoice was entered in the sales record, a check mark was placed in the Check ($\checkmark$) column following the Accounts Receivable Dr. column to indicate that the invoice will be posted directly to the account of W. O. Davenport. The invoice was then posted to Mr. Davenport's account in the accounts receivable ledger, the amount of the merchandise sold, $232.96, being entered on one line and the amount of the federal excise tax, $12.94, being entered on the next line.

At the end of each day the total amount of any checks issued, the total amount of any deposits made during the day, and the bank balance at the end of the day are entered on the daily bank statement. Since this was the first day of May, the balance on April 30, amounting to $7,591.03, was brought forward to the top of a new page. The check issued on May 1, amounting to $300, was then entered on the daily bank statement and the new balance was extended.

Tuesday, May 2

Issued checks as follows:

No. 431, Standard Battery Co., $466.81, in payment of its invoice of April 24 for $481.25, less 3% discount.

No. 432, The Office Supply Co., $48.75, in full of account.

As these checks were entered in the record of checks drawn, check marks were placed in the Check ($\vee$) column following the amounts entered in the Accounts Payable Dr. column to indicate that the checks will be posted directly from the check stubs to the proper creditors' accounts in the accounts payable ledger. In posting to the account of the Standard Battery Co., the amount of the check, $466.81, was entered on one line and the amount of the discount, $14.44, was entered on the next line.

The total of the checks issued on May 2, amounting to $515.56, was entered on the daily bank statement and the balance was extended.

Wednesday, May 3

Received the following invoices:

The Cole Tire Co., Buffalo; tires and tubes, $368, federal excise tax, $36.40; terms, May 2 — 2/10, n/30; Big Four freight collect.

National Radio Mfg. Co., Philadelphia; radios, $167.50; terms, May 2 — 3/10, n/30; B. & O. freight collect.

Powers Printing Co., City; letterheads and envelopes, $23.25; terms, May 3 — n/30.

As these invoices were entered in the invoice record, check marks were placed in the Check ($\vee$) column following the Accounts Payable Cr. column to indicate that the invoices will be posted directly to the proper creditors' accounts in the accounts payable ledger. In posting the invoice received from The Cole Tire Co., the amount of the merchandise purchased, $368, was entered on one line and the amount of the federal excise tax, $36.40, was entered on the next line.

Thursday, May 4

Issued Check No. 433 for $674.61 to The Cole Tire Co. in payment of its invoice of April 25 for $687.40, less 2% discount.

Reference to the account of The Cole Tire Co. in the accounts payable ledger showed that on April 25 merchandise was purchased amounting to $639.28 on which the federal excise tax amounted to $48.12. The purchase price of the merchandise is subject to a discount of 2%, but of course the excise tax is not subject to discount. The amount of the check was computed as follows:

Merchandise purchased......................................	$639.28
Less 2% discount..	12.79
	$626.49
Plus federal excise tax..	48.12
Net amount due..	$674.61

In posting to the account of The Cole Tire Co., the amount of the check, $674.61, was entered on one line and the discount, $12.79, was entered on the next line.

Received the following invoices:

The Cole Tire Co., Buffalo; tires and tubes, $213.07, federal excise tax, $18.53; terms, May 3 — 2/10, n/30; shipped directly to Keiffer Garage, Kingston, freight collect.

Standard Battery Co., St. Louis; batteries, $180; terms, May 3 — 3/10, n/30; Big Four freight collect.

The Office Supply Co., City; office supplies, $26; terms, May 4 — n/30.

Bryant & Wood are agents for The Cole Tire Co.; however, they do not necessarily carry in stock the entire line of tires and tubes. When an order is received for items that are not carried in stock, an order is placed with the company with instructions to ship directly to the customer, transportation charges collect. After the invoice was recorded in the invoice record and was posted to the account of The Cole Tire Co. in the accounts payable ledger, the invoice was referred to the billing clerk with instructions to bill the Keiffer Garage.

Friday, May 5

Received a check for $448.41 from B. A. Fall in payment of merchandise sold him on April 26 amounting to $420.27, less 2% discount, plus federal excise tax, $36.55.

Made charge sales as follows:

No. 816, Service Tire Shop, City; tires, $172.65, federal excise tax, $13; terms, 2/10, n/30.

No. 817, C. J. Mead, Athens; tubes, $87.63, federal excise tax, $8.67; postage, 93 cents; terms, 2/10, n/30.

No. 818, Keiffer Garage, Kingston; tires, $319.79, federal excise tax, $27.81; terms, 2/10, n/30; shipped directly from factory, freight collect.

In entering Sales Invoice No. 817 in the sales record, the postage was charged to the customer's account and was credited to Postage Stamps, Account No. 164. In posting this invoice to the account of C. J. Mead in the accounts receivable ledger, the amount of the merchandise sold, $87.63, was entered on one line; the amount of the federal excise tax, $8.67, was entered on the next line; and the amount of the postage prepaid, 93 cents, was entered on the third line. The tires billed to the Keiffer Garage on Sales Invoice No. 818 are the ones that were shipped directly by The Cole Tire Co. on May 3 and for which an invoice was received on May 4.

Issued Check No. 434 for $697.53 to the National Radio Mfg. Co. in payment of its invoice of April 26 for $719.10, less 3% discount.

Saturday, May 6

Issued Credit Memorandum No. 24 to W. O. Davenport, $3.20, for one heavy-duty tube returned; tube, $2.88, federal excise tax, 32 cents.

The tube returned was billed on Sales Invoice No. 815. This transaction was recorded in the general journal, after which the credit memorandum was posted directly to the account of W. O. Davenport in the accounts receivable ledger, the credit for the tube, $2.88, being entered on one line and the credit for the tax, 32 cents, being entered on the next line.

Made the following cash sales:

No. 416, Grant Highway Garage, City; tires and tubes, $236.07, federal excise tax, $20.53.

No. 417, C. L. Nixon, Northumberland; tires, $145.36, federal excise tax, $10.94.

At the end of each day the carbon copies of the cash sales tickets are analyzed to ascertain the total sales by departments, after which an entry is made in the record of cash receipts debiting the Bank for the total amount of cash received and crediting Cash Sales by departments for the total sales made in each department and crediting Prepaid Federal Excise Tax for the total tax.

Issued the following checks:

No. 435, $25, payable to Postage. (Cashed the check at the bank and purchased $25 worth of stamps.)

No. 436, Rubber Chain Co., $153.02, in payment of its invoice of April 27 for $157.75, less 3% discount.

No. 437, The Cole Tire Co., $197.59, in payment of merchandise purchased April 27 amounting to $183.14, less 2% discount, plus federal excise tax, $18.11.

END-OF-THE-WEEK WORK

(a) Footed the amount columns in all the books of original entry and proved the footings.

(b) Deposited $1,279.96 in the Liberty National Bank and entered the amount on the daily bank statement.

(c) Proved the bank balance in the following manner:

Balance, May 1	$7,591.03
Total receipts for the week ended May 6 per record of cash receipts	1,279.96
Total	$8,870.99
Less total checks issued during the week ended May 6 per record of checks drawn	2,563.31
Balance, May 6	$6,307.68

(d) Completed the individual posting from the books of original entry to the general ledger and the operating expense ledger accounts.

Monday, May 8

Issued Credit Memorandum No. 25 to Allegeron Dairy, $5, for two tubes returned; tubes, $4.52, federal excise tax, 48 cents.

Received the following checks:

Wyatt & Son, $613.88, in payment of merchandise sold April 28 amounting to $596, less 2% discount, plus federal excise tax, $29.80.

Allegeron Dairy, $349.10, in payment of merchandise sold April 10 for $321.25, plus federal excise tax, $27.85.

Made the following cash sales:

No. 418, R. L. Davids, Olean; batteries, $89.85; tires and tubes, $183.21, federal excise tax, $13.79; express collect.

No. 419, Kenton Garage, Kenton; tires, $90.95, federal excise tax, $6.85; called for.

Made petty cash disbursements as follows:

Typewriter repairs, $1.75. Voucher No. 56.
500 circular letters, $3.50. Voucher No. 57.

All disbursements from the petty cash fund are recorded in the petty cash disbursements record.

Issued Charge-back Invoice No. 15 to The Cole Tire Co., $34.46, for two tires returned for credit; tires purchased April 29, $31.70, federal excise tax, $2.76.

This transaction was recorded in the general journal, after which the charge-back invoice was posted directly to the account of The Cole Tire Co. in the accounts payable ledger, the charge for the tires, $31.70, being entered on one line, and the charge for the tax, $2.76, being entered on the next line.

Issued the following checks:

No. 438, The Cole Tire Co., $290.62, in payment of balance due on merchandise purchased April 29 for $275.76, less 2% discount, plus federal excise tax, $20.38.

In computing the amount of the check to be issued it was necessary to refer to the account of The Cole Tire Co. and make the following calculations:

Merchandise purchased April 29...............................		$307.46
Less merchandise returned for credit May 8....................		31.70
Amount subject to discount...................................		$275.76
Less discount @ 2%		5.52
		$270.24
Plus federal excise tax:		
Amount of tax charged on original purchase invoice.....	$23.14	
Less tax on tires returned May 8.....................	2.76	20.38
Net amount due...		$290.62

No. 439, National Radio Mfg. Co., $442.22, in payment of its invoice of April 28, $455.90, less 3% discount.

Tuesday, May 9

Received the following invoices:

Western Auto Supply Co., City; batteries, $21.50; terms, May 8 — 1/10, n/30; shipped to Union Garage, Uniontown, express collect.

The Cole Tire Co., Buffalo; tires and tubes, $517.96; federal excise tax, $45.04; terms, May 8 — 2/10, n/30; Big Four freight collect.

Office Equipment Co., City; calculator, $150; terms, May 9 — n/30.

Wednesday, May 10

Made charge sales as follows:

No. 819, Wade Garage, Gainesville; tires, $238.05, federal excise tax, $20.70; terms, 2/10, n/30; express collect.

No. 820, Courthouse Garage, Hamilton; radios and batteries, $362.80; tires, $200.38; federal excise tax, $17.42; terms, 2/10, n/30; express collect.

No. 821, B. A. Fall, Franklin; radio, $49.90; tires and tubes, $1,517.54, federal excise tax, $131.96; terms, 2/10, n/30; Pennsylvania freight collect.

No. 822, Union Garage, Uniontown; batteries, $26.50; terms, 2/10, n/30; shipped from factory, express collect.

The batteries billed to the Union Garage on Sales Invoice No. 822 are the ones that were shipped directly by the Western Auto Supply Co. on May 8 and for which an invoice was received on May 9.

Received a 30-day, 6% interest-bearing note (No. 164), dated May 9, for $750 from the Union Garage in temporary settlement of the balance due on its account May 1.

The note was recorded in the general journal and in the notes receivable register.

Issued Credit Memorandum No. 26 to the Service Tire Shop, $43.02, for two tires returned; tires, $40.26, federal excise tax, $2.76. Inasmuch as the tires were defective, they were returned immediately to The Cole Tire Co. for credit at cost, $34.46, Charge-back Invoice No. 16, tires purchased May 3, $31.70, federal excise tax, $2.76.

It will be noted that the Service Tire Shop was given credit for the wholesale price of the tires while The Cole Tire Co. was charged for the manufacturer's price.

Issued Check No. 440 to The Daily Post for $12.50 in payment of an advertisement in the Sunday edition of May 7.

Thursday, May 11

Issued Check No. 441 for $127.01 to the Liberty National Bank in payment of a dishonored check of the Four-Squares Garage, returned unpaid by the bank on which it was drawn with a notice stating the reason as "not sufficient funds."

The dishonored check was originally received in payment of sales invoice of April 19 for $129.60, less 2% discount. Bryant & Wood have arranged with the bank for all dishonored checks to be presented for reimbursement; hence, when the dishonored check of the Four-Squares Garage was presented, Mr. Bryant issued Check No. 441 in settlement and wrote A. L. Jinks, President of the Four-Squares Garage, advising him that his check of April 28 had been returned unpaid and that it had been charged back to his account.

Received the following invoices:

Powers Printing Co., City; 5M price lists, $37.50; terms, May 11 — n/30.

The Cole Tire Co., Buffalo; tires and tubes, $698.62, federal excise tax, $52.58; terms, May 10 — 2/10, n/30; Big Four freight collect.

General Auto Supply Co., Akron; tires, $207.58, federal excise tax, $15.62; terms, May 10 — 3/10, n/30; shipped directly to B. A. Fall, Franklin, freight collect.

Johnson Paper Co., City; wrapping paper, $19.50; terms, May 11 — n/30.

Western Auto Supply Co., City; batteries, $19.95; terms, May 10 — 1/10, n/30; shipped to Bishop & Wells, Marysville; express collect.

Issued the following checks:

No. 442, The Cole Tire Co., $397.04, in payment of merchandise purchased May 2 for $368, less 2% discount, plus federal excise tax, $36.40.

No. 443, National Radio Mfg. Co., $162.47, in payment of its invoice of May 2 for $167.50, less 3% discount.

Received a check for $238.10 from W. O. Davenport in payment of balance due on merchandise sold him May 1; merchandise, $230.08, less 2% discount, plus federal excise tax, $12.62.

Friday, May 12

Discounted the Union Garage note (No. 164) for $750 at the Liberty National Bank at 6% and deposited the proceeds amounting to $750.36.

This note was received on May 10. Two lines were required to record the transaction in the record of cash receipts.

Made charge sales as follows:

No. 823, Bishop & Wells, Marysville; tires, $67.53, federal excise tax, $5.87; batteries, $26.50; postage, $1.08; terms, 2/10, n/30. (The batteries were shipped directly from the factory, express collect.)

No. 824, Hope Street Garage, City; radio and batteries, $88.55; tubes, $52.78, federal excise tax, $5.22; terms, 2/10, n/30.

No. 825, B. A. Fall, Franklin; tires, $308.02; federal excise tax, $26.78; terms, 2/10, n/30; shipped directly from factory, freight collect.

No. 826, Byers Tire Shop, City; tires and tubes, $1,838.12, federal excise tax, $159.83; terms, 2/10, n/30.

Received the following checks:

Xenia Transfer Co., $357.90, in payment of our invoice of April 29, $365.20, less 2% discount.

Watson Auto Repair Co., $425.50, in full of account.

Made the following cash sales:

No. 420, J. R. Downey, El Paso; radio, $34.20; called for.

No. 421, R. L. Rockwell, Live Oak; tires, $290.72, federal excise tax, $21.88; express collect.

Issued the following checks:

No. 444, The Cole Tire Co., $227.34, in payment of merchandise purchased May 3 for $213.07, less 2% discount, plus federal excise tax, $18.53.

No. 445, Standard Battery Co., $174.60, in payment of its invoice of May 3, $180, less 3% discount.

No. 446, Mays Heater Co., $48.51, in payment of its invoice of April 14, $49.50, less 2% discount.

Saturday, May 13

Issued Check No. 447 for $118.48 to the Moore Oil Co. in payment of gasoline and oil supplied during April.

Paid $3.50 out of the petty cash fund for repairs on truck. Voucher No. 58.

Sent a corrected invoice to the Wade Garage, Gainesville, for $78.35; covering five tires at $14.55 each, plus federal excise tax, $1.12.

On Sales Invoice No. 805 dated April 25 the tires, through an error, were billed at $14.38 each, plus federal excise tax, $1.12.
In recording this transaction in the sales record, it was only necessary to debit Accounts Receivable and credit Sales, Dept. A, for 85 cents, which represented the increased amount of the corrected invoice.

END-OF-THE-WEEK WORK

(a) Footed the amount columns in all the books of original entry and the petty cash disbursements record and proved the footings.

(b) Deposited $2,715.93 in the Liberty National Bank.

(c) Proved the bank balance as follows:

Balance, May 1	$ 7,591.03
Total receipts for the period ended May 13 per record of cash receipts	4,746.25
Total...	$12,337.28
Less total checks issued during period ended May 13 per record of checks drawn...	4,564.10
Balance, May 13...	$ 7,773.18

(d) Completed the individual posting from the books of original entry to the general ledger and the operating expense ledger accounts.

Monday, May 15

Made petty cash disbursements as follows:
Water bill, $2.75. Voucher No. 59.
1M shipping tags, $3.50. Voucher No. 60.
100 sheets carbon paper, $1.50. Voucher No. 61.
Painting window sign, $2.50. Voucher No. 62.

Made the following cash sales:
No. 422, E. R. Early, City; tires and tubes, $77.56, federal excise tax, $5.84.

No. 423, J. L. Minor, Quincy; radios and batteries, $131.40; express collect.

Received the following checks:
Service Tire Shop, $139.98 in payment of balance due on merchandise sold May 5; merchandise, $132.39, less 2% discount, plus federal excise tax, $10.24.

C. J. Mead, $171.48, in full of account, less 2% discount on merchandise sold May 5 amounting to $87.63, plus federal excise tax, $8.67, and postage, 93 cents.

Keiffer Garage, $341.20, in payment of merchandise sold May 5 for $319.79, less 2% discount, plus federal excise tax, $27.81.

A. H. Day, $113.78, in full of account.

Central Garage, $269.42, to apply on account and a 60-day, 6% note (No. 165) for $500, dated May 15, in temporary settlement of the balance due.

After entering both the check and the note in the cash receipts record, they were posted immediately to the credit of the account of the Central Garage in the accounts receivable ledger. The amount of the check was entered on one line and the amount of the note on the next line.

Issued Check No. 448 for $224.40 to the Liberty National Bank, a U. S. depositary, in payment of the following taxes:

(a) Employees' income taxes (withheld during April)		$152.40
(b) F.I.C.A. taxes —		
On employees (withheld during April)	$36.00	
On the employer	36.00	72.00
Total		$224.40

Issued Check No. 449 payable to Payroll for $1,186.90.

Bryant & Wood follow the policy of paying their employees on the fifteenth and the last day of each month. They are subject to the taxes imposed under the Federal Social Security Law for both old-age insurance benefits and for unemployment purposes. They are also required to make contributions to the state unemployment compensation fund. They are required to withhold a percentage of their employees' wages for both old-age insurance benefits and for income tax purposes. In addition to the wages paid to employees, the partnership agreement provides that each partner is to receive a salary of

$400 a month, payable semimonthly. While the salaries of the partners constitute an operating expense of the business, they do not represent "wages" as defined in the social security and income tax laws; hence, such salaries are not subject to the F.I.C.A. taxes imposed upon employers and employees. Neither are such salaries subject to withholding for employees' income taxes.

On each payday the bookkeeper is supplied with a report prepared by the payroll clerk showing the total amount of wages and salaries earned during the pay period, the amount of the payroll deductions, and the net amount of cash needed for payroll purposes. The report for May 15 appears below.

A check made payable to Payroll was issued for the net amount payable. This check was then cashed at the Liberty National Bank and currency and coins in the right denominations needed to pay each employee were obtained. The bookkeeper was instructed by Messrs. Bryant and Wood to deposit their salaries in their individual bank accounts and to furnish them with duplicate copies of the deposit tickets.

The payroll check is entered in the record of checks drawn by debiting the proper salary accounts for the earnings, by crediting the proper liability accounts for the taxes withheld, and by crediting the bank account for the amount of the check issued. The payroll taxes imposed on the employer are recorded in the general journal by debiting Social Security Taxes and by crediting the proper liability accounts for the taxes imposed.

PAYROLL STATEMENT FOR PERIOD ENDED MAY 15

Classification	Total Earnings	Deductions		Net Amount Payable
		F.I.C.A. Taxes	Employees' Income Taxes	
Salaries of Store Clerks.....	440.00	8.80	39.90	391.30
Wages of Truck Driver........	100.00	2.00	3.20	94.80
Office Salaries.............	340.00	6.80	32.40	300.80
Partners' Salaries:				
J. A. Bryant...............	200.00	None	None	200.00
W. L. Wood.................	200.00	None	None	200.00
	1,280.00	17.60	75.50	1,186.90

Employer's payroll taxes:			
(a) F.I.C.A. taxes, 2% of $880..........................			$17.60
(b) Unemployment compensation taxes—			
State U.C. taxes, 2.7% of $880.......................		$23.76	
F.U.T.A. taxes, 3% of $880...................	$26.40		
Less credit for state taxes.................	23.76	2.64	26.40
Total...			$44.00

The waved lines appearing at this point in the books of original entry indicate omission of the transactions completed on the days between May 15 and 31.

Wednesday, May 31

Received the following invoices:

Western Auto Supply Co., City; battery, $12.80, express prepaid, $1.10; terms, May 31 — 1/10, n/30.

The Cole Tire Co., Buffalo; tires and tubes, $1,670.08, federal excise tax, $145.22; terms, May 29 — 2/10, n/30; Big Four freight collect.

Standard Battery Co., St. Louis; batteries, $518; terms, May 29 — 3/10, n/30; Big Four freight collect.

Office Equipment Co., City; one check writer, $35, less credit for exchange allowance on old check writer, $5; terms, May 29 — n/30.

The original cost of the old check writer was $25. Since the group method of accounting for depreciation is used, the allowance for depreciation account must be charged with the cost of the old check writer less the $5 trade-in allowance. This transaction was recorded in the invoice record by debiting Office Equipment, Account No. 19, for $35, the cost of the new check writer; by debiting Allowance for Depreciation of Office Equipment, Account No. 019, for $20, the difference between the cost and the trade-in allowance on the old check writer; by crediting Office Equipment, Account No. 19, for $25, the original cost of the old check writer; and by crediting Accounts Payable, Account No. 27, for $30, the balance due the Office Equipment Co.

Received cashier's check for $300.75 from the Evanston Bank, Evanston, in payment of Peters Garage note (No. 161) for $300 plus interest $1.50, less collection charges 75 cents.

Louis F. Dolle, attorney at law, advises that he is unable to collect the $25 owed by G. A. Wheeler and Mr. Bryant has instructed that the account be charged off.

After recording this transaction in the general journal by debiting Allowance for Bad Debts, Account No. 013, and by crediting Accounts Receivable, for $25, it was posted immediately as a credit to the account of G. A. Wheeler in the accounts receivable ledger.

Made charge sales as follows:

No. 850, W. M. Mason, City; radio, $37.95; terms, 2/10, n/30.

No. 851, Bond Service Station, Kingston; radio and batteries, $173.85; tires and tubes, $826.37, federal excise tax, $81.73; terms, 2/10, n/30; Pennsylvania freight collect.

No. 852, Courthouse Garage, Hamilton; radio and batteries, $73.70; tires and tubes, $450.86, federal excise tax, $33.94; terms, 2/10, n/30; shipped by prepaid express, $2.80.

It will be noted that the express prepaid on the merchandise sold to the Courthouse Garage at Hamilton was credited to Transportation Out, Account No. 619. Since this account is kept in the subsidiary operating expense ledger, it is also necessary to credit the freight to the general ledger control account for Operating Expenses, Account No. 61. The double posting is provided for by drawing a diagonal line throught the Acct. No. column.

Paid $2.80 out of the petty cash fund for express charges on merchandise shipped to the Courthouse Garage, Hamilton. Voucher No. 67.

Bishop & Wells have advised that the tires and tubes shipped directly from the factory on May 24 arrived by express collect, $2.75, whereas a delivered price had been quoted them. Mr. Bryant, therefore, directed that a credit memorandum (No. 29) should be issued to Bishop & Wells for the amount of the express charges.

This transaction was recorded in the general journal by debiting Transportation Out, Account No. 619, in the Operating Expense column, and by crediting Accounts Receivable for $2.75. The credit memorandum was also posted directly to the account of Bishop & Wells in the accounts receivable ledger.

Paid $4.75 out of the petty cash fund to A. B. Roberts who returned an imperfect tube purchased for cash on May 23, $4.46, federal excise tax, 29 cents (Sale No. 426). Voucher No. 68. As instructed by Mr. Bryant, the tube was returned to The Cole Tire Co. and the company was advised that its account had been charged for the cost price of the tube, $2.96, plus the federal excise tax, 29 cents. Charge-back Invoice No. 20.

In entering this transaction in the petty cash disbursements record, Sales Returns and Allowances, Dept. A, Account No. 041, was charged for the selling price of the tube, $4.46, and Prepaid Federal Excise Tax, Account No. 166, was charged for the amount of the tax, 29 cents. An entry was also made in the general journal to record the cost of the tube returned to The Cole Tire Co. In recording this transaction, Accounts Payable, Account No. 27, was debited for $3.25, Purchases Returns and Allowances, Dept. A, Account No. 051, was credited for $2.96 and Prepaid Federal Excise Tax, Account No. 166, was credited for 29 cents.

Issued the following checks:

No. 468, Citizens Garage, $20, in payment of May storage.

No. 469, Western Auto Supply Co., $20.79, in payment of its invoice of May 22, $21, less 1% discount.

No. 470, Hughes Transfer Co., $126.10, in payment of freight and drayage on incoming merchandise received during May.

According to Mr. Bryant's instructions, freight and drayage on incoming merchandise should be distributed on a basis of the value of the merchandise purchased for each department during the month. On this basis, Transportation In, Dept. A should be charged for $111.70 and Transportation In, Dept. B should be charged for $14.40.

Issued Check No. 471 payable to Payroll for $1,215.10.

PAYROLL STATEMENT FOR PERIOD ENDED MAY 31

CLASSIFICATION	TOTAL EARNINGS	DEDUCTIONS		NET AMOUNT PAYABLE
		F.I.C.A. TAXES	EMPLOYEES' INCOME TAXES	
Salaries of Store Clerks......	470.00	9.40	41.10	419.50
Wages of Truck Driver.........	100.00	2.00	3.20	94.80
Office Salaries..............	340.00	6.80	32.40	300.80
Partners' Salaries:				
J. A. Bryant................	200.00	None	None	200.00
W. L. Wood.................	200.00	None	None	200.00
	1,310.00	18.20	76.70	1,215.10

Employer's payroll taxes:
  (a) F.I.C.A. taxes, 2% of $910........................... $18.20
  (b) Unemployment compensation taxes—
      State U.C. taxes, 2.7% of $910...................... $24.57
      F.U.T.A. taxes, 3% of $910.................... $27.30
         Less credit for state taxes................ 24.57   2.73   27.30

    Total.. $45.50

Issued Check No. 472 for $34.45 payable to Petty Cash to replenish the petty cash fund.

The statement of the petty cash disbursements for May provides the information needed in recording the check in the record of checks drawn. This statement is reproduced at the top of page 478.

(Continued on page 478)

INVOICE RECORD FOR MONTH OF *May 19--*

Page 49

Dept. A	Dept. B	Federal Excise Tax	GL Amount (Dr)	GL Acct. No. (Dr)	√	Day	Date of Inv.	Inv. No.	Name	Accounts Payable	√	GL Amount (Cr)	GL Acct. No. (Cr)	√
									AMOUNTS FORWARDED					
368 00		36 40				3	5/2	91	The Cole Tire Co.	404 40	√			
	167 50					3	5/2	92	National Radio Mfg. Co.	167 50	√			
			23 25	163	√	3	5/3	93	Powers Printing Co.	23 25	√			
213 07		18 53				4	5/3	94	The Cole Tire Co.	231 60	√			
	180 00					4	5/3	95	Standard Battery Co.	180 00	√			
			26 00	163	√	4	5/4	96	The Office Supply Co.	26 00	√			
581 07	*347 50*	*54 93*	*49 25*							*1032 75*				
	21 50					9	5/8	97	Western Auto Sup. Co.	21 50	√			
517 96		45 04				9	5/8	98	The Cole Tire Co.	563 00	√			
			150 00	19	√	9	5/9	99	Office Equipment Co.	150 00	√			
			37 50	162	√	11	5/11	100	Powers Printing Co.	37 50	√			
698 62		52 58				11	5/10	101	The Cole Tire Co.	751 20	√			
207 58		15 62				11	5/10	102	General Auto Sup. Co.	223 20	√			
			19 50	161	√	11	5/11	103	Johnson Paper Co.	19 50	√			
	19 95					11	5/10	104	Western Auto Sup. Co.	19 95	√			
2005 23	*388 95*	*168 17*	*256 25*							*2818 60*				
	12 80		1 10	54	√	31	5/31	118	Western Auto Sup. Co.	13 90	√			
1670 08		145 22				31	5/29	119	The Cole Tire Co.	1815 30	√			
	518 00					31	5/29	120	Standard Battery Co.	518 00	√			
			35 00	19	√	31	5/29	121	Office Equipment Co.	30 00		25 00	19	√
			20 00	019										
8546 28	*1197 85*	*683 70*	*469 50*							*10872 33*		*25 00*		
8546 28	1197 85	683 70	469 50							1087233		25 00		
(51)	(52)	(166)	(√)							(27)		(√)		

SALES RECORD FOR MONTH OF *May* 19-- Page 57

Day	√	Accounts Receivable	Name	Sale No.	Dept. A	Dept. B	Federal Excise Tax	G.L. Acct. No.	G.L. Amount	√
			AMOUNTS FORWARDED							
1	√	245 90	W. O. Davenport	815	148 76	84 20	12 94			
5	√	185 65	Service Tire Shop	816	172 65		13 00	164	93	√
5	√	97 23	C. J. Mead	817	87 63		8 67			
5	√	347 60	Kieffer Garage	818	319 79		27 81			
		876 38			*728 83*	*84 20*			*93*	
10	√	258 75	Wade Garage	819	238 05		20 70			
10	√	580 60	Courthouse Garage	820	200 38	362 80	17 42			
10	√	1699 40	B. A. Fall	821	1517 54	49 90	131 96			
10	√	26 50	Union Garage	822		26 50				
12	√	100 98	Bishop & Wells	823	67 53	26 50	5 87	164	1 08	√
12	√	146 55	Hope St. Garage	824	52 78	88 55	5 22			
12	√	334 80	B. A. Fall	825	308 02		26 78			
12	√	1997 95	Byers Tire Shop	826	1838 12		159 83			
13	√	85	Wade Garage	805	85				2 01	√
		6022 76			*4952 10*	*638 45*	*430 20*			
31	√	37 95	W. M. Mason	850		37 95				
31	√	1081 95	Bond Service Station	851	826 37	173 85	81 73	61/619		
31	√	561 30	Courthouse Garage	852	450 86	73 70	33 94		2 80	√
		13687 35			*10555 09*	*2074 20*	*844 41*		*213 65*	
		13687 35			**10555 09**	**2074 20**	**844 41**		**213 65**	√
		(133)			(41)	(42)	(166)		(√)	

Page 78

RECORD OF CASH RECEIPTS FOR MONTH OF May 19—

Day	Received From—Description	Acct. No. (Dr)	General Ledger Amount (Dr)	√	Sales Discount	Bank Net Amount	Accounts Receivable	√	Cash Sales Dept. A	Cash Sales Dept. B	Acct. No. (Cr)	General Ledger Amount (Cr)	√
	AMOUNTS FORWARDED												
1	W. O. Davenport				7 85	418 65	426 50	√					
5	B. A. Fall				8 41	448 41	456 82	√					
6	Cash Sales					412 90			381 43		166	31 47	√
8	Wyatt & Son				11 92	613 88	625 80	√					
8	Allegeron Dairy					349 10	349 10	√					
8	Cash Sales					384 65			274 16	89 85	166	20 64	√
11	W. O. Davenport				4 60	238 10	242 70	√					
12	Bank — Note #164 disc.					750 36					131	750 00	√
12	Interest Income										71	36	√
12	Xenia Transfer Co.				7 30	357 90	365 20	√					
12	Watson Auto Repair Co.					425 50	425 50	√					
12	Cash Sales					346 80			290 72	34 20	166	21 88	√
15	Cash Sales					214 80			77 56	131 40	166	5 84	√
15	Service Tire Shop				2 65	139 98	142 63	√					
15	C. J. Mead				1 75	171 48	173 23	√					
15	Kieffer Garage				6 40	341 20	347 60	√					
15	A. H. Day					113 78	113 78	√					
15	Central Garage — Note #165	131	500 00	√		269 42	769 42						
			1400 72		265 18	12353 89	11099 88		1351 48	398 55		1169 38	
31	Evanston Bk. — Note #161	84	75	√		300 75					131	300 00	√
31	Interest Income										71	1 50	√
			1400 72		265 18	12353 89	11099 88		1351 48	398 55		1169 38	
			(√)		(82)	(111)	(133)		(41)	(42)		(√)	

RECORD OF CHECKS DRAWN FOR MONTH OF *May* 19--

DEBITS — General Ledger Acct. No.	Amount	√	Operating Expenses √	Amount	Acct. No.	Accounts Payable	√	Day	Drawn to the Order of	CREDITS — General Ledger Acct. No.	Amount	√	Purchases Discount	√	Check No.	Bank Net Amount
									AMOUNTS FORWARDED							
				300 00	631			1	H. H. Davids						430	300 00
						481 25	√	2	Standard Battery Co.				14 44		431	466 81
						48 75	√	2	The Office Sup. Co.						432	48 75
						687 40	√	4	The Cole Tire Co.				12 79		433	674 61
						719 10	√	5	Nat. Radio Mfg. Co.				21 57		434	697 53
164	25 00	√						6	Postage						435	25 00
						157 75	√	6	Rubber Chain Co.				4 73		436	153 02
						201 25	√	6	The Cole Tire Co.				3 66		437	197 59
						296 14	√	8	The Cole Tire Co.				5 52		438	290 62
						455 90	√	8	Nat. Radio Mfg. Co.				13 68		439	442 22
				12 50	611			10	Daily Post.						440	12 50
133	129 60	√						11	Liberty Nat. Bank	82	2 59				441	127 01
						404 40	√	11	The Cole Tire Co.				7 36		442	397 04
						167 50	√	11	Nat. Radio Mfg. Co.				5 03		443	162 47
						231 60	√	12	The Cole Tire Co.				4 26		444	227 34
						180 00	√	12	Standard Battery Co.				5 40		445	174 60
						49 50	√	12	Mays Heater Co.				99		445	48 51
				118 48	616			13	Moore Oil Co.						447	118 48
24	152 40	√						15	Liberty Nat. Bank						448	224 40
21	72 00	√						15			2 50					
			√	440 00	612			15	Payroll	21	17 60	√			449	1186 90
			√	100 00	613					24	75 50	√				
			√	340 00	633											
			√	200 00	614											
			√	200 00	632											
	379 00			1710 98		4080 54		15	*Amounts Forwarded*		95 69		99 43			5975 40
	379 00			1710 98		4080 54					95 69		99 43			5975 40

Page 90

RECORD OF CHECKS DRAWN FOR MONTH OF *May* 19--

DEBITS										CREDITS					
GENERAL LEDGER			OPERATING EXPENSES			ACCOUNTS PAYABLE	√	DAY	DRAWN TO THE ORDER OF	GENERAL LEDGER			PURCHASES DISCOUNT	CHECK No.	BANK NET AMOUNT
Acct. No.	Amount	√	Acct. No.	Amount	√					Acct. No.	Amount	√			
	379 00			1710 98		4080 54		15	AMOUNTS FORWARDED		95 69		99 43		5975 40
			618	20 00	√			31	Citizens Garage					468	20 00
						21 00	√	31	Western Auto Sup. Co.				21	469	20 79
53	111 70	√						31	Hughes Transfer Co.					470	126 10
54	14 40	√													
			612	470 00	√			31	Payroll	21	18 20	√		471	1215 10
			613	100 00	√					24	76 70	√			
			633	340 00	√										
			614	200 00	√										
			632	200 00	√										
53	1 00	√	611	3 50	√			31	Petty Cash Fund					472	34 45
163	1 50	√	617	3 50	√										
041	4 46	√	619	4 80	√										
166	29	√	627	7 25	√										
			634	2 75	√										
			635	1 15	√										
			643	4 25	√										
	744 85			3098 98		9266 56					381 64		243 13		12485 62
	(√)			(61)		(27)					(√)		(72)		(111)

GENERAL JOURNAL FOR MONTH OF May 19--

DEBITS										CREDITS						
Operating Expenses			Accounts Payable		General Ledger			Day	Description	General Ledger			Accounts Payable		Accounts Receivable	
Acct. No.	Amount	✓	Amount	✓	Acct. No.	Amount	✓			Acct. No.	Amount	✓	Amount	✓	Amount	✓
									AMOUNTS FORWARDED							
					041	2 88		6	W. O. Davenport —						3 20	✓
					166	32			C. M. 24						5 00	✓
					041	4 52		8	Allegeron Dairy —							
					166	48			C. M. 25							
			34 46	✓				8	The Cole Tire Co. —	051	31 70	✓				
									C. B. 15	166	2 76	✓				
					131	750 00		10	Union Garage—N 164						750 00	✓
					041	40 26		10	Service Tire Shop —						43 02	✓
					166	2 76			C. M. 26							
			34 46	✓				10	The Cole Tire Co. —	051	31 70	✓				
									C. B. 16	166	2 76	✓				
642	44 00	✓						15	Payroll Taxes	21	17 60	✓				
										22	2 64	✓				
										23	23 76	✓				
					013	25 00	✓	31	G. A. Wheeler						25 00	✓
619	2 75	✓						31	Bishop & Wells CM 29						2 75	✓
			3 25	✓				31	The Cole Tire Co. —	051	2 96	✓				
									C. B. 20	166	29	✓				
642	45 50	✓						31	Payroll Taxes	21	18 20	✓				
										22	2 73	✓				
										23	24 57	✓				
	92 25		72 17			1560 27					161 67				1563 02	
	(61)		(27)			(√)					(√)		(√)		(133)	

PETTY CASH DISBURSEMENTS FOR MONTH OF *May* 19--

DAY	DESCRIPTION	VOU. NO.	TOTAL AMOUNT	DISTRIBUTION OF CHARGES								
				#811	#617	#619	#627	#634	#635	#643	ACCOUNT	AMOUNT
1	BROUGHT FORWARD $50.00											
8	Typewriter repairs	56	1 75							1 75		
8	Circular letters	57	3 50	3 50								
13	Repairs on truck	58	3 50		3 50							
15	Water bill	59	2 75					2 75				
15	Shipping tags	60	3 50				3 50					
15	Carbon paper	61	1 50								163	1 50
15	Painting window sign	62	2 50							2 50		
			19 00	3 50	3 50		3 50	2 75		4 25		1 50
31	Express charges	67	2 80			2 80						
31	Returns, A. B. Roberts	68	4 75								041	4 46
											166	29
			34 45	3 50	3 50	4 80	7 25	2 75	1 15	4 25		7 25
			34 45	3 50	3 50	4 80	7 25	2 75	1 15	4 25		7 25
31	Balance...... $15.55											
	Rec'd in fund.. 34.45											
	Total...... $50.00											

DAILY BANK STATEMENT FOR MONTH OF May 19--

OUTSTANDING CHECKS			MEMORANDUM	DAILY BANK BALANCE			
CHECK NO.	AMOUNT	✓		DAY	DEPOSITS	CHECKS	BALANCE
			BALANCE PREVIOUS MONTH				7591 03
				1		300 00	7291 03
				2		515 56	6775 47
				3			
				4		674 61	6100 86
				5		697 53	5403 33
				6	1279 96	375 61	6307 68
				7			
				8		732 84	5574 84
				9			
				10		12 50	5562 34
				11		686 52	4875 82
				12	750 36	450 45	5175 73
				13	2715 93	118 48	7773 18
				14			
				15		1411 30	6361 88
				30			
				31	1086 55	1416 44	7458 80
Total Checks Outstanding							
Our Balance							
Bank Balance			Totals		12353 39	12485 62	

STATEMENT OF PETTY CASH DISBURSEMENTS FOR MAY

Acct. No.	Title	Amount
163	Office Supplies..	$ 1.50
166	Prepaid Federal Excise Tax......................................	.29
041	Sales Returns and Allowances, Dept. A...........................	4.46
53	Transportation In, Dept. A......................................	1.00
611	Advertising Expense...	3.50
617	Repairs on Truck..	3.50
619	Transportation Out..	4.80
627	Miscellaneous Selling Expense...................................	7.25
634	Light and Water...	2.75
635	Telephone and Telegrams...	1.15
643	Miscellaneous General Expense...................................	4.25
	Total Disbursements..	$34.45

END-OF-THE-MONTH WORK

(a) Footed the amount columns, proved the footings, entered the totals, and ruled each of the books of original entry and the petty cash disbursements record.

(b) Deposited $1,086.55 in the Liberty National Bank.

(c) Proved the bank balance as follows:

Balance, May 1..	$ 7,591.03
Total receipts for the month ended May 31 per record of cash receipts	12,353.39
Total...	$19,944.42
Less total checks issued during month ended May 31 per record of checks drawn..	12,485.62
Balance, May 31..	$ 7,458.80

(d) Completed the individual posting from the books of original entry to the general ledger and the operating expense ledger accounts.

(e) Completed the summary posting of the columnar totals of each of the books of original entry to the general ledger accounts.

PRACTICE ASSIGNMENT No. 35. The workbook contains an analysis test that should be completed at this time. Before beginning work on the test, this unit should be studied thoroughly. The narrative of transactions for May should be checked with the illustrations to see how each transaction is recorded and to note the effect of each transaction on the accounts involved. Special attention should be given to the analyses following certain transactions. Unless the procedure involved in recording the transactions completed by Bryant & Wood during the month of May is thoroughly understood, you cannot hope to make a satisfactory grade on the test.

Unit Eighteen

ACCOUNTING PROCEDURE
AT END OF MONTH

(36) MONTHLY ADJUSTMENT OF THE OPERATING EXPENSE ACCOUNTS

Periodically, the accountant should prepare financial statements and such schedules as are considered essential to sound business management. An income statement and a balance sheet are the basic financial statements included in an annual report. Much additional information may be provided by means of supporting schedules covering accounts receivable, accounts payable, operating expenses, cost of goods sold, and other accounting or statistical data.

In addition to an annual report, many firms require their accountants to prepare monthly reports setting forth the results of operations during each month and the financial condition of the business at the end of each month. Such information, provided monthly, should be a distinct aid in the conduct of a business. To wait until the end of the year to interpret the accounts and to ascertain (a) the results of current operations and (b) the financial condition of the business, may lead to serious consequences. Financial statements may be prepared at the end of each fiscal period; the fiscal period may be a year or any part of a year. Thus financial reports may be prepared on a monthly, quarterly, semiannual, or annual basis. In Part I of this course the procedure in preparing annual statements was treated in detail. In this unit the procedure in adjusting and classifying the accounts preliminary to the preparation of monthly reports is developed.

When the operating expense accounts are kept in a subsidiary ledger with a control account in the general ledger, it is usually necessary to adjust certain accounts at the end of each month in order that more accurate results of operations will be reflected. The need for adjusting certain operating expense accounts monthly arises from several factors. Certain assets depreciate continually, while other assets are consumed in the operation of a business. Depreciation is an expense that increases the cost of doing business. Supplies that are consumed in operating a business add to the cost of doing business. Prepaid insurance expires with the lapse of time and thus becomes an expense. Certain expenses may accrue; if the amount accrued is not recorded at the end of each month, the expense accounts will not reflect currently the true cost of operating an enterprise. Provision should also be made for the amount of bad debt losses anticipated. When such provision is made under the allowance method, the amount added to the allowance each month is recorded as an expense for the month.

The accounts of Bryant & Wood will be used to illustrate the procedure in adjusting the operating expense accounts monthly. The books of original entry, providing a record of some of the transactions completed during the month of May, were reproduced in the preceding unit. The following data provide the information needed in adjusting the operating expense accounts at the end of May:

BRYANT & WOOD

DATA FOR ADJUSTING THE OPERATING EXPENSE ACCOUNTS

May 31, 19--

Depreciation of store equipment.................................... $12.50
Depreciation of delivery equipment............................... 26.04
Depreciation of office equipment.................................. 20.83
Store supplies consumed during month............................. 92.75
Advertising supplies consumed during month....................... 28.35
Office supplies consumed during month............................ 57.35

Postage stamps consumed during month:
    Selling expense... $15.32
    Administration expense.................................. 15.33   30.65

Insurance expired during month:
    On merchandise... $15.00
    On delivery equipment.................................. 12.50
    On store equipment..................................... 1.25
    On office equipment.................................... 2.50   31.25

One twelfth of estimated property taxes for year..................... 30.00
Provision for bad debts, ½% of charge sales for May................ 68.44

Journalizing the Adjusting Entries. The entries required to adjust the operating expense accounts may be made on the work sheet in the manner illustrated in Unit Seven of this textbook or they may be journalized and posted to the accounts prior to making a work sheet. Bryant & Wood follow the latter practice. The adjusting entries required at the end of May are shown recorded in the general journal reproduced on page 481. By providing a special Dr. column in the general journal for

Page 22

GENERAL JOURNAL FOR MONTH OF *May* 19—

DEBITS — Operating Expenses Acct. No.	Amount	√	DEBITS — General Ledger Acct. No.	Amount	√	Accounts Payable	Day	Description	Credits — General Ledger Acct. No.	Amount	√	Accounts Payable	Accounts Receivable
								AMOUNTS FORWARDED					
							31	*Adjusting Entries:*					
625	12 50	√						Depr. of store equipment	017	12 50	√		
626	26 04	√						Depr. of delivery equipment	018	26 04	√		
641	20 83	√						Depr. of office equipment	019	20 83	√		
623	92 75	√						Store supplies consumed	161	92 75	√		
611	28 35	√						Advertising supplies consumed	162	28 35	√		
638	57 35	√						Office supplies consumed	163	57 35	√		
624	15 32	√						Postage stamps consumed	164	30 65	√		
639	15 33	√											
620	15 00	√						Insurance expired	165	31 25	√		
621	12 50	√											
622	1 25	√											
640	2 50	√						Accrued property taxes	28	30 00	√		
637	30 00	√						Provision for bad debts	013	68 44	√		
636	68 44	√											
	398 16									*398 16*			
	398 16									398 16			
	(61)									(√)			

Operating Expense Adjustments

recording operating expenses, summary posting of the monthly total to the debit of the operating expense control account in the general ledger is made possible.

Depreciation Expense. Bryant & Wood use the group method of accounting for fixed assets, separate accounts being kept in the general ledger for store equipment, delivery equipment, and office equipment. The assets charged to each of these accounts have approximately the same average useful life. In computing the amount of depreciation sustained each month, the basis is the cost of the assets owned at the beginning of the month. Depreciation is not considered on assets owned less than a month. The factors involved in ascertaining the amount of depreciation sustained during May are shown in the following schedule:

SCHEDULE OF DEPRECIATION SUSTAINED DURING MAY

FIXED ASSETS	COST	ANNUAL RATE OF DEPRECIATION	DEPRECIATION SUSTAINED DURING MONTH
Store Equipment	$1,500	10%	$12.50
Delivery Equipment	$1,250	25%	26.04
Office Equipment	2,500	10%	20.83
Total depreciation sustained during month.............			$59.37

Bryant & Wood keep separate depreciation expense accounts and allowance accounts for each group of fixed assets. These accounts are as follows:

625 Depreciation of Store Equipment
626 Depreciation of Delivery Equipment
641 Depreciation of Office Equipment
017 Allowance for Depreciation of Store Equipment
018 Allowance for Depreciation of Delivery Equipment
019 Allowance for Depreciation of Office Equipment

Keeping separate expense accounts for the depreciation sustained on different groups of fixed assets facilitates a proper classification of the expenses in the monthly and annual reports. The depreciation on each group of fixed assets is recorded by debiting the proper depreciation expense account and by crediting the proper allowance account.

Supplies Consumed. Supplies of all kinds, including store supplies, advertising supplies, office supplies, and postage stamps, constitute assets when purchased but become expenses when consumed. Instead of charging such supplies to expense at the time of purchase, they are recorded as assets and adjustments are made at the end of each month for the amounts consumed during the month in the operations of the business. The factors involved in ascertaining the amount of supplies consumed by Bryant & Wood during May are shown in the following schedule:

SCHEDULE OF SUPPLIES CONSUMED DURING MAY

SUPPLIES	ACCOUNT BALANCE END OF MONTH	AMOUNT ON HAND END OF MONTH PER STOCK RECORDS	AMOUNT CONSUMED DURING MONTH
Store Supplies	$154.00	$61.25	$ 92.75
Advertising Supplies	93.55	65.20	28.35
Office Supplies	105.95	48.60	57.35
Postage Stamps	39.45	8.80	30.65
Total supplies consumed during month........................			$209.10

Bryant & Wood keep separate expense accounts for each kind of supplies consumed. These accounts are as follows:

623 Store Supplies Consumed
611 Advertising Expense
638 Office Supplies Consumed
624 Postage (Selling)
639 Postage (Administration)

Keeping separate expense accounts for supplies consumed facilitates a proper classification of the expenses in the monthly and annual reports. The amount of each kind of supplies consumed during the month is recorded by debiting the proper operating expense account and by crediting the proper asset account. Of the total amount of postage stamps used during the month, one half was used in selling and the other half in administration. The amount used in selling was charged to Account No. 624 and the amount used in administration was charged to Account No. 639, while the total amount of stamps consumed was credited to Account No. 164.

Insurance Expired. Prepaid insurance premiums are usually recorded in the same manner as supplies. At the time of paying a premium, the amount paid is recorded as an asset; then at the end of each month the insurance expired during the month is recorded as an expense. Bryant & Wood keep separate expense accounts for the insurance expired on different kinds of property. These accounts are as follows:

620 Expired Insurance on Merchandise
621 Expired Insurance on Delivery Equipment
622 Expired Insurance on Store Equipment
640 Expired Insurance on Office Equipment

The information needed in ascertaining the amount of insurance expired on each kind of property owned was obtained from the insurance policy register. The factors involved are shown in the following schedule:

SCHEDULE OF INSURANCE EXPIRED DURING MAY

POLICY NUMBER	PROPERTY INSURED	PREMIUM PAID	TERM OF POLICY	AMOUNT EXPIRED DURING MONTH
664218	Merchandise	$45.00	One Year	$ 3.75
92368	Merchandise	45.00	One Year	3.75
372085	Merchandise	45.00	One Year	3.75
13926B	Merchandise	45.00	One Year	3.75
16431A	Delivery Equipment	15.00	One Year	1.25
67231	Delivery Equipment	45.00	One Year	3.75
62981	Delivery Equipment	90.00	One Year	7.50
369810	Store Equipment	15.00	One Year	1.25
391042	Office Equipment	30.00	One Year	2.50

Total amount of insurance expired during month................$31.25

The insurance expired on each kind of property is recorded by debiting the respective expense accounts for the proper amounts and by crediting Prepaid Insurance, Account No. 165, for the total amount of insurance expired.

Accrued Expenses. There are certain types of operating expenses that accrue during the month. If wages are paid weekly, it is probable that a few days' wage expense will have accrued at the end of most months. However, Bryant & Wood pay their employees on the last day of each month; hence, there are no accrued wages to be considered in making the monthly adjustment of the operating expense accounts.

The only accrual-type adjustment of the operating expenses necessary in the case of Bryant & Wood is for property taxes. Property taxes present a special problem. This type of tax does not accrue in the usual sense. The tax is imposed once a year upon owners of property. Whether the property has been owned for twelve days or twelve months makes no difference in the amount of the tax. It is the fact of ownership of the property on the date of assessment that subjects the owner to the tax. Generally, the tax can be paid in two equal installments.

If a business calculates net income only once a year, no problem arises with respect to property taxes in such calculations. The expense can be recorded either when the tax bill is received or when payment is made.

If the taxes are not fully paid by the end of the year, the accounts can be properly adjusted. In any event, the calculation of net income for each year should include one year's property tax expense. However, if monthly calculations of net income are made, it is only reasonable to consider that one twelfth of the total tax is an expense of each month. Accordingly, an adjusting entry should be made at the end of each month debiting Property Taxes and crediting Accrued Property Taxes Payable for one twelfth of the estimated amount of the annual tax. Payment of the tax, whenever made, should be charged to the liability account. An adjustment should be made for any difference between the estimated amount and the actual amount of the tax. This difference may be small since the tax usually can be estimated with considerable accuracy.

Bryant & Wood estimate that the total property tax expense for the current year will be $360. Thus, at the end of each month an adjusting entry is made debiting Property Taxes, Account No. 637, and crediting Accrued Property Taxes Payable, Account No. 28, for $30.

Bad Debts. Bryant & Wood use the allowance method in accounting for bad debts. By reference to the sales record at the end of each month, the accountant ascertains the amount of the charge sales for the month and multiplies this amount by ½ per cent. For the month of May the total charge sales amounted to $13,687.35. One half per cent of this amount is $68.44. This was recorded by debiting Bad Debts Expense, Account No. 636, and by crediting Allowance for Bad Debts, Account No. 013.

Posting the Adjusting Entries. The adjusting entries should be posted in the usual manner. This involves both individual posting and summary posting. In completing the individual posting, each item entered in the Operating Expenses Dr. column should be posted to the proper account in the operating expense ledger and each item entered in the General Ledger Cr. column should be posted to the proper account in the general ledger. As each item is posted, a check mark should be placed in the Check (√) column of the general journal immediately following the amount posted. The number of the general journal page from which the item is posted should also be entered in the Folio column of the proper ledger immediately preceding the amount posted.

In completing the summary posting, the total of the Operating Expenses Dr. column should be posted to the debit of the operating expense control account in the general ledger. For cross-reference purposes, the number of the operating expense control account should be entered in the general journal immediately below the amount posted, and the number of the general journal page from which the amount is posted should be entered in the Folio column of the general ledger immediately preceding the amount posted. The total of the General Ledger Cr. column need not be posted, as each item entered in this column has already been posted to the proper general ledger account. After completing the posting at the end of May, the operating expense control account in the general ledger appeared as follows:

OPERATING EXPENSES				Account No. 61		
19--				19--		
May 1 Balance		√	35,997.34	May 27	S57	2.00
31		CD 90	3,098.98	31	S57	2.80
31		GJ 21	92.25			4.80
31		GJ 22	398.16			
	39,581.93		39,586.73			

Trial Balance. After the individual and summary posting for May was completed, a trial balance of the general ledger accounts was taken. The trial balance is reproduced on page 487.

Schedules. Following the preparation of a trial balance, it is customary to prepare schedules of the account balances in each of the subsidiary ledgers as a means of proving the control account balances. Bryant & Wood keep three subsidiary ledgers; namely, an accounts receivable ledger, an accounts payable ledger, and an operating expense ledger. The schedule of accounts receivable is reproduced below and the schedules of accounts payable and operating expenses are reproduced on page 488.

BRYANT & WOOD
SCHEDULE OF ACCOUNTS RECEIVABLE
May 31, 19--

Bayless Bros..	$ 314.60
Bishop & Wells...	199.83
Bond Service Station...................................	1,081.95
Byers Tire Shop..	273.35
Central Garage...	255.35
Courthouse Garage......................................	616.85
W. O. Davenport..	370.00
A. H. Day..	196.77
B. A. Fall...	334.80
General Supply Co......................................	47.05
Hardin Farm..	254.00
Hoole Tire Co..	12.20
B. C. Jenkins & Son....................................	176.45
Lincoln Garage...	27.30
Lincoln Highway Tire Shop..............................	161.17
W. M. Mason..	37.95
Peters Garage..	325.00
Porter & Wells...	1,232.50
Service Tire Shop......................................	313.85
W. D. Trotter..	295.90
Union Garage...	26.50
Wyatt & Son..	118.50
	$6,671.87

BRYANT & WOOD

TRIAL BALANCE

MAY 31, 19--

Liberty National Bank.............................	111	$ 7,467.85	
Petty Cash Fund...................................	112	50.00	
Government Bonds..................................	12	9,900.00	
Notes Receivable.................................	131	3,203.36	
Accounts Receivable..............................	133	6,671.87	
Allowance for Bad Debts..........................	013		$ 455.94
Merchandise Inventory, Dept. A...................	14	21,847.90	
Merchandise Inventory, Dept. B...................	15	3,121.13	
Store Supplies...................................	161	31.25	
Advertising Supplies.............................	162	42.87	
Office Supplies..................................	163	48.60	
Postage Stamps...................................	164	8.80	
Prepaid Insurance................................	165	168.75	
Prepaid Federal Excise Tax.......................	166	2,506.62	
Store Equipment..................................	17	1,543.50	
Allowance for Depr. of Store Equipment...........	017		332.50
Delivery Equipment...............................	18	1,250.00	
Allowance for Depr. of Delivery Equipment........	018		476.04
Office Equipment.................................	19	2,660.00	
Allowance for Depr. of Office Equipment..........	019		400.83
F.I.C.A. Taxes Payable...........................	21		71.60
F.U.T.A. Taxes Payable...........................	22		66.54
State U.C. Taxes Payable.........................	23		90.70
Employees' Income Taxes Payable..................	24		152.20
Notes Payable....................................	25		3,500.00
Accounts Payable.................................	27		4,772.20
Accrued Property Taxes Payable...................	28		180.00
J. A. Bryant, Partner............................	31		27,000.00
J. A. Bryant, Drawing............................	311	725.43	
W. L. Wood, Partner..............................	32		27,000.00
W. L. Wood, Drawing..............................	321	436.62	
Sales, Dept. A...................................	41		102,634.44
Sales Returns & Allowances, Dept. A..............	041	1,612.40	
Sales, Dept. B...................................	42		19,585.00
Sales Returns & Allowances, Dept. B..............	042	75.00	
Purchases, Dept. A...............................	51	72,657.43	
Purchases Returns & Allowances, Dept. A..........	051		652.00
Purchases, Dept. B...............................	52	10,250.85	
Purchases Returns & Allowances, Dept. B..........	052		36.35
Transportation In, Dept. A.......................	53	1,220.70	
Transportation In, Dept. B.......................	54	175.60	
Operating Expenses...............................	61	39,581.93	
Interest Income..................................	71		119.38
Purchases Discount...............................	72		1,669.38
Interest Expense.................................	81	171.87	
Sales Discount...................................	82	1,365.33	
Charitable Contributions.........................	83	370.48	
Collection Expense...............................	84	28.96	
		$189,195.10	$189,195.10

BRYANT & WOOD

SCHEDULE OF ACCOUNTS PAYABLE

MAY 31, 19--

Bannister Mfg. Co.	$ 43.50
The Cole Tire Co.	3,843.75
Jackson Box Co.	7.50
Johnson Paper Co.	60.00
Office Equipment Co.	180.00
The Office Supply Co.	31.20
Powers Printing Co.	60.75
Standard Battery Co.	518.00
Western Auto Supply Co.	27.50
	$4,772.20

BRYANT & WOOD

SCHEDULE OF OPERATING EXPENSES

FOR THE ELEVEN-MONTHS' PERIOD ENDED MAY 31, 19--

Advertising Expense	611	$ 1,018.62
Salaries of Store Clerks	612	9,497.00
Wages of Truck Driver	613	1,950.00
W. L. Wood, Salary	614	4,400.00
W. L. Wood, Traveling Expense	615	612.50
Gas and Oil for Truck	616	784.48
Repairs on Truck	617	130.25
Garage Rent	618	220.00
Transportation Out	619	30.25
Expired Insurance on Merchandise	620	165.00
Expired Insurance on Delivery Equipment	621	137.50
Expired Insurance on Store Equipment	622	13.75
Store Supplies Consumed	623	845.10
Postage	624	481.12
Depreciation of Store Equipment	625	137.50
Depreciation of Delivery Equipment	626	286.46
Miscellaneous Selling Expense	627	138.90
Rent	631	3,300.00
J. A. Bryant, Salary	632	4,400.00
Office Salaries	633	7,400.00
Light and Water	634	82.65
Telephone and Telegrams	635	157.01
Bad Debts Expense	636	660.94
Property Taxes	637	330.00
Office Supplies Consumed	638	744.64
Postage	639	341.33
Expired Insurance on Office Equipment	640	27.50
Depreciation of Office Equipment	641	229.13
Social Security Taxes	642	942.35
Miscellaneous General Expense	643	117.95
		$39,581.93

PRACTICE ASSIGNMENT No. 36. Complete Report No. 36 in the workbook and submit your working papers to the instructor for approval. Then continue with the following study assignment until Report No. 37 is required.

(37) END-OF-PERIOD WORK SHEET

The trial balance of Bryant & Wood, taken as of May 31, will be used as the basis for illustrating the procedure in preparing a ten-column work sheet that will provide all of the information needed in preparing an income statement for the eleven-months' period ended May 31 and a balance sheet as of May 31. The completed work sheet of Bryant & Wood is reproduced on pages 492 and 493. The preparation of this work sheet involved the following procedure:

(a) The May 31 trial balance was copied on the work sheet, the debit and credit balances being recorded in the first two amount columns. It will be noted that this trial balance is the same as the one reproduced on page 487.

(b) The entries required in adjusting the account balances preliminary to preparing the financial statements were entered in the third and fourth amount columns. These columns were then footed and the footings were proved.

(c) The adjusted account balances were extended into the fifth and sixth amount columns. These columns were then footed and the footings were proved.

(d) The balances of the temporary accounts were extended into the seventh and eighth amount columns and these columns were footed. The difference between these footings, amounting to $8,056.71, was then recorded in the seventh amount column as the net income for the eleven-months' period.

(e) The balances of the remaining accounts were extended into the ninth and tenth amount columns and the columns were footed. The difference between these footings, amounting to $8,056.71, was then recorded in the tenth amount column as the net income for the eleven-months' period. The difference between the footings of the ninth and tenth amount columns was the same as the difference between the footings of the seventh and eighth amount columns.

(f) The totals of all the amount columns were then entered and the work sheet was ruled as shown in the illustration.

Adjustments. In preparing the work sheet for Bryant & Wood, it was necessary to analyze the accounts and to adjust any account balances that did not reflect the proper amount on May 31. The trial balance contains the general ledger accounts only. Since the operating expense accounts are kept in a subsidiary ledger and any necessary adjustments are made at the end of each month prior to taking a trial balance, no further adjustment of the operating expenses is required on the monthly work sheet.

Inventories. The amounts shown in the inventory accounts in the trial balance represent the calculated cost of the merchandise on hand on July 1, the start of the current fiscal year. Since a physical inventory will not be taken until June 30, the end of the fiscal year, the cost to be assigned to the goods on hand May 31 must be calculated in some other manner. It could be estimated by the gross profit method described in Unit Fifteen. However, Bryant & Wood maintain a stock record which reveals the quantities of the various items that are supposed to be on hand.

Bryant & Wood assign cost to inventories on the first-in, first-out basis, making any needed corrections to state the inventories on the basis of "cost or market, whichever is lower." After multiplying the quantity of each item in stock by the unit cost price and after ascertaining the total cost, it was necessary to add a portion of the transportation charges incurred. All transportation charges are charged to departmental transportation in accounts. At the end of each year the total transportation charges are divided by the total purchases to arrive at a rate which may be used in determining the amount of transportation charges to be added to the cost of the merchandise in stock. The rate ascertained at the end of the preceding year was found to be 1.75 per cent. Thus, the costs assigned to the inventories on May 31 were calculated as follows:

	DEPT. A	DEPT. B
Cost of merchandise on hand per stock records.....	$30,716.52	$4,417.52
Add transportation charges @ 1.75%..............	537.54	77.31
Totals..	$31,254.06	$4,494.83

When financial statements are prepared monthly, it is customary to depend upon the stock records for the inventories. In most businesses it is impractical to take a physical inventory monthly; hence, reliance is placed on the stock records for information as to the quantity of goods in stock at the end of each month. A physical inventory, however, should be taken at least at the end of each year. At that time, if the stock records are not in agreement with the physical inventories, it is customary to adjust the stock records in order to bring the book inventories into agreement with the physical inventories.

In addition to adjusting the inventory accounts, it is customary to ascertain the cost of goods sold in each department and to enter the cost on the work sheet. The procedure in adjusting the inventory accounts and in recording the cost of goods sold for each department on the work sheet was as follows:

Entry (a): The beginning inventory for Dept. A was transferred to the proper cost of goods sold account by debiting Cost of Goods Sold, Dept. A and by crediting Merchandise Inventory, Dept. A for $21,847.90.

Entry (b): The beginning inventory for Dept. B was transferred to the proper cost of goods sold account by debiting Cost of Goods Sold, Dept. B and by crediting Merchandise Inventory, Dept. B for $3,121.13.

Entry (c): The balance of the purchases account for Dept. A was transferred to the proper cost of goods sold account by debiting Cost of Goods Sold, Dept. A and by crediting Purchases, Dept. A for $72,657.43.

Entry (d): The balance of the purchases account for Dept. B was transferred to the proper cost of goods sold account by debiting Cost of Goods Sold, Dept. B and by crediting Purchases, Dept. B for $10,250.85.

Entry (e): The balance of the purchases returns and allowances account for Dept. A was transferred to the proper cost of goods sold account by debiting Purchases Returns and Allowances, Dept. A and by crediting Cost of Goods Sold, Dept. A for $652.

Entry (f): The balance of the purchases returns and allowances account for Dept. B was transferred to the proper cost of goods sold account by debiting Purchases Returns and Allowances, Dept. B and by crediting Cost of Goods Sold, Dept. B for $36.35.

Entry (g): The balance of the transportation in account for Dept. A was transferred to the proper cost of goods sold account by debiting Cost of Goods Sold, Dept. A and by crediting Transportation In, Dept. A for $1,220.70.

Entry (h): The balance of the transportation in account for Dept. B was transferred to the proper cost of goods sold account by debiting Cost of Goods Sold, Dept. B and by crediting Transportation In, Dept. B for $175.60.

Entry (i): The May 31 inventory for Dept. A was recorded by debiting Merchandise Inventory, Dept. A and by crediting Cost of Goods Sold, Dept. A for $31,254.06.

Entry (j): The May 31 inventory for Dept. B was recorded by debiting Merchandise Inventory, Dept. B and by crediting Cost of Goods Sold, Dept. B for $4,494.83.

(*Continued on page 494*)

BRYANT & WOOD
Work Sheet for Eleven-Months' Period Ended May 31, 19--

Accounts	Nos.	Trial Balance Dr.	Trial Balance Cr.	Adjustments Dr.	Adjustments Cr.	Adjusted Trial Balance Dr.	Adjusted Trial Balance Cr.	Income Statement Dr.	Income Statement Cr.	Balance Sheet Dr.	Balance Sheet Cr.
Liberty National Bank	111	7467 85				7467 85				7467 85	
Petty Cash Fund	112	50 00				50 00				50 00	
Government Bonds	12	9900 00				9900 00				9900 00	
Notes Receivable	131	3203 36				3203 36				3203 36	
Accrued Interest Receivable	132			(k) 125 27		125 27				125 27	
Accounts Receivable	133	6671 87				6671 87				6671 87	
Allowance for Bad Debts	013		455 94				455 94				455 94
Mdse. Inv., Dept. A.	14	21847 90		(i) 31254 06	(a) 21847 90	31254 06				31254 06	
Mdse. Inv., Dept. B.	15	31211 13		(j) 4494 83	(b) 31211 13	4494 83				4494 83	
Store Supplies	161	31 25				31 25				31 25	
Advertising Supplies	162	42 87				42 87				42 87	
Office Supplies	163	48 60				48 60				48 60	
Postage Stamps	164	8 80				8 80				8 80	
Prepaid Insurance	165	168 75				168 75				168 75	
Prepaid Fed. Excise Tax	166	2506 62				2506 62				2506 62	
Store Equipment	17	1543 50				1543 50				1543 50	
Allowance for Depr. of S.E.	017		332 50				332 50				332 50
Delivery Equipment	18	1250 00				1250 00				1250 00	
Allowance for Depr. of D.E.	018		476 04				476 04				476 04
Office Equipment	19	2660 00				2660 00				2660 00	
Allowance for Depr. of O.E.	019		400 83				400 83				400 83
F.I.C.A. Taxes Payable	21		71 60				71 60				71 60
F.U.T.A. Taxes Payable	22		66 54				66 54				66 54
State U.C. Taxes Payable	23		90 70				90 70				90 70
Emp. Income Taxes Payable	24		152 20				152 60				152 20
Notes Payable	25		3500 00				3500 00				3500 00
Accrued Interest Payable	26				(l) 34 42		34 42				34 42
Accounts Payable	27		4772 20				4772 20				4772 20
Accrued Property Taxes Pay	28		180 00				180 00				180 00
J. A. Bryant, Partner	31		27000 00				27000 00				27000 00

Account	No.	Trial Balance Dr.	Trial Balance Cr.	Adjustments Dr.	Adjustments Cr.	Adjusted Trial Balance Dr.	Adjusted Trial Balance Cr.	Income Statement Dr.	Income Statement Cr.	Balance Sheet Dr.	Balance Sheet Cr.
J. A. Bryant, Drawing	311	725 43				725 43				725 43	
W. L. Wood, Partner	32		27000 00				27000 00				27000 00
W. L. Wood, Drawing	321	436 62				436 62				436 62	
Sales, Dept. A	41		102634 44				102634 44		102634 44		
Sales Ret. & Allow., Dept. A	041	1612 40				1612 40		1612 40			
Sales, Dept. B	42		19585 00				19585 00		19585 00		
Sales Ret. & Allow., Dept. B	042	75 00				75 00		75 00			
Purchases, Dept. A	51	72657 43			(c) 72657 43						
Pur. Ret. & Allow., Dept. A	051		652 00	(e) 652 00							
Purchases, Dept. B	52	10250 85			(d) 10250 85						
Pur. Ret. & Allow., Dept. B	052		86 35	(f) 86 35							
Transportation In, Dept. A	53	1220 70			(g) 1220 70						
Transportation In, Dept. B	54	175 60			(h) 175 60						
Operating Expenses	61	39581 93				39581 93		39581 93			
Interest Income	71		119 38		(k) 125 27		244 65		244 65		
Purchases Discount	72		1669 38				1669 38		1669 38		
Interest Expense	81	171 87		(l) 34 42		206 29		206 29			
Sales Discount	82	1365 33				1365 33		1365 33			
Charitable Contributions	83	370 48				370 48		370 48			
Collection Expense	84	28 96				28 96		28 96			
Cost of Goods Sold, Dept. A	55			(a) 21847 90 (c) 72657 43 (g) 1220 70	(e) 652 00 (i) 31254 05	63819 97		63819 97			
Cost of Goods Sold, Dept. B	56			(b) 3121 13 (d) 10250 85 (h) 175 60	(f) 86 35 (j) 4494 83	9016 40		9016 40			
		189195 10	189195 10	145870 54	145870 54	188666 44	188666 44	116076 76	124133 47	72589 68	64532 97
Net Income								8056 71			8056 71
								124133 47	124133 47	72589 68	72589 68

It will be observed that after the foregoing adjustments were made, the balance of Cost of Goods Sold, Dept. A, which was extended to the Adjusted Trial Balance Dr. column, amounted to $63,819.97 and the balance of Cost of Goods Sold, Dept. B, which was extended to the Adjusted Trial Balance Dr. column, amounted to $9,016.40. These balances were arrived at by subtracting the sum of the credit entries from the sum of the debit entries.

Accrued Interest Receivable. It was necessary to ascertain the respective amounts of accrued interest receivable and accrued interest payable as of May 31 before the required adjustments could be made to record the interest accrued. The notes receivable register was the source of the information needed in preparing the following schedule:

SCHEDULE OF ACCRUED INTEREST ON NOTES RECEIVABLE

No.	Principal Amount	Rate of Interest	Date of Note	Days Accrued	Accrued Interest
162	$750.00	6%	April 4	57	$ 7.13
163	450.00	...	April 2	..	......
165	500.00	6%	May 15	16	1.33
166	600.00	6%	May 20	11	1.10
167	401.60	6%	May 22	9	.60
168	201.76	...	May 16	..	......
169	300.00	6%	May 25	6	.30

Total interest accrued on notes receivable...................... $10.46

In addition to the notes owned on May 31, Bryant & Wood owned 2½ per cent U. S. Treasury Bonds amounting to $9,900, acquired on December 1 of the preceding year, on which the interest is payable semi-annually June 15 and December 15. On May 31, interest on these bonds had been accruing for 167 days at 2½ per cent. Thus, the accrued interest on the bonds owned amounted to $114.81, to which was added the accrued interest on notes receivable amounting to $10.46, making the total accrued interest receivable on May 31, $125.27.

Entry (k): The interest receivable accrued on May 31 was recorded on the work sheet by debiting Accrued Interest Receivable and by crediting Interest Income for $125.27.

Accrued Interest Payable. An analysis of the notes payable account reveals that a ninety-day note for $3,500 dated April 2 and bearing interest at the rate of 6 per cent was outstanding. On May 31, interest had been accruing for a total of 59 days. The interest on $3,500 at 6 per cent for 59 days amounts to $34.42.

Entry (1): The interest payable accrued on May 31 was recorded on the work sheet by debiting Interest Expense and by crediting Accrued Interest Payable for $34.42.

Adjusted Trial Balance Columns. After the required adjustments were entered on the work sheet, the adjusted account balances were extended to the Adjusted Trial Balance columns and the columns were footed to ascertain whether the debit and credit balances were equal in amount. This is an essential step in preparing a work sheet; it is important to ascertain that the debit and credit balances of the accounts are equal in amount before the accounts are classified by extending the balances to the columns headed Income Statement and Balance Sheet, respectively.

Income Statement Columns. The balances of the temporary accounts only were extended to the columns headed Income Statement. Debit balances were entered in the left amount column, while credit balances were entered in the right amount column. After these account balances were extended, the Income Statement columns were footed, the difference between the footings was ascertained, and this difference, amounting to $8,056.71, was entered on the next horizontal line as the net income for the period. After the net income was entered, the footings of the Income Statement columns were found to be equal in amount.

Balance Sheet Columns. The last step in preparing the work sheet was to extend the balances of the remaining accounts from the Adjusted Trial Balance columns to the Balance Sheet columns. Debit balances were entered in the left amount column, while credit balances were entered in the right amount column. After these account balances were extended, the Balance Sheet columns were footed, the difference between the footings was ascertained, and this difference, amounting to $8,056.71, was entered on the next horizontal line as the net income for the period. After the net income was entered, the footings of the Balance Sheet columns were found to be equal in amount.

A work sheet prepared in proper form accomplishes the following:

(a) Serves as a medium for making the necessary adjustments of the general ledger account balances preliminary to the preparation of financial statements.

(b) Facilitates the classification of the account balances on a basis of the statements to be prepared therefrom.

(c) Makes possible the ascertainment of the net income for the period.

PRACTICE ASSIGNMENT No. 37. Complete Report No. 37 in the workbook and submit your working papers to the instructor for approval. Then continue with the next study assignment in Unit Nineteen until Report No. 38 is required.

Unit Nineteen

MONTHLY FINANCIAL STATEMENTS
AND PROCEDURE AT END OF YEAR

(38) THE INCOME STATEMENT

One of the major functions of accounting is to accumulate data to measure the progress of a business from period to period and its financial condition from time to time. The fiscal or accounting period of a business is usually a year and it is customary to prepare an annual report for the business at the end of each year. This report usually consists of an income statement and a balance sheet with various supporting schedules. While the annual report may supply all of the information wanted by most persons interested in the affairs of a business, it is not unusual for the accountant to be called upon to supply management with monthly financial statements.

In the case of Bryant & Wood, the management expects the accountant to prepare monthly income statements and balance sheets with supporting schedules of the cost of goods sold, operating expenses, accounts receivable, and accounts payable.

Form of the Income Statement. The books of Bryant & Wood are not formally closed until the end of the fiscal year, June 30. However, the amounts in the temporary proprietorship accounts accumulate from month to month. After adjusting the operating expense accounts at the end of each month and calculating the amount of the month-end inventory, a work sheet can be prepared that will provide the information needed in preparing monthly financial statements. On July 31, at the end of the first month of the fiscal year, the accountant prepares an income statement showing the results of operations for the month of July only. At the end of each succeeding month throughout the fiscal year, the accountant prepares an income statement in columnar form showing (1) the results of operations for the period extending from the beginning of the fiscal year to the end of the current month, (2) the results of operations extending from the beginning of the fiscal year to the end of the preceding month, and (3) the results of operations for the current month only. The income statement prepared in typewritten form at the end of May is reproduced on page 499. The Income Statement columns of the work sheet reproduced on pages 492 and 493 provided the information needed in stating the results for the eleven-months' period ended May 31. The results for the ten-months' period ended April 30 were copied from the income statement prepared at the end of April. The results for the month of May were ascertained by subtraction.

Form of the Schedule of Cost of Goods Sold. On July 31, at the end of the first month of the fiscal year, the accountant prepares a schedule of the cost of goods sold by departments during the month of July only. At the end of each succeeding month throughout the fiscal year, the accountant prepares a schedule in columnar form arranged to show not only the cost of goods sold by departments, but also the cost of goods sold (1) during the period extending from the beginning of the fiscal year to the end of the current month, (2) during the period extending from the beginning of the fiscal year to the end of the preceding month, and (3) during the current month only. The schedule of cost of goods sold prepared in typewritten form at the end of May is reproduced on page 500. This schedule provides the information needed for the income statement with respect to the cost of goods sold. It will be noted that the beginning inventories for Depts. A and B are the same for the eleven-months' period ended May 31 and for the ten-months' period ended April 30. This is because, in both cases, the period covered began on the same date, July 1. However, the beginning inventories for May were the same as the ending inventories on April 30.

Form of the Schedule of Operating Expenses. At the end of each month, the accountant for Bryant & Wood takes a trial balance of the general ledger accounts and prepares schedules of (a) operating expenses, (b) accounts receivable, and (c) accounts payable. One of the purposes of these schedules is to prove the balances of the control accounts kept in the general ledger. At the end of each month, beginning with the second month of the fiscal year, the accountant prepares a schedule of operating expenses in columnar form designed to show (1) the operating expenses for the period extending from the beginning of the fiscal year to the end of the current month, (2) the operating expenses for the period extending from the beginning of the fiscal year to the end of the preceding month, and (3) the operating expenses for the current month only. The schedule of operating expenses prepared in typewritten form at the end of May is reproduced on page 501. This schedule provided the information needed for the income statement with respect to the operating expenses.

BRYANT & WOOD

INCOME STATEMENT

	For 11 Mos. ended May 31, 19--	For 10 Mos. ended April 30, 19--	·For May, 19--
Operating Income:			
Department A--			
Sales..............................	$102,634.44	$90,727.87	$11,906.57
Less Returns and Allowances.........	1,612.40	1,463.26	149.14
Net Sales.............................	$101,022.04	$89,264.61	$11,757.43
Less Cost of Goods Sold.............	63,819.97	55,432.76	8,387.21
Gross Profit on Sales.................	$ 37,202.07	$33,831.85	$ 3,370.22
Department B--			
Sales..............................	$ 19,585.00	$17,112.25	$ 2,472.75
Less Returns and Allowances.........	75.00	68.18	6.82
Net Sales.............................	$ 19,510.00	$17,044.07	$ 2,465.93
Less Cost of Goods Sold.............	9,016.40	7,669.58	1,346.82
Gross Profit on Sales.................	$ 10,493.60	$ 9,374.49	$ 1,119.11
Total Gross Profit on Sales.............	$ 47,695.67	$43,206.34	$ 4,489.33
Operating Expenses...................	39,581.93	35,997.34	3,584.59
Net Operating Income....................	$ 8,113.74	$ 7,209.00	$ 904.74
Other Income:			
Interest Income........................	$ 244.65	$ 224.24	$ 20.41
Purchases Discount.....................	1,669.38	1,426.25	243.13
Total Other Income...................	$ 1,914.03	$ 1,650.49	$ 263.54
	$ 10,027.77	$ 8,859.49	$ 1,168.28
Other Expenses:			
Interest Expense.......................	$ 206.29	$ 185.06	$ 21.23
Sales Discount.........................	1,365.33	1,100.15	265.18
Charitable Contributions...............	370.48	330.48	40.00
Collection Expense.....................	28.96	26.71	2.25
Total Other Expenses.................	$ 1,971.06	$ 1,642.40	$ 328.66
Net Income..............................	$ 8,056.71	$ 7,217.09	$ 839.62

Interpreting the Income Statement. The order in which the accounts are classified in the income statement aids in its interpretation. Merchants ordinarily derive the major part of their income from sales. Such income is commonly referred to as operating income. Bryant & Wood's total gross profit on sales for the eleven-months' period ended May 31 amounted to $47,695.67. After operating expenses amounting to a total of $39,581.93 were deducted, the net operating income was found to be $8,113.74.

The income derived from other sources, amounting to a total of $1,914.03, was added to the net operating income, and other expenses amounting to $1,971.06, were subtracted from the sum to find the net income, which amounted to $8,056.71.

BRYANT & WOOD

SCHEDULE OF COST OF GOODS SOLD

	For 11 Mos. Ended May 31, 19--		For 10 Mos. Ended April 30, 19--		For May, 19--	
	Dept. A	Dept. B	Dept. A	Dept. B	Dept. A	Dept. B
Merchandise Inventory Beginning of Period	$21,847.90	$ 3,121.13	$21,847.90	$ 3,121.13	$31,040.89	$ 4,631.16
Purchases	$72,657.43	$10,250.85	$64,111.15	$ 9,053.00	$ 8,546.28	$ 1,197.85
Less Returns and Allowances	652.00	36.35	595.20	33.05	56.80	3.30
Net Purchases	$72,005.43	$10,214.50	$63,515.95	$ 9,019.95	$ 8,489.48	$ 1,194.55
Transportation In	1,220.70	175.60	1,109.80	159.66	110.90	15.94
Total Cost of Merchandise Available for Sale	$95,074.03	$13,511.23	$86,473.65	$12,300.74	$39,641.27	$ 5,841.65
Less Merchandise Inventory End of Period	31,254.06	4,494.83	31,040.89	4,631.16	31,254.06	4,494.83
Cost of Goods Sold	$63,819.97	$ 9,016.40	$55,432.76	$ 7,669.58	$ 8,387.21	$ 1,346.82

Percentage Analysis. It is common practice in analyzing an income statement on the percentage basis to let the net sales represent 100 per cent. On this basis Bryant & Wood's total gross profit on sales amounted to approximately 39.57 per cent ($47,695.67 ÷ $120,532.04). Their net operating income amounted to 6.73 per cent, while their net income amounted to 6.68 per cent. In other words, every dollar of net sales resulted in a gross profit of 39.57 cents, a net operating income of 6.73 cents, and a net income of 6.68 cents.

The income statement of Bryant & Wood reveals an unusually high rate of gross profit on sales. This was due to an increase in the prices of the products handled by Bryant & Wood during the latter part of the period. Bryant & Wood use the first-in, first-out method of costing inventories. Under this method the cost assigned to the goods in stock at the end of the period is based on the most recent purchases. As a result, the cost of the inventory is higher than normal. For example, it will be noted from the schedule of cost of goods sold that the inventory at the beginning of the year amounted to a total of only $24,969.03 while on May 31 it amounted to a total of $35,748.89. While the gross profit on sales for the period was abnormally high, there was an increase in the operating expenses for the period primarily because of increases in wages and

BRYANT & WOOD

SCHEDULE OF OPERATING EXPENSES

	For 11 Mos. ended May 31, 19--	For 10 Mos. ended Apr. 30, 19--	For May, 19--
Selling Expenses:			
Advertising Expense....................	$ 1,018.62	$ 931.00	$ 87.62
Salaries of Store Clerks................	9,497.00	8,587.00	910.00
Wages of Truck Driver...................	1,950.00	1,750.00	200.00
W. L. Wood, Salary......................	4,400.00	4,000.00	400.00
W. L. Wood, Traveling Expense...........	612.50	585.50	27.00
Gas and Oil for Truck...................	784.48	741.98	42.50
Repairs on Truck........................	130.25	125.85	4.40
Garage Rent.............................	220.00	200.00	20.00
Transportation Out......................	30.25	26.15	4.10
Expired Insurance on Mdse...............	165.00	150.00	15.00
Expired Insurance on Del. Equip.........	137.50	125.00	12.50
Expired Insurance on Store Equip........	13.75	12.50	1.25
Store Supplies Consumed.................	845.10	752.35	92.75
Postage.................................	481.12	465.79	15.33
Depr. of Store Equipment................	137.50	125.00	12.50
Depr. of Delivery Equipment.............	286.46	260.42	26.04
Misc. Selling Expense...................	138.90	130.00	8.90
Total Selling Expenses................	$20,848.43	$18,968.54	$ 1,879.89
Administrative Expenses:			
Rent....................................	$ 3,300.00	$ 3,000.00	$ 300.00
J. A. Bryant, Salary....................	4,400.00	4,000.00	400.00
Office Salaries.........................	7,400.00	6,720.00	680.00
Light and Water.........................	82.65	71.65	11.00
Telephone and Telegrams.................	157.01	139.51	17.50
Bad Debts Expense.......................	660.94	592.50	68.44
Property Taxes..........................	330.00	300.00	30.00
Office Supplies Consumed................	744.64	687.29	57.35
Postage.................................	341.33	326.00	15.33
Expired Insurance on Office Equip.......	27.50	25.00	2.50
Depr. of Office Equipment...............	229.13	208.30	20.83
Social Security Taxes...................	942.35	852.85	89.50
Misc. General Expense...................	117.95	105.70	12.25
Total Administrative Expenses..........	$18,733.50	$17,028.80	$ 1,704.70
Total Operating Expenses................	$39,581.93	$35,997.34	$ 3,584.59

taxes. As a result of the increased cost of doing business, the net income for the period amounted to only approximately 6⅔ per cent of the net sales.

The income statement for the month of May can be analyzed in the same manner as described for the eleven-months' statement. For example, the total gross profit on sales for May ($4,489.33) was 31.56 per cent of the total net sales ($14,223.36). The net income for May ($839.62) was 5.90 per cent of the total net sales for May ($14,223.36).

PRACTICE ASSIGNMENT No. 38. Complete Report No. 38 in the workbook and submit your working papers to the instructor for approval. Then continue with the following study assignment until Report No. 39 is required.

(39) THE BALANCE SHEET

Even though the books of Bryant & Wood are not formally closed until the end of the fiscal year, June 30, the management expects the accountant to prepare a balance sheet at the end of each month in order that it may have the desired information with respect to the current financial condition of the business. The balance sheet of Bryant & Wood prepared at the end of May in typewritten form is reproduced on page 503. The Balance Sheet columns of the work sheet reproduced on pages 492 and 493 provided the information needed in preparing the balance sheet. In preparing the balance sheet, the accounts are classified in accordance with standard practice. It will be noted that the assets are classified into two groups: (a) current assets and (b) fixed assets. The liabilities are classified as current liabilities. Bryant & Wood had no fixed liabilities on May 31.

Interpreting the Balance Sheet. Interpretation of Bryant & Wood's balance sheet involves an analysis of the information summarized in it. The current assets consist of cash, marketable securities, receivables, inventories, and supplies and prepaid items. The order in which these items are listed is of considerable importance. Following cash, the assets are listed in the order in which they might most readily be converted into cash. This is sometimes referred to as the order of probable liquidity. In listing notes receivable, accrued interest receivable, and accounts receivable, the amount of the provision for bad debts is shown as a deduction. The allowance is deducted from the total of all receivables because, when any of them prove worthless, the amount is charged to the allowance for bad debts account.

The items listed under the heading "Supplies and Prepayments" are classified as current assets for a special reason. There is no expectation that any of them, except prepaid federal excise tax (which is really just a part of the inventory cost), will ever be directly converted into cash. Instead, they will ordinarily be consumed in the normal operating cycle of the business. If the firm has prepaid these amounts, the amount of money that must be spent for such items in the near future will be reduced. If not actually prepaid on the date of the balance sheet, the amount owed will be included in accounts payable which is a current liability. Supplies and prepaid items are not classified as current assets because they will be converted into cash but because, if not paid in advance, they would require the use of current assets in the very near future or during the operating cycle of the business.

The amount of the prepaid federal excise tax listed among the current assets in Bryant & Wood's balance sheet represents the amount of the tax

BRYANT & WOOD
BALANCE SHEET
May 31, 19 --

ASSETS

Current Assets:

Cash		$ 7,517.85
Government Bonds		9,900.00
Notes Receivable	$ 3,203.36	
Accrued Interest Receivable	125.27	
Accounts Receivable	6,671.87	
	$10,000.50	
Less Allow. for Bad Debts	455.94	9,544.56

Merchandise Inventories:

Dept. A	$31,254.06	
Dept. B	4,494.83	35,748.89

Supplies and Prepayments:

Store Supplies	$ 31.25	
Advertising Supplies	42.87	
Office Supplies	48.60	
Postage Stamps	8.80	
Prepaid Insurance	168.75	
Prepaid Fed. Excise Tax	2,506.62	2,806.89
Total Current Assets		$65,518.19

Fixed Assets:

Store Equipment	$ 1,543.50	
Less Allow. for Depr.	332.50	$ 1,211.00
Delivery Equipment	$ 1,250.00	
Less Allow. for Depr.	476.04	773.96
Office Equipment	$ 2,660.00	
Less Allow. for Depr.	400.83	2,259.17
Total Fixed Assets		4,244.13
Total Assets		$69,762.32

LIABILITIES

Current Liabilities:

F.I.C.A. Taxes Payable	$ 71.60	
F.U.T.A. Taxes Payable	66.54	
State U.C. Taxes Payable	90.70	
Emp. Income Taxes Payable	152.20	
Notes Payable	3,500.00	
Accrued Interest Payable	34.42	
Accounts Payable	4,772.20	
Accrued Prop. Taxes Payable	180.00	
Total Current Liabilities		$ 8,867.66

PROPRIETORSHIP

J. A. Bryant, Partner

Proprietorship, July 1, Beginning of Year		$27,000.00
Net Income (1/2 of $8,056.71)....$4,028.36		
Less Withdrawals during Period.... 725.43		3,302.93
Proprietorship, May 31		$30,302.93

W. L. Wood, Partner

Proprietorship, July 1, Beginning of Year		$27,000.00
Net income (1/2 of $8,056.71)....$4,028.35		
Less Withdrawals during Period.... 436.62		3,591.73
Proprietorship, May 31		30,591.73
Total Proprietorship		60,894.66
Total Liabilities and Proprietorship		$69,762.32

applicable to the tires and tubes in stock on May 31. The tax is imposed on the manufacturer and is based on the weight of tires and tubes. It is the custom of tire manufacturers to bill the tax separately to the wholesaler, who is turn bills it separately to the retailer. Under this procedure, Bryant & Wood record the tax on tires and tubes purchased by debiting Prepaid Federal Excise Tax. When tires and tubes are sold by Bryant & Wood, the tax is credited to Prepaid Federal Excise Tax. Thus, the balance of the account always represents the tax applicable to the tires and tubes in stock. It is not practical to add the tax to the price of the tires and tubes because the tax is not subject to markup or discount.

Sometimes unused supplies and prepaid items are listed in the balance sheet as *deferred charges*. However, it is considered better practice to list them as current assets because they have either been paid for in advance or the amount owed is included in accounts payable. Any amount prepaid reduces the amount that must be spent for such items in the near future. Amounts owed for such items would be payable out of current assets in the near future. Thus, it can be seen that whether prepaid or not, the amount of such items affects the current financial position of the business.

The fixed assets of Bryant & Wood consist of three types of equipment: store equipment, delivery equipment, and office equipment. The book value of each type of equipment is shown separately. Since Bryant & Wood use the allowance method of accounting for depreciation, the credit balances of the allowance accounts are shown as deductions from the debit balances of the respective equipment accounts; thus, the net book value of each type of equipment is indicated.

All of the liabilities of Bryant & Wood are classified as current liabilities because they will mature within a comparatively short period of time. The prevailing practice is to classify as current liabilities all liabilities that are payable immediately or that will mature within the normal operating cycle of the business.

The liabilities of Bryant & Wood consist of social security taxes payable, employees' income taxes payable, notes payable, accrued interest payable, accounts payable, and accrued property taxes payable. The firm's liability for employees' income taxes payable arises from the fact that it is required to withhold a percentage of the wages of its employees and the amounts withheld are a liability until paid to the proper governmental agency.

Any debts that will not mature within the normal operating cycle of the business are usually listed in the balance sheet as fixed liabilities. Thus, long-term notes payable and mortgages payable that do not have to be paid out of current assets should be listed in the balance sheet as fixed liabilities immediately following the current liabilities.

The proprietorship section of Bryant & Wood's balance sheet is arranged to show the proprietorship of each partner at the beginning and at the end of the period beginning July 1 and ending May 31. It was necessary to take into consideration (a) each partner's proprietorship at the beginning of the period and (b) his share of the net income for the period less the amount withdrawn during the period for personal use. Partners' withdrawals are not to be confused with partners' salaries. Under the terms of the partnership agreement, the salary of each partner must be treated as an operating expense in computing the net income. Any additional drawings for personal use should be considered as drawings in anticipation of profits. Had either partner withdrawn a sum greater than his share of the net income, it would have been necessary to show the excess drawings as a deduction from his proprietorship unless he reimbursed the partnership for the excess drawings. The salaries of the partners may be treated as an operating expense in computing the net income under the terms of the partnership agreement.

Ratio Analysis of the Balance Sheet. One way to judge the financial position and structure of a business at a particular date and to make intelligent comparison with its position at an earlier date, or with other businesses of the same type, is to look at the proportionate relationship between the major classes of items in the balance sheet. These relationships can be expressed as ratios. Following is a brief discussion of a few of the most significant balance sheet ratios.

Current Ratio. A basic measure of the ability of a business to pay its current debts as they mature is the ratio between current assets and current liabilities. This ratio is called the *current ratio* or *working capital ratio*. (Working capital is usually taken to mean current assets; *net working capital* means current assets minus current liabilities.)

The current assets of Bryant & Wood on May 31 amounted to $65,518.19 and the current liabilities amounted to $8,867.66. This is a ratio of 7.39 to 1. Unless something very ususual develops, the firm should have no trouble in meeting its current obligations.

Acid-Test Ratio. A refinement of the current ratio is the ratio of *quick assets* to current liabilities. The quick assets include cash and those assets that can ordinarily be converted into cash within a relatively short time or which can readily be converted into cash with little or no loss should the need arise. The quick assets of Bryant & Wood include cash, government bonds, and receivables, which amount to a total of $26,962.41. The ratio between the total quick assets and the total current liabilities is 3.04 to 1 ($26,962.41 ÷ $8,867.66). This is called the acid-test ratio.

Ratio of Current Assets to Fixed Assets. To judge the relationship between current and fixed assets, their ratio can be calculated. On May 31, this ratio for Bryant & Wood was 15.44 to 1 ($65,518.19 ÷ $4,244.13). This indicates that a fairly small share of their total resources is tied up in fixed assets. Whether this is necessarily desirable depends upon the relative amount of their net income. If profits are adequate when judged by other standards, then it is probably desirable to have such a high ratio of current assets to fixed assets.

Ratio of Net Worth to Indebtedness. This ratio indicates the relative sources of the assets. If the ratio is high, it indicates that the owners have contributed a large share of the resources of the firm. On May 31, the net worth of the firm of Bryant & Wood was $60,894.66. The total liabilities were $8,867.66. This is a ratio of 6.87 to 1. This indicates considerable security for the creditors. The assets of the firm would have to undergo a sizable shrinkage before they would become insufficient to cover the claims of creditors.

Whether a high ratio of net worth to indebtedness is generally desirable depends upon a number of factors. Commercial banks operate with a very low ratio. The same is true of many other types of businesses. In many respects it may be good business to operate with someone else's money. On the other hand, it may be risky; a relatively small shrinkage in the assets may wipe out a large part or all of the owner's equity.

Ratio of Fixed Assets to Fixed Liabilities. In many cases the fixed liabilities of a business are secured by mortgages on the fixed assets. When this is true, the ratio of the fixed assets to fixed liabilities is a rough measure of the margin of safety to the long-term creditors. The higher the ratio, the more the security. This ratio does not apply to Bryant & Wood since this firm has no fixed liabilities.

Ratio of Net Worth to Fixed Assets. This ratio indicates the extent to which the owners of the enterprise have supplied the fixed assets and working capital. A ratio of 1 to 1 shows that the owners have supplied an amount equivalent to the fixed assets; a higher ratio would indicate that they have furnished some of the working capital. On May 31, the ratio of net worth to fixed assets for Bryant & Wood was 14.35 to 1. Since the total net worth of the firm is proportionately large, and the fixed assets relatively small, this high ratio is not surprising.

Turnover Ratios. Business men are interested in having a large volume of sales in relation to the amount invested in the business so long as more sales mean more profit. There are a few significant ratios that measure sales (or cost of goods sold) in relation to specific assets, or groups of assets. These are loosely called *turnover ratios.* In general, the ratio for one period by itself means very little; the important thing is whether the ratio is increasing or decreasing from period to period. In all cases, an increasing ratio is desirable if it is accompanied by increasing profits.

Merchandise Turnover. A merchant is vitally concerned with keeping his stock moving or "turning over." A rough measure of the speed with which the goods move, on the average, is the ratio of cost of goods sold to average inventory. (Cost of goods sold, rather than sales, must be used inasmuch as the inventories are on a cost basis. The numerator and denominator of the fraction must be on the same basis.)

For the eleven-months' period ended May 31, Bryant & Wood had a merchandise turnover of 2.4. The rate of turnover was ascertained in the following manner:

Inventories at beginning of period	$24,969.03
Inventories at end of period	35,748.89
Total	$60,717.92
Average inventory ($60,717.92 ÷ 2)	30,358.96
Cost of goods sold for the period	72,836.37

$72,836.37 ÷ $30,358.96 = 2.4

This means that, on the average, the stock turned over 2.4 times during the eleven-months' period. From July 1 through May 31 is 334 days. Three hundred thirty-four days divided by 2.4 is approximately 139 days, the average length of time the goods remain in stock.

Accounts Receivable Turnover. Accounts receivable turnover is the ratio of net sales to net notes and accounts receivable. The ratio shows the average length of the collection period which, in turn, measures the speed with which collections are made.

Bryant & Wood's net sales for the eleven-months' period ended May 31, amounted to $120,532.04. The net amount of their notes and accounts receivable on May 31, amounted to $9,419.29.* The ratio was almost 12.8 to 1 which is very good. If receivables turned over 12.8 times during 334 days, this would mean that, on the average, charges were on the books for 26 days.

---

*An average of the receivables during the period would be a more reliable figure to use.

Working Capital Turnover. Working capital turnover is the ratio of net sales to net working capital. In the case of Bryant & Wood for the eleven-months' period ended May 31, the turnover would be calculated as follows:

Net sales for period..	$120,532.04
Net working capital, May 31 * ($65,518.19 — $8,867.66)..........	56,650.53
$120,532.04 ÷ $56,650.53 = 2.13	

*An average of the working capital during the period would be a more reliable figure to use.

The figure obtained is an abstraction. Its only significance lies in its relation to the amount calculated for previous periods. An increasing figure indicates larger sales in relation to net current assets.

Fixed Asset Turnover. Fixed asset turnover is the ratio of net sales to the book value of the fixed assets. For Bryant & Wood, the ratio would be 28.4 to 1 ($120,532.04 ÷ $4,244.13) for the eleven-months' period ended May 31. As in the previous case, the figure itself means little. If comparison with similar calculations for previous periods showed an increase along with increased profits, the management could conclude that it is getting proportionately more desirable business in relation to the investment in fixed assets.

Net Worth Turnover. Net worth turnover is the ratio of net sales to net worth. It should be interpreted in much the same way as the two preceding ratios. For Bryant & Wood, the ratio would be approximately 2 to 1 ($120,532.04 ÷ $60,894.66) for the eleven-months' period ended May 31.

Ratio of Net Income to Total Assets. An important measure of the profitability of a business is the relationship between net income and total assets. The relationship can be expressed as a ratio, though stating it as a percentage is the usual practice. The net income of Bryant & Wood for the eleven-months' period ended May 31 was $8,056.71. This amounted to 11.55 per cent of the total assets of $69,762.32.

Ratio of Net Income to Net Worth. From the standpoint of the owners of a business, the relationship between net income and net worth is of prime importance. The net worth of Bryant & Wood was $60,894.66 on May 31. The net income of $8,056.71 for the previous eleven months represented a 13.23 per cent return on the partners' interest in the business.

PRACTICE ASSIGNMENT No. 39. Complete Report No. 39 in the workbook and submit your working papers to the instructor for approval. Then continue with the following study assignment until Report No. 40 is required.

(40) PROCEDURE AT END OF YEAR

As previously explained, it is the policy of the accountant for Bryant & Wood to furnish the management with a monthly income statement and a balance sheet. A work sheet is prepared as a means of compiling and classifying the information needed in preparing these statements. Preliminary to preparing the work sheet, the operating expense accounts are adjusted so that each month will be charged with its proper share of the expenses incurred. The operating expense adjustments are journalized and posted in the usual manner. In preparing the work sheet, any needed adjustments are entered in the Adjustments columns and the adjusted balances of the accounts are extended to the proper columns so that the income statement and the balance sheet may be prepared from the work sheet. These monthly adjustments are not journalized and posted to the general ledger accounts prior to the last month of the year. However, the adjustments appearing on the year-end work sheet must be journalized and posted to the proper accounts.

Adjusting the General Ledger Accounts. To illustrate the procedure in adjusting the accounts at the end of the year, it will be assumed that Bryant & Wood's work sheet prepared as of May 31 and reproduced on pages 492 and 493 represents the year-end work sheet. On this assumption, the adjusting entries appearing on the work sheet should be journalized and posted to the proper general ledger accounts. The required entries are shown in the general journal reproduced on page 510. Since the General Ledger Dr. and Cr. columns are the only amount columns used in recording the adjusting entries, these are the only amount columns reproduced in the illustration. The information needed in journalizing the adjustments was obtained from the Adjustments columns of Bryant & Wood's work sheet. For a detailed discussion of the adjustments on the work sheet see pages 489 to 495. Since these entries affected the general ledger accounts only, individual posting was required. As each item was posted a check mark was entered in the Check ($\checkmark$) column following the Amount column of the general journal and the general journal page number was entered in the Folio column of the general ledger immediately preceding the amount posted. After the adjusting entries were posted, the general ledger account balances were in complete agreement with the Adjusted Trial Balance columns of the work sheet.

Closing the Temporary General Ledger Accounts. To close the temporary accounts, it is only necessary to transfer their balances to the income summary account. Assuming that the temporary accounts of

Page 23   GENERAL JOURNAL FOR MONTH OF *May* 19—

DEBITS			DAY	DESCRIPTION	CREDITS		
GENERAL LEDGER					GENERAL LEDGER		
ACCT. No.	AMOUNT	√			ACCT. No.	AMOUNT	√
....	....		31	ADJUSTING ENTRIES	....	....	..
55	21847 90	√		To transfer beginning inventories to Cost of Goods	14	21847 90	√
56	3121 13	√		Sold, Depts. A and B......................	15	3121 13	√
55	72657 43	√		To transfer purchases to Cost of Goods Sold, Depts.	51	72657 43	√
56	10250 85	√		A and B.............................	52	10250 85	√
051	652 00	√		To transfer purchases returns and allowances to Cost	55	652 00	√
052	36 35	√		of Goods Sold, Depts. A and B.............	56	36 35	√
55	1220 70	√		To transfer transportation in to Cost of Goods Sold,	53	1220 70	√
56	175 60	√		Depts. A and B.	54	175 60	√
14	31254 06	√		To record ending inventories, Depts. A and B	55	31254 06	√
15	4494 83	√			56	4494 83	√
132	125 27	√		To adjust for accrued interest receivable..........	71	125 27	√
81	34 42	√		To adjust for accrued interest payable............	26	34 42	√
	145870 54					145870 54	
....	....	..	31	CLOSING ENTRIES	....	....	..
41	102634 44	√		Sales, Dept. A — Income Summary.............	33	102634 44	√
42	19585 00	√		Sales, Dept. B — " "	33	19585 00	√
71	244 65	√		Interest Income — " "	33	244 65	√
72	1669 38	√		Purchases Discount — " "	33	1669 38	√
33	1612 40	√		Income Summary — Sales R. & A., Dept. A....	041	1612 40	√
33	75 00	√		" " — Sales R. & A., Dept. B	042	75 00	√
33	63819 97	√		" " — Cost of Goods Sold, Dept. A	55	63819 97	√
33	9016 40	√		" " — Cost of Goods Sold, Dept. B.	56	9016 40	√
33	39581 93	√		" " — Operating Expenses.......	61	39581 93	√
33	206 29	√		" " — Interest Expense..........	81	206 29	√
33	1365 33	√		" " — Sales Discount...........	82	1365 33	√
33	370 48	√		" " — Charitable Contributions....	83	370 48	√
33	28 96	√		" " — Collection Expense........	84	28 96	√
33	4028 36	√		" " — J. A. Bryant, Drawing....	311	4028 36	√
33	4028 35	√		" " — W. L. Wood, Drawing......	321	4028 35	√
	248266 94					248266 94	
			June 1	Reversing Entries			
71	125 27	√		To reverse adjusting entries for accrued	132	125 27	√
26	34 42	√		interest.	81	34 42	√
	159 69					159 69	

Bryant & Wood are to be closed as of May 31, the work sheet reproduced on pages 492 and 493 provides the information needed in drafting the closing entries. The entries required to close the temporary general ledger accounts were made in the general journal (reproduced above) immediately following the adjusting entries.

It will be noted that the temporary accounts with credit balances were closed first, followed by the temporary accounts with debit balances. It is also necessary to distribute the net income between the partners. The partnership agreement provides that profits are to be shared equally. Accordingly, one half of the net income was transferred from Income Summary to each of the partner's drawing accounts. The partners' drawing accounts should be left open pending a decision as to whether the partners will withdraw their profits or leave all or a portion of their profits in the business. Any amount withdrawn by a partner should be recorded by debiting his drawing account and by crediting the bank account. Should the partners subsequently decide to leave all or a portion of their profits in the business as additional capital, the amount should be recorded by debiting their drawing accounts and by crediting their capital accounts.

The closing entries were posted individually to the proper general ledger accounts. As each item was posted a check mark was entered in the Check ($\sqrt{}$) column following the Amount column of the general journal and the general journal page number was entered in the Folio column of the general ledger immediately preceding the amount posted.

The Income Summary Account. In posting the closing entries to Income Summary, it is customary to identify the accounts that are being closed by itemizing them in the summary account as shown in the following illustration. The account then provides a permanent ledger record showing the results of operations for the accounting period. A comparison of the income summary account with the income statement will reveal that they provide similar information differing only in form. The income summary account is the accountant's ledger record of the operating results, while the income statement is the accountant's report of the operating results.

INCOME SUMMARY   Account No. 33

19--				19--			
May 31	Sales R. & A., Dept. A	GJ23	1,612.40	May 31	Sales, Dept. A	GJ23	102,634.44
31	Sales R. & A., Dept. B	GJ23	75.00	31	Sales, Dept. B	GJ23	19,585.00
31	Cost of Goods Sold, Dept. A	GJ23	63,819.97	31	Interest Income	GJ23	244.65
31	Cost of Goods Sold, Dept. B	GJ23	9,016.40	31	Purchases Discount	GJ23	1,669.38
31	Operating Expenses	GJ23	39,581.93				*124,133.47*
31	Interest Expense	GJ23	206.29				
31	Sales Discount	GJ23	1,365.33				
31	Charitable Contribution	GJ23	370.48				
31	Collection Expense	GJ23	28.96				
31	J. A. Bryant, Drawing	GJ23	4,028.36				
31	W. L. Wood, Drawing	GJ23	4,028.35				
			124,133.47				
			124,133.47				124,133.47

Income Summary Account Closed

Balancing and Ruling Accounts. After the adjusting and closing entries are posted, the temporary accounts will be in balance and should be ruled in the usual manner. The open accounts may also be balanced and ruled in order to prepare them to receive entries for the next fiscal period. However, accounts that have entries on only one side of the account need not be balanced and ruled.

In balancing the open accounts, it is customary to bring the balance down below the ruling on the proper side unless the page is filled, in which case the balance should be carried forward to the top of a new page.

Closing the Operating Expense Ledger Accounts. After the closing entries are posted, all of the temporary accounts that are kept in the general ledger, including the operating expense control account, will be in balance. The operating expense accounts that are kept in the subsidiary ledger should also be closed. The procedure in closing an operating expense account is illustrated below by reproducing the account with Advertising Expense. This account was closed by writing "Income Summary" in the Items column, by placing a check mark in the Folio column, by entering the balance in the Credits column, and by placing a cipher in the Balance column. All of the accounts kept in the operating expense subsidiary ledger should be closed in like manner. When the balance form of account ruling is used, it is not necessary to rule an account that is in balance, although it may be ruled if desired.

ACCOUNT ADVERTISING EXPENSE					ACCOUNT No. 611
DATE	ITEMS	FOLIO	DEBITS	CREDITS	BALANCE
19-- May 1	Dr. Balance				974.27
10		CD89	12.50		
31		CD90	3.50		
31		GJ22	28.35		1,018.62
31	Income Summary	√		1,018.62	–O–

Advertising Expense Account Closed

Post-Closing Trial Balance. After the closing entries are posted, a trial balance of the open accounts in the general ledger should be taken to test the equality of the debit and the credit balances. This trial balance is usually referred to as a post-closing trial balance. The post-closing trial balance for Bryant & Wood as of May 31 is reproduced on page 513.

Reversing Entries. The accountant for Bryant & Wood follows the practice of reversing the adjusting entries for accruals to facilitate the recording of the transactions of the succeeding fiscal period in a routine manner. The reversing entries were journalized and posted to the proper accounts. The entries are shown in the general journal reproduced on page 510. It should be noted that the reversing entries are dated June 1 which, in this case, represents the first day of the succeeding accounting period.

BRYANT & WOOD

POST-CLOSING TRIAL BALANCE

MAY 31, 19 —

Liberty National Bank	111	$ 7,467.85	
Petty Cash Fund	112	50.00	
Government Bonds	12	9,900.00	
Notes Receivable	131	3,203.36	
Accrued Interest Receivable	132	125.27	
Accounts Receivable	133	6,671.87	
Allowance for Bad Debts	013		$ 455.94
Merchandise Inventory, Dept. A	14	31,254.06	
Merchandise Inventory, Dept. B	15	4,494.83	
Store Supplies	161	31.25	
Advertising Supplies	162	42.87	
Office Supplies	163	48.60	
Postage Stamps	164	8.80	
Prepaid Insurance	165	168.75	
Prepaid Federal Excise Tax	166	2,506.62	
Store Equipment	17	1,543.50	
Allowance for Depr. of Store Equipment	017		332.50
Delivery Equipment	18	1,250.00	
Allowance for Depr. of Delivery Equipment	018		476.04
Office Equipment	19	2,660.00	
Allowance for Depr. of Office Equipment	019		400.83
F.I.C.A. Taxes Payable	21		71.60
F.U.T.A. Taxes Payable	22		66.54
State U.C. Taxes Payable	23		90.70
Employees' Income Taxes Payable	24		152.20
Notes Payable	25		3,500.00
Accrued Interest Payable	26		34.42
Accounts Payable	27		4,772.20
Accrued Property Taxes Payable	28		180.00
J. A. Bryant, Partner	31		27,000.00
J. A. Bryant, Drawing	311		3,302.93
W. L. Wood, Partner	32		27,000.00
W. L. Wood, Drawing	321		3,591.73
		$71,427.63	$71,427.63

The first entry was made to reverse the adjusting entry made to record the interest accrued on notes receivable and bonds owned as of May 31. The second entry was made to reverse the adjusting entry made to record the interest accrued on notes payable as of May 31. The reversing entries were posted in the usual manner with the result that the accounts for Accrued Interest Receivable and Accrued Interest Payable were in balance and were ruled. As a result of this procedure any interest collected and any interest paid during the ensuing fiscal year may be recorded in routine manner.

The amount credited to Accrued Property Taxes Payable is an accumulation of the monthly adjustments made to record the accrued property taxes in the operating expense ledger. It is not necessary to make a reversing entry for this accrual. On the other hand, if there had been any accrued wages payable on December 31, it would be advisable to draft a reversing entry debiting Accrued Wages Payable in the general ledger and crediting the proper salary accounts in the operating expense ledger.

The Accounting Cycle. Bryant & Wood keep their accounts on the basis of a fiscal year ending June 30. Each year constitutes a time period in which a standard accounting process takes place. The periodic repetition of this process constitutes an accounting cycle. An accounting cycle consists of a standard procedure involving the recording and analyzing of the transactions completed during the period and the reporting of the results through the medium of financial statements. Following is a brief outline of the several steps covered in the accounting cycle of Bryant & Wood:

(1) Procedure during each month:

> (a) Journalize chronologically all transactions completed.
> (b) Post to the accounts kept in the general and subsidiary ledgers.

(2) Procedure at end of each month:

> (a) Journalize and post the entries required to adjust the operating expense accounts which are kept in a subsidiary ledger.
> (b) Take a trial balance of the general ledger accounts and prepare schedules of the subsidiary ledger account balances to prove the balances of the control accounts kept in the general ledger.
> (c) Prepare a work sheet covering the period from the start of the fiscal year to the end of the current month. The purpose of this work sheet is to provide the information needed in preparing the monthly statements.
> (d) Prepare financial statements with appropriate supporting schedules.

(3) Procedure at end of fiscal year:

> Procedure same as at end of preceding months, except that a physical inventory is taken and the cost of the merchandise in stock is computed before preparing a work sheet. At end of preceding months the inventory is computed on the basis of the stock records. The following additional year-end work is also required:
>
> > (a) Journalize and post the adjusting entries.
> > (b) Journalize and post the closing entries; also close the operating expense accounts that are kept in a subsidiary ledger.
> > (c) Take a post-closing trial balance.
> > (d) Journalize and post the reversing entries as of the first day of the new fiscal period.

PRACTICE ASSIGNMENT No. 40. Complete Report No. 40 in the workbook and submit your working papers to the instructor for approval. The instructor will then give directions as to the work to be done next.

Unit Twenty

PRACTICAL ACCOUNTING PROBLEMS

The problems in this unit are supplementary to those in the workbook. They are numbered to indicate the unit of the textbook with which they correlate. For example, Problems 11-A to 11-I, inclusive, correlate with Unit Eleven. Loose-leaf stationery should be used in solving these problems.

Problem 11-A

On May 1, E. H. Christman organized a photographic equipment and supplies enterprise and opened a new set of books. Following is a list of the assets that he invested in the business:

Cash..	$ 5,212.95
Office Equipment...............................	2,650.00
Store Equipment...............................	3,195.40
Delivery Truck................................	2,480.00
Total...	$13,538.35

He owed $640 on the delivery truck that was purchased on credit.

REQUIRED: Draft the opening entry in general journal form.

Problem 11-B

HENRY GRIM

BALANCE SHEET

DECEMBER 31, 19--

ASSETS			LIABILITIES		
Cash...............		$ 2,212.75	Accounts Payable....	$2,925.70	
Accounts Receivable..	$4,216.30		F.I.C.A. Taxes Payable	35.95	
Less Allow. for Bad			Employees' Income		
Debts..........	312.48	3,903.82	Taxes Payable.....	53.12	
Mdse. Inventory......		8,196.54	Total Liabilities......		$ 3,014.77
Prepaid Insurance....		165.32	PROPRIETORSHIP		
Store Equipment.....	$3,200.00		Henry Grim, Prop....		14,373.66
Less Allow. for Depr.	290.00	2,910.00			
			Total Liabilities and		
Total Assets........		$17,388.43	Proprietorship.....		$17,388.43

Henry Grim, who has been conducting a wholesale wallpaper and paint enterprise, decides to install a new set of books as of January 2.

REQUIRED: Draft the opening entry in general journal form.

515

Problem 11-C

E. R. Duncan is engaged in the wholesale leather goods business. After closing his income and expense accounts for the calendar year ended December 31, his income summary account had a credit balance of $9,250.45. At the same time his capital account had a credit balance of $29,745 and his drawing account had a debit balance of $6,000.

REQUIRED: (a) Using the standard account form of ledger paper, open Mr. Duncan's capital account and drawing account, and an income summary account, and enter the December 31 balances. (b) Assuming that Mr. Duncan wishes to have the balances of both the income summary and drawing accounts transferred to his capital account, journalize and post the required entries. After completing the posting, total and rule the accounts and bring down Mr. Duncan's present capital below the ruling.

Problem 11-D

Mark H. Walker has been operating a wholesale hardware business as a sole proprietor. His balance sheet prepared as of September 30 is reproduced below. On October 1 of the current year he admits Charles M. Coulter as a partner with a one-half interest in the business to be conducted under the firm name of Walker & Coulter. Under the partnership agreement, Mr. Coulter invests $10,866.92 in cash. The assets of Mr. Walker become the property of the partnership and his liabilities are assumed by the partnership.

MARK H. WALKER

BALANCE SHEET

SEPTEMBER 30, 19--

ASSETS			LIABILITIES		
Cash...............		$ 3,260.12	Notes Payable........	$ 2,500.00	
Accounts Receivable..	$3,800.40		Accounts Payable....	2,100.50	
			F.I.C.A. Taxes Payable	30.00	
Less Allow. for Bad			Employees' Income		
Debts..........	390.00	3,410.40	Taxes Payable.....	50.00	
			Total Liabilities......		$ 4,680.50
Mdse. Inventory......		7,296.90	PROPRIETORSHIP		
Store Equipment.....	$2,100.00		Mark H. Walker, Prop.		10,866.92
Less Allow. for Depr.	520.00	1,580.00			
			Total Liabilities and		
Total Assets.........		$15,547.42	Proprietorship.....		$15,547.42

REQUIRED: Assuming that a new set of books is installed by the partnership, draft the necessary opening entries in general journal form to record the investments of the partners.

Problem 11-E

William A. Bence and J. A. Womack have been competitors in the wholesale drug business. On July 1 of the current year they form a partnership, to be operated under the firm name of Bence & Womack. Their balance sheets as of June 30 are reproduced below. The partnership agreement provides that the assets are to be taken over at their book value and that the liabilities are to be assumed by the partnership. The agreement also provides that Mr. Womack is to contribute a sufficient amount of additional cash to make his investment equal to Mr. Bence's investment. It is also agreed that the partners will share profits and losses equally and the assets will be distributed equally between them in case of dissolution.

WILLIAM A. BENCE
BALANCE SHEET
JUNE 30, 19--

ASSETS			LIABILITIES		
Cash..............		$3,100.95	Notes Payable.......	$ 900.00	
Accounts Receivable..	$2,850.20		Accounts Payable....	2,140.12	
Less Allow. for Bad			F.I.C.A. Taxes Payable	30.00	
Debts...........	57.40	2,792.80	Employees' Income		
			Taxes Payable.....	53.00	
Mdse. Inventory......		4,690.87			
Delivery Equipment...	$3,100.00		Total Liabilities......		$ 3,123.12
Less Allow. for Depr.	775.00	2,325.00			
			PROPRIETORSHIP		
Office Equipment.....	$1,200.00		William A. Bence, Prop.		10,586.50
Less Allow. for Depr.	400.00	800.00			
			Total Liabilities and		
Total Assets.........		$13,709.62	Proprietorship.....		$13,709.62

J. A. WOMACK
BALANCE SHEET
JUNE 30, 19--

ASSETS			LIABILITIES		
Cash..............		$ 4,200.30	Accounts Payable....	$ 2,109.65	
Accounts Receivable..	$2,100.99		F.I.C.A. Taxes Payable	29.00	
Less Allow. for Bad			Employees' Income		
Debts...........	49.60	2,051.39	Taxes Payable.....	45.46	
Mdse. Inventory......		3,240.65			
Delivery Equipment...	$2,800.00		Total Liabilities......		$ 2,184.11
Less Allow. for Depr.	700.00	2,100.00			
			PROPRIETORSHIP		
Office Equipment.....	$1,000.00		J. A. Womack, Prop..		10,108.23
Less Allow. for Depr.	300.00	700.00			
			Total Liabilities and		
Total Assets.........		$12,292.34	Proprietorship.....		$12,292.34

REQUIRED: Assuming that a new set of books is installed by the partnership, draft the necessary opening entries in general journal form to record the investments of the partners.

Problem 11-F

The Westervelt Upholstering Co., a partnership, is engaged in the wholesale upholstering business. Ownership of the firm is vested in J. C. Westervelt, R. C. Crays, A. T. Collard, and A. C. Thompson. Profits and losses are shared equally.

Mr. Collard died on July 5. His widow is entitled to receive his share in the distribution of the partnership assets. The remaining partners agreed to buy his widow's interest at 93 per cent of its book value. When the books were closed as of the date of Mr. Collard's death, his capital account had a credit balance of $8,516.20. On August 15, a partnership check was issued to Mrs. Collard in final settlement.

REQUIRED: Compute the amount to be paid Mrs. Collard under the agreement and draft the general journal entry required to record the check in the books of the partnership.

Problem 11-G

January 1. The Ideal Carpet Co. was incorporated with an authorized issue of 1,000 shares of common capital stock, par value $25 per share. Subscriptions, accompanied by checks, were received from the following:

A. D. Geissler, 300 shares, $7,500
L. F. Geissler, 300 shares, $7,500
P. G. Cameron, 200 shares, $5,000
L. L. Gleason, 200 shares, $5,000

Following is a list of the corporate accounts to be kept:

Capital Stock
Subscriptions Receivable
Capital Stock Subscribed

REQUIRED: Draft the general journal entries required to record (a) the stock subscriptions received, (b) cash received to apply on subscriptions, and (c) the capital stock issued to subscribers on January 10.

Problem 11-H

August 28. The board of directors of The Atlantic Rolling Mill Co. declared a cash dividend of $1.25 per share on its 5 per cent cumulative preferred stock, payable October 16 to holders of record September 15. There were 21,320 shares of this stock outstanding.

October 16. The company mailed dividend checks to stockholders amounting to a total of $26,650.

REQUIRED: Using standard two-column journal paper, record (a) the dividend declared on August 28 and (b) the dividend paid on October 16.

Problem 11-I

William Fuqua, Charles Lee, and Everett Hulse were engaged in business as a partnership under the firm name of Fuqua, Lee & Hulse. On January 2, The Midwest Distributing Co., with an authorized capital of $50,000, consisting of 5,000 shares of common capital stock, par value $10 per share, was organized to take over the business formerly conducted by the partnership. The following balance sheet of the partnership was prepared at the time of incorporating the business:

FUQUA, LEE & HULSE

BALANCE SHEET

DECEMBER 31, 19--

ASSETS			LIABILITIES		
Cash................		$ 6,590.42	Accounts Payable.....	$ 3,509.60	
Accounts Receivable..	$7,650.98		F.I.C.A. Taxes Payable	44.40	
Less Allow. for Bad			Employees' Income		
Debts..........	712.00	6,938.98	Taxes Payable.....	50.12	
			Total Liabilities......		$ 3,604.12
Mdse. Inventory......		11,612.30	PROPRIETORSHIP		
Office Equipment.....	$2,200.00		William Fuqua,		
Less Allow. for Depr.	700.00	1,500.00	Partner..........		9,202.12
			Charles Lee,		
			Partner..........		8,005.60
Delivery Equipment...	$3,100.00		Everett Hulse,		
Less Allow. for Depr.	1,700.00	1,400.00	Partner..........		7,229.86
			Total Liabilities and		
Total Assets........		$28,041.70	Proprietorship.....		$28,041.70

The partners subscribed for capital stock of the corporation as follows:

William Fuqua, 2,000 shares at $10 a share.......................$20,000
Charles Lee, 2,000 shares at $10 a share......................... 20,000
Everett Hulse, 1,000 shares at $10 a share....................... 10,000

The partners, as individuals, received credit toward their subscriptions for their respective equities in the assets of the partnership and issued their personal checks for the balance of their respective subscriptions. A new set of books is to be installed by the corporation.

REQUIRED: Draft entries in general journal form to record the following: (a) The partners' subscriptions to the capital stock of the corporation,

(b) the transfer of the assets and liabilities of the partnership to the corporation, (c) the receipt of cash from the partners in payment of the balances due on their respective subscriptions, and (d) the issuance of stock certificates to the partners.

Problem 12-A

Moberly & Hamilton are wholesale dealers in china and glassware. In accounting for notes, they use a notes receivable register similar to the one reproduced on pages 332 and 333. Following is a narrative of transactions involving notes received from customers during the current year:

Mar. 6. Received from Charles Lahke a 60-day, 6% note (No. 1) for $400 dated March 4 and payable at First National Bank, Cedar Rapids.

April 26. Received from Robert W. Nelson a 90-day, 5% note (No. 2) for $300 dated April 25 and payable at Second National Bank, Meadville.

May   3. Received a check for $404 from Charles Lahke in payment of his note due today plus interest.

     19. Received from Louis A. Finch a 60-day, 6% note (No. 3) for $250 dated May 18 and payable at Hyde Park Trust Company, Hyde Park.

July 17. Received a check for $252.50 from Louis A. Finch in payment of his note due today plus interest.

     24. Received a check for $303.75 from Robert W. Nelson in payment of his note due today plus interest.

Oct.   2. Received from R. K. Chapman a 90-day, 5% note (No. 4) for $460 dated October 2 and payable at Windsor State Bank.

     19. Discounted R. K. Chapman's note for $460 at the Shelby Loan & Trust Company at 6% and received credit for the proceeds.

REQUIRED: (a) Draft the entries in general journal form to record the foregoing transactions. Foot the amount columns as a means of proof. (b) Make the required entries in a notes receivable register to provide a detailed auxiliary record of the notes received by Moberly & Hamilton.

Problem 12-B

Baker & Herron operate a department store. Sometimes they find it necessary to issue notes to creditors to obtain extensions of time for payment of their accounts. Unless otherwise stated all such notes are made payable at the Shelby County State Bank, Shelbyville. Following is a narrative of transactions involving notes issued by Baker & Herron during the current year:

Feb.   1. Borrowed $500 from the bank on a 90-day, 5% note (No. 1).

Mar.   7. Issued a 60-day, 6% note (No. 2) for $295 to Alms & Doepke Co.

April 20. Issued a 60-day, 5% note (No. 3) for $320 to S. P. Nelson & Sons.

May   2. Issued a check for $506.25 to the bank in payment of note due today plus interest.

      6. Gave Alms & Doepke Co. a check for $2.95 in payment of the interest and a new note (No. 4) for $295, due in 60 days, with interest at 6%, in settlement of the note due today.

June   19. Issued a check for $322.67 to S. P. Nelson & Sons in payment of note due today plus interest.

July   1. Borrowed $1,000 from the bank on a 90-day, 5% note (No. 5).

      5. Issued a check for $297.95 to Alms & Doepke Co. in payment of note due today plus interest.

Sept.   29. Gave Shelby County State Bank a check for $12.50 in payment of the interest and a new note (No. 6) for $1,000, due in 60 days, with interest at 5%, in settlement of the note due today.

Nov.   28. Issued a check for $1,008.33 to the bank in payment of note due today plus interest.

REQUIRED: (a) Draft the entries in general journal form to record the foregoing transactions. Foot the amount columns as a means of proof. (b) Make the required entries in a notes payable register similar to the one reproduced on pages 338 and 339, to provide a detailed auxiliary record of the notes issued by Baker & Herron.

Problem 12-C

Crockett & Hyde are engaged in the wholesale distribution of dairy products. Following is a narrative of selected transactions completed by the firm:

April   18. Received a cashier's check from The National Bank of Wilmette for $216 in payment of a sight draft for $216.50 drawn April 14 on Daniel Laurence, a customer, less 50 cents collection charge.

June   9. Received an accepted time draft, dated June 7 for 30 days, for $112.92 from L. B. Ratterman in temporary settlement of his account.

July   9. Received a cashier's check from The Second National Bank for $112.42 in payment of the time draft for $112.92 drawn on L. B. Ratterman, June 7 and accepted on June 9, less 50 cents collection charge.

Aug.   23. Received trade acceptance (No. 22) dated August 17, payable September 15, from J. S. Turner for $495.16.

      26. Discounted the foregoing trade acceptance at The Atlas National Bank, at a discount of 4%, and deposited the proceeds.

REQUIRED: (a) Record the foregoing transactions in general journal form. Foot the amount columns as a means of proof. (b) Open an account with Notes Receivable, Account No. 131; post the journal entries affecting this account; foot the amount columns; and if the account is found to be in balance, rule the account.

Problem 12-D

Urban & Wiley are wholesale distributors of plate and window glass. Following is a narrative of selected transactions completed by the firm:

Mar. 28. Accepted a sight draft for $250 drawn by Pittsburgh Plate Glass Co., a creditor, and issued a check in payment.

April 19. Accepted a time draft for $316.45, dated April 17 at 30 days' sight, drawn by Kellogg & Kidd, creditors.

May 19. Issued a check for $316.45 in payment of time draft accepted April 19.

Sept. 5. Honored a trade acceptance drawn by Libbey, Owens, Ford Glass Co., a creditor, on September 2 for $210, payable on October 2.

Oct. 2. Issued a check for $210 in payment of the foregoing trade acceptance.

REQUIRED: (a) Record the foregoing transactions in general journal form. Foot the amount columns as a means of proof. (b) Open an account with Notes Payable, Account No. 25; post the journal entries affecting this account; foot the amount columns, and if the account is found to be in balance, rule the account.

Problem 13-A

Nichols & Sellers are partners engaged in the wholesale distribution of office furniture and supplies. The merchandise accounts are kept on the departmental basis, Dept. A comprising furniture and Dept. B, all other merchandise. The following general ledger accounts are affected by this problem:

17 Store Equipment	53 Purchases, Dept. A
18 Office Equipment	54 Purchases, Dept. B
25 Notes Payable	55 Transportation In, Dept. A
26 Accounts Payable	56 Transportation In, Dept. B

Following is a narrative of purchases made during February:

Feb. 1. (Tuesday) No. 206, The Shaw-Walker Co., Washington; desks, $316.40; terms, January 27 — 2/10, n/30; Pennsylvania freight collect.
No. 207, Utility Supply Co., City; memo books, $47.75; terms, January 28 — 2/10, n/30.
No. 208, Office Supply Co., Chicago; ledger outfits, $119.50; terms, January 28 — 2/10, n/60; postage prepaid and added to invoice, $6.20.
No. 209, Indian Splint, Inc., Rochester; chairs, $49.30; terms, January 28 — 3/10, n/30; New York Central freight collect.
No. 210, Hekman Furniture Co., Grand Rapids; tables, $89.55; terms, January 27 — 30 days; Pere Marquette freight collect.
14. No. 211, The Wickwede Bros. Co., Marietta; tables, $55; terms, February 11 — 30 days; Big Four freight prepaid and added to invoice, $5.20.

No. 212, Waterman's, New York City; desk sets, $198.20; terms, February 10 — 30 days; express prepaid and added to invoice, $13.95.

Feb. 21. No. 213, The Shaw-Walker Co., Washington; filing cabinets (for store use), $204; terms, February 18 — 2/10, n/30; Pere Marquette freight collect.

Received a corrected purchase invoice, dated January 27, from Hekman Furniture Co., Grand Rapids, $90.55. (See Purchase Invoice No. 210.)

No. 214, High Point Furniture Co., High Point; desks, $275; terms, February 19 — 30-day note with interest at 6%.

28. No. 215, Royal Typewriter Co., City; typewriter (for office use) $105; terms, February 26 — 30 days.

REQUIRED: As the accountant for the partnership (a) enter each invoice in an invoice record similar to the one reproduced on page 365 (except that a column will not be required for federal excise tax), and post directly to the proper creditor's account in a subsidiary accounts payable ledger; (b) complete the individual posting from the invoice record to the general ledger; (c) foot, prove the footings, enter the totals, and rule the invoice record; (d) complete the summary posting; and (e) prove the balance of the accounts payable account by preparing a schedule of the accounts with creditors as of February 28. Use standard ledger paper for the general ledger and balance-column ledger paper for the accounts payable ledger.

Problem 14-A

Beetle and Sparks are partners engaged in the wholesale distribution of musical instruments. The merchandise accounts are kept on the departmental basis. Following is a list of the general ledger accounts that are affected by this problem, with the September 1 balances indicated:

131 Notes Receivable, $700
132 Accounts Receivable, $1,125.40
41 Sales, Dept. A, $7,693.12
041 Sales Returns and Allowances, Dept. A, $375.40
42 Sales, Dept. B, $6,212.92
042 Sales Returns and Allowances, Dept. B, $113.45
619 Transportation Out, $219.40

As of September 1, Beetle and Sparks' accounts receivable had debit balances as follows:

Gaddis & Wallace, 12 Main Street, Evansville; $220
Hamilton Bros., 46 Spruce Street, Quincy; $198.40
Herron's Department Store, 1240 Main Street, Lafayette; $215.90
Moberly & Son, 262 Division Street, Janesville; $212.32
Tull's Department Store, 3315 Virginia Avenue, Decatur; $278.78

All charge sales are subject to a discount of 2% if paid within ten days from date of invoice, net 30 days.

Following is a narrative of the charge sales for September:

Sept. 1. (Friday) Sale No. 162, Tull's Department Store; Dept. A, $82.60.
2. Sale No. 163, Moberly & Son; Dept. B, $96.40. Express prepaid and added to invoice, $4.50.
5. Sale No. 164, Gaddis & Wallace; Dept. A, $42.50; Dept. B, $32.40.
8. Sale No. 165, D. D. Carpenter, 2715 Bigbee, Bowling Green; Dept. A, $104.60.
11. Sale No. 166, Hamilton Bros.; Dept. A, $76.20; Dept. B, $14.30. Freight prepaid and added to invoice, $4.65.
13. Sale No. 167, Tull's Department Store; Dept. A, $85; Dept. B, $165.30.
15. Sale No. 168, Lilly & Dunscomb Furniture Store, 12 Green Street, Fond du Lac; Dept. B, $54.20. Express prepaid and added to invoice, $2.12.
16. Sale No. 169, Herron's Department Store; Dept. A, $49.50; Dept. B, $42.60.
Sent D. D. Carpenter a corrected invoice for Sale No. 165 amounting to $106.40.
20. Sale No. 170, Carr's Victrola Shop, 22 Bloomfield Street, Paducah; Dept. A, $112.50; received 60-day, 5% interest-bearing note.
22. Sent Lilly & Dunscomb Furniture Store a corrected invoice for Sale No. 168 amounting to $57.32.
27. Sale No. 171, Tull's Department Store; Dept. A, $22.90. Parcel post charges added to invoice, $1.67.
28. Sale No. 172, Moberly & Son; Dept. A, $27; Dept. B, $32.40. Less credit for merchandise returned, Dept. A, $6.90.
30. Sale No. 173, Gaddis & Wallace; Dept. B, $92. Freight prepaid and added to invoice, $3.43.

REQUIRED:

(a) Using standard ledger paper, open the necessary general ledger accounts and enter the September 1 balances.

(b) Using balance-column ledger paper, open the necessary accounts receivable ledger accounts and enter the September 1 balances.

(c) Using a sales record similar to the one reproduced on page 389 (except that a column will not be required for federal excise tax), enter the charge sales for September and post directly to the proper customers' accounts.

(d) Complete the individual posting from the sales record to the general ledger accounts.

(e) Foot, prove the footings, enter the totals, and rule the sales record; complete the summary posting.

(f) Foot the general ledger accounts and prove the balance of the accounts receivable account by preparing a schedule of the accounts with customers as of September 30.

Problem 14-B

Wilson's Washing Machine Shop uses the installment method of accounting for sales of washing machines on an installment payment basis. The following information was obtained from the general ledger accounts at the end of the current year:

Installment Sales... $16,250.00
Cost of Goods Sold.. 13,000.00
Total down payments and collections from installment customers..... 12,250.00

REQUIRED: (a) Ascertain the amount of gross profit to be realized on the installment sales. (b) Ascertain the percentage of the gross profit to be realized on the installment sales. (c) Ascertain the amount of gross profit actually realized during the year. (d) Draft an entry in general journal form to close the installment sales account at the end of the year.

Problem 14-C

The Graybar Electric Co. distributes electric motors to local dealers on the consignment basis. Shipments to dealers on consignment are charged to the consignees at list prices. The dealer's basic compensation is a trade discount of 25% from the list prices. The dealer is also allowed an additional discount of 5% for payment in full on or before the 5th of the month for merchandise sold during the preceding month.

On October 2, The Graybar Electric Co. made a shipment of electric motors to Garvin & Son on consignment. The invoice of shipment amounted to a total of $665, computed at retail prices. During October, Garvin & Son sold all of the electric motors that were consigned to them on the October 2 shipment. On November 5, Garvin & Son rendered a statement of consignment sales to The Graybar Electric Co., at the same time remitting the proceeds which were computed as follows:

Sales... $665.00
Less:
    Commission, 25%.................................. $166.25
    Cash Discount, 5%................................. 24.94   191.19
Proceeds.. $473.81

REQUIRED: (a) As the accountant for The Graybar Electric Co. draft the entries in journal form necessary to record (1) the invoice of shipment to Garvin & Son on October 2 and (2) the sale of consigned merchandise by Garvin & Son during October, per statement received November 5 with remittance for $473.81 in payment of the proceeds. (b) Assuming that you are one of the partners of Garvin & Son and keep the books, draft the entries in general journal form required to record (1) the invoice of shipment received from The Graybar Electric Co. on October 2 and (2) the sale of consigned merchandise during October, per statement rendered November 5 with a check for $473.81 in payment of the proceeds.

Problem 15-A

Johnson Brothers are engaged in the wholesale hardware business. A stock record is kept of all merchandise handled. The following data with respect to Article X were assembled from their stock records:

On hand at beginning of period, 200 units.
First purchase during period, 250 units @ $12.50.
Second purchase during period, 180 units @ $11.
Last purchase during period, 190 units @ $13.
In stock at end of period, 175 units.

REQUIRED: Assuming that the units in stock at the beginning of the period were assigned a cost of $12 each under the FIFO method, or $12.25 each under the LIFO method, compute (a) the total cost of the units in stock at the end of the period and (b) the total cost of the units sold during the period under (1) the FIFO method and (2) the LIFO method of cost assignment.

Problem 15-B

Bush & Hayt operate a mail-order house as partners. Metered postage is used on parcel-post packages. As required, deposits are made for postage under the permit system. Postage stamps are purchased for other purposes. All prepaid postage is charged to Postage Stamps, Account No. 164, and periodically the postage used is charged to the following expense accounts:

619 Transportation Out (Parcel Post)
624 Postage on Advertising Matter
639 Postage on General Mail

Before adjusting entries had been made on April 30, the postage stamps account had a debit balance of $960.

REQUIRED: (a) Open the necessary accounts and enter the balance of the postage stamps account before adjustment. (b) Assuming that (1) during the month of April the postage used on parcel-post packages amounted to $298 and on advertising matter, $275; and (2) that on April 30 the unused stamps on hand amounted to $85 and the unused metered postage amounted to $145, make the required adjusting entry in general journal form to record all postage expense for the month. (c) Post. (d) Balance and rule the postage stamps account and bring down the balance as of May 1.

Problem 15-C

Beginning on January 3 of the current year, Kimball & Cleveland engaged as partners in the distribution of beverages. In accounting for insurance, the following accounts are used:

165 Prepaid Insurance
620 Expired Insurance on Merchandise
621 Expired Insurance on Store Equipment
640 Expired Insurance on Office Equipment

The premiums paid for insurance are charged to the prepaid insurance account. At the end of each month the expired insurance is charged to the proper expense accounts and credited to Prepaid Insurance. The firm keeps an auxiliary record of insurance in the form of a register similar to the one on pages 424 and 425.

Following is a record of the insurance transactions completed during the current year:

Jan.   3. Paid the premiums on the following insurance policies:
No. 72420 dated January 1, General Accident, Fire & Life Insurance Co.; merchandise, $30,000; term, one year; premium, $201.60.

No. 62412A dated January 1, Hardware Mutual Insurance Company of Minnesota; merchandise, $5,000; term, three years; premium, $90.

No. 247380 dated January 1, Lumbermen's Mutual Insurance Co.; office equipment, $1,500; term, one year; premium, $9.

No. 42416 dated January 1, Mutual Fire Insurance Co.; store equipment, $1,000; term, one year; premium, $7.20.

Feb.   2. Paid $60 premium on insurance policy No. 112490 dated February 1, Hartford Fire Insurance Co.; merchandise, $8,000; term, one year.

Mar.   6. Paid $18 premium on insurance policy No. 46230 dated March 1, Merrimac Mutual Fire Insurance Co.; merchandise, $1,000; term, three years.

Sept. 12. Received a check for $18 from the Hartford Fire Insurance Co. representing a refund on Policy No. 112490 canceled as of September 1.

Nov. 10. Paid $15 premium on Insurance Policy No. 16230 dated November 1, Sun Mutual Fire Insurance Co.; store equipment, $2,000; term, one year.

REQUIRED: (a) Journalize the transactions involving the premiums paid on policies purchased during January; enter the policies on the left page of an insurance register form; extend the proper proportion of the premium on each policy in effect during January to the January column on the right page of the register; foot the column in small figures. (b) Draft a journal entry to record the amount of the insurance expired during January. (c) Continue the work required each month to record any new insurance purchased during the month and to record the total insurance expired during the month. In recording the transactions for September, it will also be necessary to draft a journal entry to record the amount refunded on September 12 on Policy No. 112490. (d) As of December 31, enter the expired and unexpired insurance on each policy in the last two columns on the right page of the insurance register and foot the columns in small figures. (e) Open an account for Prepaid Insurance, Account No. 165. Post from the general journal the debit and credit entries affecting the prepaid insurance account. After completing the posting to the prepaid insurance account, foot the amount columns, ascertain the balance, and enter it on the proper side of the account in small figures. Prove your work by comparing the balance of the account with the footing of the unexpired insurance column on the right page of the insurance register.

Problem 16-A

On February 1 of the current year, Trees & Walmsley engage in the wholesale distribution of air-conditioning equipment as partners. In accounting for their fixed assets, the following accounts are used:

    17 Store Equipment
       017 Allowance for Depreciation of Store Equipment
    18 Delivery Equipment
       018 Allowance for Depreciation of Delivery Equipment
    19 Office Equipment
       019 Allowance for Depreciation of Office Equipment
    27 Accounts Payable
   625 Depreciation of Store Equipment
   626 Depreciation of Delivery Equipment
   641 Depreciation of Office Equipment

Transactions involving the purchase of fixed assets on credit are recorded in an invoice record from which they are posted to the proper general ledger accounts. Accounts with creditors are kept in a subsidiary accounts payable ledger and the posting to these accounts is done directly from the invoices and other vouchers representing transactions completed with creditors. The following is a narrative of transactions arising from the purchase of fixed assets during the year ended December 31:

Feb. 2. Invoice No. 48; purchased cabinet file for office use from The Gibson & Perin Co.; $120; terms, February 1 — 30 days. Estimated useful life, 10 years. Estimated trade-in value at end of 10 years, $30.

Mar. 6. Invoice No. 62; purchased a truck for delivery purposes from Dependable Motors, Inc.; $2,800; terms, March 4 — 30 days. Estimated useful life, 3 years. Estimated trade-in value at end of 3 years, $360.

April 8. Invoice No. 79; purchased an office desk from The H. & S. Pogue Co.; $72; terms, April 7 — 30 days. Estimated useful life, 20 years. No salvage value.

July 12. Invoice No. 104; purchased showcases from Economy Supply Co.; $360; terms, July 11 — 2/10, n/30. Estimated useful life, 15 years. No salvage value.

Aug. 18. Invoice No. 121; purchased double-pedestal desk for use in storeroom from Royal Store Equipment Co.; $90; terms, August 16 — 2/10, n/30. Estimated useful life, 20 years. No salvage value.

Sept. 19. Invoice No. 142; purchased Underwood typewriter, No. S5378852-11, from Underwood Typewriter Co.; $120; terms, September 18 — 30 days. Estimated useful life, 5 years. Estimated trade-in value at end of 5 years, $20.

REQUIRED: (a) Using an invoice record similar to the one reproduced on page 365 (except that a column will not be required for federal excise tax), record the foregoing transactions. (b) Foot the amount columns, prove the footings, enter the totals, and rule the invoice record. (c) Ascertain the annual rate of depreciation (straight-line method) applicable to each of the fixed assets purchased, compute the amount of the depreciation sustained during the current year ended December 31, and draft an entry in general journal form to record the depreciation. (d) Assuming that on January 5, after recording twenty-two months' depreciation, the delivery truck purchased on March 6 was traded in for a new truck, $1,800 in cash being paid. Draft a general journal entry to record the transaction. (No gain or loss to be recognized.)

Problem 18-A

Linger & Henderson are engaged as wholesale dealers in men's furnishings as partners. Their accounts are kept on the calendar year basis. The operating expense accounts are kept in a subsidiary ledger with a control account in a general ledger. Their accountant follows the practice of making any necessary adjustments in the operating expense accounts at the end of each month and provides the management with a monthly statement of operating expenses. The balances of the operating expense accounts on August 31, before making the monthly adjustments, were as follows:

611 Rent, $1,600
612 Salaries, $6,000
613 Advertising Expense, $452
614 Social Security Taxes, $300
616 Depreciation Expense, $248.75
617 Office Supplies Consumed, $320
618 Store Supplies Consumed, $365
619 Delivery Expense, $950
620 Bad Debts Expense, $430
621 Insurance Expense, $212
622 Heat, Light, and Water, $428.30
623 Telephone and Telegraph, $180.60
624 Traveling Expense, $1,875
625 Miscellaneous General Expenses, $183.49

Following are the numbers and titles of the general ledger accounts that will be affected by the adjusting entries:

013 Allowance for Bad Debts	161	Store Supplies
017 Allowance for Depreciation of Store Equipment	162	Advertising Supplies
018 Allowance for Depreciation of Delivery Equipment	163	Office Supplies
	164	Prepaid Insurance
019 Allowance for Depreciation of Office Equipment	61	Operating Expenses

The data for the adjusting entries at the end of August follow:

Depreciation of fixed assets during month:

Store equipment....................................	$ 7.50	
Delivery equipment.................................	22.50	
Office equipment...................................	14.80	$44.80

Store supplies consumed during month...........................	62.30
Advertising supplies consumed during month......................	61.40
Office supplies consumed during month..........................	32.95
Insurance expired during month.................................	32.12
Provision for bad debts..	50.00

REQUIRED: (a) Using standard account forms, open accounts for the foregoing operating expense accounts and record the respective balances before the monthly adjustments are made. (b) Using a sheet of columnar general journal paper ruled like the journal shown on page 475, draft the entries required to adjust the operating expense accounts as of August 31. Foot the amount columns, prove the footings, enter the totals, and rule. (c) On the assumption that the posting from the general journal to the general ledger accounts affected has already been completed, insert the necessary check marks in the Folio column of the general journal; complete the posting from the general journal to the operating expense ledger accounts. (d) Foot the accounts in the operating expense ledger and prepare a schedule of the operating expenses as of August 31. Use two-column journal paper for the schedule.

Problem 18-B

Monce & Craig are partners engaged in the operation of a wholesale mercantile business. Their accounts are kept on the calendar year basis. Accounts with customers, creditors, and operating expenses are kept in subsidiary ledgers with control accounts in the general ledger. Any needed adjustments in the operating expense accounts are made at the end of each month before taking a trial balance. Since the accountant is required to prepare monthly financial statements, he follows the practice of preparing a ten-column work sheet at the end of each month as an aid to the preparation of an income statement and a balance sheet.

REQUIRED: From the trial balance and adjustment data which follow, prepare a ten-column work sheet for Monce & Craig for the eleven-months' period ended November 30. (Allow 3 lines for Cost of Goods Sold, Account No. 55.)

The following data provide the information needed in adjusting the general ledger accounts:

Merchandise inventory November 30, per stock records, $8,634.98
Interest accrued on notes receivable, November 30, $17.50
Interest accrued on notes payable, November 30, $11.50

MONCE & CRAIG

TRIAL BALANCE

NOVEMBER 30, 19--

Second National Bank	111	$ 8,912.13	
Petty Cash Fund	112	50.00	
Notes Receivable	131	2,200.00	
Accrued Interest Receivable	132		
Accounts Receivable	133	4,170.61	
Allowance for Bad Debts	013		$ 120.00
Merchandise Inventory	15	9,334.15	
Store Supplies	161	72.60	
Office Supplies	163	57.80	
Fuel	164	46.20	
Postage Stamps	165	72.60	
Prepaid Insurance	166	319.12	
Store Equipment	17	1,500.00	
Allowance for Depreciation of Store Equipment	017		123.45
Delivery Equipment	18	2,200.00	
Allowance for Depreciation of Delivery Equipment	018		520.00
Office Equipment	19	2,100.00	
Allowance for Depreciation of Office Equipment	019		295.00
F.I.C.A. Taxes Payable	21		51.90
Employees' Income Taxes Payable	22		105.40
Notes Payable	23		100.90
Accrued Interest Payable	24		
Accounts Payable	25		2,960.32
E. H. Monce, Partner	31		8,212.80
E. H. Monce, Drawing	311	200.00	
A. E. Craig, Partner	32		8,212.80
A. E. Craig, Drawing	321	160.00	
Sales	41		61,304.80
Sales Returns and Allowances	041	920.80	
Purchases	51	45,216.20	
Purchases Returns and Allowances	051		316.05
Transportation In	53	816.31	
Cost of Goods Sold	55		
Operating Expenses	61	4,249.50	
Interest Income	71		28.40
Purchases Discount	72		612.00
Interest Expense	81	19.40	
Sales Discount	82	346.40	
		$82,963.82	$82,963.82

Problem 19-A

White & Cutshall are partners engaged in a merchandising enterprise. Their accounts are kept on the accrual basis and the books are closed at the end of the calendar year. Accounts with customers, creditors, and operating expenses are kept in subsidiary ledgers with control accounts in the general ledger. The operating expense accounts are adjusted at the end of each month. Monthly work sheets are used as an aid in preparing the financial statements. The necessary monthly adjustments in the general ledger accounts are made on the work sheet, but are not journalized and posted until the end of the year when the accounts are adjusted preliminary to closing the books.

The trial balance reproduced on the following page was taken on December 31 after making the necessary adjustments in the operating expense accounts for December.

The data for adjusting the general ledger accounts at the end of the year follow:

Merchandise inventory, per stock records, $9,057.34
Interest accrued on notes receivable, December 31, $20.54
Interest accrued on notes payable, December 31, $5.16

REQUIRED: As the accountant for White & Cutshall, (a) prepare a ten-column work sheet for the year ended December 31 (when copying the trial balance on the work sheet, allow three lines for Cost of Goods Sold, Account No. 55); (b) prepare an income statement for the year ended December 31, similar in form to the one illustrated on page 197; (c) prepare a balance sheet in account form as of December 31; (d) using a sheet of columnar general journal paper ruled like the journal shown on page 475, prepare the adjusting and closing entries required to close the books on December 31 (in closing the income summary account, one half of the net income should be transferred to each of the partners' drawing accounts); (e) using standard account forms, open the general ledger accounts and enter the balances shown in the December 31 trial balance, also open an account for Income Summary, Account No. 33, post the adjusting and closing entries, and rule the accounts that are in balance; (f) using two-column journal paper, take a post-closing trial balance to ascertain that the general ledger is in balance after closing the temporary accounts; and (g) using the same sheet of journal paper as was used for the adjusting and closing entries, journalize the entries required to reverse the adjusting entries for accrued interest, post, and rule the accounts that are in balance.

WHITE & CUTSHALL

TRIAL BALANCE

DECEMBER 31, 19--

Cash in Bank	111	$ 5,596.42	
Petty Cash Fund	112	25.00	
Notes Receivable	131	2,842.30	
Accrued Interest Receivable	132		
Accounts Receivable	133	5,997.83	
Allowance for Bad Debts	013		$ 352.85
Merchandise Inventory	15	12,742.02	
Store Supplies	161	143.96	
Office Supplies	162	133.85	
Fuel	163	56.50	
Postage Stamps	164	169.25	
Prepaid Insurance	165	487.62	
Store Equipment	17	3,600.00	
Allowance for Depreciation of Store Equipment	017		648.18
Office Equipment	18	2,100.00	
Allowance for Depreciation of Office Equipment	018		193.40
F.I.C.A. Taxes Payable	21		88.56
F.U.T.A. Taxes Payable	22		79.72
State U. C. Taxes Payable	23		179.33
Employees' Income Taxes Payable	24		162.12
Notes Payable	25		2,500.00
Accrued Interest Payable	26		
Accounts Payable	27		2,192.80
Accrued Property Taxes Payable	28		28.00
O. C. White, Partner	31		9,867.39
O. C. White, Drawing	311	612.50	
Paul Cutshall, Partner	32		9,820.39
Paul Cutshall, Drawing	321	593.85	
Sales	41		63,879.38
Sales Returns and Allowances	041	341.80	
Purchases	51	39,316.49	
Purchases Returns and Allowances	051		297.20
Transportation In	53	909.43	
Cost of Goods Sold	55		
Operating Expenses	61	14,216.45	
Interest Income	71		11.50
Purchases Discount	72		729.35
Interest Expense	81	21.25	
Sales Discount	82	948.65	
Charitable Contributions	83	175.00	
		$91,030.17	$91,030.17

THE CORPORATE ORGANIZATION

(41) ORGANIZATION AND MANAGEMENT

In 1820, John Marshall, then Chief Justice of the Supreme Court, described a corporation as follows:

"A corporation is an artificial being, invisible, intangible, and existing only in contemplation of the law."

The definition draws attention to the fact that corporations possess what is called *legal entity*. Entity means oneness — something set apart, separate and distinct — a unit. Legally a corporation is separate and distinct from its owners. A corporation can own property, enter into contracts, and incur debt in its own name. A corporation can sue and be sued.

The characteristic of legal entity does not exist for businesses existing in the form of sole proprietorships. Partnerships have only partial legal entity. The assets of businesses organized as sole proprietorships or partnerships legally belong to the proprietors or to the partners. The debts of such businesses are legally the personal debts of the owners. In accounting, every business is considered to be a separate entity regardless of whether the enterprise is a sole proprietorship, a partnership, or a corporation. In each case, the assets and the liabilities are considered to be those of the business itself. This assumption is a fiction in the case of sole proprietorships and partnerships. In the case of corporations, the assets and the liabilities are, in legal fact, those of the business.

There are more business sole proprietorships and partnerships than corporations in the United States; however, corporations, while fewer in number, do considerably more business than the other two types of organition combined. At least seventy-five per cent of the nation's business is conducted by corporations. The corporate form of organization has certain characteristics that explain its popularity and importance. Outstanding among these characteristics are the following:

(a) With the corporate form of organization it is possible to secure large amounts of capital. Certain types of businesses must be operated on a relatively large scale. In other cases, various economies are possible with large-scale operations. If large amounts of capital are to be obtained, it usually means that there must be a considerable number of investors. The corporation has been found to be the most suitable form for a business that must obtain capital from many people.

(b) The owners of corporations have *limited liability*. Ownership in a corporation is divided into shares, usually referred to as shares of capital stock. If the stock is fully paid for at the time of issuance (which is usually the case and often is required by law), the owners cannot be compelled to contribute additional capital to the company. These stockholders have no personal liability for the debts of the corporation. This condition is decidedly different from the case of sole proprietors and general partners; they have unlimited personal liability for the debts of their businesses. The limited-liability feature has been a major reason for the popularity of the corporate form of organization.

(c) Shares of stock in a corporation are transferable. Except in unusual cases, any stockholder can transfer his stock to another person without the knowledge or the consent of the other stockholders and without affecting the existence of the corporation. In contrast to this is the fact that a partner cannot transfer his interest to another without the consent of his partners. Furthermore, the withdrawal of any partner automatically dissolves a partnership.

(d) Corporations have unlimited life. A sole proprietorship ceases upon the death of the proprietor. A partnership is dissolved upon the death or the withdrawal of any partner. Corporations, however, are chartered either without any limitation upon the length of their life or with a provision for renewal if there is a limit.

(e) Capital stock may be purchased as an investment for income purposes by those who do not care to participate in the management of business enterprises. Investors in the stock of corporations provide most of the capital required by the corporations, but few of the stockholders in the larger companies actually participate in the management of the companies.

The major drawback to the corporate form of organization is the fact that corporations must pay income taxes. Sole proprietorships and partnerships, as such, do not have to pay income taxes. A sole proprietor reports the income or the loss from his business in his personal income tax return. Partnerships file tax returns but they are not required to pay income taxes. Each partner reports his distributive share of the firm's income or loss in his personal tax return. The amounts, in each case, are taken into account in calculating the tax liability of the sole proprietor or the partner. Corporations, however, are subject to a special corporation income tax, and the stockholders of corporations are subject to personal income tax on dividends they receive from their companies. The term *dividend* refers to the distribution by a corporation of cash or other property to the stockholders. Unless specifically labeled to the contrary, dividends represent income. In the usual case, the corporation is "dividing up" its earnings.

The process of taxing corporation income, both to the company that earns it and to the owners of the company who receive it, is considered by many to be unfair. Such "double taxation" has hindered the more widespread adoption of the corporate form of organization.

All states have general laws authorizing the creation of corporations by a specified number of persons who comply with the provisions of the statutes. It is not necessary that a company be incorporated in the state in which it expects to confine all or any portion of its business activities. A company may be incorporated under the laws of one state and may operate exclusively in another state. Corporations are classified as (a) domestic corporations or (b) foreign corporations. A *domestic corporation* is a company incorporated under the laws of the state in which its business is conducted. A *foreign corporation* is a company incorporated under the laws of any state other than the one in which it is doing business. It usually is necessary for a corporation to maintain an office in the state from which a certificate of incorporation is obtained, but it is not necessary to conduct the ordinary business operations of the company from that office. The maintenance of an office with an authorized agent in charge is usually sufficient. It may be necessary to keep certain corporate records in that office.

Before a corporation can do business in a state other than the one in which it is incorporated, it must obtain a license from that state as a foreign corporation. Having obtained a license as a foreign corporation in a state, a corporation is entitled to do business in that state regardless of where it is incorporated. A company may incorporate under the laws of any state and may obtain licenses as a foreign corporation entitling it to do business in all the other states.

A corporation organized under the laws of one state takes a serious risk when it transacts business within the borders of another state without first obtaining a license to do business in that state. A corporation that does not have a license to do business in a state may not have the right to take action in the courts of that state to enforce its contracts or to collect its receivables. In some states specific penalties are provided, imposing fines and imprisonment on the agents of corporations doing business without a license.

Preliminary to incorporating a company, the incorporators should familiarize themselves with the general corporation laws of the state in which they desire to incorporate. Variations in the corporation laws of the respective states make some states more attractive than others for the purpose of incorporation. Delaware is noted for the great number of companies incorporated under its laws. Following are some of the reasons often cited for the popularity of Delaware's corporation laws:

(a) Capital stock may be issued for cash, for labor done, for personal property, including patents, contracts, etc., or for real estate or leases thereof. In the absence of actual fraud, judgment of the directors as to the value of the property for which the stock was issued is conclusive, and stock so issued is fully paid.

(b) Voting power may be vested in one or more classes of stock, to the exclusion of other classes. This makes it possible for an individual or a group of individuals with an idea for a patent, or possessing a going business, to obtain capital through the sale of stock without losing control.

(c) The directors need not be stockholders. Less than a majority of the whole board of directors may constitute a quorum. When vacancies occur in the board of directors, they may be filled by a majority of the remaining directors. The right to elect all or a majority of the directors may be confined to one class of stock. The board of directors may appoint an executive committee consisting of two or more of its members who may exercise the powers of the board of directors in the management of the business.

(d) Shares of capital stock owned by persons or by corporations outside of the state are not subject to taxation. Cash and securities of the corporation may be kept on deposit in the state without the payment of any personal property taxes.

(e) The stock and transfer books are open for inspection to stockholders only and there is no state tax on the issue or transfer of stock.

Many of the foregoing provisions and others that are considered attractive will be found in the corporation laws of other states. In view of the many variations of the corporation laws of the respective states, it is advisable for the incorporators to consult a competent attorney before taking steps to obtain a certificate of incorporation from any state.

The formation of a private corporation for the purpose of engaging in a business enterprise is not as simple as the formation of a sole proprietorship or a partnership for business purposes. A corporation may be formed only with the expressed or the implied authority of government. In the United States, the power to create corporations rests largely with the respective state legislatures. All of the states have general laws authorizing the creation of corporations. Persons desiring to incorporate must comply with the laws of the state in which incorporation is desired. These provisions vary in the respective states. Under the Uniform Business Corporation Act, the incorporators may consist of "three or more natural persons of full age, at least two thirds of whom are citizens of the United States or of its territories, incorporated or unincorporated, or possessions."

Incorporators. Individuals who unite in filing an application for a certificate of incorporation are known as *incorporators*. The incorporators must be legally competent to contract, and usually each incorporator is required to be a subscriber for one or more shares of the capital stock of the corporation. In applying for a certificate of incorporation, the incorporators must file articles of incorporation or articles of association that comply with the requirements of the statutes.

Pending the election of directors, the incorporators have the direction of the affairs and the organization of a corporation and may take such steps as are proper to perfect the organization of the corporation. After the certificate of incorporation has been filed and recorded, the incorporators may hold the so-called "first meeting of incorporators" for the purpose of adopting bylaws, electing directors, and transacting such other business as may properly be brought before the meeting.

Certificate of Incorporation. When the incorporators have complied with the legal requirements, including the payment of required fees, a *certificate of incorporation* is approved by the Secretary of State or other official whose duty it is to approve certificates of incorporation that meet the requirements of the state law. A certificate of incorporation is frequently referred to as a *charter* or a *license*. Usually the incorporators must sign a certificate of incorporation and acknowledge it before a notary public or other officer authorized by law. When the certificate of incorporation has been signed and acknowledged by the incorporators, the original certificate must be filed in the office of the Secretary of State and a copy thereof, certified by the Secretary of State, should be filed with the recorder of the county where the principal office of the corporation is to be located. A third copy of the certificate should be retained by the corporation. The procedure for incorporation of a company under the laws of the different states varies as to details, but in most states it follows substantially the plan outlined in the foregoing discussion. A certificate of incorporation is illustrated on page 540.

CERTIFICATE OF INCORPORATION
OF
THE WAYMAN MANUFACTURING CO.

We, the undersigned, all being of full age, and at least two thirds being citizens of the United States and two of us are residents of the State of New York, desiring to form a corporation pursuant to the provisions of the Business Corporation Law, the General Corporation Law, and the Stock Corporation Law of the State of New York, do make, sign, acknowledge, and file a certificate for that purpose, as follows:

FIRST: The name of the said corporation shall be:
THE WAYMAN MANUFACTURING CO.

SECOND: The purposes for which said corporation is to be formed are: To manufacture, purchase or otherwise acquire, own, mortgage, pledge, sell, assign and transfer, or otherwise dispose of, to invest, trade, deal in and deal with goods, wares and merchandise and real and personal property of every class and description.

THIRD: The amount of the capital stock is Fifty Thousand Dollars ($50,000).

FOURTH: The number of shares of which the capital stock consists is Five Hundred (500) of the par value of One Hundred Dollars ($100) each, and the amount of the capital with which the corporation will begin business is Twenty-Four Thousand Five Hundred Dollars ($24,500).

FIFTH: The principal office of said corporation shall be located in the City of Olean, Cattaraugus County, New York.

SIXTH: The duration of said corporation shall be perpetual.

SEVENTH: The number of directors of said corporation shall be five.

EIGHTH: The names and post-office addresses of the directors of said corportion for the first year shall be as follows:

B. A. Wayman	516 Main St., Olean, N. Y.
C. W. Milton	1565 Chestnut St., Bradford, Pa.
G. H. Waterson	762 Mound St., Salamanca, N. Y.
B. A. Gregg	417 Mill St., Olean, N. Y.
G. J. Wayman	1216 Allen St., Olean, N. Y.

NINTH: The names and post-office addresses of the subscribers to this certificate and a statement of the number of shares of stock that each agrees to take in said corporation, are as follows:

B. A. Wayman	516 Main St., Olean, N. Y.	130 shares
C. W. Milton	1565 Chestnut St., Bradford, Pa.	50 "
G. H. Waterson	762 Mound St., Salamanca, N. Y.	50 "

In Witness Whereof, we have made, signed, acknowledged, and filed this certificate in duplicate.

Dated September 1, 19--.

B. A. WAYMAN
C. W. MILTON
G. H. WATERSON

State of New York }
County of Cattaraugus } ss.

Personally appeared before me, R. L. Watson, a notary public in and for Cattaraugus County, New York, B. A. Wayman, C. W. Milton, and G. H. Waterson, to me known and known to me to be the same persons described in and who executed the foregoing instrument, and they duly acknowledged to me that they executed the same.

R. L. Watson
Notary Public, Cattaraugus County, N. Y.

(NOTARIAL SEAL)

Certificate of Incorporation

A certificate of incorporation confers certain powers on a corporation in addition to the common-law powers. The special powers conferred are those expressed in the certificate of incorporation. In addition to the powers expressed in the certificate, such powers as are reasonably necessary to the corporation in the carrying out of its expressed powers are implied. For instance, unless prevented by the provisions of the certificate of incorporation or by the adopted bylaws, a corporation has the implied power to borrow money for use in carrying on its authorized business, to execute negotiable instruments, to issue bonds, and to mortgage or pledge its real or personal property as security for its debts.

It should be understood, however, that a corporation can exercise only such powers as are expressly or impliedly conferred by the certificate of incorporation. For instance, a corporation has the power to do only such business as is authorized by its certificate of incorporation. A natural person operating as a sole proprietor, or an ordinary partnership, may engage in any legal undertaking, but a corporation cannot engage in matters foreign to the objects for which it was incorporated and which are stated in the certificate of incorporation.

Corporation Bylaws. Rules and regulations adopted by the stockholders of a corporation are known as *bylaws*. The bylaws are for the government and regulation of members of the corporation and usually are not binding upon other persons. Reasonable bylaws, legally adopted, that are not contrary to public policy or inconsistent with the general law of the land, are binding upon all stockholders regardless of their knowledge or consent. Any bylaws that are not contrary to the laws of the state under which the company is incorporated may be adopted for the purpose of controlling the operations of a corporation. The bylaws usually provide for the time and place of holding stockholders' and directors' meetings, number of days' notice for meetings, requirements for quorum, number of directors, committees, officers, transfers of stock, signing of checks, fiscal year, annual statements, and such other matters covering the duties and the removal of officers, agents, and employees as may be decided upon from time to time.

The bylaws of a corporation are usually adopted at the first meeting of the incorporators after the filing and recording of the certificate of incorporation. Thereafter, the power to make, alter, or repeal bylaws rests with the stockholders unless in the certificate of incorporation that power is conferred upon the directors. Typical bylaws of a corporation are illustrated on pages 542 and 543.

BYLAWS
OF
THE WAYMAN MANUFACTURING CO.

Article I — Offices

1. The principal office of the company shall be in the City of Olean, County of Cattaraugus, New York.

2. The corporation may also have offices at such other places as the board of directors may from time to time see fit to establish in accord with the requirements of the business of the corporation.

Article II — Seal

1. The corporate seal shall have inscribed thereon the name of the corporation, the year of its organization, and the words "Corporate Seal, New York." Said seal may be used by causing it or a facsimile thereof to be impressed or affixed or reproduced or otherwise.

Article III — Stock

1. Certificates of stock shall be issued in numerical order, be signed by the president and secretary, and be sealed with the corporation seal.

2. Transfers of stock shall be made in the books of the corporation only by the person named in the certificate, or his duly authorized attorney, and upon surrender of the certificate therefor.

Article IV — Stockholders

1. The annual meeting of the stockholders shall be held in the principal office of the company in Olean, New York sometime during the second week of January.

2. Special meetings of the stockholders may be called at the principal office of the company at any time, by resolution of the board of directors, or upon written request of the stockholders holding one fourth of the outstanding stock.

3. Notice of regular and special meetings of the stockholders shall be prepared by the secretary and mailed to the last known post-office address of each stockholder not less than ten days before such meeting and in the case of a special meeting, such notice shall state the object or objects thereof.

4. A quorum at any meeting of the stockholders shall consist of a majority of the stock of the company represented in person or by proxy.

5. The election of directors shall take place at the time of the annual meeting of the stockholders. The election shall be by ballot and each stockholder of record shall be entitled to cast one vote for each share of stock held by him.

Article V — Directors

1. A board of five directors shall be elected annually by the stockholders for a term of one year and they shall serve until the election and acceptance of duly qualified successors. Vacancies may be filled by the board for the unexpired term.

2. Regular meetings of the board of directors shall be held in the principal office of the company in Olean, New York on the last Saturday of each month at 9 a. m., if not a legal holiday; but if a legal holiday then on the following Monday.

3. Special meetings of the board of directors to be held in the principal office of the company in Olean, New York may be called at any time by the president or by request of a majority of the directors.

4. Notice of regular and special meetings of the board of directors shall be prepared by the secretary and mailed to each member of the board not less than five days before such meeting. Notices of special meetings shall state the purposes thereof.

Corporation Bylaws

5. A quorum at any meeting of the board of directors shall consist of a majority of the entire membership of the board.

6. At the first regular meeting of the board of directors after the election of directors each year, the officers of the company shall be elected for a period of one year. The board shall fix the compensation of the officers.

ARTICLE VI — OFFICERS

1. The officers of the company shall consist of a president, a vice-president, a secretary, and a treasurer, who shall be elected for a term of one year and shall hold office until their successors are duly elected and qualified.

2. The president shall preside at all meetings and have general supervision of the affairs of the company; shall sign all certificates, contracts, and other instruments of the company as authorized by the board of directors; shall make reports to the directors and stockholders; and shall perform all such duties as are incident to his office and are properly required of him by the board of directors. In the absence or disability of the president, the vice-president shall exercise all his functions.

3. The secretary shall issue notices for all meetings of the board of directors and stockholders; shall keep minutes of such meetings; shall have charge of the seal and the corporate records; shall sign, with the president, such instruments as will require such signature; and shall make such reports and perform such other duties as are incident to his office, or are properly required of him by the board of directors.

4. The treasurer shall have the custody of all moneys and securities of the company, and shall keep regular books of account. He shall sign such instruments as require his signature, and shall perform all duties incident to his office or that are properly required of him by the board of directors. He shall give bond for the faithful performance of his duties in such sum and with such sureties as are required by the board of directors.

ARTICLE VII — AMENDMENTS

These bylaws may be amended, repealed, or altered, in whole or in part, by a three-fourths vote of the entire outstanding stock of the company, at any regular meeting of the stockholders or at any special meeting duly called for such purpose

CERTIFICATION OF BYLAWS

We, the undersigned, B. A. Wayman and C. W. Milton, respectively, the duly elected president and secretary of The Wayman Manufacturing Co., do hereby certify that the foregoing bylaws were duly adopted by the stockholders of said corporation at the first meeting held on the 10th day of September, 19--, in the principal office of the said corporation at 516 Main Street, Olean, New York.

In Testimony Whereof, we have hereunto signed our signatures and affixed the seal of said corporation this 10th day of September, 19--.

> *B. A. WAYMAN, President*
> *C. W. MILTON, Secretary*

(CORPORATE SEAL)

Corporation Bylaws

Stockholders. It has been noted already that ownership in a corporation is divided into capital stock shares. The owners receive *stock certificates* as evidence of their ownership. The owners are called *stockholders* or *shareholders*. They have certain rights and certain restrictions. Unless they own shares of a class of stock that carries no voting rights, they have a right to attend stockholders' meetings, to vote in the election of *directors*, and to vote upon such other matters as properly come before the stockholders' meetings. Each share of stock usually carries one vote. If a stockholder cannot be present at a stockholders' meeting, he can authorize another stockholder to vote for him. This is known as *voting by proxy*. A typical proxy is shown below.

Each share of stock of the same class entitles its owner to receive a proportionate amount of any dividends distributed by the corporation. Certain classes of stock usually give the holder the right to purchase a proportionate number of any new shares the corporation might issue. This is known as the *pre-emptive right*. The right is to give each stockholder a chance to maintain his proportionate equity in the corporation. The stockholder is not obliged to take advantage of this right.

In the event the corporation *liquidates* (goes out of business), each stockholder has the right to share in the distribution of the assets. The distribution is on a proportional, share-for-share basis, though there may be a rank or order of claims if the corporation has more than one class of stock outstanding.

PROXY
THE WAYMAN MANUFACTURING CO.

    The undersigned hereby appoints B. A. Wayman and C. W. Milton, and each of them, attorneys and proxies, with power of substitution, to vote at the annual meeting of stockholders of The Wayman Manufacturing Co. to be held at Olean, New York, on January 10, 19-- or at any adjournment thereof, according to the number of votes that the undersigned would be entitled to vote if personally present. Such proxies, and each of them, may vote for the directors named in the Proxy Statement received by the undersigned and on all other matters that may legally come before the meeting.

Date...........19..   ....
                                  Signature of Stockholder

                                                           152

Proxy

While stockholders are actually the owners of the corporation, they do not have the right to bind the company by a contract. This right usually belongs to the officers of the corporation. The officers may be, and often are, stockholders; but it is in their capacity as officers, not as stockholders, that they can contract in the name of the corporation.

In order to enjoy any of the rights that have been mentioned, a stockholder must have his stock properly recorded in the books of the corporation. When the stockholder acquires his shares directly from the corporation as an original issue, the capital stock certificate will, of course, be recorded in the books of the corporation. When shares of capital stock are acquired through purchase from other stockholders rather than directly from the corporation, it is necessary to have the stock transferred in the books of the corporation before the new stockholders will be entitled to vote or to share in any dividends declared.

A certificate of stock may indicate ownership of any number of shares of stock. It is not necessary for a corporation to issue a separate certificate for each share of capital stock sold; instead, one certificate may be issued to each purchaser for the total number of shares purchased.

The Uniform Business Corporation Act requires that capital stock certificates state the following:

(a) The state of incorporation.
(b) The name of the registered holder.
(c) The number and the class of shares represented.
(d) The value of each share.
(e) The number of such shares authorized to be issued.
(f) If there is more than one class of share, a summary of the rights or restrictions of each class.

Directors. The management of a corporation is usually entrusted to a *board of directors* elected by the stockholders. The number of directors to be elected and eligibility for membership on a board of directors are determined by statute, by the certificate of incorporation, or by the bylaws of the corporation. In the election of directors, as in other matters, each stockholder usually is entitled to one vote for each share of stock owned.

Directors are not allowed to vote by proxy and must personally attend meetings of the board in order to be entitled to vote. The board of directors, possessing the power of general management of the corporation, usually may appoint an executive committee to act for it between regular board meetings. The active management of a corporation usually is entrusted to the corporate officers who are elected by the board and are responsible to the board. Unless otherwise provided in the bylaws of the corporation, the board of directors has sole authority to declare dividends.

As long as the directors act in good faith, they are not liable for losses resulting from their management.

Officers. The officers usually are selected from the board of directors. Unless restricted by the bylaws, however, the officers need not be members of the board of directors nor even stockholders. The officers usually consist of a president, one or more vice-presidents, a secretary, and a treasurer. One person may hold more than one office. For example, the same person may be elected secretary-treasurer. When two or more vice-presidents are elected, each may be assigned special duties; one vice-president may be put in charge of production, one in charge of sales, and a third in charge of public relations. The officers of a corporation are merely agents who are responsible to the board of directors. The duties of the officers may be prescribed by the board of directors subject to the provisions of the certificate of incorporation and the bylaws.

PRACTICE ASSIGNMENT No. 41. Complete Report No. 41 in the workbook and submit your working papers for approval. Continue with the following study assignment until Report No. 42 is required.

(42) CORPORATE RECORDS

In recording the ordinary operating transactions of a corporation, records or books of account similar to those used by sole proprietorships and by partnerships may be used. The only records peculiar to the corporate form of organization are those required for recording the following:

    (a) Meetings of —
        (1) The incorporators.
        (2) The stockholders.
        (3) The board of directors.
    (b) Subscriptions to capital stock.
    (c) Issuance of capital stock.
    (d) Transfers of capital stock.
    (e) Retirement of capital stock.
    (f) The declaration and the payment of dividends.

State laws vary as to what corporate records must be kept. Usually a corporation is required by law to keep a minute book and a stockholders' ledger. Other corporate records may be prescribed by the bylaws. Under the laws of most states stockholders have the right to examine the corporate records, but usually such inspection is limited to the original or duplicate stock records containing the names and the addresses of the stockholders and the number of shares held by each.

Corporation Minute Book. A corporation minute book is used to record the minutes of the meetings of the stockholders and of the directors. Sometimes the minutes of the stockholders' meetings are kept in one book and the minutes of the directors' meetings in another book. Either a bound book or a loose-leaf book may be used. In most cases a loose-leaf book is used, which permits the typing of the minutes. Following are some of the plans used to prevent extraction or substitutions of sheets:

(a) The pages may be numbered consecutively and the secretary may sign each page.

(b) Watermarked paper may be used, coding each sheet with symbols consisting of letters and figures, such as "XY5AB."

(c) Keylock binders may be used, making it impossible to extract sheets, when the book is locked, without the aid of a key.

Where all minutes are recorded in a single book, it is customary to allot a portion of the book to the stockholders' meetings and another portion to the directors' meetings so that the minutes of each may be recorded consecutively. While the stockholders usually meet but once a year, the directors may meet much oftener. Sometimes the provisions of the certificate of incorporation are copied in the minute book or a copy of the certificate may be bound in the minute book. Following the certificate of incorporation, it is customary to keep a record of the bylaws adopted by the incorporators at their first meeting after the certificate is issued or by the stockholders in subsequent meetings. In recording the minutes of a meeting of the stockholders or of the directors, it is important that the following information be recorded:

(a) The character of the meeting, that is, whether it is a stockholders' meeting or a directors' meeting.

(b) The date and the place of the meeting and whether it is a regular or a special meeting.

(c) If it is a board of directors' meeting, the names of those present, indicating whether or not a quorum was present. If it is a stockholders' meeting, the name of the presiding officer, names of other officers, and either the names of the stockholders present or the number of shares represented at the meeting.

(d) A complete record of the proceedings of the meeting, which may include decisions to purchase and sell property, invest surplus funds, declare dividends, issue bonds, appropriate earnings, provide for sinking funds, adopt or amend bylaws, etc. Should any act of the board of directors or of the stockholders affect the accounting records, information concerning the action taken must be conveyed to the accountant. For instance, the

MINUTES OF FIRST MEETING OF STOCKHOLDERS
THE WAYMAN MANUFACTURING CO.

Held September 10, 19--

Pursuant to written call and waiver of notice signed by all the incorporators, the first meeting of The Wayman Manufacturing Co., was held in its principal office at 516 Main Street, Olean, New York, at 1 p. m., September 10, 19--.

Mr. B. A. Wayman called the meeting to order and was elected chairman by motion unanimously carried. Mr. C. W. Milton was elected secretary. There were present in person: B. A. Wayman, C. W. Milton, G. H. Waterson, B. A. Gregg, and G. J. Wayman.

The chairman reported that the certificate of incorporation had been filed with the Secretary of State on September 7, 19--, and that a certified copy had been filed with the County Recorder on September 8, 19--. Upon motion duly made and carried, said certificate of incorporation was accepted, the directors named therein approved, and the secretary instructed to cause a copy of such certificate to be inserted in the minute book of the company.

The secretary presented bylaws prepared by counsel, which were read, article by article. Upon motion, duly made, seconded and carried, it was resolved that the bylaws submitted be, and the same hereby are, adopted as the bylaws of this corporation, and that the secretary be, and he hereby is, instructed to cause the same to be inserted in the minute book immediately following the copy of the certificate of incorporation.

There being no further business, the meeting was declared adjourned.

B. A. WAYMAN, *Chairman*
C. W. MILTON, *Secretary*

Corporation Minutes

declaration of a dividend must be reported to the accountant in order that he may make the required entry in the books of account.

The minute book is one of the most important of the corporate records and it should be kept with the utmost care. It should be considered a permanent record of the corporation. Usually it is the duty of the secretary of a corporation to keep the minutes of all regular and special meetings of both the board of directors and the stockholders. Typical minutes of a meeting of stockholders are illustrated above.

Subscriptions Records. One who agrees to purchase capital stock of a corporation is known as a *subscriber*. A list of subscribers is known as a *subscription list*. A subscription list usually consists of one or more sheets of paper with suitable headings on which subscribers may enter their subscriptions for a specified number of shares of capital stock. One or more subscription lists may be circulated simultaneously. A common form of subscription list is illustrated on page 549. Subscriptions to capital stock may be made before or after incorporation. Since a corporation does

SUBSCRIPTION LIST

THE WAYMAN MANUFACTURING CO.

To Be Incorporated Under the Laws of New York

Capital Stock $50,000   Par Value $100 a share

We, the undersigned, hereby severally subscribe for and agree to take at par value, the number of shares of the capital stock of The Wayman Manufacturing Co. set opposite our respective signatures, said subscriptions to become due upon completion of the organization of said company, and to be then payable in cash on demand of the treasurer of the company.

Olean, New York
August 1, 19 - -

NAMES	ADDRESSES	SHARES	AMOUNT
B. A. Wayman	516 Main St., Olean, N. Y.	130	$13,000
C. W. Milton	1565 Chestnut St., Bradford, Pa.	50	5,000
G. H. Waterson	762 Mound St., Salamanca, N. Y.	50	5,000
B. A. Gregg	417 Mill St., Olean, N. Y.	10	1,000
G. J. Wayman	1216 Allen St., Olean, N. Y.	5	500

Subscription List

not exist until after a certificate of incorporation has been granted and accepted, any subscription to capital stock made before incorporation is merely an agreement to subscribe for stock. Such an agreement is a contract between the subscriber and the promoter of the corporation or its incorporators. A subscription to capital stock made after incorporation is a contract between the subscriber and the corporation. The amount due a corporation from subscribers to its capital stock represents an asset that is usually recorded in the books of account as "subscriptions receivable." A subscriber may pay for capital stock with cash or other property.

At the time of accepting subscriptions, a record should be made in the books of the corporation. When there are many subscribers, a subscription register may serve a useful purpose; but if there are only a few subscribers, their subscriptions may be recorded in an ordinary journal.

A subscription register may be either a bound book or a loose-leaf book. Usually it is ruled to provide approximately the same information as the subscription list, that is, the names and the addresses of the subscribers, the number of shares subscribed, and the amount of the subscriptions. Even when a subscription register is used, subscriptions should be recorded in the regular books of the corporation. The subscription list or any complete record of subscriptions accepted will serve to provide the information needed in making the proper entry in the regular books of account.

The accounts with subscribers may be kept in the general ledger or in a subsidiary ledger known as a *subscription ledger* or a *stock payment record*. A subscription ledger is usually used when the stock is to be paid for in installments. Unless stock is to be paid for in installments or on some deferred-payment plan, a subscription ledger will not be needed and it will not be necessary to keep accounts with subscribers. A standard form of account ruling for a subscription ledger or stock payment record is illustrated below.

STOCK PAYMENT RECORD

SHEET NO. *1*

NAME *M. H. Tunney*

ADDRESS *100 Sixth Avenue, Troy, New York*   APPLICANT

DATE	NO. SHARES PURCHASED	AMOUNT PER SHARE	Subscription No.	TOTAL DEBIT	DATE OF CREDIT	PAYMENTS WEEKLY—SEMI-MONTHLY—MONTHLY	AMOUNTS OF CREDITS
Sep 1	10	100 00	1	1000 00	Sep 1	Down Payment	100 00
					Oct 1	First Installment	100 00
					Nov 1	Second Installment	100 00
					Dec 1	Third Installment	100 00
						TOTAL $	

NAME SALESMAN		COMMISSION	% PAID	19
PAID $	IN FULL AND CERTIFICATE NO.		ISSUED	19
			SIGNATURE	AUDITOR

Subscriber's Account

Following is a narrative of the transactions recorded in the account reproduced in the illustration:

Sept. 1. M. H. Tunney subscribed for 10 shares of common stock at par value, making a down payment of $100 and agreeing to make additional payments of $100 a month until the stock is paid for in full, at which time a certificate of stock is to be issued to him.

Oct. 1. Received $100 from M. H. Tunney to apply on stock subscription.

Nov. 1. Received $100 from M. H. Tunney to apply on stock subscription.

Dec. 1. Received $100 from M. H. Tunney to apply on stock subscription.

If a subsidiary subscription ledger is kept, a control account must be kept in the general ledger. The title of such a control account usually is Subscriptions Receivable. The function of the subscriptions receivable control account and of the subscription ledger is practically the same as the function of an accounts receivable control account and an accounts receivable ledger. The balance of the subscriptions receivable control account may be proved at any time by preparing a list of the balances of the subscribers' accounts kept in the subsidiary subscription ledger. The total amount due from subscribers as shown by this list should be the same as the balance of the control account.

Stock Certificate Book. When a subscriber has paid his subscription in full, the corporation issues a certificate to him for the number of shares subscribed and paid for. The blank certificates often are bound in a book known as a *stock certificate book*. A stock certificate and its stub, representing one page of a stock certificate book, was illustrated on page 311.

In that illustration both the certificate and the stub are filled in as they should be when the certificate is ready for delivery to the subscriber. Both the certificates and the stubs should be numbered consecutively. The certificate should show the name of the stockholder, the number of shares represented, and the date of issue. It should also be signed by the president and the secretary of the corporation. The stub, when properly filled in, should show the number of shares issued, the name of the stockholder, and the date of issue. Sometimes, in the case of relatively small corporations, the stockholder is required to sign the stub as a receipt for the certificate; in the case of large corporations this procedure would be impractical. Sometimes when a certificate of stock is canceled it is pasted to the original stub from which it was detached.

Stockholders' Ledger. The general ledger of a sole proprietorship contains the capital account of the proprietor. There is a capital account for each partner in the general ledger of a partnership. In the case of a corporation, however, there is no general ledger account for each stockholder. The general ledger of a corporation contains accounts that relate to the capital of the company, but these accounts show the total amounts of each of the various types of net worth; not the name and the share of each owner. Since it is essential to have a record of the number of shares owned by each stockholder, it is common practice to maintain a *stockholders' ledger*, which contains an account for each stockholder. It is not a subsidiary ledger in the usual sense because its accounts contain information relating only to number of shares; dollar amounts usually are not shown. Inasmuch as the general ledger capital stock accounts show number of shares as well as dollar amounts, however, there is a special sort of control account-subsidiary ledger relationship.

The information recorded in each stockholder's account should include the following:

(a) The date, the certificate number, and the number of shares issued to the stockholder by the corporation.

(b) The date, the certificate number, and the number of shares transferred to the stockholder from other stockholders.

(c) The date, the certificate number, and the number of shares transferred from the stockholder to other stockholders.

(d) The balance, representing the number of shares held by the stockholder.

The stockholders' ledger is an important corporate record. It and the corporation minute book are two records that most corporations are required by law to keep.

A standard form of account ruling for a stockholders' ledger is illustrated below. Following is a narrative of transactions recorded in the account reproduced in the illustration:

July 2. Issued Certificate No. 14 for 18 shares of common stock to R. G. Walters who has paid his subscription in full.

Aug. 25. R. G. Walters surrendered Certificate No. 14 for 18 shares and requested that 4 shares of the stock be transferred to A. A. Martin. Issued a new certificate, No. 17, for 14 shares to Mr. Walters.

STOCKHOLDERS' LEDGER

NAME OF STOCKHOLDER *R. G. Walters*   ACC'T. NO. *11*

ADDRESS *1229 Glenview Ave, Wilmington, Delaware*

DATE	CERT. NOS. OLD	CERT. NOS. NEW	RECEIVED FROM	TRANSFERRED TO	NO. OF SHARES	BAL- ANCE
July 2 19		14	Original Issue		18	18
Aug 25	14	17		A. A. Martin	4	14
Sep 1	11	21	J. B. Gritz		10	24

Stockholder's Account

Sept. 1. I. B. Gritz surrendered Certificate No. 11 for 10 shares with a request that the stock be transferred to R. G. Walters. Issued Certificate No. 21 to Mr. Walters.

Stock Transfer Record. Since a stockholder has the right to transfer his stock and a corporation is required to keep a record of outstanding stock, it is advisable for a corporation to keep some sort of a stock transfer record. A standard form of transfer record is illustrated below. This record is practically a duplicate of the assignment form that ordinarily appears on the back of a stock certificate. The purpose of a transfer record is to record transfers of capital stock from one stockholder to another and to provide the information needed in keeping the stockholders' ledger. The following transaction is recorded in the illustration:

Aug. 25. R. G. Walters surrendered Certificate No. 14 for 18 shares and requested that 4 shares of the stock be transferred to A. A. Martin. Issued Certificate No. 17 for 14 shares to Mr. Walters and Certificate No. 18 for 4 shares to Mr. Martin.

When stock is transferred, the transferor must endorse the certificate and his signature must be witnessed.

Someone to whom the corporate records are properly accessible should be empowered to record the transfer of the stock. This may be the corporation secretary or a transfer agent. The person who is authorized to transfer the stock is known as the attorney, but he is not necessarily a lawyer.

It is customary for corporations to close the transfer record a specified number of days before the annual meeting or before the payment of

TRANSFER RECORD

DATE OF TRANSFER ON BOOKS	SURRENDERED		NAMES OF STOCKHOLDERS INVOLVED IN THE TRANSFER AND SIGNATURES OF ATTORNEYS MAKING THE TRANSFERS.	RE-ISSUED	
	CERT. NOS.	NO. OF SHARES		CERT. NOS.	NO. OF SHARES
Aug 25 19–	14	18	BY *R. G. Walters*	17	14
			TO *A. A. Martin*	18	4
			SIGNED *N. R. Bowen* (ATTORNEY)		

Stock Transfer Record

dividends. Stockholders must have their stock transferred and duly registered in the books of the corporation prior to the closing of the transfer records to be eligible to vote or to receive dividends, as the case may be. For instance, a corporation in notifying stockholders of the annual meeting to be held on June 21, 19-- advised that —

"In accordance with Section 40 of the corporation's bylaws, the board of directors has fixed May 31, 19-- as the record date of the stockholders entitled to notice of and to vote at said meeting and only stockholders of record at the close of business on May 31, 19-- be entitled to vote thereat."

In declaring a dividend, it is customary for the board of directors to specify not only the date of payment but also the date of record in the following manner:

"A dividend of one dollar a share is declared, payable July 1 to stockholders of record June 25."

A stockholder who acquired his stock by transfer after June 25 would not be entitled to share in this dividend.

PRACTICE ASSIGNMENT No. 42. Complete Report No. 42 in the workbook and submit your working papers for approval. Continue with the textbook discussion in Unit Twenty-two until the next report is required.

ACCOUNTING FOR CAPITAL STOCK

(43) TYPES AND VALUES OF CAPITAL STOCK

The type of stock and the number of shares that a corporation may issue are specified in its certificate of incorporation. The laws of the state of incorporation usually specify the minimum amount of capital that must be paid in before the corporation can begin business. This does not necessarily mean that all of the authorized stock must be issued at the outset. It is necessary only to issue the number of shares needed to provide the minimum amount of paid-in capital specified by law. Additional authorized shares may be issued from time to time if the corporation finds it desirable to increase its capital. After all of the authorized shares are issued and outstanding, no more shares may be issued without securing an amendment to the corporate charter.

Par-Value Stock. The *par value* (sometimes called *face value*) of a share of stock represents the minimum amount of cash or other property that the corporation can accept in exchange for the share when it is issued originally, if the share is to be fully paid. Capital stock usually is not issued until it is paid for in full. Ordinarily, stock may be paid for with cash or with other property, and sometimes with labor done or with services rendered. When stock has been fully paid for, neither the corporation nor its creditors have any further claim on the stockholders.

If stock is issued without having been fully paid for and the corporation later becomes insolvent, its creditors may force the original purchasers of the stock, if the shares are still in their hands, to pay the difference between the purchase price and the par value of the stock. Subsequent purchasers of capital stock from original subscribers may also be liable for the difference between the amount originally paid in and the face value of the stock, if it can be established that they acquired the stock knowing that the original subscriber did not pay for it in full.

The incorporators may designate any amount as the par value of the shares of a class of capital stock. It is unusual to find shares with a par value of less than 10 cents or more than $100. Par values of $1, $10, $25,

$50, and $100 are frequently specified. The number of shares authorized and the par value per share are stated in the certificate of incorporation and appear on each stock certificate. The *authorized capital* of a corporation is the par value of each share times the number of shares authorized. The certificate of incorporation of The Wayman Manufacturing Co., reproduced on page 540, specifies an authorized capital stock of $50,000 divided into 500 shares with a par value of $100 each.

There was a time when all stock issued by a corporation had to have a par value. This requirement was intended to serve as a means of protecting the interests of the creditors of corporations. Since the owners of corporations do not have personal liability for the debts of the company, it was intended that each share of stock issued should represent a capital investment of an amount equal to at least the par value of the share. The laws either forbade the issuance of stock at a discount or, if this was permitted, provided that the purchaser of the stock would be liable for the amount of such discount.

Generally, the state laws make it illegal for a corporation to pay any dividends that would result in the total assets being less than the sum of all liabilities plus the par value of all shares outstanding. Thus, any losses up to the amount of the total par value of outstanding shares will reduce the equity or interest of the stockholders but will not impair the claims of the creditors.

It should be clear that par value is strictly a legal matter. Par value does not have any direct relationship to the market value of the shares (though, unfortunately, uninformed investors often have been misled into thinking that it represents what the stock is worth). As between the shareholders, par value has little significance. Each share of stock, with or without par value, represents a proportionate interest or equity in the net worth of a corporation. If there are 10,000 shares of only one class of stock outstanding, the holder of 100 shares has a 1 per cent ownership interest. His votes count that much, he gets 1 per cent of any earnings that are distributed as dividends, and if the corporation were to liquidate, he would get 1 per cent of anything left over after all creditors were paid in full.

No-Par-Value Stock. Most states allow corporations to issue *no-par-value* stock. Shares of this type can be sold for whatever they will bring, and there will be no discount liability. The certificate of incorporation will specify the number of shares that may be issued.

Laws permitting the use of no-par shares were instituted because of certain abuses that arose in connection with par-value stock. Unscrupulous promoters and stock salesmen took advantage of the fact that some people did not understand the meaning of par value. Property accepted in exchange for stock sometimes was overvalued so that the shares issued would be fully paid. This overvaluation could occur because directors of a corporation have the power to place a value upon property accepted in exchange for stock. Oftentimes the directors were acting for the corporation in purchasing property from themselves as individuals. Sometimes they exchanged their property at a greatly exaggerated value for shares of stock that, technically, were issued as being fully paid. These stockholder-directors then would donate some of their shares to the corporation. The donated shares would be sold to raise cash with which to operate. The shares might sell for a small fraction of their par value, but the buyer would acquire no liability since the shares were fully paid when originally issued.

When no-par shares are used, there is less temptation to overvalue property received in exchange for shares. Actual and potential stockholders are less likely to be misled if the shares do not have par value. There is no problem of discount liability.

Well-established customs and legal precedents die hard, however. The laws permitting no-par stock frequently provide that each share of such stock shall be assigned a *stated value*. The corporate directors determine what this stated value is to be. Usually it is a nominal amount. A stated value of $1 may be established for shares that actually are sold for $10 or more. In such cases, the legal capital of the corporation is equal to the number of shares outstanding times the stated value per share. Stated value and par value are essentially the same thing.

In accounting for the sale of no-par shares with a stated value, some accountants credit an amount equal to the stated value to the capital stock account and the balance of the proceeds to an account usually entitled Premium on Capital Stock. The recommended procedure, however, is to credit the entire amount received to the capital stock account. The stated value of the shares can be noted parenthetically in the balance sheet.

Many of the older corporations have par stock outstanding. Corporations formed in recent years have shown some tendency to favor no-par stock, although the use of par shares still is popular.

Book Value. For purposes of comparison and analysis, the *book value* of a share of capital stock may be calculated. It represents the dollar amount of the interest or equity of each share in the assets of the corporation. It usually is calculated by using data supplied by the balance sheet.

The excess of the book value of the assets over the amount of the liabilities represents the equity of the stockholders. If one kind of stock only is issued, the book value of each share may be found by dividing the stockholders' equity by the total number of shares issued. For example, if the balance sheet of a corporation shows that its assets amount to $100,000, its liabilities amount to $40,000, and there are 1,000 shares of capital stock outstanding, the book value of each share may be computed as follows:

Book value of assets...	$100,000
Amount of liabilities...	40,000
Stockholders' equity...	$ 60,000

$60,000 ÷ 1,000 shares = $60, book value of each share.

If more than one kind of stock is issued and one kind has preference over another in the distribution of assets in case of dissolution of the corporation, it is necessary to deduct the redemption value of the preferred stock in computing the equity of the common stockholders. For example, if a corporation has 500 shares of preferred stock outstanding, par value $100 a share, and 500 shares of common stock outstanding, par value $100 a share, the redemption value of the preferred stock should be deducted from the stockholders' equity before the book value of the common stock is computed. If the balance sheet of a corporation shows that it has assets amounting to $170,000 and liabilities amounting to $90,000, the stockholders' equity is $80,000. If the preferred stock has a redemption value equivalent to its par value of $100 a share, the book value of each share of common stock may be computed in the following manner:

Total book value of assets......................................	$170,000
Amount of liabilities...	90,000
Stockholders' equity...	$ 80,000
Less redemption value of preferred stock (500 shares @ $100)......	50,000
Equity of common stockholders.................................	$ 30,000

$30,000 ÷ 500 shares = $60, book value of each share of common stock.

It must be remembered that no effort is made to have the ledger accounts and the balance sheet show the market value of most of the assets of a business. Accordingly, the book value of a share of common stock does not represent what the stockholder would receive if the corporation completely liquidated. He might receive more. As liquidation losses usually are large, however, he probably would receive less. Book value means what it says — value per the books. There is no direct relationship between par or stated value, book value, and market value. Each of these terms has a distinct meaning.

Market Value. The *market value* of capital stock is the price at which it may be bought or sold in the open market. It is a relatively simple matter to ascertain the market value of stocks *listed* on an exchange, such as the New York Stock Exchange, the American Stock Exchange, the Mid-West Stock Exchange, the San Francisco Stock Exchange, the Toronto Stock Exchange, or any other stock exchange. When the stock of a corporation is listed on any exchange, it is thereby approved for trading purposes on that exchange. *Bid and offered prices* are then tabulated daily by the exchange. The sales through the exchange are recorded and a summary of the transactions are usually published in the daily papers.

In the case of stocks not listed on any exchange, it may be more difficult to ascertain their market value. If there has been a recent sale of unlisted stock, its selling price may be considered the present market value. Certain brokers make a specialty of dealing in unlisted stocks. Through such brokers, information may usually be obtained as to the bid and offered prices of unlisted stocks. Any information that will aid in determining the price at which stock may be bought or sold will be helpful in determining the market value of such stock. Many factors affect the market value of capital stock, such as (a) the management of the company, (b) the business outlook of the company, (c) the current rate of dividends and the dividend record of the company, (d) the financial position of the company as revealed by its balance sheet, (e) the earnings of the current year as revealed by its inccme statement, and (f) the stability of the earnings of the company over a period of years.

Classes of Capital Stock. Basically, all capital stock represents an ownership equity or interest in a corporation. Unless specifically restricted by the certificate of incorporation, each share carries the same rights with respect to voting privileges, dividends, and participation in the division of assets in the event of dissolution. If there is only one class of stock outstanding, all shares will have all of these rights. The issue would be classed as *common stock*.

If there are classes of stock that carry certain specified preferences, or first claims, they are called *preferred stock*. Usually these preferences relate to either or both of the following:

> *(1) Preference as to dividends.* Shares with a dividend preference entitle their owners to receive dividends of a specified amount (often expressed as a per cent of the par value of the shares) before shares of an issue with secondary preferences or without preferences receive anything.

> *(2) Preference as to assets.* Shares with a *liquidating preference* entitle the holders to receive, in the event the corporation liquidates, a specified amount before shares with secondary preference or no preference receive anything. If there is a liquidation

preference, it is never less than the par value of the shares and is often a few dollars more. If the shares are *redeemable* or *callable* at the option of the corporation, there is usually a *call premium* involved. For example, an issue of $100 par-value preferred stock might have a preference in total liquidation of $103 per share and be callable at the option of the corporation on and after a specified date at $105 per share plus unpaid dividends, if any.

There is no promise or guarantee that there will be either any dividends or anything to distribute if the corporation liquidates, but preferred stockholders have a prior or first claim (up to a specified preference limit) upon whatever is available. It is usually provided that the preferred stock shall have no voting rights.

Corporations sometimes have more than one class of preferred stock outstanding. The issues are usually differentiated with such names as "First Preferred," "Second Preferred," etc. If the first preferred had a specified dividend rate of 4 per cent and the second preferred 6 per cent, it would mean that dividends of 4 per cent per share would have to be paid on the first preferred shares before the holders of the second preferred shares could receive any dividends and a dividend of 6 per cent would have to be paid on the second preferred shares before the common stockholders could receive any dividends.

Some corporations have more than one class of common stock outstanding. The different issues often are designated as "Class A Common," "Class B Common," etc. The differences usually relate to either dividend preferences (even though they are called common stock) or voting rights. Certain classes may entitle the holder to vote for only a limited number of directors. Such a device is used to enable the holders of one class of stock to maintain control of the corporation.

Participating or Nonparticipating Preferred Stock. Preferred stock is said to be *participating* when it is provided that, under certain conditions, the shares will be entitled to receive dividends in excess of the stated preference rate. Provisions of this sort are not found very often; nevertheless, there is a considerable variety of participation arrangements. In all cases, the preferred stock receives its regular dividend first if there are any dividends paid during the year. Usually the participation does not begin until the holders of the common stock have received a specified amount. Beyond that the preferred stock and the common stock may share according to some specified plan or ratio in any further dividends that are to be paid.

If there is an equal division of any additional dividends between the preferred shares and the common shares, without any limit to the amount the preferred shares may receive, the preferred stock is said to be *fully participating*. Often the extent of participation is limited. For example, the preferred stock might have a 6 per cent preference rate with participation up to 8 per cent. In that case the shares would never receive dividends in any year in excess of 8 per cent of their par value. If preferred dividends are limited to the specified preference rate, the stock is *nonparticipating*.

Cumulative or Noncumulative Preferred Stock. Preferred stock may be *cumulative* or *noncumulative* as to dividends. If the preferred stock is cumulative, the stockholder is entitled to a specified rate of dividend and, if the directors do not declare the dividend in any year (whether because of insufficient earnings or otherwise), the unpaid amount will accumulate until it is paid out of the earnings of subsequent years. The accumulating amounts are not a liability of the corporation, but they must be paid before the common stockholders can receive any dividends.

If the preferred stock is noncumulative and the earnings of a particular year do not warrant the declaration of dividends, there is no carryover of dividends to succeeding years. The holder of noncumulative preferred stock is only entitled to receive dividends in any year when the earnings are sufficient to pay such dividends and the board of directors declares them.

Convertible Stock. Sometimes a class of stock is issued that is *convertible* into some other class of stock. Thus, a corporation may issue a class of preferred stock that may be converted into common stock at a specified time and in a specified ratio of the number of common shares (or a fraction thereof) that may be obtained in exchange for each preferred share. This offers the stockholder the advantage of being able to convert his preferred stock into common stock should he so desire. This might be desirable if the market value of the common stock became greater than the market value of the preferred stock.

Issued and Unissued Stock. Authorized capital stock that has not been issued is known as *unissued stock*. It has no asset value and should not be listed in the balance sheet of the company as an asset. Such stock may be considered to have potential value in that it may be issued at any time for the purpose of acquiring additional capital. When a corporation sells its capital stock, certificates are issued to the stockholders and thereafter the stock is said to be outstanding. If there is no treasury stock, all shares issued would be outstanding. The total amount relating to each class of stock should be shown separately in the balance sheet. If the stock has a par value, it is shown at par. If it is no-par stock with a stated value, it is often shown at the amount of the stated value, although the recommended practice is to show the total amount received upon the issuance of the shares. The stated value may be shown parenthetically. If there is no stated value, the total amount received upon the issuance is shown and the number of shares issued is noted parenthetically.

Treasury Stock. Corporations may reacquire their own shares of capital stock by purchase or donation. If such shares are canceled and retired, they revert to the status of unissued stock. If such shares are not retired, they are considered to be *treasury stock*. As stated on page 557, the stockholders of a corporation may donate some of their stock to the corporation and such shares may be resold. Until such shares are resold they are classed as treasury stock. Treasury stock may not be voted at stockholders' meetings and does not share in dividends declared.

When a corporation reacquires its own stock by purchase, it is usually recorded at cost and is reported in the balance sheet as a deduction from the total capital of the corporation. When a corporation reacquires its own stock by donation, or at no cost, all that is needed is a notation in the Items column on the debit side of the capital stock account to show the number of shares reacquired. In preparing a balance sheet the number of donated shares held in the treasury should be noted. Since a corporation cannot own itself in whole or in part, treasury stock should not be listed in the balance sheet as an asset.

> *PRACTICE ASSIGNMENT No. 43. Complete Report No. 43 in the workbook and submit your working papers for approval. Continue with the following study assignment until the next report is required.*

(44) RECORDING CAPITAL STOCK TRANSACTIONS

The practices followed in accounting for assets, liabilities, income, and expenses of corporations are generally the same as in the case of sole proprietorships and partnerships. The peculiarities of corporate accounting relate to net worth. Accounting for typical capital stock transactions will now be considered. Following is a list of typical capital stock transactions:

(a) Capital stock authorized by certificate of incorporation.
(b) Subscriptions to capital stock.
(c) Payments received to apply on subscriptions.
(d) Capital stock issued to subscribers.
(e) Capital stock transferred.
(f) Treasury stock acquired.
(g) Treasury stock sold.

Corporate Accounts — Par-Value Stock.   In recording corporate transactions relating to capital stock with par value, some or all of the following accounts may be needed:

Capital Stock   Discount on Capital Stock
Subscriptions Receivable   Treasury Stock
Capital Stock Subscribed   Donated Capital
Premium on Capital Stock   Organization Expense

Accounting for Authorization and Issuance of Capital Stock.   The certificate of incorporation specifies the amount of the authorized capital stock of a corporation. The amount of the stock and the number of shares authorized may be recorded by means of a memorandum entry in the corporation journal. Usually a memorandum entry is also made in the capital stock account to show the amount and number of shares authorized. When more than one class of stock is authorized, there should be a separate account kept for each class. For example, suppose the XYZ Corporation is formed with the authority to issue 1,000 shares of $4\frac{1}{2}\%$ preferred stock, par value $100 per share, and 3,000 shares of common stock, par value $50 per share. Separate accounts should be kept for Capital Stock, Preferred and Capital Stock, Common and a notation of the number of shares of each class of stock authorized should be made in the Items column on the credit side of the accounts. If 800 shares of the preferred stock are sold at par for cash and 500 shares of the common stock are issued in exchange for land valued at $25,000, the transactions should be recorded as follows:

Bank... $80,000
    Capital Stock, Preferred.............................. $80,000
        Sold 800 shares of preferred stock at par for cash.

Land... 25,000
    Capital Stock, Common...............................   25,000
        Issued 500 shares of common stock at par in exchange for
        land valued at $25,000.

The capital stock section of a balance sheet of the XYZ Corporation prepared just after the preceding transactions had been recorded would appear as follows:

Capital Stock:
    Preferred Stock, $4\frac{1}{2}\%$, par $100
        (Authorized 1,000 shares) issued 800 shares............ $80,000
    Common Stock, par $50
        (Authorized 3,000 shares) issued 500 shares.............   25,000
    Total Capital Stock..................................... $105,000

If at some later date the charter is amended to permit the issuance of additional shares or to reduce the number of shares authorized, it is only necessary to make a memorandum entry in the corporation journal of the action taken and to make a similar memorandum entry in the capital stock accounts.

Sometimes accounts with Unissued Capital Stock and Authorized Capital Stock are kept. When this practice is followed, a formal entry is made debiting Unissued Capital Stock and crediting Authorized Capital Stock for the amount of the stock authorized. Subscriptions to capital stock and payments made to apply on such subscriptions are recorded in the same manner as previously explained. When the stock is issued, the transaction is recorded by debiting Capital Stock Subscribed and by crediting Unissued Capital Stock. The only difference in stating the capital stock in the balance sheet is that the amount of the unissued capital stock is shown as a deduction from the amount of the authorized capital stock to arrive at the amount of the stock issued. This method can be used only in the case of par-value stock.

Accounting for Capital Stock Subscriptions. Corporations sometimes accept subscriptions to their capital stock. The conditions of the subscription contract may call for the subscribers to make payment of the agreed amount in full at a later date or in several installments over a period of time. Subscriptions to capital stock are usually recorded by debiting Subscriptions Receivable and by crediting Capital Stock Subscribed. For example, suppose the XYZ Corporation (mentioned previously) obtained subscriptions to 1,000 shares of its common stock at par value. The entry to record these subscriptions is as follows:

Subscriptions Receivable, Common......................	$50,000	
Capital Stock Subscribed, Common....................		$50,000
Received subscriptions for 1,000 shares of common stock at par.		

It should be noted that the word "Common" appears in each of the account titles. Since the corporation has two classes of stock, separate accounts for each class are kept.

If there are a number of subscribers and the conditions of the subscription contract call for, or permit, installment payments of the purchase price, it is probable that a subsidiary subscribers' ledger will be used. See page 550 for a standard form of account for such a ledger. This ledger is controlled by the subscriptions receivable account in the general ledger.

Assume that subscribers for 500 shares pay their subscriptions in full ($25,000), while subscribers for the other 500 shares pay 20 per cent, or

$5,000, on their subscriptions. The entry to record these payments is as follows:

Bank...	$30,000	
Subscriptions Receivable, Common....................		$30,000
Received cash in full payment of subscriptions to 500		
shares of common stock and $10 per share to apply on		
subscriptions to 500 shares of common stock.		

The amounts received would be credited to the proper accounts in the subscribers' ledger. At this point the subscriptions receivable account has a debit balance of $20,000. The sum of all of the balances in the subsidiary ledger should equal this amount. If the amounts due from subscribers to capital stock represent bona fide, collectible claims, it is acceptable accounting practice to show the debit balance of the subscriptions receivable account as an asset in the balance sheet. If it is likely that the amount will be collected in the near future, the account may be classified as a current asset.

Inasmuch as the subscriptions to 500 shares have been paid in full, the certificates would be issued. The entry to record their issuance is as follows:

Capital Stock Subscribed, Common.......................	$25,000	
Capital Stock, Common...............................		$25,000
Capital stock certificates for 500 shares of common stock		
issued to subscribers who have paid in full.		

At this point the capital stock subscribed account has a credit balance of $25,000, which represents the par value of the 500 shares for which full payment has not yet been received. This account will be closed upon the issuance of the shares after full payment of the subscription price has been received.

The balance sheet of the XYZ Corporation, after all of the foregoing transactions have been recorded, would appear as follows:

XYZ CORPORATION

BALANCE SHEET

ASSETS			CAPITAL		
Current Assets:			Capital Stock:		
Cash......................	$110,000		Preferred Stock, 4½%, par $100,		
Subscriptions Receivable,			(Authorized 1,000 shares)		
Common.................	20,000		issued 800 shares.........		$ 80,000
			Common Stock, par $50,		
Total Current Assets.........		$130,000	(Authorized 3,000 shares)		
Fixed Assets:			issued 1,000 shares........	$50,000	
Land......................		25,000	Common Stock Subscribed,		
			500 shares.................	25,000	75,000
Total Assets............................		$155,000	Total Capital...................		$155,000

The common stock subscriptions receivable, instead of being shown as an asset, may be shown in the capital section of the balance sheet as a deduction from common stock subscribed. The resulting difference represents the amount actually paid in by the subscribers to common stock to the date of the balance sheet. If there is any question of the collectibility of subscriptions receivable, this treatment is mandatory. Some accountants prefer such treatment in any event.

It is not necessary to use subscriptions receivable and capital stock subscribed accounts when shares are sold outright for cash or are issued in exchange for other property. In such cases the proper asset accounts may be debited and the capital stock account may be credited directly. The subscription accounts are used in connection with subscription contracts that call for either a lump-sum payment at a later date or a series of payments over a period of time.

Discount or Premium on Capital Stock. Original issues of par-value capital stock usually are sold at par. However, the shares are sometimes sold for more than par, and, if the state law permits, they may be sold for less than par. When shares of stock are sold for more than par value, the excess is termed a *premium* and it should be credited to Premium on Capital Stock. If shares are sold for less than their par value, the difference is termed a *discount* and it should be debited to Discount on Capital Stock.

To illustrate, suppose that, at a date subsequent to the transactions already considered, the XYZ Corporation sells 100 shares of preferred stock at $103 per share and 200 shares of common stock at $48 per share. The entries to record these sales are as follows:

Bank..	$10,300	
Capital Stock, Preferred.............................		$10,000
Premium on Capital Stock, Preferred..................		300
Sold 100 shares of preferred stock at $103 per share.		
Bank..	9,600	
Discount on Capital Stock, Common...................	400	
Capital Stock, Common.............................		10,000
Sold 200 shares of common stock at $48 per share.		

Premium on capital stock is an addition to capital and the credit balance should be so reported in the capital section of the balance sheet. Discount on capital stock is a deduction from capital and should be so reported in the balance sheet. If desired, the discount account may be written off against an accumulated credit balance in the premium account. In a state where the law permits, discount on capital stock may be written off against an accumulated credit balance in the retained earnings account.

It has been mentioned that the laws pertaining to par value and stock discount have invited such subterfuges as overvaluing assets accepted in exchange for shares so that the existence of a discount is hidden. When assets are overvalued for this or any other reason, the capital stock is said to be *watered*.

Under the federal income tax law, no gain or loss arises from the original sale of capital stock by a corporation. It is immaterial whether the stock is sold at a premium or at a discount. The sale of an original issue of stock represents a capital transaction from which neither taxable gain nor deductible loss results, regardless of the selling price.

Accounting for Treasury Stock. Treasury stock refers to the shares of stock that have been reacquired by the issuing corporation and that have not been formally canceled. Treasury stock may be acquired by donation or by purchase. Accountants are not in universal agreement as to how treasury stock transactions should be recorded. The most common procedure, however, is to record treasury stock at its cost irrespective of its par value, if any. If this practice is followed, only a memorandum entry is needed if the treasury stock is acquired by donation. When the donated shares are sold, an account entitled Donated Capital may be credited. For example, suppose that 100 shares of treasury stock that had been donated by the stockholders are sold for $50 per share. The entry to record this transaction is as follows:

Bank..	$5,000	
Donated Capital.......................................		$5,000
Sold 100 shares of donated treasury stock at $50 per share.		

A corporation sometimes purchases its own capital stock for one of the following reasons:

(a) The corporation may wish to reduce the amount of capital stock outstanding, thereby reducing the capitalization of the corporation. This may occur at a time when the stock can be purchased at a discount. When the shares are formally canceled, the stock ceases to be treasury stock and reverts to the status of unissued stock.

(b) A corporation may have sold capital stock to its employees under an agreement to repurchase the shares if the workers leave the employ of the company. The price at which the shares will be repurchased usually is covered by the agreement.

(c) A corporation may purchase some of its shares to stabilize the market price of the stock.

(d) A corporation may want to obtain some of its shares to give to officers or employees as a bonus or to be sold to officers or employees under a stock option agreement.

When a corporation purchases its own stock, Treasury Stock should be debited for its cost. When treasury stock is sold at a profit, Treasury Stock should be credited for the original cost of the stock and Premium on Capital Stock should be credited for the amount of the profit. When treasury stock is sold at a loss, Treasury Stock should be credited for the original cost of the stock and Discount on Capital Stock should be debited for the amount of the loss. For example, suppose that 2,000 shares of common stock are purchased for $8 per share and later sold for $11 per share. The entries to record these transactions are as follows:

Treasury Stock, Common..............................	$16,000	
Bank..		$16,000
Purchased 2,000 shares of common stock at $8 per share.		
Bank..	22,000	
Treasury Stock, Common............................		16,000
Premium on Capital Stock..........................		6,000
Sold 2,000 treasury shares at $11 per share.		

If the stock had been sold for less than its cost, Discount on Capital Stock should have been debited for the amount of the loss.

There should be a separate treasury stock account for each class of treasury stock in the possession of the corporation. The balance of each of these accounts, representing the cost of the treasury shares on hand, is shown in the balance sheet as a deduction from the total amount of capital stock of all types. This treatment is illustrated in the capital section of the balance sheet of The Union Manufacturing Company shown on page 572.

Accountants do not consider that a corporation can make a profit or suffer a loss from dealing in its own shares. As stated on page 566, premium on capital stock is considered an addition to capital, while discount on capital stock is considered a decrease in capital and should be so stated in the balance sheet.

Organization Expense Account. In the organization of a corporation, certain expenses are incurred, such as incorporation fees, attorneys' fees, promotion expense, etc. Such expenditures are known as *organization expenses.* Organization expenses differ from ordinary operating expenses in that they apply to the entire life of a corporation rather than to one fiscal period. It is, therefore, customary to treat organization expenses as an intangible asset until such time as they may be written off. Since organization expenses represent an intangible asset and have no market value, it is common practice to write off such expenses over a period of years. If, for example, it is desired to write off organization expense over a period of five years, one fifth of the original total amount should be written off each year by debiting Income Summary and by crediting Organization Expense. Organization expense incurred prior to August 17, 1954 could not be claimed as a deduction under the federal income tax law. However, organization expense incurred after August 16, 1954 may be amortized over any period of time desired except that it may not be less than sixty months.

Accounting for No-Par-Value Stock.   Accounting for transactions involving capital stock without par value may be somewhat simpler than is the case with par-value stock. It will not be simpler if the shares have a stated value and this value is treated in the accounts as though it were par. If, however, the stated value is ignored except for balance sheet notations of its amount, or if there is no stated value, the accounting is simplified. When shares are issued, the capital stock account is credited for the amount of money or the value of property received. The number of shares issued should be noted in the account. There is no premium or discount involved.

Subscriptions to no-par stock are recorded in a manner similar to that followed in the case of par-value stock. The subscriptions receivable account is debited and the capital stock subscribed account is credited for the full amount of the subscriptions. If there are numerous subscribers, a subsidiary subscribers' ledger would be used. When the stock certificates are issued after full payment has been received, the capital stock subscribed account is debited and the capital stock account is credited for the full amount received for the stock.

The accounting for no-par treasury stock does not differ from the recording of par-value treasury stock transactions when the cost basis is used.

Capital Stock Transactions.   To illustrate the application of some of the principles of accounting for capital stock that have been discussed to this point, the entries needed to record the following narrative of corporate transactions are presented in general journal form. Only events and transactions pertaining to capital stock are included. The entries to record these transactions are shown in general journal form on page 571.

It is assumed that a subsidiary subscribers' ledger and a subsidiary stockholders' ledger are maintained. A stock transfer record, similar to the one illustrated on page 553, is used to record such transactions as those occurring on August 8, October 3 and 19, and December 6.

NARRATIVE OF TRANSACTIONS

July 1. The Union Manufacturing Company was incorporated with the authority to issue 1,000 shares of 5% preferred capital stock, par value $100, and 2,000 shares of common stock without par value.

1. At the first meeting of the incorporators, the following subscriptions to the capital stock were accepted:

A — 500 shares of preferred stock at $104 per share
B — 300 shares of preferred stock at $104 per share
C — 500 shares of common stock at $40 per share
D — 300 shares of common stock at $40 per share
E — 200 shares of common stock at $40 per share.

17. The following was received from subscribers to apply on their subscriptions to capital stock:

A — Cash, $52,000
B — Cash, $15,600
C — Cash, $2,000; land, $18,000
D — Machinery and equipment, $12,000
E — Cash, $2,000.

17. Issued stock certificates to the following subscribers, who had paid their subscriptions in full:

A — 500 shares of preferred stock
C — 500 shares of common stock
D — 300 shares of common stock.

Aug. 8. Stockholder A returned his certificate for 500 shares of preferred stock and requested that 150 shares of his stock be transferred to F. (He had sold these shares to F.) Issued a new certificate to A for 350 shares and a certificate to F for 150 shares. (No general journal entry required.)

23. Sold 200 shares of preferred stock to B at a price of $103 per share. Received cash in full payment and issued the certificate.

26. Sold 10 shares of common stock to H at a price of $35 per share. Received cash in full payment and issued the certificate.

Oct. 3. Purchased 100 shares of the preferred stock owned by A for a total of $9,800. A returned his certificate for 350 shares and was issued a new certificate for 250 shares. The shares purchased are to be held as treasury stock; accordingly, a certificate for 100 shares was made out in the name of the company.

19. Purchased 10 shares of common stock owned by H for a total of $300. The stock is to be held in the treasury.

Dec. 6. Sold the 10 shares of common treasury stock to J for $320.

General Journal

July   1. Incorporated The Union Manufacturing Company with an authorized issue of 1,000 shares of 5% preferred stock, par value $100, and 2,000 shares of common stock with no par value.

1. Subscriptions Receivable, Preferred..........................	$83,200	
Subscriptions Receivable, Common..........................	40,000	
Capital Stock Subscribed, Preferred.......................		$80,000
Capital Stock Subscribed, Common........................		40,000
Premium on Capital Stock...............................		3,200

    Received subscriptions to capital stock as follows:
    Preferred stock subscribed at $104 per share —
        A — 500 shares
        B — 300 shares
    Common stock subscribed at $40 per share —
        C — 500 shares
        D — 300 shares
        E — 200 shares.

17. Bank...	71,600	
Land...	18,000	
Machinery and Equipment...............................	12,000	
Subscriptions Receivable, Preferred.....................		67,600
Subscriptions Receivable, Common......................		34,000

    Received cash and other property in payment of subscriptions to capital stock as follows:
    To apply on preferred stock subscriptions:
        A — Cash, $52,000 (in full)
        B — Cash, $15,600
    To apply on common stock subscriptions:
        C — Cash, $2,000; land, $18,000 (in full)
        D — Machinery and equipment, $12,000 (in full)
        E — Cash, $2,000.

17. Capital Stock Subscribed, Preferred.......................	50,000	
Capital Stock Subscribed, Common.......................	32,000	
Capital Stock, Preferred...............................		50,000
Capital Stock, Common................................		32,000

    Stock certificates issued to subscribers as follows:
        A — 500 shares preferred stock
        C — 500 shares common stock
        D — 300 shares common stock.

Aug. 23. Bank...	20,600	
Capital Stock, Preferred...............................		20,000
Premium on Capital Stock..............................		600

    Sold 200 shares of preferred stock to G at $103 per share.

26. Bank...	350	
Capital Stock, Common................................		350

    Sold 10 shares of common stock to H at $35 per share.

Oct. 3. Treasury Stock, Preferred..............................	9,800	
Bank..		9,800

    Purchased 100 shares of preferred stock from A at $98 per share.

19. Treasury Stock, Common.................................	300	
Bank..		300

    Purchased 10 shares of common stock from H at $30 per share.

Dec. 6. Bank...	320	
Treasury Stock, Common...............................		300
Premium on Capital Stock..............................		20

    Sold 10 shares of treasury stock, common to J at $32 per share.

Assume that the records (not shown) of The Union Manufacturing Company disclose a net income of $5,000 for the six months ended December 31. Further assume that no dividends have been declared to that date. Accordingly, the capital section of the balance sheet of the company as of December 31 would appear as follows:

THE UNION MANUFACTURING COMPANY
BALANCE SHEET
DECEMBER 31, 19--

CAPITAL

Capital Stock:			
Preferred Stock, 5%, par $100,			
(Authorized 1,000 shares)			
issued 700 shares...............................	$70,000		
Preferred Stock Subscribed, 300 shares................	30,000	$100,000	
Common Stock, no-par, (Authorized 2,000 shares)			
issued 810 shares.................................	$32,350		
Common Stock Subscribed, 200 shares................	8,000	40,350	
Total Capital Stock.................................			$140,350
Premium on Capital Stock...........................		$ 3,820	
Retained Earnings...................................		5,000	8,820
			$149,170
Less: Treasury Stock, Preferred (100 shares, at cost)...			9,800
Total Capital..			$139,370

After completing the posting from the journal of The Union Manufacturing Company, Subscriptions Receivable, Preferred will have a debit balance of $15,600 and Subscriptions Receivable, Common will have a debit balance of $6,000. The sum of these balances may be listed among the assets in the balance sheet. If it is expected that the amounts due on subscriptions will be collected in the near future, they may be listed as a current asset. Otherwise, most accountants would probably prefer to treat Subscriptions Receivable, Preferred as a deduction from Preferred Stock Subscribed, and Subscriptions Receivable, Common as a deduction from Common Stock Subscribed in the capital section of the balance sheet.

PRACTICE ASSIGNMENT No. 44. Complete Report No. 44 in the workbook and submit your working papers for approval. Continue with the textbook discussion in Unit Twenty-three until the next report is required.

Unit Twenty-three

ACCOUNTING FOR CORPORATION EARNINGS

(45) EARNINGS RETAINED IN THE BUSINESS

There are two major sources of proprietorship or capital for every type of business: (1) capital that results from the investment of cash or other property by the owner or owners, and (2) capital that results from earnings retained in the business. In the case of sole proprietorships and partnerships, little or no effort is made to distinguish between these two types of capital. In the accounts of a sole proprietorship all of the proprietorship usually is recorded in the capital account of the proprietor. The balance in the capital account of each member of a partnership usually represents his share of the net worth of the partnership. In corporation accounting, more attention is paid to the source of the net worth, that is, to the distinction between invested capital and capital resulting from retained earnings.

Invested Capital. The original capital of a corporation is usually derived from the sale of capital stock. The amount received from the sale of capital stock represents the contributed or invested capital of the stockholders. Subsequently, the capital of a corporation may be increased by additional contributions by stockholders or by the retention of earnings for use in the business. It is important that the accounts of a corporation be kept in such a manner that they will show the sources from which the proprietary capital

---

DISCONTINUANCE OF THE USE OF THE TERM "SURPLUS"

The terminology used in the discussion of capital and earnings of corporations in this textbook is in accord with the recommendations of the American Institute of Accountants. In a bulletin issued in October, 1949, the Committee on Accounting Procedure recommended that in the balance-sheet presentation of the stockholders' equity, the use of the term *surplus* (whether standing alone or in such combination as *capital surplus, paid-in surplus, earned surplus, appraisal surplus,* etc.) be discontinued. It was further recommended that the term "earned surplus" be replaced by terms which will indicate source, such as *retained income, retained earnings, accumulated earnings,* or *earnings retained for use in the business.*

573

is derived. Invested capital, sometimes referred to as paid-in capital, should be recorded in the proper capital stock accounts to the extent of the par value or stated value of the stock. This amount usually constitutes the legal capital of a corporation. Amounts invested in excess of the par or stated value of the capital stock should be recorded in appropriate capital accounts that indicate the source of the capital. For example, if common stock is sold for more than its par value, the excess should be credited to Premium on Capital Stock. Should stock be sold for less than its par value, the difference should be debited to Discount on Capital Stock. Assuming that only common stock has been issued and that there have been no stock dividends, the amount of the contributed capital may be determined by ascertaining the sum of the amounts credited to the capital stock and premium on capital stock accounts or the difference between the amount credited to the capital stock account and the amount debited to the discount on capital stock account.

Retention of Income. Capital resulting from the retention of income should be recorded in an account with an appropriate title, such as Retained Earnings. Seldom does a corporation distribute all of its net earnings to stockholders. Usually only a portion of the earnings are distributed and the balance is retained as additional capital to help finance the growth of the business. It is not uncommon to find that a major portion of the capital of a corporation represents earnings retained in the business. Many of today's large corporations were started originally as small companies and their growth was financed primarily out of earnings. This was particularly true prior to the time of high income taxes. As income tax rates have increased, it has become more difficult for corporations to finance their growth or expansion with capital derived from earnings retained in the business. The result is that under current conditions an increasing amount of the working capital needs of corporations must be met by the sale of additional stock or by issuing bonds or other evidences of indebtedness.

The Retained Earnings Account. The net income of corporations is calculated in much the same manner as that of sole proprietorships and partnerships. At the end of the accounting period, the accounts are adjusted and the income and the expense accounts are closed into the income summary account. A credit balance in Income Summary represents net income; a debit balance signifies a net loss. Beyond this point the accounting procedures for corporations differ from those of sole proprietorships and partnerships. The balance of the income summary account of a corporation is transferred to the account with Retained Earnings.

Typical debits and credits to the retained earnings account include the following:

Debits

1. Net loss for the period (after including any unusual, nonrecurring losses or gains).
2. Corrections of errors discovered in the accounts.
3. Appropriations of earnings by the board of directors.
4. Dividends declared by the board of directors.

Credits

1. Net income for the period (after including any unusual, non-recurring losses or gains).
2. Corrections of errors discovered in the accounts.

It should be noted that the calculation of net income or net loss for a period should include any unusual, nonrecurring gains or losses. This practice is not always followed. For many years it was common practice to close only normal operating incomes and expenses into the income summary account. Unusual nonrecurring gains and losses were recorded directly in the retained earnings account. Some corporations still follow this practice. Such a procedure is not recommended, however, as it may cover up the fact that an operating profit or loss reported in the income statement was partly or wholly offset by nonoperating losses or gains recorded directly in the retained earnings account.

Stockholders tend to attach great importance to the net income or net loss figure that is shown in the income statement. They may overlook, or not bother to study, a statement of changes in retained earnings. For this reason, it is recommended that both operating and nonoperating incomes and expenses or losses be closed into the income summary account and be reported in the income statement. The statement can be arranged to distinguish clearly between the two types of income and expense. When this procedure is followed, the final net income or net loss figure gives a better indication of the total result of the activities of the period.

The list of typical debits and credits to the retained earnings account includes entries that arise from the correction of errors that are discovered in the accounts. Not all such cases involve retained earnings; but the correction of errors that had an effect on the income calculation of a prior period usually requires an adjustment in Retained Earnings. For example, suppose that after the books were closed it is discovered that the amount recorded for merchandise inventory at the end of the preceding period (the beginning of the current period) was overstated in the amount of $2,000. The entry to correct this overstatement would be as follows:

Retained Earnings...................................... $2,000
   Merchandise Inventory................................. $2,000
      Correction of overstatement of merchandise inventory as of
      December 31.

This entry not only corrects the amount shown in the ledger as the opening merchandise inventory of the present period, but it also corrects whatever amount was closed to the retained earnings account at the end of the previous period purporting to be the net income or net loss for that period.

Appropriations of Retained Earnings. Sometimes a portion of the earnings is appropriated for special purposes, such as inventory losses, patent infringement, anti-trust suit, etc. Sometimes a general appropriation is made for contingencies or contingent liabilities. The action of the directors in making such appropriations should be recorded in such a manner as to indicate what portion of retained earnings is not available for dividends. For example, if the directors should adopt a resolution appropriating $10,000 out of retained earnings for contingencies, it might be recorded by debiting Retained Earnings and crediting Appropriation for Contingencies. The account with Appropriation for Contingencies would then be shown in the balance sheet as a deduction from Retained Earnings.

The directors of a corporation have wide discretion in the matter of declaring cash dividends. In most cases, however, the amount of dividends that the directors will declare and pay is determined by the amount of cash available and considerations of policy. Even if the corporation has ample cash, the directors may not feel that it is wise to pay large dividends. They may want to use some of the money to expand the business or to reduce liabilities. They may want to invest the money in marketable securities that could be converted into cash very quickly in case of emergency. Most corporations do not regularly distribute all of their earnings as dividends.

The result of successful operations for a period of years coupled with a moderate dividend policy is an increasing balance in the retained earnings account. It is extremely unlikely that there would be a parallel increase in the size of the bank balance. The money probably will have been used to purchase various assets or to reduce liabilities. Such a corporation is said to be *growing from within*.

When the directors have no intention of paying dividends to the extent of the balance of Retained Earnings, they may reduce the balance of the account by distributing a stock dividend or they may appropriate a portion of the earnings. The latter amounts to nothing more than formally passing a resolution at a directors' meeting instructing the accountant to transfer a certain amount of the credit balance of the retained earnings account to a designated appropriation account, such as Appropriation for Contingencies, Appropriation for New Construction, or Appropriation for Expansion.

Such appropriations have no effect on the assets, the liabilities, or the total net worth of a corporation. The appropriations amount to nothing more than renaming a portion of retained earnings. This procedure is sometimes described as earmarking part of the retained earnings. Recording such appropriations in the suggested manner serves to advise the readers of a balance sheet that the directors have no present intention of distributing more than an amount equal to the unappropriated earnings as dividends.

Statement of Retained Earnings. In order to explain the change in the amount of retained earnings between two successive balance sheet dates, it is customary to prepare a statement of earnings retained for use in the business. To illustrate the relationship between such a statement and the balance sheet of a corporation, a condensed balance sheet and a detailed statement of income retained for use in the business are reproduced (page 578) from a recent annual report of a well-known company which is referred to here as The X Machinery Company.

The balance sheet shows that the capital contributed by the stockholders amounts to $13,612,440 ($10,862,440 + $2,750,000), while the capital resulting from earnings retained in the business amounts to $14,603,861 ($700,000 + $13,903,861). The statement of income retained for use in the business provides an analysis of the retained earnings for the year under consideration. It will be noted that there was a special write-off of $50,000 in the book value of trade-marks and goodwill during the year. Cash dividends of $2 a share, amounting to a total of $1,086,244, were paid to the stockholders during the year. After making these deductions, there was a balance at the end of the year of $13,903,861 of income retained for use in the business. Of this amount $700,000 had been appropriated for contingencies and the balance was unappropriated. The amount of the appropriation for contingencies must have been made in a prior year; otherwise, it would appear as a deduction in the current statement of income retained for use in the business. It should be noted further that the amount appropriated for contingencies is listed as a subdivision of income retained for use in the business. The action taken by the directors in making this

THE X MACHINERY COMPANY
BALANCE SHEET
DECEMBER 31, 19—

Total Assets.........................			$34,361,337

Total Liabilities....................			$ 6,145,036
Stockholders' Equity:			
Common stock, $20 par value, (Authorized 900,000 shares) outstanding 543,122 shares.........		$10,862,440	
Premium on capital stock............		2,750,000	
Income retained for use in the business:			
Appropriated for contingencies......	700,000		
Unappropriated, per statement........	13,903,861	13,903,861	
			28,216,301
Total Liabilities and Capital........			$34,361,337

THE X MACHINERY COMPANY
INCOME RETAINED FOR USE IN BUSINESS
DECEMBER 31, 19—

Balance, beginning of year...................			$13,859,292
Net income for year.........................	$1,180,813		
Provision for reduction of trade-marks and goodwill..	50,000	1,130,813	
			$14,990,105
Cash dividends — $2.00 per share.............			1,086,244
Balance, December 31, end of year...........			$13,903,861

appropriation indicates that the amount appropriated is not available for dividends. While the amount of the unappropriated retained income is technically available for dividends, it is not to be taken for granted that the entire amount will be distributed to the stockholders.

The fact that such an amount of income has been retained for use in the business is an indication that more than half of the capital requirements of the corporation has been provided through earnings retained in the business. As a result of this policy, the stockholders' equity has grown until their stock has a book value of $51.95 a share although its average issue price was only $25.06 a share.

Appreciation in Corporate Assets. Sometimes it is deemed advisable to increase the book value of the fixed assets of a corporation. An expert appraisal of the assets may reveal that their actual value is greater than their book value. This may be the result of an increasing market value of a firm's fixed assets. To record any appreciation in the fixed assets of a business involves debits to the particular assets affected and offsetting credits to an appropriate account which must be reflected in stating the stockholders' equity in the balance sheet. Any appreciation included in the stockholders' equity as a result of an appraisal of the fixed assets should be designated by such terms as *appreciation of fixed assets*, or *excess of appraised value of fixed assets over cost*. Such an item should appear as an addition to restricted capital rather than to unappropriated earnings. While the formal recognition of increases in the value of assets is sometimes warranted by special circumstances, the general practice of recording such increases in the accounts are opposed by most accountants. Records are supposed to show the cost (less depreciation, if any) of the assets owned by a corporation — not opinions of what they are worth. There is a general rule in accounting that forbids the recognition of unrealized gains. Realization occurs when there is an actual sale or exchange of property. In the absence of such realization, it ordinarily is considered to be improper to record so-called appreciation.

Recapitalization. With full knowledge and consent of its stockholders, a corporation may secure an amendment to its charter to permit it to change the legal value of its stock. Usually the change is to a lower par value or to no par value. Generally this involves calling in the old stock certificates and issuing new certificates. A major reason for reducing either the par value or the stated value of capital stock without increasing the number of shares outstanding is to eliminate an accumulated deficit. If a corporation is operated at a loss over a prolonged period of time, it may result in a deficit showing up in the balance sheet. This means that the amount of the liabilities is greater than the excess of the assets over the capital of the corporation. Officers, directors, and stockholders of corporations dislike having the balance sheet of their companies show a deficit; hence, take steps to eliminate it. One way of accomplishing this is to recapitalize the corporation and to reduce the par or stated value of its capital stock.

Assume that the Acme Coal Company had a deficit of $200,000 as shown by the following condensed balance sheet:

THE ACME COAL COMPANY
BALANCE SHEET

Total Assets......	$1,200,000	Total Liabilities...	$ 400,000

CAPITAL

		Capital Stock.....	$1,000,000	
		Less: Deficit....	200,000	800,000
Total Assets.....	$1,200,000	Total L. and C....		$1,200,000

There were 10,000 shares of capital stock outstanding with a par value of $100 per share. In order to eliminate the deficit of $200,000 it was decided to obtain an amendment to the articles of incorporation to permit an exchange of its old shares of capital stock for an equal number of new shares with a par value of $50 per share. The exchange of stock certificates was recorded in the following manner:

Capital Stock (Old)................................	$1,000,000	
Capital Stock (New).............................		$500,000
Deficit...		200,000
Premium on Capital Stock.........................		300,000

Premium on capital stock is credited for the excess valuation because the new stock has actually been issued at a premium. The par value of the old stock was $1,000,000, whereas the par value of the new stock is only $500,000. After writing off the deficit of $200,000, the balance represents the premium on the new stock.

After recording the exchange of shares in the manner suggested, the capital section of the balance sheet of the company would appear as follows:

CAPITAL

Capital Stock........................	$ 500,000	
Premium on Capital Stock.............	300,000	$ 800,000
Total Capital........................		$1,200,000

The exchange of shares had no effect upon the assets or the liabilities. It will also be noted that the total capital after exchanging the stock and writing off the deficit is the same as before. The book value per share of stock was not affected. There are still 10,000 shares of stock outstanding and the total capital of the company is still $800,000; hence, the book value of each share of stock is $80 a share. A reduction of the legal capital and the elimination of the deficit in the accounts were the only results of these events.

It must be understood that corporate recapitalizations have various purposes and take a variety of forms. Sometimes a recapitalization amounts to a reorganization of the company. Recapitalizations may involve the elimination of one or more classes of stock and, sometimes, bonds. Not infrequently a so-called *stock split* takes place. A stock split refers to an exchange of one share of an old issue for more than one share of a new issue of essentially the same class of stock. The usual purpose of a stock split is to increase the total number of shares outstanding so as to improve the marketability of the shares by reducing their market price and to make possible a wider ownership of the stock.

> *PRACTICE ASSIGNMENT No. 45. Complete Report No. 45 in the workbook and submit your working papers for approval. Continue with the following study assignment until Report No. 46 is required.*

(46) EARNINGS DISTRIBUTED TO STOCKHOLDERS

A pro-rata distribution of property by a corporation to its stockholders is known as a dividend. When the dividend represents a distribution of earnings, it is usually paid in cash, though it may consist of the distribution of other property. Sometimes corporations issue additional shares of their own stock to the stockholders on a pro-rata basis. Such a distribution is termed a *stock dividend*. When a corporation is being dissolved and any property is distributed among the stockholders, the distribution is known as a *liquidating dividend*.

Cash Dividends. Most corporation dividends are paid in cash and represent the distribution of corporate earnings. Some corporations are able to pay regular dividends periodically, that is, annually, semiannually, or quarterly. Other corporations pay dividends irregularly. It has been noted that the size and the frequency of dividend distributions depends upon earnings, the amount of cash available, and the plans and policies of the directors.

Three dates are involved in the declaration and the payment of dividends: (1) the date of declaration, (2) the record date, and (3) the date of payment. The record date is the day on which the names of stockholders entitled to receive the dividend will be determined. For example, a board of directors might meet on January 25 and declare a dividend of $2 a share on common stock, payable on February 15 to stockholders of record on February 5.

The result of such a declaration is to make the corporation liable for the dividend at the time of declaration on January 25. However, the dividend will not be paid until February 15. To be eligible to receive the dividend, a stockholder must have his stock recorded in his name in the books of the corporation not later than February 5. Thereafter any stock of the corporation that may be transferred is said to be transferred *ex-dividend*. This means that anyone acquiring the stock after February 5 will not be entitled to share in the dividend declared on January 25 even though the dividend is paid after the stock is acquired.

Usually each dividend declared is given a number to distinguish it from those that have been declared in the past. Dividends on different classes of capital stock should be accounted for separately. To illustrate, assume that the board of directors declares a semiannual dividend of $2.50 per share on 3,000 shares of preferred stock outstanding and a dividend of $4 per share on 10,000 shares of common stock outstanding. Assume that this is the 37th dividend on the preferred stock and the 28th on the common stock. These declarations would be recorded as follows:

Retained Earnings...	$ 7,500	
Preferred Dividend Payable, No. 37.....................		$ 7,500
Declared a dividend of $2.50 per share on 3,000 shares of preferred stock outstanding.		
Retained Earnings...	40,000	
Common Dividend Payable, No. 28.....................		40,000
Declared a dividend of $4 per share on 10,000 shares of common stock outstanding.		

When the dividends are paid, the dividend payable accounts will be debited and Bank will be credited. If a balance sheet were prepared on some date between the time the dividends were declared and the time they were paid, the balances of the two dividend payable accounts would be included among the current liabilities.

Sometimes large corporations with many stockholders draw a single check to cover a particular dividend and deposit the check in a special bank account. This transaction is recorded by a debit to the special dividend checking account and a credit to the general checking account.

Special check forms probably will be used in paying the dividend. The individual dividend checks may be recorded in a special dividend check register or in a dividend record similar to the one shown below. No other record need be made until the canceled checks are received from the bank together with a statement covering the special dividend deposit account. At that time the sum of the checks paid and canceled by the bank may be recorded by debiting Dividend Payable and by crediting the special dividend checking account. After all the dividend checks have been paid by the bank and the proper entries have been made in the books of the corporation, the dividend payable account and the special dividend checking account will be in balance.

In some instances dividend checks may be returned unclaimed or they may never be presented for payment to the bank on which they are drawn. Any checks that are unclaimed may be canceled when they are returned. Payment may be stopped on any checks not returned and not presented to the bank for payment within a reasonable length of time. The total of such unclaimed and uncashed checks may be recorded by debiting Dividend Payable and crediting Unclaimed Dividends. At the same time the unused portion of the dividend checking account should be transferred back to the general checking account. The account with Unclaimed Dividends will have a credit balance as long as any dividend checks remain unpaid. This balance will be reported in the balance sheet as a current liability.

Stock Dividends. A pro-rata distribution of shares of a corporation's own stock to its stockholders is termed a stock dividend. Corporations may distribute this type of dividend for one or more of several reasons.

DIVIDEND RECORD

DIV. NO	DATE DECLARED	RATE	NO. OF SHARES	AMOUNT	NAME OF STOCKHOLDER	HOW PAID	DATE PAID
1	Jan. 15 19–	$1.00	130	130 00	B. A. Wayman	Check	Jan 31 19–
1	15	$1.00	50	50 00	C. W. Milton	"	31
1	15	$1.00	50	50 00	G. H. Waterson	"	31
1	15	$1.00	10	10 00	B. A. Gregg	"	31
1	15	$1.00	5	5 00	G. J. Wayman	"	31

Dividend Record

The company may be short of cash and may be unable or unwilling to borrow to pay a cash dividend. It may be to the stockholders' interest to have more shares with a lower market price, as low-priced shares usually are more readily marketable. A greater number of shares outstanding makes wider ownership possible, and wide ownership may be desired in some cases. The corporation may have a large credit balance in Retained Earnings and the directors may deem it advisable to transfer a portion of the retained earnings to the category of restricted capital for purposes of subsequent balance sheet presentation.

Some corporations pursue a policy of distributing a portion of their earnings to stockholders in cash and a portion in stock each year. This policy may be justifiable under conditions where the directors deem it advisable to retain cash for use in the business instead of distributing it in dividends to stockholders. This is likely to be true in the case of a rapidly growing business where more and more funds must be invested in the assets of the business, such as inventory, accounts receivable, and fixed assets.

When a stock dividend is declared by the board of directors, an entry may be made debiting Retained Earnings and crediting Stock Dividend Payable for the total par or stated value of the shares to be distributed. Stock Dividend Payable is not a liability account since no money is owed. The balance of the account would be reported in the capital section of a balance sheet prepared after the dividend declaration but before the shares were issued. When the shares are distributed, Stock Dividend Payable is debited and Capital Stock is credited. If treasury stock is distributed, the treasury stock account should be credited.

A stock dividend does not affect the assets, the liabilities, or the total capital of the corporation. The transaction merely transfers part of the retained earnings to a capital stock account. Such a transfer serves to destroy the distinction between invested capital and earned capital, but that is not considered to be a serious matter in this case.

The amount of a common stockholder's interest in a corporation is not affected by a stock dividend of the same class of shares. He will have more shares, but the book value of each one will be proportionately reduced. The owner of 100 out of 1,000 shares of common stock has a 10 per cent interest in the total equity that belongs to the common shareholders. If a 25 per cent common stock dividend is distributed, he would own 125 out of 1,250 shares. He would still have a 10 per cent interest. He actually has no more or less than he had before the dividend. For this reason, the income tax laws do not regard a "common on common" stock dividend as income to the stockholder if there is only one class of common stock.

A dividend of one class of stock distributed to another class of shareholders may change the relative equity of those who receive the shares. Stock dividends of this type may constitute taxable income to the recipient to the amount of the fair market value of the shares received.

Liquidating Dividends. A liquidating dividend is very different from an ordinary cash dividend. An ordinary cash dividend is a distribution of earnings, a return *on* the stockholders' investment. A liquidating dividend represents a return *of* the stockholders' investment. The liquidation of the firm need not be completed before liquidating dividends are paid. As assets are converted into cash, the money may be distributed to the stockholders. Mining companies sometimes pay partial liquidating dividends as their ore reserves are depleted. They may pay dividends that represent partly earnings and partly a return of capital.

When a corporation is being completely dissolved or liquidated, the liabilities must be paid in full first. If there are outstanding preferred shares that have a preference as to assets, the holders of such shares must receive the full amount to which they are entitled (including unpaid dividends if the stock is cumulative) before the common stockholders receive anything. Whatever is left is distributed on a pro-rata basis to the common stockholders. Usually all such distributions are in cash. Sometimes, however, property other than cash is distributed to the stockholders. Upon receiving the final distribution, the stockholders will return their stock certificates. When articles of dissolution are filed with the proper state official, the corporation ceases to exist.

Application of Principles. As a means of illustrating the principles involved in recording dividends declared and paid, the following selected transactions completed by The Johnson Manufacturing Company are shown recorded in general journal form on the following page.

NARRATIVE OF TRANSACTIONS

Jan. 10. The board of directors declared dividends as follows:

On preferred stock: quarterly dividend of $1 a share on 2,000 shares (No. 21).

On common stock: 20 cents a share on 30,000 shares (No. 11). Both dividends are payable in cash on February 1 to stockholders of record on January 20.

29. The shares of preferred stock are held by a very few people, while the shares of common stock are held by a large number of people. Checks in payment of preferred dividends are drawn on the regular checking account. Special checks drawn on a dividend checking

account are used to pay common stock dividends. Accordingly, the treasurer drew a check for $6,000 on the regular bank account and deposited it in the dividend checking account.

Jan. 30. Checks drawn on the regular bank account in payment of the preferred dividend were prepared and mailed. Special checks drawn on the dividend checking account in payment of the common dividend were prepared and mailed.

Feb. 28. A statement covering the dividend checking account was received from the bank together with the canceled checks. It was noted that all checks issued had been paid.

Mar. 15. The board of directors declared a special dividend of $150,000 payable to the common stockholders in common stock on the basis of one share for every two shares held. The stock will be distributed on April 5 to common stockholders of record on March 25.

Apr. 5. Certificates for a total of 15,000 shares were issued to the common stockholders in payment of the dividend declared on March 15.

GENERAL JOURNAL

Jan. 10.	Retained Earnings....................................	$ 2,000	
	Preferred Dividend Payable, No. 21....................		$ 2,000
	Declared $1 per share dividend on 2,000 shares of preferred stock outstanding.		
	10. Retained Earnings....................................	6,000	
	Common Dividend Payable, No. 11....................		6,000
	Declared a dividend of 20 cents a share on 30,000 shares of common stock outstanding.		
	29. First National Bank, Dividend Account....................	6,000	
	First National Bank, General Account..................		6,000
	Transferred $6,000 to special dividend account.		
	30. Preferred Dividend Payable, No. 21......................	2,000	
	First National Bank, General Account..................		2,000
	Paid preferred dividend, No. 21.		
Feb. 28.	Common Dividend Payable, No. 11......................	6,000	
	First National Bank, Dividend Account.................		6,000
	Dividend checks issued January 30, in payment of common dividend No. 11, paid by bank per statement of this date.		
Mar. 15.	Retained Earnings....................................	150,000	
	Common Stock Dividend Payable.....................		150,000
	Declared a dividend to common stockholders payable in common stock on the basis of one share for every two held.		
Apr. 5.	Common Stock Dividend Payable......................	150,000	
	Capital Stock, Common..............................		150,000
	Issued 15,000 shares of common stock in payment of stock dividend declared March 15.		

PRACTICE ASSIGNMENT No. 46. Complete Report No. 46 in the workbook and submit your working papers for approval. Continue with the following study assignment in Unit Twenty-four until Report No. 47 is required.

ACCOUNTING
FOR CORPORATION BONDS

(47) ACCOUNTING FOR BONDS SOLD AND BOND INTEREST EXPENSE

To supplement the funds provided by the stockholders of a corporation, additional funds may be obtained by issuing bonds. A *bond* is similar to a long-term note in that it is an interest-bearing, negotiable instrument, under seal, in which the maker promises to pay a certain sum in money at a definite or determinable future date. It usually is secured as to either principal or interest, or both, by a pledge of certain properties, real or personal.

The right to borrow money is implied in the charter of a corporation. The board of directors usually decides when and how much to borrow. If only a small amount of money is needed or if the money will be repaid in a short time, notes usually will be issued. The notes may be secured or unsecured. If the corporation has a good credit standing, it may be able to borrow on its unsecured notes. If this is the case, the liability that arises is recorded as Notes Payable. If the notes are secured by a mortgage, the liability is recorded as Mortgage Payable.

When a corporation borrows a large sum of money for a long period of time, say from five to fifty years or more, it is customary to issue bonds instead of notes. A bond issue usually consists of a number of bonds. All of the bonds comprising the issue need not have the same denomination. Some may be for $1,000 or less, while others may have face values of $5,000 or $10,000, and sometimes more.

If bonds are secured, all the bonds in a particular issue usually will be secured alike under one deed of trust. A *deed of trust* is a mortgage on certain specified property. The deed is placed in the hands of a trustee who represents the bondholders. The deed of trust states the terms and the conditions under which the bonds are issued and under which the property for their security is held. Reference is made in the bonds to the deed of trust by which they are secured. It will be seen, therefore, that both the deed of trust and the bonds issued refer to each other in such a manner that all terms and conditions are clearly stated in both instruments. The trustee has the right to act in behalf of the bondholders and may bring foreclosure proceedings if it becomes necessary to do so in order to safeguard the interest of the bondholders.

Classification of Bonds. Bonds are commonly classified (a) as to purpose of the issue, (b) as to security of the bonds, (c) as to payment of the interest, or (d) as to payment of the principal.

As to Purpose of Issue. When bonds are issued with a view to acquiring funds for a specific purpose, the bonds may be classified as follows:

(a) Improvement bonds.
(b) Purchase-money bonds
(c) Refunding bonds.
(d) Adjustment bonds.

When the purpose of issuing bonds is to acquire funds for the construction of new buildings, such as an office building, a warehouse, a power plant, or other types of permanent structures, the bonds may be classified as *improvement bonds*.

When bonds are issued in exchange for property or as part payment of the purchase price of property that has already been constructed, the bonds may be classified as *purchase-money bonds*.

When a new series of bonds is issued for the purpose of raising funds to be used in paying off an old series of bonds that is soon to mature or to retire outstanding bonds prior to maturity, the bonds may be classified as *refunding bonds*. In recent years, under favorable market conditions, many corporations have issued new bonds at lower rates of interest and used the proceeds to retire outstanding bonds bearing a higher rate of interest. For example, a corporation that has an issue of 6 per cent bonds outstanding amounting to $1,000,000 might, under favorable market conditions, issue new bonds bearing 4 per cent interest and use the proceeds to retire the 6 per cent bonds, thus saving 2 per cent interest on $1,000,000, or $20,000 a year.

When companies that are in financial difficulties are being reorganized, new types of securities may be issued to the holders of securities already outstanding. For instance, bondholders may be given new bonds bearing a lower rate of interest in exchange for their old bonds. If a corporation is unable to pay the interest on its outstanding bonds because of reduced earnings, the bondholders may agree to take a new issue of bonds bearing a lower rate of interest in exchange for the old bonds. Such an issue of bonds may be classified as *adjustment bonds*.

As to Security. Bonds are often classified on the basis of the security offered. Such bonds may be classified as follows:

(a) Mortgage bonds.
(b) Collateral-trust bonds.
(c) Guaranteed bonds.
(d) Income bonds.
(e) Debenture bonds.

When bonds are secured by a mortgage on property, such as real estate, equipment, or leaseholds, they may be designated as *mortgage bonds*. Such bonds are sometimes designated as first-mortgage bonds, second-mortgage bonds, etc., according to the lien by which they are secured. Thus, a first-mortgage bond is a first lien on the property covered by the mortgage. For example, the Kentucky Utilities Company issued $20,000,000 of first-mortgage bonds on February 29, 1940. These are 4 per cent bonds due to mature in 1970.

When bonds are secured by a deposit of stocks, bonds, mortgages, or other collateral with a trustee under a trust agreement, they may be classified as *collateral-trust bonds*.

When bonds of subsidiary or affiliated corporations are guaranteed as to payment of principal or interest, or both, by the parent company, or another affiliated company, they may be known as *guaranteed bonds*. To be effective, the guarantee must be in writing and must either be written on the bond itself or be attached to it.

Usually interest on bonds must be paid to the bondholders before dividends may be paid to stockholders. When the payment of interest on bonds is contingent upon the net income of the company and is payable at the discretion of the board of directors, the bonds may be classified as *income bonds*. Income bonds may be cumulative or noncumulative as to interest and the principal may be secured or unsecured. Such bonds differ from preferred stock only from the standpoint that their principal is an absolute obligation of the issuing company and must be paid at maturity.

When no security is offered other than the general credit of the corporation issuing the bonds, the bonds may be classified as *debenture bonds*. Usually a debenture bond is merely a formal promise to pay a definite sum of money at a stated time — thus it may be a promise to pay a specified rate of interest annually and to pay the principal at a specified maturity date — but the payment is not secured by a lien or mortgage on any specific assets of the corporation.

As to Payment of Interest. Bonds may be classified according to how the interest on them is to be paid. In this respect they are classified as:

(a) Registered bonds.

(b) Coupon bonds.

If the bonds are *registered*, it means that a record must be kept of the names and the addresses of the bondholders. Sometimes the corporation keeps the record; sometimes the record is kept by the trustee. Some form of bond register is used. This will show the number and the denomination of each bond, to whom it was issued, to whom it was transferred, etc. Checks for the amount of interest due to each registered bondholder are mailed to the bondholders periodically in accordance with the terms of the bond contract, often called the *bond indenture*.

Very often bonds are issued with a number of interest coupons attached. Each coupon is, in itself, a promise to pay a specified sum of money on the date stated. Coupon bonds usually are *bearer bonds*. This means that the corporation will pay the face amount of the bonds to whoever presents them at the maturity date. Likewise the corporation will pay the interest to whoever presents the interest coupons on or after the maturity of each one. Bond interest may be paid quarterly, semiannually, or annually. Most coupon bonds pay interest semiannually on specified dates, such as January 1 and July 1, or March 15 and September 15. A 20-year, 4 per cent, $10,000 coupon bond with interest payable semiannually would be issued with 40 coupons for $200 each attached to it. Each coupon would have its own maturity date. As each interest date arrives, the owner of the bond detaches the coupon and presents it for payment. Many bondholders have their banks act as their agents in collecting on bond coupons. Coupons should not be detached until they come due because they might be lost or because the owner of the bond might want to sell it to someone else.

As to Payment of Principal. Bonds are sometimes classified in accordance with the provisions made as to the payment of the principal. Such bonds may include the following:

(a) Sinking-fund bonds.

(b) Serial bonds.

(c) Convertible bonds.

(d) Redeemable bonds.

The designation *sinking-fund bonds* applies when the terms of the bond issue require the issuing corporation to make periodic payments into a so-called sinking fund. Usually the fund is held by a trustee. The fund consists of investments purchased with the money paid in by the corporation and the earnings on such investments. The size of the payments to the fund must be large enough to permit the accumulation of the amount needed to pay the bonds at maturity and, sometimes, the interest on the bonds.

When bonds are issued in series so that a specified amount of the principal matures each year, the bonds may be classified as *serial bonds*. This is a means of providing for the paying off of a bond issue on the installment basis. Serial bonds may be secured or unsecured. If unsecured, they are similar to debenture bonds. If secured by a mortgage on certain properties covering the entire issue, provision may be made for the relinquishment of portions of the security after the redemption of each series; otherwise, all of the property mortgaged may be tied up until the last series of bonds is redeemed.

When bonds are issued with a provision that the holder has the option of exchanging his bonds for capital stock, the bonds may be classified as *convertible bonds*. Such a privilege may become a valuable one should the market value of the capital stock rise above the market value of the bonds. The basis upon which the conversion may be made is usually stipulated and the time within which the conversion must be made is often limited.

When bonds are issued with a provision that they may be called for redemption before the date of maturity fixed by the deed of trust, they may be classified as *redeemable bonds*. In the case of many bond issues, such a provision is made. Thus, twenty-year bonds may be issued with a provision that they are subject to call for redemption at any time after ten years from date of issue.

There are many other types of bonds issued, such as *consolidated bonds, reorganization bonds, terminal bonds, car-trust bonds, profit-sharing bonds, junior-lien bonds*, etc., each of which may be classified similarly to the bonds previously discussed. Such terms are merely descriptive and may have no other significance.

On page 592 is a reproduction of a first-mortgage, 5½ per cent, $1,000 bond of The Wilmington Rapid Transit Company. The issue date of the bond was April 15, 1952; the maturity date, April 15, 1977. It is a coupon bond. When it was issued, it had fifty coupons attached. Coupon No. 10 is reproduced on page 593. The other coupons were identical except for their number and date.

Bonds and stocks often are mentioned in the same breath, but basically they are very different. A bond is an obligation of the issuing corporation

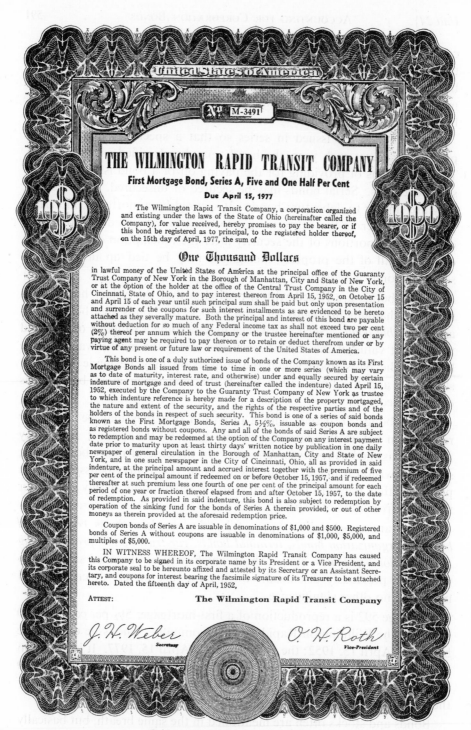

No. 10 $27.50

Coupon for $27.50, lawful money of the United States of America, payable to bearer on the fifteenth day of April, 1957, at the principal office of the Guaranty Trust Company of New York in the Borough of Manhattan, City and State of New York, or at the option of the holder at the office of the Central Trust Company in the City of Cincinnati, State of Ohio, without deduction for taxes, for six months' interest due on that day on the $1,000 First Mortgage, 5½% Bond, Series A, of The Wilmington Rapid Transit Company, No. M-3491, subject to the terms of said bond, and of the indenture dated April 15, 1952.

HERMAN B. TAYLOR
Treasurer

Bond Interest Coupon

— a promise to pay a definite sum of money on a certain date. Stock represents corporate ownership or proprietorship; there is no promise to pay any definite amount at any stated time. Bondholders are creditors of a corporation; stockholders are owners.

Accounting for Bonds Issued. The decision of the board of directors to borrow by the use of bonds would be detailed in the official minutes of their meeting. When the bonds are issued, the resulting liability is recorded in a bonds payable account. The account title may be more descriptive if desired. A more descriptive account title would be necessary if the corporation had more than one issue outstanding. There would be a separate account, properly identified, for each issue. Bonds Payable is credited with the face or maturity value of the bonds issued, regardless of the amount that was received upon their issuance. In the balance sheet, bonds payable usually are classified as fixed liabilities because the amount may not be due for many years.

It is the universal custom to speak of the sale of bonds. The expression is not incorrect, but it must be understood that the issuing corporation is actually borrowing when it "sells" its own bonds. It is selling documents containing its promise to pay specified amounts of money on specified dates to the holders of the bonds. When the owner or holder of a bond sells it to someone else, the transaction is a sale in the usual sense of the word.

Bonds sometimes sell for exactly the amount of their face or maturity value. More often they sell for more or less than face value. If the bonds sell for more than face value, the excess is termed *premium*. If the bonds sell for less than face value, the difference between the face value and the amount received is termed *discount*. Premium or discount usually represents an adjustment of the contractual rate of interest. If the rate promised by the bonds is higher than the going or market rate for bonds of a similar quality, the issue will sell at a premium. If the contractual rate is below the going rate, the bonds will sell at a discount. For this reason, the issuing corporation considers a premium to be a partial offset to the amount of interest that must be paid, while a discount represents bond interest expense in addition to the contractual interest that is paid.

Sale of Bonds for Face Amount. Most corporations sell issues of bonds to bankers or underwriters who, in turn, sell them to investors. If a $100,000 issue of first-mortgage bonds is sold for exactly this amount, the entry to record the transaction would be as follows:

Bank	$100,000	
First Mortgage Bonds Payable		$100,000
Sold mortgage bonds at face value.		

If the above bonds were sold directly to the investing public on a subscription basis, a bond subscription record similar to a stock subscription record might be maintained. In such case, accounts should be kept with Bond Subscriptions Receivable, Bonds Subscribed, and Bonds Payable to record the transactions arising from subscriptions, payments received to apply on subscriptions, and issuance of the bonds. The transactions arising from the sale of the bonds on a subscription basis may be recorded in general journal form as follows:

Bond Subscriptions Receivable	$100,000	
First Mortgage Bonds Subscribed		$100,000
Received subscriptions to mortgage bonds at face value.		
Bank	100,000	
Bond Subscriptions Receivable		100,000
Received payments on bond subscription contracts.		
First Mortgage Bonds Subscribed	100,000	
First Mortgage Bonds Payable		100,000
Mortgage bonds issued to subscribers.		

It is necessary to keep bond subscription accounts only when subscriptions are taken in advance of payment. When the bonds are sold outright and payment is received immediately, there is no need for keeping subscription accounts.

Sale of Bonds at a Premium. When bonds are sold for more than face value, such excess is credited to Premium on Bonds. If the bonds referred to above were sold at 102,* the transaction should be recorded in the manner illustrated on page 595.

*Bond prices are quoted on the basis of $100 even though most bonds have larger denominations. A $1,000 bond selling at 102 would bring $1,020; if the price were 99, it would bring $990; etc.

Bank... $102,000
    First Mortgage Bonds Payable....................... $100,000
    Premium on Bonds..................................   2,000
        Sold mortgage bonds at 102.

Sale of Bonds at a Discount. When bonds are sold for less than face value, the difference between the face value and the amount received is debited to Discount on Bonds. If the bonds in question were sold at 97, the transaction would be recorded as follows:

Bank... $ 97,000
Discount on Bonds..................................   3,000
    First Mortgage Bonds Payable....................... $100,000
        Sold mortgage bonds at 97.

It will be noted that the bonds payable account is credited for the face or maturity value of the bonds, regardless of the amount received upon their issuance.

Sale of Bonds Between Interest Dates. All of the preceding examples involved the sale of bonds on the very day interest began. The entries shown would have been equally correct if the bonds had been sold on any interest date. When bonds are sold between interest dates, the buyer must pay for the amount of interest that has accrued since the last interest date. Bond prices are quoted at a certain amount plus accrued interest. The buyer will get back the interest he has purchased on the first regular interest date following his purchase.

For example, suppose a corporation has a $100,000 issue of 4½ per cent bonds printed. The bonds are dated April 1, with interest coupons maturing semiannually. The first coupons mature October 1. Further suppose that delays arise so that the bonds are not sold until May 31 following the issue date. Since the purchasers will be able to cash their first coupons for six months' interest only four months later, they will have to pay the corporation 60 days' interest accrued when the bonds are purchased. If the issue sold at 103 plus accrued interest, the total amount received would be $103,750. The sale would be recorded as follows:

May 31. Bank... $103,750
        First Mortgage Bonds Payable....................... $100,000
        Premium on Bonds..................................   3,000
        Bond Interest Expense.............................   750
            Sold first-mortgage bonds at 103 plus accrued interest,
            April 1–May 31.

The additional amount received May 31 because of the interest accrued since April 15 is recorded as a credit to Bond Interest Expense. By crediting the accrued interest to Bond Interest Expense, that account will show the proper amount of interest expense incurred when it is debited for the interest paid on the bonds October 1 amounting to $2,250 ($2,250 — $750 = $1,500).

If coupon bonds are originally sold a considerable time after the issue is dated, all of the coupons that matured before the bonds were sold would be detached. Therefore, the purchasers of the bonds are required to pay for the interest accrued since the last interest date only. Thus, if a $1,000 coupon bond dated July 1 were not sold until April 1 of the following year, the buyer would have to pay for interest accrued from January 1 only. The first interest coupon matured January 1 and would be detached prior to the sale of the bond on April 1.

Bond Interest Expense. The interest on bonds may be payable annually, semiannually, or at other periods. Interest payment on a semiannual basis is probably the most common. The method used in recording bond interest expense is not necessarily affected by the kind of bonds issued; that is, the interest on registered bonds may be recorded in the same manner as the interest on coupon bonds. It is desirable to record bond interest expense separately from the interest on other obligations. The semiannual interest on the issue of 4½ per cent, first-mortgage bonds, principal amount $100,000, dated April 1, may be recorded in general journal form as follows:

Oct. 1. Bond Interest Expense.................................... $2,250
          Bank... $2,250
              Made semiannual payment of interest on 4½% bonds out-
              standing.

At the close of each accounting period an adjusting entry should be made to record any interest accrued on bonds payable. For example, in the case of the bonds referred to above, as of December 31, 91 days' interest has accrued (October 1 to December 31). This amounts to $1,137.50.

It is, therefore, necessary to adjust the accounts as follows:

Dec. 31. Bond Interest Expense................................ $1,137.50
          Accrued Bond Interest Payable...................... $1,137.50
             Accrued bond interest.

After the posting is completed the bond interest expense account will have a debit balance of $2,637.50 and the account with Accrued Bond Interest Payable will have a credit balance of $1,137.50. The balance of the bond interest expense account represents the total interest expense incurred since the bonds were sold on May 31. The balance of the account with Accrued Bond Interest Payable represents the amount of the accrued liability on December 31.

In the case of coupon bonds, it is common practice to have a *coupon register*. This register is usually arranged so that a page is devoted to each bond issued. Usually the number, the amount, and a brief description of the bond are entered at the top of the page. The remainder of the page is divided into spaces of the same size as the coupons, each space with a number corresponding to the coupons originally attached to the bond. When a coupon is paid, it is marked "Canceled" and is pasted in the proper space of the register. Reference to the coupon register at any time will show which coupons have been paid and which are outstanding.

Amortization of Bond Premium or Discount. If bonds are sold at either a premium or a discount, the amount of interest that is actually paid each year is not the real interest expense of the year. The bond interest expense account must be adjusted for a pro-rata share of the original premium or discount. This process is called *amortization* of the premium or discount. (Technically, premium is amortized, while discount is accumulated; but the term *amortization* often is used to describe the procedure in both cases.) Premium or discount can be amortized on a compound-interest basis. This method is the most accurate from a theoretical standpoint; but in most cases a simple, so-called straight-line method is satisfactory. Under the straight-line method, the total original discount or premium is divided by the number of months or years between the date on which the bonds were issued and the date on which they are to mature. The quotient is the amount of premium or discount to be written off each month or year.

For example, suppose that an issue of 4 per cent, 10-year bonds with a face value of $500,000 is sold at 103 on January 1 (the day interest begins). The entry recording this sale would include a credit to Premium on Bonds in the amount of $15,000. Since the bonds mature in 10 years, one tenth of this premium should be written off each year by means of the following entry:

Dec. 31. Premium on Bonds...	$1,500	
Bond Interest Expense..................................		$1,500
Amortization of premium on bonds for one year.		

After recording the amount of the bond interest paid during the year and the amount accrued at the end of the year, the bond interest expense account will have a debit balance of $20,000 which is the contractual interest for the year. After posting the entry made to amortize one tenth of the premium on the bonds, the bond interest expense account will have a debit balance of $18,500. This amount is the true bond interest expense for the year. It will be closed into the income summary account and will be reported in the income statement for the year.

The justification for considering $18,500 to be the proper bond interest expense for each year is provided by the following analysis:

Face value of the bonds that the corporation must pay at maturity....	$500,000
Total interest that must be paid ($20,000 a year for 10 years)........	200,000
Total expenditures with respect to both bonds and interest..........	$700,000
Less: Amount realized upon sale of bonds......................	515,000
Excess of total expenditures over total receipts....................	$185,000

$185,000 ÷ 10 years = $18,500.

To illustrate the amortization of discount on bonds, the following case is presented: 3½ per cent, 20-year bonds with a face value of $200,000 are sold at 98 on October 1 (the day interest begins). The entry recording their sale includes a debit of $4,000 to Discount on Bonds. At the end of the first year, no interest would have been paid (since the bonds would have been outstanding for only 91 days), but an adjusting entry would be made debiting Bond Interest Expense and crediting Accrued Bond Interest Payable for $1,769.44 ($200,000 @ 3½% for 91 days). The discount of $4,000 must be charged off to the bond interest expense account on a pro-rata basis over the 20-year life of the bonds. This would amount to $200 a year. At the end of the first year, however, the bonds would have been outstanding for only three months, so the amortization at the end of that year would be $50. The entry to record this would be as follows:

Dec. 31. Bond Interest Expense.....................................	$50	
Discount on Bonds......................................		$50
Amortization of discount on bonds for three months.		

After posting such an entry, the bond interest expense account would have a debit balance of $1,819.44 representing the bond interest expense for the three months from October 1 to December 31. This amount would be closed into the income summary account and would be reported in the income statement for the year. For each of the following full years that the bonds are outstanding, the total bond interest expense would be $7,200. This can be calculated as follows:

Face value of the bonds that the corporation must pay at maturity....	$200,000
Total interest that must be paid ($7,000 a year for 20 years)..........	140,000
Total expenditures with respect to both bonds and interest..........	$340,000
Less: Amount realized upon sale of bonds......................	196,000
Excess of total expenditures over receipts...........................	$144,000

$144,000 ÷ 20 years = $7,200.

Simple straight-line amortization of premium or discount is suitable only in cases where all of the bonds comprising the issue are issued at the same time and all mature on the same date. If all of the bonds are not outstanding for the same length of time, the amortization of any premium or discount must be in proportion to the total amount of bonds outstanding each year or fraction of a year.

It should be apparent that the credit balance in the premium account or the debit balance in the discount account will be reduced year by year, until no balance is left on the date the bonds mature. Balance sheets prepared during the time the bonds are outstanding will report bond discount as a deferred charge or bond premium as a deferred credit.

Deferred Charges. There are certain expenditures that are expected to benefit a number of fiscal periods. Supplies and certain prepaid items, such as prepaid insurance and prepaid interest, which will ordinarily be consumed within the current operating cycle of a business, are generally treated as current assets. On the other hand, expenditures for services or benefits that are properly allocable to a number of fiscal periods should be capitalized and the cost distributed over the periods benefited. The cost of issuing bonds, including any commissions paid to brokers, underwriting fees, or discounts, represents such an expenditure. Experimental and development costs may also represent such expenditures. Accounts of this type are usually classified as *deferred charges*. Such account balances may be grouped together under the title of deferred charges or may be itemized under the heading of deferred charges in the balance sheet. It is customary to list deferred charges last among the assets.

Deferred Credits. Sometimes income is received or collected in advance of the period in which it is earned. Goods may be sold on installment terms and it may be considered desirable to distribute the profit over the periods in which the installment payments are collected. When an issue of bonds is sold at a price in excess of their par value, the premium should be distributed over the life of the bonds. Accounts of this type are usually classified as *deferred credits*. Such account balances may be grouped together under the title of deferred credits or may be itemized under the heading of deferred credits in the balance sheet. It is customary to list deferred credits last among the liabilities.

PRACTICE ASSIGNMENT No. 47. Complete Report No. 47 in the workbook and submit your working papers for approval. Continue with the textbook discussion until Report No. 48 is required.

(48) ACCOUNTING FOR BONDS RETIRED

Bonds issued by a corporation usually are redeemed at face value upon their maturity. By that date the entire amount of any premium or discount should have been written off. To record the redemption, Bonds Payable is debited and Bank is credited. The retired bonds are usually marked "Canceled" and are stored away until they are checked over by the company auditors; after that the bonds are destroyed.

Corporations may redeem some or all of a bond issue before maturity. In some cases a corporation may force the bondholders to surrender their bonds by taking advantage of an option to call the bonds before they mature. Unless the terms of the issue include such an option, however, this procedure is not possible. Without such an option, a corporation can purchase its bonds if it has the money and if the holders of the bonds are willing to sell.

Redemption of Bonds Originally Sold at Face Value. Usually there is either a gain or a loss involved in the redemption of bonds before their maturity date. If the bonds were originally sold at face value and the corporation pays more than this when the bonds are redeemed, there is a loss. For example, a corporation sells a $100,000 issue of bonds at face value. Some years later, but prior to the date of maturity, $10,000 of the issue is redeemed on an interest date at 102. The bonds were sold for $10,000 and were redeemed for $10,200; therefore, the corporation sustained a loss of $200. The entry to record this transaction would be as follows:

Bonds Payable	$10,000	
Loss on Bonds Redeemed	200	
Bank		$10,200
Redeemed bonds with face value of $10,000 at 102.		

If bonds that originally were sold at face value are redeemed for a lesser amount, a gain results. If, in the preceding case, the price paid had been 98 instead of 102, there would have been a gain of $200. In this case the entry to record the transaction would be as follows:

Bonds Payable	$10,000	
Bank		$ 9,800
Gain on Bonds Redeemed		200
Redeemed bonds with face value of $10,000 at 98.		

Redemption of Bonds Originally Sold at a Premium. If a corporation redeems some or all of its bonds that originally were sold at a premium, the calculation of the gain or the loss involved must take into account the premium amortization from the date of issue to the date of redemption. For example, suppose that an issue of 20-year bonds with a face value of $100,000 had been sold at 103. Eight years later the corporation redeems $10,000 of the issue at a price of 102. If this redemption were made at the end of the fiscal period, the amortization of the premium on the bonds would be up to date. If the redemption were made at some other time, it would be necessary to record the amortization of the premium relating to the bonds for the time elapsed since the last regular premium write-off entry had been made. The proper amount should be debited to the premium account and credited to the bond interest expense account — the same accounts that are involved in the regular periodic premium-amortization entry.

After any needed entry is made to record the up-to-date amortization of the premium relating to the bonds being redeemed, the *unamortized premium* pertaining to these bonds would be $180. (These bonds sold for $10,300 eight years before. Eight twentieths, or $120, of the $300 premium would have been written off, leaving $180 unamortized.) The adjusted issue price of these bonds is, then, $10,180. Their redemption for $10,200 results in a loss of $20. The entry to record this transaction would be as follows:

Bonds Payable	$10,000	
Premium on Bonds	180	
Loss on Bonds Redeemed	20	
Bank		$10,200
Redeemed bonds with face value of $10,000 at 102.		

It will be noted that this entry writes off the portion in the premium account that relates to the bonds that are being retired. When the bonds themselves are taken out of the accounts, any unamortized premium that relates to such bonds must also be removed. The balance of the premium account represents the unamortized premium on the bonds still outstanding.

It should be apparent that the treatment of the premium would be the same no matter what price was paid when the bonds were redeemed. If these bonds had been redeemed at a price of 101½ instead of 102, a gain of $30 would have resulted. The entry in this case would be as follows:

Bonds Payable	$10,000	
Premium on Bonds	180	
Bank		$10,150
Gain on Bonds Redeemed		30
Redeemed bonds with face value of $10,000 at 101½.		

Redemption of Bonds Originally Sold at a Discount. If a corporation redeems some or all of its bonds that originally were sold at a discount, the calculation of the gain or the loss involved must take into account the discount amortization from the date of issue to the date of redemption. For example, suppose that an issue of 20-year bonds with a face value of $100,000 had been sold at 98. Fifteen years later the corporation redeems $10,000 of the issue at a price of 99. Before recording the redemption, the amortization of the discount pertaining to the bonds must be brought up to the date of purchase. If the date of purchase was the end of the fiscal period, the amortization would be up to date. If this was not the case, the amount of discount amortization since the last regular discount write-off would have to be calculated and recorded. This amount would be debited to the bond interest expense account and credited to the discount account — the same accounts that are involved in the regular periodic discount-amortization entry.

After any needed entry is made to record the up-to-date amortization of the discount relating to the bonds being redeemed, the unamortized discount pertaining to these bonds would be $50. (These bonds sold for $9,800 fifteen years before. Fifteen twentieths, or $150, of the $200 discount would have been written off, leaving $50 unamortized.) The adjusted issue price of these bonds is, then, $9,950. Their redemption for $9,900 results in a gain of $50. The entry to record this transaction is as follows:

Bonds Payable..	$10,000	
Bank..		$ 9,900
Discount on Bonds.....................................		50
Gain on Bonds Redeemed.............................		50
Redeemed bonds with a face value of $10,000 at 99.		

It will be noted that this entry writes off the portion in the discount account that relates to the bonds that are being retired. When the bonds themselves are taken out of the accounts, any unamortized discount that relates to such bonds must also be removed. The remaining balance of the discount account represents the unamortized discount on the bonds still outstanding.

If these bonds had been redeemed at a price of 101, a loss of $150 would have resulted. The proper entry in this case is as follows:

Bonds Payable..	$10,000	
Loss on Bonds Redeemed...............................	150	
Discount on Bonds.....................................		$ 50
Bank..		10,100
Redeemed bonds with a face value of $10,000 at 101.		

In all of the preceding discussion, it was assumed that the bonds were redeemed on an interest date. Presumably the interest on all of the bonds being purchased had been paid in the usual manner. If the bonds had been redeemed between interest dates, the price in each case would have been plus accrued interest. The entry in each case would have included a debit to the bond interest expense account for the amount of the interest accrued, and the credit to Bank would have been correspondingly larger. It was noted that, with respect to the bonds being redeemed, a special adjustment is needed to record the amortization of premium or discount for the time elapsed since the date of the last regular adjustment of the accounts. Thus, the correct interest expense on these bonds for whatever portion of the year they were outstanding would be reflected in the bond interest expense account.

All of the foregoing procedures pertaining to the redemption of bonds and the treatment of premiums, discounts, and interest are in accord with the federal income tax regulations.

Bond Sinking Funds. A sinking fund consists of cash and investments that are being accumulated and held for some specific purpose. When the purpose is to accumulate money, or assets that can be converted into money, to redeem bonds at their maturity, it is termed a *bond sinking fund*. Realizing the need for advance planning and action, corporations may voluntarily establish bond sinking funds to provide the cash when it will be needed to redeem bonds at their maturity. In most cases, however, bond sinking funds exist because they are required under the terms of the bond contract or indenture. The corporation agrees to make payments into such a fund for the reason mentioned and because the promise of such a fund may act as an inducement to potential bond buyers. The security afforded to bondholders by a sinking fund requirement may make it possible for the corporation to borrow the money at a lower rate of interest. Sometimes it is provided that the bond interest, as well as the principal, shall be paid out of a sinking fund.

Usually the sinking fund is held and administered by a trustee who represents the bondholders. Banks and trust companies often act in such a capacity. The amount the corporation must pay into the sinking fund each year may depend upon the earnings of the company or it may be a fixed minimum sum. If it is to be the latter, the size of the payments will depend, in part, upon the rate of earnings that the sinking fund assets are expected to yield.

For example, suppose a corporation issues 10-year bonds with a maturity value of $500,000. The bond indenture requires that the corporation make annual payments into a sinking fund. If it is anticipated that all money put into the fund can immediately be invested to earn 3 per cent, ten annual contributions of $43,615.25 made at the end of each year for ten years will accumulate to $500,000 by the end of the tenth year. When the amount needed, the number of periods, and the rate of interest are known, the size of the periodic payments can be determined by the use of an appropriate formula. Bankers, and others who frequently have occasion to calculate such things, save time and effort by referring to annuity tables that facilitate such computations.

If the earnings on fund assets are not as large as anticipated, the corporation will have to make larger payments to the fund in later years. Instead of this arrangement, it is sometimes required that the corporation make larger payments in the early years when the fund earnings are smaller. In the above example, the bond indenture might have provided that the corporation should pay $50,000 a year, less the amount earned by the fund assets during the past year. That would mean a full $50,000 payment the first year. If the fund earned $1,500 during the next year, the second payment would need to be only $48,500, etc.

Accounting for Sinking Funds. A sinking fund is an asset of the corporation regardless of whether the property in the fund is held and administered by the company itself or whether the fund is handled by a trustee. If there is no trustee, as may be the case with a voluntary fund, it is probable that there will be several accounts relating to the fund. There are likely to be such asset accounts as Bank — Sinking Fund, Sinking Fund Investments, and Accrued Interest on Sinking Fund Investments. There also will be an income account, Sinking Fund Income. In the balance sheet, all of the fund assets may be shown together under the caption "Sinking Fund." The adjusted balance of the sinking fund income account would be reported in the income statement under the classification "Other Income."

For example, assume that a corporation voluntarily decides to establish a sinking fund to accumulate money to redeem an issue of bonds maturing several years later. The following transactions and events relating to the fund occur during the first year:

(a) A special sinking fund checking account is opened at the First National Bank, and $20,000 is withdrawn from the regular checking account and deposited therein.

(b) The sum of $19,500 is invested in shares of preferred stock of a utility company and bonds of a railroad. (The bonds were purchased at face value on an interest date.)

(c) The sum of $490 is received in cash as dividends and interest on the sinking fund investments and is immediately deposited in the sinking fund checking account.

(d) At the end of the year, interest of $160 has accrued on the bonds in the sinking fund.

The journal entries to record the foregoing transactions would be as follows:

(a) First National Bank — Sinking Fund Account...........	$20,000	
First National Bank — General Account.............		$20,000
Transferred cash to sinking fund bank account.		
(b) Sinking Fund Investments..........................	19,500	
First National Bank — Sinking Fund Account........		19,500
Purchased investments for sinking fund.		
(c) First National Bank — Sinking Fund Account..........	490	
Sinking Fund Income.............................		490
Received interest and dividends on sinking fund investments.		
(d) Accrued Interest on Sinking Fund Investments...........	160	
Sinking Fund Income.............................		160
Interest accrued on sinking fund investments as of December 31, 19--.		

After all of these entries were posted, the sinking fund income account would have a credit balance of $650. This balance would be closed into the income summary account and would be reported in the "Other Income" section of the income statement. The balances of the asset accounts of the fund would be as follows:

First National Bank — Sinking Fund Account......................	$ 990
Sinking Fund Investments...	19,500
Accrued Interest on Sinking Fund Investments......................	160
Total...	$20,650

Sinking fund assets are usually classified as "Investments" among the assets in the balance sheet. Such assets may be itemized under the caption "Bond Sinking Fund" or the total may be shown as a single item.

The sinking fund investments would be converted into cash just before the maturity date of the bonds. The conversion might involve profits or losses upon the sale of the securities. Any needed addition to the sinking fund cash account would be made so as to bring the deposit up to the amount required to redeem the bonds. When the bonds are redeemed, an entry would be made debiting Bonds Payable and crediting First National Bank — Sinking Fund Account.

Premium and Discount on Sinking Fund Investments. Just as premium or discount represents a component of the interest expense to the corporation issuing the bonds, it similarly represents an adjustment of interest income to the buyers of the bonds who expect to hold them to maturity. In the preceding example there was no such problem, as it was stated that the railroad bonds were purchased at face value. If they had been purchased at either a premium or a discount and if they will mature within the expected life of the sinking fund, such premium or discount should be amortized. It should be clear that there is no accurate basis for calculating amortization unless it is intended that the bonds will be held to maturity. There is no way of knowing what the bonds might bring should they be sold prior to maturity.

It is not necessary to use separate accounts for premium or discount on long-term investments; the total cost of the securities may be debited to the investment account. When the periodic amortization entry is made, the proper amount will be debited to the investment account, if a discount is being amortized, or credited to the investment account, if a premium is being written off. The offsetting credit or debit is made to the sinking fund income account.

Sinking Fund Handled by a Trustee. When a sinking fund is held and administered by a trustee, the records relating to the fund that are kept by the corporation can be very simple. A single asset account entitled Sinking Fund and an account for Sinking Fund Income are all that are required. When payments are made to the trustee, the amount of the payment is debited to the sinking fund account. At least once a year the trustee will submit a report that summarizes the affairs of the fund for the period just ended. The report will list the assets of the fund as of that date. In the records of the corporation an entry will be made debiting the sinking fund account and crediting the sinking fund income account for the amount of the increase in the fund from its net earnings. On the basis of the trustee's report, the corporation could set up accounts for the various types of fund assets, such as Sinking Fund Cash, Sinking Fund Investments, etc., but this is not essential.

Frequently the trustee of a bond sinking fund will purchase bonds of the very issue to which the fund relates. Usually these bonds are treated as ordinary fund assets. The trustee collects interest from the corporation and amortizes any premium or discount involved in the purchase of the bonds. If the fund was held and administered by the corporation itself and some of its own bonds were purchased, it is probable that the corporation would retire and cancel the bonds. As a matter of usual practice, and sometimes because of technicalities in the provisions relating to required sinking funds, however, fund trustees usually treat such bonds as they would any other fund investment.

By the date the bonds mature, the assets of the sinking fund should be equal to the face value of the bonds. The trustee will convert the investments of the fund into cash (except, of course, any bonds of the issue involved). The conversion may involve liquidation gains or losses. The corporation will have to contribute any additional cash that is needed. In all probability the trustee will handle the redemption of the bonds. When they have all been redeemed, he will submit a final report to the corporation and will return the bonds. An entry should then be made in the corporation books debiting Bonds Payable and crediting Sinking Fund.

Sinking-Fund Provisions. Making payments to a sinking fund causes a periodic drain on the cash of a corporation. If the operations of a company are profitable, the balance of the retained earnings account may be increasing but a shortage of cash may make it unwise, if not impossible, to pay large dividends. Accordingly the directors may decide to appropriate a portion of the earnings each year for sinking-fund purposes. Sometimes the terms of the bond indenture require a corporation to appropriate a specified amount each year out of earnings for sinking-fund purposes. In such cases, an account with Provision for Sinking Fund Requirements should be kept and the amount appropriated each year should be recorded by debiting Retained Earnings and by crediting Provision for Sinking Fund Requirements.

The amount of earnings appropriated for sinking-fund purposes is clearly a segregation of retained income which should be included in the balance sheet as part of the stockholders' equity. Making such a provision for sinking-fund purposes does not in itself provide any money. It only serves to reduce the balance of the retained earnings account and, in an indirect way, may help to conserve cash by forestalling the demands for dividends that might otherwise be made upon the corporation directors by the stockholders. When the bonds are redeemed, there is no further need for maintaining a sinking-fund provision. Its balance may then be transferred back to the retained earnings account. Thus, providing for sinking-fund requirements by periodically making appropriations out of retained earnings does not affect the stockholders' equity; it merely has the effect of earmarking a portion of the earnings to be retained until such time as the bonds are redeemed, after which the amount so retained should be transferred back to Retained Earnings where it will be available for dividends or other corporate purposes at the will of the directors.

Application of Principles. To illustrate further the accounting for bond sinking funds and bond sinking-fund provisions, the following example is presented: The Niagara Utilities Company issued first-mortgage, 10-year, 4 per cent bonds, principal amount $100,000. Interest was payable semiannually on January 1 and July 1. The deed of trust provided that the corporation should make payments into a sinking fund to be used to redeem the bonds at maturity. The payments were to be made to the sinking-fund trustee at the end of each year. At the end of each of the first nine years, the payments were to be $9,000. At the end of the tenth year, the corporation was to pay an amount sufficient to bring the fund up to $100,000. Annual appropriation of retained earnings was to be made for sinking-fund purposes.

NARRATIVE OF TRANSACTIONS AND EVENTS

First Year

Jan.   2. The entire issue of bonds, principal amount $100,000, was sold to an underwriting syndicate at a price of 101.

July   1. Semiannual interest of $2,000 was paid.

Dec. 31. Accrued interest on bonds, $2,000.
Premium to be amortized, $100.
Payment to trustee, $9,000.
Appropriation of earnings for sinking-fund purposes, $9,000.

Second Year

Jan.   2. Semiannual interest of $2,000 was paid.

July   1. Semiannual interest of $2,000 was paid.

Dec. 31. Accrued interest on bonds, $2,000.
Premium to be amortized, $100.
Trustee reported $260 net earnings for year on investments in sinking fund.
Payment to trustee, $9,000.
Appropriation of earnings for sinking-fund purposes, $9,260.

Tenth Year

(NOTE: As of January 1 of this year the balances of the sinking fund and the sinking-fund provision accounts were both $92,350. The premium on bonds payable account had a balance of $100.)

Jan.   2. Semiannual interest of $2,000 was paid.

July   1. Semiannual interest of $2,000 was paid.

Dec. 28. Trustee reported that, after liquidating all of the investments except bonds of The Niagara Utilities Company, he had a total of $94,720 (cash and bonds of the issue).

Dec. 31. Accrued interest on bonds, $2,000.

         Premium to be amortized, $100.

         Payment to trustee, $5,280.

         Appropriation of earnings for sinking-fund purposes, $7,650.

Eleventh Year

Jan. 2. Semiannual interest of $2,000 was paid.

     10. Trustee reported that all bonds of the issue were redeemed.

     10. Directors authorized the cancellation of the bond sinking-fund provision.

    The entries to record these transactions are recorded in general journal form as follows:

GENERAL JOURNAL

1st Year

Jan. 2. Bank...	$101,000	
First Mortgage Bonds Payable.........................		$100,000
Premium on Bonds....................................		1,000
Sold ten-year, 4% bonds with face value of $100,000 at 101.		
July 1. Bond Interest Expense................................	2,000	
Bank...		2,000
Paid semiannual interest on bonds.		
Dec. 31. Bond Interest Expense...............................	2,000	
Accrued Bond Interest Payable.......................		2,000
Six-months' interest accrued on bonds payable.		
31. Premium on Bonds....................................	100	
Bond Interest Expense...............................		100
Amortization of premium on bonds.		
31. Bond Sinking Fund...................................	9,000	
Bank...		9,000
Payment to trustee for sinking fund.		
31. Retained Earnings...................................	9,000	
Provision for Sinking Fund Requirements.............		9,000
Appropriation of earnings for sinking-fund purposes.		

2nd Year

Jan. 1. Accrued Bond Interest Payable..........................	2,000	
Bond Interest Expense...............................		2,000
Reversing entry for accrued bond interest.		
2. Bond Interest Expense................................	2,000	
Bank...		2,000
Paid semiannual interest on bonds.		
July 1. Bond Interest Expense................................	2,000	
Bank...		2,000
Paid semiannual interest on bonds.		
Dec. 31. Bond Interest Expense...............................	2,000	
Accrued Bond Interest Payable.......................		2,000
Six-months' interest accrued on bonds payable.		
31. Premium on Bonds....................................	100	
Bond Interest Expense...............................		100
Amortization of premium on bonds.		

Dec. 31.	Bond Sinking Fund...................................	$ 260	
	Sinking Fund Income...............................		$ 260
	Earnings on sinking-fund investments per report of trustee.		
31.	Bond Sinking Fund...................................	9,000	
	Bank...		9,000
	Payment to trustee for sinking fund.		
31.	Retained Earnings...................................	9,260	
	Provision for Sinking Fund Requirements..............		9,260
	Appropriation of earnings for sinking-fund purposes.		

10th
Year

Jan. 1.	Accrued Bond Interest Payable...........................	2,000	
	Bond Interest Expense...............................		2,000
	Reversing entry for accrued bond interest.		
2.	Bond Interest Expense.................................	2,000	
	Bank...		2,000
	Paid semiannual interest on bonds.		
July 1.	Bond Interest Expense...............................	2,000	
	Bank...		2,000
	Paid semiannual interest on bonds.		
Dec. 28.	Bond Sinking Fund...................................	2,370	
	Sinking Fund Income...............................		2,370
	Earnings on sinking fund per report of trustee.		
31.	Bond Interest Expense...............................	2,000	
	Accrued Bond Interest Payable......................		2,000
	Six-months' interest accrued on bonds payable.		
31.	Premium on Bonds...................................	100	
	Bond Interest Expense...............................		100
	Amortization of premium on bonds.		
31.	Bond Sinking Fund...................................	5,280	
	Bank...		5,280
	Final payment to trustee for bond-sinking fund.		
31.	Retained Earnings...................................	7,650	
	Provision for Sinking Fund Requirements..............		7,650
	Appropriation of earnings for sinking-fund purposes.		

11th
Year

Jan. 1.	Accrued Bond Interest Payable...........................	2,000	
	Bond Interest Expense...............................		2,000
	Reversing entry for accrued bond interest.		
2.	Accrued Bond Interest Payable...........................	2,000	
	Bank...		2,000
	Final payment of semiannual interest on bonds.		
10.	First Mortgage Bonds Payable...........................	100,000	
	Bond Sinking Fund...................................		100,000
	Payment of first-mortgage bonds at maturity by trustee with sinking-fund proceeds.		
10.	Provision for Sinking Fund Requirements..................	100,000	
	Retained Earnings...................................		100,000
	Cancellation of bond sinking-fund provision.		

PRACTICE ASSIGNMENT No. 48. Complete Report No. 48 in the workbook and submit your working papers for approval. Continue with the following study assignment in Unit Twenty-five until Report No. 49 is required.

ACCOUNTING FOR INTANGIBLE AND WASTING ASSETS

(49) ACCOUNTING PROCEDURE

Not infrequently a firm will own one or more assets of a type described as intangible. Certain types of businesses acquire and exploit what are termed wasting assets. Following is a discussion of the major features of accounting for intangible assets and wasting assets.

Intangible Assets. In an accounting sense, the term *intangible* has come to have a very limited meaning. The word itself is broad enough to include all types of assets that lack physical substance. Amounts on deposit in a bank, receivables of all types, prepaid insurance, and securities are all assets that have no physical substance. The fact that some of these assets are evidenced by documents or certificates of various types does not make the properties tangible. However, none of these assets is included in the category of intangibles as the term is used in accounting. Instead, the term is used to refer to a limited group of certain valuable legal or economic rights that a firm may acquire. All of the items classified as intangibles have the common characteristic of being comparatively long lived; they are usually considered to be fixed assets. Major examples of intangibles include patents, copyrights, leases, leasehold improvements, franchises, trade-marks, and goodwill.

Patents. A *patent* is a grant by the Federal government to an inventor giving him the exclusive right to produce and sell his invention for a period of seventeen years. A firm may acquire a patent by original grant or by purchase from a prior patent owner. If a patentable invention is developed in the operation of a business, the cost associated with the patent may be very nominal or a considerable amount depending upon various circumstances. A manufacturing company that carries on regular research activities may treat the costs of such activities as current expenses. If patents are secured on any inventions that result, the cost of the patents is considered to be only the fees paid to the government and probably certain fees paid to patent attorneys whose services were used. In many cases these fees are considered as ordinary expenses of the period in which they were incurred. The patents may become very valuable, but they are not treated as assets in the accounting records.

In other cases a record may be kept of all of the costs and expenses connected with a certain research project. These costs, together with any legal fees, are treated as a cost of the patent that is obtained. An asset account, Patents, is charged with the total of these costs.

In many cases patents are acquired by purchase and their cost is debited to Patents. If numerous patents are owned, a subsidiary or supplementary record showing the nature, life, and cost of each one may be maintained.

Since the life of a patent is specifically limited, its cost, if any, should be prorated over no more than the number of years that the patent right will exist. The greatest number of years would be seventeen if the firm acquired the patent at original issuance. If a patent that had already run five years were acquired, its cost should be apportioned over a period of twelve years. In many cases, however, it is expected that the effective or economic life of a patent may be something less than its legal life. In this event, the cost is prorated over the expected useful or economic life.

If the cost of a patent is to be written off on a straight-line basis, the charge-off each year is determined by dividing the cost of the right by its expected life. Suppose, for example, that a patent with thirteen years to run was purchased at a cost of $5,000. Further suppose that the buyer expects that the effective life of the patent will be only ten years. In that event, $500 ($5,000 ÷ 10) would be treated as expense for each of the ten years. The $500 is called the periodic amortization of the cost. As used in accounting, the term amortization means to write off a certain amount gradually. The adjusting entry to record the amortization for a year would be as follows:

Patent Expense	$500	
Patents		$500
Amortization of patent.		

Sometimes an account entitled Amortization of Patents is debited for the amount written off. On rare occasions the credit is to an account entitled Allowance for Amortization of Patents. The latter account is identical in nature to an allowance for depreciation account. In most cases, however, the credit is made directly to the asset account rather than to a contra account. This is not consistent with the accounting for depreciation of most tangible fixed assets. Depreciation write-offs are almost always credited to an allowance for depreciation account; the amortization or write-off of intangible fixed assets is nearly always credited directly to the asset account.

Patent expense is usually treated as a manufacturing expense. Patents are an asset; their unamortized cost is reported in the balance sheet as an intangible asset.

Copyrights. A *copyright* is similar in many respects to a patent. It consists of a Federal grant to the exclusive right to the reproduction and sale of a book, drawing, design, formula, photograph, musical composition, or certain other creations. A copyright is granted for 28 years with the privilege to renew for another 28 years. The cost of obtaining a copyright in the first place is very nominal and would be treated as an ordinary and incidental expense by the one who secures it. However, if an existing copyright is purchased, the cost might be large enough and the expected future value sufficient to warrant charging the cost to an asset account entitled Copyrights. If a number of copyrights are owned, a suitable subsidiary or supplementary record may be maintained.

It would be a rare case if it were expected that a copyright would have an economic life as long as its legal life (56 years at the most). In most cases the cost of a copyright is written off in a very few years. The write-off can be on a straight-line basis or in the proportion of the actual sales of the copyrighted article during the period to the total expected sales. The amount of the write-off for each period, however calculated, is debited to Copyright Expense (or Amortization of Copyrights) and credited to Copyrights. The expense is reported in the income statement and any unamortized portion of the cost of copyrights is reported in the balance sheet as an intangible asset.

Leases. A *lease* is a contract wherein the owner of certain property (commonly real estate) agrees to let another party use it for a certain length of time in return for specified payments, usually monthly rental payments. In most cases the original lessee (the party who will use the property) acquires a lease at no cost apart from the monthly rental payments that must be made as the property is used. Such payments are treated as ordinary expenses when paid.

Most leases are transferable. Any of several circumstances may cause a long-term lease to become valuable. Thus, it may happen that the original lessee can sell his rights under a lease to another party. The buyer acquires an asset with a life that can be measured exactly. For example, suppose that a business buys what is left of a twenty-year lease on a certain store five years after the lease started. The lease may call for monthly rental payments of $200. However, the buyer considers the location to be so desirable that he is willing to pay more than that. Assume that he buys the lease (which has 15 years to run) for $18,000. He may record the purchase by a debit of $18,000 to the account Leasehold and a credit to Bank.

If the lease had exactly 15 years, or 180 months, to run, the cost would be allocated over this length of time. The sum of $18,000 divided by 15 years is $1,200 a year, or $100 a month. An adjustment would be made either monthly or annually to amortize the proper amount. If the adjustment was made at the end of each month, the entry would be as follows:

Rent Expense	$100	
Leasehold		$100
Amortization of leasehold.		

The debit was made to the rent expense account since the cost of the lease was really the same thing as the prepayment of rent. The rent expense account would already have been debited for the $200 cash rent paid to the owner of the property at the start of the month. It should be apparent, however, that the real rent expense to the tenant is $300 each month — $200 cash rent plus 1/180 of the $18,000 cost of the 180-month lease. Some accountants might prefer to debit the $100 to an account entitled Amortization of Leasehold rather than Rent Expense but, in most cases, this serves no useful purpose.

The unamortized portion of the cost of the lease should be reported in the balance sheet as an intangible asset.

Leasehold Improvements. The party using property under a long-term lease may decide that it is to his interest to incur costs to improve the property. In most cases whatever is left of any improvements or additions will belong to the owner of the property at the termination of the lease. In the records of the lessee, the cost of any long-lived improvements is charged to an account entitled Leasehold Improvements. This cost will be written off as expense over the number of years that it is expected to benefit the lessee. If the benefit from the improvements is expected to be exhausted before the lease expires, the cost is amortized over the expected economic life of the improvements. If, however, it is expected that the benefit from the improvements will extend beyond the life of the lease, then the cost of the improvements is written off over the remaining period of the lease.

Suppose, for example, that three years after taking over the lease on the store mentioned previously, the lessee spends $2,880 restyling the front of the store and installing various modern features. Let it be assumed that these improvements are expected to benefit the property for fifteen to twenty years. However, they will become a permanent part of the store and the lessee's right to use the property will end in twelve years. Thus, the cost of the improvements should be amortized over the twelve-year period. The adjusting entry at the end of each year would be as follows:

Amortization of Leasehold Improvements......................	$240	
Leasehold Improvements...................................		$240
Annual amortization of leasehold improvements.		

Amortization of Leasehold Improvements is an expense similar to depreciation and should be so reported in the operating section of the income statement. The unamortized portion of the cost of leasehold improvements should be reported in the balance sheet as an intangible asset. It may be noted that the leasehold improvements usually have physical substance but, since they become a part of property owned by someone else, they are not considered to be a tangible asset of the lessee.

The original lessee of property might have leasehold-improvement cost to account for even though he had incurred no cost for the lease itself.

Franchises. A *franchise* is a grant of certain rights or privileges for either a specified time, indefinitely, or forever. In many cases franchises are granted to businesses by governments. Examples of governmental franchises include the right to operate buses or street cars on city streets, and the monopoly right to operate a power company or a telephone company. Business organizations sometimes enter into contracts that are called franchises. A manufacturer, for example, may give a franchise to a certain dealer that gives the latter the exclusive right to sell the manufacturer's product in a specified geographic area. A franchise of this type is often called a *dealership*.

Quite often there is no cost to the party who originally secures a franchise right. However, if the right becomes valuable and its terms allow it to be transferred, a subsequent buyer of the franchise will have something to account for. The cost of a purchased franchise should be debited to a franchise account. Whether this cost should be written off and, if so, how fast depends upon various circumstances. If the franchise has a specified term with no renewal option, the cost should be written off over a period no longer than that length of time. The period of the write-off might be less than the legal life if there were reason to think that the economic value would disappear before the right legally ends. Even if there is no reason to think that the value of an indefinite or perpetual franchise is diminishing, many accountants favor a policy of amortizing the cost in the interest of conservatism.

The amortization adjustment at the end of each period would be similar to that made for other intangibles. In this case the debit might be to an expense account entitled Amortization of Franchise and the credit should be to the franchise account. The amount of the expense should be reported in the income statement and the unamortized portion of the franchise cost should be reported in the balance sheet as an intangible asset.

Trade-Marks. The manufacturer or seller of a product frequently wishes to identify his merchandise in some unique fashion. The practice of using *trade-marks* or trade names is widespread. The Federal government offers legal protection to such designations by permitting them to be registered with the United States Patent Office. As long as the trade-mark or trade name is continuously used, the courts will protect the owner of a registered trade-mark by preventing others from using it, or by assessing damages against those who infringe upon such rights.

The person or firm who originally registers a trade-mark may have incurred little or no cost in its creation or, by contrast, may have incurred sizable cost in its development. Since trade-marks and trade names can be sold, a buyer will have cost to account for. Inasmuch as a trade-mark or trade name does not expire as long as it is used, the question arises as to whether any cost of such an asset should be amortized and, if so, over what period of time. The future value of a trade-mark or trade name is highly uncertain. Conservatism suggests that any cost should be written off within a few years.

The periodic adjusting entry to record the amortization involves a debit to Amortization of Trade-Marks (or Trade Names) and a credit to Trade-Marks (or Trade Names). The amount written off should be reported as a nonoperating expense in the income statement. It should be mentioned, however, that some accountants would make the write-off directly against the retained earnings account in the first place, and not include the expense in the income statement. The federal income tax law does not permit a deduction for the amortization of trade-marks and trade names. Any unamortized portion of the cost of trade-marks or trade names should be reported in the balance sheet as an intangible asset.

Goodwill. Goodwill is usually defined as the value of excess earning capacity. Just exactly what is meant by "excess" and how to calculate such value is difficult. Usually, goodwill is not recorded as an asset unless it has been purchased. In that case its amount is known or can be determined.

Goodwill cannot be purchased by itself. It arises in connection with such transactions as the admission of a new partner into a partnership (see Unit Eleven) and in connection with the purchases of all of the assets of one business by another. If the price paid for the net assets of the business that is "selling out" is larger than the reasonable value of the identifiable assets being purchased, the excess is regarded as the amount paid for the goodwill of the terminated business.

For example, suppose that James Wells, who owns and has been successfully operating the Wells Supply Company, decides to sell his business. The officers of the Acme Corporation want to buy Wells' business and merge it with their own business. The corporation officers inspect the assets of the Wells Supply Company and decide that the property has the following values:

Accounts Receivable	$ 22,500
Merchandise Inventory	15,600
Furniture and Fixtures	12,900
Land	9,000
Building	45,000
Total	$105,000

Mr. Wells will pay all liabilities of the business and withdraw any cash that is left. He agrees that the values placed on the assets are fair, but refuses to sell unless he receives $125,000. If the Acme Corporation decides to buy at this price, it will be paying $20,000 ($125,000 − $105,000) for the goodwill that relates to Mr. Wells' business. Obviously the buyer would not pay the price asked unless he thought he was getting something of value. In this example, the directors of the Acme Corporation may feel that $20,000 is not too much to pay for the business contacts, patronage, and prestige that Mr. Wells has built up. If the offer is accepted and the price of $125,000 is paid in cash, the entry to record the transaction in general journal form would be as follows:

Accounts Receivable	$22,500	
Merchandise Inventory	15,600	
Furniture and Fixtures	12,900	
Land	9,000	
Building	45,000	
Goodwill	20,000	
Bank		$125,000
Purchased the assets of the Wells Supply Co.		

If goodwill has been purchased and charged to an asset account, the question arises as to whether it should be written off and, if so, how fast. Goodwill has no legal life; its economic life is uncertain. Since a logical basis for prorating the cost of goodwill is lacking, conservatism dictates that it should be written off in a very few years. If it were decided that the goodwill purchased by the Acme Corporation is to be written off over five years, the adjusting entry at the end of each of these years might be as follows:

Amortization of Goodwill............................	$4,000	
Goodwill..		$4,000
Amortization of goodwill.		

If the write-off was made in this form, the amortized portion should be reported in the income statement as a nonoperating expense. Instead of handling the matter in this way, some accountants would charge the amount written off each year to Retained Earnings. Amortization of goodwill is not deductible for federal income tax purposes. The unamortized portion of goodwill should be reported in the balance sheet as an intangible asset.

Other Intangibles. The intangible assets that have been discussed are the major examples of this type of property. Other examples include organization expenses (necessary costs incurred in launching an enterprise), secret processes or formulae, and subscription lists. The usual practice is to amortize the costs of such property within a few years after its acquisition.

Under the federal income tax law, organization expense is allowed as a deduction provided it is charged off over a period of not less than sixty months, beginning with the month in which the corporation begins business. The amount written off each year is usually recorded by debiting Amortization of Organization Expense and by crediting Organization Expense.

A common practice in regard to many intangibles is to write off all of their cost but $1 as soon as possible. The $1 is carried in the accounts and reported in the balance sheet indefinitely. This serves to call the attention of the readers of the balance sheet to the existence of such assets and the fact that the company has followed the conservative practice of amortizing their cost. To find "Patents, Trade-Marks, and Goodwill . . . $1" listed among the assets in the balance sheet of a hundred-million dollar corporation is not uncommon.

Wasting Assets. The term *wasting asset* is applied to real property which is acquired for the purpose of removing or extracting the valuable natural resource on or in the property. Stands of timber, mines, oil wells, gas wells, or land acquired in the belief that the property contains minerals, oil, or gas that can be extracted, are examples of this type of asset. The adjective "wasting" is applied because, in most cases, it is expected that the valuable product will be removed eventually so as to leave the property relatively valueless. In the case of many types of mines and wells, only the valuable material below the surface is owned. The land, as such, may not be owned by the mining, oil, or gas company.

Depletion. The consumption or exhaustion of wasting assets is called *depletion.* Apart from income tax considerations, the accounting problem is to apportion the cost of such assets to the periods in which they are consumed. The procedure is very similar to that involved in computing depreciation on an output basis. The cost of the property is reduced by estimated salvage or residual value, and the difference is divided by the estimated number of units that the property contains. The result is the depletion cost or expense per unit. This amount times the number of units extracted during the period will give the depletion expense for the period.

The following example is used to illustrate both the method of computing depletion and the proper accounting procedure:

> A coal mine is acquired at cost of $200,000. No salvage value is expected. The estimated number of units available for production is 1,000,000 tons. During the current year 145,000 tons of coal are mined and sold.

COMPUTATION OF AMOUNT OF DEPLETION

$200,000 ÷ 1,000,000 units = 20¢, unit cost.
145,000 tons × 20¢ per ton = $29,000, amount of depletion.

The depletion may be recorded by means of the following general journal entry:

Depletion...	$29,000	
Allowance for Depletion of Coal Mine.................		$29,000
Depletion based on 145,000 tons of coal at a unit rate of		
20¢ a ton.		

The difference between the cost of the coal mine and the amount of the allowance for depletion is the book value of the property.

Cost of coal mine..	$200,000
Less allowance for depletion.................................	29,000
Book value of mine..	$171,000

It is customary to show the allowance for depletion as a deduction from the property account in the balance sheet so as to indicate the book value of the property. Depletion is a temporary account that is closed into Income Summary at the end of the accounting period. The amount is reported as an operating expense in the income statement.

Not infrequently the estimate of the quantity of the resource that is contained in the property has to be changed. The usual practice is to make the calculation for the depletion per unit each year starting with the book value of the property and dividing that amount (less estimated salvage value, if any) by the number of units extracted during the year plus the current estimate of the number of units remaining. For example, the mine mentioned in the previous illustration had a book value of $171,000 at the start of the second year. During that year 200,000 tons were extracted and at the end of the year the engineers estimate that 700,000 tons remain. The calculation of the revised depletion cost per unit would be as follows:

$$\frac{\$171,000}{200,000 \text{ tons} + 700,000 \text{ tons}} = 19\cancel{c} \text{ per ton}$$

200,000 tons × 19¢ = $38,000, depletion for the second year.

Depletion for Federal Income Tax Purposes. Special rules govern the amount of the deduction for depletion that can be taken for federal income tax purposes. The taxpayer may compute the amount in the manner explained in the preceding paragraphs. However, taxpayers who own and operate oil and gas wells and certain types of mines may take deductions equal to certain specified percentages (which vary from 5% to 27½%) of the amount of the sales of the period subject to stated maximum and minimum limits. This is commonly known as *percentage depletion.* These provisions of the law do not purport to have any relation to good accounting; they were enacted to promote the production of certain products by giving an income tax advantage or subsidy to the producers of the products.

PRACTICE ASSIGNMENT No. 49. Complete Report No. 49 in the workbook and submit your working papers for approval. Then continue with the next study assignment in Unit Twenty-six until Report No. 50 is required.

Unit Twenty-six

THE VOUCHER SYSTEM OF ACCOUNTING

(50) PRINCIPLES OF VOUCHER ACCOUNTING

Many business organizations use a method of handling cash disbursements known as the *voucher system*. This system is useful for controlling expenditures. Under this method written authorization is required for each cash disbursement. For example, the secretary of a corporation may be the one authorized to approve all expenditures, while the cashier may be the one authorized to issue the checks. Such a system usually involves the use of vouchers, a voucher register, a vouchers payable account in the general ledger, voucher checks, and a check register, although in some cases ordinary checks are used and are recorded in a simple cashbook or in a cash disbursements journal. There is no one standard procedure in voucher accounting. Like most bookkeeping and accounting processes, the voucher system is adaptable to various situations.

Verification of Invoices. All invoices received, whether they represent the cost of goods, materials, or other property purchased or the cost of services rendered, are verified by the proper parties. The receiving clerk usually verifies the receipt of all property purchased as to quantity and quality. The purchasing agent usually verifies prices, grades, sizes, and terms of payment. Clerks in the accounting department usually verify the mathematical accuracy of the extensions and the amounts. The chief accountant or auditor may indicate the accounts to be charged. Invoices for services usually are checked by the department receiving the service or incurring the expense.

On the following page is shown an invoice received by The King Manufacturing Co. from The Office Supply Company. This invoice represents the purchase of office supplies on account. The receipt of the supplies has been verified by the receiving clerk, the prices have been verified by the purchasing agent, the extensions and the amount of the invoice have been verified by an accounting clerk, and the chief accountant has indicated that Account No. 181 should be charged for the amount of the invoice.

621

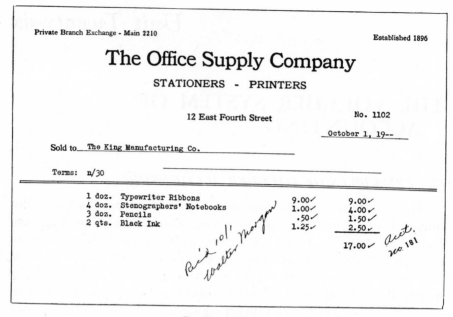

Private Branch Exchange - Main 2210   Established 1896

The Office Supply Company
STATIONERS - PRINTERS

12 East Fourth Street   No. 1102

October 1, 19--

Sold to __The King Manufacturing Co.__

Terms: n/30

1 doz.	Typewriter Ribbons	9.00	9.00
4 doz.	Stenographers' Notebooks	1.00	4.00
3 doz.	Pencils	.50	1.50
2 qts.	Black Ink	1.25	2.50
			17.00

Paid 10/1 Walter Morgan   Acct. no. 181

Purchase Invoice

Preparation of Vouchers. As used in this connection, the term *voucher* refers to a business paper or document that provides space in which to record information relating to goods or services purchased, accounts to be charged, and authorization for payment. There is also space in which to record the date of payment and the number of the check issued.

A voucher should be prepared for each invoice except those representing minor expense items that may be paid out of a petty cash fund. There is no standard form of voucher, the form varying depending upon the nature of the business, the classification of accounts, and the distribution desired. The vouchers are usually prepared by a voucher clerk to whom the invoices are referred after they have been verified.

On page 623 is shown a voucher that was prepared by the voucher clerk for The King Manufacturing Co. The information recorded on this voucher was obtained from the invoice shown above. After the voucher was prepared, the invoice was attached to it and both were referred to the accounting department to be recorded. When the voucher was paid, the date of payment, the check number, and the amount of the check were recorded in the spaces provided for this information on the back of the voucher form.

VOUCHER

THE KING MANUFACTURING CO.

No. __101__   DATE ISSUED __Oct. 1,__ 19__   TERMS __n/30__   DUE __Oct. 31,__ 19__

To __The Office Supply Co.__

ADDRESS

INVOICE DATE	DESCRIPTION	AMOUNT
10/1	Office Supplies	17 00

AUTHORIZED BY

L. G. Wolf

PREPARED BY

W. O. Day

VOUCHER CLERK

(Front of Voucher)

DISTRIBUTION

RAW MATERIALS	DIRECT LABOR	MANUFACTURING EXPENSES		SUNDRY ACCOUNTS	
		ACCOUNT	AMOUNT	ACCOUNT	AMOUNT
				181	17 00

PAYMENT

DATE OF PAYMENT __November 1,__ 19__ CHECK NO __185__ FOR $ __17.00__

CERTIFICATION

THIS VOUCHER HAS BEEN AUDITED CAREFULLY AND IS CORRECT IN EVERY RESPECT

B. C. Whitman

ACCOUNTANT

(Back of Voucher)

Voucher

Recording of Vouchers. After the invoices have been properly verified and vouchers have been prepared for them, the vouchers should be recorded in a *voucher register*. This register can best be described as an expanded purchases journal; it is used to record the purchases of all types of property and services.

The ruling and the columnar headings of a voucher register depend upon the nature of the business and the desired classification of purchases and expenses. One form of voucher register is shown on page 625. Reference to that illustration will show that voucher No. 101, which is reproduced on page 623, was recorded by debiting Office Supplies, Account No. 181, and by crediting Vouchers Payable for $17.

Following is a description of the vouchers that are shown recorded in the voucher register:

Oct.　1.　No. 101, The Office Supply Company, 12 East Fourth Street; office supplies, Account No. 181, $17; terms, October 1 — n/30.

　　　2.　No. 102, Stevens Truck Co., 1869 Colerain Ave.; factory lift truck, $187.50; terms, October 2 — 2/15, n/30. (Charge to Factory Equipment, Account No. 23.)

　　　2.　No. 103, Landis & Co., Morristown; raw materials, $1,052; terms, October 1 — 2/10, n/30.

　　　2.　No. 104, Scott & Scott, 63 Millsdale Ave.; factory supplies, Account No. 183, $52.10; terms, October 2 — n/30.

　　　2.　No. 105, Day Machine Works, 1146 Gilbert St.; repairs on machinery, Account No. 747, $92.75; terms, cash.

　　15.　No. 106, Factory Payroll, $635.05.　Distribution: Direct Labor, $500.70; Indirect Labor, Account No. 741, $134.35. Taxes withheld: Employees' Income Taxes, Account No. 32, $82.51; F.I.C.A. Taxes, Account No. 311, $14.29.

Note: The amount of the F.I.C.A. taxes being withheld from employees' wages by The King Manufacturing Co. is computed on a basis of 2¼ per cent of the taxable wages of each employee. A similar tax is also imposed on the employer.

Voucher No. 106 was based on a report of the payroll clerk. The amount payable is the net amount of the factory payroll after deducting the taxes withheld. The total wages earned during the pay period ended October 15 amounted to $635.05 of which $500.70 represented direct labor and $134.35 represented indirect labor. It should be noted that two lines were required to record this transaction in the voucher register. This was because of the two entries in the Sundry Accounts Cr. columns required to record the employer's liability for the taxes withheld. It was also necessary to record the social security taxes imposed on the employer. The entry t

(Continued on page 626)

VOUCHER REGISTER FOR MONTH OF October 19--

Raw Material Purchases Dr.	Direct Labor Dr.	Mfg. Expenses Dr. Acct. No.	Amount	✓	Sundry Accts. Dr. Acct. No.	Amount	✓	Day	Vchr No.	To Whom Issued	Sundry Accts. Cr. Acct. No.	Amount	✓	Vouchers Payable Cr.	Disposition Date	Ck. No.
					181	17 00	✓	1	101	The Office Supply Co.				17 00		
					23	187 50	✓	2	102	Stevens Truck Co.				187 50	10/17	87
1052 00								2	103	Landis & Co.				1052 00	10/11	85
					183	52 10	✓	2	104	Scott & Scott				52 10		
		747	92 75	✓				2	105	Day Machine Works	32	82 51	✓	92 75	10/2	84
	500 70	741	134 35	✓				15	106	Factory Payroll	311	14 29	✓	538 25	10/15	86
1052 00	500 70		227 10			256 60						96 80		1939 60		

CHECK REGISTER FOR MONTH OF October 19--

Vouchers Payable Dr. No.	Amount	Day	Drawn to the Order of	Purchases Discount Cr.	Bank Cr. Ck. No.	Amount
105	92 75	2	Day Machine Works		84	92 75
103	1052 00	11	Landis & Co.	21 04	85	1030 96
106	538 25	15	Factory Payroll		86	538 25
102	187 50	17	Stevens Truck Co.	3 75	87	183 75
	1870 50			24 79		1845 71

record these taxes was made in the general journal, the entry being as follows:

Social Security Taxes.......................................	$33.34	
F.I.C.A. Taxes Payable...................................		$14.29
State U.C. Taxes Payable................................		17.15
F.U.T.A. Taxes Payable..................................		1.90
Employer's social security taxes.		

When the voucher system is used with a voucher register and a check register having columnar arrangements similar to those illustrated on page 625, the procedure in recording wages may be as follows:

(a) The gross earnings of each employee for the pay period is ascertained from the time record of the employee. A summary report is then prepared by the payroll clerk showing: (1) a proper classification of the wages earned and the titles or numbers of the accounts to be charged; (2) the amount of the total earnings to be charged to each account; (3) the total deductions to be made for taxes withheld, and for any other purposes; and (4) the net amount of wages payable.

(b) A voucher is prepared for the payroll and is recorded in the voucher register by debiting the proper labor accounts and by crediting the proper liability accounts for the taxes withheld, and by crediting Vouchers Payable for the net amount payable.

(c) A check is issued in payment of the payroll voucher. This check is usually made payable to Payroll and it may be cashed at the bank on which it is drawn to obtain the funds needed to meet the payroll, or it may be deposited in a special payroll checking account and an individual pay check may then be issued to each employee. The check issued for the net amount of the payroll should be recorded in the check register by debiting Vouchers Payable and by crediting the proper bank account.

(d) An entry is made in the general journal to record the employer's liability for the social security taxes imposed on the employer. Sometimes the social security taxes imposed on the employer are recorded at the end of each month instead of each payday.

When the social security taxes become due, vouchers should be prepared authorizing the payment of such taxes. These vouchers should be recorded in the voucher register by debiting the proper liability accounts and by crediting Vouchers Payable. When checks are issued to pay the taxes, the checks should be recorded in the check register by debiting Vouchers Payable and by crediting the proper bank account.

In a manufacturing enterprise, separate expense accounts may be kept to record the social security taxes imposed on factory wages, administrative salaries, and sales salaries. In recording such taxes, it will be necessary, of course, to debit the proper expense accounts.

To prove the voucher register, it is only necessary to ascertain that the sum of the debit footings is equal to the sum of the credit footings. The footings should be proved before the totals are forwarded and before the summary posting is completed.

Posting from the Voucher Register. Both individual posting and summary posting from the voucher register are required. The individual posting involves posting each item entered in the Manufacturing Expenses **Dr.** Amount column to the proper account in the manufacturing expense subsidiary ledger. It is also necessary to post each item entered in the Sundry Accounts **Dr.** and **Cr.** Amount columns to the proper account in the general ledger. As each item is posted, a check mark should be placed beside it in the Check ($\sqrt{}$) column of the voucher register. The page number of the voucher register should also be entered in the Folio column of the ledger account to which the amount is posted.

The summary posting of the voucher register required at the end of each month involves the following procedure:

(a) The total of the column headed Raw Material Purchases **Dr.** should be posted to the debit of the raw material purchases account in the general ledger.

(b) The total of the column headed Direct Labor **Dr.** should be posted to the debit of the direct labor account in the general ledger.

(c) The total of the column headed Manufacturing Expenses **Dr.** Amount should be posted to the debit of the manufacturing expenses account in the general ledger.

(d) The total of the column headed Vouchers Payable **Cr.** should be posted to the credit of the vouchers payable account in the general ledger.

As the total of each column is posted from the voucher register, the account number should be written immediately below the total. The page of the voucher register should also be written in the Folio column of the ledger account to which the amount is posted. A check mark should be placed below the totals of the Sundry Accounts **Dr.** and **Cr.** Amount columns in the voucher register to indicate that these totals are not posted.

Filing Vouchers. After the vouchers are recorded in the voucher register, they may be filed alphabetically in an unpaid vouchers file or

---

No. __104__   November 1,   19--

FIRST NATIONAL BANK 88-1809 / 1131

Pay to the order of __The Office Supply Co.__ $ __17.00__

Seventeen and no/100 - Dollars

THE KING MANUFACTURING CO.

Walter Wolfe, Pres.

DETACH THIS BRIEF BEFORE DEPOSITING CHECK

RETAIN THIS STATEMENT
ENDORSEMENT ON VOUCHER CHECK
IS SUFFICIENT RECEIPT

THE KING MANUFACTURING CO.   DATE November 1, 19--

ATTACHED VOUCHER CHECK IS FULL SETTLEMENT OF THE FOLLOWING

INVOICE DATE	NUMBER	DESCRIPTION	INVOICE AMOUNT	DEDUCTIONS FOR	AMOUNT	NET AMOUNT
10/1	1102	Office Supplies	17 00			17 00

IF THE ABOVE STATEMENT IS NOT CORRECT RETURN IT AND ATTACHED CHECK FOR CORRECTION

Voucher Check

they may be filed numerically according to due date. If the vouchers are not filed according to due date, it may be advisable to use a tickler file as an aid in determining which vouchers need to be paid on certain dates. Invoices should be paid according to their terms. Delay in payment may result in discounts being lost or in loss of credit standing.

Paying Vouchers. At or before maturity, the vouchers should be approved by the one authorized to approve expenditures and should be presented to the proper disbursing officer for payment. Ordinary checks may be used. In some cases, however, a special form of *voucher check* is used that provides suitable space for copying data from the invoice or other information concerning the voucher to which the check relates. In the above illustration a voucher check issued to The Office Supply Company in payment of its invoice of October 1 is reproduced. The form of the check is the same as an ordinary check. The statement attached to it provides a description of the invoice, including its date, number, description, amount, deductions, and net amount. The information given on the statement attached to the check is for identification purposes and is given for the benefit of the payee of the check. Usually the canceled check is filed with the voucher and the original invoice.

Recording Checks. All checks issued in payment of vouchers may be recorded in a *check register*. When the charges pertaining to each voucher have been recorded in the voucher register, it is not necessary to make provision for distribution of charges in the check register. It is not unusual, however, to find that columns are provided in the check register to record deductions that may be made at the time of payment. The form of check register shown on page 625 has a column for cash discount deductions. At the time of recording checks in the check register, an entry should also be made in the Disposition columns of the voucher register to show that the voucher has been paid. This entry serves the same purpose as a debit entry in a creditor's ledger account.

Following is a description of the checks that are shown recorded in the check register reproduced on page 625:

Oct. 2. No. 84, Day Machine Works, $92.75, in payment of Voucher No. 105.
11. No. 85, Landis & Co., $1,030.96, in payment of Voucher No. 103 for $1,052, less 2% discount.
15. No. 86, Factory Payroll, $538.25, in payment of Voucher No. 106.
17. No. 87, Stevens Truck Co., $183.75, in payment of Voucher No. 102 for $187.50, less 2% discount.

To prove the check register, it is only necessary to ascertain that the sum of the credit footings is equal to the footing of the Vouchers Payable Dr. column. The footings should be proved before the totals are forwarded and before the summary posting is completed.

Posting from the Check Register. No individual posting from the check register is required. It is only necessary to complete the summary posting at the end of each month. The procedure is as follows:

(a) The total of the column headed Vouchers Payable Dr. should be posted to the debit of the vouchers payable account in the general ledger.

(b) The total of the column headed Purchases Discount Cr. should be posted to the credit of the purchases discount account in the general ledger.

(c) The total of the column headed Bank Cr. Amount should be posted to the credit of the bank checking account in the general ledger.

As the total of each column is posted from the check register, the account number should be written immediately below the total. The page of the check register should also be written in the Folio column of the ledger account to which the amount is posted.

Filing Canceled Checks.   When a canceled check is received from the bank on which it was drawn, it may be filed with the original invoice and the voucher.   Sometimes a file is kept for paid vouchers and sometimes a separate file is kept for each creditor in order that all invoices, vouchers, and canceled checks may be filed under the name of the creditor.

Proving Vouchers Payable.   When a trial balance is prepared, the balance of the vouchers payable account should be verified by preparing a list of the unpaid vouchers.   The total of this list should, of course, be equal to the balance of the account.

The use of the voucher system of accounting is not advisable under all conditions, but it usually may be used to advantage under the following circumstances:

(a) When transactions involving purchases and expenses are sufficiently numerous to justify the use of a special register.

(b) When the nature of the business is such that it is desirable to record expense invoices at the time they are received rather than when payment is made.

(c) When it is the custom of the firm to pay all invoices in full at maturity instead of making partial or installment payments.

Purchases Returns and Allowances.   When the voucher system of accounting is used, purchases returns and allowances must be recorded in such a way that the accounts will show correctly the effect of such transactions and the voucher register will show the proper amounts payable. When credit is received for a return or for an allowance on an invoice, the amount of the unpaid voucher is thereby reduced.

There are several possible ways of recording a return or an allowance. If the item relates to an invoice vouchered and recorded during the current month, a correction entry can be interlined in the voucher register.   The amount of the allowance can be written in just above both the amount in the Raw Materials Purchases Dr. column and the amount in the Vouchers Payable Cr. column that relate to the vouchered invoice that is being reduced.   Some accountants use red ink to indicate that these amounts are offsets.   Instead of this, dark ink can be used and the amounts can be circled to explain their nature.   A notation of the reduction is made on the affected voucher and the credit memo is attached to it.   Such offset items are totaled separately in each column of the register.   The sum of any such items in the Raw Materials Purchases Dr. column is posted as a credit to the purchases returns and allowances account.   The sum of such negative items in the Vouchers Payable Cr. column is posted as a debit to the vouchers payable account.

If the return or the allowance relates to an invoice that was vouchered and recorded during a prior month, the foregoing treatment could not be used. Some accountants do not favor it in any case. Instead, a general journal entry can be made to cancel the old voucher and to record the return or the allowance, and a new voucher for the adjusted amount can be prepared and recorded. A notation of the cancellation is made in the Disposition columns of the register following the amount of the original voucher.

Another treatment that is often quite satisfactory is (1) to make a notation of the return or the allowance on the voucher that is affected and to attach the credit memo to the voucher; (2) to make a notation of the reduction in the voucher register beside the amount of the voucher that is being reduced; and (3) formally to record the transaction by a general journal entry. A return of, or an allowance relating to, a merchandise or materials purchase would require a debit to Vouchers Payable and a credit to Purchases Returns and Allowances. If the return or the allowance related to the purchase of a fixed asset or to some expense that had been incurred, the credit in the entry would be to the proper asset or expense account.

Corrected Invoices. Sometimes a corrected invoice is received after the original invoice has been recorded in the voucher register. The corrected invoice may involve either an increase or a decrease in the amount of the original voucher. An entry should be made in the general journal to record the change in the amount of the original voucher. If the amount is increased, the entry will involve a debit to the account that was charged for the amount of the original invoice and a credit to Vouchers Payable. If the amount is decreased, the entry will involve a debit to Vouchers Payable and a credit to the account that was charged for the amount of the original invoice. The corrected invoice should then be attached to the original invoice and voucher, and a notation should be made in the voucher register to indicate that this amount has been changed. As in the case of returns and allowances, some accountants would cancel the original voucher and issue a new voucher for the proper amount, while others would interline the correction in the voucher register if the latter had not been posted.

Partial Payments. The voucher system is not generally used when it is the custom of a business to make partial or installment payments on invoices. When such situations do arise in the case of a company using the voucher system, special handling is required. If it is known at the outset that an invoice will be paid in installments, separate vouchers for each installment should be prepared in the first place. If it is decided to make a partial payment on an invoice already vouchered and recorded, it is recommended that the original voucher be canceled and that two or more new ones be issued. The total amount of the new vouchers would be equal to that of the old voucher. The debit may be to Vouchers Payable on the new vouchers. When they are recorded in the voucher register, the new debit to Vouchers Payable will offset the credit to that account recorded from the old voucher. The original debit to the proper account will stand from the old voucher. A note should be made in the Disposition columns indicating that the old voucher has been canceled and showing the numbers of the new vouchers. Payments of the new vouchers would be recorded in the usual manner.

Notes Payable. When a note is given in temporary settlement of a voucher, it may be recorded in the general journal as a debit to Vouchers Payable and a credit to Notes Payable. At the same time, an entry should be made on the original voucher to show that it has been settled temporarily with a note. An entry should also be made in the voucher register to indicate the settlement of the voucher. When the note becomes due, a new voucher should then be issued authorizing the payment of the note and interest. The new voucher should be recorded in the voucher register, and the check issued in payment of the voucher should be recorded in the check register. The entry in the voucher register will involve a debit to Notes Payable for the face of the note, a debit to Interest Expense for the amount of the interest on the note, and a credit to Vouchers Payable for the amount of the check to be issued. The entry in the check register will involve a debit to Vouchers Payable and a credit to the bank account for the amount of the check issued.

If a new note is issued in settlement of an old note plus the interest accrued thereon, the entry may be made in the general journal debiting Notes Payable for the face of the old note, debiting Interest Expense for the amount of the interest on the old note, and crediting Notes Payable for the amount of the new note. A voucher would not be prepared until it was time to pay the new note and any interest thereon.

If a check is issued in payment of the interest and in partial payment of the principal of an outstanding note payable and a new note is issued for the balance, a voucher should be prepared authorizing the amount to be paid in cash. This voucher should be recorded in the voucher register debiting Interest Expense for the amount of the interest, debiting Notes Payable for the amount to be paid on the principal, and crediting Vouchers Payable for the total. A check should then be drawn in payment of the voucher and it should be recorded in the check register in the usual manner. The new note issued for the balance should be recorded in the general journal debiting Notes Payable and also crediting Notes Payable for the amount of the new note. The debit entry cancels the unpaid portion of the old note and the credit entry records the liability for the new note.

The Unpaid Vouchers File as a Subsidiary Ledger. When the voucher system is used, it is possible to dispense with a subsidiary accounts payable ledger. The file of unpaid vouchers serves as the detail to support the balance of the vouchers payable account after all posting has been completed. The voucher register itself partially performs this function. Every blank in the Disposition columns of the register shows that the indicated voucher is unpaid. The unpaid vouchers file can be consulted if more detail about any item is needed.

If a subsidiary accounts payable ledger is not maintained and unpaid vouchers are filed according to due date, there is no way of quickly finding out how much is owed to a particular creditor. This may not be considered important, however. Businessmen using the voucher system tend to think in terms of unpaid invoices rather than being primarily concerned with the total amount owed to each of their creditors. If the latter information is needed, the vouchers, or copies thereof, can be filed according to the names of the creditors. A subsidiary creditors' ledger can be maintained, however, if it is desired. It may be wanted for the sake of furnishing a detailed history of dealings with each creditor.

Petty Cash Fund. The maintenance of a petty cash fund eliminates the need for writing checks for small amounts. There are two methods of handling such a fund: one is known as the imprest method and the other as the journal method. Under the *imprest method* (which was discussed in some detail in Unit Four, pages 112–116) disbursements from the petty cash fund are recorded in a petty cash record, which is treated as an auxiliary record. The entries in this book are not posted directly. When the fund is replenished, a check is issued for the necessary amount and, when this check is recorded in the check register, the proper expense accounts are debited for the amount that has been paid out of the fund. Under this plan, the amount of money in the petty cash fund plus the sum of the receipts for payments should always be equal to the balance in the petty cash fund account in the general ledger.

Under the *journal method*, amounts paid from the petty cash fund are recorded in a petty cash disbursements journal. Each payment is recorded as a debit to the proper account and as a credit to Petty Cash Fund. Special columns may be provided in this journal to facilitate the desired classification of expenditures. If special columns are not provided, each item must be posted separately; if special columns are provided, summary posting of the totals will be possible. When the fund is exhausted, additional money is obtained by issuing another check. Each check issued for petty cash fund purposes is recorded in the check register as a debit to Petty Cash Fund and as a credit to the proper bank account.

The use of the voucher system of accounting does not affect the handling of a petty cash fund except that a voucher must be prepared for the check issued to create the fund and for each check issued thereafter to replenish the fund. These vouchers must, of course, be recorded in the voucher register. If the imprest method is used, the voucher issued to create the fund is recorded in the voucher register by debiting Petty Cash Fund and by crediting Vouchers Payable. At the same time, the check is recorded in the check register by debiting Vouchers Payable and by crediting the proper bank account. Each voucher issued subsequently to replenish the fund is recorded in the voucher register by debiting the proper expense accounts and by crediting Vouchers Payable.

If the journal method is used, each voucher issued for petty cash fund purposes is recorded in the voucher register as a debit to Petty Cash Fund and as a credit to Vouchers Payable. Checks issued in payment of petty cash vouchers under this method should be recorded in the same manner as when the imprest method is used; that is, by debiting Vouchers Payable and by crediting the proper bank account.

PRACTICE ASSIGNMENT No. 50. Complete Report No. 50 in the workbook and submit your working papers for approval. Continue with the next study assignment in Unit Twenty-seven until Report No. 51 is required.

ACCOUNTING FOR MANUFACTURERS

(51) TYPICAL MANUFACTURING ACCOUNTS

The manufacturer makes the merchandise that he sells, while the merchant buys the merchandise that he sells. In the manufacturing process certain types of transactions are completed that differ from those completed by a merchant. The transactions that are typical of the manufacturing enterprise may be classified as follows:

(a) Those relating to raw materials.
(b) Those relating to factory labor.
(c) Those relating to manufacturing expenses.

Raw Materials. Certain materials are needed in the manufacture of a product. A manufacturer of automobiles requires sheet metal, bar steel, cloth, tires, and numerous other articles. A manufacturer of clothing requires cloth, thread, buttons, and various other articles. The only distinction between raw materials and finished goods, in many instances, is their relation to a particular manufacturer. The finished goods of one manufacturer may be the raw materials of another manufacturer. Thus, flour is finished goods to a miller but raw material to a baker; silver may be the finished product to a mining company but may constitute raw material to a manufacturer of silverware. Manufacturing materials may be classified as follows:

(a) Direct materials.
(b) Indirect materials.

Direct materials include those that enter into and become a part of the finished product. Thus, the leather trimmings and the linings used in the manufacture of shoes are direct materials. Similarly, the sheet metal, bar steel, cloth, and other materials used in the manufacture of an automobile are direct materials.

Indirect materials include those used in the manufacturing process that do not become a part of the finished product. Thus, oil and grease used in the operation of machinery are indirect materials. Such materials are more often referred to as factory supplies.

Labor. Wages paid to factory workers constitute a part of the cost of the finished product. Supervisors, skilled mechanics, and ordinary laborers usually are employed in the operation of a factory. The wages paid to the skilled and unskilled employees of a factory represent the cost of labor. The employees of a factory may be divided into two classes as follows:

(a) Those who devote their time to converting the raw materials into finished goods. Such workers may do handwork or may operate factory machinery. The wages paid to such workers are directly chargeable to the cost of the products being manufactured. This type of labor usually is referred to as *direct labor*.

(b) Those who devote their time to supervision or to work of a general nature. Such workers may include superintendents, foremen, inspectors, timekeepers, engineers, repairmen, receiving clerks, and general laborers. The wages paid to such workers cannot be charged directly to the cost of the products being manufactured, but must be included in the overhead expenses of the factory. This type of labor usually is referred to as *indirect labor*.

Recording Labor Costs. While there are many different methods employed in the handling of payrolls, the final results are much the same. Separate ledger accounts should be used for direct factory labor, indirect factory labor, sales salaries, office salaries, administrative salaries, etc. The payroll should be classified to facilitate the distribution of labor charges. When labor cost is properly analyzed and recorded so as to distinguish between direct and indirect labor, and between labor employed in the factory and in other departments, the accounts will provide the information needed in preparing manufacturing and income statements.

Manufacturing Expenses. To the costs of direct material and direct labor, sometimes called the *prime costs*, must be added all of the expenses incurred in manufacturing in order to ascertain the total cost of goods manufactured. Manufacturing expenses may be divided into three general classes as follows:

(a) Indirect materials.
(b) Indirect labor.
(c) Other indirect expenses.

Indirect materials and indirect labor have already been discussed. Other indirect expenses include all other costs that are incurred in the manufacturing process. Outstanding examples of this type of expense include those listed at the top of the following page.

(a) Depreciation of factory buildings and equipment.
(b) Repairs to factory buildings and equipment.
(c) Insurance on factory buildings and equipment.
(d) Property taxes applicable to factory buildings and equipment.
(e) Social security taxes applicable to factory wages.
(f) Factory supplies used.
(g) Heat, light, and power consumed.

The accounts kept to record the manufacturing costs of different firms vary extensively. The information desired in the manufacturing statement and in such other reports as may be required determine what accounts should be kept. Obviously, each distinct type of any sizable expense should be recorded in a separate account. Manufacturing expenses are sometimes referred to as factory *overhead expenses* or *burden*.

As manufacturing expenses are incurred, they should be recorded as debits to the proper accounts. Expenses that are wholly chargeable to manufacturing should be recorded in separate accounts. Repairs to factory buildings and equipment is an example of this type of expense. There are certain other expenses of a general overhead nature that cannot be charged wholly to manufacturing or to any other single department. Each of these must be prorated or apportioned on some equitable basis. Power expense, for example, may be distributed on the basis of the amount of power consumed by the various departments. Property taxes on land and buildings may be allocated in relation to the space occupied in the buildings. Property taxes on furniture, fixtures, and equipment may be apportioned in relation to the value of the property in each department. A reasonable basis of distribution must be found for each expense of this type.

Inventories of a Manufacturing Company. The inventory of a merchant consists of finished goods only. In contrast to this, a manufacturer usually has three inventories: (1) raw materials, (2) goods in process, and (3) finished goods. It is necessary to know the amount of the inventories of raw materials and goods in process at the beginning and at the end of the period in order to determine the cost of goods manufactured. The beginning and the ending inventories of finished goods must be known in order to calculate the cost of goods sold. The relationship between these elements is as follows:

COST OF GOODS SOLD = Beginning Inventory of Finished Goods
+ COST OF GOODS MANUFACTURED
− Ending Inventory of Finished Goods

COST OF GOODS
   MANUFACTURED   = Beginning Inventory of Goods in Process
                       + COST OF RAW MATERIALS USED
                       + Direct Labor
                       + Manufacturing Expenses
                       − Ending Inventory of Goods in Process

COST OF RAW
   MATERIALS USED   = Beginning Inventory of Raw Materials
                       + Raw Material Purchases (Net)
                       − Ending Inventory of Raw Materials

Bases of Inventory Valuation. In calculating the amount of an inventory, either of two bases of valuation is usually used:

(a) Cost basis.

(b) Cost or market, whichever is lower.

For federal income tax purposes either basis is acceptable as long as it is consistently followed.

Inventories at Cost. In the case of a merchant, cost means the inventory price of goods on hand at the beginning of the year and the cost of merchandise purchased since the beginning of the year. The cost of merchandise purchased is the invoice price plus transportation or other necessary charges incurred in acquiring possession of the goods. The usual practice is to deduct trade discounts and to use the net invoice price. Cash discounts for early payment usually are not deducted from the invoice price.

In the case of a manufacturer, cost has the same meaning when applied to raw materials as it has when applied to merchandise by a merchant. When applied to either goods in process or to finished goods, cost means (a) the cost of raw materials and supplies entering into or being consumed in production, (b) expenditures for direct labor, and (c) indirect expenses incurred in the manufacturing process. Indirect expenses include a reasonable proportion of management expenses, but should not include any cost of selling the product. The cost of finished goods, therefore, is the actual production cost of the goods when fully manufactured and ready for sale. The cost of goods in process is the actual cost of the raw materials plus the cost of the direct labor and the indirect expenses applicable to goods in the process of being manufactured at the end of the year or at the time of taking the inventory.

Without the use of cost accounting procedures, it may be difficult to determine the costs that relate to the goods that are in process. The difficulty may be insurmountable if the company has a large number of different products in various stages of completion at the end of the period. There usually is no difficulty in determining the total cost of raw materials and direct labor used, as well as the total manufacturing expenses incurred during the period. The problem is to allocate or apportion these costs and expenses between the goods completed during the period and the goods in process at the end of the period. Often the assignment of costs involves a considerable element of estimation, especially with respect to the degree of completion of unfinished products.

Considerable accuracy is attainable in some cases, however. The nature of the product and the method of manufacture or processing may make it possible to compute the cost of the materials and the direct labor that have gone into the goods that have been finished and into those that are incomplete at the end of the period. The manufacturing expenses may be apportioned on some reasonable basis. Sometimes they are allocated in proportion to direct labor. For example, suppose that the accounts of a manufacturer disclose the following information relative to a year just ended:

Cost of goods in process, first of year	$12,000
Cost of raw materials used during year	40,000
Direct labor for year	60,000
Manufacturing expenses for year	42,000

Manufacturing expenses amounted to 70 per cent of direct labor ($42,000 ÷ $60,000). If it was determined that $8,000 was the cost of direct labor in the goods in process at the end of the year, it might be reasonable to consider that $5,600 (70% of $8,000) of the manufacturing expenses related to those goods. If $9,000 was determined to be the cost of raw materials in the incomplete goods, the allocation of all of these costs and expenses between finished and unfinished goods would be as follows:

	TOTAL	COST APPORTIONED TO	
		GOODS FINISHED DURING YEAR	ENDING INVEN-TORY OF GOODS IN PROCESS
Opening Inventory of Goods in Process	12,000	12,000	.....
Materials used	40,000	31,000	9,000
Direct labor	60,000	52,000	8,000
Manufacturing expenses	42,000	36,400 (1)	5,600 (2)
	154,000	131,400	22,600

(1) 70% of $52,000
(2) 70% of $ 8,000

There is a special problem involved in calculating the cost of an inventory if several lots of identical goods or materials have been purchased at different prices at different times during the period. This problem sometimes confronts both merchants and manufacturers. Often there is no way of knowing the specific cost of the items that have been sold or used and the specific cost of the unsold or unused items that are on hand at the end of the period. Similarly, it may not be possible to know the exact cost of the materials that are a part of the goods in process or finished goods inventories.

In the case of goods or materials included in an inventory that cannot be identified in relation to specific invoices or cost records, the *first-in, first-out* rule (frequently referred to as the Fifo method) is usually applied. This rule is based upon the presumption that the goods first purchased or produced were the ones first used or sold and that the goods on hand are the ones most recently purchased or produced.

In some cases, the *last-in, first-out* rule (often called the Lifo method) is applied. Under this method, goods on hand at the close of the accounting period are treated as being: (a) those included in the inventory at the beginning of the period in the order of acquisition plus, perhaps, (b) those acquired during the period, also in the order of acquisition.

In times of changing prices, the two methods may give different results. In some cases, costs are averaged for the purpose of inventory valuation.

Inventories at Cost or Market, Whichever is Lower. Under ordinary circumstances, the term "market," as used in relation to inventories, means the current bid price prevailing at the date of the inventory for the particular merchandise in the volume in which it is usually purchased. Where the inventory is valued on the basis of cost or market, whichever is lower, the market value of each article on hand should be compared with the cost of the article and the lower of such values should be taken as the inventory value of the article. In certain situations it is proper to use the lower of either the total cost of all items in the inventory or the total market value of all the items.

When the "cost or market, whichever is lower" rule is applied to the goods in process and finished goods inventories of a manufacturer, the term "market" has to be specially interpreted. Usually there is no market in which he could purchase either partly or wholly finished goods exactly like those that he manufactures. Instead of market, *cost to replace* must be used. The rule becomes "cost or cost to replace, whichever is lower." Cost to replace may have to be estimated. Sometimes the cost of the latest lot of goods finished can be used as a measure. If there has been no change in any of the cost elements since such goods were completed, their unit cost may be considered as the unit cost to replace.

To illustrate the application of the rule, assume that a manufacturer has 3,000 units of Product A on hand at the end of the period. On the basis of first-in, first-out, 1,200 of the items cost $1 each and 1,800 units just completed cost 90 cents each. Further assume that there has been no change in the prices of raw materials, rates of labor, or other expense elements since the last lot of goods was completed. Thus, it would be proper to consider that the replacement cost is 90 cents per unit or $2,700 for the 3,000 units. The cost of this inventory was $2,820 (1,200 items at $1 plus 1,800 at 90 cents). The manufacturer would consider $2,700 to be the value of the inventory if he were following the "cost or cost to replace, whichever is lower" rule. If replacement cost had been higher, he would use cost. If there had been a recent change in the prices of raw materials, the rates of labor, or the items of manufacturing expense, the latest actual costs could not be used as a measure of replacement cost. The manufacturer would have to estimate what the cost to replace would be under the new conditions.

The practice of valuing inventories on the basis of the rule of cost or replacement cost, whichever is lower, has been widely followed. The popularity of this rule stems from the fact that it is conservative. The use of the rule results in the recognition of losses in the periods in which values have fallen rather than when the goods are sold.

Book Inventories. A *book inventory*, sometimes called a perpetual or running inventory, is a continuous record of the amount of materials or goods on hand. This type of record is a useful device for control. Merchants and manufacturers like to know the quantity and the cost of goods on hand at all times without the delay incident to taking stock. If they feel that such information is worth the extra bookkeeping expense that it entails, they will maintain book inventories.

When a book inventory of raw materials is kept, there is no raw materials purchases account in the ledger. Instead, all such purchases are debited to the raw materials inventory account. A record must be kept of the quantity and the cost of all materials used or returned. This amount is credited to the raw materials inventory account. After all posting has been completed, the balance of the account shows the cost of the goods that are presumed to be on hand.

Usually the raw materials inventory account controls a subsidiary ledger, called a *stores ledger*. This ledger has an account (frequently in the form of a card) for each type of material. The card shows the quantity and the cost of materials received, the quantity and the cost of materials issued, and the resulting balance. The postings to these accounts are kept up to date so that reference to the card for each type of material will show the quantity and the cost of the item on hand at that time. Often the form of the stores ledger cards (accounts) includes a memorandum column in which to record the quantity of goods ordered but not yet received.

Unless a manufacturer has a suitable cost accounting system, it is not likely that he will be able to have a book inventory of goods in process. Without cost accounting it usually is difficult to keep an accurate book inventory of finished goods, though this may be possible under certain circumstances. In some cases, records of raw materials, goods in process, and finished goods are kept in terms of quantities alone. When the record is in this form, it is purely supplementary and there is no control account; nevertheless, this type of record may be helpful in inventory control.

The use of book inventories does not eliminate the necessity for periodically making a count of the materials or goods on hand. The book inventory shows what should be on hand. The record may be wrong in that errors may have been made or goods may have been lost, destroyed, or stolen. Some types of goods are subject to physical shrinkage. At least once a year a physical inventory should be taken. If the quantity of goods on hand is found to be more or less than the quantity shown by the inventory records, an adjustment of the accounts is needed. For example, if the balance of the raw materials inventory account showed the cost of goods on hand to be $8,000 but a costing of the goods found to be on hand by physical count totaled only $7,500, an adjusting entry would be needed debiting Manufacturing Summary and crediting Raw Materials Inventory for $500. The discovery of an overage or a shortage of finished goods would require an adjustment to the income summary account.

When book inventories are maintained, it is not necessary to take an inventory of everything at the same time. One particular type of goods can be counted and the finding compared with the stores or stock card for that item. Another type can be inventoried at a different time. Adjustments can be made as shortages or overages are discovered. In such cases, inventory over and short accounts can be used. They are closed at the end of the period. Some large companies have the inventorying process going on continuously.

PRACTICE ASSIGNMENT No. 51. Complete Report No. 51 in the workbook and submit your working papers for approval. Continue with the following study assignment until Report No. 52 is required.

(52) THE CHART OF ACCOUNTS AND RECORDS OF A MANUFACTURER

The chart of accounts of The King Manufacturing Co. is reproduced on the following page. The King Manufacturing Co. is a small manufacturing concern whose operations are confined to manufacturing and selling a single product. No merchandise is purchased for resale in its original form. The company does not have a cost accounting system nor does it keep book inventories. The costs attached to the inventories of raw materials and finished goods are calculated on the basis of a physical count made at the end of each fiscal period. The cost of the inventory of goods in process is estimated.

There is a similarity in the titles of certain manufacturing expense, administrative expense, and selling expense accounts. For example, there are three depreciation expense accounts, including Depreciation of Factory Property, Account No. 745, Depreciation of Office Property, Account No. 814, and Depreciation of Delivery Equipment, Account No. 835. It is necessary to classify such expenses by recording them in appropriate accounts so that the proper information may be set forth in the annual reports. Obviously, depreciation of factory property is a manufacturing expense, while depreciation of office property is an administrative expense, and depreciation of delivery equipment is a selling expense. Taxes and insurance on property must also be apportioned among the proper expense accounts.

Ledgers. While all of the accounts shown in the chart of accounts of The King Manufacturing Co. might be kept in one general ledger, it has been found advantageous to keep the accounts with customers, the accounts with manufacturing expenses, and the accounts with stockholders in subsidiary ledgers with control accounts in the general ledger. Following are the names of the subsidiary ledgers and the titles of the control accounts that are kept in the general ledger:

Subsidiary Ledgers	Control Accounts
Accounts Receivable Ledger	133 Accounts Receivable
Manufacturing Expense Ledger	74 Manufacturing Expenses
Stockholders' Ledger	51 Capital Stock

The King Manufacturing Co. uses a balance-column account form in the general ledger, accounts receivable ledger, and manufacturing expense ledger. The account form used differs slightly from that previously

(*Continued on page 645*)

THE KING MANUFACTURING CO.

CHART OF ACCOUNTS

I Current Assets

  11 Cash

    111 First National Bank
    112 Petty Cash Fund

  12 Government Bonds

  13 Receivables

    131 Notes Receivable
    132 Accrued Interest Receivable
    133 Accounts Receivable
      013 Allowance for Bad Debts

  16 Inventories

    161 Raw Materials
    162 Goods in Process
    163 Finished Goods

  18 Supplies and Prepayments

    181 Office Supplies
    182 Advertising Supplies
    183 Factory Supplies
    184 Prepaid Insurance

II Fixed Assets

  21 Office Equipment
    021 Allow. for Depr. of Office Equip.
  22 Delivery Equipment
    022 Allow. for Depr. of Del. Equip.
  23 Factory Equipment
    023 Allow. for Depr. of Fcty. Equip.
  24 Building
    024 Allow. for Depr. of Building
  25 Land
  26 Intangibles
    261 Patents

III Current Liabilities

  31 Social Security Taxes Payable

    311 F.I.C.A. Taxes Payable
    312 F.U.T.A. Taxes Payable
    313 State U.C. Taxes Payable
  32 Employees' Income Taxes Payable
  33 Corporation Income Taxes Payable
  34 Notes Payable
  35 Accrued Interest Payable
  36 Vouchers Payable
  37 Dividends Payable
  38 Accrued Property Taxes Payable

IV Fixed Liabilities

  41 Mortgages Payable
  42 Bonds Payable

V Capital

  51 Capital Stock
  52 Retained Earnings
  53 Income Summary

VI Income

  61 Income from Sales

    611 Sales
      0611 Sales Returns and Allow.
      0621 Cost of Goods Sold

  63 Other Income

    631 Interest Income
    632 Purchases Discount

VII Manufacturing Costs

  71 Raw Material Purchases
    071 Raw Material Returns and Allow.
  72 Transportation In
  73 Direct Labor
  74 Manufacturing Expenses
    741 Indirect Labor
    742 Utilities Expense
    743 Factory Supplies Consumed
    744 Factory Building Maintenance
    745 Depr. of Factory Property
    746 Expired Ins. on Factory Prop.
    747 Factory Repairs
    748 Patent Expense
    749 Taxes on Factory Property
    750 Social Security Taxes — Factory
    751 General Factory Expenses
  76 Manufacturing Summary

VIII Operating Expenses

  81 Administrative Expenses

    811 Office Salaries
    812 Officers' Salaries
    813 Office Supplies Consumed
    814 Depr. of Office Property
    815 Expired Ins. on Office Property
    816 Taxes on Office Property
    817 S. S. Taxes — Administrative
    818 General Office Expenses

  83 Selling Expenses

    831 Sales Salaries
    832 Traveling Expense
    833 Advertising Expense
    834 Delivery Expense
    835 Depr. of Delivery Equipment
    836 Expired Ins. on Delivery Equip.
    837 Bad Debts Expense
    838 Expired Ins. on Finished Goods
    839 Taxes on Delivery Equipment
    840 Social Security Taxes — Sales
    841 General Selling Expenses

IX Other Charges

  91 Interest Expense
  92 Sales Discount
  93 Charitable Contributions
  94 Corporation Income Taxes

NOTE: Items set in *italics* indicate classification; they are not account titles.

introduced in this textbook. It is illustrated below. A few items have already been posted to illustrate the proper use of the form. This account form is especially well suited for general ledger use because it provides a means of indicating whether the balance of each account is a debit balance or a credit balance. This is important because some general ledger accounts normally have debit balances, while other accounts normally have credit balances. The Description column is seldom used; however, it may be used for writing an explanation of the entry for any unusual transaction. For example, in the illustration the word "Balance" is inserted in the Description column to explain that the entry on January 1 represents the balance of the account which has been brought forward from another page. The notation "90-day note" is an explanation of the entry of January 27. It signifies that a customer has been given credit for a note tendered with a view to obtaining an extension of time on his account. A Check ($\sqrt{}$) column is provided immediately following each amount column for checking purposes.

When this account form is used in an accounts receivable ledger it is customary to extend the balance following each entry. This is done because of the need for credit information in handling current sales on account. When this account form is used in a general ledger or in a manufacturing expense ledger, the balance need be extended only at the end of each month or when taking a trial balance. The procedure is as follows:

(1) Foot the Debits and Credits amount columns.
(2) Compute the new balance.
(3) Enter the new balance in the Balance column.

ACCOUNT   *Accounts Receivable*   ACCOUNT NO. *133*

DATE 19--		DESCRIPTION	FOLIO	DEBITS	$\sqrt{}$	CREDITS	$\sqrt{}$	DR. OR CR.	BALANCE	$\sqrt{}$
Jan.	1	Balance	$\sqrt{}$					Dr.	16668 17	
	12		GJ31			23 50				
	12		GJ31			357 15				
	21		GJ32			8 25				
	27	90-day note	GJ36			1000 00				
	31		S44	25576 09						
	31		C47			19771 96		Dr.	21083 40	
						21160 86				

When entering the balance, the abbreviation Dr. or Cr. should be inserted in the column preceding the Balance column as illustrated. After all posting has been completed, the balance of the control account for Accounts Receivable, Account No. 133, may be proved by preparing a schedule of accounts receivable from the information provided in the subsidiary ledger. The balance of the control account for Manufacturing Expenses, Account No. 74, may be proved by preparing a schedule of the manufacturing expenses from the information provided in the subsidiary ledger.

The stockholders' ledger used by The King Manufacturing Co. is of the same design as the account illustrated on page 552. This account differs from other account forms in that it does not provide any information as to the value of the shares owned by each stockholder; instead, it provides information as to the number of shares owned. The control account for the stockholders' ledger is Capital Stock, Account No. 51. The control account shows the total par value or stated value of the stock issued. The balance of the control account may be proved by preparing a schedule of the shares issued to stockholders from the information provided in the stockholders' ledger and multiplying the total number of shares issued by the par value or stated value of each share.

Since The King Manufacturing Co. uses the voucher system of accounting, a subsidiary accounts payable ledger is not kept. The voucher register not only supplants a purchases journal, but it also provides information regarding vouchered liabilities. Further detail can be secured by maintaining files of unpaid and paid invoices. The management of the company feels that the voucher register and these files provide all of the information needed with respect to transactions with creditors.

Journals. The number, the nature, and the variety of the transactions of The King Manufacturing Co. warrant the use of the following journals:

(a) Voucher register.
(b) Sales record.
(c) Record of cash receipts.
(d) Check register.
(e) General journal.

The forms of the voucher register and the check register used by this company are similar to those illustrated on page 625. A sales record with the following amount columns is used:

General Ledger Dr.
Accounts Receivable Dr.
Sales Cr.
General Ledger Cr.

It is not necessary to provide for the recording of sales taxes as a manufacturing firm is not subject to retail sales taxes. The nature of the business of The King Manufacturing Co. is such that no federal excise taxes are imposed on its products; hence, there was no need to provide for the recording of either sales taxes or federal excise taxes in the sales record. Neither was there any need for providing for a departmental distribution of sales.

A cash receipts record with the following amount columns is used:

General Ledger Dr.
Sales Discount Dr.
Bank Dr.
Accounts Receivable Cr.
Cash Sales Cr.
General Ledger Cr.

There is no need for providing for a departmental distribution of cash sales.

The company uses a general journal with three amount columns. The first of these columns is used to record amounts to be posted to subsidiary ledger accounts. The second and the third columns are used to record amounts to be debited and credited to general ledger accounts. The use of this form of journal is discussed on page 663 and illustrated on pages 664–668.

It must be understood that the types and the forms of journals and subsidiary ledgers used in keeping the financial records of a business are determined by such factors as the nature of the undertaking, the volume of business done, the amount of information required by the management, the number of employees required to keep the records, etc. It is important to keep in mind that all transactions should be recorded in some book of original entry or journal. The use of special columns facilitates the classification of the desired information and saves time in posting. Timesaving is important, for accounting is one of the operating expenses of a business and it can be unduly expensive if the accounting department is not efficiently organized and if a sound accounting system is not maintained.

Auxiliary Records. It has been noted at several points in this course that various auxiliary records are usually kept by businesses. These are supplementary to the journals and ledgers. Such auxiliary records may include the following:

(a) Petty cash disbursements record.
(b) Fixed assets record.
(c) Insurance policy register.
(d) Notes receivable register.
(e) Notes payable register.
(f) Payroll record.
(g) Employees' earnings record.

The purpose of auxiliary records is to supply the detailed information needed in the operations of an enterprise. For example, the fixed assets record should provide a detailed record of office equipment, delivery equipment, factory equipment, and buildings owned; showing date acquired, cost, rate of depreciation, and total amount of accumulated depreciation. The insurance policy register should provide a detailed record of all insurance policies carried, with provision for distributing the premium uniformly over the life of each policy. This information will facilitate the recording of the expired insurance with a proper classification of the insurance expense. The preparation and maintenance of formal payrolls and employees' earnings records is mandatory for companies subject to the requirements of the Federal Fair Labor Standards Act (the wages and hours law) and the social security laws.

It may be assumed that The King Manufacturing Co. keeps most, if not all, of the auxiliary records listed. Since this company does not keep any type of book inventories, it does not have formal subsidiary stores and stock ledgers, or even auxiliary records that show only the physical quantities of the materials and goods on hand.

PRACTICE ASSIGNMENT No. 52. Complete Report No. 52 in the workbook and submit your working papers for approval. Continue with the next study assignment in Unit Twenty-eight until Report No. 53 is required.

ACCOUNTING
FOR MANUFACTURERS (Concluded)

(53) THE WORK SHEET OF A MANUFACTURER

The procedure in preparing the financial statements for a corporation engaged in manufacturing is similar to that for a mercantile enterprise. The statements may be prepared monthly, quarterly, semiannually, or annually. Most accountants use a work sheet as a means of summarizing and classifying the information needed in preparing the income statement, the manufacturing statement, and the balance sheet. The required adjustments of the general ledger accounts are made on the work sheet, but usually these entries are not recorded in the accounts unless the books are to be closed. Most companies close their books at the end of the year only, at which time the adjusting entries are journalized and posted to the proper accounts. The procedure in preparing the work sheet is much the same whether the statements are being prepared monthly or annually. The discussion in this unit relates to the preparation of annual statements.

A twelve-column work sheet prepared for The King Manufacturing Co. for the year ended December 31 is shown on pages 650 and 651. This work sheet is designed to provide the information needed (a) in preparing an income statement for the year ended December 31, (b) in preparing a manufacturing statement for the year ended December 31, (c) in preparing a balance sheet as of December 31, (d) in journalizing the adjusting entries required to bring the general ledger accounts into agreement with the statements as of December 31, (e) in journalizing the entries required to close the temporary accounts as of December 31, and (f) in journalizing the entries required to reverse the adjusting entries for accruals as of January 1, the beginning of a new fiscal year.

Trial Balance. The first pair of amount columns contains the trial balance figures. The purpose of the trial balance is to ascertain that the totals of the debit and the credit balances of the accounts are equal.

Adjusting Entries. The second pair of amount columns contains the entries required to adjust the general ledger account balances.

(Continued on page 652)

THE KING MANUFACTURING CO.
Work Sheet for the Year Ended December 31, 19--

Accounts	No.	Trial Balance Dr.	Trial Balance Cr.	Adjustments Dr.	Adjustments Cr.	Adjusted Trial Balance Dr.	Adjusted Trial Balance Cr.	Manufacturing Dr.	Manufacturing Cr.	Income Statement Dr.	Income Statement Cr.	Balance Sheet Dr.	Balance Sheet Cr.
First National Bank	111	10407 03				10407 03						10407 03	
Petty Cash Fund	112	100 00				100 00						100 00	
Government Bonds	12	5000 00				5000 00						5000 00	
Notes Receivable	131	2448 50				2448 50						2448 50	
Accrued Interest Rec.	132			(g) 24 46		24 46						24 46	
Accounts Receivable	133	19552 90				19552 90						19552 90	
Allow. for Bad Debts	013		491 06		(r) 455 29		946 35						946 35
Raw Materials Inv.	161	12774 47		(d) 12248 16	(a) 12774 47	12248 16						12248 16	
Goods in Process Inv.	162	2216 22		(e) 1986 28	(b) 2216 22	1986 28						1986 28	
Finished Goods Inv.	163	14819 62		(f) 14327 63	(c) 14819 62	14327 63						14327 63	
Office Supplies	181	302 67			(j) 228 57	74 10						74 10	
Advertising Supplies	182	250 00			(k) 175 00	75 00						75 00	
Factory Supplies	183	409 94			(l) 335 04	74 90						74 90	
Prepaid Insurance	184	707 90			(q) 329 27	378 63						378 63	
Office Equipment	21	2950 00				2950 00						2950 00	
Allow. for Depr. of O. E.	021		965 00		(m) 295 00		1260 00						1260 00
Delivery Equipment	22	2600 00				2600 00						2600 00	
Allow. for Depr. of D. E.	022		1400 00		(n) 650 00		2050 00						2050 00
Factory Equipment	23	29000 00				29000 00						29000 00	
Allow. for Depr. of F. E.	023		3900 00		(o) 2900 00		6800 00						6800 00
Building	24	40000 00				40000 00						40000 00	
Allow. for Depr. of Bldg.	024		7700 00		(p) 800 00		8500 00						8500 00
Land	25	5000 00				5000 00						5000 00	
Patents	261	1200 00			(s) 300 00	900 00						900 00	
F.I.G.A. Taxes Pay.	311		194 80				194 80						194 80
F.U.T.A. Taxes Pay.	312		155 84				155 84						155 84
State U.C. Taxes Pay.	313		350 65				350 65						350 65
Emp. Inc. Taxes Pay.	32		462 28				462 28						462 28
Corp. Inc. Taxes Pay.	33				(t) 7272 14		7272 14						7272 14
Notes Payable	34		15171 89				15171 89						15171 89
Accrued Interest Pay.	35				(h) 175 00		175 00						175 00
Vouchers Payable	36		14370 43				14370 43						14370 43
Dividends Payable	37		1450 00				1450 00						1450 00
Accrued Prop. Taxes Pay.	38				(i) 1080 00		1080 00						1080 00
Mortgages Payable	41		14000 00				14000 00						14000 00
Capital Stock	51		29000 00				29000 00						29000 00
Retained Earnings	52		26939 89				26939 89						26939 89
Sales	611		115723 94				115723 94				115723 94		
Sales Returns and Allow.	0611	437 74				437 74				437 74			
Interest Income	631		66 65		(g) 24 46		91 11				91 11		

Twelve-column work sheet (concluded):

Account	No.	Trial Balance Dr	Trial Balance Cr	Adjustments Dr	Adjustments Cr	Adjusted Trial Balance Dr	Adjusted Trial Balance Cr	Cost of Goods Mfd Dr	Cost of Goods Mfd Cr	Income Statement Dr	Income Statement Cr	Balance Sheet Dr	Balance Sheet Cr
Purchases Discount	632		393 04				393 04		393 04				
Raw Material Purchases	071	13555 75				13555 75		13555 75					
Raw Material R. and A.	071		238 03				238 03		238 03				
Transportation In	072	1159 34				1159 34		1159 34					
Direct Labor	073	1829147				1829147		1829147					
Manufacturing Expenses	74	5862 62		756 00 (i); 335 04 (l); 2900 00 (o); 700 00 (p); 188 40 (q); 300 00 (s)		11042 06		11042 06					
Office Salaries	811	6004 40				6004 40				6004 40			
Officers' Salaries	812	18400 00				18400 00				18400 00			
Office Supplies Consumed	813			228 57 (j)		228 57				228 57			
Depr. of Office Prop.	814			100 00 (p); 295 00 (m)		395 00				395 00			
Exp. Ins. on Office Prop.	815			56 95 (q)		56 95				56 95			
Taxes on Office Prop.	816			216 00 (j)		216 00				216 00			
S. S. Taxes — Adm.	817	1281 23				1281 23				1281 23			
General Office Expenses	818	113 99				113 99				113 99			
Sales Salaries	831	6891 85				6891 85				6891 85			
Traveling Expense	832	1530 00				1530 00				1530 00			
Advertising Expense	833	2300 00		175 00 (k)		2475 00				2475 00			
Delivery Expense	834	3010 19				3010 19				3010 19			
Depr. of Delivery Equip.	835			650 00 (n)		650 00				650 00			
Exp. Ins. on Del. Equip.	836			40 94 (q)		40 94				40 94			
Bad Debts Expense	837			455 29 (r)		455 29				455 29			
Exp. Ins. on Fin. Goods	838			42 98 (q)		42 98				42 98			
Taxes on Del. Equipment	839			108 00 (i)		108 00				108 00			
S. S. Taxes — Sales	840	361 82				361 82				361 82			
General Selling Expenses	841	2856 27				2856 27				2856 27			
Interest Expense	91	173 32		175 00 (h)		348 32				348 32			
Sales Discount	92	804 26				804 26				804 26			
Charitable Contributions	93	200 00				200 00				200 00			
Corporation Inc. Taxes	94			7272 14 (t)		7272 14				7272 14			
Cost of Goods Sold	0621			14327 63 (c); 12774 47 (a); 2216 22 (b)		14819 62				14819 62			
Manufacturing Summary	76			1248 16 (d); 1986 28 (e)									
		232973 50	232973 50	73392 15	73392 15	275187 46	275187 46	59039 31	59039 31	130179 27	147147 59	130535 72	130535 72
Cost of Goods Mfd									44566 84				
Net Income											16968 32		16968 32
										147147 59	147147 59	130535 72	130535 72

THE KING MANUFACTURING CO.
DATA FOR ADJUSTING THE ACCOUNTS
DECEMBER 31, 19--

Inventories:

Raw materials..		$12,248.16
Goods in process...		1,986.28
Finished goods...		14,327.63

Accruals:

Accrued interest receivable................................		24.46
Accrued interest payable..................................		175.00
Accrued property taxes payable:		
On factory property (70%)........................	$756.00	
On office property (20%).........................	216.00	
On delivery equipment (10%)....................	108.00	1,080.00

Office supplies consumed......................................		228.57
Advertising supplies consumed..............................		175.00
Factory supplies consumed.................................		335.04
Depreciation of office equipment, 10%.....................		295.00
Depreciation of delivery equipment, 25%..................		650.00
Depreciation of factory equipment, 10%...................		2,900.00
Depreciation of building, 2%:		
$7/8$ charged to factory............................	$700.00	
$1/8$ charged to office............................	100.00	800.00

Insurance expired:

On factory property.................................	$188.40	
On office property.................................	56.95	
On delivery equipment.............................	40.94	
On finished goods..................................	42.98	329.27

Provision for bad debts, $1/2$% of credit sales.....................		455.29
Amortization of patents.......................................		300.00
Provision for corporation income taxes........................		7,272.14

The quantities of raw materials and finished goods on hand at the end of the year were determined by actual count and their cost was calculated on a first-in, first-out basis. Since a cost accounting system was not maintained, the cost of the goods in process at the end of the year was estimated.

Before recording the new or year-end inventories on the work sheet, the old or beginning inventories were transferred to the proper summary accounts. The old inventories of raw materials, $12,774.47, and goods in process, $2,216.22, were transferred to Manufacturing Summary, Account No. 76 (adjustments *a* and *b*). The old inventory of finished goods, $14,819.62, was transferred to Cost of Goods Sold, Account No. 0621 (adjustment *c*). The new inventories of raw materials, $12,248.16, and goods in process, $1,986.28, were recorded by debiting the proper inventory accounts and by crediting Manufacturing Summary (adjustments *d* and *e*). The new inventory of finished goods, $14,327.63, was recorded by debiting Finished Goods Inventory, Account No. 163, and by crediting Cost of Goods Sold (adjustment *f*).

The accrued interest receivable, amounting to $24.46 at the end of the year, was ascertained by computing the interest accrued on notes receivable and government bonds owned. The amount accrued was entered on the work sheet by debiting Accrued Interest Receivable, Account No. 132, and by crediting Interest Income, Account No. 631 (adjustment *g*).

The accrued interest payable, amounting to $175 at the end of the year, was ascertained by computing the interest accrued on notes payable and mortgages payable. The amount accrued was entered on the work sheet by debiting Interest Expense, Account No. 91, and by crediting Accrued Interest Payable, Account No. 35 (adjustment *h*).

The accrued property taxes payable at the end of the year, amounting to $1,080, was the amount assessed against the property owned on December 10. Of the total amount of the assessment, 70 per cent or $756 was chargeable to the factory, 20 per cent or $216 was chargeable to administration, and 10 per cent or $108 was chargeable to selling. These taxes were entered on the work sheet by debiting Manufacturing Expenses, Account No. 74, (because the account for taxes on factory property is kept in the subsidiary manufacturing expense ledger) for $756; debiting Taxes on Office Property, Account No. 816, for $216; and debiting Taxes on Delivery Equipment, Account No. 839, for $108; and by crediting Accrued Property Taxes Payable, Account No. 38, for the total, $1,080 (adjustment *i*).

The cost of office, advertising, and factory supplies consumed during the year was ascertained by making a physical count of the supplies of each type that were on hand at the end of the year, ascertaining their cost, and subtracting the amounts of these inventories from the balances of the accounts with Office Supplies, Account No. 181, Advertising Supplies, Account No. 182, and Factory Supplies, Account No. 183. Office Supplies Consumed, Account No. 813, was debited for $228.57, the cost of the office supplies used. Advertising Expense, Account No. 833, was debited for $175, the cost of the advertising supplies consumed. Manufacturing Expenses, Account No. 74, was debited for $335.04, the cost of the factory supplies consumed (because the account for factory supplies consumed is kept in the manufacturing expense subsidiary ledger). The proper supplies account was credited in each case (adjustments *j*, *k*, and *l*).

The depreciation of office equipment, $295, was recorded by debiting Depreciation of Office Property, Account No. 814, and by crediting Allowance for Depreciation of Office Equipment, Account No. 021 (adjustment *m*). The depreciation of delivery equipment, $650, was recorded by debiting Depreciation of Delivery Equipment, Account No. 835, and by crediting Allowance for Depreciation of Delivery Equipment, Account No. 022 (adjustment *n*). The depreciation of factory property account is kept in the manufacturing expense subsidiary ledger; hence, factory depreciation of $2,900 was debited to Manufacturing Expenses, Account No. 74, and credited to Allowance for Depreciation of Factory Equipment, Account No. 023 (adjustment *o*). The depreciation of the building was distributed on the basis of $7/8$ to manufacturing and $1/8$ to administration. The amount chargeable to manufacturing, $700, was debited to Manufacturing Expenses, Account No. 74. The portion chargeable to administration, $100, was debited to Depreciation of Office Property, Account No. 814. The sum of the two amounts was credited to Allowance for Depreciation of Building, Account No. 024 (adjustment *p*).

The amount of the insurance expired during the year was ascertained from the insurance policy register. Separate expense accounts are kept for the insurance expired on each kind of property. The expired insurance on factory property, $188.40, was debited to Manufacturing Expenses, Account No. 74 (because the expired insurance on factory property account is kept in the subsidiary ledger). The expired insurance on office property, $56.95, was debited to Expired Insurance on Office Property, Account No. 815. The expired insurance on delivery equipment, $40.94, was debited to Expired Insurance on Delivery Equipment, Account No. 836. The expired insurance on finished goods, $42.98, was debited to Expired Insurance on Finished Goods, Account No. 838. Prepaid Insurance, Account No. 184, was credited for the total amount of insurance expired, $329.27 (adjustment *q*).

The company has been following the practice of crediting Allowance for Bad Debts, Account No. 013, at the end of each year, with an amount equal to $1/2$ per cent of the credit sales for the year. This amount was $455.29 for the year just ended. The debit was to Bad Debts Expense, Account No. 837 (adjustment *r*).

The patents were acquired five years ago by purchase at an original cost of $2,400. At the time of purchase, the patents had a remaining life of eight years, hence $1/8$ of the cost or $300 is being written off each year. This amount was recorded on the work sheet by debiting Manufacturing Expenses, Account No. 74, and by crediting Patents, Account No. 261 (adjustment *s*).

The income tax for the year just ended was estimated to be $7,272.14 on the basis of the prevailing rates. This amount was recorded on the work sheet by debiting Corporation Income Taxes, Account No. 94, and by crediting Corporation Income Taxes Payable, Account No. 33 (adjustment *t*).

Adjusted Trial Balance. The third pair of amount columns contains the adjusted balances of the accounts. In two cases, the debits and the credits to the account, rather than the resulting balance, are extended into the columns. These cases are Cost of Goods Sold, Account No. 0621, and Manufacturing Summary, Account No. 76. The debits and the credits to these accounts are beginning and ending inventories. Subsequently the inventory amounts opposite Cost of Goods Sold are extended into the Income Statement columns, and the amounts opposite Manufacturing Summary are extended into the Manufacturing columns. As a result, these columns will contain the items needed in the preparation of the manufacturing and income statements.

Manufacturing Accounts. The fourth pair of amount columns contains the balances of the accounts that will be reported in the manufacturing statement. The detailed breakdown of the elements that constitute manufacturing expenses must be obtained from the accounts in the subsidiary manufacturing expense ledger, taking into consideration the adjustments of these accounts that would not have been posted at this point. A schedule of manufacturing expenses may be prepared in the following form:

SCHEDULE OF MANUFACTURING EXPENSES

Account	No.	Unadjusted Balance, Dec. 31	Adjustment Debits	Adjusted Balance, Dec. 31
Indirect Labor...............	741	$ 2,360.00	......	$ 2,360.00
Utilities Expense.............	742	1,679.89	......	1,679.89
Factory Supplies Consumed......	743	......	$ 335.04	335.04
Factory Building Maintenance...	744	327.50	......	327.50
Depreciation of Factory Property...................	745	......	{2,900.00 700.00	3,600.00
Expired Insurance on Factory Property..................	746	......	188.40	188.40
Factory Repairs...............	747	160.00	......	160.00
Patent Expense...............	748	......	300.00	300.00
Taxes on Factory Property......	749	......	756.00	756.00
S. S. Taxes--Factory...........	750	1,084.20	......	1,084.20
General Factory Expenses.......	751	251.03	......	251.03
		$ 5,862.62	$ 5,179.44	$11,042.06

The difference between the footings of the Manufacturing columns on the work sheet represents the cost of goods manufactured during the year. In this case the amount was $44,566.84. The columns are balanced by entering that amount in the credit column. The same amount is also entered in the Income Statement Dr. column.

Income Statement. The fifth pair of amount columns contains the balances of the accounts that will be reported in the income statement. The difference between the footings of these columns represents the net income for the year after provision for corporation income taxes. In this case the amount was $16,968.32. The columns are balanced by entering that amount in the debit column. The same amount is also entered in the Balance Sheet Cr. column.

Balance Sheet. The sixth pair of columns contains the balances of the accounts that will be reported in the balance sheet. The only exception is in the case of the retained earnings account — the amount of retained earnings shown in the balance sheet will be equal to the sum of the amount shown in the work sheet plus the amount of the net income after provision for corporation income taxes. The totals of the Balance Sheet columns are equal when the amount of the net income after taxes is entered in the credit column.

PRACTICE ASSIGNMENT No. 53. Complete Report No. 53 in the workbook. Do not submit the report at this time. Since Reports Nos. 53, 54, and 55 are related, you should retain the working papers until you have completed all three reports. Continue with the next study assignment until Report No. 54 is required.

(54) *THE ANNUAL REPORT OF A MANUFACTURER*

The annual report of a corporation always includes an income statement and a balance sheet. A statement of retained earnings is usually included. If the corporation is engaged in manufacturing, it is probable that there will be a manufacturing statement also. Such other supporting schedules as are considered necessary may be included. The prime purpose of the annual report is to provide the officers of the corporation and its stockholders with information as to the financial position of the company at the end of the year and the results of operations for the year. The company's bondholders, creditors, banks, and certain taxing authorities may also be interested in the annual report. The form of the statements comprising the annual report of a corporation should conform to standard accounting practice. The nature of the business conducted and the volume of the business done by the corporation will have little or no effect upon the form of the statements. Following is a discussion of the statements comprising the annual report of The King Manufacturing Co. Most of the data in these statements were obtained from the work sheet reproduced on pages 650 and 651.

The Income Statement. The income statement of The King Manufacturing Co. for the year ended December 31 is reproduced on page 658. This statement was prepared from the data found in the Income Statement columns of the work sheet. The statement is presented in a form that shows (a) gross profit on sales, (b) net operating income, (c) net income before provision for income taxes, and (d) net income after provision for income taxes.

Interpreting the Income Statement. An analysis of the income statement of The King Manufacturing Co. shows that the gross profit on sales amounted to $70,227.37, or approximately 60 per cent of net sales. The total operating expenses amounted to $45,118.48, which was approximately 39 per cent of net sales. The net operating income of $25,108.89 was nearly 22 per cent of net sales. The net income before provision for income taxes was $24,240.46, or 21 per cent of net sales. After the provision for income taxes, the net income amounted to $16,968.32, or 14.72 per cent of net sales.

The rate of finished goods turnover was slightly over 3. This was calculated by dividing the cost of sales for the year by the average inventory of finished goods. In this case the average inventory was determined by adding the beginning and the ending inventories of finished goods and

(*Continued on page 659*)

THE KING MANUFACTURING CO.

INCOME STATEMENT

FOR THE YEAR ENDED DECEMBER 31, 19--

Operating Income:

Sales..		$115,723.94	
Less Sales Returns and Allowances.............		437.74	
Net Sales.....................................		$115,286.20	
Less Cost of Goods Sold:			
Inventory of Finished Goods, beginning of year	$14,819.62		
Plus Cost of Goods Manufactured during year...	44,566.84		
Finished Goods available for sale..............	$59,386.46		
Less Inventory of Finished Goods, end of year.	14,327.63	45,058.83	
Gross Profit on Sales.........................			$70,227.37

Operating Expenses:

Administrative Expenses:

Office Salaries..............................	$ 6,004.40		
Officers' Salaries..........................	18,400.00		
Office Supplies Consumed.....................	228.57		
Depreciation of Office Property..............	395.00		
Expired Insurance on Office Property.........	56.95		
Taxes on Office Property.....................	216.00		
Social Security Taxes--Administrative........	1,281.23		
General Office Expenses......................	113.99		
Total Administrative Expenses...............		$ 26,696.14	

Selling Expenses:

Sales Salaries..............................	$ 6,891.85		
Traveling Expense............................	1,530.00		
Advertising Expense..........................	2,475.00		
Delivery Expense.............................	3,010.19		
Depreciation of Delivery Equipment...........	650.00		
Expired Insurance on Delivery Equipment.......	40.94		
Bad Debts Expense............................	455.29		
Expired Insurance on Finished Goods..........	42.98		
Taxes on Delivery Equipment..................	108.00		
Social Security Taxes--Sales.................	361.82		
General Selling Expenses.....................	2,856.27		
Total Selling Expenses......................		18,422.34	
Total Operating Expenses......................			45,118.48
Net Operating Income..........................			$25,108.89

Other Income:

Interest Income...............................		$ 91.11	
Purchases Discount............................		393.04	
Total Other Income..........................			484.15
			$25,593.04

Other Charges:

Interest Expense..............................		$ 348.32	
Sales Discount................................		804.26	
Charitable Contributions......................		200.00	
Total Other Charges.........................			1,352.58
Net Income before provision for Income Taxes......			$24,240.46
Less Corporation Income Taxes..................			7,272.14
Net Income after provision for Income Taxes.......			$16,968.32

dividing by two. The rate of turnover indicates that the average amount invested in inventories was turned a little over three times during the year.

The Manufacturing Statement.   The manufacturing statement of The King Manufacturing Co. for the year ended December 31 is reproduced on page 660. This statement was prepared from information found in the Manufacturing columns of the work sheet reproduced on pages 650 and 651 and in the schedule of manufacturing expenses reproduced on page 655. This statement supplements the income statement. The manufacturing statement is arranged to show the three elements of manufacturing cost: (1) direct materials, (2) direct labor, and (3) manufacturing expenses. The total of these amounts, $44,336.90, is the *manufacturing cost* for the year. Of this sum, the cost of raw materials placed in process was $15,003.37, or 33.84 per cent of the total cost; direct labor was $18,291.47, or 41.26 per cent of the total cost; and manufacturing expenses were $11,042.06, or 24.90 per cent of the total. When the amount of the beginning inventory of goods in process is added and the amount of the ending inventory of goods in process is subtracted, the result is the cost of goods completed during the year.

The Balance Sheet.   The balance sheet of The King Manufacturing Co. as of December 31 is reproduced on page 661. This statement was prepared from information found in the last two columns of the work sheet. The statement is arranged in account form. Both assets and liabilities are classified as to current and fixed items. The capital elements are grouped together following the liabilities.

Interpreting the Balance Sheet.   As of December 31 the total current assets of The King Manufacturing Co. amounted to $65,751.24 and the total assets amounted to $127,591.24. The total current liabilities amounted to $40,683.03 and the total liabilities amounted to $54,683.03. The ratio of current assets to current liabilities is approximately 1.6 to 1, while the ratio of total assets to total liabilities is slightly less than $2\frac{1}{3}$ to 1. The current position of the company as indicated by the ratio of current assets to current liabilities is somewhat unsatisfactory. The total cash, government bonds, and net receivables amount to $36,586.54, while the current liabilities amount to $40,683.03. It is possible that the company may have to acquire additional working capital from some source to be able to meet its current obligations.

THE KING MANUFACTURING CO.

MANUFACTURING STATEMENT

FOR THE YEAR ENDED DECEMBER 31, 19--

Raw Materials:

Inventory, beginning of year	$12,774.47	
Purchases	13,555.75	
Transportation In	1,159.34	
	$27,489.56	
Less Returns and Allowances	238.03	
Total Cost of Available Materials	$27,251.53	
Less Inventory, end of year	12,248.16	
Cost of Materials Placed in Process during year		$15,003.37
Direct Labor		18,291.47

Manufacturing Expenses:

Indirect Labor	$ 2,360.00	
Utilities Expense	1,679.89	
Factory Supplies Consumed	335.04	
Factory Building Maintenance	327.50	
Depreciation of Factory Property	3,600.00	
Expired Insurance on Factory Property	188.40	
Factory Repairs	160.00	
Patent Expense	300.00	
Taxes on Factory Property	756.00	
Social Security Taxes--Factory	1,084.20	
General Factory Expenses	251.03	
Total Manufacturing Expenses		11,042.06
Total Manufacturing Costs incurred during year		$44,336.90
Add Inventory of Goods in Process, beginning of year		2,216.22
		$46,553.12
Less Inventory Goods in Process, end of year		1,986.28
Cost of Goods Manufactured during year		$44,566.84

The investment in fixed assets amounts to a total of $61,840, while the total capital of the corporation amounts to only $72,908.21. It is apparent, therefore, that the company should retain a rather large portion of its earnings for working capital purposes. Otherwise, it may be necessary to sell additional stock or to borrow additional funds by issuing bonds. The company's real estate is already mortgaged to the extent of $14,000 and the company's current position is not such as to encourage bankers to make short-term loans.

There are 290 shares of common capital stock outstanding with a total par value of $29,000, and a total book value of $72,908.21 or $251.41 a share. Earnings retained for use in the business amounted to $43,908.21, or $151.41 a share. At a meeting of the board of directors on December 15, a cash dividend of $5 a share was declared, payable on January 5 to stockholders of record on December 31. This dividend amounted to $1,450

(*Continued on page 662*)

THE KING MANUFACTURING CO.

BALANCE SHEET

DECEMBER 31, 19--

ASSETS

Current Assets:

Cash.............................		$10,507.03	
Government Bonds..........		5,000.00	
Notes Receivable............	$ 2,448.50		
Accrued Interest Receivable	24.46		
Accounts Receivable........	19,552.90		
	$22,025.86		
Less Allow. for Bad Debts	946.35	21,079.51	

Inventories:

Raw Materials..............	$12,248.16	
Goods in Process...........	1,986.28	
Finished Goods.............	14,327.63	28,562.07

Supplies and Prepayments:

Office Supplies.............	$ 74.10	
Advertising Supplies.......	75.00	
Factory Supplies...........	74.90	
Prepaid Insurance..........	378.63	602.63
Total Current Assets......		$ 65,751.24

Fixed Assets:

Office Equipment...........	$ 2,950.00		
Less Allowance for Depr.	1,260.00	$ 1,690.00	
Delivery Equipment........	$ 2,600.00		
Less Allowance for Depr.	2,050.00	550.00	
Factory Equipment.........	$29,000.00		
Less Allowance for Depr.	6,800.00	22,200.00	
Building..................	$40,000.00		
Less Allowance for Depr.	8,500.00	31,500.00	
Land......................		5,000.00	
Patents...................		900.00	
Total Fixed Assets........		61,840.00	
Total Assets..............		$127,591.24	

LIABILITIES

Current Liabilities:

Social Security Taxes Payable:

F.I.C.A. Taxes..	$194.80		
F.U.T.A. Taxes..	155.84		
State U. C. Taxes..	350.65	$ 701.29	
Employees' Income Taxes Pay..		462.28	
Corporation Income Taxes Pay..		7,272.14	
Notes Payable...........		15,171.89	
Accrued Interest Payable		175.00	
Vouchers Payable.......		14,370.43	
Dividends Payable.......		1,450.00	
Accrued Property Taxes Pay..		1,080.00	
Total Current Liabilities...			$ 40,683.03

Fixed Liabilities:

Mortgages Payable...........		14,000.00
Total Liabilities.............		$ 54,683.03

CAPITAL

Capital Stock (Authorized 1,000 shares) issued 290 shares.....	$29,000.00	
Retained Earnings............	43,908.21	
Total Capital...............		72,908.21
Total Liabilities and Capital...		$127,591.24

and it will be noted that it is classified as a current liability in the balance sheet.

Statement of Retained Earnings. A statement of earnings retained for use in the business by The King Manufacturing Co. is shown below. The information needed in preparing the statement was obtained in part from the account with Retained Earnings (not shown) and in part from the work sheet reproduced on pages 650 and 651. The purpose of the statement is to explain the difference between the amount of retained earnings reported in the balance sheet prepared at the end of the previous year (not shown) and the amount reported in the balance sheet as of the end of the current year (reproduced on page 661). In this case, the $15,518.32 increase in retained earnings was due to the net income for the year amounting to $16,968.32, less the cash dividend of $1,450 declared on December 15.

THE KING MANUFACTURING CO.

STATEMENT OF RETAINED EARNINGS

DECEMBER 31, 19--

Balance, January 1, beginning of year.	$28,389.89
Add: Net income for year after making provision for corporation income taxes amounting to $7,272.14.	16,968.32
	$45,358.21
Less: Cash dividend declared December 15 ($5 a share on 368 shares of capital stock outstanding).	1,450.00
Balance, December 31, end of year.	$43,908.21

PRACTICE ASSIGNMENT No. 54. Complete Report No. 54 in the workbook. Do not submit the report at this time. Since Reports Nos. 53, 54, and 55 are related, you should retain the working papers until you have completed all three reports. Continue with the next study assignment until Report No. 55 is required.

(55) *CLOSING THE BOOKS OF A MANUFACTURER*

At the end of the fiscal year the accounts should be adjusted and the temporary accounts should be closed. Some concerns adjust and close their accounts at the end of each quarter, or sometimes each month. Many businesses prepare monthly or quarterly statements (often called *interim statements*) without formally adjusting and closing their accounts. They prepare such statements by taking the needed adjustments into consideration, usually on a work sheet. At the end of the year the adjustments for the entire period are formally recorded and the temporary accounts are closed.

In some cases, the manufacturing expense accounts are adjusted at the end of each month. This is especially appropriate when a subsidiary manufacturing expense ledger is used and when monthly statements are prepared. The accountant for The King Manufacturing Co. could have followed this practice. Since monthly or quarterly statements are not prepared, however, it is felt that end-of-year adjustments are sufficient.

Adjusting the Accounts. The adjustments shown in the Adjustments columns of the work sheet are recorded in the general journal and posted to the proper general ledger and subsidiary ledger accounts. The King Manufacturing Co. uses a general journal with three amount columns. The second and the third amount columns are used to record debits and credits to general ledger accounts. The first amount column is headed "Detail" and is used to record amounts that are to be posted to subsidiary ledger accounts. The names of the subsidiary ledger accounts that are to be debited are placed immediately below the name of the general ledger control account that is to be debited. In a similar fashion, the names of subsidiary ledger accounts that are to be credited are placed just below the name of the general ledger control account that is to be credited.

The journal entries to record the adjustments as of December 31 are reproduced on pages 664 and 665. When these entries are posted, the balances in the general ledger accounts will be the same as those shown in the Adjusted Trial Balance columns of the work sheet. The total of the balances of the accounts in the manufacturing expense subsidiary ledger will be equal to the adjusted balance of the manufacturing expenses control account.

Closing the Temporary Accounts. The preparation of closing entries is facilitated by the use of the work sheet. There are four steps involved in closing the temporary accounts. These steps are discussed on page 669.

GENERAL JOURNAL

Page 14

DATE	DESCRIPTION	ACCT. NO.	DETAIL	DEBIT	CREDIT
Dec. 31	*Adjusting Entries*				
	Manufacturing Summary	76		12774 47	
	Raw Materials Inventory	161			12774 47
	Manufacturing Summary	76		2216 22	
	Goods in Process Inventory	162			2216 22
	Cost of Goods Sold	0621		14819 62	
	Finished Goods Inventory	163			14819 62
	Raw Materials Inventory	161		12248 16	
	Manufacturing Summary	76			12248 16
	Goods in Process Inventory	162		1986 28	
	Manufacturing Summary	76			1986 28
	Finished Goods Inventory	163		14327 63	
	Cost of Goods Sold	0621			14327 63
	Accrued Interest Receivable	132		24 46	
	Interest Income	631			24 46
	Interest Expense	91		175 00	
	Accrued Interest Payable	35			175 00
	Manufacturing Expenses	74		756 00	
	Taxes on Factory Property	749	756 00		
	Taxes on Office Property	816		216 00	
	Taxes on Delivery Equipment	839		108 00	
	Accrued Property Taxes Payable	38			1080 00
	Office Supplies Consumed	813		228 57	
	Office Supplies	181			228 57
	Advertising Expense	833		175 00	
	Advertising Supplies	182			175 00

Account	No.			
Manufacturing Expenses	74	335 04		
Factory Supplies Consumed	743		335 04	
Factory Supplies	183			335 04
Depreciation of Office Property	814		295 00	
Allowance for Depr. of Office Equipment	021			295 00
Depreciation of Delivery Equipment	835		650 00	
Allowance for Depr. of Delivery Equipment	022			650 00
Manufacturing Expenses	74	2900 00		
Depreciation of Factory Property	745		2900 00	
Allowance for Depr. of Factory Equipment	023			2900 00
Manufacturing Expenses	74	700 00		
Depreciation of Factory Property	745		700 00	
Depreciation of Office Property	814		100 00	
Allowance for Depreciation of Building	024			800 00
Manufacturing Expenses	74	188 40		
Expired Insurance on Factory Property	746		188 40	
Expired Insurance on Office Property	815		56 95	
Expired Insurance on Delivery Equipment	836		40 94	
Expired Insurance on Finished Goods	838		42 98	
Prepaid Insurance	184			329 27
Bad Debts Expense	837		455 29	
Allowance for Bad Debts	013			455 29
Manufacturing Expenses	74	300 00		
Patent Expense	748		300 00	
Patents	261			300 00
Corporation Income Taxes	94		7272 14	
Corporation Income Taxes Payable	33			7272 14

GENERAL JOURNAL

Page 15

DATE	✓	DESCRIPTION	ACCT. NO.	DETAIL	✓	DEBIT	✓	CREDIT	✓
		Closing Entries							
Dec. 31		Manufacturing Summary	76			44048 62	✓		
		Raw Material Purchases	71					13555 75	✓
		Transportation In	72					1159 34	✓
		Direct Labor	73					18291 47	✓
		Manufacturing Expenses	74					11042 06	✓
		Indirect Labor	741	2360 00					
		Utilities Expense	742	1679 89	✓				
		Factory Supplies Consumed	743	335 04	✓				
		Factory Building Maintenance	744	327 50	✓				
		Depreciation of Factory Property	745	3600 00	✓				
		Expired Insurance on Factory Property	746	188 40	✓				
		Factory Repairs	747	160 00	✓				
		Patent Expense	748	300 00	✓				
		Taxes on Factory Property	749	756 00	✓				
		Social Security Taxes — Factory	750	1084 20	✓				
		General Factory Expenses	751	251 03	✓				
		Raw Material Returns and Allowances	071			238 03	✓		
		Manufacturing Summary	76					238 03	✓
		Cost of Goods Sold	0621			44566 84	✓		
		Manufacturing Summary	76					44566 84	✓
		Sales	611			115723 94	✓		
		Interest Income	631			91 11	✓		
		Purchases Discount	632			393 04	✓		
		Income Summary	53					116208 09	✓

Date		Account	No.		Debit	Credit
Dec.	31	Income Summary	53	✓	99239 77	
		Sales Returns and Allowances	0611	✓		437 74
		Cost of Goods Sold	0621	✓		45058 83
		Office Salaries	811	✓		6004 40
		Officers' Salaries	812	✓		18400 00
		Office Supplies Consumed	813	✓		228 57
		Depreciation of Office Property	814	✓		395 00
		Expired Insurance on Office Property	815	✓		56 95
		Taxes on Office Property	816	✓		216 00
		Social Security Taxes — Administrative	817	✓		1281 23
		General Office Expenses	818	✓		113 99
		Sales Salaries	831	✓		6891 85
		Traveling Expense	832	✓		1530 00
		Advertising Expense	833	✓		2475 00
		Delivery Expense	834	✓		3010 19
		Depreciation of Delivery Equipment	835	✓		650 00
		Expired Insurance on Delivery Equipment	836	✓		40 94
		Bad Debts Expense	837	✓		455 29
		Expired Insurance on Finished Goods	838	✓		42 98
		Taxes on Delivery Equipment	839	✓		108 00
		Social Security Taxes — Sales	841	✓		361 82
		General Selling Expenses	842	✓		2856 27
		Interest Expense	91	✓		348 32
		Sales Discount	92	✓		804 26
		Charitable Contributions	93	✓		200 00
		Corporation Income Taxes	94	✓		7272 14
		Income Summary	53	✓	16968 32	
		Retained Earnings	52	✓		16968 32

GENERAL JOURNAL

Page 16

DATE		DESCRIPTION	ACCT. NO.	DETAIL	√	DEBIT	√	CREDIT	√
		Reversing Entries							
Jan.	1	Interest Income	681			24.46	√		
		Accrued Interest Receivable	132					24.46	√
		Accrued Interest Payable	35			175.00	√		
		Interest Expense	91					175.00	√
		Accrued Property Taxes Payable	38			1080.00	√		
		Manufacturing Expenses	71					756.00	√
		Taxes on Factory Property	749	756.00	√				
		Taxes on Office Property	816					216.00	√
		Taxes on Delivery Equipment	889					108.00	√

(1) The balances of the accounts that enter into the calculation of cost of goods manufactured are transferred to Manufacturing Summary, Account No. 76. The beginning and the ending inventories of raw materials and goods in process were entered in this account when the adjusting entries were posted. In closing, it is necessary to transfer the balances of Raw Material Purchases, Account No. 71; Raw Material Returns and Allowances, Account No. 071; Transportation In, Account No. 72; Direct Labor, Account No. 73; and Manufacturing Expenses, Account No. 74, to the manufacturing summary account.

(2) The balance of the manufacturing summary account, which is the cost of goods manufactured, is transferred to Cost of Goods Sold, Account No. 0621. Since the beginning and the ending inventories of finished goods have already been posted to this account, its balance will be the cost of goods sold during the year.

(3) The balance of the cost of goods sold account and the balances of all of the other accounts that enter into the calculation of net income are transferred to Income Summary, Account No. 53.

(4) The balance of the income summary account is transferred to Retained Earnings, Account No. 52.

The general journal entries to close the temporary accounts of The King Manufacturing Co. are reproduced on pages 666 and 667. In posting to the summary accounts, however, many accountants follow the practice of *posting in detail*. This means that they make separate debits and credits for each item that is being transferred to the summary account, rather than posting the total of several debits or credits as shown in the journal entry. Each item is labeled in the Description column of the account. This practice makes these summary accounts more informative. The manufacturing summary, cost of goods sold, and income summary accounts are reproduced on page 670 with the postings in detail.

Post-Closing Trial Balance. After all of the closing entries are posted, the accounts in the subsidiary manufacturing expense ledger and all of the temporary and summary accounts in the general ledger will be in balance. It is customary to take a trial balance of the open accounts in the general ledger at this point. If all the work has been done correctly, it will be found that the accounts have the same balances as those shown in the balance sheet. A post-closing trial balance is actually an unclassified balance sheet. The post-closing trial balance of the general ledger of The King Manufacturing Co. is reproduced on page 671.

ACCOUNT   *Income Summary*   ACCOUNT NO. 53

Date 19--		Description	Folio	Debits	√	Credits	√	Dr. or Cr.	Balance	√
Dec.	31	Sales	GJ15			115723 94				
	31	Interest Income	GJ15			91 11				
	31	Purchases Dis.	GJ15			393 04				
	31	Sales R. & A.	GJ15	437 74		116 208 09				
	31	Cost of Goods Sold	GJ15	45058 83						
	31	Office Salaries	GJ15	6004 40						
	31	Officers' Salaries	GJ15	18400 00						
	31	Office Sup. Con.	GJ15	228 57						
	31	Depr. of O. P.	GJ15	395 00						
	31	Ex. Ins. on O. P.	GJ15	56 95						
	31	Taxes on O. P.	GJ15	216 00						
	31	S. S. Taxes — Adm.	GJ15	1281 23						
	31	Gen. Office Ex.	GJ15	113 99						
	31	Sales Salaries	GJ15	6891 85						
	31	Traveling Ex.	GJ15	1530 00						
	31	Adv. Expense	GJ15	2475 00						
	31	Del. Expense	GJ15	3010 19						
	31	Depr. of D. E.	GJ15	650 00						
	31	Ex. Ins. on D. E.	GJ15	40 94						
	31	Bad Debts Ex.	GJ15	455 29						
	31	Ex. Ins. on F. G.	GJ15	42 98						
	31	Taxes on D. E.	GJ15	108 00						
	31	S. S. Taxes — Sales	GJ15	361 82						
	31	Gen. Selling Ex.	GJ15	2856 27						
	31	Interest Expense	GJ15	348 32						
	31	Sales Discount	GJ15	804 26						
	31	Char. Contributions	GJ15	200 00						
	31	Income Taxes	GJ15	7272 14				Cr.	16968 32	
				99239 77						
	31	Ret. Earnings	GJ15	16968 32				—0—		

ACCOUNT   *Cost of Goods Sold*   ACCOUNT NO. 0621

Dec.	31	F. G. Inv., beg.	GJ14	14819 62						
	31	F. G. Inv., end.	GJ14			14327 63				
	31	Mfg. Summary	GJ15	44566 84				Dr.	45058 83	
				59386 46						
	31	Income Summary	GJ15			45058 83		—0—		

ACCOUNT   *Manufacturing Summary*   ACCOUNT NO. 76

Dec.	31	R. M. Inv., beg.	GJ14	12774 47						
	31	G. in P. Inv., beg.	GJ14	2216 22						
	31	R. M. Inv., end.	GJ14			12248 16				
	31	G. in P. Inv., end.	GJ14			1986 28				
	31	R. M. Purchases	GJ15	13555 75						
	31	Transportation In	GJ15	1159 34						
	31	Direct Labor	GJ15	18291 47						
	31	Mfg. Expenses	GJ15	11042 06						
				59039 81						
	31	R. M. R. & A.	GJ15			238 03		Dr.	44566 84	
						14472 47				
	31	Cost of Goods Sold	GJ15			44566 84		—0—		

THE KING MANUFACTURING CO.

POST-CLOSING TRIAL BALANCE

DECEMBER 31, 19--

First National Bank	111	$ 10,407.03	
Petty Cash Fund	112	100.00	
Government Bonds	12	5,000.00	
Notes Receivable	131	2,448.50	
Accrued Interest Receivable	132	24.46	
Accounts Receivable	133	19,552.90	
Allowance for Bad Debts	013		$ 946.35
Raw Materials Inventory	161	12,248.16	
Goods in Process Inventory	162	1,986.28	
Finished Goods Inventory	163	14,327.63	
Office Supplies	181	74.10	
Advertising Supplies	182	75.00	
Factory Supplies	183	74.90	
Prepaid Insurance	184	378.63	
Office Equipment	21	2,950.00	
Allowance for Depreciation of Office Equipment	021		1,260.00
Delivery Equipment	22	2,600.00	
Allowance for Depreciation of Delivery Equipment.	022		2,050.00
Factory Equipment	23	29,000.00	
Allowance for Depreciation of Factory Equipment..	023		6,800.00
Building	24	40,000.00	
Allowance for Depreciation of Building	024		8,500.00
Land	25	5,000.00	
Patents	261	900.00	
F.I.C.A. Taxes Payable	311		194.80
F.U.T.A. Taxes Payable	312		155.84
State U.C. Taxes Payable	313		350.65
Employees' Income Taxes Payable	32		462.28
Corporation Income Taxes Payable	33		7,272.14
Notes Payable	34		15,171.89
Accrued Interest Payable	35		175.00
Vouchers Payable	36		14,370.43
Dividends Payable	37		1,450.00
Accrued Property Taxes Payable	38		1,080.00
Mortgages Payable	41		14,000.00
Capital Stock	51		29,000.00
Retained Earnings	52		43,908.21
		$147,147.59	$147,147.59

Reversing Entries. The accountant for The King Manufacturing Co. follows the usual practice of reversing the adjusting entries for accruals after closing the books at the end of each year. This practice facilitates the recording of the transactions of the succeeding fiscal year in a routine manner. The reversing entries are journalized in the manner shown on page 668.

It should be noted that the reversing entries are dated January 1 which is the first day of the succeeding accounting period. It should also be noted that the reversing entries are just the opposite of the adjusting entries for accruals made on December 31. In the case of accrued property taxes payable, the amount accrued on December 31 was recorded as an adjustment, the accrued taxes being distributed to the proper expense accounts. The amount accrued was the amount assessed against the property on tax listing day which was December 10. Since the amount of the assessment had not been recorded prior to the end of the month, it was recorded as an adjustment on December 31. Thus, the proper amounts of tax expense are reflected in the manufacturing and income statements and the proper amount of the liability incurred because of the assessment for taxes is reflected in the balance sheet.

The accountant for The King Manufacturing Co. might not have reversed the adjusting entry for accrued property taxes, in which case it would be necessary to issue a voucher for the accrued taxes payable when due and this voucher would be recorded in the voucher register by debiting Accrued Property Taxes Payable and by crediting Vouchers Payable. The check issued in payment of the voucher would be recorded in the check register by debiting Vouchers Payable and by crediting the bank account. However, the accountant prefers to reverse the adjusting entries for accrued property taxes in exactly the same manner as the adjusting entries for accrued interest receivable and accrued interest payable are reversed. This makes it possible to record the subsequent payment of the taxes in a routine manner. When the taxes become due, a voucher should be issued for the amount payable and this voucher should be recorded in the voucher register by debiting the proper expense accounts and by crediting Vouchers Payable. The check issued in payment of the voucher should be recorded in the check register by debiting Vouchers Payable and by crediting the bank account.

The reversing entries should be posted in the usual manner after which the accounts with accruals will be in balance and should be ruled.

PRACTICE ASSIGNMENT No. 55. Complete Report No. 55 in the workbook and submit your working papers for Reports Nos. 53, 54, and 55 for approval. Continue with the next study assignment in Unit Twenty-nine until Report No. 56 is required.

Unit Twenty-nine

ACCOUNTING
FOR BRANCH OPERATIONS

(56) RECIPROCAL ACCOUNTS AND RECORDING PROCEDURE

In an effort to sell more goods or services and thus to increase their profits, business organizations sometimes establish branches. The term *branch* covers a variety of different arrangements. Sometimes such units have many of the characteristics of complete and independent businesses. A branch may have its own bank account, receivables, merchandise inventory, fixed assets, and various liabilities. The manager of a branch may have wide authority in the management of all phases of the operations of his unit. In other cases, a branch may be nothing more than a sales office. The branch manager may confine his activities to attempting to secure orders for goods that will be shipped from the main plant or home office. He may not have the authority to bind the company in any but sales contracts.

The size of a branch, the nature of its operations, and various other factors will determine what type of records it will keep. In some cases, the branch keeps no permanent formal records. Daily or weekly summaries of branch activities are sent to the home office where all formal records are maintained. The branch may have a revolving cash fund to use in making such disbursements as are not made by the home office. This fund may be accounted for and reimbursed periodically by the home office in a manner similar to the procedure followed in the case of petty cash funds. In other cases, the branch may maintain a complete set of records of its operations. From an accounting standpoint the branch may be a separate entity, keeping its own books of original entry and at least a general ledger, and preparing its own periodic financial statements.

Reciprocal Accounts. When formal records are kept at a branch office, it is common practice to follow a procedure that causes the general ledger of the branch and the general ledger of the home office to be *interlocking* or *reciprocal* to each other. In the ledger of the home office there should be an account entitled "Branch Office." This account will have a debit

673

balance and will show the amount for which the branch is accountable to the home office. In the ledger of the branch there should be an account entitled "Home Office." This account will have a credit balance and will show the amount for which the branch is accountable to the home office. The balances of these two accounts should be equal, but opposite; the debit balance in the one account should offset the credit balance in the other account. The two accounts are reciprocal. The relationship is illustrated by the following diagram:

BRANCH LEDGER 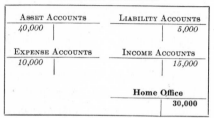 HOME OFFICE LEDGER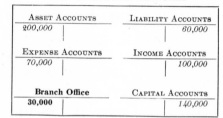

Transactions between the home office and the branch require entries in both ledgers. Such entries will involve the reciprocal accounts. If, for example, the home office remits $4,000 to the branch, the entry in the home office ledger will be a debit to Branch Office and a credit to Bank. In the branch ledger, Bank will be debited and Home Office will be credited. At the end of the period the branch will adjust its accounts and close the income and the expense accounts into Income Summary. The balance of Income Summary will be closed to Home Office, a debit indicating a loss or a credit indicating a profit. When the branch income statement reaches the home office, the home office accountant will make an entry debiting Branch Office and crediting Branch Profit if there was a profit, or debiting Branch Loss and crediting Branch Office if there was a loss.

If the business is engaged in selling merchandise, there probably will be another pair of reciprocal accounts: *Shipments to Branch* in the home office ledger and *Shipments from Home Office* in the branch ledger. When the home office sends goods to the branch, the home office accountant debits Branch Office and credits Shipments to Branch. The branch accountant records the receipt of the goods by a debit to Shipments from Home Office and a credit to Home Office. If the branch gets all of its merchandise from the home office, the shipments from home office account replaces a purchases account in the branch records. It must be understood, however, that branches sometimes purchase goods from outsiders and in such cases they may have a purchases account in addition to, or in place of, a shipments from home office account.

Branch Accounting Procedure. In most respects the usual accounting procedures are followed by both the home office and the branch. Each uses books of original entry, each has its general ledger, and each may have as many subsidiary ledgers as circumstances warrant. It has been indicated that the peculiarities of branch accounting arise in connection with transactions or events that affect both home office and branch office accounts, that is, the reciprocal accounts that have been described. The following example is presented to illustrate branch accounting procedure. In each instance, the transaction or event is given first, followed by the entries (all in general journal form) that should be made in the books of the branch and in the books of the home office. It will be observed that each transaction is recorded simultaneously on the books of both the home office and the branch office without regard to dates, whereas, in actual practice there usually would be some lapse of time between the dates on which the transactions are recorded in the books of each office.

1. On January 1, the general ledger accounts of The Quality Sales Co. had the following balances:

Bank...................................	$ 22,000	
Accounts Receivable.........................	30,000	
Allowance for Bad Debts.....................		$ 500
Merchandise Inventory.......................	20,000	
Prepaid Insurance...........................	640	
Furniture and Fixtures.......................	6,000	
Allowance for Depr. of Furniture and Fixtures...		2,400
Building....................................	50,000	
Allowance for Depreciation of Building........		28,000
Land.......................................	6,000	
Vouchers Payable............................		21,000
Capital Stock...............................		50,000
Retained Earnings...........................		32,740
	$134,640	$134,640

On January 2, the corporation established a branch in the town of Smithville and turned over to the manager of the branch $5,000 in cash, furniture and fixtures that had just been purchased at a cost of $1,000, and merchandise that cost $6,000. (The fixed assets used at a branch can be recorded in either the branch ledger or the home office ledger. In this illustration the fixed assets used at the branch are recorded in the branch ledger.)

BRANCH OFFICE BOOKS:			HOME OFFICE BOOKS:		
Bank.................	$5,000		Branch Office...........	$12,000	
Furniture and Fixtures..	1,000		Bank................		$5,000
Ship. from Home Office	6,000		Furniture and Fixtures		1,000
Home Office........		$12,000	Shipments to Branch..		6,000

2. The branch manager purchased additional furniture and fixtures for $4,000 cash, paid $300 rent on the branch store, and paid a premium of $150 on a three-year fire insurance policy.

BRANCH OFFICE BOOKS:			HOME OFFICE BOOKS:
Furniture and Fixtures..	$4,000		No entry.
Operating Expenses*....	300		
Prepaid Insurance......	150		
Bank...............		$4,450	

3. The home office purchased goods on account for $90,000 and incurred operating expenses in the amount of $28,000.

BRANCH OFFICE BOOKS:	HOME OFFICE BOOKS:		
No entry.	Purchases..............	$90,000	
	Operating Expenses.....	28,000	
	Vouchers Payable.....		$118,000

4. The home office shipped goods costing $40,000 to the branch.

BRANCH OFFICE BOOKS:			HOME OFFICE BOOKS:		
Ship. from Home Office.	$40,000		Branch Office..........	$40,000	
Home Office........		$40,000	Ship. to Branch......		$40,000

5. During the year the branch had cash sales of $4,200 and sales on account of $41,000.

BRANCH OFFICE BOOKS:			HOME OFFICE BOOKS:
Bank..................	$ 4,200		No entry.
Accounts Receivable....	41,000		
Sales...............		$45,200	

6. During the year the home office had cash sales of $18,000 and sales on account of $93,000.

BRANCH OFFICE BOOKS:	HOME OFFICE BOOKS:		
No entry.	Bank..................	$18,000	
	Accounts Receivable....	93,000	
	Sales...............		$111,000

7. The branch incurred additional operating expenses during the year (rent, wages, light, telephone, advertising, etc.) in the amount of $15,700. The items were vouchered. Total payments on vouchers were $14,500.

BRANCH OFFICE BOOKS:			HOME OFFICE BOOKS:
Operating Expenses.....	$15,700		No entry.
Vouchers Payable.....		$15,700	
Vouchers Payable.......	$14,500		
Bank...............		$14,500	

---

*For the sake of brevity in this example, all expenses are charged to the single account, Operating Expenses.

8. Cash collections on the branch accounts receivable were $20,000.

BRANCH OFFICE BOOKS:			HOME OFFICE BOOKS:
Bank.................	$20,000		No entry.
Accounts Receivable..		$20,000	

9. Cash collections on the home office accounts receivable were $80,000, and accounts in the amount of $400 were determined to be worthless.

BRANCH OFFICE BOOKS:	HOME OFFICE BOOKS:		
No entry.	Bank.................	$80,000	
	Allow. for Bad Debts...	400	
	Accounts Receivable..		$80,400

10. Home office payments on vouchers payable were $95,000.

BRANCH OFFICE BOOKS:	HOME OFFICE BOOKS:		
No entry.	Vouchers Payable.......	$95,000	
	Bank................		$95,000

11. The branch office borrowed $4,000 at its bank giving a 90-day note at $4\frac{1}{2}$ per cent interest.

BRANCH OFFICE BOOKS:			HOME OFFICE BOOKS:
Bank.................	$ 4,000		No entry.
Notes Payable........		$ 4,000	

12. The branch returned to the home office for credit, goods costing $300.

BRANCH OFFICE BOOKS:			HOME OFFICE BOOKS:		
Home Office...........	$ 300		Ship. to Branch.........	$ 300	
Ship. from Home Office		$ 300	Branch Office........		$ 300

13. Branch accepted notes from customers in temporary settlement of their accounts, $3,000.

BRANCH OFFICE BOOKS:			HOME OFFICE BOOKS:
Notes Receivable.......	$ 3,000		No entry.
Accounts Receivable..		$ 3,000	

14. Home office accepted notes from customers in temporary settlement of their accounts, $4,500.

BRANCH OFFICE BOOKS:	HOME OFFICE BOOKS:		
No entry.	Notes Receivable.......	$ 4,500	
	Accounts Receivable..		$ 4,500

After posting the foregoing transactions, the branch office accounts appeared as shown in the following "T" accounts:

BRANCH OFFICE ACCOUNTS

	BANK		
(1)	5,000	(2)	4,450
(5)	4,200	(7)	14,500
(8)	20,000		*18,950*
(11)	4,000		
14,250	*33,200*		

	NOTES RECEIVABLE	
(13)	3,000	

	ACCOUNTS RECEIVABLE		
(5)	41,000	(8)	20,000
18,000		(13)	3,000
			23,000

	PREPAID INSURANCE	
(2)	150	

	FURNITURE AND FIXTURES	
(1)	1,000	
(2)	4,000	
	5,000	

	NOTES PAYABLE		
		(11)	4,000

	VOUCHERS PAYABLE		
(7)	14,500	(7)	15,700
			1,200

	HOME OFFICE		
(12)	300	(1)	12,000
		(4)	40,000
		51,700	*52,000*

	SALES		
		(5)	45,200

	SHIPMENTS FROM HOME OFFICE		
(1)	6,000	(12)	300
(4)	40,000		
45,700	*46,000*		

	OPERATING EXPENSES	
(2)	300	
(7)	15,700	
	16,000	

The following trial balance of the branch office accounts was taken at the end of the year:

THE QUALITY SALES CO. — SMITHVILLE BRANCH
TRIAL BALANCE
DECEMBER 31, 19--

Bank...	$ 14,250	
Notes Receivable....................................	3,000	
Accounts Receivable.................................	18,000	
Prepaid Insurance...................................	150	
Furniture and Fixtures...............................	5,000	
Notes Payable.......................................		$ 4,000
Vouchers Payable....................................		1,200
Home Office...		51,700
Sales...		45,200
Shipments from Home Office..........................	45,700	
Operating Expenses..................................	16,000	
	$102,100	$102,100

After posting the transactions, the home office accounts appeared as shown in the following "T" accounts:

HOME OFFICE ACCOUNTS

BANK

Bal.	22,000	(1)	5,000
(6)	18,000	(10)	95,000
(9)	80,000		
20,000	*120,000*		*100,000*

NOTES RECEIVABLE

| (14) | 4,500 | | |

ACCOUNTS RECEIVABLE

Bal.	30,000	(9)	80,400
(6)	93,000	(14)	4,500
38,100	*123,000*		*84,900*

ALLOWANCE FOR BAD DEBTS

| (9) | 400 | Bal. | 500 |
| | | *100* | |

MERCHANDISE INVENTORY

| Bal. | 20,000 | | |

BRANCH OFFICE

(1)	12,000	(12)	300
(4)	40,000		
51,700	*52,000*		

PREPAID INSURANCE

| Bal. | 640 | | |

FURNITURE AND FIXTURES

| Bal. | 6,000 | (1) | 1,000 |
| *5,000* | | | |

ALLOWANCE FOR DEPR. OF FURN. & FIX.

| | | Bal. | 2,400 |

BUILDING

| Bal. | 50,000 | | |

ALLOWANCE FOR DEPR. OF BUILDING

| | | Bal. | 28,000 |

LAND

| Bal. | 6,000 | | |

VOUCHERS PAYABLE

(10)	95,000	Bal.	21,000
		(3)	118,000
		44,000	*139,000*

CAPITAL STOCK

| | | Bal. | 50,000 |

RETAINED EARNINGS

| | | Bal. | 32,740 |

SHIPMENTS TO BRANCH

(12)	300	(1)	6,000
		(4)	40,000
		45,700	*46,000*

SALES

| | | (6) | 111,000 |

PURCHASES

| (3) | 90,000 | | |

OPERATING EXPENSES

| (3) | 28,000 | | |

The following trial balance of the home office accounts was taken at the end of the year:

THE QUALITY SALES CO. — HOME OFFICE

TRIAL BALANCE

DECEMBER 31, 19--

Bank...	$ 20,000	
Notes Receivable..................................	4,500	
Accounts Receivable...............................	38,100	
Allowance for Bad Debts...........................		$ 100
Merchandise Inventory.............................	20,000	
Branch Office.....................................	51,700	
Prepaid Insurance.................................	640	
Furniture and Fixtures.............................	5,000	
Allowance for Depr. of Furniture and Fixtures...........		2,400
Building..	50,000	
Allowance for Depr. of Building......................		28,000
Land...	6,000	
Vouchers Payable..................................		44,000
Capital Stock.....................................		50,000
Retained Earnings.................................		32,740
Shipments to Branch...............................		45,700
Sales..		111,000
Purchases..	90,000	
Operating Expenses................................	28,000	
	$313,940	$313,940

PRACTICE ASSIGNMENT No. 56. Complete Report No. 56 in the workbook and submit your working papers for approval. Then continue with the following study assignment until Report No. 57 is required.

(57) WORK AT CLOSE OF FISCAL YEAR

The books of the home office and of the branch office should be closed in the usual manner at the end of each fiscal year.

Accounting Procedure in Closing Branch Office Books. Following is a step-by-step analysis of the usual procedure in closing the books of a branch office:

(1) Prepare a work sheet as a means of compiling and classifying the data needed in the preparation of financial statements. In preparing the work sheet it will be necessary to make the usual adjustments to record (a) the merchandise inventory at end of year, (b) the portion of any prepaid expenses consumed during the year, (c) any provision for bad debts, (d) the depreciation of fixed assets, and (e) any accruals. The adjusted trial balance figures appearing on the work sheet will then provide the proper amounts to be used in preparing an income statement and a balance sheet.

The data for adjusting the accounts of the Smithville Branch of The Quality Sales Co. at the end of the year are as follows:

Merchandise inventory, end of year, $20,000
Insurance expired, $50
Provision for bad debts, $400
Depreciation of furniture and fixtures (10%), $500
Accrued interest on notes receivable, $24
Accrued interest on notes payable, $30

The work sheet prepared for the Smithville Branch of The Quality Sales Co. is reproduced on page 682. The merchandise inventory at end of year amounting to $20,000 was recorded in the Adjustments columns of the work sheet by debiting Merchandise Inventory and by crediting Shipments from Home Office. After making this adjustment the balance of the account with Shipments from Home Office represented the cost of goods sold by the branch. Under this procedure there is no need for keeping a summary account with Cost of Goods Sold in the branch office ledger.

(2) Prepare an income statement showing the results of operating the branch during the year and send a copy to the home office. The Income Statement columns of the work sheet are the source of the information needed in preparing this statement. The income statement of the Smithville Branch of The Quality Sales Co. is reproduced on page 683.

(3) Prepare a balance sheet showing the financial status of the branch at the end of the year and send a copy to the home office. The balance sheet of the Smithville Branch of The Quality Sales Co. is reproduced on page 683.

THE QUALITY SALES CO. — SMITHVILLE BRANCH
Work Sheet For Year Ended December 31, 19——

Accounts	Trial Balance Dr.	Trial Balance Cr.	Adjustments Dr.	Adjustments Cr.	Adj. Trial Balance Dr.	Adj. Trial Balance Cr.	Income Statement Dr.	Income Statement Cr.	Balance Sheet Dr.	Balance Sheet Cr.
Bank	14,250				14,250				14,250	
Notes Receivable	3,000				3,000				3,000	
Accrued Interest Receivable			(c) 24		24				24	
Accounts Receivable	18,000				18,000				18,000	
Allowance for Bad Debts				(b) 400		400				400
Merchandise Inventory			(a) 20,000		20,000				20,000	
Prepaid Insurance	150			(b) 50	100				100	
Furniture and Fixtures	5,000				5,000				5,000	
Allowance for Depreciation of F. & F.				(b) 500		500				500
Notes Payable		4,000				4,000				4,000
Accrued Interest Payable				(d) 30		30				30
Vouchers Payable		1,200				1,200				1,200
Home Office		51,700				51,700				51,700
Sales		45,200				45,200		45,200		
Shipments from Home Office	45,700			(a) 20,000	25,700		25,700			
Operating Expenses	16,000		(b) 950		16,950		16,950			
Interest Income				(c) 24		24		24		
Interest Expense			(d) 30		30		30			
	102,100	102,100	21,004	£1,004	103,054	103,054	42,680	45,224	60,374	57,830
Net Income							2,544			2,544
							45,224	45,224	60,374	60,374

THE QUALITY SALES CO. — SMITHVILLE BRANCH
INCOME STATEMENT
FOR THE YEAR ENDED DECEMBER 31, 19--

Operating Income:			
Sales..			$45,200
Less Cost of Goods Sold:			
Shipments from Home Office......................		$45,700	
Less Inventory, December 31.....................		20,000	25,700
Gross Profit on Sales..................................			$19,500
Operating Expenses..			16,950
Net Operating Income....................................			$ 2,550
Other Income:			
Interest Income..			24
			$ 2,574
Other Charges:			
Interest Expense......................................			30
Net Income..			$ 2,544

THE QUALITY SALES CO. — SMITHVILLE BRANCH
BALANCE SHEET
DECEMBER 31, 19--

ASSETS			LIABILITIES		
Cash.................		$14,250	Notes Payable..........		$ 4,000
Notes Receivable.......	$ 3,000		Accrued Interest Pay....		30
Accrued Interest Rec....	24		Vouchers Payable.......		1,200
Accounts Receivable....	18,000		Home Office..........	$51,700	
	$21,024		Plus Net Income......	2,544	54,244
Less Allow. for Bad					
Debts.............	400	20,624			
Merchandise Inventory..		20,000			
Prepaid Insurance......		100			
Furniture and Fixtures..	$ 5,000				
Less Allow. for Depr..	500	4,500			
Total Assets...........		$59,474	Total Liabilities........		$59,474

(4) Journalize and post the entries required to adjust the accounts of the branch. The Adjustments columns of the work sheet are the source of the information needed in drafting the adjusting journal entries. The entries required to adjust the accounts of the Smithville Branch of The Quality Sales Co. are as follows:

Merchandise Inventory....................................	$20,000	
Shipments from Home Office...........................		$20,000

Operating Expenses	$ 950	
Prepaid Insurance		$ 50
Allowance for Bad Debts		400
Allowance for Depreciation of Furniture and Fixtures		500
Accrued Interest Receivable	24	
Interest Income		24
Interest Expense	30	
Accrued Interest Payable		30

(5) Journalize and post the entries required to close the temporary accounts in the branch books. The entries required to close the temporary accounts of the Smithville Branch of The Quality Sales Co. are as follows:

Sales	$45,200	
Interest Income	24	
Income Summary		45,224
Income Summary	42,680	
Shipments from Home Office		25,700
Operating Expenses		16,950
Interest Expense		30
Income Summary	2,544	
Home Office		2,544

The last entry was made to close the income summary account and to transfer the net income to the home office account.

(6) Prepare a post-closing trial balance of the branch ledger accounts. Following is the post-closing trial balance of the Smithville Branch of The Quality Sales Co.:

THE QUALITY SALES CO. — SMITHVILLE BRANCH

POST-CLOSING TRIAL BALANCE

DECEMBER 31, 19--

Bank	$14,250	
Notes Receivable	3,000	
Accrued Interest Receivable	24	
Accounts Receivable	18,000	
Allowance for Bad Debts		$ 400
Merchandise Inventory	20,000	
Prepaid Insurance	100	
Furniture and Fixtures	5,000	
Allowance for Depr. of Furniture and Fixtures		500
Notes Payable		4,000
Accrued Interest Payable		30
Vouchers Payable		1,200
Home Office		54,244
	$60,374	$60,374

(7) Journalize and post the entries required to adjust the reversing entries for accruals. The entries required to reverse the entries for accruals in the books of the Smithville Branch of The Quality Sales Co. are as follows:

Interest Income..	$24	
Accrued Interest Receivable....................................		$24
Accrued Interest Payable.......................................	30	
Interest Expense...		30

Accounting Procedure in Closing Home Office Books. Following is a step-by-step analysis of the usual procedure in closing the books of the home office:

(1) Prepare a work sheet as a means of compiling and classifying the data needed in the preparation of financial statements. In preparing the work sheet it will be necessary to make the usual adjustments to record any changes in the accounting elements that have not been entered in the accounts in the routine recording of the transactions completed during the year.

The data for adjusting the accounts of the home office of The Quality Sales Co. at the end of the year are as follows:

Merchandise inventory, $13,000
Insurance expired, $420
Provision for bad debts, $750
Depreciation of furniture and fixtures (10%), $500
Depreciation of building (4%), $2,000
Accrued interest on notes receivable, $45
Branch office profit, $2,544
Corporation income taxes, estimated, $10,421

The income statement received from the branch office is the source of the information as to the amount of the branch office profit.

It is necessary to adjust the accounts for the amount of the branch office profit in order to bring the account with Branch Office in the home office books into agreement with the account with Home Office in the books of the branch office. After making these adjustments, the home office accounts reflect the total income of the enterprise for the year.

The work sheet prepared for the home office of The Quality Sales Co. is reproduced on page 686. A summary account with Cost of Goods Sold was kept in the home office ledger. This account was debited for (a) the beginning inventory amounting to $20,000 and (b) purchases amounting to $90,000, and was credited for (c) shipments to branch amounting to $45,700 and (d) the ending inventory amounting to $13,000. After making these adjustments the balance of the account amounted to $51,300.

(*Continued on page 688*)

THE QUALITY SALES CO. — HOME OFFICE
WORK SHEET FOR YEAR ENDED DECEMBER 31, 19—

Accounts	Trial Balance Dr.	Trial Balance Cr.	Adjustments Dr.	Adjustments Cr.	Adj. Trial Balance Dr.	Adj. Trial Balance Cr.	Income Statement Dr.	Income Statement Cr.	Balance Sheet Dr.	Balance Sheet Cr.
Bank	20,000				20,000				20,000	
Notes Receivable	4,500				4,500				4,500	
Accrued Interest Receivable			(f) 45		45				45	
Accounts Receivable	38,100				38,100				38,100	
Allowance for Bad Debts		100		(e) 750		850				850
Merchandise Inventory	20,000		(d) 13,000	(a) 20,000	13,000				13,000	
Branch Office	51,700		(g) 2,544		54,244				54,244	
Prepaid Insurance	640			(e) 420	220				220	
Furniture and Fixtures	5,000				5,000				5,000	
Allowance for Depreciation of F. & F.		2,400		(e) 500		2,900				2,900
Building	50,000				50,000				50,000	
Allowance for Depreciation of Building		28,000		(e) 2,000		30,000				30,000
Land	6,000				6,000				6,000	
Vouchers Payable		44,000				44,000				44,000
Corporation Income Taxes Payable				(h) 10,421		10,421				10,421
Capital Stock		50,000				50,000				50,000
Retained Earnings		32,740				32,740				32,740
Shipments to Branch		45,700	(c) 45,700							
Sales		111,000				111,000		111,000		
Purchases	90,000			(b) 90,000						
Operating Expenses	28,000		(e) 3,670		31,670		31,670			
Interest Income				(f) 45		45		45		
Branch Office Profit				(g) 2,544		2,544		2,544		
Corporation Income Taxes			(h) 10,421		10,421		10,421			
Cost of Goods Sold			(a) 20,000 (b) 90,000	(c) 45,700 (d) 13,000	20,000 90,000	45,700 13,000	20,000 90,000	45,700 13,000		
	313,940	313,940	185,380	185,380	343,200	343,200	152,091	172,289	191,109	170,911
Net Income							20,198			20,198
							172,289	172,289	191,109	191,109

THE QUALITY SALES CO. — HOME OFFICE
INCOME STATEMENT
FOR THE YEAR ENDED DECEMBER 31, 19--

Operating Income:			
Sales...			$111,000
Less Cost of Goods Sold:			
Inventory, beginning of year......................	$ 20,000		
Purchases.....................................	90,000		
	$110,000		
Less Shipments to Branch.....................	45,700		
Merchandise Available for Sale.....................	$ 64,300		
Less Inventory end of year.......................	13,000	51,300	
Gross Profit on Sales.................................		$ 59,700	
Operating Expenses...................................		31,670	
Net Operating Income................................		$ 28,030	
Other Income:			
Interest Income......................................		45	
Net Income — Home Office............................		$ 28,075	
Branch Office Profit..................................		2,544	
Total Net Income before provision for Income Taxes......		$ 30,619	
Less Corporation Income Taxes......................		10,421	
Net Income after provision for Income Taxes.............		$ 20,198	

THE QUALITY SALES CO. — HOME OFFICE
BALANCE SHEET
DECEMBER 31, 19--

ASSETS			LIABILITIES		
Cash.................		$ 20,000	Vouchers Payable.......	$ 44,000	
Notes Receivable.......	$ 4,500		Corp. Income Taxes Pay..	10,421	
Accrued Interest Rec....	45				
Accounts Receivable....	38,100		Total Liabilities........		$ 54,421
	$42,645		**CAPITAL**		
Less Allow. for Bad			Capital Stock..........	$50,000	
Debts............	850	41,795	Retained Earnings......	52,938	
Merchandise Inventory..		13,000	Total Capital..........		102,938
Branch Office...........		54,244			
Prepaid Insurance......		220			
Furniture and Fixtures..	$ 5,000				
Less Allow. for Depr..	2,900	2,100			
Building..............	$50,000				
Less Allow. for Depr..	30,000	20,000			
Land.................		6,000			
Total Assets...........		$157,359	Total Liabilities and Cap.		$157,359

(2) Prepare an income statement showing the results of operating the home office during the year. The Income Statement columns of the work sheet are the source of the information needed in preparing this statement. The income statement of the home office of The Quality Sales Co. is reproduced on page 687.

(3) Prepare a balance sheet showing the financial status of the home office at the end of the year. The balance sheet of the home office of The Quality Sales Co. is reproduced on page 687.

(4) Journalize and post the entries required to adjust the home office accounts. The Adjustments columns of the work sheet are the source of the information needed in drafting the adjusting entries. The entries required to adjust the home office accounts of The Quality Sales Co. are as follows:

Cost of Goods Sold....................................	$20,000	
Merchandise Inventory...............................		$20,000
Cost of Goods Sold....................................	90,000	
Purchases...		90,000
Shipments to Branch...................................	45,700	
Cost of Goods Sold.................................		45,700
Merchandise Inventory.................................	13,000	
Cost of Goods Sold.................................		13,000
Operating Expenses....................................	3,670	
Prepaid Insurance....................................		420
Allowance for Bad Debts.............................		750
Allowance for Depreciation of Furniture and Fixtures.....		500
Allowance for Depreciation of Building.................		2,000
Accrued Interest Receivable............................	45	
Interest Income......................................		45
Branch Office...	2,544	
Branch Office Profit.................................		2,544
Corporation Income Taxes............................	10,421	
Corporation Income Taxes Payable....................		10,421

(5) Journalize and post the entries required to close the temporary accounts in the home office books. The entries required to close the temporary accounts of the home office of The Quality Sales Co. are as follows:

Sales..	$111,000	
Interest Income.......................................	45	
Branch Office Profit...................................	2,544	
Income Summary....................................		$113,589
Income Summary......................................	93,391	
Cost of Goods Sold.................................		51,300
Operating Expenses.................................		31,670
Corporation Income Taxes............................		10,421
Income Summary......................................	20,198	
Retained Earnings...................................		20,198

(6) After posting the closing entries, a post-closing trial balance should be taken. The post-closing trial balance for The Quality Sales Co. follows:

THE QUALITY SALES CO. — HOME OFFICE
POST-CLOSING TRIAL BALANCE
DECEMBER 31, 19--

Bank..	$ 20,000	
Notes Receivable..............................	4,500	
Accrued Interest Receivable...................	45	
Accounts Receivable...........................	38,100	
Allowance for Bad Debts.......................		$ 850
Merchandise Inventory.........................	13,000	
Branch Office.................................	54,244	
Prepaid Insurance.............................	220	
Furniture and Fixtures........................	5,000	
Allowance for Depreciation of Furniture and Fixtures.....		2,900
Building......................................	50,000	
Allowance for Depreciation of Building........		30,000
Land..	6,000	
Vouchers Payable..............................		44,000
Corporation Income Taxes Payable.............		10,421
Capital Stock.................................		50,000
Retained Earnings.............................		52,938
	$191,109	$191,109

(7) After taking a post-closing trial balance, any adjusting entries for accruals should be reversed. The following entry is required to reverse the adjusting entry for accrued interest receivable in the home office books of The Quality Sales Co.:

Interest Income...................................	$45	
Accrued Interest Receivable...................		$45

PRACTICE ASSIGNMENT No. 57. Complete Report No. 57 in the workbook and submit your working papers for approval. Then continue with the following study assignment until Report No. 58 is required.

(58) CONSOLIDATED FINANCIAL STATEMENTS

While separate financial statements of the home office and the branch office provide useful information for the management, *consolidated statements*, in which the results of operations and the financial data are combined, provide more complete information regarding the business as a whole. The preparation of consolidated statements is facilitated by the use of special work sheets. The work sheet that was used in preparing a

(*Continued on page 691*)

THE QUALITY SALES CO.
HOME OFFICE AND SMITHVILLE BRANCH
Work Sheet for Consolidated Income Statement
For Year Ended December 31, 19--

	Home Office		Smithville Branch		Eliminations		Consolidated Income Statement	
	Dr.	Cr.	Dr.	Cr.	Dr.	Cr.	Dr.	Cr.
Sales		111,000		45,200				156,200
Cost of Goods Sold:								
Merchandise Inventory, January 1	20,000						20,000	
Purchases	90,000						90,000	
Shipments from Home Office			45,700			45,700		
Shipments to Branch		45,700			45,700			
Merchandise Available for Sale	64,300		45,700				110,000	
Merchandise Inventory, December 31		13,000		20,000				33,000
Cost of Goods Sold	51,300		25,700				77,000	
Gross Profit on Sales		59,700		19,500				79,200
Operating Expenses	31,670		16,950				48,620	
Net Operating Income		28,030		2,550				30,580
Add Interest Income		45		24				69
				2,574				30,649
Less Interest Expense			30				30	
Net Income before Taxes		28,075		2,544				30,619
Branch Profit Transferred to Home Office		2,544	2,544					
Total Net Income before Taxes		30,619						30,619
Income Taxes	10,421						10,421	
Net Income after Taxes		20,198						20,198

consolidated income statement for The Quality Sales Co. and its Smithville Branch is reproduced on page 690. The data in the first column were obtained from the income statement of the home office. The data in the second column were obtained from the income statement of the branch office. The columns headed "Eliminations" are used to offset reciprocal accounts. In this case the only reciprocal accounts are Shipments from Home Office and Shipments to Branch.

The following consolidated income statement for The Quality Sales Co. and its Smithville Branch was prepared from the information provided in the last column of the work sheet:

THE QUALITY SALES CO.
HOME OFFICE AND SMITHVILLE BRANCH
CONSOLIDATED INCOME STATEMENT
YEAR ENDED DECEMBER 31, 19--

Sales..		$156,200
Less Cost of Goods Sold:		
Merchandise Inventory, January 1..................	$ 20,000	
Purchases...	90,000	
Merchandise Available for Sale.......................	$110,000	
Less Merchandise Inventory, December 31...........	33,000	77,000
Gross Profit on Sales.................................		$ 79,200
Less Operating Expenses		48,620
Net Operating Income.................................		$ 30,580
Other Income:		
Interest Income....................................		69
		$ 30,649
Other Charges:		
Interest Expense...................................		30
Net Income before provision for Income Taxes............		$ 30,619
Less Corporation Income Taxes......................		10,421
Net Income after provision for Income Taxes.............		$ 20,198

The work sheet that was used in the preparation of the consolidated balance sheet of The Quality Sales Co. and its Smithville Branch is reproduced on page 692. The data in the first column were obtained from the balance sheet of the home office. The data in the second column were obtained from the balance sheet of the branch office. The columns headed "Eliminations" are used to offset reciprocal accounts. In this case the only reciprocal accounts are Home Office and Branch Office.

THE QUALITY SALES CO.
HOME OFFICE AND SMITHVILLE BRANCH
WORK SHEET FOR CONSOLIDATED BALANCE SHEET

DECEMBER 31, 19--

	Home Office		Smithville Branch		Eliminations		Consolidated Balance Sheet	
	Dr.	Cr.	Dr.	Cr.	Dr.	Cr.	Dr.	Cr.
Cash	20,000		14,250				34,250	
Notes Receivable	4,500		3,000				7,500	
Accrued Interest Receivable	45		24				69	
Accounts Receivable	38,100		18,000				56,100	
Allowance for Bad Debts		850		400				1,250
Merchandise Inventory	13,000		20,000				33,000	
Branch Office	54,244					54,244		
Prepaid Insurance	220		100				320	
Furniture and Fixtures	5,000		5,000				10,000	
Allowance for Depreciation of F. & F.		2,900		500				3,400
Building	50,000						50,000	
Allowance for Depreciation of Building		30,000						30,000
Land	6,000						6,000	
Income Taxes Payable		10,421						10,421
Notes Payable				4,000				4,000
Accrued Interest Payable				30				30
Vouchers Payable		44,000		1,200				45,200
Home Office				54,244	54,244			
Capital Stock		50,000						50,000
Retained Earnings		52,938						52,938
	191,109	191,109	60,374	60,374	54,244	54,244	197,239	197,239

The following consolidated balance sheet for The Quality Sales Co. and its Smithville Branch was prepared from the information provided in the last column of the work sheet:

THE QUALITY SALES CO.
HOME OFFICE AND SMITHVILLE BRANCH
CONSOLIDATED BALANCE SHEET
DECEMBER 31, 19--

ASSETS			LIABILITIES		
Cash.................		$ 34,250	Notes Payable..........	$ 4,000	
Notes Receivable.......	$ 7,500		Accrued Interest Payable	30	
Accrued Interest Rec.....	69		Vouchers Payable.......	45,200	
Accounts Receivable....	56,100		Corp. Income Taxes Pay.	10,421	
	$63,669				
Less Allow. for Bad			Total Liabilities.........		$ 59,651
Debts............	1,250	62,419	CAPITAL		
Merchandise Inventory..		33,000			
Prepaid Insurance.......		320	Capital Stock..........	$50,000	
Furniture and Fixtures..	$10,000		Retained Earnings......	52,938	
Less Allow. for Depr..	3,400	6,600	Total Capital..........		102,938
Building..............	$50,000				
Less Allow. for Depr..	30,000	20,000			
Land.................		6,000			
Total Assets...........		$162,589	Total Liab. and Capital..		$162,589

Accounting for Merchandise Billed to Branch in Excess of Cost.

Sometimes a home office bills its branch for an amount greater than the cost of the merchandise shipped to the branch. This practice may be followed in order to conceal the actual costs and therefore the actual branch profit or loss from the branch manager and others. In some cases the branch is billed at the selling price of the goods. This practice will not only conceal the cost, but it may facilitate control of the stock at the branch. When the count of goods is made at the end of the period, it usually is easier to value them at sales prices. Furthermore, the sum of the prices of goods on hand plus the amount of sales during the period should equal the opening inventory of goods at selling price plus the total amount of shipments from the home office during the period (assuming no changes in selling prices). Any discrepancy not caused by changes in selling prices after the goods were received indicates the need for investigation and closer control of stock.

If the branch is billed for the sales price of goods shipped, the home office may credit an account entitled *Provision for Overvaluation of Branch Inventory* for the difference between the cost and the sales price of the goods sent to the branch. For example, assume that the home office ships goods costing $30,000 to the branch and bills the branch for $50,000, the sales price of the merchandise. This shipment could be recorded in the home office books as follows:

Branch Office...	$50,000	
Shipments to Branch...................................		$30,000
Provision for Overvaluation of Branch Inventory..........		20,000
Goods shipped to branch:		
Sales price $50,000, Cost $30,000.		

The branch would record the shipment by a debit to Shipments from Home Office and a credit to Home Office in the amount of $50,000.

Under such circumstances the branch will never show a profit on its records since its sales and reported cost of goods sold will be equal. It will report a loss equal to the amount of its expenses. Assume that the branch in the case mentioned above had no beginning inventory, received only the one shipment, and sold 70 per cent of those goods. Assume also that the operating expenses of the branch were $10,000. The branch would report sales and cost of goods sold of $35,000, expenses of $10,000, and a loss of $10,000. Its balance sheet would show $15,000 as the amount of unsold goods on hand.

Actually the branch had a net profit of $4,000. (Sales, $35,000, less actual cost of goods sold, $21,000, less expenses, $10,000, equals net profit, $4,000.) The actual cost of the inventory at the branch is $9,000 (60% of $15,000). Since the branch debited $10,000 to Home Office when it closed its Income Summary, the home office must credit that amount to Branch Office in its ledger. At the same time the home office will want to record the actual branch profit of $4,000 and reduce the Provision for Overvaluation of Inventory from $20,000 to $6,000 (the overvaluation of the goods now on hand at the branch). This can be accomplished if the home office makes the following entry to record the loss reported by the branch:

Provision for Overvaluation of Branch Inventory............	$14,000	
Branch Office..		$10,000
Branch Profit..		4,000
Reported loss of branch, $10,000 (caused by $14,000 over-		
statement of cost of goods sold).		

In the process of preparing consolidated statements for the home office and the branch, the overvaluations in the accounts can be eliminated or offset so that the consolidated statements will show actual costs and profit.

In some cases a home office may bill its branch at an amount in excess of cost, though not as high as the selling price of the goods shipped. This procedure may not be any help in keeping control of the branch inventory, but it will conceal the true results of the branch operations from the manager and others at the branch. The branch may show a profit, but such profit will be understated to the extent that the recorded cost of goods sold is overstated. The mechanics of accounting for shipments and the handling of statement consolidation in such situations are similar to the procedures used when the goods are billed at selling price.

Several Branches. Frequently a company has more than one branch. If each branch has its own ledger, the home office ledger will contain an account for each branch. Preferably the branches will not have accounts with each other. Any transaction between two or more branches will be recorded as though each of them dealt with the home office. For example, suppose that the home office decides to transfer $2,000 from Branch Office No. 1 to Branch Office No. 2. To record this transfer of cash the following entries should be made in the books indicated:

BOOKS OF BRANCH OFFICE NO. 1
Home Office...	$2,000	
Bank...		$2,000
$2,000 transferred to Branch No. 2.		

BOOKS OF BRANCH OFFICE NO. 2
Bank...	2,000	
Home Office...		2,000
$2,000 received from Branch No. 1.		

HOME OFFICE BOOKS
Branch Office No. 2......................................	2,000	
Branch Office No. 1...................................		2,000
$2,000 transferred to Branch No. 2 by Branch No. 1.		

Reconciliation of the Reciprocal Accounts. While the branch office account in the home office ledger and the home office account in the branch office ledger will have balances of the same amount after all transactions between the units have been recorded properly, it is probable that the balances of the two accounts will not be exactly equal at all times. Apart from discrepancies because of errors, one or more of four circumstances may result in temporary differences between the balances of these accounts. These circumstances are as follows:

(1) The home office has charged the branch, but the branch has not yet credited the home office. For example, a discrepancy of this type could exist during the interval between the date that goods were shipped by the home office and the date the goods were received by the branch.

(2) The branch has credited the home office, but the home office has not yet charged the branch. For example, a discrepancy of this type could exist just after the branch had transferred a credit balance from its income summary account to the home office account, but before the home office recorded the branch profit.

(3) The home office has credited the branch, but the branch has not yet charged the home office. For example, suppose a customer of the branch sent the home office a check in payment of his debt to the branch. The home office deposited the money in its own bank account and sent a letter (or a credit memo) to the branch instructing it to credit the account of the customer and to debit the home office. The balances of the reciprocal accounts would be unequal until the branch made the proper entry upon receipt of the letter or memo.

(4) The branch office has charged the home office, but the home office has not yet credited the branch. For example, suppose the branch has recorded a remittance to the home office, but the home office has not yet received it; hence, has not recorded it.

Any difference in the balances of the reciprocal accounts must be accounted for before the statements of the home office and the branch can be consolidated. When the reasons for any differences are known, any needed correcting or adjusting entries can be made on the consolidated statement work sheets and, if needed, in the books of the home office, the branch, or both. Sometimes the reciprocal accounts are reconciled at frequent intervals in order to cross-check the accuracy of the branch and the home office records.

PRACTICE ASSIGNMENT No. 58. Complete Report No. 58 in the workbook and submit your working papers for approval.

Unit Thirty

PRACTICAL ACCOUNTING PROBLEMS

The problems in this unit are supplementary to those in the workbook. Each problem is numbered to indicate the unit of the textbook with which it correlates. Loose-leaf stationery should be used in solving these problems.

Problem 21-A

The Union Manufacturing Co. is a corporation, organized under the laws of Missouri, with an authorized capital of $100,000 divided into 1,000 shares of common stock, par value $100 a share. The company uses a standard form of stockholders' ledger. Following is a list of selected stock transactions:

Mar. 1. Issued Stock Certificate No. 14 for 40 shares of common stock to James A. Brown, 2138 Auburn Avenue, Dayton, Ohio. This stock is fully paid and nonassessable.

April 1. Issued Stock Certificate No. 18 for 30 shares of common stock to Mrs. Richard Betzing, Route 3, Hamilton, Ohio.

June 15. Mrs. Betzing surrendered Certificate No. 18 for 30 shares of common stock and requested that 15 shares be transferred to Mr. Brown. Issued Certificate No. 21 for 15 shares to Mr. Brown and Certificate No. 22 for 15 shares to Mrs. Betzing.

Sept. 1. Mr. Brown surrendered Certificate No. 14 for 40 shares and Certificate No. 21 for 15 shares and requested that 50 shares be transferred to Arthur J. McNeil, 206 West 10th Street, Columbus, Ohio. Issued Certificate No. 23 for 50 shares to Mr. McNeil and Certificate No. 24 for 5 shares to Mr. Brown.

REQUIRED: Open accounts in the stockholders' ledger for Mr. Brown, Mrs. Betzing, and Mr. McNeil, and record the foregoing transactions directly in the accounts.

Problem 21-B

The Union Manufacturing Co., referred to in the preceding problem, uses a standard transfer record to record all transfers of its capital stock. This record is kept by the secretary of the company. Following is a narrative of stock transfers for the month of December:

Dec. 2. Charles A. Patman, 1315 Alabama Street, Gainesville, Florida surrendered Certificate No. 11 for 20 shares of common stock and requested that it be transferred to Arthur Raible, 3446 Belle Crest, Tampa, Florida. Issued Certificate No. 31 for 20 shares to Mr. Raible.

Dec.   5. Harold B. Jordan, 835 Villa Avenue, Indianapolis, Indiana surrendered Certificate No. 16 for 12 shares and requested that 6 shares of the stock be transferred to Carl E. Roehmer, 511 Indiana Avenue, Muncie, Indiana. Issued Certificate No. 32 for 6 shares to Mr. Roehmer and Certificate No. 33 for 6 shares to Mr. Jordan.

      15. Mr. Raible surrendered Certificate No. 31 for 20 shares and requested that it be transferred to his daughter, Miss Elsie Raible, 3446 Belle Crest, Tampa, Florida. Issued Certificate No. 34 for 20 shares to Miss Raible.

      21. Roy T. Fishback, 1214 Center Street, Wray, Colorado surrendered Certificate No. 17 for 60 shares and requested that 20 shares be transferred to the First National Bank, Wray, Colorado. Issued Certificate No. 35 for 20 shares to the First National Bank and Certificate No. 36 for 40 shares to Mr. Fishback.

REQUIRED: (a) Record the foregoing transactions in the stock transfer record of The Union Manufacturing Co. (b) Open the necessary accounts in the stockholders' ledger and post the entries from the transfer record to the stockholders' ledger. In opening the stockholders' accounts record the following balances as of December 1:

First National Bank	0 shares
Roy T. Fishback	60 shares
Harold B. Jordan	12 shares
Charles A. Patman	20 shares
Arthur Raible	50 shares
Elsie Raible	0 shares
Carl E. Roehmer	4 shares

(c) After posting the stock transfers for December, prepare a list of the stockholders showing the number of shares held by each as of December 31.

Problem 22-A

J. B. Brown and L. C. Smith were partners. They decided to incorporate their business. On January 2, the company was incorporated under the name of The Eclipse Company. The authorized capital was $800,000 divided into 80,000 shares of common stock, par value $10 each.

Brown and Smith decided to transfer all of the assets except cash and all of the liabilities of the partnership to the corporation in exchange for 41,000 shares of stock at par. The corporation was to accept the assets and the liabilities at their net book value in each case. Brown and Smith divided the cash of the partnership and the stock of the corporation in the ratio of their capital interests in the partnership.

The balance sheet of the partnership on December 31 appeared as follows:

BROWN & SMITH
BALANCE SHEET
DECEMBER 31, 19--

Assets			Liabilities	
Cash............................		$ 10,000	Notes Payable.................	$100,000
Accounts Receivable.............		150,000	Accounts Payable..............	40,000
Materials Inventory.............		100,000		
Machinery & Equip.....	$120,000		Total Liabilities.................	$140,000
Less Allow. for Depr..	20,000	100,000		
			Capital	
Buildings.............	$200,000		J. B. Brown, Partner............	252,000
Less Allow. for Depr..	40,000	160,000	L. C. Smith, Partner............	168,000
Land.........................		40,000		
Total Assets...................		$560,000	Total Liabilities and Capital.......	$560,000

REQUIRED: (a) Draft an entry in general journal form to record the acquisition of the partnership assets and liabilities in exchange for stock. (b) Calculate the number of shares of stock each partner received.

Problem 22-B

The City Manufacturing Co. is organized under the laws of Illinois with authority to issue 2,000 shares of preferred stock, par value $100 a share, and 8,000 shares of common stock with no par value.

Feb. 1. Subscriptions for capital stock, payable on demand, were accepted as follows:

> 1,000 shares of preferred stock at par
> 2,500 shares of common stock at $50 a share

Mar. 1. Cash is received from subscribers in full payment of their subscriptions accepted February 1 and stock certificates are issued to all subscribers.

July 1. Issued Certificate No. 11 for 100 shares of common stock to George L. Sherman in payment of land valued at $5,000 to be used as a site for a new factory.

Oct. 1. George L. Sherman sold 50 shares of the common stock owned by him to C. E. Harrison and requested that the transfer be made on the records of the company. Certificate No. 11 for 100 shares was canceled and Certificates Nos. 12 and 13 were issued to Mr. Sherman and Mr. Harrison for 50 shares each.

REQUIRED: Record the foregoing corporate transactions in the general journal of The City Manufacturing Co.

Problem 22-C

The City Refrigeration Co. is incorporated with an authorized capital of $250,000 of which $100,000 is preferred stock and $150,000 is common stock. Par value of shares, $100 each. All of the preferred stock is sold for cash at par value, but it is found that the common stock cannot be sold at par and the purchasers of the preferred stock donate $50,000 of their stock to the company to be given as a bonus to purchasers of the common stock. All of the common stock is then sold at par value, each subscriber receiving one share of preferred stock free as a bonus in connection with the purchase of three shares of common stock at par value.

REQUIRED: Draft the entries in general journal form to record the following transactions:

(a) Sale of preferred stock.
(b) Donation of preferred stock to the issuing company.
(c) Sale of common stock.

Problem 22-D

The Capital City Manufacturing Co. is incorporated on January 2 with the authority to issue 500 shares of preferred stock with a par value of $100 per share and 10,000 shares of common stock with a par value of $10 per share.

January 4. All of the common stock is given to the founders of the corporation in exchange for patents valued at $100,000.

January 5. The common stockholders donate 2,000 shares to the corporation to be sold to raise working capital.

January 26. All of the donated shares are sold for cash at $6 per share.

February 8. Three hundred shares of the preferred stock are exchanged for machinery and equipment valued at $34,000.

December 31. The income and expense accounts are closed to the income summary account, giving the latter a credit balance of $18,500.

REQUIRED: Draft the entries in general journal form to record the foregoing transactions and to close the income summary account.

Problem 23-A

The Lone Star Oil Co. is incorporated with an authorized issue of 500 shares of 6% preferred stock, par value $100 a share, and 1,000 shares of common stock without par value. At the time of the annual meeting of the board of directors on July 1, all of the preferred stock had been issued and was outstanding and 500 shares of the common stock had been issued at a price of $10 a share, the entire selling price having been credited to the capital stock account. The balance sheet submitted showed that the company had retained earnings amounting to $16,000.

After declaring a cash dividend (No. 11) of 6% on the preferred stock outstanding, the board declared a dividend (No. 7) on the common stock, payable in cash at the rate of $1 a share and in unissued common stock at the rate of one share for each 10 shares of common stock held. The cash dividends declared on the preferred stock and on the common stock are payable August 1 to stockholders of record July 25, and the stock dividend is to be distributed on September 1 to stockholders of record August 25. The cash dividends were paid by drawing an individual check against the regular checking account of the corporation in The Ranger National Bank for the amount due each stockholder. The common stock issued as a dividend is to be valued at $10 a share.

REQUIRED: As the accountant for The Lone Star Oil Co., record the declaration and payment of both the cash and stock dividends. Make the entries in general journal form.

Problem 23-B

The following information was taken from a recent annual report of a corporation engaged in business as a magazine publisher:

Balance of earnings retained in the business at beginning of period, $12,713,183.
Net earnings for the year ended June 30, $4,047,146.
Appropriation for replacement of publishing equipment, $305,000.
Cash dividends paid during the year on common stock, $1,935,000.
The amount appropriated for replacement of publishing equipment represents the difference between accumulated depreciation based on original cost and accumulated depreciation based on prevailing replacement cost as determined by independent appraisal.

REQUIRED: From the foregoing information prepare a statement of earnings retained for use in the business showing the balance of retained earnings at end of period.

Problem 24-A

July   1. Snow Brothers, Inc. received $488,450, representing the proceeds from the sale of $500,000 of 3½% first-mortgage bonds. The issue matures 25 years from this date. Interest is payable semiannually on January 1 and July 1.

Dec. 31. Bond interest accrued to December 31 is to be recorded.

   31. The proper amount of discount is to be amortized.

   31. The bond interest account is to be closed into Income Summary.

Jan.   1. Reverse the adjusting entry for bond interest accrued December 31.

REQUIRED: (a) Draft the entries in general journal form to record the foregoing. (b) Show calculations to prove that the balance of the bond interest account (before closing) is the proper interest expense for the first year.

Problem 24-B

It is January 1. Exactly 24 years ago The Johnson Manufacturing Co. sold an issue of 25-year, 5%, sinking-fund bonds with a maturity value of $100,000. They received $105,000 for the bonds. The interest is payable on January 1 and July 1. The conditions of the issue required that the corporation pay $2,953.03 to a sinking-fund trustee on December 31 of each year. (Twenty-five such payments, if invested to earn 5%, would accumulate to $100,000 by the date the bonds mature.) At the end of each year, the trustee reports on the earnings of the fund. A sinking-fund appropriation, equal to the amount in the fund, was required.

All interest has been paid when due. At the end of each calendar year the proper adjustments (including the amortization of the bond premium) have been made. Twenty-four payments of the proper amount have been made to the sinking-fund trustee. Sinking-fund earnings reported by the trustee have been correctly recorded. The sinking-fund appropriation has been maintained. Accordingly, as of the start of business on January 1, the general ledger of the corporation included the following accounts with the balances shown:

Bond Sinking Fund (Dr.)	$ 90,283.69
Bonds Payable (Cr.)	100,000.00
Premium on Bonds Payable (Cr.)	200.00
Bond Interest Expense (Cr.)	2,500.00
Provision for Bond Sinking Fund (Cr.)	90,283.69

The following transactions and events are to be recorded:

Jan.   1. Paid semiannual interest, $2,500.

July   1. Paid semiannual interest, $2,500.

Dec. 31. The sinking-fund trustee reports that net fund earnings during the past year were $4,462.13. (Since this brings the fund assets to only $94,745.82, the corporation will have to pay $5,254.18 to provide the required amount.)

Dec. 31. $5,254.18 is paid to the trustee.

31. The directors authorized an increase in the sinking-fund appropriation of $9,716.31.

31. $2,500 bond interest accrued.

31. The remaining balance of the premium account is to be written off.

31. The bond interest expense account and the sinking fund income account are to be closed.

Jan. 1. (Next year) Paid semiannual bond interest, $2,500.

10. The trustee reports that all bonds were redeemed and returns the bonds.

10. The directors authorized the cancellation of the sinking-fund appropriation.

REQUIRED: Prepare the entries, in general journal form, to record the foregoing transactions and events.

Problem 24-C

R. V. Williams has been operating The Williams Manufacturing Co. as a sole proprietor. He has decided to form a new company which is to be incorporated, under the name of The General Manufacturing Co. The corporation is to take over The Williams Manufacturing Co. acquiring all the assets, except cash, and assuming the existing liabilities. Mr. Williams is to be allowed a price equal to the present worth of The Williams Manufacturing Co. (after deducting cash), with no allowance for goodwill or other intangible assets.

The General Manufacturing Co. was incorporated January 1, with an authorized capital stock of $4,000,000, consisting of 10,000 shares of 7% cumulative preferred stock, par value $100 a share, and 30,000 shares of common stock, par value $100 a share.

Following is a summary of the operations of the corporation for the year ending December 31, after incorporation:

(a) Subscriptions to the capital stock were as follows:

R. V. Williams — 5,000 shares common and 5,000 shares preferred stock
A. B. Opfer — 2,000 shares common and 1,000 shares preferred stock
H. W. Henry — 1,000 shares preferred stock
C. H. Bowser — 5,000 shares common stock
Maude E. Barnes — 1,500 shares common and 1,500 shares preferred stock
Ruth E. Forry — 2,000 shares common and 1,500 shares preferred stock
R. O. Wiggins — 5,000 shares common stock
E. W. Atkinson — 5,500 shares common stock

The stock was subscribed for at par, payment to be made upon demand. Certificates of stock are not to be issued until subscriptions are paid in full.

(b) A firm of certified public accountants was engaged to audit the books of The Williams Manufacturing Co. and to prepare a balance sheet showing the amount of Mr. Williams' equity in the business. The accountants submitted the following certified balance sheet which reveals an equity of $1,671,000:

THE WILLIAMS MANUFACTURING CO.
BALANCE SHEET
DECEMBER 31, 19--

Assets			Liabilities		
Cash....................		$ 69,330	Notes Payable, Bank..	$ 590,000	
Notes Receivable.....	$ 24,340		Notes Payable, Trade.	57,000	
Accounts Receivable..	98,181		Accounts Payable....	416,344	
	$ 122,521		Total Liabilities..............		$1,063,344
Less Allow. for Bad			*Proprietorship*		
Debts..........	8,925	113,596	R. V. Williams, Proprietor.......		1,671,000
Merchandise Inventory........		223,258			
Furniture & Fixtures..	$ 8,976				
Less Allow. for Depr.	816	8,160			
Machinery, Tools, and					
Equipment	$1,356,000				
Less Allow. for Depr.	226,000	1,130,000			
Buildings		690,000			
Land		500,000			
Total Assets.................		$2,734,344	Total Liab. & Proprietorship....		$2,734,344

After deducting cash, Mr. Williams' equity amounts to $1,601,670. In view of the fact that Mr. Williams has decided to purchase bonds to be issued by the corporation, it is agreed that any amount due him, after crediting his subscription account with the amount he owes the corporation on account of subscriptions to common and preferred stock, will be credited to his personal account until the details of the bond issue may be completed. Stock certificates are issued to Mr. Williams immediately.

(c) C. H. Bowser and R. O. Wiggins pay their subscriptions to the capital stock by conveying to the company title to patents valued at $1,000,000. Stock certificates are issued.

(d) Following the organization of The General Manufacturing Co., it was decided to issue bonds as follows: (maturity value, $1,000 each).

First Mortgage Bonds, 5%, 20 years, $120,000
Second Mortgage Bonds, 6%, 15 years, $398,000
Debenture Bonds, 5%, 10 years, $153,000

R. V. Williams purchased the entire bond issue at par, thereby canceling his account against the company, he paying the difference, $69,330, in cash.

(e) Upon demand, the following subscribers to the capital stock paid their subscriptions in full in cash and stock certificates were issued:

A. B. Opfer.....................................	$300,000
H. W. Henry....................................	100,000
Maude E. Barnes................................	300,000
Ruth E. Forry..................................	350,000
E. W. Atkinson.................................	550,000

REQUIRED: Record the foregoing transactions in general journal form.

Problem 25-A

Construction Enterprises, Inc. owns a sand pit that had been purchased a few years before for $15,000. The accountant has been calculating depletion on the basis of 3 cents for every cubic yard of sand excavated. At the beginning of the current year the balance of the allowance for depletion account was $1,780. During the first four months of this year 10,000 cubic yards of sand were excavated and on May 2 the pit was sold for $13,400 cash.

REQUIRED: Draft entries, in general journal form, to record (a) the depletion for the first four months of the year, and (b) the sale of the sand pit.

Problem 25-B

A corporation acquired by purchase a lease on a tract of land at a cost of $14,000. Under the terms of the lease, the corporation is required to pay the lessor an annual rental of $12,000. The lease will expire in 10 years. Immediately upon acquiring the lease, improvements were made at a total cost of $2,000.

REQUIRED: Record the following in general journal form:

(a) The payment for the lease.
(b) The cost of the improvements assuming that they were paid for in cash.
(c) The annual rent paid to the lessor.
(d) The portion of the leasehold cost to be amortized at the end of the first year.
(e) The amortization of the leasehold improvements at the end of the first year.

Problem 26-A

The Charleston Mfg. Co. uses the following books of original entry:

Voucher register
Sales record
Record of cash receipts
Check register
General journal

The general journal is of the ordinary two-column type.

Following is a narrative of the transactions completed during the month of May that should be recorded in the general journal:

May 5. Received a credit memorandum for $54.80 from the William Anderson Company for raw materials returned that were originally included on Voucher No. 687.

     7. Received a 60-day, 6% note for $350 from Henry S. Moore and Co. in temporary settlement of their account.

    10. Issued a credit memorandum for $25.65 to H. R. Martinson Bros. for finished goods returned on their purchase of May 1.

    12. Received a corrected invoice from the Stewart Supply Company for raw materials amounting to $118.75. The amount of the original invoice represented by Voucher No. 635 was $128.75. (A new voucher was not issued.)

    15. Issued a 60-day, 6% note for $835 to Barnham and Crow in temporary settlement of their invoice of April 15. Voucher No. 583.

    19. Issued a credit memorandum for $11.75 to C. H. Frederick as an allowance on defective goods received by him on May 10.

    22. Received a 30-day, 5% note for $475 from John L. Thomas and Company in settlement of their invoice of March 30.

    26. Received a credit memorandum for $43.80 from the Masters Foundry Co. representing an allowance on raw materials covered by Voucher No. 632.

    29. Issued a 30-day, 6% note for $625 to the American Supply Company in settlement of invoice of April 25. Voucher No. 615.

REQUIRED: Using two-column paper, record the foregoing transactions in general journal form, assuming that the following accounts are kept, among others:

Vouchers Payable	Sales Returns and Allowances
Raw Material Returns and Allowances	Purchases
Notes Receivable	Notes Payable
Accounts Receivable	

Problem 26-B

The Jubilee Radio Mfg. Co., a corporation just organized, plans to use a voucher register and a check register similar to those shown on page 625.

NARRATIVE OF TRANSACTIONS

(Assume that checks were issued in payment of invoices, subject to discount, on the day preceding the last day of the discount period.)

Oct. 1. Issued Voucher No. 1 for $50 to establish a petty cash fund, and cashed Check No. 1 for that amount. (Petty Cash Fund, Account No. 112.)

1. Received an invoice for $75 from the Churchill Real Estate Co., 55 West Fifth St., for rent. Issued Check No. 2 in payment of the invoice. (Rent Expense, Account No. 814.)

2. Received an invoice for $1,687.50 from the Morrison Radio Manufacturers, Inc., Detroit, Michigan, for raw materials. Date of invoices September 30; terms, 1/10, n/30.

5. Received a freight bill for $84.30 from the B. & O. Railway Company, the charges on the materials shipped by the Morrison Radio Manufacturers, Inc. Paid the bill with Check No. 3. (Transportation In, Account No. 72.)

5. Received an invoice for $150 from Reade Equipment Co., 120 East Fourth St., for an office desk purchased. Date of invoice, October 3; terms, net 30 days. (Office Equipment, Account No. 21.)

6. Received a bill for telephone service from the Citizens Telephone Co., 104 Chestnut St., and issued Check No. 4 for $15.25 in payment. (General Office Expense, Account No. 818.)

7. Received a bill for office supplies from Frederick A. Glenco & Co., 508 Walnut St., and issued Check No. 5 for $48.50 in payment. (Office Supplies, Account No. 181.)

9. Received an invoice for $937.25 from W. M. Clark & Sons Co., Cleveland, for a shipment of raw materials. Of this amount $42.70 represented prepaid freight charges. Date of invoice, October 8; terms, 2/15, n/60.

12. Received an invoice for $76.35 from the National Advertising Co., 709 Union Central Building, for advertising service. Issued Check No. 7 in payment. (Advertising Expense, Account No. 823.)

13. Received an invoice for $41.50 from the Gibraltar Insurance Co., 2411 Carew Tower, for insurance. Issued Check No. 8 in payment. (Prepaid Insurance, Account No. 184.)

14. Received an invoice for $1,805.35 from the Goldtone Radio Mfg. Co., Chicago, for a shipment of radio parts. Date of invoice, October 11; terms, 1/10, n/30.

15. Received from the New York Central Railway a freight bill for $94.35, the charges on the radios shipped by the Goldtone Radio Mfg. Co. Paid the bill with Check No. 9.

Oct. 15. Issued Payroll Voucher No. 13 covering wages earned for the half month as follows:

> Direct labor, $810
> Indirect labor, $72.50
> Office salaries, $650
> Sales salaries, $500

Taxes withheld:

> F.I.C.A. taxes, $45.73
> Employees' income taxes, $252

Issued Check No. 10 in payment of Payroll Voucher No. 13.

The following accounts will be affected in recording the payroll:

> 111 Bank
> 311 F.I.C.A. Taxes Payable
> 32 Employees' Income Taxes Payable
> 36 Vouchers Payable
> 73 Direct Labor
> 741 Indirect Labor
> 811 Office Salaries
> 821 Sales Salaries

17. Issued a voucher for $50 to be used in purchasing stamps for use in the office. Cashed Check No. 11 for this amount and obtained the stamps. (Charge to Office Supplies, Account No. 181.)

19. Received from the First National Bank a notice of the maturity of a $500 note dated September 21 and discounted at the bank. Issued Check No. 12 for that amount. (Notes Payable, Account No. 34.)

20. Received an invoice from the Henderson Repair Shop, 238 East Third St., for $21.75, the cost of repairs on factory machinery. Issued Check No. 13 in payment. (Factory Repairs, Account No. 747.)

22. Received an invoice for $2,518.70 from Gradison Bros., Pittsburgh, for a shipment of raw materials. Of this amount $105.65 represented prepaid freight charges. Date of invoice, October 20; terms, 1/10, n/30.

23. Received an invoice for $138.25 for factory supplies purchased from the Marx Box Co., 54 Elm St. Terms, on account. (Factory Supplies, Account No. 183.)

26. Received an invoice from the R. C. Mollison Co., Dayton, for $165, the cost of a lift truck for use in the factory. Terms, net 30 days. (Factory Equipment, Account No. 23.)

29. Received an invoice for $912.40 from the Campton Mfg. Co., Inc., Akron, for a shipment of raw materials. Of this amount $62.70 represented prepaid freight charges. Date of invoice, October 28; terms, 2/10, n/30.

31. Issued Payroll Voucher No. 21 covering wages earned for the half month as follows:

> Direct labor, $790
> Indirect labor, $84
> Office salaries, $650
> Sales salaries, $500

Taxes withheld:

> F.I.C.A. taxes, $45.54
> Employees' income taxes, $259

Issued Check No. 17 in payment of Payroll Voucher No. 21.

Required: (a) Record the foregoing transactions in the voucher register and check register. (b) Foot and prove the footings of both the voucher register and the check register. (c) Open an account for vouchers payable and post the footings of the Vouchers Payable columns in the voucher register and the check register. (d) Prove the balance of the vouchers payable account by preparing a schedule of the unpaid vouchers from the voucher register.

Problem 27-A

The Ajax Manufacturing Company uses three raw materials designated A, B, and C. Data relative to inventories, purchases, and market prices of these materials are as follows:

MATERIALS

	A	B	C
Opening Inventory	6,000 @ $1.00	20,000 @ $.08	500 @ $30.00
Purchases (in order)	12,000 @ 1.10	80,000 @ .09	1,000 @ 28.00
	20,000 @ 1.15		2,000 @ 32.00
	4,000 @ 1.30		
Ending Inventory	5,000 units	15,000 units	1,800 units
Market price, end of period	$1.35	$.085	$32.00

Required: (a) On a first-in, first-out basis, calculate the total cost of the ending inventory of each of the three items. (b) Compute the market value of the ending inventory of each of the three items. (c) If the "cost or market, whichever is lower" rule is to be followed, what is the total value of the ending inventory of raw materials?

Problem 27-B

The Superior Machine Tool Co. is a manufacturer of machine tools. Following is a list of the accounts used in recording manufacturing costs. You are required to assign appropriate numbers to these accounts.

VII Manufacturing Costs
    Raw Material Purchases
      Raw Material Returns and Allowances
    Transportation In
    Direct Labor
    Manufacturing Expenses
      Indirect Labor
      Light, Heat, and Power
      Factory Supplies Consumed
      Factory Building Maintenance
      Depreciation of Factory Equipment
      Depreciation of Factory Building
      Expired Insurance on Factory Property
      Factory Repairs
      Patent Expense
      Factory Property Taxes
      Social Security Taxes — Factory Wages
    Manufacturing Summary

Problem 28-A

The Madison Manufacturing Co. operates on the basis of a fiscal year ending June 30. Following are the adjusted balances of the accounts affecting the cost of goods manufactured:

Raw Materials Inventory (beginning of year).....................	$31,500
Goods in Process Inventory (beginning of year).................	14,800
Raw Material Purchases......................................	85,750
Raw Material Returns and Allowances.........................	1,970
Transportation In...	2,430
Direct Labor...	71,200
Indirect Labor...	13,800
Light, Heat, and Power......................................	10,500
Maintenance and Repairs....................................	5,790
Factory Property Taxes......................................	3,600
Depreciation of Machinery and Equipment.....................	11,500
Depreciation of Factory Building.............................	3,500
Factory Supplies Used.......................................	4,890
Expired Insurance on Machinery and Equipment................	1,080
Expired Insurance on Factory Building........................	720
Social Security Taxes, Factory...............................	3,825
Sundry Factory Expense.....................................	1,300

Inventories, end of year:

Raw Materials...	$37,830
Goods in Process..	19,500

REQUIRED: Prepare a manufacturing statement showing the cost of goods finished during the year. Follow the form of the statement shown on page 660.

Problem 28-B

The Hagan Manufacturing Co. keeps its accounts on the calendar year basis, but the accountant prepares monthly statements. Data for adjustment of the accounts are assembled and entered on a work sheet at the end of each month, although adjustments of the general ledger accounts are recorded only at the end of each year. The manufacturing expense accounts, however, are formally adjusted at the end of each month. This group of accounts is kept in a subsidiary ledger, controlled by the manufacturing expenses account in the general ledger. The following trial balance was taken on December 31 after the manufacturing expense adjusting entries for the month had been posted. (It will be noted that a few of the accounts have no balances. These accounts are included because they will be affected by the adjusting entries required on the work sheet.)

THE HAGAN MANUFACTURING CO.
TRIAL BALANCE, DECEMBER 31, 19--

Account	No.	Debit	Credit
American National Bank	111	$ 12,580.00	
Petty Cash Fund	112	50.00	
Notes Receivable	131	1,678.00	
Accrued Interest Receivable	132		
Accounts Receivable	133	5,744.00	
Allowance for Bad Debts	013		$ 148.00
Subscriptions Receivable	134	5,000.00	
Raw Materials Inventory	161	2,165.00	
Goods in Process Inventory	162	1,672.00	
Finished Goods Inventory	163	4,213.00	
Office Supplies	181	278.00	
Factory Supplies	183	513.00	
Prepaid Insurance	184	525.00	
Office Equipment	21	1,950.00	
Allowance for Depreciation of Office Equipment	021		186.00
Delivery Equipment	22	2,500.00	
Allowance for Depreciation of Delivery Equipment	022		625.00
Machinery and Equipment	23	25,000.00	
Allowance for Depreciation of Machinery and Equipment	023		7,800.00
Building	24	37,000.00	
Allowance for Depreciation of Building	024		7,500.00
Land	25	4,000.00	
F. I. C. A. Taxes Payable	311		177.33
F. U. T. A. Taxes Payable	312		141.86
State U. C. Taxes Payable	313		319.19
Employees' Income Taxes Payable	32		560.00
Corporation Income Taxes Payable	33		
Notes Payable	34		3,890.00
Accrued Interest Payable	35		
Vouchers Payable	36		10,397.00
Dividends Payable	37		75.00
Mortgage Payable	41		3,500.00
Capital Stock	51		38,000.00
Capital Stock Subscribed	52		12,500.00
Retained Earnings	54		12,234.00
Sales	611		92,134.24
Sales Returns and Allowances	0611	525.00	
Cost of Goods Sold	0621		
Interest Income	631		88.00
Purchases Discount	632		649.00
Raw Material Purchases	71	21,346.00	
Raw Material Returns and Allowances	071		237.00
Transportation In	72	1,976.00	
Direct Labor	73	27,138.00	
Manufacturing Expenses	74	11,951.53	
Manufacturing Summary	76		
Officers' Salaries	811	8,400.00	
Office Salaries	812	2,135.00	
Office Supplies Consumed	813		
Depreciation of Office Equipment	814		
Expired Insurance on Office Equipment	815		
Social Security Taxes (Adm.)	816	553.09	
General Office Expenses	817	434.00	
Sales Salaries	831	6,000.00	
Advertising Expense	832	1,917.00	
Depreciation of Delivery Equipment	833		
Expired Insurance on Delivery Equipment	834		
General Delivery Expense	835	1,776.00	
Bad Debts Expense	836		
Expired Insurance on Finished Goods	837		
Social Security Taxes (Sales)	838	315.00	
General Selling Expenses	839	635.00	
Interest Expense	91	247.00	
Sales Discount	92	945.00	
Corporation Income Taxes	93		
		$191,161.62	$191,161.62

The following schedule of manufacturing expense accounts was prepared after posting the adjusting entries for December:

SCHEDULE OF MANUFACTURING EXPENSES
DECEMBER 31, 19--

Indirect Labor	741	$ 3,615.00
Light, Heat, and Power	742	2,800.00
Maintenance and Repairs	743	418.00
Depreciation of Factory Property	744	2,870.00
Expired Insurance on Factory Property	745	308.00
Social Security Taxes (Factory)	746	1,614.53
General Factory Expenses	747	326.00
		$11,951.53

The following information is provided: (Bear in mind that the manufacturing expense accounts have already been adjusted.)

DATA FOR YEAR-END ADJUSTMENT OF GENERAL LEDGER ACCOUNTS
DECEMBER 31, 19--

Inventories:		
Raw materials		$1,875.00
Goods in process		1,400.00
Finished goods		4,510.00
Accruals:		
Accrued interest receivable		7.00
Accrued interest payable		26.00
Office supplies consumed		225.00
Depreciation of office equipment		395.00
Depreciation of delivery equipment		625.00
Insurance expired:		
On office equipment	$22.00	
On delivery equipment	37.00	
On finished goods	34.00	93.00
Provision for bad debts		450.00
Provision for corporation income taxes		1,422.79

REQUIRED: (a) Using twelve-column analysis paper, prepare an end-of-year work sheet as a means of summarizing and classifying the information needed in preparing financial statements.

(b) Prepare an income statement for the year ended December 31.

(c) Prepare a manufacturing statement for the year ended December 31.

(d) Prepare a balance sheet as of December 31 in account form.

(e) Prepare a statement of retained earnings for the year ended December 31. (Dividends paid during the year amounted to $1,900.)

(f) Journalize the adjusting and closing entries.

(g) Using balance-column ledger paper, open the following accounts:

132 Accrued Interest Receivable
35 Accrued Interest Payable
53 Income Summary
54 Retained Earnings
0621 Cost of Goods Sold
631 Interest Income
76 Manufacturing Summary
91 Interest Expense

Post the adjusting and closing entries that affect these accounts.

(h) Journalize the entries required to reverse the adjusting entries for accruals and post to the accounts affected.

Problem 29-A

The ledger accounts of The Miller Appliance Co. had the following balances on January 1:

Bank	$ 16,100	
Accounts Receivable	19,400	
Allowance for Bad Debts		$ 600
Merchandise Inventory	13,500	
Prepaid Insurance	200	
Furniture and Fixtures	12,000	
Allowance for Depreciation of Furniture and Fixtures		5,800
Building	40,000	
Allowance for Depreciation of Building		8,000
Land	5,000	
Vouchers Payable		11,300
Capital Stock		60,000
Retained Earnings		20,500
	$106,200	$106,200

On January 2, the company established two branches, one in the northern part of the state, called the North Branch, and another in the western part of the state, called the West Branch.

Following is a narrative of transactions completed by the home office and the two branches: (Many of the transactions are given in summary form.)

(1) Home office sent $5,000 to North Branch.

(2) Home office sent $6,000 to West Branch.

(3) Total purchases of merchandise at home office, $150,000 (on account).

(4) Total shipments of merchandise to North Branch (at cost), $38,000.

(5) Total shipments of merchandise to West Branch (at cost), $46,000.

(6) Furniture and fixtures purchased for cash at North Branch, $4,000; insurance premium paid, $150.

(7) Furniture and fixtures purchased for cash at West Branch, $4,800; insurance premium paid, $160.

(8) Sales at home office: cash, $33,000; on account, $77,000.

(9) Sales at North Branch: cash, $14,000; on account, $31,000.

(10) Sales at West Branch: cash, $10,000; on account, $40,000.

(11) Operating expenses vouchered at home office, $18,400.

(12) Operating expenses vouchered at North Branch, $8,900.

(13) Operating expenses vouchered at West Branch, $9,600.

(14) Collected on accounts receivable at home office, $80,000; accounts written off as worthless, $500.

(15) Collected on accounts receivable at North Branch, $25,000.

(16) Collected on accounts receivable at West Branch, $20,000.

(17) Cash sent by North Branch to West Branch, $10,000.

(18) Cash payments on vouchers at North Branch, $8,200.

(19) Cash payments on vouchers at West Branch, $9,300.

(20) Cash sent to home office by North Branch, $18,000.

(21) Cash sent to home office by West Branch, $27,000.

(22) Cash payments on vouchers at home office, $160,000.

REQUIRED: (a) Using two-column journal paper, journalize the foregoing transactions as they should be recorded in the books of the home office and both branch offices. Since dates are purposely omitted, it will be advisable to number each journal entry to correspond with the number of the transaction.

(b) Using plain paper, 8½″ x 11″, rule 26 "T" account forms (eight to a page arranged in 2 columns) under the heading Home Office Ledger. In addition to the 13 accounts appearing in the trial balance at beginning of year, the following accounts will be needed: North Branch, West Branch, Purchases, Shipments to North Branch, Shipments to West Branch, Sales, Operating Expenses, Cost of Goods Sold, North Branch Profit, West Branch Profit, Corporation Income Taxes, Corporation Income Taxes Payable, and Income Summary. Enter the opening balances.

Rule 13 "T" account forms under the heading North Branch Ledger. Also rule 13 "T" account forms under the heading West Branch Ledger. In each case the following accounts are needed: Bank, Accounts Receivable, Allowance for Bad Debts, Merchandise Inventory, Prepaid Insurance, Shipments from Home Office, Furniture and Fixtures, Allowance for Depreciation of Furniture and Fixtures, Vouchers Payable, Home Office, Sales, Operating Expenses, and Income Summary.

Post the journal entries to the "T" accounts of each ledger. Number each entry to correspond with the number of the journal entry.

(c) Take a trial balance as of December 31 of the accounts kept for each office.

(23) End-of-year adjustments for North Branch:

   (a) Merchandise inventory, $7,000.
   (b) Depreciation of furniture and fixtures, $400.
   (c) Insurance expired, $50.
   (d) Provision for bad debts, $800.
       (Charge *b*, *c*, and *d* to Operating Expenses.)

Journalize the adjusting entries and post to the accounts affected. Also journalize the entries required to close the temporary accounts and to transfer the net profit to the home office account.

(24) End-of-year adjustments for West Branch:

   (a) Merchandise inventory, $12,000.
   (b) Depreciation of furniture and fixtures, $480.
   (c) Insurance expired, $60.
   (d) Provision for bad debts, $1,200.
       (Charge *b*, *c*, and *d* to Operating Expenses.)

Journalize the adjusting entries and post to the accounts affected. Also journalize the entries required to close the temporary accounts and to transfer the net profit to the home office account.

(25) End-of-year adjustments for home office:
    (a) Transfer the opening inventory and the balances of purchases and shipments to branch accounts to Cost of Goods Sold.
    (b) Ending inventory, $14,000.
    (c) Depreciation of furniture and fixtures, $1,200.
    (d) Depreciation of building, $1,000.
    (e) Insurance expired, $170.
    (f) Provision for bad debts, $1,650.
        (Charge *c, d, e*, and *f* to Operating Expenses.)
    (g) Record the net profits of the branch offices in the home office books.
    (h) Provision for corporation income taxes, estimated, $10,400.

Journalize the adjusting entries and post to the accounts affected. Also journalize the entries required to close the temporary accounts and to transfer the net profit to Retained Earnings.

Prepare a work sheet for a consolidated income statement. The form of this work sheet should be similar to that illustrated on page 690. Prepare a consolidated income statement similar to the one illustrated on page 691.

Prepare a work sheet for a consolidated balance sheet. The form of this work sheet should be similar to that illustrated on page 692. Prepare a consolidated balance sheet similar to the one illustrated on page 693.

Problem 29-B

The Cooper Company bills its branch at 20% above cost for goods shipped to it. The home office credits the difference between the cost and the billed price to Provision for Overvaluation of Branch Inventory. At the start of the year, the branch inventory (at billed price) was $16,800. Accordingly, the provision account in the home office books had a credit balance of $2,800. During the year the cost of goods shipped to the branch was $125,000; the billed price was $150,000.

At the end of the year the branch submitted an income statement showing cost of goods sold to be $142,800 and net profit to be $13,000. The branch balance sheet showed the ending inventory to be $24,000.

REQUIRED: (a) Compute the actual cost of goods sold by the branch office.

(b) Compute the actual net profit of the branch office.

(c) Compute the actual cost of the goods in the branch office inventory at end of year.

(d) Draft a journal entry to record, in the home office books, the actual branch profit and to adjust the Provision for Overvaluation of Branch Inventory.

INDEX

A

PAGE

A.B.A. Numbers.................... 99
Accommodation Endorsement........ 333
Account.......................... 15
  Advertising Expense............... 512
  Balance-Column Form............. 151
  Bank............................ 109
  Cash............................ 81
  Checking........................ 97
  Clearing........................ 204
  Cost of Goods Sold................ 213
  Income Summary.................. 511
  Notes Payable.................... 337
  Notes Receivable.................. 331
  Organization Expense.............. 568
  Purchases........................ 50
  Purchases Returns and Allowances... 51
  Retained Earnings................. 574
  Sales.......................56, 402
  Sales Returns and Allowances....... 57
  Savings......................... 111
  Standard Form................... 16
  Subscriber's.................550, 552
  "T" Form....................... 17
Accounting
  Accrual Basis.................... 139
  Cash Basis...................... 229
  Cycle.......................228, 514
  Elements........................ 10
  Equation........................ 12
  Methods.....................229–264
  Payroll.....................117–138
  Procedure........27–48, 65–80, 139, 158
  vs. Bookkeeping.................. 10
Accounting for
  Bad Debts....................... 144
  Bond Interest Expense..........587–599
  Bonds Issued.................... 593
  Bonds Retired................600–610
  Bonds Sold....................587–599
  Branch Operations..............673–696
  Capital Stock..................555–572
  Capital Stock Subscriptions........ 564
  Cash..........................81–116
  Corporation Bonds.............587–610
  Corporation Earnings...........573–586
  Depreciation.................... 146
  Intangible and Wasting Assets....611–620
  Interest Expense................. 148
  Interest Income.................. 142
  Inventory and Prepaid Expenses..411–430
  Investments..................... 250
  Manufacturers.................635–672
  Merchandise....................49–80
  Merchandise Billed to Branch in Excess of Cost.................... 693
  No-Par-Value Stock.............. 569
  Notes and Drafts.............321–350

PAGE

Notes Payable.................148, 335
Notes Receivable..............142, 326
Prepaid Expenses................. 146
Proprietorship.................289–320
Purchases.....................351–376
Retail Store...................139–184
Sale of Real Property............. 254
Sales.........................377–410
Securities....................... 255
Sinking Funds................... 604
Tangible Fixed Assets..........431–446
Treasury Stock.................. 567
Wages and Wage Deductions....... 130
Wholesale Merchant...........447–478
Accounting Period.................. 21
  Calendar Year................... 21
  Fiscal Year...................... 21
Accounting Procedure
  End of Month.................479–496
  End of Year..................409–514
Accounting Procedure in Closing
  Books of a Manufacturer.......... 663
  Branch Office Books.............. 681
  Home Office Books............... 685
Accounting, Voucher System of....612–634
Accounts
  Adjusting....................... 663
  Balancing....................... 511
  Chart of........................ 30
  Closing Temporary................ 663
  Contra......................141, 231
  Control......................... 152
  Corporate....................... 563
  Footing.......................24, 41
  Interlocking..................... 673
  Manufacturing................... 655
  Merchandise..................... 50
  Payable.......................10, 52
    Control...................... 152
    Ledger....................158, 455
    Schedule of..............55, 371, 488
  Permanent Proprietorship.......... 203
  Proprietary..................... 294
  Proving the Balances.............. 42
  Receivable.....................10, 60
    Control...................... 152
    Ledger....................158, 454
    Schedule of............64, 394, 486
    Turnover..................... 507
  Reciprocal...................... 673
    Reconcilation of................ 695
  Ruling.....................217, 222, 511
  Temporary Proprietorship......... 21
  Transportation.................. 373
Accounts with
  Creditors....................... 150
  Customers...................... 150

PAGE

Accrual
  Adjustments...................... 224
  Basis of Accounting.............. 139
Accrued
  Expenses......................... 484
  Interest Payable...149, 188, 227, 340, 494
  Interest Receivable.143, 188, 226, 338, 494
Acid-Test Ratio.................... 505
Adjusted Trial Balance............189, 655
Adjusting
  Accounts......................... 663
  Entries...............209–214, 246, 649
    Journalizing.................210, 480
    Posting.....................213, 485
  General Ledger Accounts.......... 509
Adjusting and Closing Accounts at End
  of Accounting Period...........209–228
Adjustment Bonds................... 588
Adjustment Columns................. 187
Adjustments........................ 489
  Accrual.......................... 224
  Deferral......................... 428
  End-of-Period.................... 140
Advances on Behalf of Clients...... 231
Advertising Supplies............... 422
Amortization...................432, 597
  Bond Premium..................... 597
  Copyrights....................... 613
  Discount......................... 597
  Goodwill......................... 618
  Leasehold........................ 614
Annual Report of a Manufacturer...657–662
Application for Social Security Account
  Number........................... 123
Application of Accounting Principles
           156–184, 447–478, 585, 608
Appreciation Bonds................. 255
Appreciation in Corporate Assets... 579
Appreciation of Fixed Assets....... 579
Appropriations of Retained Earnings... 576
Articles of Copartnership.........295–297
Assessments........................ 433
Asset Valuation Accounts........... 446
Assets.............................9, 10
  Current.......................... 199
  Fixed............................ 202
  Intangible....................... 611
  Quick........................205, 505
  Wasting.......................... 611
Assets, Liabilities, and Proprietorship...9–14
Authorization of Capital Stock..... 563
Authorized Capital................. 556
Automatic Teller Machines.......... 101
Auxiliary Records...114, 158, 239, 456, 648
Average Costing.................... 414

B

Back Orders........................ 355
Bad Debts......................144, 485
  Expense.......................... 144
  Loss from........................ 144
Balance-Column Account Form........ 151

PAGE

Balance of Income Summary Account,
  Disposition of................... 294
Balance Sheet........45, 198, 502–508, 656
  Analysis......................... 205
  Classification of Data........... 199
  Columns.......................... 190
  Corporate Accounts in the........ 319
  Form of.......................... 198
    Account.....................198, 200
    Report......................198, 201
  Importance of.................... 198
  Interpreting.................502, 659
  Ratio Analysis................... 505
Balances
  Credit........................... 24
  Debit............................ 24
Balancing
  Cashbook......................... 87
  Open Accounts.................... 222
Balancing and Ruling Account....... 511
Bank
  A.B.A. Numbers................... 99
  Account.......................... 109
  Automatic Teller Machines........ 101
  Checkbook........................ 103
  Checking Account................. 97
  Deposit Ticket................... 98
  Reconciling Balance.............. 108
  Savings Account.................. 111
  Service Charges.................. 109
  Signature Card................... 98
  Statement of Account............. 107
Banking Procedure...............97–111
Bases of Inventory Valuation....... 638
  Cost............................. 638
  Cost or Market, Whichever is Lower . 638
Bearer Bonds....................... 590
Bid and Offered Prices............. 559
Bill of Lading..................... 358
Billing............................ 381
Blank Endorsement.................. 333
Board of Directors.............308, 545
Bond............................... 587
Bond Interest Expense.............. 596
Bonds.............................. 255
  Adjustment....................... 588
  Appreciation..................... 255
  Bearer........................... 590
  Callable......................... 560
  Collateral-Trust................. 589
  Convertible...................... 591
  Corporation..................255, 259
  Corporation First Mortgage....... 592
  Coupon........................... 590
  Current Income................... 255
  Debenture........................ 589
  Government...................255–259
  Guaranteed....................... 589
  Improvement...................... 588
  Income........................... 589
  Indenture........................ 590
  Mortgage......................... 589

	PAGE
Public	255
Purchase-Money	588
Record of	262
Redeemable	591
Refunding	588
Registered	590
Serial	591
Sinking-Fund	590, 603
U. S. Savings	255
U. S. Treasury	257
Bonds, Classification of	588
As to Payment of Interest	590
As to Payment of Principal	590
As to Purpose of Issue	588
As to Security	589
Bonds Issued, Accounting for	593
Bonds Retired, Accounting for	600–610
Book	
Inventories	641
Stock Certificate	551
Value	202, 311, 557
Book of Original Entry	28, 156
Books of Final Entry	156
Branch Accounting Procedure	675
Branch Office Books	
Balance Sheet	683
Closing	681
Income Statement	683
Ledger	678
Post-Closing Trial Balance	684
Trial Balance	678
Work Sheet	682
Branch Operations, Accounting for	673–696
Buildings	251, 431–438
Burden	637
Business Enterprises	229
Business Papers	27
Bylaws	541

C

	PAGE
Calendar Year	21
Canceled Insurance	427
Capital	11
Authorized	556
Invested	573
Stock	260, 310
Accounting for	555–572
Discount	566
Premium	566
Subscriptions	564
Transactions	569
Types of	555–562
Values of	555–562
Watered	567
Working	206
Case Docket	240
Cash	
Account	81
Accounting for	81–116
Basis of Accounting	229
Disbursements	82
Journal	83
Records of	81–97

	PAGE
Discounts	356
Dividends	581
Over and Short	87
Proving	86
Purchases	372
Receipts	81
Sales	377–396
Cashbook	83
Advantages of	85
Balancing	87
Footing	87
Illustrated	83
Posting from	89
Ruling	87
Cashier's Check	321
Cash Payments Journal	83
Cash Receipts	81
Journal	82
Records of	81–97
Certificate of Stock	311
Certificate of Incorporation	539, 540
Certified Check	321
Certified Public Accountant	10
Charge	17
Charges, Deferred	599
Charter	308, 309, 539
Chart of Accounts	30, 66, 141, 232, 455, 644
Chart of Accounts and Records of a Manufacturer	643–648
Check	
Cashier's	321
Certified	321
Recording	629
Register	83, 625, 629
Posting	629
Travelers'	322
Voucher	628
Writer	105
Checkbook	103, 458
Checking Account	97
Checks	104
Counter	108
Dishonored	101
Postdated	102
Writing	104
Classes of Capital Stock	559
Common	559
Preferred	559
Clearing Account	204
Closing	
Accounts at End of Accounting Period	209–228
Accounts	
General Ledger	509
Operating Expense Ledger	512
Books of a Manufacturer	663–672
Entries	215, 248, 666
Procedure	214–228
Temporary Accounts	663
Collateral-Trust Bonds	589
Collection Docket	242
Collection Fees	233
Collect on Delivery	378
C.O.D. Purchases	359, 372

PAGE

C.O.D. Sales........................ 394
Combined Cash-Journal...........90, 159
  Footing......................... 94
  Form of........................ 90
  Illustrated..................... 91
  Mercantile Enterprise.......168–169
  Personal Service Enterprise......... 238
  Posting from.................... 94
    Individual.................... 94
    Summary..................... 95
  Proving......................... 93
  Ruling.......................... 94
Commission on Consignment Sales.... 407
Common Stock.............260, 310, 559
Compensation of Partners............ 302
Composite Rate of Depreciation....... 435
Compound Journal Entry............ 132
Computing Wages................... 118
Consignee.......................... 402
  Books........................... 408
Consignment Sales..............402–410
  Accounting for.................... 404
  Commission.................... 407
  Consignee...................... 402
  Consignor...................... 402
  Invoice of Shipment.............. 402
  Statement of.................403, 405
Consignor.......................... 402
  Books........................... 406
Consolidated Financial Statements. .689–696
Contingent Fee..................... 231
Contingent Liability................. 329
Contra Accounts................141, 231
Control Accounts................... 152
Convertible Bonds.................. 591
Convertible Stock.................. 561
Copyrights.....................431, 613
Corporate
  Accounts....................312, 563
    Balance Sheet, in the............ 319
  Assets, Appreciation in........... 579
  Organization.................535–554
  Records....................546–554
  Transactions.................... 312
Corporation....................307–320
  Board of Directors............... 308
    Executive Committee........... 310
  Bonds.......................255, 259
    Accounting for.............587–610
  Bylaws.....................541–543
  Certificate of Stock............... 311
  Charter....................308, 309
  Directors........................ 309
  Domestic........................ 537
  Earnings, Accounting for........573–586
  First Mortgage Bonds............. 592
  Foreign......................... 537
  Minute Book.................... 547
  Officers........................ 310
  Organization of.................. 307
  Ownership of a.................. 308
  Stockholders.................... 308
  Stocks.......................... 260
Corrected Invoices................. 631

PAGE

Correcting Errors................... 79
Cosignor.......................... 333
Cost Apportionment................ 416
Cost of Goods Sold Account......... 213
Cost of Goods Sold, Schedule of....498, 500
Counter Checks.................... 108
Coupon Bonds..................... 590
Coupon Register................... 597
Credit
  Advice......................106, 330
  Approval........................ 381
  Balances........................ 24
  Memorandums................154, 361
  Sales......................377–396
Creditors, Accounts with............. 150
Credits........................... 17
  Deferred....................... 599
Cumulative Preferred Stock.......... 561
Current Assets..................... 199
Current Income Bonds.............. 255
Current Liabilities.................. 203
Current Ratio..................... 505
Customers, Accounts with............ 150
Cycle, Accounting...............228, 514

D

Daily Bank Statement...........458, 477
Dealership......................... 615
Debenture Bonds................... 589
Debit Balances..................... 24
Debits............................ 17
Declaration of Dividends............ 313
Deed of Trust..................... 587
Deferral Adjustments............... 428
Deferred Charges................504, 599
Deferred Credit..................401, 599
Deferred Income................... 407
Deficit............................ 313
Depletion.....................432, 619
  For Federal Income Tax Purposes... 620
  Percentage..................... 620
Deposits.......................... 98
  By Mail......................... 102
  Night.......................... 102
Deposit Ticket..................... 98
Depositary Receipt................. 137
Depreciation....................... 433
  Accounting for.................... 146
  Calculating..................... 434
    Methods of................... 434
      Declining Balance..........434, 437
      Fixed Percentage of Diminishing
        Value..................... 437
      Straight-Line............... 434
      Sum-of-the-Year's Digits....434, 438
      Unit Output...............434, 436
    Unit Basis.................... 439
  Causes of...................... 433
  Expense........................ 482
  Functional...................... 434
  Physical....................... 433
  Recording...................... 441
  Reducing-Charge Method.......... 147
  Straight-Line Method.............. 147

PAGE

Direct Labor................... 636
Directors................544, 545
　Board of.................... 545
Disbursements, Cash........... 82
　Recording................... 82
Discarding Fixed Assets........ 441
Discount..................566, 593
　Capital Stock............... 566
　Purchases.................. 150
Discounting.................. 148
Discounting a Note............ 326
Discounts.................... 385
　Cash...................... 356
　Trade..................... 355
Dishonored Checks............ 101
Disposition of Fixed Assets...... 441
Dissolution of a Partnership...... 304
Dividend.................310, 537
　Cash...................... 581
　Declaration of.............. 313
　Ex-...................... 582
　Liquidating............581, 585
　Record.................... 583
　Stock.................581, 583
Docket
　Case...................... 240
　Collection................. 242
Domestic Corporation......... 537
Double-Entry Process........15-26
Down Payment............... 396
Drafts..................341-350
　Bank..................... 341
　Commercial................ 342
　　Sight................... 342
　　　Order Bill of Lading...... 344
　　Time.................342, 346
　　　Honored.............. 347
　　Trade Acceptances.......342, 348
　　　Honored.............. 347
Drafts and Trade Acceptances....341-350
Drawee.................... 342
Drawer.................... 342
Drayage Bill................ 361

E

Earned Surplus.............. 312
Earnings
　Distributed to Stockholders....581-586
　Retained in the Business......573-581
　Retained Statement.......... 662
Elements of Accounting........9-26
Employees, Earnings Record..... 127
Employees' Income Taxes Payable..... 131
End-of-Period Adjustments...... 140
End-of-Period Work Sheet......185-194
Endorse.................... 333
Endorsements............... 100
　Accommodation............ 333
　Blank.................... 333
　Full..................... 333
　Restrictive................ 100

PAGE

Entries
　Adjusting.209-214, 480-486, 509, 649, 664
　　Journalizing............. 210
　　Posting................. 213
　Closing..........215, 248, 663, 664
　　Journalizing............. 215
　　Posting................. 216
　Compound Journal.......... 132
　Opening...............291, 296
　Readjusting............... 224
　Reversing.........224, 512, 668, 671
　　Journalizing............. 225
Equation, Accounting.......... 12
Equipment..............431-438
Equity.................... 291
Errors
　Correcting................ 79
　Finding.................. 78
Excess of Appraised Value of Fixed
　Assets Over Cost........... 579
Exchange Allowance.......... 443
Exchange of Fixed Assets...... 443
Ex-Dividend................ 582
Expense................... 20
　Depreciation.............. 482
Expenses
　Accrued.................. 484
　Real Property............. 253
Expired Insurance............ 424

F

Face Value................. 555
Federal Depositary Receipt...... 137
Federal Excise Taxes.......... 358
Federal Insurance Contributions Act
　(F.I.C.A.) Taxes Payable...... 131
Fifo Inventory............413, 640
Filing Canceled Checks........ 630
Filing Returns and Paying Payroll Taxes 136
Filing Vouchers.............. 627
Financial Statements.....44-48, 79, 195-208
　Balance Sheet......45, 198, 247, 502-508
　　Account Form.........198, 200
　　Report Form..........198, 201
　Income Statement...45, 195, 246, 497-501
Finding Errors.............. 78
First-In, First-Out Costing...... 413
Fiscal Year................ 21
　Work at Close............. 681
Fixed Asset
　Accounts................. 439
　Records.................. 439
　Turnover................. 508
Fixed Assets............... 202
　Acquisition of............. 432
　Discarding............... 441
　Disposition of............. 441
　Exchange of.............. 443
　Fully Depreciated.......... 445
　Retiring................. 441
　Selling.................. 442
Fixed Liabilities............. 203

PAGE

Footing
  Accounts........................24, 41
  Cashbook........................ 87
Foreign Corporation................. 537
Forms
  Miscellaneous..................... 358
  Standard......................... 362
  450............................. 137
  SS-4............................ 130
  SS-5............................ 123
  W-2............................. 128
  W-4............................. 120
Franchises.....................431, 615
Freight Bill...................... 360
Full Endorsement.................. 333
Fully Participating Stock............. 561

G

General Journal.........64, 453, 475, 510
  Proving......................... 453
  Posting......................... 453
General Ledger.................157, 454
General Ledger Accounts
  Adjusting....................... 509
  Closing......................... 509
Goodwill..................301, 431, 616
Government Bonds.................. 255
Gross Earnings
  Deductions from.................. 119
  Determination of................. 118
Gross Margin..................... 196
Gross Profit...................... 196
Guranteed Bonds.................. 589

H

Home Office Books
  Balance Sheet.................... 687
  Closing......................... 685
  Income Statement................ 687
  Ledger......................... 679
  Post-Closing Trial Balance.......... 689
  Trial Balance.................... 680
  Work Sheet..................... 686

I

Imprest Method.................114, 633
Improvement Bonds................ 588
In Balance....................... 24
Income.......................20, 589
  Deferred........................ 407
  Investment...................... 253
  Real Property................... 252
  Retention of.................... 574
  Self-Employment................ 264
  Statement.................44, 195, 656
    Interpreting................... 657
  Taxes.......................... 119
Income and Expense Statement........ 195
Income and Self-Employment Taxes.... 264

PAGE

Income Statement........44, 195, 497–501
  Analysis........................ 196
  Columns........................ 190
  Exhibiting Investment Income....... 263
  Form of.......................196, 497
  Importance of................... 195
  Interpreting..................... 499
Income Summary Account........... 511
Income Tax Withholding Table........ 121
Incorporating a
  Partnership..................... 317
  Sole Proprietorship............... 316
Incorporators.................307, 539
Indenture Bonds.................. 590
Independent Contractors............. 117
Indirect Labor.................... 636
Individual Posting............94, 370, 390
Installment Sales................396–401
  Account Form................... 399
  Accounting for.................. 397
    Accrual Basis.................. 397
    Installment Basis............... 398
Insurance
  Canceled....................... 427
  Expired......................424, 483
  Parcel Post...................375, 382
  Policy.......................... 423
    Register....................424–426
  Premium....................... 423
    Annual Rate.................. 424
    Term Rate.................... 424
  Short-Term Rate................ 427
Intangible Assets................431, 611
  Other.......................... 618
Interest
  Calculating..................... 322
  60-Day, 6 Per Cent Method....... 324
  Prepaid........................ 427
Interest Expense, Accounting for...... 148
Interest Income, Accounting for...... 142
Interest Payable, Accrued.........227, 494
Interest Receivable, Accrued......226, 494
Interlocking Accounts.............. 673
Inventories.....................50, 490
  Assigning Cost to the............. 413
  At Cost........................ 638
  At Cost or Market, Whichever is
    Lower........................ 640
  Average Costing................. 414
  Bases of Valuation............... 638
  Book.......................... 641
  Comparison of Methods.......... 415
  Cost or Market, Whichever is Lower. 416
  First-In, First-Out Costing.....413, 640
  Last-In, First-Out Costing......414, 640
  Manufacturing Company.......... 637
  Merchandise.................411–419
  Perpetual...................... 419
  Physical........................ 411
  Retail Method.................. 418
  Sheet.......................... 412
  Taking......................... 411
Invested Capital.................. 573
Investment Income................ 253

PAGE

Investments, Accounting for.......... 250
Investments in Securities, Accounting for 255
Invoice........................... 353
   Corrected...................... 631
   Method......................... 52
   Preparation of.................. 622
   Purchase.....................51, 353
      Corrected.................. 363
   Record..................363, 365, 450
   Sales.......................... 353
   Verification of................. 621
Invoice of Shipment................. 402
Issuance of Capital Stock........... 563
Issued Stock....................... 561

J

Journal........................27, 646
   Cash Disbursements............. 83
   Cash Payments................. 83
   Cash Receipts................. 82
   Combined Cash................90, 157
      Footing.................... 94
      Posting.................... 94
      Proving.................... 93
      Ruling..................... 94
   General..............64, 453, 475, 510
   Method........................ 634
   Proving....................... 36
   Purchases....................49, 157
      Posting.................... 55
   Sales.......................61, 157
      Posting.................... 63
Journalizing..................27, 30, 76
   Adjusting Entries..............210, 480
   Closing Entries............... 215
   Employers' Payroll Taxes........ 136
   Payroll Transactions........... 131
   Transactions..................27–37
Journals, Multicolumn.............. 97

L

Labor.............................. 636
   Costs, Recording.............. 636
   Direct........................ 636
   Indirect...................... 636
Land.............................. 250
Land, Buildings, and Equipment....431–438
Last-In, First-Out Costing........... 414
Leasehold Improvements............. 614
Leaseholds........................ 431
Leases............................ 613
Ledger................37, 366, 387, 643
   Accounts Payable..............158, 455
   Accounts Receivable...........158, 454
   Balance-Column................ 151
   General.....................157, 454
   Operating Expense............. 456
   Stockholders'................. 551
   Subscription.................. 550
   Subsidiary.................... 151
Ledger Account Method............53, 60
Legal Entity...................... 535

PAGE

Legal Fees......................... 233
Liabilities.......................9–14
   Current....................... 203
   Fixed......................... 203
Liability, Contingent............... 329
Liability, Limited.................. 536
License........................... 539
Lifo Inventory..................414, 640
Limited Liability.................. 536
Liquidates........................ 544
Liquidating Dividend............581, 585
Liquidating Preference.............. 559
Listed............................ 559
Loss from Bad Debts................ 144

M

Management...................535–546
Manufacturer
   Annual Report...............657–662
   Closing the Books...........663–672
Manufacturers, Accounting for.....635–672
Manufacturing Accounts............. 655
Manufacturing Expenses............. 636
   Burden........................ 637
   Overhead...................... 637
   Prime Costs................... 636
Market Value...................... 311
Marketable Securities.............. 202
Materials
   Direct........................ 635
   Indirect...................... 635
   Raw.......................... 635
Merchandise, Accounting for........49–80
Merchandise Accounts............... 50
Merchandise, Consigned
   Sold at Market Prices.......... 404
   Sold at Stipulated Prices........ 406
Merchandise Inventory...........411–419
Merchandise Inventory Account....... 50
Merchandise Turnover............... 507
Merchant
   Retail........................ 49
   Wholesale..................... 49
Micro-Film Method of Accounting.... 390
Minute Book, Corporation.......... 547
Minutes, Corporation............... 548
Miscellaneous Forms................ 358
Monthly Adjustment of the Operating
   Expense Accounts.............479–488
Monthly Financial Statement and Pro-
   cedure at End of Year.........497–514
Mortgage.......................... 203
   Bonds........................ 589
Multicolumn Journals............... 97

N

Narrative......................... 31
Natural Business Year.............. 411
Negotiable Instruments............. 321
   Checks....................... 321
   Drafts....................... 321
   Notes........................ 321
   Trade Acceptances............. 321

PAGE

Net Income............................ 20
  From Real Estate Investment....... 253
Net Loss............................. 20
Net Operating Profit.................. 196
Net Sales............................ 196
Net Working Capital................. 505
Net Worth........................... 11
Net Worth Turnover.................. 508
Night Deposits....................... 102
Noncumulative Preferred Stock....... 561
Nonparticipating Stock............... 560
No-Par-Value Stock.................. 556
  Accounting for.................... 569
Notes..........................321–340
  Discounted Prior to Maturity....... 328
    Contingent Liability............. 329
  Discounting...................148, 326
  Dishonored....................... 334
  Endorsement of................... 333
    Accommodation................. 333
    Blank.......................... 333
    Full........................... 333
  Issued as Security................. 335
  Issued in Exchange for Merchandise.. 335
  Issued to Creditors................ 335
  Negotiable....................... 322
  Paid at Maturity................330, 336
  Payable Account.................. 337
  Payable Register...............337–339
  Present Value.................... 325
  Present Worth.................... 325
  Promissory....................... 142
    Interest-Bearing................. 142
  Receivable Account................ 331
  Receivable Register.............331–333
  Renewed at Maturity...........331, 337
  Transferred Prior to Maturity....... 328
Notes Payable....................11, 632
  Accounting for.................148, 335
Notes Receivable.................... 10
  Accounting for.................142, 326
  From Customers.................. 327
  From Employees.................. 327
  In Exchange for Merchandise....... 327
Notice of Maturity.................. 336

O

Obsolescence........................ 434
Offered Prices....................... 559
Office Equipment.................... 449
Office Supplies...................... 420
Officers............................ 546
Open Accounts
  Balancing........................ 222
  Ruling........................... 222
Opening Entries...................291, 296
Operating Expense Accounts
  Ledger........................... 456
  Monthly Adjustment............479–488
Operating Expenses, Schedule of...... 488
Operating Statement................. 195

PAGE

Order
  Back............................ 355
  Bill of Lading.................... 344
  Purchase........................ 352
Organization
  Corporate.....................535–554
  Expense Account................. 568
  Expenses........................ 568
Organization and Management.....535–546
Organization of a Partnership......... 295
Original Records.................... 27
Overdraft.......................... 105
Overhead Expenses.................. 637
Ownership.......................... 289

P

Parcel Post Insurance............375, 382
Partial Payments.................... 631
Participating Stock.................. 560
Partners, Compensation............. 302
Partnership......................295–306
  Accounts in the Balance Sheet....... 306
  Admitting a New Partner.......... 300
  Allocation of Profits and Losses..... 303
  Dissolution of a.................. 304
  Incorporating a.................. 317
  Organization of a................. 295
Par Value.......................310, 555
  Stock..........................555, 563
Patents.........................431, 611
Pay Check.......................... 127
Payee.............................. 342
Paying Vouchers.................... 628
Payroll Accounting...............117–138
  Importance of.................... 117
Payroll Records..................... 123
Payroll Taxes
  Filing Returns and Paying.......... 136
  Imposed on the Employer.......132–138
  Paying.......................... 136
Percentage Method Withholding Table. 119
Periodic Summary................185–208
Permanent Investments............. 202
Permanent Proprietorship Accounts.... 203
Perpetual Inventory................. 419
Personal Property................... 431
Personal Service Enterprise........229–264
  Adjusting Entries................. 246
  Balance Sheet.................... 247
  Business......................... 229
  Cash Basis of Accounting.......... 229
  Closing Entries................... 248
  Financial Statements.............. 246
  Professional...................... 229
  Work Sheet...................... 242
Petty Cash
  Disbursements Record..........113, 239
    Proving the..................... 113
  Fund.......................112–116, 633
    Establishing a................... 112
    Imprest Method.............114, 633
    Journal Method................. 634
    Voucher....................... 112

PAGE

Petty Cash Disbursements 476
   Statement of 478
Physical Inventory 411
Postage Stamps 422
Post-Closing Trial Balance . 223, 249, 512, 669
Postdated Checks 102
Posting 37, 76
   Adjusting Entries 213, 485
   Cashbook 89
   Closing Entries 216
   Combined Cash-Journal 94
   Individual 94, 370, 390
   Machines 390
   Procedure 366, 388
   Purchases Journal 55
   Sales Journal 63
   Summary 55, 95, 371, 393
Posting and the Trial Balance 37–48
Posting from
   Books of Original Entry 153
   Check Register 629
   Other Documents 153
   Voucher Register 627
   Vouchers 153
Posting in Detail 669
Posting to
   Individual Accounts with Creditors . . 153
   Individual Accounts with Customers . . 154
Practical Accounting Problems
   265–288, 515–533, 697–715
Pre-emptive Right 544
Preferred Stock 260, 311, 559
   Cumulative 561
   Fully Participating 561
   Noncumulative 561
   Nonparticipating 560
   Participating 560
Premium 566, 593
   On Capital Stock 566
   Unamortized 601
Prepaid Expense 146
Prepaid Expenses, Accounting for 146
Prepaid Interest 427
Preparation of Invoices 622
Prepayments 420–430
Present Worth 325
Prices
   Bid 559
   Offered 559
Prime Costs 636
Principles of Voucher Accounting . . . 621–634
Professional Enterprises 229
Profit
   Gross 196
   Net Operating 196
Profit and Loss Statement 195
Promissory Note 142
Proprietary
   Accounts 294
   Transactions 293
Proprietorship 9–14, 203
   Accounting for 289–320
   Accounts 290
      Permanent 290
      Temporary 290

PAGE

Sole 289–295
Proving
   Balance of Accounts 42
   Cash 86, 93
   Combined Cash-Journal 93
   Journal 36
   Petty Cash Disbursements Record 113
   Vouchers Payable 630
   Work Sheet 191
Proxy 544
   Voting by 544
Purchase
   Invoice 51, 353
      Corrected 363
   Orders 352
      Billing 381
      Checking Accuracy 381
      Credit Approval 381
      Handling Incoming 380
      Interpretation 380
      Transportation 380
   Requisition 351
Purchase-Money Bonds 588
Purchases
   Account 50
   Cash 372
   C.O.D. 359, 372
   Discount 150
   Journal 49–56, 157
      Posting from 55
   Returns and Allowances 376, 630
      Account 51
Purchases and the Purchases Journal . . 49–56
Purchasing Procedure 351–362
   Accounting 362–376

Q

Quick Assets 205, 505

R

Ratio 205
   Acid-Test 505
   Analysis 206, 505
   Current 505
   Current Assets to Fixed Assets 506
   Fixed Assets to Fixed Liabilities 506
   Net Income to Net Worth 508
   Net Income to Total Assets 508
   Net Worth to Fixed Assets 506
   Net Worth to Indebtedness 506
   Turnover 507
   Working Capital 505
Raw Materials 635
Real Estate Investment, Net Income . . . 253
Real Property 250, 431
   Expenses 253
   Income 252
Recapitalization 579
Receipt, Federal Depositary 137
Receipts, Cash 81
   Recording 82
Receivable, Accounts 60
Reciprocal Accounts and Recording
   Procedure 673–680

	PAGE
Reconciliation of Reciprocal Accounts	695
Reconciling the Bank Balance	108
Record	
Auxiliary	456
Cash Receipts	450, 472
Posting	451
Proving	451
Cash Receipts and Disbursements	81–97
Checks Drawn	452, 473, 474
Posting	452
Proving	452
Employees' Earnings	127
Invoice	450, 470
Petty Cash Disbursements	476
Sales	386, 389, 450, 471
Individual Posting	390
Proving	387
Summary Posting	393
Stock	457
Recording	
Bank Transactions	105
Capital Stock Transactions	562–572
Checks	629
Vouchers	624
Records	
Auxiliary	114, 158, 239, 648
Cash Disbursements	81–97
Corporate	546
Payroll	123
Stock Payment	550
Stock Transfer	553
Stocks and Bonds	262
Subscription	548
Redeemable Stock	560, 591
Redemption of Bond Originally Sold	
Discount	602
Face Value	600
Premium	600
Refunding Bonds	588
Register	
Check	625, 629
Posting from	629
Coupon	597
Notes Payable	337
Notes Receivable	331
Voucher	624, 625
Posting from	627
Registered Bonds	590
Report Form	198
Report of Earnings	195
Restrictive Endorsement	100
Retail Merchant	49
Retail Method of Inventory	418
Retail Sales Tax	57
Retail Store, Accounting for a	139–184
Retained Earnings	573–581
Account	574
Appropriations of	576
Statement of	577
Retention of Income	574
Retiring Fixed Assets	441
Return Notice	101
Returns and Allowances	385
Purchases	376
Sales	395

	PAGE
Revenue and Expense Statement	195
Reversing Entries	224, 512, 668, 671
Journalizing	225
Ruling	
Accounts	511
Cashbook	87
Closed Accounts	217
Combined Cash-Journal	94
Merchandise Inventory Account	213
Open Accounts	222
Purchases Account	213
Work Sheet	191

S

	PAGE
Sale of Bonds	
Between Interest Dates	595
Discount	595
Face Amount	594
Premium	594
Sale of Real Property	254
Accounting for	254
Sale, Terms of	377
Sales	
Account	56, 402
Accounting for	377–410
Cash	377–396
C.O.D.	378, 394
Consignment	402–410
Credit	377–396
Installment	396–401
Invoice	353
Corrected	387
Journal	56–65, 157
Posting from	63
On Account	378
On Approval	379
Record	386, 389, 450
Individual Posting	390
Summary Posting	393
Returns and Allowances	395
Account	57
Ticket	58
Method	60
Will Call Sales	379
Sales and the Sales Journal	56–65
Savings Account	111
Savings Bond Deductions Payable	131
Schedule of	
Accounts Payable	55, 371, 488
Accounts Receivable	64, 394, 486
Accrued Interest on Notes Receivable	494
Cost of Goods Sold	498, 500
Depreciation	482
Operating Expenses	488, 498, 501
Supplies	483
Securities	255
Bonds	255
Appreciation	255
Corporation	255, 259
Current Income	255
Government	259
U. S. Savings	255
U. S. Treasury	257
Stocks	255, 260
Self-Employment Income	264

PAGE

Self-Employment Taxes.............. 264
Selling Fixed Assets................. 442
Serial Bonds....................... 591
Service Charges..................... 109
Shareholders....................... 544
Signature Card..................... 98
Sinking Fund...................... 590
  Accounting for................. 604
  Handled by a Trustee............. 606
  Investments.................... 606
    Discount..................... 606
    Premium..................... 606
  Provisions..................... 607
Social Security Account Number, Application for..................... 123
Social Security Taxes............... 132
Sole Proprietorship...............289–295
  Incorporating a................. 316
  Organization of a............... 289
Standard Account Form............. 16
Standard Forms.................... 362
Stated Value...................... 557
Statement
  Daily Bank..................458, 477
  Earnings Retained.............577, 662
  Income......................... 656
  Interim........................ 663
  Manufacturing.................. 659
  Withholding Tax................ 128
Statement of
  Account....................... 155
  Assets......................... 198
  Condition...................... 198
  Liabilities..................... 198
Statements
  Financial.....................79, 195
  Income......................... 195
    Importance of................. 195
  Income and Expense.............. 195
  Operating...................... 195
  Profit and Loss................. 195
  Report of Earnings.............. 195
  Revenue and Expense............ 195
Statements, Consolidated............ 689
  Balance Sheet.................. 692
  Income......................... 691
  Work Sheet.................... 690
Stock
  Book Value.................... 557
  Capital......................260, 310
  Certificate...................311, 544
    Book....................... 551
  Common................260, 310, 559
  Convertible.................... 561
  Corporation................... 260
  Cumulative.................... 561
  Dividend....................581, 583
  Face Value..................... 555
  Fully Participating.............. 561
  Issued......................... 561
  Market Value.................. 559
  Noncumulative................. 561
  Nonparticipating............... 560
  No-Par-Value.................. 556
  Participating................... 560

PAGE

Par-Value....................555, 563
Payment Record................... 550
Preferred....................260, 311
Record................262, 457, 559
Split............................ 581
Stated Value..................... 557
Transfer Record.................. 553
Treasury........................ 562
Unissued........................ 561
Stockholders..................308, 544
  Earnings Distributed...........581–586
  Ledger.......................551, 552
Store Supplies..................... 421
Stores Ledger..................... 641
Straight-Line Method.............. 147
Subscriber........................ 548
Subscriber's Account.............. 550
Subscription
  Ledger........................ 550
  List........................548, 549
  Records....................... 548
Subscriptions, Stock............... 312
Subsidiary Ledgers................ 151
Summary Posting.........55, 95, 371, 393
Supplies and Prepayments........420–430
  Asset Method of Accounting....... 420
  Expense Method of Accounting..... 428
Supplies Consumed................ 482
Surplus.......................... 573

T

"T" Account Form................. 17
Tax
  Employer's F.I.C.A.............. 133
  Employer's F.U.T.A............. 133
  Retail Sales.................... 57
Taxes
  Federal Excise.................. 358
  F.I.C.A. Payable................ 131
  F.U.T.A. Payable............... 134
  Income........................ 119
  Payroll........................ 132
  Self-Employment............... 264
  Social Security................. 132
  State U. C..................... 134
  State U. C. Payable............. 135
Temporary Investments............. 202
Temporary Proprietorship Accounts.... 21
Term Rate........................ 424
Terms........................... 358
Terms of Sale.................... 377
  Cash.......................... 377
  C.O.D......................... 378
  On Account.................... 378
  On Approval................... 379
  On Consignment................ 402
  On Installment................. 396
  Will Call...................... 379
Ticket
  Deposit....................... 98
  Sales......................... 58
Trade Acceptances..............341–350
Trade Discounts................... 355
Trade-Marks..................431, 616

	PAGE
Trade Names	616
Transactions	13
Capital Stock	569
Recording	562–572
Journalizing	27–37
Payroll	131
Proprietary	293
Transportation	380
Accounts	373
Charges	372, 394
Collect	373
Prepaid	372
Travelers' Checks	322
Treasury Stock	562
Accounting for	567
Trial Balance	23, 41, 78, 486, 649
Adjusted	189
After Closing	223
Columns	186
Adjusted	189
Post-Closing	223, 249, 512, 669
Working	185
Turnover	207
Accounts Receivable	507
Fixed Asset	508
Merchandise	507
Net Worth	508
Ratios	507
Working Capital	508
Type of Business Organization	447
Types and Values of Capital Stock	555–562
Typical Manufacturing Accounts	635–642
Labor	636
Manufacturing Expenses	636
Raw Materials	635

U

Unamortized Premiums	601
Unissued Stock	561
Unit Basis of Depreciation	439
U. S. Savings Bonds	255
U. S. Treasury Bonds	257
Unpaid Vouchers File as a Subsidiary Ledger	633
Unrealized Gross Profit on Installment Sales	401

V

Value	
Book	311, 557
Face	555
Market	311, 559
No-Par	556
Par	310, 555
Stated	557
Values of Capital Stock	555–562
Vendor	352

	PAGE
Verification of Invoices	621
Voting by Proxy	544
Voucher Check	628
Voucher System	621
Accounting	621
Principles of	621
Vouchers	622
Filing	627
Payable, Proving	630
Paying	628
Recording	624
Register	624, 625
Posting from	627

W

Wage Deductions	117–132
Wages	130
Computing	118
Wages and Wage Deductions	117–132
Accounting for	130
Wasting Assets	432, 611, 618
Watered Stock	567
Waybill	360
Wholesale Merchant	49
Will Call Ledger	379
Will Call Sales	379
Withdrawals, Making	103
Withholding Employees' Taxes	
F.I.C.A.	122
Income	119
Withholding Exemptions	119
Certificate	120
Withholding Table	
Income Tax	121
Percentage Method	119
Withholding Tax Statement	128
Work at Close of Fiscal Period	242
Work at Close of Fiscal Year	681–689
Working Capital	206
Ratio	505
Turnover	508
Working Trial Balance	185
Work Sheet	185, 245, 492
End-of-Period	185, 489–496
Function of	185
Mercantile Business	186
Nature of	185
Of a Manufacturer	649–656
Personal Service Enterprise	242
Proving	191
Ruling	191
Totaling	191

Y

Year	
Calendar	21
Fiscal	21
Natural Business	411